Nathalie Prézeau

Third edition

TORONTO

FUN
PLACES

The family-tested guide
to over 400 outings in and around
the Greater Toronto Area

Word
— of —
Mouth
Production

This book is dedicated
to my mother Raymonde Taillefer,
who never ceases to appreciate
the pleasure and beauty
in her daily life!

Published by Word-of-Mouth Production
299 Booth Avenue
Toronto, Ontario M4M 2M7, Canada
Tel.: (416) 462-0670   Fax: (416) 462-0682
mail@torontofunplaces.com

www.torontofunplaces.com

Writing and photos: **Nathalie Prézeau**
Illustrations: **Johanne Pepin** (450) 456-3980
Design and layout: **Publisher Friendly** (416) 465-6060
Proofreading: **Kerstin McCutcheon**
Printing: **AGMV Marquis** (514) 954-1131

Library and Archives Canada Cataloguing in Publication

Prézeau, Nathalie, 1960 –
Toronto fun places: the family-tested guide to over 400 outings
in and around the Greater Toronto Area – Third edition

Includes index.
ISBN 0-9684432-3-0

Second edition published in 2001
First edition published in 1999 under title:
Toronto: the family-tested guide to fun places

1. Family recreation – Ontario – Toronto Region – Guidebooks.
2. Toronto Region (Ont.) – Guidebooks. I. Title.

FC3097.18.P74 2004   917.13'541044   C2004-903924-5

A word from the author

I just celebrated my son's eleventh birthday, my daughter recently turned seven, and my "last born" is now in its third edition.

It's been interesting to watch my children and my guide grow and see how it affected our journey. Indoor playgrounds have given way to skateparks (hence a new section!). As my kids were maturing and getting more able to grasp certain aspects of real life, a new Charity chapter took form.

I've refined my table of contents and split all high-energy activities between the Sports and the Amusement Centres chapters. I've divided these and the Arts & Culture chapter into more categories for quicker reference, and reorganized the seasonal outings into a Holiday Outings chapter.

Finally, I have included a Totally Arbitrary Section with no other goal than to pass on the addresses of a few interactive stores, original suppliers and fun restaurants I have come across over the years.

It took me nine years to visit all the places described in this guide and six months to write this user-friendly third edition. As a result, it should hopefully take you only a few minutes to find the perfect outing for your family.

Make sure to read the "How to use this guide" information on the inside cover to make this reference guide work for you.

All the information was accurate at the time of print but things change! My best advice is to always call to confirm the opening hours of an attraction before you go, to avoid disappointment.

Have fun with your loved ones!

Nathalie Prézeau
(with great help from my R & D team: François, my husband, and our two children Laurent and Roxane)

Thank you so much to... *François, for great "one-liners" that made me laugh through the pressure, like the day I felt so overwhelmed by the idea of one more meal to cook or more homework to supervise, preventing me from focusing on the writing of this guide, that I burst out: "That's when I wish I had a wife!" To which he quietly commented: "Me too." (For those who might wonder, yes, he does his share: laundry, dish washing, garbage, etc. The man just can't cook!)*

TOURIST CORNER

Toronto Fun Places was written for parents living in Southern Ontario, but it can be very useful for tourists.

Having visitors over? Log on to the <u>Tourist Corner</u> on our web site **www.torontofunplaces.com** for the author's suggestions of itineraries to make the most out of their stay, with or without you!

Here's what a grateful visitor sent us: "Your excellent guide book was loaned to us by my wife's cousin who lives in Mississauga. My son Ian (10) says it was the best holiday he has ever had."
- S. W., *Northern Ireland*

TABLE OF CONTENTS

AMUSEMENT CENTRES

ANIMALS

ARTS & CULTURE

SPORTS

General tips about
Amusement centres:

- Always check height requirements before waiting in line! Most amusement parks are really strict about those and, no, fluffing your kid's hair over her head won't do.
- Be ready to spend a lot on all the extra costs in most amusement parks: the cost of food in their snack bars can be double what you would expect. They usually charge an additional fee for tube rentals. There's always a popular attraction with its cost not included in the admission fee.
- In most cases, if you intend on visiting a specific attraction more than twice during the season, consider a seasonal pass.

AMUSEMENT
CENTRES

See **StoryBook Gardens** on p. 30.

ONTARIO PLACE

In the first place

Ontario Place is an excellent waterpark as well as theme park. The numerous rides offer adrenalin rushes for young and old. It is also entertaining, with Imax movies and numerous musical shows on different stages. Finally, it is like a conservation area, with paddle boats, large green spaces and the surrounding lake.

Many things have changed here since 2001. No more Haida warship (it was moved to Hamilton). Also gone is the Children's Village on the east side of Ontario Place but don't worry! Kids will have even more fun in the new Go Zone located in the western part of the park.

For those who have never visited it, Ontario Place's architecture is an attraction in itself. Children enjoy watching people from the bridges linking the huge white pods built atop the water. You'll find the Imax theatre in the sphere attached to the white structure.

Riding one of the paddle boats from Bob's Boat Yard (included with the Play-All-Day pass) is a great way to admire it all. The Play-All-Day pass actually gives visitors unlimited access to all the rides, including the regular Cinesphere screenings (somewhat hard on young eardrums by the way).

Kids like to take control so younger children will love the Mini Bumper Boats (3 years+, 49" max.), while the older ones will want to ride on the bigger boats (48"+), now located on the western side of Ontario Place.

Those who can reach the foot pedals will have access to the Whiz Kids' battery-powered go-karts (min. 4 years old, 52" max.) at the east end. Expect a long line-up. While you wait, you might as well stuff yourselves with Beaver Tails, a treat sold on the premises. A few other rides located in that section will thrill the younger kids.

At the western end, the new O.P. Driving School (for drivers 5-12 years old) comes with real traffic lights! The smile on their faces...

We really were excited by the Atom Blaster, located a bit further. There, parents become the favourite target for foam balls launched by air cannons. The less combative kids prefer to feed the balls into a huge cannon which eventually will blow them to the ceiling in a spectacular blast. Microkids offers similar fun on a lower scale, for pre-schoolers.

The H_2O Generation Station is an impressive structure composed of towers linked by tunnels. Some transparent ones are way up high!

In that area is the Wilderness Adventure Ride (42"+): a raft ride through canyons that features animated characters with a final 40-foot drop. The Megamaze is a multi-level labyrinth consisting of 7 mazes with optical illusions, puzzling for younger children. The Mars

TIPS (fun for 2 years +)
• More on **Ontario Place** water park on page 32.
• Ground admission is the cheapest way to visit if you just intend to accompany a young child to the waterpark and to the kiddie rides. It allows you to watch shows on outdoor stages or even the **Canadian International Air Show** and the **fireworks**. You can always upgrade your ground admission to a Play-All-Day pass on the site if you change your mind.
• A footbridge connects the western tip of Ontario Place to the West entrance. It's a good shortcut back to the parking lot on the west end side. There usually is a water shuttle linking both ends of the park. It offers a quick access to the East entrance. Check to see if this service is maintained in 2005.
• If you go on the Wilderness Adventure Ride, bring a garbage bag to cover yourself if you want to stay dry!
• The international firework competitions don't exist anymore but Ontario Place has revived its spirit, offering three major **firework** displays during the summer. Expect one on **Canada Day** and the others during the week before or after. Call for exact dates.
• There's a free shuttle bus running from Union Subway Station during Ontario Place operating hours (except for weekdays in June).

Simulator Ride (36"+) includes moving seats and a big screen creating fun effects. The "Artefacts from Mars" display beside the line-up is hilarious.

The Super Slide, next to the Festival Stage by the waterpark, is the perfect way to kill time before the next show.

Ontario Place (416) 314-9900 www.ontarioplace.com	**J-10 Downtown** Toronto 10-min.

Schedule: Open on Victoria Day weekend. Open daily from the following weekend until Labour Day, then weekends only September through Thanksgiving. Most attractions open 10 am to 8 pm in July and August. ATTENTION: shorter hours in June and in the fall!

Admission: Play-All-Day Pass (including the ground admission) is $29/6-64 years, $17/65 years and up, $15/4-5 years, FREE for children 3 and under (prices vary during CNE). Ground admission is $13 (only $5 after 5 pm). If you plan on going more than once ask about their season pass. Parking costs: $10/daytime, $5/non-event evenings ($15 or more on event days or evenings).

Directions: 955 Lake Shore Blvd., Toronto (on the waterfront between Strachan Ave. and Dufferin St.).

NEARBY ATTRACTIONS
Harbourfront Centre (10-min.)......p. 68
Historic Fort York (5-min.)............p. 400

CANADA'S WONDERLAND

Do your kids measure up?

Children measuring less than 40 inches tall have access to eighteen small rides, several shows, a large playground and the big water park. When children reach 44" tall, two-thirds of the rides become accessible to them. As soon as the children are 48" tall, they're allowed on most of Wonderland's 60 rides.

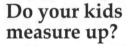

Last visit, my son had hit 54" and all of a sudden, he was on all the gut-wrenching rides: Drop Zone, Psyclone, Cliffhanger and the likes.

Children's rides

The Candy Factory is a great playground where kids can use up lots of energy. Near it are two areas for children 8 years and under. If your children are comfortable with the Taxi Jam roller coaster in Kidzville (probably too much for children 3 years and under) you might want them to try the Ghoster Coaster (40"+) in Hanna-Barbera Land.

Our other favourite rides in those sections include the Frequent Flyers' Parachutes, the turning cups of the Flavourator and the bumper cars of the Boulder Bumpers.

Gone are the slow racing cars of the Hot Rock Raceway, the Flinstone picnic tables and the Bedrock Tent with its seal shows in Hanna-Barbera Land.

The new section Nickelodeon Central has been added for the very young. Its new rides, and most of the other rides in Kidzville and Hanna-Barbera Land are pretty tame and seem too short to endure long line-ups.

The Zoom Zone features more exciting rides for young thrill seekers. There's Silver Streak, the long suspended coaster, Blast Off where kids rise and drop on a rocket ship, and Jumpin' Jet, flying riders through looping spins.

In the Medieval section is the Speed City Raceway (cars run on 9 hp engines), for riders 40"+.

We love the gorgeous animals on the large antique carousel (36"+) in the Grande World Exposition of 1890. On the way out, young and old watch with fascination the "crazies" who leap from the top of the Xtreme Sky Flyer tower (48"+), the one you jump off with a bungee cord; a show in itself.

Now, it was my own son with his life hanging by one thread! "You have to try it!" he claimed after his jump. Yeah, sure!

Shows

The Playhouse Theatre in Kidzville usually runs an excellent little musical show several times a day. The theatre is covered and provides welcome shade in the midst of summer.

Throughout the summer, there's a host of international festivals going on on various interior and exterior stages. Aquatic shows are available at Arthur's Baye and professionals dive daily from atop the mountain waterfall.

Furthermore, there's the Paramount Action FX Theatre (44"+), a motion simulator with seats that move in sync with the action on the screen. Check their daily schedule.

TIPS (fun for 3 years +)
• More on **Canada's Wonderland** water park on p. 34.
• Note for 2004! Wonderland offers their best deal in years: save $15 off $50 admission when buying it from one of the Blockbuster video stores. Otherwise, there are different sponsors every month. Call their guest services to find out their current partner: (905) 832-8131.
• I saw several children crying their hearts out after a long wait for a ride, as they were finding out they weren't tall enough. Consult the table with height requirement, available at the park entrance.
• The best way to enjoy the Wonderland experience is to arrive at opening time and go straight to your favourite ride! Then, spend some time studying the map and schedule of shows, available at the entrance, to plan your day.
• The Deluxe-12 tickets option is to be considered if you only intend to get on a few rides or access the water park and watch the outdoor shows.
• Canada's Wonderland will please children of all ages but for children measuring under 44", I recommend sticking to **Ontario Place** (p. 12) for a while.
• There are two **fireworks** displays: Sunday of **Victoria Day** weekend and **Canada Day** at around 10:30 pm.
• Closest **campground** is **Yogi Bear's Jellystone Park**, (905) 775-1377, www.jellystonetoronto.com. Also check the Plan a visit section on Wonderland's web site for a list of accommodations offering packages.
• There are snack bars everywhere.

More big rides
Our first choice is the Thunder Run, going through the mountain (40"+). It puts you in good spirits for the day! Further on, you're sure to get wet (if you haven't covered yourself with a garbage bag) at the White Water Canyon and the Timberwolf Falls (both 40" +)!

From Splash Works, we can hear the cries (of hysteria, I presume) of thrill seekers riding at full speed on the Mighty Canadian Minebuster (48"+) and those (of horror, I suspect) of the SkyRider passengers, tracing loops with their feet hanging in the air. For roller coaster fans, there are many other options including the new Tomb Raider in which you are hung under a hang glider-like structure. A few are accessible to children of 44"+.

Need anything else with that? Every year usually brings a new attraction.

Courtesy of R.Giddings

Paramount Canada's Wonderland
G-10
North of Toronto
40-min.

• Vaughan
(905) 832-7000
www.canadaswonderland.com

 Schedule: Open on weekends starting the first Sunday in May right through to Thanksgiving and daily from Victoria Day to Labour Day. Open from 10 am to 10 pm minimum (closing times vary).
Admission: (taxes not included) $50/7 to 59 years (48"+), $25/3 to 6 years and seniors, FREE for 2 years and under. If you consider going more than once, ask about their season pass! Parking is $7.50.
Directions: 9580 Jane St., Vaughan. Take Hwy 401, then Hwy 400 North. Exit Rutherford Rd. (exit #33) eastbound.

SPORTSWORLD

Worth the trip

It took us 75 minutes to get there from downtown Toronto but the kids played non-stop for seven hours! The least I could say is that it was well worth the trip.

Sportsworld's water park in itself is nice enough to justify a visit (see p. 41), but the variety of other activities it offers in a small setting makes for a great outing. Here, you won't have to walk miles to get from one activity to the next.

Most rides are in the spirit of a local fair, with lots of inflatable structures.

The small train on real tracks going through a tunnel was a hit with my still not-too-big 7-year-old.

The large Swing and giant Ferris Wheel I saw a few years ago are gone. They've been replaced by the Cobra, a spinning ride more to the taste of the dare-devils (42" +).

I was impressed by the wide outdoor climbing wall with different degrees of difficulty. There are electric bells you can ring when you reach the top. The huge indoor climbing room, accessible from the Galaxy Game Centre, was even more breathtaking.

We all enjoyed going down on our carpets over the big bumps of the Big Dipper Slide (30"+). The Magestic Bumper Cars (42"+) offered young pilots a good rough ride.

My kids were too small to drive their own go-kart (56"+), but they enjoyed the ride by my side (kind of... I was not driving fast enough for them!).

TIPS (fun for 2 years +)

• If you're just accompanying your kids, a waterpark pass plus a few tickets for rides will suffice.

• The spread of activities throughout the amusement park makes it tough for only one adult to manage children of different age groups still requiring supervision. My advice is to have a ratio of one adult per age group so nobody gets frustrated.

NEARBY ATTRACTIONS
Children's Museum (15-min.)........p. 260
Shade's Mill (20-min.)...................p. 281

Sportsworld • Kitchener 1-800-393-9163 or (519) 653-4442 www.sportsworld.on.ca	**D-1** **West** **of Toronto** **75-min.**

Schedule: Waterpark opens daily from early June to Labour Day, 10 am to 8 pm (rides and games close at 9 pm). Rides and games open on weekends after Labour Day until end of December (weather permitting), 12 noon to 6 pm. Call to confirm.

Admission: (tax not included) The Power Passport (including unlimited access to waterpark, midway rides, one go-kart lap and one wall climb) costs around $28/adults, $24/seniors and 5-11 years, $9/2-4 years old and $20/person after 4 pm. FREE under 2 years old. Extra fees apply to some activities. Waterpark only is around $17/adults, $12/seniors and 5-11 years, $2/2-4 years, $10/person after 4 pm. You can buy individual coupons for the rides (around $2.50 + tax per ride).

Directions: From Hwy 401 West, take exit #278/Hwy 8 northbound. Then take the first exit to Sportsworld Dr.

THE DOCKS

Surprising family fun

I had heard about the wet T-shirt and swimsuit contests and the loud music. I had seen the bikini-clad gals on the advertising. Family fun was unlikely in this waterfront entertainment complex... but it is exactly what we found!

The sight of a go-kart track, minigolf and driving range, rock climbing wall, gladiator jousting game and boot camp excited my kids. What really did the trick for me was the 40,000 square foot waterfront patio. At last! A place from which to admire Lake Ontario!

There's action to observe from the Stoker's Patio Bar and Grill: police boats, tall ships, ferries, with Ward's Point in Toronto's Islands as a backdrop on one side and the CN Tower by the lake-shore on the other. We warmed up to the place with a go-kart ride right next to the parking lot on Polson. Costly, but the big smiles on my young partners' faces made it worth it.

The gladiator jousting game was a blast. Helmets on, my son and his cousin fought over an inflated mattress with sticks that look like giant Q-tips. They could play for a while since nobody was waiting in line.

My thrill-seeker begged me to try the 125-foot-high Scream'n Demon

Swing, where up to four people can jump off a platform in a cocoon attached to bungee cords. I resisted, unsuspecting that his dad would take him a few months later at Wonderland!

Another attraction really caught our attention: the Confidence Course, an impressive army-like training camp with some 30 obstacles on sand. We opted for Higher Ground's Rock Climbing and its 40-foot wall. There are also batting cages.

My kids also wanted to swim in the octagonal pool in the middle of the patio. Denied! Me? Paying to be among the only ones to play, in a bathing suit, in a fenced pool surrounded by customers leisurely watching? I don't think so!

There is more but I want you to know there's a drive-in theatre in downtown TO! In the Spring, weather permitting, The Docks' driving range turns into a drive-in some nights, screening a double-feature of the latest movies.

TIPS (fun for 8 years +)

• Children must be 3 feet high to try the Swing. They must be 12 years old and 52 inches tall to drive a go-kart but kids of all ages can accompany an 18-year-old driver.
• The Confidence Course birthday package would make for a super party for 12 years and older! Call (416) 778-6321.
• Kids are allowed on the patio until 9 pm. More on **Stoker's Patio Grill** on p. 430.

More on **Stoker's Patio Grill** on p. 430.

The Docks (416) 461-3625 www.thedocks.com	J-10 **Downtown** Toronto 5-min.

Schedule: The driving range is open year-round. The other outdoor activities start in Spring, weather permitting. The patio is open from noon, no kids are allowed after 9 pm.

Costs: Go-Kart Racing: $4.50 per run, $14 for 4. Swimming Pool: $8/adults, $6/children ($10/person on weekends). Jousting game: $12/two players for 5 minutes. Rock Climbing: $10/two climbs. Giant Swing: $25/swing. Mini Putt: $4/children, $6/adults ($2 extra on the weekends). Batting cages: $2/10 balls. Drive-in theatre: Open Tuesday, Friday and Saturday. Screening starts after 9:30 pm. $13/adults, $4/3-12 years old (half-price on Tuesdays).

Directions: 11 Polson St., Toronto. Turn south on Cherry St., accessible from Lake Shore Blvd going eastbound, turn west on Polson.

NEARBY ATTRACTIONS

PLAYDIUM MISSISSAUGA

Jump-start into adolescence

My son steps in front of the grey, naked wall. Its smooth metal splits in two before his eyes. In awe, he proceeds into a cold-coloured corridor. This leads him under an interstellar-like canopy with noisy machines scattered around. Then, his eye is caught by sculptures reaching towards a black ceiling with coloured dots; luminous floor drawings dance to background music.

Unfortunately, I am so terrible at these games that I keep "dying" within 60 seconds. That's another story with my son and his buddies!

In the IMAX Ridefilm room, I fasten my seat belt and hold on to the handles beside me. Soon, the seats move in sync with the film. It features a spaceship flying at full speed, with accidents and cata-strophes galore. The 3-D illusion is perfect, and I giggle all along. My companions choose the Max Flight simulating a roller coaster. And they spend a long time competing against each other in the Indy 500 race cars.

Many games are physically fun to ride. The demos shown on their screens are entertaining enough for little ones so you won't have to spend a penny!

My daughter's favourite is the double-seat rafter. Be ready to sweat as you row.

Outdoors batting cages and go-kart track awaited. We opted for the latter. Riders need to be 52"+ and 11 years old (they'll ask you your date of birth!).

Last but not least, there's a whole section of games redeeming coupons kids can exchange for trinkets. Don't grind your teeth, it comes with the territory.

TIPS (fun for 5 years +)
• Call before you go. All or part of Playdium may be closed for a private function.
• The noise level is very high!
• Don't hesitate to ask the attendants how the games work. If you have had troubles with a game, they might even credit it for you.
• You can't take personal belongings along to the IMAX show, but there's a free cloakroom at the Playdium entrance.
• You may buy snacks and decent fast food on the premises.

NEARBY ATTRACTIONS	

Playdium Mississauga
· Mississauga
(905) 273-9000
www.playdium.com

I-8 West of Toronto 35-min.

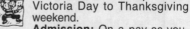

Schedule: Open year-round, Monday to Thursday, 12 noon to midnight, Friday, 12 noon to 2 am, Saturday, 10 am to 2 am and Sunday, 10 am to midnight. Outdoor attractions open from Victoria Day to Thanksgiving weekend.

Admission: On a pay-as-you-play basis debited from your Play Card. Family Power Play-Pack offers 120 credits for $17.50 instead of $20 (min. 3 family members). The average game costs 6 credits.

Directions: 99 Rathburn Rd., Mississauga (just south of Hwy 403 and west of Hurontario).

DAVE & BUSTER'S

For big... and small kids

What is this place exactly? Isn't it for adults? Can kids go? Is it big? Is it fun? Is it a restaurant? All of the above, and a little bit more.

Some of you might have heard about this entertainment complex... at the office. It is actually a popular corporate outing and primarily an adult establishment with alcohol license and smoking allowed in designated areas. But their arcade section is such a "natural" fit for kids that they have come up with a house policy to suit all ages.

Basically, guests under 19 years old (the legal drinking age) must be accompanied by a parent or a guardian 25 years or older. One guardian can accompany no more than three young guests.

Entering this establishment feels like entering a casino. A large portion of the complex hosts a posh restaurant with bars and pool tables (as well as an amazing indoor golf simulator you can rent by the hour). All the action for kids (small and big) takes place in what they call the Midway section.

From your children's perspective, passing its threshold will be like entering Alibaba's den. There are some 250 games, all competing for your attention so expect noise!

A huge counter bar greets you at the entrance. Around the bar area are retro black-lacquered booths lined with red vinyl. We grabbed one and it became our meeting point for the next three hours.

A third of the floor, to the left, is covered with games rewarding players with coupons they can exchange for trinkets or something fancy (remember, it's an adult place).

To the right, one finds all the virtual games technology can exploit: riding (race cars, 18-wheelers, motorcycles, planes, tanks, helicopters), sports (surfing, snowboarding, skiing, skating, football, basketball, hockey, golf, bowling, horse racing), hunting (alien, dinosaurs... even turkeys!). I even noticed a virtual theatre where four players can work together to beat up aliens in some galaxy.

TIPS (fun for 5 years +)

• They use a Power Card system on which you can put the amount of money you want to spend and on which they also can enter the number of coupons you have redeemed, instead of handing you a paper voucher. You can combine all the family's coupons on one single card to increase your bartering power at the Winner's Circle (their gift counter).

• When we visited, it was not busy at all so we had the chance to play on the funny horse-race track (against a wall to the left) where the winner gets 50 coupons. Since it was only our family playing, one of us was sure to win!

• The midway section offers an affordable kids' menu and edible adult food.

NEARBY ATTRACTIONS
Putting Edge (1-min. walk)........... p. 21
Sportsville (10-min.)..................p. 369

Dave & Buster's
· Vaughan
(905) 760-7600
www.
daveandbusters.com

**H-10
North
of Toronto
35-min.**

 Schedule: Open from 11:30 am to midnight or later. Kids can stay until 9 pm.

 Costs: $5 on the Power Card will give you 3 chips, $20 gives 100 chips (what they recommended for each of my kids),

 plus $2 for processing the card. **Directions:** 120 Interchange

 Way, Vaughan. Take Hwy 400 North. Turn east on Rutherford, then south on Jane St. and west on Interchange.

LASER QUEST

Tag!

On our way back in the car from Laser Quest, my friend and I can't get a word in edgewise. Our three boys aged 7 to 9 are still beaming from their first experience with the laser game that even their mothers thoroughly enjoyed. Aerobic exercise has never been more fun!

Our little warriors are rehashing the game to its last detail, record sheet in hand. It lists who they tagged, who tagged them, how many shots they fired and how they ranked in the group of sixteen.

At the front desk, each player was invited to choose a nickname. Being a pacifist at heart, I went for "Positive". The kids chose (what else!) Pokemon names. On our second tour, the names get funnier. One of the fathers becomes "Save Me" and my friend, at other times a refined woman with excellent manners, picks the misleading name of "Tralala" and turns into an aggressive amazon ranking third at the end of the game.

In the science-fiction airlock where we put on our equipment, our ranger briefs us on the few rules and we enter the vast two-level maze of walls riddled with large holes. Except for splats of paint lit by black light, we're in the dark and the fog, with loud music matching the pounding of our hearts! I lose the kids in a flash and find them afterwards, teaming up against the adults, from the highest lookout in the room.

The laser beams reach as far as we want them to, amazingly bright and precise. Whenever one hits the flashing lights on our equipment, we are neutralized for 5 long seconds, preventing us from tagging our adversaries.

After 25 minutes of playing, our laser device indicates "Game over" and we follow the arrows on the floor to find our way out of the maze. Laser Quest is exactly what it claims to be: a 21st century combination of two old-fashioned games, tag and hide & seek.

TIPS (fun for 6 years +)

• You may call ahead to reserve. Most players play twice, but there should be half an hour between the two games. The kids will be red-faced and thirsty after the first one.

• We played solo (each on our own). Larger groups play in teams, in which case each team's equipment bears a different colour of lights, and players can't neutralize a player on their own team.

Laser Quest
www.laserquest.com

Schedule: In general, they are at least open Tuesday to Thursday, 5 to 9 pm, Friday, 5 to 11 pm, Saturday, noon to 11 pm, Sunday, noon to 6 pm. Many are open on Mondays and several have longer hours. Call to confirm.

Admission: $7.50/per game.

Directions:

Brampton: 241 Clarence St., (905) 456-9999 (H-8 on map).

Kitchener: 45 Walter St. South, (519) 579-9999 (D-1 on map).

London: 149 Carling St., (519) 660-6000 (off E-1 on map).

Mississauga: 1224 Dundas St. East, (905) 272-8000 (I-8 on map).

Richmond Hill: 9625 Yonge St., (905) 883-6000 (H-10 n map).

Toronto East: 1980 Eglinton Ave. East, (416) 285-1333 (I-11 on map).

PUTTING EDGE

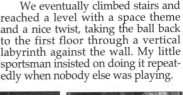

We eventually climbed stairs and reached a level with a space theme and a nice twist, taking the ball back to the first floor through a vertical labyrinth against the wall. My little sportsman insisted on doing it repeatedly when nobody else was playing.

They'll be glowing with joy!

Walking through the dark place is like being on the set of a children's production. Tall houses in funny shapes seem to lean over the players. Every detail covered with glow-in-the-dark paint contrasts with the darkness of all that wasn't painted. The greens are... black and we are golfing in the dark. Rocks are bright red and yellow. Trees are green and turquoise, with a whole forest glowing in the background.

On the first green, when one of my enthusiastic 7-year-old partners hit his ball and made it fly to the third hole (bouncing on its way off four different vertical props), I realized that watching over them would be quite a challenge!

As we left the forest, we entered an aquatic zone where a whole green takes the shape of a shark. The colour theme switched to blues and pinks. Fish shapes were cut out in the walls and schools of fish were painted on the murals. There was even a treasure glimmering in the middle of a green.

From the flowers painted on the ground and the psychedelic whale hanging from the ceiling to the fluorescent balls and clubs, the attention to detail made this outing a real success.

TIPS (fun for 6 years +)

• Each Putting Edge offers different murals and themes so it is fun visiting different ones.
• You don't have to pay if you just prefer to accompany your children, keeping an eye on them so they won't step into other people's games.
• A maximum of four players per group is permitted. It is suggested you allow faster groups to play through.
• The whole game took us forty minutes to play.

Putting Edge
www.puttingedge.com

Schedule: In general, they are at least open Monday to Thursday, 2 to 9 pm, Friday, noon to midnight, Saturday, 10 am to midnight, Sunday, 10 am to 8 pm. Some have longer hours.
Admission: $8.50/adults, $7.50/youth, $5/6 years and under ($7/person before 6 pm, except on Holidays).

Directions:
Barrie: 34 Commerce Park Dr., (705) 737-2229 (B-2 on map).
Brampton: 90 Courtneypark Dr. East, (905) 564-8808 (H-8 on map).
Burlington: 1250 Brant St., (905) 315-9155 (E-2 on map).
London: 149 Carling St., (519) 660-6000 (off E-1 on map).
Oakville: 2085 Winston Park Dr., (905) 829-4055 (I-7 on map).
Richmond Hill: 9625 Yonge St., (905) 508-8222 (H-10 on map).
St. Catharines: 221 Glendale Ave. at Hwy 406, (905) 685-3343 (E-3 on map).
Vaughan: 60 Interchange Way, (905) 761-3343 (H-10 on map).
Whitby: 75 Consumer Dr., Unit 4, (905) 430-3206 (C-4 on map).

BOWLERAMA

Little kingpin

Young hands drop the balls more often than they manage to throw them. The tiny bowler stamps his feet, jumps up and down and huddles with anticipation. Adults' mute prayers and crossed fingers change to cries of joy, as the ball miraculously knocks down one of the five pins! A young champion is born, amidst the excitement of Bowlerama.

The day we visited, our group consisted of seven adults, three preschoolers and two babies. It was our first family bowling experience. Excitement was in the air as pins and balls rolled down 60 shining lanes, knocking noisily against one

another. It's a challenge to have little busy bodies try on bowling shoes! The ones my little lad put on didn't close properly, while his friend's were simply too large. Not to worry, it didn't hold anyone back from the game.

We registered. Up to six players can play on one lane. After a somewhat chaotic first round, we finally understood the key procedures, and were better able to focus on our delighted kids. They understood the idea: with three balls, you try to knock down five pins.

Of course, many other aspects of the game will elude them, such as respecting the line between two alleys, not running after the ball, waiting their turn... etc. Besides, little kingpins are different from adults. It was great to see their faces as they watched their ball roll towards its goal. Will it hit... or not? Well, it's hard to miss when you're bumper bowling!

TIPS (fun for 5 years +)

• **Thorncliffe Bowlerama** doesn't belong to the same owners. The web site is about the other Bowleramas; print a $5 off coupon for these from the web. They all offer glow-in-the-dark bowling!

• When calling to reserve, mention you'll be bowling with children in order to get an alley lined with bumpers. Make sure you reserve a 5-pin lane, with the smaller balls.

• Accompany children to the washroom before registering, since bowling alleys are rented by the hour... If you play beyond your allotted time, you'll be charged an additional hour.

• As a souvenir, you can ask for a printout of your scores.

Bowlerama
www.bowlerama.com

 Schedule: Variable. Some are open 7 days a week, 24hrs a day. Call to confirm

 Admission: On average, $20-$22/per lane, per hour ($1/children and $3/adults for shoe rental). Bowling shoes are mandatory.

Directions:

 Bowlerama Newtonbrook: 5837 Yonge St. North, North York, (416) 222-4657 (H-10).

 Bowlerama Rexdale: 115 Rexdale Blvd., Etobicoke, (416) 743-8388 (H-9 on map).

Bowlerama West: 5429 Dundas West, Etobicoke, (416) 239-3536 (I-9).

Thorncliffe Bowlerama: 45 Overlea Blvd., East York, (416) 421-2211 (I-10).

CENTREVILLE AMUSEMENT PARK

Old fashioned way

Did you know that an amusement park existed in 1800 at the very same place today's Toronto Island Airport sits?

Maybe it's not by chance that Centreville has the charm of a turn-of-the-century village. It is a small-scale amusement park. With its 24 small rides, Centreville is perfect for young families!

Our small group really loved the beautiful carousel, a feast for the eyes! It includes ostriches, zebras, lions, pigs, cats, giraffes, as well as the traditional horses. The animals are laid out in three rows and turn rapidly as they go up and down to the sound of lively music.

The little ones are fascinated by the train that rides through a long tunnel, by the antique cars set on tracks which they drive "themselves" and by the Swan Ride on the pond. They're also pretty excited by the Bumble Bee Ride at the entrance.

Older children appreciate the bumper boats and cars, the Lake Monster Coaster and the train of the Haunted Barrel ride.

Those who like heights will want to try the Sky Ride cable-car or the Ferris wheel. Don't hesitate to try the Saugeen Lumber Co. Log Flume Ride, even with the smaller kamikazes.

A small farm and a lovely wading pool are found on site. Don't forget the bathing suits!

TIPS (fun for 2 years +)

• More on **Toronto Ferry** terminal and **Toronto Islands** on p. 268.
• A reader wrote to me with a good tip! If you arrive at opening time and there's a line-up at the entrance, don't buy your tickets there. Enter the park (there's no admission fee), there are more ticket booths inside with no line-up.
• Most people eat in the park outside Centreville Amusement Park's walls. It has picnic tables, a playground and... numerous geese.
• **Westin Harbour Castle** usually offers a Family Fun Package with Centreville Amusement Park. Call (416) 869-1600.
• There are snack bars inside the amusement park.

NEARBY ATTRACTIONS
Ward's Beach (15-min. walk).......p. 269

Centreville Amusement Park (416) 203-0405 www.centreisland.ca	J-10 Toronto Islands 15-min.

Schedule: Open weekends in May and September and daily from Victoria Day to Labour Day, weather permitting. Open from 10:30 am to 8 pm during July and August. Closes between 5 pm and 7 pm the rest of the season.

Admission: The All-Day-Ride Pass is $16.50 for visitors 48" and under, and $23 for others. $72/family of 4.Tickets for each ride can be bought individually.

Directions: Directly accessible by Centreville Ferry line, then a 10-min. walk from Centre Island dock.

THE CNE... AND BEYOND

Midway stop

With the large rides located close to the Princes' Gate, and the younger children's section, the Kids' Midway, located on the site's opposite side by Dufferin Gates, CNE is indeed a children's paradise!

There is a great variety of rides at the Kids' Midway: a merry-go-round, a Ferris wheel, a small and medium-sized roller coaster, the bumble bee, flying helicopter and planes, jeep and construction trucks that went round and round, tossing submarines, shaking strawberries and more. Most of these rides are for children 42 inches or less. In this area, there are also games of dexterity for an additional cost, where children are guaranteed a prize. That's all they ask for!

The **midway** closer to the Princes' Gate is more interesting for kids 8 years and up. Most require a minimum height of 42 to 48 inches.

Activities at Kids' World, located by the Kids' Midway, are of another kind, but equally entertaining. Among them, a great petting zoo and elephant

rides. Don't miss the original Backyard Circus Show, very interactive for young children. When we visited, it ended with a parade of huge puppets held by the parents themselves!

It usually features the booth from

Science North, packed with widgets to touch and experiments to observe and Junk Joint (a place where you can create original objects made from recycled material).

To this, add the Super Dogs performances, a big favourite, where dogs compete on an obstacle course.

The Farm exhibits in the Automotive Building feature more animals and antique farm equipment. In the Children's Area, they have daily demonstrations such as goat milking, rope making or sheep shearing.

There's more action in the National Trade Building (closer to Strachan Avenue). Hall B features an International Stage on which are presented over 150 performances throughout the CNE. Heritage Court is the place to check out flowers and vegetables entered in a competition.

Every night during the CNE, huge **fireworks** lasting over 10 minutes start at 10:30 pm (9:30 pm on Labour Day Monday).

You can also watch the **Air Show** (which always takes place on the Labour Day weekend) from the grounds of **Exhibition Place**.

Also at Exhibition Place

More events take place at **Exhibition Place** throughout the year. Everyone knows about the **Medieval Times** show mixing dinner with chivalry (see p. 398).

Every **Halloween** brings back **Screemers**. It consists of six different attractions plus rides (probably indoor rides starting this year). Expect extreme rides, a haunted house and a haunted castle with monsters in every corner, a 3-D maze, a black hole, a maniac maze and an executioner theatre... You get the idea! When I visited it a few years ago, they had activities for young children. Not anymore, this event is strictly for visitors 10 years and over.

The same people who are responsible for **Screemers** have created a new **March Break** event for the whole family called **Wizard World**. This one is intended for children 2 to 12 years old. Expect a magical Wizard's Castle, a 3-D maze with dragons, fairies and dwarves, crafts and interactive play area, mechanical rides and inflated bouncing structures. There's also a laser tag game, magic shows, reptile show and more.

The **CHIN Picnic** returns every year. Organized by the multicultural radio broadcaster, this free event includes non-stop multicultural community shows, rides, circus, petting zoo, World food kiosks and Bazaar booths.

TIPS (fun for 2 years +)

• It could cost you approximately $17 to park your car on the **Exhibition Place** site during main events. Try neighbourhood parking on Fleet Street, east of Strachan Avenue.
• During the **CNE**, express shuttles transport you free of charge across the site. Take advantage of this service as it easily takes 20 minutes to walk from one side to the other.
• Instead of buying **CNE** Magic Passes for the whole family, you can purchase a magnetic ride pass and pay for a specific number of "ride units". You can get more than one card sharing the same "rides credit" so your family can split, each group with its own card. Each time you swipe your card before entering a ride, the machine tells you what's left in your shared account.

NEARBY ATTRACTIONS

Canadian National Exhibition (CNE) (416) 263-3800 www.theex.com	J-10 Downtown Toronto 10-min.

Schedule: Open for 18 consecutive days ending on Labour Day Monday, 10 am to 10 pm. The big midway closes at midnight. The Kids' World activities close at 8 pm but rides remain open as long as there are customers. (CNE 2004: August 20 to September 6.)
Admission: Fun Pass (admission only) is $10, or $7 if bought in advance. Magic Pass (admission and unlimited rides) is $35, or $25 if bought in advance. Call or check the web site to find out where to buy advance tickets, sold until the day before the CNE.
Directions: Exhibition Place, Toronto. Take Lake Shore Blvd. and turn north on Strachan Ave. Princes' Gate entrance is on the west side.

CHIN Picnic
(416) 531-9991
www.chinradio.com
Schedule: Usually from Thursday to Sunday around Canada Day.
Admission: FREE (extra cost for rides).
Directions: Around the Bandshell Park, in the south-west part of Exhibition Place.

Wizard World
(416) 585-9263
www.wizardworld.ca
Schedule: On weekends before and after the March Break and on March Break weekdays, 10 am to 6 pm.
Admission: $17/person for unlimited access to the activities and the rides.
Directions: In the Better Living Centre by Ontario Dr. at Exhibition Place.

Screemers
(416) 979-3327
www.screemers.ca
Schedule: Open for 13 consecutive nights ending October 31, 7 to 11 pm (closes at midnight of Friday and Saturday).
Admission: $25/person, including one ticket for each of the six attractions plus unlimited rides. Print $5 off coupon from their web site.
Directions: In the Horticultural Building by Saskatchewan Rd. at Exhibition Place.

FANTASY FAIR

Courtesy of K.McCutcheon

Footloose at the Fair

On the verge of panic, I alerted the Woodbine Centre security guards. I was searching for my young fugitive, lost in Fantasy Fair. I eventually saw him as he was getting expelled from the little train he had illegally hopped on without a passport bracelet on his wrist.

The 200-shop **Woodbine Centre** includes two storeys linked by several escalators. It is connected to a huge parking area by large, easily opened doors so I recommend being extra careful if you go there on a busy day. Having said this, the place is very pleasant.

Thanks to skylights and bay windows, Fantasy Fair is bathed in natural light. The fair offers nine rides and a giant play area, over three storeys high. It does-

n't sound like much, but it is plenty for children 8 years and under.

Among other things, there's a magnificent antique carousel, bumper boats (max. 54"), red and white airplanes that give young pilots a surprisingly realistic feeling (36" to 54"), Ship's Ahoy spinning ride and Spinners (min. 36" and under 54" must be accompanied).

The train running through the park is a youngster's favourite attraction. Avoid the Ferris wheel if the waiting line is long (the ride is slow).

The bumper car ride is for drivers min. 54" and passengers min. 36".

Last time we visited, the play structure could already hold kids' attention for more than an hour. Since, they've rebuilt it. It is 5,500 sq. ft. with purple climber, observation ball over 30 feet in the air, touch and play music floor and High Ballocity, a dynamic section with interactive foam shooters!

It includes a Toddler Zone for kids under four.

TIPS (fun for 2 years +)
- See **Woodbine Centre** on page 188.
- The carousel admission is FREE for accompanying adults.
- On busy days, bring snacks to pass the time while waiting, instead of planning a sit-down meal. The wait for each ride can be as long as 20 minutes. (A reader told me there were no line-ups on a PA day in December!)
- There's a **McDonald's** on site and a **Rainbow movie theatre** in the lower level of the mall, (416) 213-1998, www.rainbowcinemas.ca

---

NEARBY ATTRACTIONS

Fantasy Fair
(416) 674-5437
www.fantasyfair.ca

H-9
N-W
of downtown
30-min.

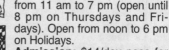

Schedule: Open year-round, from 11 am to 7 pm (open until 8 pm on Thursdays and Fridays). Open from noon to 6 pm on Holidays.

Admission: $14/day pass for child 36" to 54", $12/day pass for visitor over 54" or under 36", $45/pass for a family of 4, $25/30 tickets.

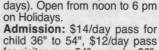

Directions: Woodbine Centre, Toronto. Take Hwy 427 North, exit at Rexdale Ave. East, turn left on Queen's Place Dr. At Woodbine Centre, park between The Bay and Sears.

THE BIG APPLE

Have a bite!

While I'm busy taking a picture of my children having fun at the Big Apple playground, I feel something applying gentle pressure on my feet. Looking down, I discover a cute bunny chewing calmly on my straw handbag!

The Big Apple, located on the south side of Highway 401, is worth the stop when driving in the corridor between Montreal and Toronto.

The apple dessert counter inside the major building will make your mouth water: cookies, muffins, tarts, dumplings, buns... Large windows allow visitors to look inside the kitchen, where the bakers are in action all dressed in white. The outdoor playground is fun and the bunny rabbits are adorable. If you look closely, you can see more than a dozen of them roaming freely on the site.

The Big Apple, well, is big! It stands more than 10 metres high and you can climb to the top from inside, while viewing a few apple-theme displays.

Children want to reach the tiny bal-cony located at the top of the apple. The scenery offers nothing outstanding, but you can see far away.

You may rent clubs in the gift shop to play in the new and much improved miniature golf or get a ride in the small train for a small fee.

Small dens are inhabited by deer, sheep and llamas. They can be fed with grains from vending machines. Behind them, you will find a few small trails, one of them pretty with wild flowers. Perfect to stretch small legs before continuing your journey.

TIPS (fun for 2 years +)

• Think of bringing baby carrots so children can enjoy offering a real treat to the rabbits.

• The big gift shop is filled with Canadian souvenirs and trinkets.

• You can have a meal in the huge fast-food restaurant but the tasty apple desserts and snacks are the main reason to stop at the Big Apple.

The Big Apple
• Colborne
(905) 355-2574

C-6
East
of Toronto
90-min.

 Schedule: Open year-round, 7:30 am to 7 pm (closes at 9 pm from April 1 to October 31).

Admission: FREE.

 Directions: Big Apple Dr., Colborne. From Hwy 401 East, take exit #497 southbound, then turn west on Big Apple Dr.

SANTA'S VILLAGE

Santa in short sleeves

The beard and smile are authentic. Mrs. Claus stands close by. Holiday melodies accompany birds singing. Reindeer rest in their pen. Children are having their picture taken in a sleigh. Others are sucking on candy canes while waiting to sit on the friendly old man's lap.

When summer arrives, Santa trades in his heavy suit for a red vest and short-sleeved shirt. Cooled off by a few fans, he greets children in his village in Bracebridge, in the Muskoka region.

The roller coaster hidden behind the trees by the entrance was the most exciting ride for young thrill-seekers and myself. Rudolph adorns its front car. The coaster goes around the track twice only (which allows children who don't enjoy the ride to get off quickly but disappoints the others). You might want to save this ride for last.

I suggest you start by feeding the deer inside their pen and then hop on the small train circling the Village. It gives a good overview of the activities on the site.

Santa awaits the kids inside his cottage, along with Mrs. Claus (children can hop on her lap too). It's time to take out the camera, if the white beard doesn't scare your little elves! All children get a notepad from Santa. You can purchase a picture if you don't have your camera.

A path leads to the ride area. All the rides are included in the one-day pass. Enjoy the Ferris wheel with cabins shaped like Christmas tree decorations, a carousel, small planes, pedal boats and floating swans. Don't miss the ride on the big boat.

This area also offers the Jumpin' Star ride. It gives a great view of the village from up high before it drops. Any child accompanied by an adult can try it.

Later, you can go to Elves Island, the playground area linked to Santa's Village by a narrow strip of land. An enormous array of nets allows kids to climb way up high. Behind the nets, an ingenious labyrinth made out of nets and tubes presents a challenge to little adventurers. In fact, it can bewilder a child of 3 years or less. I had to rescue my little one who was walking behind her brother and lost his tracks.

There's an inflated, bouncing chamber shaped like Santa's head.

To calm down, you can visit the farm or see a musical show for children by the deer pen.

Before leaving, we had an ice cream by the exit. To top it all off, we went to the gift shop to choose a little toy. The shop is surprisingly large and it offers a tremendous amount of trinkets priced at $5 on average. You can easily spend half an hour there to check everything out. Indeed, Santa does things well!

Courtesy of K.McCutcheon

Courtesy of Santa's Village

Water games

Kids can hop from the wading pool topped with giant candy canes spraying water to the spray pad with spraying rings.

Sportsland

Sportsland is beside Santa's Village and is managed by the same organization. It is an area designed with older kids in mind. The place has less character than the village, but is well adapted to its clientele. Expect noisy video games, a laser tag room, a go-kart track, another track for in-line skating, a miniature golf course and a batting cage.

My pre-preteen tremendously enjoyed a go-kart ride along with his Dad (no minimum height for the passenger). Two laser-gun fights helped reinforce their male bonding even more.

TIPS (fun for 2 years +)

• I know Santa's Village is far from Toronto, but it's so well designed that I never regretted driving back and forth on the same day. To create excitement, ask your little copilots to watch for Santa signs lining the road. Don't worry about the way back. They'll have played so hard all day they'll be sleeping like logs in no time.

• The Village itself is fun for children 8 years and under. Sportsworld is fine for kids 5 years and over.

• You can print a $2 off coupon from Santa's Village web site (not valid from mid-July to mid-August).

• Even during busy weekends, there's hardly a 10-minute wait for attractions. On weekdays, you rarely wait!

• If it's not windy, bring insect repellent. The Muskoka region is paradise for mosquitoes!

• The **Whispering Pines Campground** is located across the road from the Village. It usually offers an attractive package (including 2 nights camping and 2 days family admission to Santa's Village) for approx. $125. You can reach the campground at (705) 645-5682, www.muskokacamping.com.

• There are many snack bars on the premises.

NEARBY ATTRACTIONS
High Falls (20-min.).....................p. 305

Santa's Village & Sportsland
· Bracebridge
(705) 645-2512
www.santasvillage.on.ca

A-3
North
of Toronto
2 1/4 hrs

  Schedule: Open daily mid-June to Labour Day, plus the following weekend, from 10 am to 6 pm. Sportsland closes at 9 pm (except on Sundays when it closes at 6 pm).

Admission: (taxes not included) The Village: $19/5 years and up, $14/ children 2 to 4 years old and seniors, FREE for children under 2. Sportsland is a pay-as-you-play zone (pay half price from 7:30 pm to closing on weeknights).

Directions: Take Hwy 400 North, continue on Hwy 11. Take exit #4 (Muskoka Rd./Hwy 118). Turn left on Santa's Village Rd., at the first light after the bridge in Bracebridge.

STORYBOOK GARDENS

The whole story

Millions have been injected into the place. Ambitious new playgrounds, gorgeous spray pad, different characters, more vegetation. Add a new path which turns into an ice skating trail in the winter and you get a clue to another major change: the attraction is now open year-round.

For more than 40 years now, the StoryBook Gardens have been one of London's feature attractions. With a collection of farm and exotic animals, living in cages and paddocks, it could almost qualify as a small zoo but as its name indicates, its primary mission is to display within gardens, various decorative sets inspired by children's fairy tales.

A Cheshire Cat greeted us at the entrance, smiling through a screen of smoke coming from a well. Humpty Dumpty awaited us to our left. To our right, we entered through the mouth of a large whale to see the treasure she had swallowed.

Many animals were missing when we visited, due to the renovations. It gave us more time to admire the seven sea lions playing in the large pool. We got pretty close to them so we could enjoy their frolics.

A bit farther, two otters were swimming to and fro their small pond.

Deeper into the park, the kids tried the small climbing walls but the immense red spider web was even more challenging. It connected three poles, each offering anchorage for children to climb up. Don't try this barefoot!

There was a 3-storey-high slide, a large wooden structure and an impressive pirate ship, a treehouse and a maze.

After all that playing, the Slippery's Great Escape was most welcome: a large colourful spray pad with water cannons, bucket dumps and sprays of all sorts. Kids all ages had a blast.

TIPS (fun for 2 years +)

• There eventually will be a special birthday party area in StoryBook Gardens. Call to find out when it is available.

• You can catch the **bicycle trail** bordering the Thames River directly from StoryBook Gardens' parking lot. It runs amidst pretty scenery and will lead you to the University in 12 km.

• Within half an hour walk to your right on that trail, you'll find a lovely café under the trees by the water.

• In the winter, the refrigerated path can hold ice for a fun skating experience through the gardens, weather permitting. Animal exhibits are open. During the **March Break**, expect crafts, small shows and roller skating (if the ice has melted).

• Check **www.londontourism.ca** for their section <u>Where to stay</u>. We took advantage of the **Hilton**'s family package to spend one night in the area. It allowed us to wind down completely. What a perfect little getaway!

• The **Fanshawe Conservation Area** on the eastern edge of London includes a campground. Call 1-866-668-2267.

• The attraction's snack bars are conveniently located by the water games.

• The cute restaurants and cafés in London are found along Richmond Street by Victoria Park in London.

• You could combine your outing with a visit to the new local water park **Wally World** (equipment from the old Wally was relocated) in East Park, east of Highbury Avenue, on Hamilton Road. Admission cost is reduced after 4 pm. For information, call (519) 451-2950, www.eastparkgolf.com. East Park also includes go-karts, batting, 36 holes of mini-golf, indoor rock climbing, bumper cars and a kids' jungle gym.

• The **London Balloon Festival** (the largest hot air balloon festival in English Canada) always takes place during the Simcoe Day weekend in Harris Park, check www.londonballoonfestival.com.

• Victoria Park, downtown London, hosts two free musical events: **Sunfest**, a four-day festival usually held around the second weekend in July (call to confirm); and the **Fiesta del Sol**, always on Labour Day weekend; check www.sunfest.on.ca or call (519) 672-1522.

After they'd cooled down, we watched a little show put together by the young staff, a (free and funny) interactive adaptation of *Hansel & Gretel.*

Kids always like to watch the large carp and ducks from the covered bridge overlooking the pond. The renovations continue. This pond is being rejuvenated. I predict it will become the cutest little nook.

The thin strip of forest up the hill, where deer used to live, will be turned into an Enchanted Forest. Can't wait!

Outside of the attraction's gate, a miniature steam train with its railroad track stretching over one kilometre, adds to the fun. So does the carousel by the water.

NEARBY ATTRACTIONS

StoryBook Gardens	E-1
· London	S-W
(519) 661-5770	of Toronto
www.storybook.london.ca	2 1/2 hrs

 Schedule: Now open year-round! From May 1st to Thanksgiving, open from 10 am to 8 pm (closes at 4 pm the rest of the year).

 Admission: $8.25/adults, $5.75/11-17 years, $5.25/5-10 years, $2.50/2-4 years, FREE under 2. Train or carousel ride is $1.25. From mid-October to April 30, only $8.25 per family.

 Directions: Take Hwy 401 West, exit # 183 to Hwy 402 westbound. Turn north at Colonel Talbot Rd. Stay on that road until it ends at the entrance to Springbank Park. StoryBook is in the park.

Ontario Place

Watch out!

Here, children armed to the teeth, show no mercy and obey no law. Instinctively, they know how to choose their victims in order to derive maximum enjoyment from their hunt. Their favourite target: grownups.

In the back of Ontario Place awaits Waterplay, designed for children aged 12 and under (measuring less than 60 inches). Think you'll stay dry while accompanying a child to this spray-pad? Guess again! A gush from one of the water guns bound to the main fortress nearly yanked my camera from my hands (it was a disposable, luckily!).

Waterplay seems like a large miniature golf course, except that the blue of the various small basins full of water replaces the green. The site is well adapted for young children due to its shallow depth. It's also very entertaining for older kids, thanks to its numerous activities.

TIPS (fun for 1 year +)

• More on **Ontario Place** on page 12.
• Accompanying adults only need ground admission to be with their children. If you wish, a park admission can be upgraded to a Play All Day Pass at many booths throughout the site.
• You can rent a locker for a loonie in the water park.
• Eating is forbidden in the waterplay area. Those exiting the area can get their hand stamped and return after eating. The snack bar by the lake offers a few tables with a view under the shade of umbrellas.

Children cross a suspension bridge, climb on ropes or go from one basin to the other via tunnels (parents must sprint into the water to pick up their explorer on the other side). Kids also pass under a cascade before throwing themselves into one of two waterslides.

Little ones can hop on a swing in the water, while their older counterparts pump water into water guns by pedalling on a bicycle. Older kids will go for more intense water games such as the Rush River Raft Ride, which spans 873 feet (42"+), or the Pink Twister (48"+) and the Purple Pipeline waterslides (42"+), plunging them into the darkness with their enclosed flumes.

There is also the 50 kph ride down a gigantic bowl in Hydrofuge (48"+), ending with a 12-foot drop into the water.

I passed on that one!

Ontario Place (416) 314-9900 www.ontarioplace.com	**J-10** **Downtown** **Toronto** **10-min.**

Consult **Ontario Place** information box on p. 13 for schedule, costs, directions and nearby attractions.

WILD WATER KINGDOM

Wild indeed!

Waist-deep in water, hordes of swimmers dance away with the encouragement of a DJ and his music. My 6-year-old can't resist the invitation and jumps in (chest-deep), dancing the Macarena with his newfound friends. There is no lack of ambience at Wild Water Kingdom's Caribbean Cove pool!

Wild Water Kingdom, Canada's largest water park, may actually include less slides than the water games section of Canada's Wonderland amusement park, but it is half the price. If you plan to play in the water all day, this is certainly your best bet, especially with children 48" and over!

Since our last visit, they have added the Wild Water Wall, an exciting 25-foot rock-climbing wall... where you get soaked. They've also put up the Spacewalker in which you evolve, strapped in, 25 feet above the ground.

In addition, thirteen body and tube slides, two 7-storey speed slides along with a wave pool, a lazy river and the entertaining pool, are enough to satisfy the legions of teenagers invading the site daily. All slides have a 48" minimum height requirement, except the Cork Screw, Side Winder and Little Twister, which are accessible to children from 42" in height.

Younger children will thoroughly enjoy the large Dolphin Bay water playground. It offers beach-like access, small water slides passing through a mushroom, a fish and a frog, a splashing structure with sprays and a tube slide plus wading spots link it all. Then there's the Big Tipper with large buckets emptying tons of water over the willing visitors.

Next to the water park are pay-as-you-play activities: a mini-golf course, batting cages, bumper boats and volleyball courts.

TIPS (fun for 2+ years)

• Managed by Toronto Region Conservation Authority, **Indian Line Campground** offers 240 sites and is located along the Claireville Reservoir, right next to the water park. Call 1-800-304-9728 or check www.trca.on.ca.

• No coolers are allowed on the site (exception is made for parents with babies). We had to take our cooler back to our car. You will find on-site lockers, snack bars and a shop.

NEARBY ATTRACTIONS

Wild Water Kingdom | H-8 N-W of Toronto 40-min.
• Brampton
(416) 369-9453
www.wildwaterkingdom.com

 Schedule: Weather permitting, opens early June to Labour Day, from 10 am to 6 pm (closes at 8 pm from end of June to end of August).

 Admission: $25.50/10 years and up, $19/seniors and children under 10, $15/after 4 pm, FREE 3 years and under. Parking is around $6.

 Directions: 7855 Finch Ave., Brampton. Take Hwy 427 North, turn west on Finch Ave., follow the signs.

CANADA'S WONDERLAND

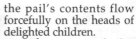

Splash!

It was not with a light heart that I watched my assertive little boy drag his huge tire for the first time, way up to the launching board of the Whirl Winds. He was so thrilled with his ride that he could not wait to get back in line to do it again! If your child is tall enough and already shows some dare-devil inclinations at the local pool, you might want to let her try it too.

Splash Works includes 16 water slides, some of which are 8 storeys tall. They all require a minimum height of 48", except for the Whirl Winds in which adventurers measuring 40" or more slide solo on a large tire.

The Barracuda Blaster ends up with a twist around the vertical walls of a giant bowl before being flushed into the Lazy River.

All the kids like the Pumphouse located at the heart of Splash Works. It features a large coloured structure full of surprising water sprays. It is topped by a gigantic pail that gradually fills up with 3,500 litres of water. Every five minutes,

the pail's contents flow forcefully on the heads of delighted children.

The water park also boasts a wide and long Lazy River (36"+) on which an adult and child can float on the same tire and a large wave pool (36"+) equipped with lounge chairs.

For the little ones, there's an entertaining wading pool and mini water slides.

TIPS (fun for 3 years +)
- More on **Canada's Wonderland** on page 14.
- Children's life jackets are available for free. Lockers, beach shop and snack bar are found within the water park as well.

Paramount Canada's Wonderland
• Vaughan
(905) 832-7000
www.canadaswonderland.com

G-10
North
of Toronto
40-min.

Splash Works is open on weekends beginning end of May, and daily from end of June to Labour Day, from 11 am to 8 pm (closes at 7 pm after mid-August. Consult Canada's Wonderland information box on p.15 for schedule, costs, directions and nearby attractions.

CEDAR PARK RESORT

Refreshing complement

Being the only place with water games in the Bowmanville area, Cedar Park is a great complement to a visit to one of the local attractions, for a full-day outing in the region.

My 7-year-old and his older cousin spent most of the visit between the three giant waterslides (48"+) and a good playground on a large patch of sand in the vicinity.

I followed my little one in the pretty wading pool and on the small water slides. I even dared accompany her in the cold water of the shallow section of their huge pool.

We eventually rejoined the whole party to eat a hot dog and a slush. We would have tried the mini-golf had we not planned to visit a zoo in the neighbourhood.

At the time of print, I was told the kids' water play section would be expanded. Even better!

TIPS (fun for 2 years +)

• The pool's regulations are strict! In order for young swimmers to be allowed in the bigger part of the pool, they have to line up for a test requiring them to swim across the width of the pool and back (and it is a big one!). When I realized that, it was too late, they were in line to do the test. My two big guys could not do it at the time and they really suffered the "humiliation" of failing the test, with tears in their eyes and all. Had I known...

• The water park is attached to a trailer park.

NEARBY ATTRACTIONS
Bowmanville Zoo (10-min.)............p. 52
Jungle Cat World (15-min.)............p. 53

Cedar Park Resort
· Hampton
(905) 263-8109

C-4
East
of Toronto
60-min.

 Schedule: Open 7 days, mid-June to Labour Day, 10 am to 7 pm.

 Admission: (cash only) Ground admission and pool access is $5.50/adults, $4/3-12 years, FREE 2 and under. Mini-golf is an extra $4, water slides are an extra $6.50 per visitor.

Directions: 6296 Cedar Park Rd., Bowmanville. From Hwy 401 East, take exit #431/Regional Rd. 57 northbound. Turn east on 6th Concession, then north on Cedar Park Rd.

Also check **Beaches** in the **NATURE'S CALL** chapter (pp. 267-289) as well as **Spray pads** (pp. 380-381) and **Swimming** (pp. 382-385) in the **SPORTS** chapter.

WILD WATERWORKS

The large pool for very young bathers is quite fun with its unusual shape framed by stairs. The water temperature is comfortably lukewarm and doesn't go higher than the knees.

It is full of small fountains that squirt intermittently and little roofs streaming with water.

Go out with a splash!

You can observe children in almost all directions from the comfortable green turf by the wave pool which sits in the heart of the action.

From the bounty of water activities offered and the new huge slides accessible to children of all ages, to the immense wave pool, you will find Wild Waterworks leaves nothing to be desired.

The Lazy River (a sinuous water path on which you can flow down atop an inner tube), is the only one I know of that comes equipped with side showers, fountains and nooks and crannies. My son and his father chose a double ring to float on and bump me!

The two Demon Slides are some six storeys high, much to the delight of swimmers minimum 48" tall. I tried them both and found them surprisingly smooth, a little like a gentle toboggan ride.

There are new giant tubeslides offering a 480-foot-long drop (in solo or with a friend) with no minimum height requirement.

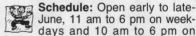

TIPS (fun for 2 years +)

• We visited on a warm but cloudy Saturday afternoon and found the place enjoyably quiet. We never waited more than 5 minutes for a ride on the slides.
• A suggestion for parents with younger non-swimmers wishing to try a large slide. Go down first so that you can assist them when they reach the bottom. There is always a lifeguard on duty.
• There is a colourful playground within **Confederation Park**.
• There is a **campground** in **Confederation Park**. Call (905) 578-1644 for information.
• There are two snack bars on site. We found a shady spot by the large boulders and trees separating the kiddie section from the wave pool area.

Wild Waterworks	E-2
• Hamilton 1-800-555-8775 or (905) 561-2292 www. conservationhamilton.ca	S-W of Toronto 50-min.

Schedule: Open early to late-June, 11 am to 6 pm on weekdays and 10 am to 6 pm on weekends. From end of June until mid-August, open 7 days from 10 am to 8 pm. Open mid-August to Labour Day (weather permitting), 10 am to 6 pm.
Admission: $13.75/adults, $8.75/seniors and 4-10 years, FREE 3 years and under, $7.25/visitor after 4 pm. Vehicle entrance to Confederation Park is $6.75. There is an extra fee to rent an inflatable tube to play in the wave pool.
Directions : From QEW West, take exit #88/Centennial Pkwy.-Hwy 20. Turn north towards the Lake, follow signs to Confederation Park.

NEARBY ATTRACTIONS
Steam Museum (10-min.)..............p. 243
Children's Museum (10-min.)....... p. 259

EMERALD LAKE

A little gem!

This natural setting is utterly unique in the region. This is your chance to swim in the pristine green water of a spring-fed lake. This is your kids' opportunity to jump off a diving board into a real lake. This is definitely a great reason to escape the city.

The lakeshore is not the usual beach created around a reservoir like in most conservation areas. It consists of natural rock plates descending into the water like some man-made stairs. The water doesn't have the usual muddy texture of the small lakes with sandy bottoms. This one sits on pale bedrock, hence the nice emerald shade.

Emerald Lake is a trailer resort and water park doing its job to entertain the customers with: a 200-foot water slide with small receiving pool (48"+), a large kids pool with deck and water sprays, many volleyball courts, paddle boat and kayak rentals. Nothing too fancy.

But when I swam in the farthest part of the pollution-free lake, enclosed by overhanging boughs of trees, it felt like Eden...

From the water, I had a great spot to observe the daredevils, my 8-year-old included, jumping from the board off the small cliff.

Later on, we rented a paddle boat and explored another section of the small lake with weeds and... big snails! My kids enjoyed jumping from the paddle-boat and were glad to rest on it for a while.

This year, the management is adding a 3,400 sq ft splash pad between the slide and the pool. The rock plates on the lake's shore don't offer a gradual entrance into the water and they are slippery. I found that section stressful for parents of toddlers. The new spray pad is solving this problem. Toddlers will be more than happy to stick to the water games area. Good old-fashioned fun!

TIPS (fun for 2 years +)

• The water is a bit cool. It's spring-fed, remember?

• We visited on a weekday in August and it was not too crowded but judging from their promotional flyers, it can get quite busy during the hottest weekends.

• The trailer resort also includes family **campsites** for tents. Call them to reserve one month in advance if you want to get a space during a long weekend.

• There's a snack bar on site. There are some BBQ pits throughout the park, (bring your own charcoal).

NEARBY ATTRACTIONS

Emerald Lake
· Puslinch
1-800-679-1853
(905) 659-7923
www.emerald-lake.com

E-2
West
of Toronto
60-min.

 Schedule: Open on Victoria Day weekend and then from June 1st to Labour Day, 10 am to 8 pm.

 Admission: $9/adults, $7/5-12 years ($1 less on weekdays, seniors always pay $5).

Directions: Gore Rd., R.R. #2, Puslinch. From Hwy 401 West, take exit #299/Hwy 6 South. Turn west (right) West Flamborough Concesion 11, go up approx. 5 km, the lake is on your right hand side.

WILD WATER & WHEELS

one 210-foot-long double spiral flume (min. 42") and there's no pool to cool down for those who don't use the slides.

Still, the bumper boat ride (min. 48") was the longest we had ever done; so was the ride on the merry-go-round. The mini-golf is large and adorned with life-sized jungle animals. The giant carpet slide, 145 feet long and 35 feet high, with five huge bumps, was equally fun for the whole family.

We stayed away from the seven batting cages and did not get to try the go-kart circuit.

The real surprise was the Pipeline Express Coaster! It is a metal toboggan rolling on tracks on a structure five storeys high and 850 feet long. The view from the top is amazing... and the drop at the beginning of the ride is breathtaking!

Curious?

The sign for Wild Water & Wheels teased me every time I drove on Hwy 401 around Bowmanville, so I just had to go and check it out with the kids. Good news: it is worth advertising! Bad news (if, like me, you think an attraction should not be too far from the sign advertising it on the highway): you'll have to drive an additional 45 minutes to get there.

Wild Water & Wheels is a collection of entertaining activities oddly juxtaposed, but each activity taken individually was thoroughly enjoyed by my little inspectors and myself.

This is more of an amusement park than a water park per say as it offers only

TIPS (fun for 4 years +)
• I would not drive almost two hours only to visit this attraction, but it is well worth adding to your itinerary if you are visiting the Peterborough area.
• My 3-year-old trooper rode with me on the Pipeline Express. She even went back with her brother but I am still not sure I would recommend it for kids younger than 4 years old.
• The snack bar is air-conditioned. I insisted we make a stop there every 45 minutes in order to cool down my red-faced kids.

NEARBY ATTRACTIONS
Riverview Park & Zoo (15-min.).....p. 65

Wild Water & Wheels • Peterborough (705) 876-9292 (seasonal)	B-5 N-E of Toronto 2 hrs

Schedule: Open beginning of April until last Sunday in September, 10 am to 9 pm (end of June to Labour Day) and at least from 12 noon to 6 pm before that.

Admission: Approximately $6 for each ride and $15 for the water slides. Ask for their Summer Value Pack.

Directions: Chemong Rd., Peterborough. From Hwy 401 East, take exit #436 (Hwy 35/115) northbound. Follow Hwy 115 to Hwy 28 northbound. At Fowlers Corners, turn eastbound (right), then right again on Chemong.

SPORTSWORLD

In the swim

Sportsworld's water park in itself is nice enough to justify a visit. Good news is that it comes with a whole amusement park!

I found the two-level kiddies' water section, located near the wave pool, to be original. There were stepping rocks, net tunnels and swinging tires and a palm tree to top it off. They've added a bucket dump and sprinklers since my last visit.

The wave pool was definitely a hit with my 8-year-old companions. From my position by the pool, I would see their heads bobbing in and out of view. Part of the fun was to jump as the waves headed towards them, stabalizing each other by holding hands.

The three middle slides of the Flash Flood Waterslides finish off steeply but I noticed the ones to the far ends offered a smoother entrance into the water. For all five of these slides, kids have to be able to swim in the 4-foot-deep catch pool.

In the Waikiki Express Maui (46" +), you slide down on a double raft tube. I personally prefer slides with tubes. Sliding without a tube can sometimes hurt, not that I ever heard a child complain!

I was absolutely NOT tempted by the 12-foot fall down the Deep Dive tube-slide, but my young kamikaze declared it absolutely… safe (I can't wait to see what he'll do when he's a teenager!).

Sportsworld
· Kitchener
1-800-393-9163
or (519) 653-4442
www.sportsworld.on.ca

**D-1
West
of Toronto
75 min.**

Consult Sportsworld information box on p. 16 for schedule, costs, directions and nearby attractions.

General tips about
Animals:

- A great free outing to do with kids is a visit to a big box pet store. Don't underestimate these! Some are amazing, with rabbits, snakes, hamsters, fish, dogs, cats, ferrets, parrots and so on.
- I recommend one of the six **Big Al's Aquarium Services**. They don't belong to the same owner but all offer the same concept. A huge quantity of aquariums are displayed in dark rooms so we can admire the colourful fish like little jewels in a black velvet case. Most of them host a shark aquarium and invite us to observe a feeding session once a week. They're located in Scarborough (416) 757-3281, North York (416) 223-2161, Mississauga (905) 276-6900, Brampton (905) 454-1174, Newmarket (905) 895-7677 and Whitby (905) 725-3474.

ANIMALS

See **Kortright Waterfowl Park** on p. 56.

WOOFSTOCK AT THE DISTILLERY

Humans allowed

They come in all kinds, with assorted masters: pocket dogs with funny hairdos, fabulous royal poodles, good old golden retrievers with kids attached. Dog owners really are in their element at this festival.

If you have not yet had a chance to visit The Distillery Historic District, use this event as an excuse! Opened in 2003, The Distillery is becoming a Toronto landmark with its gorgeously renovated buildings from the 1880's, paved streets, art galleries and a roster of events.

During Woofstock, 60 exhibitors and vendors compete at every corner for the attention of dog owners. Dogs (not kids!) get free cookies, samples, and gifts. In one of the booths, a portrait artist is painting a dog. There's a playground for dogs...

The event is obviously for dog owners but frustrated dog lovers like me (who can't have one because of an allergic family member) will enjoy the display of breeds... and masters' comments. "This is for crazy dogs, not like us" explains a woman to her little pet in front of the obstacle course open to the public before an agility show. The event includes modest dog contests of all kinds: Stupid Dog Tricks, Cutest Dog, Smallest Dog, Dog-Most-Like-Its-Owner...

Another great event to attend with kids is the **Wolf Howl Event** during which we saw a wolf mask exhibit, native drummers and dancers. We also made wolf masks and did a howling session.

The glass gallery is amazing. Some glass sculptures, lit for a dramatic effect, are breathtaking. Artsy children will appreciate the bouquets of giant anemones, glass fish in vases or incredibly fine engravings inside clear cubes.

TIPS (fun for 5 years +)

• All dogs must be on leash. Dogs are not allowed in the restaurants (indoor or patio) or in art galleries. You may eat on the patios and attach your pet outside the fence.
• Other attractions at **The Distillery**: the impressive two-storey Balzac Café, the paved plaza with over 150 tables often featuring live music, the Brick Street Bakery and the Mill Street Brewery.
• I can't keep up with all their festivals! Check their web site. I heard good things about their kids' activities during their jazz festival.

• **Doggie Day Afternoon Festival** is a local dog festival which usually takes place on the third Saturday in September, at **Jimmie Simpson Park** (Queen Street East and Booth Avenue). For more information call Jimmie Simpson R. C. at (416) 392-0751.

NEARBY ATTRACTIONS	
The Docks (5-min.)	p. 17
Cherry Beach (5-min.)	p. 272

The Distillery	J-10
(416) 410-1310 or (416) 364-1177 (Distillery) www.woofstock.ca www.thedistillerydistrict.com	Downtown Toronto 10-min.

 Schedule: The Distillery is open year-round. Woofstock usually on first weekend in June, from 10 am to 6 pm. Call to confirm.
Admission: FREE.
Directions: The Distillery, 55 Mill St., Toronto. Between Cherry St. and Parliament, south of Front St.

RIVERDALE FARM

Fieldmouse in the city

At Riverdale Farm, there are cows of all types, goats, sheep and large pigs. There are hens, roosters, geese and large turkeys. All this in the heart of the city!

Personally, what brings me back to Riverdale Farm is its turn-of-the-century atmosphere and the beautiful flowery and softly steeped setting.

A path brings us to a lower level and a natural pond, our favourite spot. There, a small house sits with mesh-covered windows, around which my kids like to imagine they're in a prison. During the summer, the pond is covered by natural algae that hides the fish and makes the ducks seem like they are gliding on a green carpet.

The cattle paddock by the farm's entrance, with its huge hairy cows, welcomes visitors. On the other side of the gates, the horse paddock and the Francey Barn await you. That's where you might get a chance to see demonstrations such as ice cream making, horse grooming and cow or goat milking. In the barn you'll find sheep, goats and donkeys. In late spring, you might have the chance to glimpse a cute new-born.

There's also the pig and poultry barn and further down, another pond beautifully surrounded by flowers. Make sure you drop by the Meeting House right in front. It offers children a play area with miniature farm animals and machines, and, usually, craft material for a make-and-take activity.

TIPS (fun for 1 years +)

• More on special events taking place at the farm and surroundings on p. 132.
• There's a wading pool in the park adjacent to the farm.
• There are drop-in sessions at Riverdale Farm Meeting House. Last time I checked, families could come Monday, Friday and Saturday from 1:30 to 4:30 pm and parents with kids 3 years and under could come Monday, Wednesday and Friday from 10:30 am to 12:30 pm. Call to confirm.
• In Simpson House is the Farm Kitchen, selling beverages and snacks (open daily 10 am to 3 pm). There's also a small shop with a surprising selection (closed on Mondays).

NEARBY ATTRACTIONS
Allan Gardens (5-min.) .... p. 309

Riverdale Farm	I-10
(416) 392-6794	**Downtown**
www.	**Toronto**
friendsofriverdalefarm.	**15-min.**
com	

Schedule: Open year-round, from 9 am to 5 pm (closes at 6 pm from May 1 to October 31).
Admission: FREE.
Directions: 201 Winchester St., Toronto. Take Parliament St., go north of Carlton St., turn eastbound on Winchester.

TORONTO ZOO

Kid-friendly all year long

Sometimes, we adults tackle an itinerary through the zoo as if it were a shopping list. We just have to see all 5000 animals between lunch and naptime. Orangutan? Been there! Giraffes? Done that! Hippo?... "Darn! We missed the hippo!" And while we stand there, confounded in the midst of such a tragedy, we miss the sounds of our young explorers laughing in front of a small otter's cage.

It would take more than eight hours to tour all the trails shown on the zoo's map. How many of us have ever reached the Grizzly Bear den located more than a one-hour walk from the admission gate? (The Zoomobile is actually the way to go!)

The zoo fascinates each child in a different way. It seems logical to adapt the visit according to their interest of the moment. The Visitor's Guide handed out at the admission gate is packed with useful information and includes a map, which will help you locate your child's favourite animals.

Splash Island

The Splash Island is so much fun that it could become the main reason we go to the zoo, with the animals as a bonus! It is located on the way to the Australasia Pavilion.

The spray pad is simply gorgeous. The giant animals seem to be popping out of the water. Kids run from the lake to the wetlands, the river (with water slides), and back to the ocean with whales and polar bear. All of these gen-erously sprayed us when we least expect it.

At the time of print, a very promising Kids Zoo was being constructed near the water games. We were told to expect a two-level tree house with animal costumes, story telling, puppet shows, crafts, giant spider web to climb and more. Add to this the new Waterside Theatre with animal shows... I'm speechless!

(daily May to October and weekends). They take place not too far from the Splash Island.

Around the corner, beside the Australasia pavilion, don't miss the free-flying birds in the Lorikeet Feeding Aviary. They brushed our hair with their wings! Past the pavilion is another neat attraction: the Aussie Walkabout. It is a fenced section where we're allowed to walk on a path, amidst dozens of kangaroos (unfortunately, you can't expect them to come really close).

The Conservation Connection Centre (located beside the Indomalaya Pavilion) goes one step further and offers hands-on activities: Computer Corner, Kid's Corner, Pondering Pond, Bat-Box building and a resource library.

Interactive zoo

There's more to the Toronto Zoo than just walking and spying on animals. At the entrance, take a few seconds to check out the day's schedule for feedings and encounters with animal keepers.

Over 70 keepers take care of the animals; many of them meet visitors daily. From them, you'll learn the animals' names, what and how much they eat and the answers to any other questions the children might have.

Kesho Park (a 15-minute walk from the admission gate) is beautiful. Large bay windows allow you to watch the animals through rock walls. Along the trail, kids can go right inside a large baobab tree, peek inside a termite mound, look at footprints, spy zebras and touch elephant tusks.

You can try a **camel ride** for $5

Indoor zoo

The Malayan Woods, Indomalaya, Africa, Americas and Australasia pavilions, make it possible to spend most of your visit indoors. With their jungles and tropical surroundings, they offer a great outing during very cold days and they're perfect on rainy days.

Personally, I really like these pavilions because they're enclosed spaces. Animals are within arm's reach... and so are the kids! Plus, they are perfect for winter outings.

In the Indomalaya pavilion, have a close look into the amazingly intelligent eyes of the orangutan. In Americas, children are fascinated by the incessant moves of the lively otters. In Australasia, you meet eye to eye with a Tasmanian Devil.

Inside the Africa pavilion awaits the huge gorilla. Don't miss the intriguing (and very ugly) naked mole rats, which can be observed in their cross-sectioned maze of tunnels.

The Round the World Tour trail encompasses them all, including the outdoor polar bear pool with a wonderful underwater viewing window.

Right off this trail, near the restaurant, you'll find another great attraction: the Fur Seal pool. Both attractions always fascinate visitors.

TIPS (fun for 2 years +)

• More on the **Toddle for Tots** in September on p. 125.

• Fall colours are great at the zoo when the trails are covered with leaves.

• **Halloween** time brings back the **Ghostly Ghoulish Gala** (a few days when children follow a special trail and have a passport stamped to get treats.

• During the **Christmas** Treat Walk organized every Boxing Day (December 26), starting at 10 am, visitors walk with the keepers from one den to the next to watch them offering certain animals their favourite treat. Admission is free with a food bank donation. When we attended this event, three hundred people were gathering around the dens, leaving not much space for children to see anything. We had a good look at the tiger when everybody followed the keeper to the next animal. It had waited for the crowd to leave. The beast slowly walked to its treat, had a sniff at its red steak, and went back to sleep. Not exactly what we expected. The kids were frozen; we headed towards a pavilion to enjoy the tropical climate.

• The keepers swear elephants, lions and tigers love to play in the snow.

• On **Easter** Sunday, children are also invited to collect stamps in order to get treats.

• During **March Break**, children are admitted free and there are more daily feedings and meetings with the keepers. Parking is free.

• The zoo's gift shop is huge and filled with animal-related items.

• The Zoomobile (a trackless train) runs through the zoo in 45 minutes. You hop on and off of it all day long when you buy the $5 pass. BEWARE! You can't get on with a stroller. It runs daily from

Victoria Day until Thanksgiving and on weekends in April and October.

• Your family could sleep overnight during the family nights in the **Bush Camp**. See **About camping** on p. 164.

• **Glen Rouge Campground** is the closest campground to the zoo. It is located at 7450 Kingston Road in Scarborough. Call (416) 392-2541.

• On their web site, the zoo advertizes a package with the hotel **Crowne Plaza**. Call 1-877-474-6835 for more information.

• There are several snack bars throughout the site.

Toronto Zoo
· Scarborough
(416) 392-5900
www.torontozoo.com

I-12
N-E
of downtown
25-min.

Schedule: Open year-round. (Last admission always one hour before closing time.) From March Break, 9 am to 6 pm. From Victoria Day to Labour Day, closes at 7:30 pm. The rest of the year, open 9:30 am to 4:30 pm. Splash Island: weather permitting, open weekends in June and daily from end of June to end of August; then, weekends only until mid-September.

Admission: $18/13-64 years, $12/65 years +, $10/4-12 years, FREE for 3 years and under. Parking is $8 (cash only, FREE from November to end of April). If you plan to go more than once in the year, ask about membership!

Directions: Take Hwy 401 East. ATTENTION! Follow the signs to Morningside exit and stay in the collector lanes (you can't take exit at Meadowvale directly from the express lanes).Then follow Meadowvale Rd. (exit #389) northbound.

NEARBY ATTRACTIONS

HUMBER CONSERVATORY

A well kept secret!

Butterflies are around us on plants, in trees and on the ceiling. We see chrysalis of Monarchs, and watch the accelerated clip of an insect emerging from its cocoon.

Humber Butterfly Conservatory is set in the back of the largest garden centre I have ever seen. We walk through life size bronze nymphs and marble furniture before reaching a screened area with double doors to keep butterflies in.

Basically, the conservatory is a showcase of garden plants attracting butterflies. Add the nice information centre and it makes a great oasis to observe these beautiful insects all year round.

We finish our tour with a visit to the pond in the fish section where twenty small pools await us, some of them housing impressive gold fish.

Humber Nurseries Butterfly Conservatory · Brampton (905) 794-0555 www.humbernurseries.com	H-9 N-W of Toronto 35-min.

 Schedule: The conservatory is open 7 days from May 1 to September 30. The store is open year-round, at least from 9 am to 5 pm, with variable hours.
Admission: $3/adults,$2/16 years and under.
Directions: 8386 Hwy 50, Brampton. Take Hwy 427 North. Turn west on Hwy 7, then south on Hwy 50. The store is on the west side.

REPTILIA

 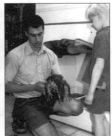

Need a pet?

As the manager sets his Nile Monitor Lizard free on the floor, she rushes towards my 3-year-old like a nosey dog, licking her with a blue-forked tongue. Interesting sight from a mother's point of view!

Reptilia is an education centre, breeding facility and retail store for those who keep reptiles or intend to do so. All the animals are displayed in great terrariums: lizards, alligators, snakes, salamanders, frogs, geckos, turtles and a chameleon.

The kids press their faces against the glass of the terrarium to observe the lizards, and get down on all fours to have a better look at snakes.

There's no guarantee that visitors will be able to actually touch the animals. This might happen when staff have to take a reptile out of its cage for a demonstration in the private Birthday room, in which case they allow kids in the store to touch it afterwards.

Reptilia · Vaughan (905) 761-6223 www.reptilia.org	H-10 North of Toronto 35-min.

 Schedule: Monday to Friday, 10 am to 8 pm, Saturday and Sunday, 10 am to 5 pm.
 Admission: FREE.
Directions: 91 Fernstaff Court, Unit #8, Vaughan. Take Allen Rd. North from Hwy 401. It becomes Dufferin St. Turn west on Fernstaff Cr. (north of Langstaff Rd.).

OSHAWA ZOO

Farm animals?

A cute lemur with fluffy white ears holds out his little paw to delicately pick the popcorn off my daughter's hand. He quietly starts to eat it while staring at her with interest. We are in the peaceful little Oshawa Zoo and enjoy every minute of it.

Despite its small size, the Oshawa Zoo holds a few surprises, the most awkward being the sight of a camel in the shade of a mature tree with lazy black and white cows grazing in the background! Thankfully, most enclosures are set in the middle of green pastures, adding to the quaint atmosphere of the place.

Further, we notice colourful pheasants on a grassy outcrop. The zoo counts an interesting variety of animals, including donkeys, llamas, goats, zebra and even a breed of rabbits from Argentina that look like kangaroos.

While it doesn't take long to complete your visit, children can take as much time as they want to feed the animals (popcorn is sold at the entrance for this purpose).

TIPS (fun for 1 year +)

• You'll find picnic tables on site. We chose, however, to go back on pretty Columbus Road, westbound and down to Simcoe Street where we found a chip truck selling decadent fries and hamburgers by a gas station. We took our scrumptious lunch to the playground beside the adjacent church.

NEARBY ATTRACTIONS	

Oshawa Zoo
· Oshawa
(905) 655-5236

C-4
East
of Toronto
40-min.

Schedule: Open 7 days, end of May to Labour Day, 10 am to 5 pm. May open on weekends during Easter weekend and in May when weather is nice. Call to confirm.

Admission: (cash or Interac) $7/adults, $6/seniors and students, $4/3 years and up, FREE for children 2 years and under, $22/family. Popcorn bags cost $1.50.

Directions: From Hwy 401 East, take exit #419/Harmony Rd. northbound. Turn right on Columbus Rd. then left on Grandview St. North. The zoo is on the left hand side.

NORTHWOOD SANCTUARY

Nose to nose with the beast

North of Port Perry, a small, surprising private zoo can be found. It hosts tigers and lions, only separated from visitors by an iron fence doubled with electrical wires. It's a rare occasion to look straight in the eye of a tiger, and to see its teeth from up close! Whether young or old, visitors are impressed.

The zoo includes many lions and other felines in those cages allowing you to be closer than you ever will to these wild animals.

Kids enjoyed the monkeys for a while and made me wonder how really different from a monkey is a 5-year-old?

We then headed towards the huge buffalo den at the top of a hill.

I loved the feeling by the wolf and elk pens which boasted plenty of trees.

There were eagles, ostriches, goats and grizzly bears.

Some cages aren't really large or even original, but the zoo is very well maintained.

TIPS (fun for 5 years +)
• Since younger children aren't aware that it should be frightening to stand a metre away from a lion, I would recommend the visit to this remote zoo to those accompanying children 5 years and over, old enough to be thrilled.
• They usually feed the animals at around 3 pm daily during the summer.
• They sell animal feed on site.

NEARBY ATTRACTIONS
Cullen Gardens (25-min.).............p. 116

Northwood Exotic Animal Sanctuary
• Seagrave
(905) 985-2738
www.northwoodranch.com

B-4
N-E
of Toronto
60-min.

Schedule: Open daily from mid-May until Thanksgiving from 10 am to 5 pm.
Admission: (cash only) $10/adults, $9/seniors, $8/3-12 years old, FREE 2 years and under.
Directions: 2192 Cookson Lane, Seagrave. From Hwy 401 East, take exit #412/Thickson Rd. northbound. Turn east on Winchester Rd. and north on Simcoe St. (Hwy 2). Turn left on River St. then watch for signs.

BOWMANVILLE ZOO

Please feed the animals

"Not in your mouth!" For the umpteenth time, my friend catches her little one as he is about to eat an animal treat. True, the biscuits in the greasy brown paper bag do look very appetizing. Undoubtedly, the Bowmanville Zoo gives its residents the royal treatment.

Unlike the Toronto Zoo, Bowmanville Zoo (the oldest private zoo in North America) gives visitors the opportunity to feed most of the animals, much to the delight of children. In fact, without supervision, kids would likely give their entire feed bag to the hungry and plump little goats that await them in the first compound located across the bridge.

TIPS (fun for 1 year +)
• A board at the entrance indicates the day's performances and other demonstration schedules.
• I recommend you buy a minimum of one animal feed bag per child (sold at the entrance for $2.50).
• **Elephant rides** are offered for $5. A few small mechanical rides are located near the entrance. They are included with the admission fee in July and August.
• We had a picnic under the trees, but there is an air-conditioned snack bar near the entrance, with washrooms, tables and an aquarium to entertain visitors. Their gift shop is well stocked.

NEARBY ATTRACTIONS	
Cedar Park Resort (15-min.)......p. 35	
Petticoat Creek (15-min.).............p. 385	

The Bowmanville Zoo also contrasts with its big brother by its smaller size (42 acres compared to 710 acres at Toronto Zoo), and a more modest sampling of animals (only 220 animals). The upswing however, is the convenience of touring the zoo in a single visit and interacting with the animals.

The broad paths that criss-cross the zoo are generally well shaded by the bordering mature trees; a real plus on hot summer days. There is a lovely country feel to the site. We began our tour with the parrots, camels, reptiles, monkeys and llamas. We then crossed a small bridge over a river, that brought us to the elephants, lions and zebras.

There are bisons, various kinds of horned animals, large birds with impressive calls, intriguing large rodents and roaming peacocks, geese and ducks. A separate enclosure we're allowed in is a refuge to many fallow deer.

Two to three daily performances involving lions, elephants or the many other kinds of animals, are presented in the impressive 400-seat indoor Animatheatre. Animal encounters also take place in and around an outdoor cage.

Bowmanville Zoo
• Bowmanville
(905) 623-5655
www.bowmanvillezoo.com

C-4
East
of Toronto
45-min.

  Schedule: Open daily from end of April to end of September, and weekends only in October, weather permitting. Opens at 10 am, closes at 6 pm on June weekends and daily in July and August. Closing time varies from 4 pm to 5 pm the other days. Shows daily in July and August, weekends only May through October.

Admission: $15.25/adults, $12/seniors and students, $8.75/2-12 years, FREE under 2 years.

Directions: 340 King St. E. (Hwy 2), Bowmanville. From Hwy 401 East, exit #432/Liberty St. northbound. Turn east on King St.

JUNGLE CAT WORLD

ly houses the "baby" of the moment. When I visited for the first time in 1996, I was surprised to discover a German Shepherd pup and a baby lion cohabiting like the best of friends. During my most recent visit, there was a young leopard gnawing a stuffed teddy.

We particularly enjoyed the otters and the small rabbit enclosure. Generally, the cages are relatively small, except those of the Siberian tigers (with its large pond) and the white wolves.

Mommy is there!!!

"What's she doing?" a girl is cooing to a couple of tame tigers in a back cage, as her friend the keeper cleans their main cage. The big "kitties" brush their backs against the wired fence, allowing the girl to touch their beautiful fur. Then they engage in a friendly fight. Intimacy is the operative word in this privately owned zoo, which is one of a few to be accredited by the Canadian Association of Zoological Parks and Aquariums.

Visitors are welcomed to Jungle Cat World by the strident "Hello" of a real parrot. A cage, located close to the zoo entrance, general-

However, I saw grizzly bears, wolves and tigers squabble happily. Among the zoo's many tenants, you'll also find lions, bobcats, leopards, cougars, lynx, a black jaguar, gibbons and marmoset monkeys, many of them born on site.

Jungle Cat World also features a small playground with free-roaming deer, pygmy goats, donkeys, sheep and peacocks. There was even a goat interested in joining my kids in the mini merry-go-round! You can purchase a bag of grain to feed the animals.

TIPS (fun for 2 years +)

• Felines stay put during summer's hot days. However, count on daily feeding sessions at 1:30 pm to see them in action.

• The best way to view the marmoset monkeys is to kneel at their level while they stand on the bottom of their cage. When we visited, they stared curiously at the colourful soother in my daughter's mouth, with their heads bent to one side then the other.

• More about their **Night Safari** experience allowing groups to sleep over in **About camping** on p. 164.

• I recommend you eat at the **New Dutch Oven** instead of the zoo's snack bar. It is a family restaurant located across from the zoo, (905) 983-5001.

NEARBY ATTRACTIONS

Jungle Cat World

C-5 East of Toronto 55-min.

• Orono
(905) 983-5016
www.junglecatworld.com

Schedule: Open year-round, 7 days, 10 am to 5 pm. Closes at 4 pm in the winter.

Admission: $12/adults, $9/ seniors and students, $6/2-13 years, FREE for children under 2.

Directions: 3667 Concession Rd. 6, Orono. Take Hwy 401 East to Hwy 35/115 (exit #436) northbound. The zoo is on the southeast corner of Hwy 35/115 and Taunton Rd.

DANIEL'S ARK

Close encounter

The still cougar licks its lips as it stares at the baby in her mother's arms, the end of its tail wagging energetically. To its defense, I must say the infant looks really yummy in her little peach and pink outfit.

This cat is no pet. It is a wild animal, with a special relationship with Daniel, its caregiver. When he approaches, the feline brushes its head against the cage to be pet. All of a sudden, it looks like a big purring cat. Daniel has hand-raised and named most of the animals in the preserve: orphans or injured and unfit to go back to the wild.

Years ago, he opened this non-profit licensed wildlife centre to care for cougars, lynx, timber wolves, fox and mink.

He's been busy ever since, adding

to the fun with summer day camps for children and events such as the Saturday evenings session of **Timber Cry Wolf Howl**.

The owner's nice wooden house is right in the middle of the action, which gives quite an intimate feeling to the outing, like visiting an original uncle. Around the house, a few smaller cages house rabbits or raccoons. Farther, bigger cages are home to the larger mammals.

We notice some animals "sleeping" on the grass further in the back yard. Two dead deer! Thanks to an agreement with the local Roads Department, road kill is brought to the preserve where it becomes the wild animals' lunch. The circle of life takes a new meaning!

There's a stocked quarry lake 70 feet deep in which we can fish for a fee. They don't rent gear but they sell bait. They even rent canoes, with life jackets, for $10 for 30 minutes.

We opt to have our picnic here and I make a mental note to come back with my young fisherman.

TIPS (fun for 5 years +)

• For $10, you can have your picture taken with a baby fox or lynx (depending on the babies handy at the time!) in a souvenir frame.

• Family fishing is $45 for a family of four. It includes a tour of Daniel's Ark and the cost of the fish you catch! You don't need a license but you have to comply with the legal catch limit.

• Ice fishing is available, weather permitting, from January to March. They can drill the holes for you. Ask about their **Ice Fishing Derbies**! Same rates as summer fishing apply.

NEARBY ATTRACTIONS
Downey's Farm (15-min.)..............p. 141
Albion Orchards (15-min.)............p. 142

Daniel's Ark Wildlife Preservation Alliance
· Bolton
(905) 857-9874
www.danielsark.org

F-10
N-W
of Toronto
55-min.

 Schedule: Open daily from May 1 to September 31, 10 am to 6 pm. Wolf Howl evenings, Saturday, 7:30 to 9:30 pm, starting Victoria Day weekend. Call for ice fishing in the winter.

Admission: $8/adults, $6/seniors and youth, $4/3-12 years old.

Directions: 14616 The Gore Rd., Bolton. Take Hwy 400 North, exit at King Rd. westbound, and turn north on The Gore Rd.

WHITE ROCK OSTRICH FARM

Now, that's interesting!

What has three pairs of eyelids, two toes and one toenail? An ostrich! Want to see for yourself? Go to this ostrich farm!

It seems that health-conscious North Americans are turning to low-cholesterol protein sources. In this light, ostrich meat is gaining in reputation. This could explain the ostrich farms that are popping up here and there. But not all are open to the public.

The owners of this farm housing some 40 big birds obviously have fun with their unusual herd. In the gift shop, you can sample ostrich stew or admire carved ostrich eggs (watch the kids, as these are an expensive item to break!).

Visitors are not allowed to roam freely on the site. They are invited on a bumpy hay-wagon ride to the fields.

As the ostriches are called, the children are given some grass to feed the huge birds. When the bravest bird sneaks its head through the wire fence, we can appreciate the flexibility of that long, muscled neck.

On our way out, we were given a small ostrich feather as a souvenir.

TIPS (fun for 2 years +)

• The visit is not very long (approximately half an hour). It's a good stop to combine with an outing to another regional attraction.
• Usually over three weekends during **Halloween** time, the farm hosts a **Screamfest**. It seems to have gotten quite ambitious over the years with actors, intense sound and light effects, computers and pneumatic props. Suitable for 8 years and over, $8/12 years and older, $6/8-11 years. Check the web site for more details.
• Frozen ostrich meat can be bought on the premises. If you wish to take some home, it would be a good idea to bring a cooler. Ostrich burgers and hot dogs are sold on weekends.

NEARBY ATTRACTIONS
Long Lane Orchards (15-min.)..... p. 146
Rockwood C.A. (20-min.)............. p. 340

White Rock Ostrich Farm • Rockwood (519) 856-1487 www.screamfest.info	**D-2 West of Toronto 55-min.**

Schedule: Open 10 am to 5 pm, weekends from Easter weekend to Victoria Day and from Thanksgiving until Christmas. Open Wednesday to Sunday from Victoria Day to Thanksgiving. Tours offered on weekends only from Victoria Day to Thanksgiving.
Admission: FREE admission. Hay-wagon tours:$5/adults, $3/children 2 years and up.
Directions: 13085 4th Line, Rockwood. From Hwy 401 West, take exit #320/Hwy 25 northbound. Turn west on Regional Rd. 12, then north on 4th Line.

KORTRIGHT WATERFOWL PARK

Quacky corner

At the Kortright Waterfowl Park, in Guelph, the flock of birds walking towards us believes my son is Dr. Doolittle... Kids understand they hold power in their hands while they give out golden grains. If we manage to restrain their first impulse (giving out all the food at once), we'll easily spend an hour observing the feathered population frolicking.

At the end of the winding boardwalk, a path leads to the park's entrance: a door cut into a high wire-mesh fence. We're here to observe all classes of web-footed birds that we already hear squawking from afar.

Following the concert, we head for the meeting point of all free-roaming species: the big pond. Some birds were adopted by the centre and had feathers removed to prevent them from flying away. Other wild birds came here on their own free will. Rare specimens stay confined in pens.

Like any other Torontonians, we were a bit blasé as we watched the flock of Canada geese greeting us. However, we found their friends, the large black swans, quite ravishing. When stretched out, the tallest one's big muscular neck was the same height as my five-year-old son. I was quite impressed!

Each species gives out a very different call: from the trumpet blaring out a wild jazz tune to the small toy horn. When they all compete to attract our attention, the result is a joyous cacophony.

Beaks come in all styles: green, pink, red or black, and long, short or curled up. Feet, song and sizes are as varied. I had no idea that there were so many types of ducks and geese. The Sanctuary houses over 90 different species, though not all are on display to visitors.

We even spot a pudgy groundhog, rabbits and a deer family hiding in the undergrowth.

TIPS (fun for 2 years +)
• In late spring (usually by mid-May) we can admire cygnets, goslings and ducklings!
• During the fall only, bags of corn (the only food allowed) are usually sold at the entrance. I recommend that you buy at least one per child. It's great to watch the birds scheme while they approach us or protect their territory. Certain ones are shy; others have eaten out of my young ornithologist's hand.

NEARBY ATTRACTIONS
Springridge Farm (15-min.).........p. 143
Crawford Lake (20-min.)..............p. 410

Kortright Waterfowl Park · Guelph (519) 824-6729	D-1 West of Toronto 60-min.

Schedule: Weekends and Holidays, from March 1 until October 31, from 10 am to 5 pm.

Admission: $2.50/adults, $2/seniors and students, $1/4 to 14 years old, FREE for children under 4.

Directions: 305 Niska Rd., Guelph. From Hwy 401 West, take exit Hwy 6 North. Turn westbound on Kortright St. Niska St. is on the right.

THE FALCONRY CENTRE

In a flash

The small falcon leaves its stand in a flash. It takes us a few moments to locate it above the woodland at the back of the outdoor theatre. As the master falconer raises his arm, meat in his gauntlet, the bird dives back at amazing speed to catch its prey. Remarkably, the bird dismisses freedom, and this is telling of the complex relationship between falcon and master.

Don't go to the Falconry Centre expecting medieval costumes and references to chivalry. Instead, the centre serves primarily as a breeding centre for endangered or threatened birds of prey, with approximately a hundred birds hatching there each year.

Now open to the public, the centre offers self-guided visits via an audio commentary, programmed to be heard throughout the site. I learned it takes twelve weeks for a baby Bald Eagle the size of a chicken egg to reach its full size and an eight-foot wing span!

With cages made of particle board, the centre is no fancy zoo either. Strong odours are to be expected, as anyone owning a bird as a pet will know. Our visit to the mews, where rare wild birds are kept (along with hundreds of chicks used for feeding the birds of prey), proved to be quite trying for that reason. The falcon chambers brought a welcome contrast. Previously trained breeding birds live there, undisturbed by visitors. You can look at them comfortably through a series of narrow windows (kids need to be lifted to see).

Other spectacular sights of birds can be found along a pathway that runs a mere two metres away from an open site, where some twenty proud birds remain, simply tied to their stands.

TIPS (fun for 5 years +)
• The best time to see newly hatched birds is from May to July.
• You may buy raptor chow to feed the birds near the path.
• Check their web site to print the $1 off coupon.

NEARBY ATTRACTIONS

The Falconry Centre	C-2
• Tottenham	N-W
(905) 936-1033	of Toronto
www.falconrycentre.com	60-min.

Schedule: Open 7 days from Victoria Day to Thanksgiving, 10 am to 4 pm. One show daily at 2 pm in May, June, September and October. Two shows daily at 12:30 pm and 3 pm in July, August.

Admission: $9/adults, $8/seniors, $6/3-12 years, $26/family.

Directions: 2nd Line, Tottenham. From Hwy 400 North, take exit #55/Hwy 9 westbound. Turn north on Tottenham Rd. and take first road westbound.

AFRICAN LION SAFARI

Close encounters of the animal kind

Go figure why children are so attracted to animals! They're happy visiting a traditional zoo, but become literally ecstatic when encountering the fantastic opportunities offered by African Lion Safari. The park is huge and offers the unique opportunity to drive through the animals' living quarters, with your car windows as the only screen between your children and the animals.

African Lion Safari houses over 1000 exotic animals and birds of 132 species. When we drove through the seven large game reserves, we first encountered big birds such as emus.

We then watched sleeping lions that didn't lift an eyebrow. The tigers were just as lethargic. The whole scenery lacked action... then a crowd of baboons started to jump on our car!

If you're able to live with the idea of a monkey's "little present" decorating the hood of your car, I strongly recommend using your own vehicle instead of the zoo's bus. Children become delirious with joy with baboons perched on the windshield.

Having tried both, I see some disadvantages to the bus option. First, you don't control the amount of time spent watching each animal

(the Safari Tour Bus ride takes approximately 1 hr 15-min.; in your own vehicle, it lasts as long as you please).

Second, the bus offers little grip for the monkeys, while cars make comfortable perches.

Bears were strolling among the monkeys. Quite a mixed company!

You'll meet among others: a few tall giraffes (rather impressive from up close), some albino rhinoceros, zebras and antelopes. My kids went wild when the tall giraffe licked our windshield with her black tongue.

Further on, you can witness the elephant's bath, pet the animals at the Pets Corner, watch shows by parakeets and birds of prey and see other trained animal performances.

You can cross the pond on board the small boat named African Queen and ride the small train.

In the summer, children will enjoy playing in interactive water games at the Misumu Bay, located close to the restaurant's terrace.

You can also visit the Discovery Centre, including skulls, claws, teeth, eggs and more to touch.

Courtesy of African Lion Safari

TIPS (fun for 2 years +)

• Don't forget the bathing suits!
• Check their web site for a list of hotels offering a package.
• The park's restaurant and gift shop are well stocked and affordable. In the gift shop, look carefully at the T-shirts. Some of them were painted by the elephants! Now, that's a unique souvenir.

African Lion Safari
• Cambridge
1-800-461-9453
www.lionsafari.com

E-2
S-W
of Toronto
75-min.

Schedule: Open end of April to Thanksgiving, 10 am to 4 pm. Closes at 5 pm during weekends until end of June. Closes at 5:30 pm daily from July to Labour Day. Ground remains open for 1 1/2 hours.

Admission: (taxes not included) $24/13-54 years, $21/seniors, $19/3-12 years, FREE for children 2 years and under ($3 less during Spring and Fall). Tour bus costs approx. $5 extra per person.

Directions: From Hwy 401 West, take exit #299/Hwy 6 southbound for 14 km and turn west (right) on Safari Rd.

NEARBY ATTRACTIONS

WINGS OF PARADISE

The butterfly effect

We had just spent fifteen minutes focusing on the impressive hatchery inhabited by dozens of still cocoons so it was quite a contrast to return to the path with free-flying butterflies where we were literally cut by reckless flyers zooming by. It felt like this was the highway and we had to be careful.

There's action in the butterfly conservatory: babbling brooks, small cascading waterfalls and close to two thousand butterflies, many of them frolicking about.

It is fascinating to observe the chrysalis set in different hatching stages in the hatchery. The cocoons come from Costa Rica and Malaysia. Nearby are resting specimens of the amazing Atlas Moth, a nocturnal insect wider than the face of a ten-year-old. Everywhere else, patient ones could

locate over thirty species of butterflies.

We have to watch where we walk to avoid crushing butterflies on the floor. A staff member explains it's a sign they are getting weaker and closer to the end of their life cycle. Small quails stroll under the bushes. Their job is to clean up the place, that is... to eat the insects in terminal phase.

The weak beauties accept our hand as a perch when they are laid in front of them. The children understand intuitively how to behave with the fragile butterflies.

The vegetation surrounding us is tropical. The humid air smells of flowers and fruit (butterfly meals on plates). The controlled weather under the glassed roof ranges from 24 to 28 degrees Celsius. After a while, a visit to the cooler galleries is most welcome.

A large number of butterflies are framed in the "Flying Jewels" exhibit room. Some are endangered species. The "Insects of the World" includes intriguing displays of dead insects as well as a few live specimens such as a humongous centipede. Yuck!

TIPS (fun for 4 years +)

• When we were visiting, there was not much vegetation in the conservatory gardens. They will be designed over the next few years. A butterfly garden and a labyrinth are planned.
• Ask about their **Bugfeast** event from the last week in December through early January. A lifetime opportunity to taste chocolate-dipped crickets!
• They offer additional drop-in activities during the **March Break**.
• The gift shop is well stocked with butterfly-themed toys, books, clothes and trinkets. My kids went crazy for chocolate butterfly lollypops.
• The **Paradise Café** is open daily for snacks and light lunch, 10 am to 4 pm.

| Wings of Paradise Butterfly Conservatory | D-1 West of Toronto 85-min. |

· Cambridge
(519) 653-1234
www.wingsofparadise.com

Schedule: Open year-round from 10 am to 5 pm. Closed Dec. 24, 25, 26 and Jan. 1st.

Admission: $8.25/adults, $7.25/students, $4.25/3-12 years, FREE under 3 years.

Directions: 2500 Kossuth Rd., Cambridge. From Hwy 401 West, take exit #282/Hespeler Rd. North-Hwy 24. Turn west on Kossuth Rd. and follow signs. Niska St. is on the right.

NEARBY ATTRACTIONS

BUTTERFLY CONSERVATORY

fruit plates are left for the hungry butterflies, so that we may admire them while they feed. We can also observe their cocoons in each phase of development, suspended from the shelving in front of a large window with openings. A few iguanas share the space!

Butterfly-friendly attraction

The visit begins with the viewing of a short film. It is followed by a leisurely walk around the greenhouse for as long as we want. The conservatory layout includes trees, bushes and flower clumps, as well as a small waterfall. The hot and humid air contributes to the overall exotic feel of the place.

We are told that nearly fifty butterfly species live freely at the Niagara Butterfly Conservatory. I couldn't tell most of them apart, yet I saw at close range all sorts of exotic kinds including blue, black, red, yellow and orange ones. Here and there,

The beautiful winged insects are quite tame. In truth, they were born in this environment and have grown accustomed to the crowds that regularly and respectfully visit the hothouse.

My little naturalist miraculously stops moving for a minute, hoping that one of the two thousand butterflies in the greenhouse will mistake him for a flower and land on him.

A woman, looking through her camera, waits for the perfect moment to snap a picture, unaware that a wonderful specimen is resting on her head. I take my time to capture (on film) a superb green and black butterfly standing 10 centimetres away from me.

Don't miss the interactive stations in the entrance hall.

TIPS (fun for 4 years +)
• More on the **People Movers** transportation system on p. 302.
• Purchase your tickets as soon as you arrive at the conservatory, as only then will the time of your visit be assigned (often one hour later in the high season).
• If you arrive at opening time, chances are there will be many butterflies on the floor.
• Washrooms at the conservatory are less busy than those at the snack bar.
• You can end your outing with a visit to the adjacent outdoor gardens (the Conservatory sits at the centre of a botanical garden), have a bite at the snack bar or browse in the large gift shop.

Niagara Parks Butterfly Conservatory
| E-4 Niagara Region 90-min.

• Niagara Falls
(905) 371-0254
1-877-642-7275
www.niagaraparks.com

 Schedule: Open from March Break to December 31, 9 am to 5 pm (last admission 30 min. prior to closing time).

Admission: $10/adults, $6/6 to 12 years, FREE for 5 years and under.

Directions: 2405 Niagara Pkwy., Niagara Falls. From QEW towards Niagara, take Hwy 405 towards Queenston, then exit at the Niagara Pkwy. southbound (right). The conservatory is on the right.

MARINELAND

Not just another fish story...

As soon as kids try to feed one of the hundreds of deer Marineland is swarming with, they're swept away amidst a sea of white spots with dozens of wet noses and velvety antlers tickling their faces.

When you think of Marineland, the first thought that comes to mind is the sight of killer whales splashing the crowd. Yet this attraction offers plenty of other activities too: a huge fish-feeding pond, a bear pit, a deer park, rides, a roller coaster and of course, a pool allowing a closer view of the killer whales and a whole new team of dolphins.

Performances

As soon as you arrive, head for the theatre where the next performance will be held. Schedules for the shows are posted at the site's entrance. It's better to get there 15 minutes before performances begin. The animal shows last approximately half an hour.

Killer whale and sea lion shows are presented in the King Waldorf Theatre, left of the entrance. We walked along the amphitheatre's edge and reached a ramp that lead to the top of the auditorium and found seats in one of the last rows (where we had a good view of the show).

Inside their glass basin, the killer whales are gigantic. The first sight I had

of them left me standing open-mouthed. It is incredible to watch these impressive forces of nature perform their number in unison. However, the best way to watch these beasts is to go to Friendship Cove, with fabulous underwater viewing windows.

For above water viewing, it's also surrounded by walkways. You might even get a chance to touch the whales. Friendship Cove is located a 15-minute walk away from the admission gate.

Since my last visit, they've added a separate beluga whale habitat called the Artic Cove.

The Aquarium Theatre features a show starring sea lions and dolphins. Unfortunately, the theatre was full when we got there. If this happens to you, don't despair! You can still see the dolphins perform thanks to the wide underwater viewing windows located in the basement of the theatre. Freshwater aquariums are also located at this level.

One, two, three, GO!

There are three other points of interest not to be missed at Marineland: the fish pond, the bear pit and the deer park. For the best effect, visit them in that order. A detailed map is given to visitors at the entrance.

You'll be surprised by the number of deer greeting you at the back of the deer park. Most of the 500 animals stay close to the stand where deer food is for sale.

When heading towards these attractions, you'll pass by the Kiddie Rides area. It includes a small roller coaster, especially designed for the younger crowd, that we really enjoyed. There's a Viking Boat carousel for the whole family, a Ferris wheel and the Space Avenger.

Beyond Friendship Cove, you can find the more elaborate rides, some way too testing for me!

TIPS (fun for 3 years +)

• During the summer, try to arrive no later than 10 am to avoid long line-ups, especially if you want to try the rides.

• Marineland's parking lot is set up lengthwise. If you're parked at one of the extremities, you'll have to walk more than 5 minutes before reaching the park entrance. Furthermore, Marineland is vast. You'll require a stroller for young children. Dolphin-shaped strollers can be rented on site for around $6.

• There's barely any shade on the Marineland site. Don't forget water bottles, hats and sunscreen!

• If you sit in the first ten rows of the killer whale show, bring a change of clothes and hide your camera!

• Don't do what my friend and I tried: to prop our children's caps up on their heads in order to make them reach the required height for a certain ride! The employee took a good 30 seconds to measure them carefully, then refused them access without batting an eye.

• The gift shop is huge and filled with small souvenirs. And by the entrance, there's a noisy (but air-conditioned) video arcade, with games galore.

• The closest **campground**, **King Waldorf's Tent & Trailer Park** is located behind Marineland at 9015 Stanley Avenue, (905) 295-8191.

• Click on <u>Hotels</u> in their web site for a list of accommodations offering packages.

• For lunch, expect to pay about $7 for a hamburger with fries at the Marineland cafeteria. You'll find large indoor and outdoor areas with tables by a playground, perfect for picnics.

• At last! A 326,000 sq. ft. aquarium is being built! It will consist of four domes. I was told the largest will house an interactive dolphin habitat! The others will host the Terrors of the sea (with sharks and stingrays), the Discovery Reef (with species from the Caribbean) and the Forest Lagoon (with fresh water fish from around the world). Still a few years to wait...

Marineland
• Niagara Falls
(905) 356-9565
www.
marinelandcanada.com

**E-4
Niagara
Region
90-min.**

Schedule: Open from Victoria Day until Thanksgiving. From Victoria Day to late June, open from 10 am to 5 pm. In July and August, open daily from 9 am to 6 pm. Then, open from 10 am to 5 pm until Thanksgiving. All park activities remain in operation until dusk, after the admission gate closes.

Admission: (taxes not included) From the end of June until beginning of September:$33/10-59 years, $28/5 to 9 years and seniors. Call them for their brochure including a $3 off coupon.

Directions: 7657 Portage Rd., Niagara Falls.Take QEW west towards Niagara Falls, then take McLeod Rd. exit and follow signs.

NEARBY ATTRACTIONS

ELMVALE JUNGLE ZOO

I spy...

If your child swears she is seeing a zebra in the woods as you drive along Hwy 27, she speaks the truth!

Elmvale Jungle Zoo houses more than 300 zoo-reared animals that have known no life in the wild: lemurs, tigers, snakes, flamingos, kangaroos, giraffes and more.

I really enjoyed the design of this small zoo. Trees everywhere make it the perfect place to hang out on a very hot day. Some cages are very nicely set along shaded trails in the woods. We bought bags of peanuts to feed the animals.

The trout pond has a small island inhabited by ducks and has a fountain that throws water way up in the air. We could feed the fish to generate some action. Parrots were fun to watch as they tried to grab the shells with their beaks.

There's a snack bar and playground on the premises.

Elmvale Jungle Zoo • Elmvale (705) 322-1112 www. elmvalejunglezoo.com	A-2 Midland Region 60-min.

Schedule: Open late May to end of June, weekdays, 9:30 am to 5 pm, weekends, 9:30 am to 6 pm. From July to Labour Day, 7 days, 9:30 am to 7 pm. (Open until Thanksgiving, 10 am to 5 pm, weather permitting. Last admission one hour before closing time.)

Admission: $11.50/adults, $9.50/seniors and students, $6/3-12 years, FREE for 2 years and under.

Directions: From Hwy 400 North, take exit #98/Hwy 26 northbound. Follow Hwy 26 into Hwy 27, to Elmvale.

BERGERON'S EXOTIC SANCTUARY

Discovery zone

Around the lane are big cages housing bigger animals: felines, bear, white wolves, fox and… goats, just to remind us that we are on a farm, after all. And the goats are getting along with llamas, just to remind us that we are not on a traditional farm.

In one lane, small cages are prettily invaded by wild plants and decorated with the domestic touch of flower pots. On the ground of a cage, my daughter spots a mother cat carrying her litter by the neck, one after the other. The kittens seem just like regular pets, but the adult looks like a tiny puma. They are jungle cats and are fed raw meat as we watch.

By the entrance, ducks roam free and chickens peck over a pile of fruit and vegetable crop rejects. On a cage next to this, we see Akira, a female timber wolf rejected by her pack and hand-raised by the owners. Many animals here were rejected by zoos.

Bergeron's Exotic Animal Sanctuary • Picton (613) 476-4212 www.bergerons.ca	C-6 East of Toronto 2 1/2 hrs

Schedule: March Break to October 31, 10 am to 6 pm. During Christmas, December 26 to early January, 11 am to 3 pm.

Admission: (cash only) $10/adults, $8/students and seniors, $5/3-12 years, FREE 2 years and under.

Directions: From Picton: Go east on Main St., it becomes County Rd 49. Turn left on County Rd 6, then right onto County Rd 5. They're at #967.

RIVERVIEW PARK & ZOO

On the right track

What a unique combination: a great outdoor playground and a beautiful little zoo. It comes with a small train ride along Otanabee River as a bonus. A definite must if you are in the Peterborough area.

Some of the 27 exhibits are lovely and offer a habitat well-adapted to the animals! I am not the only one to think so, since the Peterborough Zoo was declared one of the two most ethical zoos in Canada by Zoocheck, a Toronto-based organization.

Yaks, various monkeys, snakes, camels, parrots, reindeer, ducks in a huge pond, pot-bellied pigs and other farm animals are nice. But if you ask my children, the playground is even nicer!

Kids are attracted like magnets to the cable ride, which allows them to fly above the ground over a distance of 15 metres. There's a long flume slide that stretches among wild flowers, many climbing structures and a spray pad.

We walked past the duck pond towards the train track, passing by a real plane jacked up on a post. We unfortunately missed the last train. The ride seemed like fun; it crosses over Otanabee River, goes through a tunnel, takes a loop and returns.

We reached the Monkey House and strolled on the trail along the river, back to the playground for more cable rides.

TIPS (fun for 2 years +)

• Bring insect repellent if you want to go on the trails. Don't forget the bathing suits for the spray pad.
• It took us approximately 20 minutes to walk from the parking lot to the train stop at the other end of the park.
• From May to August, there are eight open-air concerts on Sunday afternoon at 1:30 pm.
• There's an on-site snack bar and a gorgeous picnic spot down from the playground by the river, where we can walk to a tiny island across a small bridge.

NEARBY ATTRACTIONS
Wild Water & Wheels (15-min.).....p. 40

Riverview Park & Zoo
• Peterborough
(705) 748-9300, ext. 2304
www.
puc.org/files/zoo/zoo.html

B-5 N-E of Toronto 2 1/4 hrs

Schedule: Open year-round 8 am to 8:30 pm in the summer (closes at 4 pm the rest of the year).Train operates from Victoria Day to Labour Day.
Admission: FREE, $1/train ride.
Directions: 1230 Water St. North, Peterborough. From Hwy 401 East, take exit #436/Hwy 35/115. Near Peterborough, exit at The Parkway., turn right on Lansdowne St. West, turn left on George St. South, turn right on Water St.

General tips about
Arts & culture:

- BEWARE! If you buy tickets through services such as Ticket Master, there could be an extra charge of up to $5 per ticket! And they won't deliver if you buy at the last minute. You can usually buy tickets directly from the venue's box office to save the extra cost.

- You will find the seating maps of most of Toronto's major theatres and venues in the **Telus** phone directory. Call 1-877-987-8737 to get a copy.

- Consult our calendar of events on p. 445 for an idea of the schedule of attractions listed in this guide. For an exhaustive listing of family events in the GTA, go to **www.toronto4kids.com**, click <u>Events & Entertainment</u>, then <u>Monthly Listings</u>.

- For a calendar of the festivals held in Ontario, check the web site **www.festivals-events-ont.com**.

ARTS
& CULTURE

Make-up done with material from **R. Hiscott Beauty & Theatrical Supplies**, p. 440.

HARBOURFRONT CENTRE

At all times you can view at no cost an eclectic selection of art works at the York Quay Gallery and along the main building's corridors. The Power Plant is wholly dedicated to exhibits of modern art enjoyed with admission fee.

Then there is the Harbourfront Centre for children, which prides itself on helping children become familiar with the world of culture and the arts. Among others: **Toronto Festival of Storytelling**, camps, **International Children's Milk Festival**, **Music with Bites**, Canadian Thanksgiving celebration, **Christmas** fairs and a host of other free cultural fairs.

A family affair

Harbourfront Centre sits on the edge of the water. Its waterfront terrace with panoramic views of Lake Ontario on one side and CN Tower on the other, the long promenade along the piers with its many choices of harbour cruises, and most of all, the over 4000 large and small events taking place year-round, explain the site's huge popularity. In a word, it is one of the best ways to enjoy Toronto's waterfront.

For the inquisitive mind, the Craft Studio allows visitors to watch artists in action as they are crafting glass, metal, ceramics or textiles. Children are generally impressed by the glassblower's prowess with the large red ball coming out of the oven's belly, and its patient transformation into a shapely vase with handles.

There is the Harbourfront Centre for adults, with its ambitious programs including dance, music and theatre festivals, conferences and visual arts exhibits.

During the summer weekends, visitors will sample different cultures when looking at the crafts at the International Marketplace and tasting the World cuisine at the World Cafe near Harbourfront Centre's main stage (currently called the CIBC Stage), with world music as a bonus.

Entering the World Café tent is a bit like experiencing Caravan, condensed under one roof. Most of the food is too spicy for kids but adults can taste a wide variety of meals.

Throughout the summer there's a different festival every weekend. When we showed up, in the middle of July, the Ritmo y Color event was going on. Kids made masks, maracas and ponchos to get ready for a

parade behind giant puppets. Activities may differ from one year to the next.

I was thrilled by the opportunity to make my daughter taste fresh coconut juice directly from a machete-cut shell. Later on, we had tropical fruit on a stick.

During the afternoon, a clown was trying to convince us to follow his dance lessons in the middle of the park. Kids were the first to join in, attracted by the pile of percussion instruments he had laid on the ground.

TIPS (fun for 5 years +)

• It is possible to rent canoes and kayaks from **Harbourfront Canoe & Kayak Centre Toronto** to paddle on Lake Ontario. The centre rents them for $20/hour or $40 for the day ($50 for the kayaks, extra fee for tandem). It takes 20 minutes to paddle to Toronto Islands. Check www.paddletoronto.com or call (416) 203-2277 for more information. They are located west of Harbourfront Centre, at 283A Queen's Quay West.

• Open-air movie screenings called **Free Flicks** are presented on the main stage (currently CIBC Stage) on Wednesday nights from early July to mid-August, when it gets dark enough.

• See **Kajama (tall ship)** on p. 230.

• See **Milk International Children's Festival** on p. 70.

• See **Music with Bites** on p. 102.

• More on the superb outdoor artificial ice rink currently called **Natrel Rink** on p. 372.

• **Queen's Quay Terminal** just east of Harbourfront Centre is small. This beautiful shopping centre is worth a visit. It includes various specialty stores: dolls, musical boxes, kites, toys, candy and more. It also hosts a restaurant Il Fornello with patio by the water.

• The **Lakeside EATS** terrace is great during the warmer days and on cold days after skating. The restaurant's menu at the counter is affordable. During the summer, there's also the **Splash** patio between the pond and the lake, serving food and alcohol.

• See the restaurant **Pier 4** on p. 430.

NEARBY ATTRACTIONS

Harbourfront Centre (416) 973-4000 www. harbourfrontcentre.com	J-10 Downtown Toronto 5-min.

Schedule: Open year-round with variable opening and closing hours depending on the events.
Admission: FREE ground admission.

Directions: 235 Queen's Quay West (west of York St.), Toronto.

MILK INTERNATIONAL FESTIVAL

The Milk gives!

This Festival of the Arts is literally a showcase for the best theatre, dance, music and acrobat shows created for children worldwide.

Over the years, I have been able to appreciate the constant high calibre of the performances presented at the Milk Festival. I saw amazing shows: two artists creating characters with their knees, shins and feet, a performer turned into a giant baby exploring the musical potential of his giant playpen (with the help of digital technology)!

The festival generally includes a number of acrobatic performances which young and energetic audiences really enjoy. Beware! Kids will want to try this at home! The day we were there, acrobats transformed themselves into human sculptures, executing contortions and jumps to the sound of wild African music.

I can't say enough about the site's exciting ambience, thanks to the musical performances that take place on the stage in the Ann Tindal Park, at the heart of the festival, as well as the myriad of interactive activities under tents going on throughout the site.

Young artists can try their hand at some funky crafts usually involving the creation of something they tend to wear for the rest of the day.

You can usually count on some percussion jams everyone can join, percussion instruments and coaching provided. Those are always appreciated!

TIPS (fun for 3 years +)
• The majority of performances last one hour.
• Several shows rely on body language instead of the spoken word.
• If a specific performance catches your fancy, it is advisable to purchase your tickets in advance, as seating is limited. It will cost $1 per ticket, a small fee to reduce the stress level on site! You also may buy tickets on site. A board by the ticket booths will indicate which show is sold out and what is currently available.
• You may call **Harbourfront Centre** Box Office to get a festival program through the mail.

Milk International Children's Festival of the Arts (416) 973-4000 www.harbourfront.on.ca	J-10 Downtown Toronto 5-min.

Schedule: Goes on for eight days, from Sunday of Victoria Day weekend to following Sunday.
Admission: Festival Fun Pass (ground activities only) is $9/person. Moola Lah Pass (activities + one performance) is $12.50/person (or $9 from Tuesday to Friday). Milky Way Pass (activities + two performances) is $15.50/person.
Directions: Harbourfront Centre, 235 Queen's Quay West, Toronto (east of York St.).

CARIBANA

Irresistible!

We are mesmerized by the explosion of colourful spandex, tulle, lace, sparkles, fringes and pompoms, in what has to be Toronto's hottest street celebration and North America's largest such festival.

When the large float finally reaches us (we heard its loud music from blocks away) everybody is consumed by an irresistible euphoria. Lost in the engaging rhythms of calypso, the crowd joins the contagious lead of tireless street dancers. A baby claps enthusiastically while a young girl throws in the occasional whistle blow, perched atop her father's shoulders.

Adorable little girls walk in the procession, adjusting accessories and pink leotards too big for them, while some kids catch their breath on a float before jumping again.

When we reach the parade's finish point (at Dowling Avenue and Lake Shore Boulevard), some 3.5 km away from Exhibition Place, at around 1:30 pm, we are right on time to see it arriving.

The north side of Lake Shore Boulevard was not crowded as most spectators favour the south side and its line-up of food stands. At no time did we feel overwhelmed by large crowds.

Many pedestrian access points open up during the parade to allow easy passage from the north and south sides of the boulevard.

TIPS (fun for 5 years +)

• Bring the fun up a notch and equip your youngsters with their own whistle.
• Remember to bring bottles of water, hats and sunscreen on sunny days.
• Rain or shine, Caribana takes place. I've attended the celebrations under a torrential downpour and admired participants' determination to continue.
• Be warned, music from the floats can be deafeningly loud to young ears.
• Caribana is notorious for starting later than scheduled, and there can be up to 30 minutes between floats.
• The best way to catch sight of the many fabulous costumes (and snap a few pictures), is at **Exhibition Place**. At 3 pm, dancers are still there waiting for their turn in the procession.
• There is a **Junior Caribana** celebration for participants aged 4 to 16 years old. It usually happens one week prior to Caribana. Call for details.

NEARBY ATTRACTIONS	
Ontario Place (5-min.)...............p. 12	
Fort York (5-min.)........................p. 400	

Caribana (416) 466-0321 www.caribana.com	I-9 **Downtown Toronto** 5-min.

 Schedule: Usually the Saturday of the first weekend in August, from 10 am. (For 2004: July 31.)
Admission: FREE ($15 for premium seating at Exhibition Place).
Directions: Starting point at Exhibition Place (at the corner of Strachan Ave. and Lake Shore Blvd.). Runs west-bound along Lake Shore Blvd. up around Dowling Ave.

CANADIAN ABORIGINAL FESTIVAL

Dance competitions, commonly known as the "SkyDome Pow Wow", are the heart of the Festival, attracting over 800 dancers competing in different categories.

They are accompanied by the rhythm of several live drummers and singers who perform around what is known as "the circle of dance".

The "Women's Jingle Dress Dance" is a high point with the clattering sounds of dresses covered with over 300 sewn-in

Regalia of sound and colours

Strolling the open space at the Sky-Dome during the Festival reminds me of the activity and excitement backstage of a show. Whether standing in a food line-up, checking out the market's many stalls or tidying fringes and feathers, dancers clad in beautiful traditional regalia are everywhere and mingle informally with visitors before the competitions.

TIPS (fun for 4 years +)
• More on the **SkyDome** on p. 356.
• Toronto is an aboriginal word meaning "the gathering place."
• You'll find interesting things at the marketplace. We bought a nice wooden set of bow and arrows ($9), as well as a leather quiver ($9), on which an artist burned my daughter's name along with drawings of rabbits and beavers.
• Most activities are adult-oriented: traditional teachings, art exhibition and fashion show. Check the schedule at the entrance to find out more about the children's activities such as storytelling and games.
• See the **Six Nations Fall Festival** on p. 79.

tin cones. Similarly, men move around with tiny bells attached around their ankles.

Most visitors prefer to stand near the "circle of dance" in the **SkyDome** stadium. This allowed my 3-year-old great freedom to roam around without annoying spectators.

In fact, children can stroll easily all over the grounds. But most of all, it was playing with newfound friends inside the large teepee that captivated my little papoose most.

Canadian Aboriginal Festival (519) 751-0040 www.canab.com	I-9 Downtown Toronto 10-min.

 Schedule: Usually last Friday to Sunday in November.
Admission: $10/adults, $5/4-12 years, FREE for 3 years and under. $25/family of 4. Parking is approximately $13 across Bremmer Blvd.
Directions: SkyDome, Toronto (at the northeast corner of Front and John St., north of Bremmer Blvd.). Buy tickets at Gate 7.

NEARBY ATTRACTIONS
CN Tower (2-min. walk).................p. 110
CBC Museum (5-min. walk)......... p. 112

ST. PATRICK'S DAY PARADE

Visit the Land of the Leprechaun with

Green power

This has to be the easiest parade a family could attend, with subway stations, and enough room on the sidewalk all along its circuit.

The appeal of any parade is the anticipation. What surprise is awaiting us around the corner?

Bands can be majestic (especially the bagpipers playing and walking in perfect sync). Floats can be interesting and often funny with original details.

At the St. Patrick's Day Parade, we saw a "castle" with beautifully costumed lords. There was another one with barbarians feasting at the king's court. This float was followed by peasants pushing their wheelbarrows filled with straw. The parade ended with St. Patrick "himself" waving at us from inside a glass box, not unlike… the Pope himself.

The real appeal of the parade for children is the music from bands and floats. They create ambience and are a reason to wave flags and shake it!

The interaction with the parade's marchers also contributes a lot to the fun

of the experience: a clown on a wacky bicycle, two walkers on stilts and a teasing leprechaun, dressed in green with the trademark hat, throwing chocolate coins to the crowd.

Right after the parade, marchers reunited at the **Hilton Hotel** on Richmond Street in a ballroom, for a beer and some dynamic Celtic music. Anyone can attend; it gives you a chance to have a closer look at Miss St. Patrick and some of the costumed marchers.

When we left, children were starting to flood the dance floor to skillfully try a few Celtic dance steps.

TIPS (fun for 3 years +)
• This is no Santa Claus Parade. Don't go expecting elaborate floats.
• The parade started at noon, at the corner of Bloor and St. George Streets. When we got to the intersection of Yonge and Queen Streets at 1:45 pm, the parade was already there, and went on until 3 pm.

St. Patrick's Day Parade
(416) 487-1566
www.topatrick.com

**J-10
Dowtown**
Toronto
10-min.

Schedule: If March 17 falls on a Friday, Saturday or Sunday, the parade takes place the Sunday of that weekend, from noon to 3 pm. Otherwise, the parade is on the preceding Sunday.
Admission: FREE.
Directions: Goes from Bloor St. (at Devonshire) eastbound, southbound on Yonge St. then west on Queen St. The parade ends at University.

NEARBY ATTRACTIONS
Royal Ontario Museum (1-min.)...p. 252
Bata Shoe Museum (1-min.)........p. 254

Caravan

Around the world

Visiting any of Caravan's pavilions makes anyone a tourist in Toronto. You get to taste food you can't name and buy the crafts you would buy, were you to visit the countries represented here. You also mingle with Toronto's cultural communities, each very well represented among the audience in the pavilion that showcases their heritage.

Caravan has been a Toronto tradition for over 30 years. During Caravan, each pavilion (approximately 20 of them) marks the event by selling special foods. Some we recognize and others, we don't: Rasanali (boiled cheese soaked in sugar syrup with rosewater), melomakarono (dough fingers flavoured with orange juice), tulumbi (decadent batter in honey sauce), pavlova (meringue and kiwi cake). So many exotic desserts to discover!

Caravan is also about music and dance. Some performers are as young as two and quite cute to watch. Others are seasoned professionals who will delight you with exotic dances involving Ukrainian red boots, Polynesian grass skirts, Filipino bamboo tinikling, flamenco's castanets and belly-dancing's bells.

More activities are on the program. During my visit, children particularly enjoyed the Ukrainian pavilion, where they could learn to paint their own egg using wax in the old-fashioned way. Everybody loved to join in the circle of dance at the Native pavilion! I thought the sari demonstration at the New Delhi pavilion was fascinating.

Pavilions vary from one year to the next but the festive spirit remains with over 200 shows in nine days.

TIPS (fun for 5 years +)

• At the time of print, the future of Caravan was uncertain (for lack of funds). There was the possibility that it could all take place under the same roof instead of offering pavilions spread all over the city. I can only recommend that you call or check their web site for the 2004 event. In 2005, check the update section on www.torontofunplaces.com for the latest news regarding this outing.

• Mississauga has had its own event called **Carassauga**, for some 20 years. It is held in May, with around 20 pavilions. The 3-day passport costs $10 (FREE for 12 years and under); (905) 615-3010, www.carassauga.com.

• Brampton's version, also over 20 years old, is called **Carabram**. Usually held in July over three days, it includes a dozen pavilions. The 3-day passport costs $10 (FREE under 12 years); check www.carabram.org or call (416) 452-4917.

Caravan (416) 977-0466 www.caravan-org.com	**Toronto** **various** **locations**

 Schedule: Usually from the end of June to beginning of July during the evenings plus weekend afternoons. ATTENTION: later for 2004, READ TIPS!
Admission: 9-day Passport for unlimited access to the pavilions is $25/person. READ TIPS!
Directions: READ TIPS!

See **March Break** at **AGO** on p. 92.

PACIFIC MALL

Ticket to Hong Kong

I have heard from several friends of Chinese friends, who've actually lived in Hong Kong, that going to Pacific Mall would be the closest to experiencing the real thing without catching a plane. Good enough for me! So I grabbed my 10-year-old and took him on a trip... to Markham.

I'm surprised by how small most stores are in the mall (self-proclaimed as the largest Pacific mall in North America). It includes some 300 indoor outlets plus 100 more outdoor stores and restaurants surrounding the building.

Clothes in the windows differ from what you see in the big retail chains. We can't understand one word anybody says and most signs are not in English.

It is all really exotic to us! But the truth is, we feel quite at ease being the visible minority in this environment.

My son thinks he's in heaven when he spots a store selling the collection cards in fashion at the moment, with a dozen guys challenging each other at tables (**Pacific Gifts**, first floor, number E61).

I can't resist buying the cutest Chinese outfit for my 18-month-old niece, pink and gold with the Chinese buttons and collar ($35, tax included in the price, cash only; many stores carry these). Adorable toddlers are actually wearing these colourful clothes in the mall.

We try bubble tea. Our pastel drinks are topped with huge straws and stocked with black spheres at the bottom. These

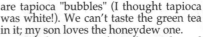
Courtesy of M. Prézeau

are tapioca "bubbles" (I thought tapioca was white!). We can't taste the green tea in it; my son loves the honeydew one.

We buy tons of nicely packaged snacks at **Ding Dong** (a large convenience store located in front of the Asian Bank on the first floor), little cookies shaped like mushrooms covered with chocolate, litchee-flavoured chewy candies, flat marshmallows with a yellow filling mimicking eggs, to name a few. I make a mental note to come back to stock up on these for my daughter's next birthday party!

The second floor is where we find the most exotic section of the mall. Shops are even smaller. The entrance is adorned with dark wood and dragons greet us on large murals.

Our nostrils are caught by the wonderful odour of intriguing doughnut-like pastries, deep-fried under our eyes. Farther, I discover a tiny store (#C-210) filled with gadgets you can personalize with miniature pictures.

In the small foodcourt, we eat a Japanese meal served in gorgeous bento boxes where everything has its own little compartment. Not your usual cafeteria tray; those same boxes are sold for $35 at **Japan, the Art of Tableware**, on the same floor.

Also on the second floor is the **Orbit Entertainment Centre**, a cool arcade my son just had to see. It feels like any other arcade except for the teenage crowd assembled around an improvised band consisting of aspiring musicians playing along with the machines on electronic guitar, keyboard and drums.

My personal biggest find in this mall is the **MHQ Karaoke Box** (second floor, # F33)! Behind a spectacular silver wall of brushed metal with portholes showing Chinese video clips, are corridors with a series of doors leading to small rooms. These are furnished with sofas and a huge television set. Movie buffs will remember seeing such rooms in the film *Lost in Translation* with Bill Murray! You can rent those booths by the hour to sing karaoke with your friends. They offer a huge catalogue of English songs to choose from, in addition to the obvious selection of Chinese songs.

It does not get more exotic than that on this side of the planet!

TIPS (fun for 5 years +)
• Some stores only take cash.
• **First Markham Place**, the other big Chinese mall you'll find in Markham (on Hwy #7, east of Woodbine Avenue, 905-944-1629), is smaller and less exotic but with similar merchandise. It includes the arcade **Jipoh's** and

Fantasy Focus (store #67), a place filled with intriguing photo booths offering a wide variety of treatment. Young customers seem to love these. They even have membership cards! There's a whole line-up of Asian restaurants out of this mall as well as a host of big-box stores and the **Cineplex Odeon First Markham Place**, (905) 474-5101.

NEARBY ATTRACTIONS	
Sandylion Stickers (15-min.)	p. 440

Pacific Mall
· Markham
(905) 947-9560
www.
pacificmalltoronto.com

H-11
N-E
of Toronto
40-min.

Schedule: Sunday to Thursday, 11 am to 8 pm. Friday and Saturday, 11 am to 9 pm.
Admission: FREE.
Directions: In Markham. Take Hwy 404 north, turn east on Steeles Ave. The mall is at the northeast corner of Steeles and Kennedy Rds.

MISSISSAUGA FESTIVAL

Room to move

Missed the Milk Festival at Harbourfront Centre? Try the Mississauga International Children's Festival taking place in and around the Living Arts Centre. The concrete environment doesn't compare with Harbourfront's enchanting waterfront setting, but it is not as crowded: a real advantage!

Our outing starts with a craft activity at Civic Square (next to the City Centre), where my budding artist joins other children in the creation of a spaghetti tree. Meanwhile, a storyteller dances on the outdoor stage while kids in nearby tents are busy craft-ing frames or playing with toys on display.

We make a short stop at the greenhouse as we walk through the City Centre to get to the Living Arts Centre, the festival's performance hotbed.

Outside the Living Arts Centre, an inflatable structure and mini-golf greens are installed beside a most welcomed ice cream stand.

That day, we enjoyed a show by a Swiss artist who gives life to characters made from a giant roll of Kraft paper and we were tickled by a duo of crazy cooks from Alberta, whose full-size kitchen is electronically wired to create a giant drum set.

The year we visited, lots of interactive activities were also offered on the premises between shows. Among other things, kids could build structures with straws or K'Nex and create complicated tubular circuits for golf balls.

The activities vary from one year to the next, depending on the budgets...

TIPS (fun for 3 years +)

• We didn't have trouble getting tickets for the weekend shows we wanted on the day of their presentation.
• To reserve weekend tickets in advance, call the **Living Arts Centre** at (905) 306-6000.
• Underground parking on the premises is free.

Mississauga Int'l Children's Festival
week: (905) 897-8955
weekend: (905) 306-6000
www.kidsfestival.org

I-8
N-W
of Toronto
35-min.

 Schedule: Usually early June, from Wednesday to Saturday. Call to confirm.

 Admission: $8/first show, $7/second show, $10/Saturday performance. Free parking.

 Directions: Living Arts Centre, Mississauga. From Hwy 403 West, exit Hurontario St. southbound. Turn west on Burnhamthorpe Rd.

SIX NATIONS ANNUAL FALL FAIR

Light feet in action

We hear the live singers and musicians as soon as we arrive at the fairground. In order to reach the dance circle, we have to cross a gravel road that has been blocked. With other visitors, we patiently wait (wondering why exactly). All of a sudden, a four-horse wagon flashes by, leaving a huge cloud of dust behind. Now I get it: crossing the road in the middle of the chuck wagon race of the Six Nations Fall Fair would be a perilous affair!

Once the race is over, the gate is opened and we walk to the base-ball diamond turned into the perfect spot for a great **Pow Wow**.

The dance circle is surrounded by sets of bleachers where all visitors can get a good look at participants, dressed in colourful regalia. We are close enough to appreciate the intricate steps per-formed with such light feet that the

dancers seem to never rest their full weight on the ground.

Teenagers and grandparents, preschoolers and adults, male and female alike, all participate in the dance competitions.

I am really pleased that my daughter sees how great the kids are doing. She actually beco-mes so enthu-sed that I have to restrain her from joining the Pow Wow (which should never be con-fused with a dancing party). I tell her she could dance outside of the s t a d i u m instead. After enjoying the dance competi-tion, we spent a full hour alter-nating between the midway (offering some fifteen rides on a pay-as-you-play basis) and the food lane. Lasting a few days, the out-door **Pow Wow** includes a birds of prey demonstration, a rodeo, a demolition derby and even fireworks on Friday.

TIPS (fun for 4 years +)
• You may want to complete your outing with a visit to the longhouse and adjoining **Kanata**, 17th century Iroquois lifestyle interpretation centre, (440 Mohawk Street, Brantford, (519) 752-1229, www.kanatavillage.net).
• Check the **Canadian Aboriginal Festival** on p. 72.

NEARBY ATTRACTIONS
Warplane Museum (20-min.)........p. 245

Six Nations Fall Fair	E-2
• Ohsweken	S-W
(519) 445-0783	of Toronto
	90-min.

 Schedule: Always the weekend following Labour Day weekend (In 2004, September 9 to 12).
Admission: (cash only) Approximately $6/adults, $4/seniors, $2/7-11 years, FREE for 5 years and under. (Pay-per-ride midway.)
Directions: Take QEW then follow Hwy 403 towards Hamilton. Exit Hwy 18 southbound, follow Hwy 54 past Onondaga. Turn right on Chiefswood Rd. to 4th Line.

Oktoberfest Parade

Yodoheleeetee!

There is a great ambience on the street as we wait for the Oktoberfest Parade to start. The crowd is keen; everyone likely got up at the crack of dawn so as not to miss a minute of what must be Canada's earliest parade!

The event, also known as the Thanksgiving Parade, begins in Waterloo at 8:30 am and runs a five-kilometre stretch along King Street. It ends in Kitchener at approximately 10 am. Coming from Toronto, we decide to catch the parade at the end of its journey in Kitchener.

We easily find affordable parking on a public lot. It is 9 am and the crowd keeps pouring in. East of St. Francis Street (where King Street narrows and becomes prettier), there is still plenty of room on the sidewalks. By the Kitchener City Hall, kids burn off some energy jumping on an inflatable structure, while others warm up inside.

By 9:30 am, we find a spot at the corner of Ontario Street next to a family clad in the traditional feathered Bavarian hats. A few minutes later, forty policemen on motorcycles appear in a roar, blasting sirens and all, followed by the first band, from Michigan.

Composed of over 20 bands and some 30 floats, the hour-and-a-half parade boasts a line-up of public officials: mayors, judges, Miss Oktoberfest, the mascot Onkel Hans, as well as members of various German clubs, outfitted in Tyrolian shorts and low-cut dresses. Some really catch children's attention as they flip their whips in the air and yodel. So do the dancers, holding their partners by the waist, feet up in the air and spinning fast.

The floats, although modest, were fun to watch. There was a huge bear drumming on a turtle, a 2-storey-high inflated clown, a 40-foot inflated lion and a big turkey. Shoppers Drug Mart's trademark giant bear was so huge it had to be pulled down to slip under traffic lights.

After the parade, we take in a number of street entertainers at the Wilkommen Platz, downtown Kitchener.

TIPS (fun for 3 years +)

• No wonder Oktoberfest is so strong in that region. In 1873, Kitchener, with a population of 3,000, was still called Berlin!

• The Oktoberfest-Thanksgiving Parade is broadcast live on CTV.

• Call or check the web site to find out more about the Oktoberfest program.

Kitchener-Waterloo Oktoberfest Thanksgiving Day Parade
D-1 West of Toronto 70-min.
1-888-294-4267
www.oktoberfest.ca

 Schedule: Held on the Thanksgiving Monday, starting at 8:30 am.
Admission: FREE.
Directions: From Hwy 401 West, exit #278/Hwy 8 northbound. Follow King St. to downtown. The Parade runs southbound from Waterloo to Kitchener along King St.

DUSK DANCE

The concept is clever: the public is led from one station to the next through a public park, to enjoy a series of 10-minute choreographies inspired by the natural surroundings. Some pieces are more traditional; others are quite experimental or even hilarious. The great dancers are often within arms-reach from the wide-eyed kids. You can see many children impulsively mimicking the movements of the dancers.

Dance to another tune

Going to the park takes on new meaning when the Dusk Dance event is on. Kids are in for a surprise! They might see white-clad people hiding in the forest under the spell of strange music, graceful women running around the field with flowing scarves, acrobat dancers jumping from trees...

Dusk Dance provides quite a refreshing approach to modern dance and clearly is an original way to expose our kids to contemporary dance.

Even the presentation between

choreographies is funny. As we walked to the next performance, our host suggested, tongue in cheek, that we do a collective sound: "Lets all say b a h h h h h !" Hundreds of us did; picture that!

TIPS (fun for 3 years +)

• Don't install yourself too comfortably before the event because you will keep changing places to watch the next choreography somewhere else in the park. A thick blanket could be useful.
• Dusk Dance is sometimes presented as well at **Dufferin Grove Park** (p. 324).
• This amazing urban event is organized by **Corpus**, a most dynamic dance company also involved in the creation and presentation of its work around the world (their trademark humorous dance A Flock of Flyers has delighted audiences for years!). This explains why the Dusk Dance cannot be considered as a yearly rendez-vous. Dates might vary from one summer to the next. The event might even skip a summer from time to time according to the company's tight schedule. Nevertheless, I really wanted to include it in the guide because it is bound to come back now and then, an event not to be missed.
• **Corpus** also organizes a yearly fundraising indoor event during which they present their great creations. Call the company for details.

Dusk Dance (416) 516-4025 www.corpus.ca	**I-10** **Downtown** Toronto 20-min.

 Schedule: Usually several evenings in a row, starting end of June or beginning of July depending on Corpus' schedule. Always at 7:30 pm. Call to confirm.
Admission: Pay-as-you-can.
Directions: Traditionally held in two parks. Withrow Park, south of Danforth, between Carlaw Ave. and Logan Ave. Dufferin Grove Park, on Dufferin, south of Bloor St. West.

Famous People Players

In the dark

Taking your child to Famous People Players' dinner theatre is as close as you'll get to a grown-up outing without incurring the cost of a sitter.

Your only concern here may be to maintain children's appropriate behaviour during the elaborate hour-long dinner. After the show, all guests come back to the dining room for a tasty dessert.

It is likely the white-gloved waiter serving your meal in the dining room will also perform on stage that evening. This you won't find out though until all performers remove their black hoods for the closing salute.

All productions are presented in black light, that is with performers who remain unseen to the public because they are dressed in black against a black backdrop, and who manipulate various fluorescent props that seemingly "float" around with a life of their own. Light-hearted, the shows often include tall puppet characters (controlled by three performers), lip-syncing to original musical scores, and humourously designed objects miming scenes in a lively choreography.

Various musical productions are presented throughout the year, with some involving a story, while others simply present a series of great songs. All use the same concept.

I attended a **Christmas** show with two boys aged 7 and 9, and both just loved it. Musicals are appropriate for any child who likes lively songs.

Parents will be moved when they learn this company's mandate is to present world class stage productions and integrate, through training, people who are developmentally challenged. Between the reception, the restaurant, and the performance, these people run the whole show!

As the founder of the company, Diane Dupuy, puts it: "What you see is sensational... What you don't see is inspirational."

TIPS (fun for 7 years +)

• Stars' photos you'll see on the walls aren't there just for decorating purposes. These famous actors and singers have actually made financial contributions to Famous People Players.

NEARBY ATTRACTIONS	
Ontario Place (10-min.)	p. 12
Fort York (10-min.)	p. 400

Famous People Players Dine & Dream Theatre
(416) 532-1137
www.fpp.org

**I-10
Downtown
Toronto
10-min.**

Schedule: Open year-round from Tuesday to Saturday. Dinner shows: arrival 6 pm to 6:45 pm, dinner at 7 pm, show at 8 pm, dessert at 9:15 pm. Lunch shows: arrival at 11am-11:45 am, lunch at noon, show at 1 pm, dessert at 2:15 pm.
Admission: (tax not included) $49/adults, $43/seniors, $35/12 years and under.
Directions: 110 Sudbury St., Toronto. From Lake Shore Blvd., take Strachan northbound. Turn westbound on King St. and turn right on Sudbury St. (just west of Shaw St.).

MYSTERIOUSLY YOURS

Guess what?

Around dessert time, the extroverted members of a noisy family pour into the restaurant from every angle, entering into individual conversations with diners, in a joyous cacophony. A piano player swiftly replaces the taped music in the background and all of a sudden, we are in the midst of the Godfather's retirement party.

A nervous black-eyed man with unbuttoned tuxedo shirt asks my wide-eyed son if he has seen a little plastic bag somewhere while the Godfather, his dad, graciously welcomes "dear friends" at the next table. In the vicinity, his sister is fishing for compliments on her Versace party dress while a pink satin-clad woman is kissing an "old boyfriend" she had just "recognized" among the guests.

TIPS (fun for 10 years +)
• The restaurant opens at 6:30 pm but action only starts at around 8 pm. The mystery is solved before 10:30 pm.
• Drinks and soft drinks are not included in the fixed price of the meal.
• Most items offered on the menu won't appeal to the average child. You may arrive a bit before 8 pm and pay only for the play. Note there's a **Mandarin** at 2200 Yonge Street, in Canada Square, four blocks north of the theatre (with well-priced parking at the top of Canada Square). Reservations are a must, as you don't want to be late for the show; call (416) 486-2222.
• Matinee presentations are offered at least two Wednesdays each month at the **Toronto Historic Old Mill** Restaurant (lunch at 11:30 am, mystery at 12:45 pm); $53/lunch and show, $35/show only. See **Old Mill** on p. 438.

People of all ages attend the show. The nice (and young) grandparents at our table are quick to offer repartees to the actors who come to visit us. The more we improvise, the funnier it gets. My companion is thrilled to watch adults play make-believe!

It doesn't take long for a murder to occur (the Godfather's son) and for Lieutenant Carumbo to appear, bearing an unmistakable resemblance to Peter Falk's Colombo. The subsequent interrogation launches into quick and witty dialogue between the comedians evenly spread throughout the restaurant.

Many of us end up acting a small staged part, adding to the interactive nature of the attraction (my 10-year-old was turned into a mobster offering his condolences to the Godfather, cigar in mouth). Throughout the play, clues are given away; little details that will help those who listen carefully solve the mystery. We are too busy laughing to pay attention.

The murders staged by Mysteriously Yours keep changing. Over thirty plays were created over the last seventeen years. You can expect a different mystery roughly every six months, investigated by the likes of Hercule Poirot, Miss Marple or Sherlock Holmes.

Mysteriously Yours (416) 486-7469 www. mysteriouslyyours.com	I-10 Downtwn Toronto 25-min.

Schedule: Year-round, Thursday, Friday and Saturday (dinner from 6:30 pm, mystery at 8 pm).
Admission: (including tax) $75/dinner and show, $45/show only ($5 more on Saturdays).
Directions: 2026 Yonge St., Toronto. Located four blocks south of Eglinton, on the west side.

STAGE WEST

Go West!

A buffet instead of a fixed menu makes a big difference, especially with young children. It allows them to stretch their legs, returning again and again to explore the exciting display of food. Then, they're ready to settle down to watch the show.

We remain at our table in the elegant theatre restaurant to enjoy the performance. Many seats in the large multi-level room are horse-shoe-shaped booths. I love the cozy feeling of those and they were a great hit with my daughter. Covered with a long tablecloth, it made for a nice little fort to hide under with her little friend after dessert, before the play.

If you can't book a booth, don't worry. Conveniently, you'll have a good view of the stage from any of the well-padded seats.

The children's productions are lunch shows presented during the March Break and Christmas time. I've seen three different ones; they all lasted a bit less than one

hour. While I found some better than others, my kids were equally thrilled by the whole experience on all three occasions.

All year-round, they also produce dinner musicals and concerts, many suitable for families. Impersonators regularly return with tributes to the Beatles, Abba and other legendary singers. They look like the real thing! I suspect these would be fun for pre-teens.

Courtesy of Stage West

To give you an idea of the kind of plays they produce: in 2005, they will present *Joseph and the Amazing Technicolour Dream Coat* from February to April and *Anne of Green Gables* from April to July.

Stage West is also a hotel! Their family packages are popular among the local families who just want a change in scenery. Must be the hotel's pool with a 3-storey-high water slide!

TIPS (fun for 3 years +)

• Their **Christmas** Hotel Package for a family of 4 includes: Saturday night in a suite, 4 tickets to Saturday kids' lunch show, access to the pool, 2 tickets for the Sunday Brunch show (for mom and dad) plus babysitting and lunch for the kids (around $300 plus tax).

• Their **March Break** Package for a family of 4 includes: 2 nights in a suite, 4 tickets to the kids' lunch show and access to their great pool, craft room, ping pong room, Kiddies Bingo and free shuttle to **Square One** (around $300 plus tax).

NEARBY ATTRACTIONS

Stage West Theatre Restaurant
(905) 238-0042
1-800-263-0684
www.stagewest.com

I-8
N-W
of Toronto
35-min.

 Schedule: Lunch from 12:30 pm, show at 1:45 pm. Christmas shows on Saturdays, from mid-November to the first week of January. March Break shows on Saturdays in March and during the March Break weekdays (except Wednesday). Check their web site or call for the year-round program of concerts or plays.

 Admission: Kids lunch shows around $25 per person plus tax. Other dinner shows around $50 plus tax.

 Directions: 5400 Dixie Rd., Mississauga (south of Hwy 401, turn west on Matheson Blvd to access entrance).

TODAY'S PARENT KIDSUMMER

One treat a day

On a Kidsummer day, one might experience soap bubbles like never before, get the "inside scoop" on how ice cream is really made, enjoy a 1-hour tour of the Toronto Harbour or check out how animals are cared for at a veterinary hospital.

For the past 17 years, Kidsummer's mission has been to give children access to fun events during the summer months, by sponsoring substantially reduced entry fees at established venues and attractions, or by simply organizing its own events.

Under the auspices of Canadian magazine *Today's Parent*, the yearly summer-long event provides a myriad of activities all across the Greater Toronto Area. Its biggest focus is the free admission to specific attractions offered to children 12 years and under on certain days. Accompanying adults pay regular admission fees, yet it can represent great savings for a family.

To date, Kidsummer days have been offered at many attractions included in this guide: Ontario Place, Hockey Hall of Fame, Cullen Gardens, Toronto Zoo and the likes. You'll have to consult this year's calendar to find out what's being offered this summer.

Kidsummer also offers the opportunity for exceptional hands-on activities you otherwise might miss. Mind you, they require a bit of organization since you need to pre-register to secure a space at these specific events.

In past years, young visitors have enjoyed a theatre performance followed by a meeting with the actors and a visit to the prop shop at the children's theatre. Some children have learned to tap their feet to the flamenco beat, with the Academy of Spanish Dance. Others have met the people behind the scenes at YTV, done a special tour of CBC or visited 98.1 CHFI studios.

The year I participated with my family, drop-in activities were offered at the Orthopaedic and Arthritic Hospital. It turned out to be interactive, fun and educational. My son ended up with a cast! Last year, Kids could visit the Willowdale Animal Hospital.

Some kids had the chance to be involved in a workshop with Rona Homes & Gardens.

TIPS (fun for 3 years +)

• Kidsummer is under *Today's Parent* administration. You will find the Kidsummer calendar and pre-registration information in their magazine's July issue (as well as in *Chatelaine*).

• Call to check availability of activities and reserve. Better yet, check online, you'll know right away if the activity you want is available.

Today's Parent Kidsummer
1-866-363-5437
(seasonal number)
www.kidsummer.com

Greater Toronto Area

Schedule: July 1 to August 31 (hours vary for different events).
Admission: Most events are FREE for children 12 years and under. Some adult fees apply. Pre-registration fees to some activities are $5.
Directions: All over the Greater Toronto Area.

THOMAS FOSTER PICNIC

A gift from Heaven

"Free pizza?" ask the incredulous passers-by. **"And the pony ride is also free?"** Yes it is, along with refreshments, cotton candy, miniature golf and other activities planned for the occasion.

For over 50 years, the Thomas Foster Annual Picnic has created cheerful effervescence in the district where it arrives almost without warning, on a beautiful weekend day. I should know, it has been held on my own street!

The story is moving. Upon his death, Thomas Foster, a Toronto businessman, left a bequest to the city, dedicating it to the organization of an annual neighbourhood picnic, until the funds run out (but it seems that the well-administered money keeps on regenerating).

TIPS (fun for 3 years +)

• Thomas Foster became a butcher in Cabbagetown, served as Mayor of Toronto from 1925 to 1927 and made a large fortune from real estate. His unusual will included funds to feed Toronto birds in winter, for needy newsboys in the city and to plant trees.

We can expect it to be held again for many years to come. Few people know about the nature of this event. When it is announced that the picnic is held in a certain area, people don't really understand that it's a great party until they see it before their eyes.

This unexpected gift makes everyone happy. By word of mouth, news of the picnic circulates. Neighbours waiting in line recognize each other.

Every time his picnic is taking place, I'm sure Thomas Foster is smiling in his grave.

City of Toronto
(416) 338-2614
www.city.toronto.on.ca

Schedule: The annual picnic is usually held the second Saturday in June, from noon to 4 pm. Call to confirm exact date of next picnic.

Admission: FREE.

Directions: The event can be held in any park managed by the City of Toronto. Call for exact location of next picnic.

TORONTO STREET FESTIVAL

Street smart!

During the Toronto Street Festival, Yonge Street is transformed. A short section of Canada's longest street becomes traffic free and takes on the appearance of a fun fair including trapeze artists balancing against the backdrop of skyscrapers, a large inflated dragon engulfing happy children and people gathering around one of the many outdoor performances. The street becomes an extravagant display of colour and excitement.

When we were there, children were enjoying improvised sandboxes sitting next to a large sandcastle under construc-tion. Nearby, professional divers were jumping off high diving boards into a small pool. At one inter-section, passengers bounced on board a large inflated replica of the Titanic. At another, chil-dren bounced in more inflated structures.

Down the road, visi-tors embarked on a ride inside the elevated cabin of an Ontario Hydro truck's hydraulic arm, while others enjoyed making crafts in one of the many tents along the street.

Further down, a good selection of rides (for a fee) attracted visitors, as did performances by acrobats and trained dogs participating in an obstacle race.

Add street performers and an impressive flow of visitors to the mix and you get a good idea of this fun-packed, high-density event. While activities change from year to year, the same spirit remains.

TIPS (fun for 3 years +)

• You would need one hour to walk the section of Yonge Street where activi-ties take place. A convenient alternative is to purchase a day pass from the TTC (Toronto Transit Commission), as it gives you unlimited entry to all subway stations including those along Yonge Street.

• When we visited, most activities were free except the midway rides (at Eglinton) for which we purchased indi-vidual tickets. Expect long line-ups for the free children's activities at Lawrence.

• You will find a list of activities on-site for the two-day festival and a series of discounts coupons to Toronto's main attractions.

• In the spirit of the new **WinterCity Festival** (see p. 90), the gourmet event Summerlicious is attached to the street festival, with prix fixe menus available at over 100 restaurants city-wide.

• See **Eggspectation** on p. 436.

Celebrate Toronto Street Festival (416) 338-0338 www. toronto.ca/special_events	I-10 5 locations 15-30 min.

Schedule: Usually held first or second weekend in July, Friday evening (Dundas Square only). Saturday, noon to 11 pm and Sunday noon to 8 pm.

Admission: FREE (extra charge for midway rides).

Directions: Along Yonge St., at the intersection of Dundas St., Bloor St., St. Clair Ave., Eglinton Ave. and Lawrence Ave. (all serviced by a subway station).

OAKVILLE WATERFRONT FESTIVAL

Courtesy of E.Ritson

As good as it gets

Coronation Park during the Oakville Waterfront Festival is my kind of walkabout! The crowd, big without reaching Toronto's proportions, spreads comfortably over the huge waterfront site. The event is extremely well organized, down to the free shuttle buses from the free parking lots at Oakville, Bronte and Sheridan College Go Stations.

It takes us fifteen minutes to ride the shuttle bus from Oakville Go Station to **Coronation Park**. We get to see how the whole town is celebrating.

Not long after we pass the gates at Coronation Park, we come across children involved in a collective clay creation. Next door, others are making big soap bubbles. Further, tents are bursting with activities of cookie decoration, mask making, play dough creation and more.

Children get their share of cardio on the inflatable structures and burn more

energy yet on the two playgrounds. Our kids are thrilled to cool down in the colourful spray pad. Animal shows are the norm at this festival. Last time I checked, there was going to be parrot and dog shows. Past the sponsors' tents, a dynamic band galvanizes the audience at the big Waterfront Stage which will host a roster of great shows throughout the Festival.

Since my last visit, they've added a pay-as-you-play theme park with kiddie rides and major big rides such as a portable 110-foot-high Drop-Zone!

To top it all, **fireworks** are presented at 10 pm on Friday and Saturday.

There is more to the Oakville Festival than a family can handle in a day. In summary: this is as good as it gets!

TIPS (fun for 2 years +)
• Don't forget bathing suits, sunscreen and bottles of water.
• To find out about the schedule of activities, check their web site.
• See **Coronation Park** on p. 381.
• See **Whimpy's** and **Fire Hall** restaurants on pp. 434-435.

Oakville Waterfront Festival
• Oakville
(905) 847-7975
Or (905) 847-1216
www.oakvillefestival.com

D-2
West
of Toronto
35-min.

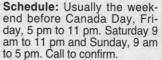

Schedule: Usually the weekend before Canada Day, Friday, 5 pm to 11 pm. Saturday 9 am to 11 pm and Sunday, 9 am to 5 pm. Call to confirm.

Admission: $12/person in advance or $18 at the gate for the three days ($12 if you show up on Sunday). FREE for 5 years and under. You can buy tickets on-line.

Directions: Coronation Park, Oakville. From QEW West, take exit #118/Trafalgar Rd. southbound. Turn west on Cross Ave. to Oakville GO Station. Take the Festival shuttle bus to Coronation Park.

TORONTO BUSKERFEST

Real urban fun

A menacing gladiator slowly walks towards my son and stops one foot short of his face. My son bravely sustains the look, at the same time shy and amused by the attention while people start to gather around us. Little did he know that he was about to be held hostage, serving as a shield between the heartless warrior and his enemy.

Now, we know first hand the BuskerFest qualifies as an interactive event! In the next two hours as we walked from one attraction to the next, my 9-year-old keener took part in a sword fight, he shook hands with an extraterrestrial, he was involved in a balloon sculpture contest and he passed the hat for a wacky cowgirl. I think his blond hair had something to do with being selected at every corner.

Among other skits, we saw a wacky black-belt performer from New York, the most interactive Men in Tights from Toronto and a cowgirl from California who claimed she would "milk us for all we were worth" at the end of her act.

The following year, we saw a naughty Australian contortionist covered with tattoos, amazing break-dancers from New York, out-of-control acrobat dancers from the UK and a local favourite, Mark Cmor, who will grab your cell phone if it rings during his performance and engage in a conversation with your unsuspecting friend. Shy people beware! Expect great interaction and lots of jokes and teasing from these free-spirited street performers.

It is quite interesting to see how humour differs from one country to the next. Over the years, I have noticed that Australians are the most provocative, UK performers play with the absurd, Americans are more politically correct and Canadians have a tendency to downplay their act to better surprise you with something bold when you're off guard.

Initially confined to Nathan Phillips Square, the street event has moved to Front Street near the St. Lawrence Market and should remain there for years.

TIPS (fun for 5 years +)

• Make sure you bring a handful of loonies to the event. The shows are free but hats circulate at the end of every performance. Kids like to contribute their share. Buskers are not paid to perform during the event. Our donation is their bread and butter.

• The donations you make at the entrance to the car-free zone goes to **Epilepsy Toronto**. Toronto BuskerFest is actually an awareness event organized by this not-for-profit charity.

• The event now includes free little workshops under tents allowing kids to learn more about the art of mime, drama, magic and more.

• See **Le Marché Mövenpick** on p. 437.

NEARBY ATTRACTIONS
St. James Cathedral (1-min. walk) p. 113
Hockey Hall (10-min. walk)............ p. 362

Toronto BuskerFest (416) 964-9095 www. torontobuskerfest.com	J-10 Downtown Toronto 10-min.

Schedule: The organizers want to stick to the weekend before Labour Day, in August (including the Thursday and the Friday preceding this weekend), from noon to midnight (closes at 5 pm on Sunday). Call to confirm.
Admission: Donations for Epilepsy Toronto at the entrance. Pay-what-you-can for individual busker performance.
Directions: Front St., between Church and Jarvis. There's a public parking lot on Church, south of Front.

WinterCity Festival

New tradition...

Remember Toronto Winterfest with its host of indoor and outdoor family shows and activities evenly spread between two poles of the city? Now it's time to forget it all and adapt to a new version with a new name, new concept and new ambition.

Some will miss the old concept: the midway, the indoor and outdoor craft activities, the numerous family shows. The core of the event has switched to downtown Toronto, with the **Eaton Centre**, **Dundas Square** and **Nathan Phillips Square** offering most of the program, with a few family shows still presented at **Mel Lastman Square**. At the time of print, they were considering adding more locations.

The WinterCity Festival has the ambition to turn the ex local attraction into a high-profile urban and tourist event, in the spirit of Montreal's successful Festival des Lumières. Hence the Winterlicious part involving prix fixe menus in numerous restaurants throughout the city. Time to get a babysitter!

Families can still count on outdoor weekend shows. We saw the Kratt Brothers (famous for their *Zaboomafoo* television shows) at the **Dundas Square**. Sesame Street, Babar and Strawberry Shortcake were also featured during the festival.

Everyone can enjoy top-calibre evening shows. Last winter, the opening ceremony was a spectacular affair involving thrilling percussion and showers of fireworks. Another ambitious show featured a giant human mobile 35 metres in the air. We saw great acrobats in action from the mezzanine of the **Eaton Centre**. Everyone could have skating fun accompanied by live music at **Nathan Phillips** rink on many occasions. WinterCity is bound to evolve. It takes time for an event to become a tradition.

TIPS (fun for 3 years +)

• WinterCity offers getaway package deals with hotels and a series of discounts at Toronto's main attractions. You can print discount coupons from their web site or get them in the brochure distributed on the site of the major attractions of the festival.

• Small restaurants and coffee shops around **Dundas Square** and Yonge Street sold hot chocolate to warm the spectators during the shows.

• Check **Eggspectation** on p. 436.

NEARBY ATTRACTIONS
Hockey Hall/Fame (10-min.walk) p. 362

WinterCity Festival
(416) 338-0338
www.
toronto.ca/special_events

I-10
2 locations
15-35 min.

 Schedule: Two weeks in February (usually including Friday, Saturday and Sunday of the second weekend). Call for exact dates and hours.

 Admission: FREE. You can download coupons for participating attractions from the web site or get them in the official Festival brochure.

Directions: Locations throughout the city, most probably including Dundas Square, Eaton Centre, Nathan Phillips Square and Mel Lastman Square. Call or check web site for exact locations.

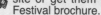

MORE WINTER FESTIVALS

The white stuff

Most of the winter festivals take place around February when the probability of iced lakes and snowfalls is at the highest. They all have the right stuff to bring us fun in the cold.

What first comes to my mind when I think about winter festivals are the hilarious cardboard toboggan races of Penetang's **Winterama Carnival**. They come in all shapes.

So much effort was put into building the toboggans, with such little results on the hill! The giant snowman would slide sideways, in danger of crossing paths with the UFO and the heavy life-size jeep. The first explorers' slow-moving canoe was running against the military tent complete with fire pit, both totally ignoring aerodynamic laws.

When visiting this 55-year-old carnival, we also saw the Centennial Museum, took a helicopter ride, watched snow sculptures and participated in a kids' ice-fishing derby. Check their web site for a list of accommodations.

Richmond Hill Winter Carnival has been going on for over 36 years. I have not visited it but we have skated at **Mill's Pond** (p. 374) and the setting is perfect for such an event.

We enjoyed **Barrie Winterfest's**

dogsled rides on the lake. We also saw snowmobiles and sailboards mounted on skates.

In Heritage Park, parents were "curling" on the ice formed over the water, using their laughing children as "rocks". Kids had fun in the ice maze and going down the snow tubing slide built for the occasion. There were also artists sculpting from huge ice blocks. We visited this carnival on our way back from **Snow Valley Tubing** (p. 378); it was a perfect combination.

Orillia Winter Carnival's highlight was its 1,200 sq. ft ice castle. Also expect Kid's tent, snow sculpture, dogsled rides, petting zoo, lumberjack show, and a midway.

TIPS (fun for 3 years +)

• Activities vary from one year to the next, call or check the winter festivals' web sites.

• Call on the day of the event to check the weather conditions (different from the GTA's)! Some activities could be cancelled if weather gets too cold, making it unbearable, or too mild, making activities on ice unsafe.

Winter festivals:
• **Richmond Hill Winter Carnival**
(905) 771-5478 (H-10 on map)
www.wintercarnival.net
When: Usually the first full weekend of February
• **Orillia Winter Carnival**
(705) 329-2333 (A-3 on map)
www.orilliawintercarnival.ca
When: Usually the second weekend of February (In 2005: February 11-13)
• **Barrie Winterfest**
(705) 739-4285 or 1-800-668-9100
www.city.barrie.on.ca (B-2 on map)
When: Usually the first full weekend of February (In 2005: February 5-6)
• **Penetanguishene Winterama**
(705) 549-2232 (A-2 on map)
www.town.penetanguishene.on.ca
When: Usually in mid-February (In 2005: February 18-19)

ART GALLERY OF ONTARIO

Off the Wall!

My little artist's jaw drops once his tiny drawing on a minuscule plastic square is placed into a slide and changed into a huge and flamboyant mural that appears like magic on the dark wall. That's how AGO turns the newest generation into artists.

As you enter the **Off the Wall!** discovery zone for children, you can't miss the treehouse that serves as the drawing corner. Behind, a large mural inspired by the Group of Seven welcomes us with the image of a lake and a real canoe.

Once the kids have selected from the dozens of costumes and accessories found in the You're Framed section, they get on stage. Behind them, the set is made of a large canvas reproduction of a master's painting. In front of them, their image is projected on a large screen, creating a stunning visual.

During the Family Sundays, the AGO opens its studio to the public: a huge room with high ceilings, the perfect environment to nurture the whole family's creativity. Different tables offer all the material for printing or sculpting activities. A whole section on the floor is used for painting.

Every first Sunday of the month, Family Sundays adds performers and special tours to the program.

As for the rest of the AGO, you're pretty sure to find intriguing installations in the Contemporary Gallery. Don't miss **The Grange**, the historical building at the back of the museum.

I suggest you visit the other galleries with a theme in mind: children, animals, winter... It will turn the tour into a scavenger hunt.

TIPS (fun for 3 years +)

• At the time of print, the AGO was undergoing renovations, to be completed by the end of March 2005. **Off the Wall!** will remain open until the end of 2004. Call to confirm the situation for 2005.

• The AGO is a sure bet for a successful **March Break** outing! **Off the Wall!** is open all week and craft activities, linked to the special exhibition at the time are offered. Performers are invited. Special activities are presented in the different galleries and the museum offers extended hours.

• The AGO's gift shop is fabulous and includes many great children's toys. A fancy snack bar is right next to it.

NEARBY ATTRACTIONS

Art Gallery of Ontario (AGO)
(416) 979-6615
or (416) 979-6649
www.ago.net

I-10
Downtown
Toronto
10-min.

Schedule: Closed on Mondays. Open Saturday and Sunday, 10 am to 5:30 pm; Tuesday, Thursday and Friday, 11 am to 6 pm; Wednesday, 11 am to 8:30 pm. Off the Wall! is open Saturdays and Sundays, 1 to 5 pm and Tuesday to Friday during the March Break. Family Sundays offered from early November to end of March.

Admission: $12/adults, $6/6-15 years old, $25/family of 7, FREE 5 years and under. FREE on Wednesdays from 6 to 8:30 pm. Does not include admission to temporary exhibits.

Directions: 317 Dundas St. West, Toronto (between McCaul and Beverley).

McMichael Art Collection

Inspired hands-on

There is no better way to initiate kids to art appreciation than by taking them to a Drop-in Studio activity in the heart of the McMichael gallery on a Family Sunday. Who knows what awaits them? They might create their own sketch book or cut and layer coloured tissue paper into a landscape.

When we were visiting, one hands-on workshop was held in the little studio located in front of the gallery. Our youngster got to choose from a mountain of socks adorned with glass eyes and rubber noses and made her own animal puppet.

No other painters have better depicted nature than Tom Thompson and the Group of Seven. The museum holds more than 2000 of their masterpieces.

Seeing Group of Seven reproductions on placemats and stamps has never given me the feeling of being overexposed to their art. Each time, I rediscover them with the eyes of a child. But seeing these paintings with a child is another story, I must admit.

An easy way to do it is to select a theme and have them look for it in the paintings. This treasure hunt may lead to cries of excitement when they spot their theme but... galleries are not churches after all!

We criss-crossed all the rooms, looking for autumn leaves on the canvases. The gallery's walls seemed to my son like storybook pages on which he was looking for coloured trees. Meanwhile, he was noticing that certain landscapes were covered in snow and that people were drawn on others. It became a great observation exercise on the sly.

Wide windows, framing the same nature painters seek to capture, are another reason to appreciate the gallery. Just looking through them makes us want to go outside and play. That's exactly what we did after our tour. A wide path, lined with little trails, undulates through the site. On our way to the parking lot, we stopped to pet a few bronze wolves resting by the path!

TIPS (fun for 4 years +)

• For a great **March Break** off the beaten track, the gallery offers special craft activities, hands-on activities and entertainment in the lobby and in different galleries.

• The snack bar at the path's entrance by the parking lot, was turned into a classroom. The restaurant inside the gallery used to be quite posh but now caters to families, selling snacks and light lunches.

NEARBY ATTRACTIONS	

McMichael Canadian Art Collection · Kleinburg (905) 893-1121 www.mcmichael.com	**C-3 N-W of Toronto 45-min.**

 Schedule: Open daily from May 1 to October 31, 10 am to 5 pm (close at 4 pm rest of the year). Family Sundays are held on the second Sunday each month, 11 am to 4 pm.

 Admission: $15/adults, $12/6-18 years and seniors, $30/family of 5, FREE for 5 years and under. Parking is $5.

 Directions: 10365 Islington Ave., Kleinburg. From Hwy 400 North, take exit #35/Major Mackenzie Dr. westbound, then follow the signs to Kleinburg.

TORONTO PUBLIC LIBRARY

Kids flip... the pages

Through the Toronto Public Library, over 12 million items are put at our disposal: books, videos, CDs, CD-ROMs, cassettes, magazines and newspapers, in more than 100 languages. It is an invaluable free service.

To obtain a library card, go to any branch and bring identification on which your name and address appear.

We can borrow as many books as we want, for a 21-day period, a manageable time limit for busy parents. Three videos can be borrowed at no charge for a 7-day period.

Only videos have to be returned to

the same branch where they were borrowed. Thanks to a computerized system, the books can be borrowed from and returned to any branch (which can be useful when visiting another part of the city). You can also request books to be shipped to your local branch from any of the 98 branches.

Library activities

Books are just the tip of the iceberg. You need to flip through a copy of the Toronto Public Library publication *What's On* to grasp the extent and variety of the free activities that take place at the different branches, many of which are drop-in activities. Most programs are less than one hour long.

Many branches offer programs for children: Babytime (for babies 0-18 months) or Toddler Time (19-35 months). Preschool Storytime is for those who are ready to be on their own in a group. Family Preschool Storytime is for children 1 to 5 with their parents or caregivers.

I have attended many activities with my children. Each time, we stayed afterwards to read books and came back with piles of them.

Lillian H. Smith Library

The Lillian H. Smith branch (located at 239 College Street, east of Spadina, (416) 393-7746) offers thousands of illustrated book titles, including hundreds of books for toddlers.

Younger children love to go there to see the spiral staircase and to sit in the pleasant reading corner for kids.

TIPS (fun for 1 year +)

• Obtain a library card under your child's name. The late fine is much lower for children than for adults! Take a sturdy bag to the library to bring back all the books the children want.

• Your child can hear a story on the phone 24 hours a day with the Dial-A-Story service! Stories for different age groups are told in over five languages: (416) 395-5400.

• Toronto Public Library pays special attention to the **March Break**. In the *What's On* issue of January to March, you may consult the March Break Highlight pages or check the programs scheduled for each branch to find out about entertaining and free activities involving Reptilia, Stylamanders, Mad Science or clowns, to name a few cool options.

• Many branches also offer activities during **Halloween**.

Toronto Public Library
(416) 393-7131
www.tpl.toronto.on.ca

Schedule: Varies according to branch.

Costs: The late fine for library items is 30¢ per day up to a maximum of $12 per item for adults, and 10¢ per day up to a maximum of $4 per item for children 12 years and under. To replace a lost card, it is $2/adults and $1/children (cash or cheques only).

Directions: Various locations around the GTA.

TORONTO FRENCH BOOK FAIR

French connection

Here's one for parents of children in immersion schools! A bit like the "Word on the Street" event but indoor and spread over four days, this event gathers under one big roof the best publishers of French books, with a strong presence of children's literature. Time to stock up!

Book fairs have been a tradition for years in Quebec so it was natural to import the concept to Toronto over ten years ago. Like its sisters in Montreal and Ottawa, the Toronto French Book Fair (Le Salon du livre de Toronto) provides a space where visitors can buy French books, meet with authors and assist in round table discussions.

The Toronto version offers an obvious additional advantage in a city with very few options for buying French literature. You'll find many big names among the exhibitors such as: Boréal, Casterman, La courte échelle, Gallimard, Hachette, Héritage Jeunesse, J'ai lu and Nathan. You'll find comic books, youth literature, picture books, novels, reference books or guides in all price ranges.

The book show also puts together workshops for the thousands of students flocking from the French and immersion schools all around the GTA. Indeed, the busiest time to visit the book fair is Thursday and Friday during the day. Younger kids are happy to hug popular characters such as Franklin the Turtle (Benjamin la tortue, in French!)

In the latest years, the Salon has started to offer a daycare service for the 2- to 8-years-old, complete with storytelling, drama sessions, craft activities and other means to amuse them… in French.

Adult francophiles will of course find the French classics and latest novels from francophone authors of all origins. French immersion at its best!

TIPS (fun for 6 years +)

• **Librairie Champlain**, the major French bookstore in Toronto, is open year-round. It is located at 468 Queen Street East, east of Parliament Street, (416) 364-4345, www.librairiechamplain.com. This large bookstore includes an exhaustive selection of children's books.

NEARBY ATTRACTIONS
NFB Mediatheque (5-min. walk)..p. 101
CBC Museum (2-min. walk)........p. 112

Salon du livre de Toronto (416) 498-6275 www. salondulivredetoronto.ca	**J-10 Downtown** Toronto by CN Tower

 Schedule: Usually the first or second week in October. Call to confirm (2004: September 30 to October 3).
Admission: $5/adults, $3/children, FREE for children 5 years and under.
Directions: Metro Toronto Convention Centre, 255 Front St. West (east of John St.).

WORD ON THE STREET

Street smart

In the large Kidstreet section, you may catch an old-fashioned puppet show, see favourite children's hosts on the stage, hug Caillou, Franklin the Turtle or other popular characters.

But more importantly, savvy young readers can see in the flesh Canadian Children's authors and browse through all the important children's book publishers and bookstores' booths.

For one day, book lovers of all ages take over the street. Some 170,000 visitors take advantage of this great cultural event every fall. They have done so for the last fifteen years. They know they can always rely on over 250 exhibitors under tents: book and magazine publishers, bookstores and more.

TIPS (fun for 3 years +)

• For a site map and exhibitors listing check the *Toronto Star* the day before the event (Saturday).
• *Toronto Fun Places* has had a booth at the Word on the Street since 1999. Come to meet the author (me!). I take advantage of this event to offer bookmarks and a discount on the retail price of my guide. See you there!
• Word on the Street also takes place in Kitchener on the same day.
• There will be a food vendors' section offering picnic-style eating in and around the park.
• The first **Great Ontario Book Break** took place early April 2004 at Harbourfront Centre. A new tradition?

NEARBY ATTRACTIONS	
ROM (2-min. walk)	p. 252
Yorkville Park (10-min. walk)	p. 308

ATTENTION! The event has changed its location! It is now held around Queen's Park.

The event was getting too crowded and participants had difficulty getting to the tables to make their purchases or pass along the jammed sidewalks. In addition, it was becoming hard for the organization to meet the City of Toronto's fire and emergency access regulations. Since Word on the Street could not spread further, it would have had to cancel Kidstreet (an option nobody wanted to consider seriously!).

The new location will run on both sides of Queen's Park Circle, from Wellesley to Charles Streets, just south of the Royal Ontario Museum as well as in the park.

Whatever the location, it takes a while to stroll through it all, so many parents will choose to stick to the Kidstreet section with their children. Many won't resist checking out the rest of the booths and reading tents. You can also count on a great ambience around the main stage in Queen's Park.

Word on the Street
(416) 504-7241
www.
thewordonthestreet.ca

**I-10
Downtown
Toronto
15-min.**

Schedule: Rain or shine. Usually on the last Sunday of September, from 11 am to 6 pm.
Admission: FREE.
Directions: The new location will run on both sides of Queen's Park Circle, from Wellesley to Charles St., just south of the Royal Ontario Museum as well as in the park. The Kidstreet section is located on the northwest side of Queen's Park Cr. Closest subway access is Museum station.

DRIVE-IN THEATRES

Don't remain seated

Some families are real pros at making themselves at home at the drive-in. One of them has parked its mini-van with open hatchback facing the screen, allowing two teenagers to lay down on their bellies to watch the movie. Their parents are comfortably seated wrapped in blankets on foldable chairs, beside the vehicle, feet up on a footstool and small dog on their lap.

Where else can your kids leave their seat to stretch their legs while watching a movie? At home, watching a video?… That's true. But here, you get to see the latest movies and you have a chance to socialize. Plus, smokers find an obvious advantage to the outdoor drive-ins.

To get to the 5-Drive In in Oakville, we drive through farmland (maybe not for long considering the way developments are catching up).

A big 5-Drive In neon sign glows in the twilight. "Why do you call it 5-Drive-In if you have only three screens?" enquires my son. The man at the booth laughs and explains: "Cause we're located near Dundas, still called Hwy 5 by some!"

The three screens are placed back to back in a triangle. The biggest, Starlite(#1), can park 520 cars while the Sunset (#2) and Cosmic (#3) theatres respectively accommodate 330 and 150 cars with smaller screens.

It's 7:40 pm. We have to wait until the sun sets, at around 8:30 pm (we attended on a warm night in September). Kids play ball under the Sunset screen. My son is engaged in a game with new friends.

We admire a magnificent sunset, another advantage to a drive-in, and the double feature begins. Oops! I realize I should have brought Windex to clean my windshield!

TIPS (fun for 5 years +)

• You will catch the movie sound track on your car radio, through a local radio frequency, motor off. Don't worry, it won't drain your battery.
• You can play volleyball while you wait for the movie to start.
• There is a snack bar with the long and narrow look of diners from the 50's in the Starlite section. During the summer, it includes a BBQ pit from which you can get corn on the cob, sausages, chicken. Signs advise "No outside food allowed"… No comments…
• See p. 17 for information on the only drive-in in Toronto at **The Docks**.
• The 3-screen **North York Drive-in Theatre**, in Newmarket, is located at 893 Mount Albert Rd. West, (905) 836-4444. Check www.northyorkdrivein.com.

NEARBY ATTRACTIONS	
Shell Skate Park (15-min.)	p. 371
Coronation Park (15-min.)	p. 381

5-Drive In • Oakville (905) 257-8272 www.5drivein.com	**I-7** **West** **of Toronto** **35-min.**

Schedule: During the summer, open seven days, first feature starting at sundown. (Starts earlier closer to the fall.)
Admission: Double feature is $10/person, FREE for 12 years and under, $5 on Tuesdays. 3-feature nights are $11.
Directions: 2332, 9th Line in Oakville. Take QEW, exit at Ford Dr. North. It becomes the 9th Line. The drive-in is on the east side.

IMAX AND OMNIMAX

Super-sized movie experience

You're flying over mountains, almost touching the rocky tops. Then the breathtaking sea reveals itself in all its splendour and you feel your plane taking a plunge until it levels a few metres above the waves. For a while, you can admire coral reefs through the turquoise water just before you dive under to follow a school of sharks...

I think Imax technology is used at its best when revealing an environment very few of us will ever get to see. My son disagrees, more inclined to appreciate Imax the most when it depicts extreme speed and sports.

Whatever the artistic themes behind the Imax movies, what makes them different from regular theatres is the technology. The film used to shoot the images is three times larger than standard film used in Hollywood productions. The resulting frame is 10 times bigger than the 35mm used in regular theatres.

In Imax theatres, a person's head in the row in front of you reaches your knee level. There's no question you'll have a perfect view of the 8-storey-high screen.

Imax screens are painted silver to better reflect the images and they are perforated with hundreds of thousands of tiny holes to let the sound go through perfectly.

The best place to understand the Imax technology is the **Omnimax Theatre** located under the noticeable dome of the **Ontario Science Centre** (p. 256). In the back of the Science Centre's lobby, you'll find large bay windows overlooking the impressive Imax projection room.

All Imax screens are designed to encompass our peripheral vision but it is at the **Omnimax Theatre** that the impression is the strongest. Its curved screen spreads over more than half of the vast surface of the dome. This allows the image to reach as high above and far to the right and the left as your eyes can normally see without moving your head!

Omnimax Theatre is also the only place screening a 15-minute presentation before the movies, an attraction in itself! It allows us to see the apparently solid dome disappear over our heads to reveal the 44 speakers. Sound effects will make you think an airplane is taking off right in front of you. Visual effects will make your kids throw their arms in a Superman fashion to fly through the universe in a tunnel of light.

Cinesphere at **Ontario Place** (p. 12) was the first Imax theatre to open in the world, in 1971. It is the biggest theatre, with 752 seats. **Imax Paramount**'s 90-foot screen is the tallest.

TIPS (fun for 5 years +)

• Documentaries with landscapes are more interesting than the ones with lots of close-ups. Watching the 3,600 sq. ft. image of a gorilla can be nauseating, especially on a curved screen.

• **Niagara Falls Imax Theatre** is the second largest theatre with 620 seats (see Niagara Falls on p. 302).

• **Western Fair Imax Theatre**, located in London, is 5 storeys high. (519) 438-4629.

Imax Theatres
www.imax.com

Omnimax Theatre
(416) 696-3127
www.ontariosciencecentre.com

Ontario Place Cinesphere
(416) 314-9900
www.ontarioplace.com

Famous Players Imax
www.famousplayers.com
- **Imax Paramount/Toronto**
  (416) 368-6089
- **Imax Coliseum/Mississauga**
  (905) 275-4748
- **Imax Colossus/Woodbridge**
  (905) 851-6400

BABY-FRIENDLY THEATRES

No more cabin fever

When I was on maternity leave, I sneaked into matinee screenings with my baby. Sometimes, I was lucky and he would sleep through the whole presentation. Other times, I had to leave the theatre with a screaming baby. But that was before a trend that would fulfill the needs of a forever-grateful niche: movie buffs with babies.

The first to understand this craving new mothers have to just get out and see the latest movie was **Movies for Mommies**, which showed its first Toronto screening in 2001. From the beginning, this film event producer has favoured small independent cinemas, more suitable for moms networking, with their intimate environment.

On the day I attended one of their presentations in The Beaches Fox Cinema, there was a line-up of moms with strollers waiting to get in. The back of the theatre was packed with strollers. A table offered free diapers, baby wipes, bottle warmer and free welcome packs were given by sponsors to first-time attendees.

During the screening, we could hear the babies cooing because there was no Dolby sound to bury their noise. When a baby cried, his mom would walk up and down the aisle and he would usually settle down. Of course, when they don't, the civil thing to do is to step out into the lobby, guilt-free, until the little one has quieted down.

I could see little heads sticking out behind the arms of nursing mothers. Some infants were jumping on their parent's knees (some dads were in the audience). Five moms stood in the aisles, rocking their babies to sleep as they watched the movie. One mom was even sitting in the aisle with her young toddler. All sorts of things mothers would not dare to try during regular presentations.

Another producer, **Mini Matinees**, involving different independent cinemas, has followed the trend.

Of course, the major movie theatre chains joined in. Cineplex Odeon offers **Stars & Strollers** (www.cineplex.com). Famous Players presents **Famous Babies** (www.famousplayers.com).

Whatever the location, always count on reduced sound. New locations are added periodically.

Bring on the popcorn!

TIPS (non-walking babies)

• You can bring toddler siblings if you feel they can sit through an adult movie (but bear in mind that most films screened are meant for adults).

• Food concessions are not necessarily open for those special screenings in the independent cinemas (in which case they will allow you in with your own coffee and popcorn).

• Check **www.cinemaclock.com** for current movie descriptions, theatre listings and more. You can also call (416) 444-FILM (3456) for similar information and to buy tickets in advance.

Movies for Mommies
(905) 707-8866
www.moviesformommies.com
Schedule/locations: At 1:30 pm.
• Mondays at **Rainbow Cinema**/Promenade Centre, (905) 764-3247.
• Wednesdays at **Fox Cinema**/2236 Queen St. E., (416) 691-7330.
• Thursdays at **Rainbow Cinema**/80 Front St. E., (416) 214-7006.
Admission: $7.50 to $8/adults.

Mini Matinees
(416) 531-3130
www.minimatinees.com
Schedule/locations: At 1 pm.
• Mondays at **Revue Cinema**/400 Roncesvalles Ave., (416) 531-9959.
• Tuesdays at **Kingsway Theatre**/3030 Bloor St. W., (416) 236-1411.
Admission: $8/adults, $4/seniors and 2-12 years old, FREE under 2 years.

SPROCKETS FILM FESTIVAL

Reel fun

"Didn't we get the ticket already?" inquires a four-year-old girl standing in line in front of us at the Festival. **"Yes sweetheart"**, replies her dad, **"but that was the parking ticket".**

TIPS (fun for 3 years +)

• When we visited, the doors opened at 9:45 am and some 10 am presentations were already sold out. It is better to reserve tickets on-line or by calling. Program information is available both ways. They start selling tickets by the end of March. You can order on the same day. They'll give you a confirmation number to present at the theatre.

• The English subtitles for many foreign language films are read aloud by a narrator.

• Sprockets has created the **Globe-trotter Series** to allow us to see great international children's movies when the festival is over. Suitable for children 8 years and over, each monthly presentation comes with a detailed introduction to explain the film topics. The series goes on the first Saturday from January to June at 10 am ($14.50/adults, $12.50/children or $125/all 6 movies for one adult and one child). Call for exact location in 2005.

• If the festival remains at Canada Square, you might want to know there's a **Mandarin** all-you-can-eat Chinese restaurant in the building, (416) 486-2222.

• **Hot Docs** is a 10-day international festival of documentaries held around the last week of April. It includes some documentaries interesting for children (RealKids, RealTeens Screenings). Presented in various locations; $10/adults, FREE for students and children. Check www.hotdocs.ca or call (416) 203-2155.

First held in 1998, the Sprockets Festival is the little brother of the famous Toronto International Film Festival. It aims to present the best films from around the world, made for children 4 to 17 years of age.

I am not one to think that big commercial successes are automatically lacking depth and meaningful messages, but it is a great opportunity to take a break from Disney!

In many of the films for children 8 years and older, young viewers can relate to the way the young characters learn to overcome their difficulties.

Some films include animation in various forms: claymation, digital, puppet or multi-media animation.

Children 3 to 6 years old will be thrilled by the Reel Rascals presentations held between 10 am and 12 noon. These one-hour long screenings usually include around eight different shorts.

Looking for the next Atom Egoyan? Jump Cuts is another original event under the Toronto Film Festival Group umbrella, screening films and videos made by Ontarians from grade 3 to 12 (usually two presentations).

Sprockets Toronto International Film Festival for Children
(416) 968-3456
www.bell.ca/sprockets

I-10 Downtown Toronto 15-min.

Schedule: Usually runs 10 consecutive days from mid-April, 10 am to 9 pm, including an opening night for the whole family on Friday, two weekends open to the public and 5 weekdays open to the schools (call to confirm exact dates).

Admission: (2004 rates) $10.75/adults, $7/under 18. $7/person for Reel Rascals and Jump Cuts. $14.50/adults, $9.25/under 18 for opening night $77/10 tickets for regular screenings.

Directions: Was held at the Famous Players in Canada Square (south of Eglinton Ave.) for the last few years but you need to call to confirm 2005 location!

NFB MEDIATHEQUE

Courtesy of NFB

Culture doesn't get cooler than this!

My young movie buff casually slides behind a console in the cozy parlour, as if he had lived in this kind of futuristic environment all his life. Down goes the headrest with enclosed speakers, up goes the volume, tap-tap knock the fingers on the touch screen and off he boldly goes, in the universe of Canadian cinematic culture.

"Free? We don't have to pay to use the viewing stations?" The staff member shakes his head and laughs as he gives us an access code to enter into the console. He must get that all the time. The fact is, our tax dollars have allowed Canadian creators to explore their art for decades and the free Mediatheque is National Film Board's way of giving something in return while celebrating Canadian productions.

I did not expect such a selection! Over 800 animated, documentary, short and feature films (roughly 10% of the entire NFB inventory), including over 200 in French. And they keep adding choices on a weekly basis.

The NFB went even further to stimulate the young visitors by offering $5 animation workshops where grateful parents watch their kids absorbed in the production of a real segment in claymation (remember Wallace and Gromit?) or other type of animation. Offered Saturdays and Sundays from 1 to 3 pm, the workshops can be combined with the free screening of a host of shorts in the 79-seat theatre on the second floor (also on Saturdays and Sundays, from 2 to 4 pm). Kids 3 to 5 years can rely on similar $5 workshops on Saturdays, from 10:30 am to 12 noon. Theirs includes a special screening in a small viewing room on the first floor.

We attended the workshop. Every time a child finished his animation, the friendly and patient professional staff would play it on the two monitors and large screen for the benefit of everybody. And each time it never failed: every one in the room would cheerfully applaud the new production and its proud creator.

You can also rent or buy NFB productions at the Mediatheque.

TIPS (fun for 3 years +)

• When viewing shorts with children at the consoles, it is better to select the <u>Children's Material</u> category under the <u>Film Genre</u> section. Il will direct you to all productions appropriate for children.

• The animation workshop is a drop-in activity but it is very popular. It is better to reserve in advance if you want to secure a place. It is better to arrive at the beginning of the workshop to ensure that your child will have enough time to complete his animation. An adult must accompany children.

• You can bring a VHS tape to take home a copy of his animated short! Kids get to take home their clay creation.

• No food is allowed on the premises. Get a snack at **Indigo**, across the street.

NFB Mediatheque (416) 973-3012 www.nfb.ca	J-10 **Dowtown** Toronto 1-min.

 Schedule: The Mediatheque is open Mondays and Tuesdays, 1 to 7 pm. Wednesdays, 10 am to 7 pm. Thursdays to Saturdays, 10 am to 10 pm and Sundays, 12 noon to 5 pm.

 Costs: FREE use of viewing stations. The workshops cost $5 per child.

Directions: 150 John St., Toronto. The Mediatheque is at the corner of Richmond St., just south of Queen St.

NEARBY ATTRACTIONS	
CN Tower (7-min. walk)	p.110
CBC Museum (5-min. walk)	p.112

MUSIC WITH BITE

A bit of this, a bite of that

"Perfect setting for a pillow fight, isn't it? If you want to do it, I'll join you... but after the concert" insists the smiling pianist to the bunch of kids slumped on the cushions by the stage. **Acclaimed piano genius Ian Parker will give us a taste of his medicine for the next 45 minutes with as much cool interaction with the young spectators as will allow a piano concert.**

I observe my six-year-old daughter with her friends. They carved themselves a comfortable niche in the cushions... Maybe too comfortable, I wonder? Now, they seem ready for a sleepover! A quick look at the other kids reassures me; they all do!

The musician serves us a sonatina. His fingers create magic right under our nose. I see very young kids fidgeting their little fingers along with him. One toddler is mimicking Parker's way of lifting the hands between musical phrases.

He will explain how to appreciate moments of silence (all the parents are with him!) in a Chopin's Mazurka: "They hold you in the clouds." He helps kids discern the spring wheel in a Schubert's piece and the rhythmic waves supporting the melody created by Liszt. He even shows how to play the piano without touching the keys, by brushing the cords to set a mood.

During the question session, young pianists ask the funniest questions. "Don't your fingers get really tired?" "How many minutes do you practice every day?" Every adult who has had to time 10-minute piano practice sessions roars with laughs hearing that one. How about five hours!

Once the concert is over, children are allowed to play on the grand piano, quite a treat for young pianists. My kids prefer the treat of cookies and milk offered in the back of the room.

Every show in the Music with Bite program is a co-production with Jeunesses Musicales of Ontario. They present an eclectic roster. During the 2004 season, we could hear a guitar trio one Sunday and musician-performers combining music, dance and theatre the next. We could even listen to opera singers interpreting the story of *Bilbo the Hobbit*. What better way to make kids hungry for more!

TIPS (fun for 5 years +)

- See **Harbourfront Centre** on p. 68.
- Kids in the process of learning to use the instrument starring in a specific show will be thrilled by those shows. My friend's two young pianists were enthralled by Ian Parker's performance and left with a renewed motivation to improve their art.
- Parents don't have to sit on cushions. The large Brigantine Room is filled with tables and chairs for the occasion.

NEARBY ATTRACTIONS
Toronto Music Gardens (2-min.)..p. 307
Little Norway Park (4-min.)..........p. 321

Music with Bite
(416) 973-4000
www.
harbourfrontcentre.com

J-10
**Dowtown
Toronto**
10-min.

Schedule: The program runs from September to May. It includes eight concerts presented on different Sundays at 1 pm. Call to confirm dates.

Admission: (2004 rates) $8/person or $25/family of 4.

Directions: At Harbourfront Centre, on Queen's Quay West, at the foot of Lower Simcoe St. Exact room varies depending on nature of performance. You can access the parking lot from Lower Simcoe going northbound.

Toronto Symphony Orchestra

A classic outing

A dark-clad man is testing his tuba, casually sitting on the edge of the stage and beating the tempo with his legs. Musicians and spectators alike are slowly reaching their respective seats and the joyous cacophony of a full orchestra tuning before the show fills the air.

I tease the two mature women in front of us who did not feel they needed to be accompanied by a child as an excuse to attend the Young People's Concert which is about to delight us. We came to see the animated movie based on Raymond Briggs' touching book *The Snowman*, with live music from the TSO!

On the program are printed *Jingle Bells* and *Frosty the Snowman* songs, for the sing-along part of the show. Among other things, we will also be treated to excerpts from a full orchestra version of the theme song of *Hockey Night in Canada* and Vivaldi's *Winter* enriched by the conductor's reading of Vivaldi's comments on the original score.

Storytelling, theatrical situations, dramatic conductors or even puppets, nothing is ruled out by the Young People's Concerts series in order to initiate children to the world of classical music. The roster varies from one year to the next but it always includes a **Christmas** show. Another TSO Christmas tradition is their Handel's *Messiah*, performed with the **Toronto Mendelssohn Choir**. (Check with Roy Thomson Hall, this choir usually gives us a great Festival of Carols in December.)

The younger body of TSO, the **Toronto Symphony Youth Orchestra,** involves musicians 22 years and under; a great model for young spectators! They perform throughout the season.

TIPS (fun for 5 year +)
- Children 5 years and older with purchased tickets are welcome to any TSO performance.
- TSO offers the **tsoundcheck** price of $10 on certain performances for spectators 15-29 years old. Check www.tsoundcheck.com on Mondays to find out what tickets are currently available at this price.
- Also performing at the Roy Thomson Hall is the **Toronto Children's Chorus.** We saw their **Christmas** show. Most memorable was the 300 children's passionate expressions as they sang carols. And what parent wouldn't wish for the level of attention these children so easily give their conductor!
- Fancy frozen deserts and refreshments are usually sold during intermission.

NEARBY ATTRACTIONS
AGO (5-min.)....................................p. 92

Toronto Symphony Orchestra (416) 598-3375 (TSO) (416) 593-4828 (Roy Thomson Hall) www.tso.ca	**J-10 Dowtown Toronto 5-min.**

 Schedule: Young People's Concerts run from September to June.

Costs: $22/person, all 5 concerts for $95 (or $60 at the balcony level).

 Directions: 60 Simcoe St., Roy Thomson Hall, Toronto (southwest corner at King St.).

THEATRE VENUES

Solar Stage

(416) 368-8031
www.solarstage.on.ca
Concourse Level of
Madison Centre, 4950 Yonge St.,
North York. **Tickets:** $12 + tax.

H-10
North
of downtown
40-min.

Live it up!

What a treat it is to watch children engaging with something other than a screen for a change. The palpable energy that comes from good live performances is simply irreplaceable.

Yearly events such as the **Milk Festival** (p. 70) or the **Mississauga Festival** (p. 78) are like a smorgasbord of high quality children's productions. They are a treat we can indulge in over a few consecutive days.

The rest of the year, you can count on other options to get your fix.

It is sometimes difficult from simple descriptions to know if performances involve actors or puppetry, if it's a musical or a simple storytelling. Better call the theatre beforehand to avoid any disappointment.

Solar Stage

Most plays at **Solar Stage** are intended for children aged 2 to 8; some however are appropriate for children up to 10 years old.

The younger crowd gathers in front of **Solar Stage**'s intimate stage, comfortably seated on floor cushions. Parents of young children attending for the first time shouldn't worry about letting their child sit by themselves. Sooner or later most little ones join their parents during the performance; it's part of the deal and performers know it.

TIPS (fun for 3 years +)

• There is no snack bar open on Sundays in the Madison Centre where Solar Stage is housed. You'll find a **Second Cup** on Yonge Street, south of the building.

Lorraine Kimsa Theatre for Young People

Courtesy of LKTYP

Lorraine Kimsa Theatre for Young People (LKTYP) can be seen as the next level up in theatre initiation as it can also serve an older audience. The bigger stage allows for more ambitious productions. While their season is intended primarily for children 8 years and older, some productions, usually presented on a smaller stage, will interest younger audiences.

Here, my young designer has discovered wondrous theatre sets and props; my little animal lover has seen giant butterflies magically flying in the air. Both have been captivated by harmless villains, introduced to the magic of elegant puppetry and to the mystery of ancient tales (with a little help from pyrotechnic and sound effects).

TIPS (fun for 3 years +)

• When attending with younger children, I suggest you avoid the front rows of the balcony section as the railing sits at their eye level.
• To ensure LKTYP is accessible to all audiences, a limited number of seats are reserved for specific performances at Pay-What-You-Can. These tickets can be purchased in person (cash only) and they go on sale at 10 am on the day of the show. Call the theatre for more information.
• There's a snack bar with tables at the lower level.

LKTYP

(416) 862-2222
www.lktyp.ca
165 Front St. East, Toronto.
Tickets: $19-$29.

J-10
Downtown
Toronto
5-min.

Family series

Many performing arts centres are committed to affordable and quality family shows at a cost of approximately $15 per show.

Popular productions are often booked in more than one venue during the same season. If you've missed a favourite show at your local theatre, call other performing arts centres on the listing to see if it is being presented at any of them. They will mail their season's program upon request.

Performing Arts Centres:
• **Lester B. Pearson Theatre/ Bramalea**
(905) 874-2800
www.city.brampton.on.ca
150 Central Park Dr.
• **Living Arts Centre/Mississauga**
(905) 306-6000
www.livingarts.on.ca
4141 Living Arts Dr.
(west of Square One)
• **Meadowvale Theatre/Mississauga**
(905) 615-4720
www.mississauga.ca
6315 Montevideo Rd.
• **Markham Theatre**
(905) 305-7469
www.markham.ca
171 Town Centre Blvd.
(north of Hwy 7, west of Warden Ave.)
• **Oakville Centre**
(905) 815-2021
www.oc4pa.com
130 Navy St.

TIPS (fun for 3 years +)

• Check **www.toronto.com** for a calendar of shows in all the performing arts centres in the GTA. Click on <u>Arts</u> and look up their <u>Events by calendar</u> section. They also provide a list of locations by neighbourhood.
• **The Fringe** is Toronto's Theatre festival including Kidsvenue, a selection of family theatre. Usually held for 12 days including the first week in July. For details, call (416) 966-1062 or check www.fringetoronto.com.

Arts in the school

Did you know that as a parent, you can help to bring a production to your school via its school council (the parents association)?

As a member of my kids' school parents' association, I know that the schools' administration stretch the envelope as much as they can to create extracurricular activities, but there's just so much you can do with the kind of budget our education system allows.

I also know that our school council has the power to decide how it will spend money collected through fundraising. We often choose to pay for tickets and transportation for our students to enjoy performances in major venues.

As a member of the board of Prologue to the Performing Arts, I know first hand that this non-profit organization is a less costly way to ensure kids have access to performing arts: by skipping the transportation costs and bringing subsidized performances to the school.

Prologue to the Performing Arts is committed to ensuring equal access to the arts for young audiences across Ontario. For over 38 years, it has been assisting parents, teachers, school boards and professional artists in creating and touring shows suitable for the schools.

The company provides a detailed catalogue (with booking information) upon request. Performances are presented under different categories such as: dance, music, puppet theatre, theatre, storytelling, etc.

Schools can enjoy considerable savings as they can book shows for an average cost of $3 or less per student. Some school councils book as many as ten shows every year! Many share the costs with their school's administration.

The benefits are obvious. The school presentations enhance the curriculum, injecting arts back into the programs. They reduce out-of-class time and expenses.

It gives a break from routine programs and exposes many kids to performing arts they might not experience otherwise, for lack of money or time!

Prologue to the Performing Arts
(416) 591-9092
www.prologue.org

55 Mill St., The Case Goods Building, Suite 201, Toronto, ON, M5A 3C4.

SHAKESPEARE IN THE ROUGH

Smooth theatre

I watch a little boy strolling along the park's path, unaware that a Shakespearean play is taking place right next to it. I laugh as I observe his astonished look when two big men engage in a fight. It caught the attention of other passers-by who decide to join in the crowd already following the play.

Withrow Park offers a perfect setting for an outdoor theatre. Two mature tress frame the stage, small pickets with lines mark imaginary aisles and spectators sit on the small slope, ensuring a good view.

When we attend, *Othello* is playing.

The fact that we could see him coming from the grass field added a realistic touch impossible to recreate in an indoor theatre. Later on, as the scenes unfold, we can still watch a naughty Casio running after a playful Bianca in the far-away background.

Open-air plays also mean we can observe the actors "behind the scene". What I mistook for a flea market clothing sale was actually the actors' costume rack!

Some spectators come fully equipped to enjoy the show. The man in front of me brought his folding chair and coffee in a thermos. A mother of three offers an endless supply of snacks to her kids. Babies are quietly sleeping in their parent's arms. There's even a master petting a happy dog by his side.

The actor's voices are strong, which is a good thing with all those cicadas singing in the background!

TIPS (fun for 7 years +)

• Refreshments and snacks are sold on the premises.

• **Withrow Park** includes a gorgeous playground with wading pool much appreciated by local families. Danforth Avenue offers a wide choice of restaurants east and west of Logan over and above the obvious Greek restaurants usually popular with kids.

• **Dream in High Park** takes place all summer long at the Amphitheatre in High Park; www.canstage.com, (416) 367-1652. Costumes and decors are more ambitious and the stage allows for dramatic lighting effects but it runs later and it is harder to leave the premises if your younger child loses interest. (Pay-what-you-can, they strongly suggest $15 per person, and free for 14 years and under). Shakespeare in the Rough offers parents of younger kids a better chance to enjoy the whole performance.

• There's also the new **Shakespeare-Works** at the Beaches, on p. 271, and **Shakespeare Under the Stars** on Bradley House Museum's grounds, on p. 156.

Shakespeare in the Rough (416) 536-0916 www.sitr.ca	**I-10 East** of downtown 20-min.

Schedule: Normally presented from the long weekend in August (around Simcoe Day) to Labour Day weekend, Wednesdays to Saturdays at 7 pm and Sundays at 2 pm. Call to confirm.

Admission: Pay-what-you-can, suggested price $10 per adult.

Directions: Withrow Park in Toronto, south of Danforth, between Carlaw Ave. and Logan Ave.

CLIFFHANGER PRODUCTIONS

A positive Guild trip

We had just seen a great children's play set under the mature trees. It involved many actors playing several roles, including a black bear paddling a canoe around the clearing. "Were you the bear?" asked a boy to one of the actresses in the questions' session following the show. As an answer, she lifted her long skirt to reveal big furry legs, generating shrieks of delight from the crowd.

TIPS (fun for 3 years +)
• The Guild Inn hotel has closed down but the gardens remain accessible.
• If there's a question of rain, call to confirm if the play will be presented.
• They usually present a children's play during the weekdays and Sunday matinees as well as an evening adult play. ATTENTION! There will only be daytime children's performances in 2004 (suitable for children 3 to 10 years old). Evening plays will return in 2005 along with daytime shows.
• Every year on the weekend following Simcoe Day, the Scarborough Arts Council organizes the **Art Naturally Festival** at the **Guild Inn Gardens**. It involves music, theatre, small activities for children and artistic exhibitors. Cliffhanger Productions traditionally performs during the evenings of the festival. Check www.scarborougharts.com or call (416) 698-7322.
• Bring a thick blanket or lawn chair; snacks and washrooms available on site.
• There's a **Lick's** restaurant not too far away, at 2383 Kingston Road.

Good children's theatre is a treat in itself. When it is presented in such a setting as the **Guild Inn Gardens**, it becomes a unique experience. We thoroughly enjoyed the show. Exploring the architectural fragments all around us was as much fun. And we topped it off with a stroll along the westbound trail bordering the cliff.

Cliffhanger Productions' mandate is to bring world mythology to life for audiences of all ages so it was quite appropriate to choose a setting meant to save part of Toronto's historical past. In the 50s, when Toronto began to tear down the downtown area to make room for the new, there was not much concern about preserving historical buildings. The owners of the Guild, already offering an outdoor sculpture garden, decided to collect the pieces of historical sites they came across.

Nowadays, among other things, you can admire fragments of the Imperial Bank of Canada, built in 1928, and the Toronto Star Building, erected in 1929. But the pièce de résistance is the central entrance to the Bank of Toronto, built in 1912 and turned into the impressive Greek Theatre where Cliffhanger Productions usually presents evening performances.

The Greek Theatre offers no shelter from the summer sun, daytime performances are presented in a shady clearing closer to the lake and the trail access. You just follow the signs.

Cliffhanger Productions	J-11 East of downtown 30-min.
• Scarborough	

(416) 264-5869
www.cliffhangerproductions.ca

Schedule: Daytime performances only for summer 2004, from July 19th to August 5th, Monday to Thursday, at 11 am and 2 pm. Call to confirm for following years.
Admission: $6/person.
Directions: The Guild Inn Gardens, 201 Guildwood Pkwy., Scarborough. Take Kingston Rd. East to Guildwood Pkwy. and turn south.

General tips about
Buildings:

- **Doors Open**, usually held the first weekend of May, offers free tours in many buildings listed in this guide. Consult **www.doorsopenontario.on.ca** for details. Click <u>Events</u> on this web site for a list of over 30 Doors Open events held in Ontario, including the main one Doors Open Toronto encompassing over 150 buildings throughout the city.

BUILDINGS

See **CN Tower** on p. 110.

CN TOWER

Broaden their horizons

With kids, you have to think big and tall... as tall as the CN Tower! It's great to see them looking up over and over again, attempting to make out the top of the 550-metre-high tower! It's well worth stopping at the base, just to see the great view from down there.

Arriving from Front Street, we walk over several railroad tracks via a sheltered bridge. This location is an excellent vantage point to see the sculptures of giant characters in their **SkyDome** balconies. Inside, before getting to the elevators, we walk across a spacious mezzanine housing displays and interactive computers.

Closer to the elevators, visual simulators located on three screens give us the impression we are flying with a hangglider, jumping with a bungee cord or walking on a high wire (all extreme sports used by real eccentric athletes in the past to link their fame to the CN Tower).

Up! Up! And away!

Then comes the famous ride up the elevator: it's a one-minute climb on a fair day (over an hour if you climbed the 1760 stairs), but it can take up to four minutes in high wind. Let your children go close to the glass door. The view will blow them away.

The elevator leads to the interior observation deck, 346 metres (1136 feet) from ground level, from where we can admire Lake Ontario and the four corners of the city. Children are allowed inside the **Horizons Café** located at this level.

One floor down is the fascinating glass floor surrounded by a beautiful mural depicting a construction site in the sky. When he was five, my little one didn't show any fear while walking on the glass floor. At six, he joined the rank of grown-ups cautiously remaining on the edge of the glass.

If you're wondering how such a surface can support visitors, a sign states that this glass floor can hold the weight of 14 large hippos!

We can read lots of interesting and fun information on large panels around the room, such as the fact that the CN Tower holds the world record for longest egg fall (... and tallest standing structure in which man can climb).

At this level, you can also access the exterior observation deck, to better feed your vertigo. We didn't feel the need to pay extra to go up to the Sky Pod. I suggest you do it only if there's no line-up. I must admit 100 metres more make a difference. The Skydome really looks smaller from up there!

Special effect

We completed the visit with a stop at the FX Shop. That was fun! My teenager companions were thrilled to act scared in front of the camera as they "fell" from atop the tower. A staff member worked on her computer to add their picture to the background of their choice. (Have a look at p. 109 to see the different background chosen by my son and nephew). It costs $20 for 2 photos and is worth it!

Other activities are offered at the base of the CN Tower. Films are presented in a mini-theatre equipped with seats that move to the rhythm of the movie projected on screen. There's also an arcade. Very few games are suitable for smaller children, but my little one had a great time driving the motorcycles. And he and I teamed up, frantically rowing on a rubber dinghy, while attempting to avoid dangerous situations. I sweated up a storm and we laughed the whole time.

... and out!
For a better viewpoint of the tower in all its loftiness, stand on the outside terrace located between the Tower and the **SkyDome**. You'll have to lay down on the ground to take a picture!

A bit farther, you'll notice a pretty fountain with metal salmon swimming up the stream. Towards the east, look for a giant woodpecker on a tall pole.

TIPS (fun for 5 years +)
• Avoid very windy days, when access to the outside observation deck and to the Sky Pod is forbidden. Also avoid foggy days, otherwise you'll be paying a lot just to have your head in the clouds...

• Try to visit the CN Tower before or after the summer rush. We had a perfect visit during the **March Break** when it was not crowded by tourists. The CN Tower offers special activities for the occasion.

• The **Horizons Café** is not the expensive revolving restaurant but a fixed one underneath, with affordable menu (see p. 428). There's also a **Planet Hollywood** restaurant by Front Street.

CN Tower
(416) 868-6937
www.cntower.ca

J-10
Downtown
Toronto
at CN Tower

Schedule: Open year-round, 9 am to 10 pm, closes at 11 pm on Fridays and Saturdays (extended hours during the summer).

Admission: (taxes not included) $19/adults, $17/seniors, $14/4-12 years, FREE for children 3 years and under. (Extra fees for Simulator Rides and Sky Pod.)

Directions: 301 Front St. W. (corner of John St.).

CBC MUSEUM & GUIDED TOURS

Behind the scenes

"That's what I like about this job" our guide tells us, "you never know what to expect!" Walking into the Canadian Broadcasting Corporation's largest studio (the Big Red Box), we come face to face with a huge half-constructed pyramid, a modern 25-metre-high statue and several walls of look-alike blue ice, all made of styrofoam.

Before entering the 14,000 sq. ft. studio with a high ceiling, you travel through corridors of fake bricks, fake cement and tapestry. We learn the fake bricks are cast from real ones and the paint is peeled off the floors after each production. "How could we make it more real?" asks our guide of the children in our group. "With some bird sounds?" tries a pint-size artistic director.

The tour takes us through the unfinished set of a new soap opera, then out to the studio where the Royal Canadian Air Farce is taped in front of live audiences. We are initiated to the workings of a teleprompter used in reading the news in front of robotic cameras.

From the glassed-in elevator going up to the 10th floor, we admire the Atrium's grandiose architecture and the spectacular skylight. We then carry on by ourselves to visit the free CBC Museum. In the display by the entrance, I recognize the castle and costume of the *Friendly Giant* of my childhood (I'm giving myself away here). *Sesame Street, Mr. Dress-up* and other kids shows' props can be seen. A large selection of clips from CBC programs for adults or kids can be watched.

In the back of the little museum are a series of displays explaining how they did the sound effects for the radio, with computer clip demonstrations. Kids can even listen to the sound they create by manipulating different objects.

| CBC Museum
(416) 205-5574
www.cbc.ca/museum | J-10
Downtown
Toronto
2-min. walk |

CBC Guided Tours
(416) 205-8605

TIPS (fun for 8 years +)

• The tour is not suitable for younger children. It starts to make sense when they are old enough to be interested in how things work. The museum is fun for younger kids but better for older ones.
• The Behind-the-Scenes guided tour doesn't include a visit to the make-up and props departments.

Schedule: The tour schedule varies year-round. You need to call to find out about the month's schedule. The museum is open Monday to Friday from 9 am to 5 pm, Saturday from 12 noon to 4 pm.
Admission: FREE admission to the Museum. Tours admission is $7/adults, $5/seniors, students and children 6 years and over (cash only).
Directions: 250 Front St. West (across from the CN Tower), Toronto.

St. James Cathedral

The sound of music

I glance sideways at my little lad, amused by his reaction as music from the 87 ranks and 5000 pipes of the St. James Cathedral's grand organ surrounds us.

Short concerts to broaden children's musical horizons, a lovely church to show them things of beauty grown-ups sometimes create and a cute little garden to stretch their legs; St. James Anglican Cathedral is one of those best

kept secrets I'm glad to share with you.

With its huge and gorgeous stained glass artwork framing the pulpit, and twelve colourful triptychs adorning the side walls, St. James is a beautiful cathedral of gothic architecture and proportions.

It is topped by a set of twelve ringing bells (the only such ring of 12 in North America). These are heavy bells, ranging from 631 lbs to 2418 lbs! Bell ringing practices take place every Monday at 6 pm. Visitors might have a chance to tour the bell tower afterwards (call in advance to let them know).

Free lunch-time concerts are offered on Tuesdays during the year and free summer concerts are presented on Sundays in July and August. During **Christmas** time, we are usually treated to a concert from the **Toronto Mendelssohn Youth Choir** (admission fees apply).

Got a cherished pet? St. James offers the **Blessing of the Animals** in October! The special service usually gathers over 300 people with their pets (outside of the church of course), plus the Toronto Police on horseback, working dogs and exotic animals from Bowmanville Zoo.

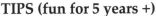

TIPS (fun for 5 years +)
* See the **Crèche Exhibition** (p. 194) organized by **St. James Archives and Museum**.
* Check the **Sculpture Garden** right across King Street. It usually displays eye-catching outdoor installations!
* While in the area, take a five-minute walk down Church Street southbound, then Front Street westbound until you reach the small park by Scott Street, to view the huge trompe-l'oeil mural adorning the **Flatiron Building**.

NEARBY ATTRACTIONS
Hockey Hall (15-min.walk)..........p. 362

St. James Cathedral
(416) 364-7865
www.
stjamescathedral.on.ca

**J-10
Downtown
Toronto
15-min.**

Schedule: Lunch concerts from September through June, Tuesdays at 1 pm. Summer concerts in July and August, Sundays at 4 pm. Blessing of the Animals usually on first or second Saturday in October, call to confirm.
Admission: FREE.
Directions: 65 Church St. (at the corner of King and Church), Toronto.

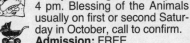

CASA LOMA

"I'm the king of the castle..."

Glancing at Casa Loma from the outside is enough to excite young minds. No mistake, we're about to enter a "real" castle. Inside, it seems like the fairy godmother waved her magic wand to transform the whole castle. It has regained the splendour of its younger days and a magical look worthy of Cinderella's Christmas. Those who visit Casa Loma at other times don't get to appreciate how great it is during the Christmas period and March Break.

During the **Christmas** holidays, the grandeur of Casa Loma awaits us. A 15-metre-high fir tree doesn't quite reach the main hall ceiling. Illuminated chandeliers and tinsel garlands contribute to the ambience of opulence, absent at other times of the year.

Between two performances, characters in the brief musical, produced for the occasion, mingle within the impressive decor.

One year, **Christmas** at Casa Loma was celebrated with Cinderella as a theme. We could see the handsome prince dressed in royal velvet answer a child's question in a gentlemanly fashion. The fairy godmother, in a cloud of pink tulle, held an ecstatic little girl in her arms. Farther in the room, Cinderella's cruel sisters, seemingly not as mean as their reputation and splendid in their period dress, were flirtatious with visitors. On the three occasions I saw a show at Casa Loma, actors were always very nice with the little ones who were looking at them lost in wonder. And they never stepped out of character.

So far, we've seen Snow White, Robin Hood and Cinderella spread their magic. I didn't expect such high-quality musicals, presented several times daily in the castle library. Even if we're off-off-Broadway, voices are quite strong and well modulated, the five actors expressive and smart, the songs original and the musical arrangements harmonious. There are amusing, interactive dialogues aimed at the parents. The sets, mounted on curtains, compensated for the stage's limited size.

In the beautiful marble-floor conservatory, a second good clown or magic show is usually performed several times daily.

Walking up the imposing grand staircase, we arrive in a wide, richly decorated corridor lined with costumes or cut-out props. Kids can step behind them

to have their pictures taken. Little adventurers will be thrilled when they find out they can also use the secret staircase hidden behind the wood panelling in Sir Henry's office!

From there, we can visit the former rooms of Sir Henry Mill Pellatt (the romantic Toronto financier who had the castle built in 1911) and his wife. These are also decorated along the year's theme.

On the top floor, during **Christmas** time, Santa awaits us in a room filled with multicoloured gifts and stuffed animals. You have time to take a picture of your little elves... if they cooperate.

Staircases located on the top floor lead to the castle's two towers, where you can enjoy a great view of the city. During **March Break**, the weather is usually nice enough to sit on the Norman Tower's outside terrace, which is closed in winter.

A 250-metre tunnel links the castle with the stables. The tunnel's entrance faces the Gift Shop located on the lower level of the castle. (Frankly, this level isn't more exotic than any basement, but nevertheless, it intrigues children.)

Furthermore, it leads to impressive stables. Their mahogany stalls and Spanish tile floors attest to Sir Henry's taste for luxury.

TIPS (fun for 3 years +)

• Parking is available on site. After 11:30 am, it is sometimes full, but spots free up rapidly at any hour.
• It is less interesting to visit Casa Loma when children's shows are not scheduled (the admission fee remains the same and the castle isn't decorated). On the plus side, the place is not as crowded.
• **March Break** is as much fun as **Christmas**. The same concept applies.
• The admission counter is inside a portico too small to contain the whole waiting line. Dress warmly!
• In the room where the musical performances are presented, the audience sits on the floor (there are a few chairs for adults). It is better to arrive fifteen minutes before a performance. Shows only last half an hour.
• In the winter, the long tunnel is definitely cold. It's better to put on your coat before walking through there.
• Santa Claus arrives on the first day the castle presents its **Christmas** performances, and stays until December 24th.
• You can print a $2 off coupon from their web site.
• A cafeteria located in the castle's basement offers an affordable menu with little variety. At the same level, the unfinished pool lies inside an enclosure. Decorations pertaining to the current theme are often displayed in it.

Casa Loma
(416) 923-1171
www.casaloma.org

I-10
North
of downtown
20-min.

Schedule: The Christmas show is presented daily from end of November to early January, from 9:30 am to 5 pm, excluding December 25th and January 1. On December 24, the Castle closes at 1 pm. During March Break, the show is performed every day, from 9:30 am as well. (Last admission always at 4 pm.)

Admission: At all times, even when shows for children are performed, $12/adults, $7.50/ seniors and students, $6.75/ 4-13 years. FREE for children 3 and under. Parking max. is $8.25.

Directions: 1 Austin Terrace, Toronto. (southbound from St.Clair Ave., Spadina Rd. becomes Austin Terrace).

CULLEN GARDENS

Tiny, but not trivial...

I found the country cottage of my dreams, only half an hour away from Toronto. It stands at number 77 on a country road in Whitby's Cullen Gardens. It is just perfect: right by a lake, with a shingled roof, adornments of Victorian inspiration and a large veranda. The only problem... it's no more than one metre wide!

What refined precision in the construction of these small buildings (approximately a hundred); all exact replicas of existing buildings you will find outlined in the small plan of the site handed out at the entrance.

The site includes a number of Toronto landmarks, such as an office building located at 98 Queen Street East, Duncan Farm (Don Mills and York Mills), A. Parrel & Mr. Music stores, a gas station (York Mills and Yonge Street), a stone residence located at the crossing of Highway 401 and Kennedy Road, and a dock of blue boats at Queen's Quay.

The small village includes a main road, a residential area, a few estates, a large resort, many secondary residences, a gas station, a church, a fire station and even a campground; all populated with created-to-scale citizens. The postman, the painter and the travelling circus entering the town; the myriad of everyday life details is awesome.

The town's vibrant energy during the summer stimulates the imagination. With children playing in the schoolyard, firemen extinguishing a fire (check the real smoke and smell of burn coming out of the house), paramedics looking for a plane wreck; these little scenarios will enthuse children old enough to recognize them.

There's more to enjoy, with trains and locomotives whistling to announce their arrival on various tracks while children run at their side, yachts sailing, a ferry and many cars travelling the highway. Here and there, the familiar sounds of farm animals, sirens, church bells, planes and even the "woush-woush" of a campground's toilet resonate, adding to the scene's realism.

The site's gorgeous floral displays are an attraction in their own right, with landscaping enhancing the small residences and their well trimmed bushes. The gardens evolve with changing seasons; 80,000 tulips and 300 rhododendron bushes in springtime, 10,000 roses announcing summer, 1,200 mums in the fall. They are adorned with dinosaurs, elephants and other animals sculpted out of the bushes.

There is a large valley with a pond and covered bridge, opening onto a small forest that shades a playground. There, a long suspension bridge will appeal to small children.

You will also find a maze, a large structure to climb, a miniature golf (extra $3) and a pedal karts path ($2). Next to it, you can cool off at a double wading pool with lovely water slides. You can also catch a pioneer wagon ride on the weekends, watch exotic birds in cages and throw a penny in a wishing well.

Since my last visit, Cullen has added a "forest fort" in the playground area as well as a wagon ride through Petal Pets Valley with interactive (computer-chip equipped) petal characters, and a super-size bug and flower blacklight room in the main building.

On the site, you will find picnic tables. Don't miss the mini fairground.

Expect more entertainment from July to Labour Day.

TIPS (fun for 2 years +)
• Don't forget the kids' bathing suits!
• A visit to **Lynde House** is included in your entry fee. The residence recreates daily life in 1856 and is outfitted with animated mannequins. During **Halloween** and **Christmas** time, the decor changes in an entertaining way.
• There are **fireworks** on **Victoria Day**, **Canada Day** and **New Year's Eve**.
• We loved visiting the place during **Halloween** when the gardens and miniature village were decorated for the occasion. The real action started at the covered bridge with stroboscope lights. Woods were inhabited by scary creatures and (pre-taped) sounds. A large part of the valley was turned into a cemetery and kids could collect treats at different stations throughout the site.
• During **Easter** Friday and Saturday, they offer Easter Egg Hunts (hiding plastic eggs with messages to unscramble in order to exchange for treats.
• During the summer, you can buy hot dogs, fries and ice cream next to the playground. The Village Snack Bar located next to the entrance is open throughout the year.
• See **Cullen Gardens** in the winter on p. 202.

NEARBY ATTRACTIONS

Cullen Gardens & Miniature Village
· Whitby
(905) 686-1600
www.cullengardens.com

C-4 East of Toronto 45-min.

Schedule: Open 7 days from Easter weekend to early January, 9 am to 8 pm during the summer, 10 am to 6 pm during spring and fall and 10 am to 10 pm during the winter.

Admission: $12.50/adults, $9/seniors and students, $5.50/3-12 years, $40/family of 5, FREE 2 years and under.

Directions: 300 Taunton Rd. West, Whitby. Take Hwy 401 East, exit Brock St. (Hwy 12/exit #410) northbound. Turn west on Taunton Rd.

SHARON TEMPLE

A temple of light

While driving on Leslie Street, I look around for the temple. Despite having read comments regarding its amazing architecture, I don't quite know what to expect. Then it appears, with its dazzling whiteness contrasting with the blue autumn sky. Wow! The place holds its promise. Even my little adventurer, usually not inclined towards contemplation, recognizes that this building is different.

The Children of Peace, a sect fascinated by the spiritual value of art and music, built Sharon Temple between 1825 and 1832.

Everything here is symbolic. The three stories stand for the Holy Trinity. In the centre, the four columns surrounding the Ark of the Covenant are engraved with the words Hope, Faith, Love and Charity. The twelve pillars bear the apostles' names. On Jacob's ladder, the bars supporting the ramp gradu-

ally reduce in height and width as we go up, giving the impression of rising towards Paradise.

I was impressed by the natural light shining through all the windows. There is no pulpit; priests didn't preach here. People came to meditate and listen to music while sitting in the mezzanines. The temple's acoustics are in fact remarkable, as my miniature pianist appreciated when he played a few notes on the large piano, encouraged by the tour guide.

We tour the 1819 house belonging to the builder-architect. At the back of the house, there's a small, peculiar round house. My little rascal was intrigued when he found out it was the architect's toilet, made in such a way "because the Devil hides in corners".

My son, being crazy about the movie *Back to the Future*, was impressed by photographs in the Wright Exhibit Hall. First, we see the temple as it was in 1832 (without any vegetation around it), then as it is now, surrounded by mature trees, and finally as it could become if no one takes care of it (abandoned, with broken windows and peeling paint).

TIPS (fun for 5 years +)

• Some sect traditions, highlighting the temple's inspired architecture and beauty, have been preserved. For example, in summer and autumn, shows featuring chamber music or choirs are held here. The Musical Illumination ceremony is still held on the evening of the first Friday of September. These events, though, are not suitable for children.

• There are picnic tables on the site.

Sharon Temple
• East Gwillimbury
(905) 478-2389
www.sharontemple.ca

C-3
North
of Toronto
45-min.

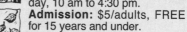

Schedule: Open mid-May to mid-October, Thursday to Sunday, 10 am to 4:30 pm.
Admission: $5/adults, FREE for 15 years and under.
Directions: 18974 Leslie, Sharon. From Hwy. 404 North, exit on Davis Dr. westbound, then turn north on Leslie St. The temple is on the southwest corner of Leslie and Mount Albert Sideroad.

CASTLE VILLAGE

Take a peek!

Slightly off the beaten track in the Georgian Bay area, the Castle is an intriguing sight in itself. But the little village hidden in its backyard was an even bigger surprise to us when we stopped there on our way back from a great weekend by the beach.

Delightful little houses awaited us, with inviting windows to peek through. Inside, we could see the Teddy Bears' Tea Party, Goldilocks and the Three Bears, Little Red Riding Hood and her grandmother and Mother Goose at reading time.

Since our last visit, Snow White with the Seven Dwarfs' house and Merlin the Magical Wizard's Tower were added. All the beautiful small interiors are skillfully decorated with painstaking attention to original detail.

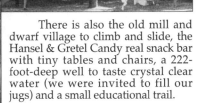

There is also the old mill and dwarf village to climb and slide, the Hansel & Gretel Candy real snack bar with tiny tables and chairs, a 222-foot-deep well to taste crystal clear water (we were invited to fill our jugs) and a small educational trail.

TIPS (fun for 2 years +)

• The Castle houses a large gift shop and two indoor attractions: a series of small prisons inhabited by a few horror characters ($1) and a section showcasing medieval arms ($2). I was personally more impressed by the craft involved in the creation of the Enchanted Kingdom.

NEARBY ATTRACTIONS	
Wye Marsh (10-min.)	p. 320
Discovery Harbour (15-min.)	p. 418

Castle Village · Midland (705) 526-9683 www.castlevillage.ca	A-2 Midland Region 90-min.

Schedule: The outdoor Enchanted Kingdom is open on weekends from early May to late October and daily from mid-June to Labour Day, 10 am to 5:30 pm (11 am to 5 pm on Sundays). The Castle itself is open from early April to December 31.

Admission: Enchanted Kingdom access is $2/person, FREE under 2.

Directions: 701 Balm Beach Rd., Midland. From Hwy 400 North, take exit #147/Hwy 12 westbound. Turn north on Hwy 93 and west on Balm Beach Rd.

General tips about
Charities:

- This chapter is meant to help you introduce to your kids the notion that they have the power to make a difference in someone's life by giving time, money (or toys). You're planting the seed...

CHARITIES

See **Bell Walk for Kids** on p. 123.

LIST OF CHARITIES

Action... reaction

One of the first tough lessons kids have to learn is to share their toys. Once they've gotten over the pain of letting go, they discover the power of making someone happy. Here's a list of charities that could help them better understand the next step: that they truly can make a difference.

Big Brothers Big Sisters (p. 126) and **Youth Assisting Youth** (p. 127) are obvious pet charities for me since they encourage outings with kids. But I also favour charity events combining fundraising with an activity, such as **Paws in the Park** for the Toronto Humane Society (p. 124), **Toddle for Tots** for the Ronald McDonald House (p. 125) and **Bell Walk for Kids** for the Kids Help Phone service (p. 123).

It is through **Operation Christmas Child** (p. 128) that I initiated my kids to the notion of giving to strangers. It was easy for them to imagine the impact of their gift at the receiving end.

I also think that the closer to home, the clearer they will see how their actions bring result. Imagine using **Kerstin's Idea** (p. 129) to collect money to buy an aquarium for your child's classroom! (Schools can issue income tax receipts.) The charities I chose to list here are more options to initiate kids to charity. I think they support causes that a child can relate to.

Two good sources of information related to charities are Canada's supersite **www.charityvillage.com** with 3,000 pages of information for donors, volunteers, executives and staffers and **www.canadian-charities.com** listing Canadian charities alphabetically or by subject.

If you would like to volunteer, contact the **Volunteer Centre of Toronto** at www.volunteertoronto.on.ca or (416) 961-6888.

Toronto Zoo Foundation
(416) 392-9114
www.torontozoo.com
The funniest way to support the Toronto Zoo is through their Adopt-An-Animal Program. For $25 +, your child gets a personalized certificate of adoption, his animal's fact sheet, a newsletter and a gift card. For $100 +, he gets the current colour Zoo Animal Calendar and an invitation to the special Parents' Day at the zoo. The Wild Walk Program is also cool: for $250, you can have a 3-line message (15 characters max per line) on one of the walkway bricks inside the zoo's main gate!

Tim Horton Children's Foundation
(519) 448-1248
www.timhortons.com
This one is dedicated to providing a fun-filled camp environment for children from economically disadvantaged homes. They own 5 camps in Canada and one in the US.

Sunshine Foundation of Canada
1-800-461-7935
www.sunshine.ca
This foundation makes dreams come true for children aged 3 to 18 who are challenged by severe physical disabilities or life-threatening illnesses (also presented as Sunshine Dreams for Kids).

Starlight Children's Foundation Canada
(905) 752-7827
www.starlightcanada.org
This non-profit organization provides creative and fun entertainment therapies to seriously ill children and their families, both in and out of the hospital.

The Hospital for Sick Children Foundation
(416) 813-7771
www.sickkids.on.ca
Your donation can help to purchase toys and games or music therapy programs to help hospitalized kids cope with the stress of their illness. It can help to pay accommodation for out-of-town families (among other things).

BELL WALK FOR KIDS

Walk your talk

"It's downhill. I can do down-hill!" jokes a man at the 2.5km checkpoint. Next to him, a six-year-old is anxious to get his sticker. He wants to be the first to get all the stickers distributed at each checkpoint. "It's not really a race!" his mom reminds him.

I arrived before 9 am, when there was no line-up at registration. There are lots of Bell employees getting ready for the walk designed to raise money for the great organization **Kids Help Phone**. What better cause for a telephone company to support?

TIPS (fun for 5 years +)

• In the morning, the waterfront is much cooler than the city. Bring shirts you can peel off later.
• Make sure the kids use the portable toilets before a line-up starts to build in front of them (at around 9:40 am).
• It takes a little over an hour to walk 5 km at adult speed. I noticed some golf carts strolling along the walk to carry participants who might experience some problems (like a small kid at the end of her rope) and need a lift back to Coronation Park.
• **Kids Help Phone** is Canada's only 24-hour, toll-free, bilingual, confidential phone counselling and Internet service for children 4 to 19 years old. It handles approximately 1,000 calls and on-line questions every day. Kids can call 1-800-668-6868 or check http://kidshelp.sympatico.ca. This web site offers a very useful resource section for parents, on a variety of delicate subjects.

When the departure is officially announced, everyone is excited to start walking their 5 or 10 km circuit. Many brought their dogs along. Some participants use walking sticks, others will run. Parents are equipped with wagons, strollers, kids with scooters and even roller blades. They start on their feet but many of the youngest will pass the finish line on dad's shoulders or sleeping in the stroller.

We walk along Ontario Place, not open yet for the season. We pass the huge windmill. When we reach the Lake Shore, we form an impressive stretch of pilgrims on the sidewalk.

At each checkpoint, we're given bottled water, rice krispies squares and other goodies. Now, I am convinced my ever-hungry 10-year-old would have loved this walk. At the finish line (also the starting point of the walk) a greeting committee welcomes us with more treats, cheering in a way that makes us feel great!

There's action in the background: volunteers doing face painting, music on the stage, an inflatable structure to jump into and prize tables according to the amount of your pledges.

Bell Walk for Kids 1-866-WALK-4-KIDS (1-866-9255-4-5437) www.bellwalkforkids.com	**J-9 Downtown Toronto 15-min.**

 Schedule: Usually on the first Sunday of May, call to confirm. The event takes place, rain or shine, starting at 10 am.

 Admission: No registration fees. There's parking for $8 on the Exhibition grounds in front of the park.

Directions: In Toronto, at Coronation Park along Lake Shore Blvd. West, at the foot of Strachan Ave.

PAWS IN THE PARK

Gone to the dogs

As the participants and their dogs undertake the 6 km Dogwalk, they are cheered loudly by numerous volunteers armed with noise makers and pompons. The ambience is contagious; everyone there shares the same love for dogs.

Every September, close to 4000 dog owners stroll through **Sunnybrook Park** with their four-legged companions. The event's purpose is to raise money for more than 20,000 abandoned, neglected or abused animals in the care of the **Toronto Humane Society**.

Beautiful pure breeds, dynamic pooches, skinny four legged things, big shaggy dogs, even a three-legged one; we see

them all as they cross the departure line under a colourful balloon arch. Some masters carry their miniature dogs in their arms, others push their old hounds in a stroller.

My heart breaks when, having asked a family about the dog picture attached to their stroller, I find out their furry friend used to participate in this event and died this year... In fact, I notice more dogless walkers with similar pictures.

In the park, a band appropriately plays Elvis Presley's *Hound Dog* song while trained dogs demonstrate their skills in an open space.

A dog-free zone is reserved for cats, turtles, rabbits and ferrets. Some lucky dogs enjoy a massage in a nearby dog clinic! Some pets are dressed for the Best Costume contest, which eventually takes place alongside the Look-Alike contest. These are entertaining but short.

Without a doubt the event attracts the most obedient of canines and their well-heeled owners. There are hundreds of leashed dogs present... and the grounds remain immaculate!

TIPS (fun for 5 years +)

• If you come by car, you may have to drive to the last parking lot in **Sunnybrook Park**. It is a 20-minute walk back to the Dogwalk departure, located in the first park on the left, as you enter **Sunnybrook Park** from Leslie Street. There's a shuttle service for pets and humans from Sunnybrook parking lots to the starting point.

• It is preferable to ask the owner's permission before petting a dog. These are not professionals used to dealing with the public.

• Over $250,000 from the Paws in the Park fundraising effort goes to the **Toronto Humane Society**.

Paws in the Park	**I-10**
• North York	**North**
(416) 392-2273, ext. 2157	**of downtown**
www.pawsinthepark.com	**20-min.**

Schedule: Usually a Sunday in September (September 26 in 2004). Registration at 9 am.
Admission: No registration fee. Walkers are asked to raise at least $100 in pledges.
Directions: Sunnybrook Park, off Leslie St. (north of Eglinton).

TODDLE FOR TOTS

Sweet charity

Held at the Toronto Zoo, rain or shine, this fundraising activity is perfect for children. It invites kids to collect pledges and accumulate animal stickers on a special map along a course inhabited by genuine creatures. As they enjoy themselves, they're raising money for out-of-town sick children and their families living in Toronto's Ronald McDonald House.

TIPS (fun for 3-12 years)
• Registered children are given a hot dog, a soft drink and a Popsicle. For a small cost, non-registered children can purchase the same lunch.
• With a minimum of $30 in pledges, participants get a free T-shirt.
• Children aged 12 years and under that didn't collect pledges can still participate, by paying the registration fee.
• Registration forms can be picked up and dropped off at any Greater Toronto Area Toys'R'Us, LCBO or Loblaws.
• See **Toronto Zoo** on page 46.

NEARBY ATTRACTIONS	
Whittamore's Farm (15-min.).......p. 135	
Rouge Park (5-min.)....................p. 348	

Registration provides children with a Zoo day pass, a Toddle Bag stuffed with goodies, a barbecue lunch, and a Toddle Map. They also collect stickers and participate in amusing activities at each checkpoint, prepared by generous participating corporations.

You don't return empty-handed from these checkpoints! We got a T-shirt, containers, toys and other gadgets. My sweet-toothed son was also delighted by the tons of treats he got.

Most checkpoints offer activities as well. In fact, children are so thrilled by the games, gifts and stickers, they forget to look at the animals!

Toddle For Tots	**I-12**
• Scarborough	**N-E**
(416) 977-0458	**of downtown**
www.rmhtoronto.org	**25-min.**

 Schedule: Usually on a Saturday in September from 9 am to 3 pm (September 18 in 2004).
 Admission: Early registration for children 11 years and under is $14. Same day registration rises to $17. Non participants pay the Zoo admission.
Directions: See Toronto Zoo on p. 46.

BIG BROTHERS BIG SISTERS

Make a big difference

Studies found that children who benefit from a special relationship with a Big Brother or Sister go on to graduate from high school at a rate of 20% higher than the national average; 78% of them who came from a social assistance background no longer rely on this form of income and a disproportionately high number of former Little Brothers or Sisters graduate from college or university compared to others in their age group. Those volunteers make a difference!

Big Brothers and Big Sisters used to be two separate organizations but they've decided to amalgamate to become stronger by leveraging their infrastructure and to increase their ability to develop programs for both girls and boys.

Big Brothers Big Sisters (BBBS) of Canada is now the leading child and youth serving organization providing mentoring programs across the country with over 170 local agencies (some 80 in Ontario alone). You can call the head office or check their web site to find the agency closest to you.

Currently, over 17,000 children are matched with adults in their original one-to-one programs. But they still have to find matches for the 7,000 kids on their waiting lists!

Their original and best-known program gives volunteers 18 years and older the chance to build a one-on-one relationship with a child/youth 6 to16 years old. Big Brothers or Sisters commit to meet with their match at least 2 hours per week or 4 hours every two weeks, for one year. Those meetings are spent simply listening, talking and having fun while doing an activity of their choice.

There are also several fun sponsored events provided throughout the year such as **Soap Box Derby Races at High Park** (see p. 232) or the annual Holiday Party for all Big and Little Brothers and Sisters.

In response to the different needs and demands of children, youth, and volunteers alike, BBBS has created new programs: In-School Mentoring (1 hour/week), Group Programs, for those kids on the waiting lists (4 hours/month), Couples for Kids, Cross Gender Matching, Internet Mentoring and the new Life Skills Program.

Each offer different kinds of commitment that could better match your life style if you feel the original program isn't for you. Call your local agency for details.

All you need is the desire to give some quality time.

TIPS

• If you work so much that you don't even have time for your own kids, maybe your corporation can do something! Many companies sponsor programs, projects or special events designed by local or national BBBS for fundraising or to create awareness. You can make Big and Little Brothers and Sisters benefit from a new product or service launch, test marketing at a regional or local level at the same time. You could give access to unused facilities or privileges.

BBBS of Canada
1-800-263-9133
www.bbbsc.ca
Consult them to find your local agency.

BBBS of TORONTO
(416) 925-8981
www.bbbst.com

YOUTH ASSISTING YOUTH

I don't know about you but I'm impressed. It seems the positive youth role model thing works!

The youth volunteers are referred to as "seniors". They commit to spend approximately 3 hours a week with a "junior" for at least a year. An orientation session and a pre-match workshop are offered before accepting a "senior". The matched volunteers receive

Match-makers

For over 25 years, Youth Assisting Youth has assisted in building special friendships between youth volunteers 16 to 29 years and children ages 6 to 15, on a rewarding one-on-one basis. Surely something to applaud!

It costs taxpayers $100,000 to keep a child in the juvenile justice system for one year. It costs Youth Assisting Youth (YAY) $1,600 a year to keep the same child out of the system.

It's all about prevention. The "at risk" children

Photos: Courtesy of YAY

YAY matches with a young volunteer are often exposed to gangs, drugs or violence. Since 1976, the mentoring organization has helped more than 10,000 children and youth and it has actually been 98% successful in keeping its young clientele in schools and out of trouble.

support in the form of personal connections with YAY staff, "seniors-only" events to get to know other peer-volunteers, newsletters and large YAY outings.

YAY sponsors a wide variety of free monthly events for their "seniors" and "juniors" as well as annual gatherings, camping trips and summer camps.

The organization is strong in developing partnerships with other foundations dedicated to the well-being of children such as: the **Raptors Foundation**, the **Go Leafs Foundation** or the **Ontario Trillium Foundation**.

TIPS

• 100% of the contribution dollars go directly to help youth. Money contributions can help recruit youth volunteers, send kids to YAY summer camps, among other things. Send a cheque to the attention of Youth Assisting Youth to the address listed on this page. A receipt will be issued for tax purposes for donations $20 and over.

• To become a volunteer, call the office for the next orientation session in your area. The list of kids waiting for a match is long!

Youth Assisting Youth
(416) 932-1919
www.yay.org

Head office: 5734 Yonge St., Suite 401, Toronto, ON, M2M 4E7

OPERATION CHRISTMAS CHILD

Irresistible operation

Imagine a child, somewhere in the world, rummaging about in a garbage dump for anything that could be recycled and sold to help his family survive. Then, imagine that same child's astounded look as he receives a colourful shoe box filled with surprises carefully chosen by your own child...

TIPS (fun for 4 years +)

• Call or check their web site to find out where the collection site is closest to you.
• You can put a picture of your family in the shoe box to personalize it.
• Wrapped candies are appreciated. Stay away from anything that could melt under warm weather or anything containing liquids. Don't send anything sharp, breakable, war-related or needing batteries.
• Plastic shoe box-size containers are accepted. I prefer the Rubbermaid kind with attached lid, from a mom to another...
• A sample of things we have sent: flute, diary with lock, hair clips, beads, kid's jewelry, magnets, marbles, bouncing balls, whistles, small cars, balloons, stickers, paper pads, plush toys, clothes...
• Your family can help sort out the boxes (min. 14 years old to volunteer) at the general distribution warehouse for Ontario. Call to find out its current location.
• The **Toronto Star Santa Claus Fund** (since 1906!) puts together its own Christmas boxes for families in need within the GTA, with the help of our donations. Contact (416) 869-4847, www.thestar.com/santaclausfund. **CHUMCity Christmas Wish**, in its 38th year, collects new unwrapped toys and donations. Contact (416) 926-4199 or www.thewish.ca.

When I first heard about this operation, I was seduced by the opportunity for my kids to discover they could create a magical moment in the life of another child. It seems I'm not the only one!

Last time I checked, in a year, Canadians alone had donated nearly 740,000 shoe boxes, involving over 10,000 volunteers, 1,100 schools, 3,400 churches, 2,000 community groups and 1,200 collection sites.

Courtesy of Operation Christmas Child

Word-wide, six million children in over 95 countries had received a gift box.

The concept is simple: 1) Your child chooses if she wants to give to a girl or a boy. 2) She selects an age group (2-4 years, 5-9 years or 10-14 years). 3) You wrap the box, lid-separately. 4) She fills the box with age-related small toys, treats and useful objects. 5) You insert an envelope with a $5 cheque in the box and place a rubber band around the box and lid, along with a coupon detailing the sex and age group selected.

The boxes are distributed through a volunteer project created in 1993 by the Christian organization **Samaritan's Purse**. Orphanages, hospitals, refugee camps, schools and churches serve as distribution centres, regardless of their religious affiliation. The boxes get there by plane, then by boat, donkey, trucks or even helicopters.

Operation Christmas Child
1-800-303-1269
www.samaritanspurse.ca

Schedule: Deadline normally mid-November, call to confirm.
Costs: Each box must be sent along with a $5 cheque to the attention of Samaritan's Purse (to help cover shipping and related costs).
Directions: Call or check their web site to find the closest collection site according to your postal code.

KERSTIN'S IDEA

The gift of kindness

A few years ago, in my mother's group, we were talking about birthday parties. "Last birthday, my daughter played with maybe one gift and the rest got tossed away!" lamented one of us. "And they open the gifts so mechanically when there's fifteen of them!" added another sickened mom. "Well, we've found a solution!" claimed Kerstin.

Parents of toddlers will shriek at the notion (the first birthdays are as much fun to them as they are to their child). This concept is for parents with school-age kids, especially those in well-knit neighbourhood schools where it gets almost impossible not to invite the whole class to every party.

My friend had already thrown eight of those parties for her daughter and son. And she had bought gifts for the dozens of other parties her kids were invited to by their classmates. Add to this a family birthday party and possibly a small celebration to mark the exact day of birth and it only takes a few years before you feel things are getting out of control. So Kerstin came up with a daring solution.

She tried it on her son who was warm to the idea. She coached him to choose a charitable cause that suited his interests. Then, they prepared an invitation stating: "No gift please. If you would like, please consider bringing a donation, of no more than $15, to the **United Way** and Mark will deliver it."

Parents of the guests were saved a trip to the toy store and the agony of choosing yet another gift. The dollar amount suggested on the card took all the guess work away.

In the loot bags, Kerstin included a thank you note announcing that $180 was raised for the day. Mark was really proud to personally deliver the money himself.

Jess, his older sister, thought she would chose the **World Wildlife Fund (WWF)** and she collected $195. When she delivered it, it turned out to be a very rewarding choice! Her donation allowed her to "adopt" a wolf pup and to receive an adoption kit including a plush wolf, an adoption certificate (min. donation of $40). She also got a gorgeous 16-month calendar because her donation exceeded $80. (See www.wwf.ca or call (416) 489-8800 for details.) In the same spirit, see the **Toronto Zoo Foundation** on p. 122.

> Mark's 7th Birthday
>
> THANK YOU!
> $_____ was raised today at the 2002 Olympics for the UNITED WAY.
>
> Thanks for coming.
>
> Mark

TIPS (fun for 7 +)
• Casually explain the concept to your child and see how she reacts (reminding her how little she has played with last birthday's gifts). You'll be surprised how easily kids can enthuse over the notion that they could help others. The trick is to confirm that they will still get a wrapped gift from you and that they can always go back to the old way of doing things on the next birthday.
• Check p. 122 for a list of potential charities.

Photos: Courtesy of Kerstin

General tips about
Farms:

- Two good web sites to find a pick-your-own farm in your area are: **www.ontberries.com** (click Find a patch) and the web site **www.harvestontario.com** (click Pick-Your-Own).
- Here's a crop calendar for different Ontario fruit and vegetables. Always call to check the current crop report of the farms you want to visit. Mother Nature sometimes plays tricks on us! I remember picking a pumpkin from under a snow fall.

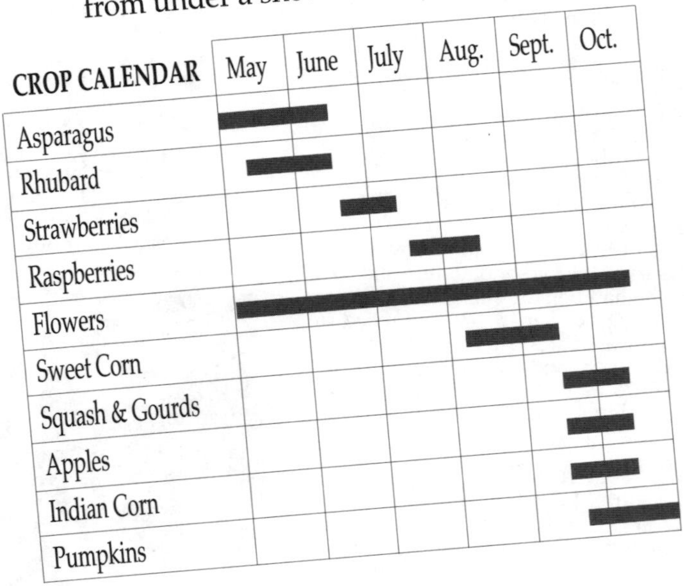
CROP CALENDAR
May
June
July
Aug.
Sept.
Oct.
Asparagus
Rhubard
Strawberries
Raspberries
Flowers
Sweet Corn
Squash & Gourds
Apples
Indian Corn
Pumpkins

FARMS

See **Springridge Farm** on p. 143.

RIVERDALE FARM FALL FESTIVAL

Best of the crop

Twelve kids have already given their attempt at the chicken-calling contest. My son stands next in line. I've never heard him imitate a hen. I see him whispering something to the host, who nods, smiling, announcing this contestant has requested permission to call a rooster. After a resounding try, he leaves with the second-best caller ribbon!

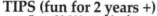

TIPS (fun for 2 years +)

• Over 30,000 people show up during this dual event so parking is hard to find around Cabbagetown. Come early or be prepared to walk. Get the small wagon out.

• The local residents have been organizing the **Forsythia Festival** on the first Sunday of May for over 30 years. It consists of a popular parade starting in front of Riverdale Farm at around 10 am (people arrive at around 9:30 am). Participants are asked to wear yellow and decorate their bike, stroller or dog! The parade heads to **Wellesley Park**, located a 5-minute walk north of the farm, and continues until 1:30 pm in the lovely park, with entertainment and food stands. To access this park, walk north on Sumach and turn east on Amelia. Call **Cabbagetown Preservation Association** at (416) 410-4259 for details.

• The farm usually organizes one day of **Halloween** activities, suitable for kids 10 years and under. For **Christmas**, they usually offer an evening of tree lighting, carolling and marshmallow roasting and a morning with Santa and treats. Call for exact date.

• More on **Riverdale Farm** on p. 45.

The farm gets very lively during the Fall Harvest Festival. Not only do they offer a wide range of activities within the farm's gates but **Cabbagetown Arts & Crafts Sale** takes place in the adjacent park at the same time.

Last year, the festival included line dancing, clowning, antique farm tools display, several demonstrations, kids crafts, potato-sack race, egg and spoon relay, horseshoe pitch, straw jump, hog and chicken calling contest, storytelling and more. Smaller kids could "fish" for little prizes, they

could touch reptiles and admire scarecrows. On Sunday morning, they serve $5 pancake breakfasts.

In the park, we could admire the work of artisans and listen to musicians. When visiting, we even got to watch a children's play in the small chapel north of the farm! For more details, check www.cabbagetownartsandcrafts.org.

Riverdale Farm (416) 392-6794 www.friendsof riverdalefarm.com	I-10 **Downtown** **Toronto** **15-min.**

 Schedule: The **Fall Harvest Festival** takes place on the weekend after Labour Day, from 10:30 am to 7 pm on Saturday and from 9:30 am to 4 pm on Sunday. Call to confirm dates of other seasonal events.

 Admission: FREE.
Directions: See p. 45.

  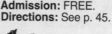

NEARBY ATTRACTIONS
Allan Gardens (5-min.)..................p. 309

ROYAL WINTER FAIR

Fair enough!

If you think this nearly 80-year-old fair is all about livestock and show-jumping competitions, you're in for a surprise when you first visit this huge event!

Strolling around, watching animals lined up in preparation for competitions is not particularly stimulating for younger children, yet, they are impressed when they meet large furry cows (nose to nose). Here, you'll find the obvious Dairy Cattle section (where we saw young beasts being lead by 10-year-old farmers), and a bit further, the large Beef Cattle stalls, along with the Swine (there are cute piglets to see), Rabbits and Poultry sections.

There's also the Royal Horse Palace to the extreme west side of the site, with its imposing stalls, some heavily decorated with champions' medals; a world in itself.

Other animals can be touched at the petting farm. There are also paddocks where goats and sheep are competing for titles.

When visiting, we saw interesting demonstrations in one of the rings, such as the large animal Vet check-ups, which allows young aspiring veterinarians to listen to a huge horse's heartbeat with a stethoscope. It also was the stage for live auction simulations and sheep-shearing sessions. Activities and floor plan change every year but you get the picture.

There usually are some horse shows included with general admission. During our visit, there was lots of action when the staff prepared the ring after the jumping competition. It took them less than 10 minutes to put away all the obstacles and make way for shiny large carriage demonstrations. Now, THAT was entertainment(!), according to my young builder.

Throughout the fair there are several educational displays, such as maple syrup making, egg grading, honey production and animal and sheep wool care. Kids can grind wheat into flour or crush canola seeds to extract oil.

Not to be missed are the butter sculptures. When we visited, over 12 creations were kept in a refrigerated room.

Of course, the Royal Fair is about seeing animals in action. Dog shows are included with admission. You can often see a keen dog barking enthusiastically at its master, begging her to start the routine through a series of obstacles. They seem to live for that kind of action. Check the schedule for the day as soon as you get to the fair.

TIPS (fun for 3 years +)
• Not all activities are presented daily. Call or check their web site to select the best day to visit.
• The giant vegetable competition takes place during the first days. (They're deflated by the end of the fair!)
• In the Coliseum, you will have to leave your stroller at the foot of the bleachers.
• Snack bars are found on site.

NEARBY ATTRACTIONS
Music Gardens (10-min.)............p. 307
High Park (15-min.)......................p. 322

Royal Agricultural Winter Fair
(416) 263-3400
www.royalfair.org

J-10
Downtown
Toronto
10-min.

Schedule: 10 days long, usually from the first Wednesday in November, 9 am to 9 pm (closes at 8 pm on Sunday).
Admission: Around $16/adults, $11/seniors and 5 to 17 years, FREE under 5, $38/family of 4. Parking around $13.
Directions: National Trade Centre in Exhibition Place. Take Lake Shore Blvd., go north on Strachan Ave. The entrance is to your left.

SOUTHBROOK FARM

Attention shoppers!

The drive is busy with cars lining up to enter the farm's parking lot or slowing down to figure out what's attracting so many people. We're on the last patch of country road in an area that has experienced major residential development in the last few years. And this working farm is flooded by city dwellers starving for fresh and locally grown produce and a little piece of natural setting.

In the fall, you can't miss the tall silo with an orange pumpkin face and the large hay bales painted with funny faces at the entrance.

Southbrook is more market-oriented than activity-oriented. Sure, you can grab a wagon ride to the gigantic pumpkin field but there is no maze, or hay jumping and all the other things one can

do at a farm. It is a place to spend money: at the farm market, at the **Halloween** shop (or Christmas Gift Store later in the season) and at the small kiddy midway during **Halloween**.

Their **Halloween** shop alone is worth the stop! It took us half and hour to explore it all.

The huge barn offers an extensive selection of costumes and accessories of all prices that can compete with the best suppliers in town. In addition, the barn is the perfect setting for some ambitious decorations. Inside, you'll find a large graveyard turned into a picnic spot for witches.

The market smells of fresh pies and fudge. It displays an abundance of produce, baked products, preserves as well as herbs, flowers, decorative items and snacks. Those caramel apples are hard to resist.

TIPS (fun for 3 years +)
• Pick-your-own strawberries, raspberries and pumpkins.
• Their boutique winery offers whites, reds, some ice wines and award-winning fortified dessert wines made with raspberries, blueberries or blackcurrants, developed for them by one Niagara vineyard. Ask about their tasting sessions and fancy dinners.

Southbrook Farm & Winery
• Richmond Hill (Maple)
(905) 832-2548
WWW.southbrook.com

H-10 North of Toronto 35-min.

Schedule: Farm store and winery open daily from May to Christmas. Winery open weekends only from Christmas to May.

Admission: FREE.
Directions: 1061 Major Mackenzie Dr., Maple. North of Hwy 7, west of Bathurst St.

WHITTAMORE'S FARM

Snack time at the farm

The frozen yogurt sign caught my ever-hungry son's attention. I was really happy we made that stop!

Not only was the snack bar's food delicious, the farm's market was well stocked with preserves, giftware and baked goods and it had an entertaining playground, complete with chickens and goats.

During their **Pumpkinland** event, you can catch a wagon ride through their **haunted forest**, enjoy corn, straw and kiddies' mazes and inflated structure. There is also a straw pyramid, log walk, nature trail and more.

We went back to pick strawberries in their huge fields. Here, you can pick your own strawberries, raspberries, peas, peppers, tomatoes and pumpkins, each in their own season. Call for crop updates!

Whittamore's Farm · Markham (905) 294-3275 www.whittamoresfarm.com	I-12 N-E of Toronto 35-min.

  Schedule: The market is open early May to October 31. Pumpkinland open weekends from end of September to Halloween, 10 am to 5 pm.
Admission: FREE ($5 access to Pumpkinland).
Directions: 8100 Steeles Ave. East, Markham. From Hwy 401 West, take exit #389/Meadowvale Rd. northbound. Turn east on Steeles.

WATSON FARMS

twigs, a slide, as well as a horse and rabbits to pet.

Throughout the strawberry season and on weekends during apple season, wagon rides are provided to and from the fields.

You can pick your own strawberries, peas, raspberries, beans, apples and pumpkins.

Surprise!

Out of sight, a great surprise awaits us in the middle of the fields at Ted Watson Farms. You find it by driving along a small road past the large farm's small produce market, on the side of the road.

When in Bowmanville, don't miss the unique free playground set up amidst Watson Farms. It is small but well laid out.

When we visited, there was a tractor to climb on, a haystack shaded by a canopy to jump into, a large wooden structure to climb, a cottage made of

Watson Farms · Bowmanville (905) 623-7252	C-4 East of Toronto 50-min.

  Schedule: The market is open end of June until October 31. Pick your own weekdays from 8:30 am to 8:30 pm (until 5:30 pm on weekends).
Admission: FREE.
Directions: 2287 Hwy # 2, Bowmanville. From Hwy 401 West, take exit #431 northbound, turn west on Hwy 2/King St.

MAGIC HILL TREE FARM

"O, Christmas Tree"...

After our wagon ride had taken us, ax in hand, to the heart of the fir tree farm, we pulled our little green elf at full speed in his toboggan. Then, we stopped to assess the potential of the tree in front of us. "What do you think, pumpkin?" With all the conviction in the world, the miniature expert replies: "It's PERFECT!"

Cutting your own tree is a great family activity. It brings kids in close contact with the great outdoors. After helping to select and cut the tree, my son looked at our **Christmas** tree with new eyes.

There's more to the adventure. A tractor-pulled cart shuttles the young lumberjacks to the field every 15 minutes. An impressive bonfire burns to warm the families in the fields.

On your way back, you may buy a hot chocolate and cookies at the snack bar. You can play in the big barn hayloft. You can see Santa in his workshop, and there is also a magic show you can watch.

The tree-wrapping machine stringing the evergreens to reduce their volume was a good show in itself!

Finally, visitors have access to some of the attractions Magic Hill Farm normally only offers to private functions: Giant playground, Rule-less Square, Catwalk Park, Sandpit Playground...

TIPS (fun for 3 years +)

• It's colder here than in Toronto. Dress warmly, but not too elegantly, because sticky mud is often present on the paths. I had to undress my son before he entered the car. A warm change of clothes could be useful.
• Sleighs are provided for transporting trees. They can lend you tools but you might have to wait for some to become available. It is better to bring your own tools to cut your tree.
• While you're at it, bring your own toboggan as there are hills on the site.
• Cutting your own tree doesn't save money! You have a better chance of finding a deal at your local corner store. I like to consider the cost of the tree we cut ourselves as the admission fee to a great family outing.
• More about **Magic Hill Haunted Adventure** during **Halloween** on p. 185.

NEARBY ATTRACTIONS
Forsythe Farm (15-min.)..........p. 140

Horton's Magic Hill Tree Farm
· Stouffville
(905) 888-1738
www.hortontreefarms.com

G-12
N-E
of Toronto
30-min.

Schedule: Open weekends in December up to weekend prior to Christmas, 9 am to 4:30 pm.
Admission: FREE for tree buyers (Cut-your-own trees cost $30. Premium pre-cut trees are $35 and up).
Directions: 13953, 9th Line, Stouffville. From Hwy 404 North, take exit #41/Bloomington Rd. eastbound. Turn north at 9th Line.

BROOKS FARMS

You'll have a blast!

Most of the farms around Toronto are strongly feeling the pressure of residential development. Not this one. It still stands in the middle of farmland, without one townhouse ruining the horizon, which is a good thing. You wouldn't want those pumpkin cannons disturbing a baby's nap!

Once you walk past the entrance, you can assess in a glimpse the wide range of activities going on here: pig races, pumpkin cannon demonstrations, "train" ride to the pumpkin field, straw jumps, corn maze, really funny haunted ride in the daylight and my kid's favourite, the zip lines.

Wondering what a zip line is? It's a suspended metal line going downhill, with sliding handles kids hang from as they launch from a small platform. There's sand underneath so nobody gets hurt if they fall. The announcement of the cannon blast about to take place could not lure many young acrobats away from this activity!

Wondering how pumpkin cannons work? With propane gas and some crazy guys loading wet newspapers and pumpkins into the cannons. These are aimed at some scarecrows, far away. The anticipation before each blast is just too much for the very excited kids. The

TIPS (fun for 3 years +)
• Pick-your-own strawberries, raspberries and pumpkins.
• Their store sells pumpkins, jams, decorative corn and straw bales.
• They have a small snack bar which makes hot dogs and tasty small doughnuts on site (12 for $4). Bring a blanket to sit on the ground to eat lunch (not many tables around).

NEARBY ATTRACTIONS
North York Drive-in (15-min.).......p. 97

strange muffled explosion doesn't disappoint them.

For the pig races, the same crazy guys encourage the crowd to cheer the pigs with resounding "Sew-Wee" combined with a ridiculous dance step they demonstrate.

The haunted ride in broad daylight through a dried-out cornfield wasn't so scary that all kids under six would cry. The farm staff goes for fun scare more than anything... Although the sight of masked chainsaw-wielding individuals approaching have an effect on some people...

We went on Thanksgiving. Three hours went by in a flash at this most dynamic farm! It's a shame I had to take everybody back. I still had a turkey to cook, my first!

Brooks Farms
• Mount Albert
(905) 473-3920
www.brooks-farms.com

C-3
N-E
of Toronto
45-min.

 Schedule: Fall Fun runs from last weekend of September to October 31, Saturdays and Sundays 10 am to 6 pm, and on Thanksgiving Day. Pick-your-own from end of June to mid-August.

 Admission: Around $6/person for one haunted ride and all activities. FREE under 3 years.

 Directions: 122 Ashworth Rd., Mount Albert. Take Hwy 404 North, exit at Vivian/Mulock eastbound. Turn north on Hwy 48, then Mount Albert Rd. East. Drive to Durham 30 and Ashworth Rd.

PINGLE'S FARM MARKET

Big field trip

At Pingle's Farm Market, the pumpkins are mighty impressive! There must be 10,000 of them, sitting in an amazing patch. We enter armed with a wheelbarrow, and pass through a winding corridor of lovely pumpkins standing at attention. It's well worth the trip, if only to take a look.

The farm's setting was nicely decorated for the season when we visited in the fall. An old wooden witch eyed my little one, and friendly scarecrows stared at us mischievously.

We visited the farm on a weekend during the **Fun Fall Harvest** when the outdoor playground was transformed into a Fun Farm Area accessible for a fee.

Kids bounced in the inflated structure, they rode on an amusing tricycle race track and they played funny bowling where they used small pumpkins as balls. Kids enjoyed the musical puppet shows presented on those weekends.

The messy bowling with pumpkin activity has been replaced by a pumpkin cannon show. The farm now has a Bunnyville (with rabbit inhabiting houses in a small fenced space). Then there's the elevated goats walk and mini-maze.

For an additional fee, you could carve or paint a small pumpkin or get your child's face painted.

TIPS (fun for 3 years +)

• Pick your own strawberries, fall raspberries, apples and pumpkins.
• During the **Easter** weekend, (excluding Monday) Pingles offers Easter egg hunts for around $7: kids decorate their basket then fetch plastic eggs hidden by the Easter Bunny, which they trade for chocolate eggs and pot and seed to plant, earth provided on site.
• Pingles has created an 8-acre-wide corn **maze** which opens mid-August. It could take 1hr to complete and find the letters forming a secret word (additional fees apply).
• You can buy snacks and baked goods in the relatively large market or fast food under a large tent.

NEARBY ATTRACTIONS

Jungle Cat World (10-min.).........p. 53
Cullen Gardens (25-min.)............p. 116

Pingle's Farm Market	C-4 East of Toronto 50-min.
· Hampton (905) 725-6089 www.pinglesfarmmarket.com	

 Schedule: Opens for Easter, then daily, May 1 to October 31, 10 am to 5 pm. (Call to check if reopens during Christmas time.) Fun Fall event is offered during October weekends and Thanksgiving Monday, from 11 am to 4 pm.

 Admission: Extra fees apply during Fun Fall and for Easter Egg Hunts. Call to confirm.

 Directions: 1805 Taunton Rd.. East, Hampton. From Hwy 401 East, take exit #425/Courtice Rd. northbound. Turn east on Taunton Rd..

ARCHIBALD ORCHARDS

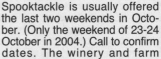

Starring Mr. Johnson

Every fall at Archibald Orchards, something happens to Mr. Johnson, recognizable by his pumpkin head. Last time we saw him, he was looking for a wife. The season before that, he was looking... for his head. God knows what he'll be looking for next fall!

Hidden behind a rustic country road, you'll find Archibald Orchards. The farm is small, the orchard huge, the location great. It is a treat to find yourself basking in the calm of the country, amidst this intimate and lovely farm.

Halloween Spooktackle is a wacky little show usually offered before **Halloween**. It tells the story of Mr. Johnson, as we are taken on a 15-minute wagon ride through the orchard.

We all sat in the barn to hear the story's introduction. Mr. Archibald, a very patient man with the young audience, welcomed us and briefed us on Mr. Johnson's situation. He then invited us to hop on the wagon for a ride to find a wife for Mr. Johnson as the driver took her place behind the wheel.

Kids did not notice Mr. Archibald run like crazy. Neither did they recognize him under a wig and apron at our first stop along the wagon ride. He played the part of a homely woman making pies, trying to convince us that she would be a suitable wife. She succeeded, until she started to smash into a pumpkin with a hammer.

We saw a couple more unsuitable wives until we caught Mr. Johnson kissing a woman in a wedding dress, bearing a pumpkin head too.

This was a refreshing **Halloween** attraction for younger children: hilarious yet not really scary. Then, there's the pedal-kart racetrack and the wooden maze in the Children's Area.

TIPS (fun for 3 years +)
- Pick your own apples.
- Children's entertainment offered on weekends in September and October.
- The orchard is also a winery selling great fruit wine all year in their store (ask to have a sip!). They offer Food & Wine Tasting events.
- Since our last visit, they've rebuilt the winery and farm market under one roof... and they've added a 9-hole golf course in the orchard!
- In the well-stocked market, you can observe the making of cider, and everyone can taste this fresh apple nectar. You can buy snacks and fast food.

NEARBY ATTRACTIONS

Archibald Orchards Estate Winery	**C-4**
• Bowmanville	**East**
(905) 263-2396	**of Toronto**
www. archibaldswinery.com	**50-min.**

Schedule: The Halloween Spooktackle is usually offered the last two weekends in October. (Only the weekend of 23-24 October in 2004.) Call to confirm dates. The winery and farm market is open daily May through December, 10 am to 6 pm. It opens weekends in April.
Admission: $1/person for Spooktackle.
Directions: 6275 Liberty St. North, Bowmanville. From Hwy 401 East, take exit #432/Liberty St. northbound.

FORSYTHE FAMILY FARMS

Come to your senses

Multicoloured flower baskets, delicious warm pies, smooth stacks of hay, apple turnovers fresh out of the oven, candied apples and children's laughter in the playground. You're at Forsythe Family Farms.

This farm-market isn't only a cornucopia of farm products, it also goes to great lengths to make us return to nature.

When we arrived at Forsythe Farms, we were struck by the beauty of the large, rustic market.

Farther along, a decorated slide and a pony-shaped swing made from a recycled tire, helped to entertain the little ones while we waited for the cart ride leading to the **Enchanted Forest**.

A 10-minute cart ride brought us to the entrance of a tiny forest, where we were greeted by a funny face painted on a tree. A few wagons are put at the disposal of visitors at the edge of the forest.

Lovely paths carpeted with twigs

criss-cross the woods. From time to time they reveal scenes from several popular fairy tales.

For little ones, the simple act of taking a stroll in the woods is impressive in itself. I suggest to those accompanying bigger kids that they ask them to identify the depicted fairy tales.

After the ride, there's the tricycle track. Further, by the parking lot, the owners have added the Barnyard Adventure.

It includes Bunnyville, a big pen incorporating a house, (you may buy food to feed the animals) and a straw tunnel made of large square bails. There are also beehives in this section.

TIPS (fun for 2 years +)

• Pick-your-own strawberries, peas, beans and pumpkins.

• Each weekend in October is **Harvest Festival** with **Halloween** activities (inflated pumpkin for jumping, scarecrow making) for an extra fee.

• During **Christmas** time, free hot cider is offered at the farm's market and the farm sells Christmas trees. Their store includes gift items and seasonal decorations.

• You may buy snacks at the farm's market. There's an outdoor snack bar (call to confirm if open when visiting).

Forsythe Family Farms
• Unionville
(905) 887-1087
www.forsythefamilyfarms.com

| H-11 |
| N-E |
| of Toronto |
| 30-min. |

Schedule: Enchanted Forest is open weekends only from May 1 until first week of November, weather permitting. The farm is open weekends only in May and November. It opens daily from early June to October 31 and all December until December 24. Variable hours depending on crops. Call to confirm.

Admission: Weekend admission to the Fun Area is $4/visitor, FREE 2 years and under ($2 only on weekdays). FREE in December.

Directions: 10539 Kennedy Rd., Unionville. From Hwy 404 North, take exit #31/Major Mackenzie eastbound, turn north on Kennedy Rd..

DOWNEY'S FARM MARKET

Mountain goats, sea of pumpkins

Navigating in an orange ocean, my tiny adventurer thinks he's dreaming. Then, we get into the action: jumping on hay-covered mattresses, visiting the haunted barn and the destabilizing black hole, racing on huge balloons, exploring the big cornfield maze and sending feed to the mountain goats perched high above our heads.

We had a good laugh in the cowshed, due to the surprising bouncing effect of the hay-covered mattresses carpeting the floor. I tried it myself, and found it delightfully soft.

During our visit, the Black-Hole Barn was a great attraction. Completely black inside, it included a trip through a turning cylinder, all black as well and studded with stars, with sound effects to boot. We literally lost our balance. My little one also lost her boot and we had problems finding it in the dark.

There were giant tires, bales of hay, knotted ropes to climb on, a strolling pumpkin character and more. For an additional fee, you can make a big scarecrow, a great project for the whole family to create together!

The petting farm section is safe for children of all ages. It is filled with beautiful animals. We particularly enjoyed petting a small white goat with a soft coat. My little menace loved to chase the poor ducks.

Other farms have climbing goats but no other place has such an ambitious setting for them. At the crossing of four wooden corridors mounted on stilts, hungry goats bleat at us. The intelligent animals started to move only when I had filled a dish fastened to a rope and my little engineer had enthusiastically hauled it up using the pulley system.

Pony rides are offered for a fee on weekends from end of June to end of October.

TIPS (fun for 2 years +)

• Pick-your-own strawberries, raspberries (wagon ride to the berry patch) and corn in August and September.
• The goats and the Kritter Corral are there from May to December. However, the best time to visit is during the events.
• During **Easter**, their Easterfest includes egg hunts with the Easter Bunny, egg decorating, wagon rides, puppet shows and children's entertainers.
• They celebrate **Canada Day** with entertainment (free admission).
• The farm's market is brimming with goodies. We indulged ourselves with cheese bread, pumpkin doughnuts and pretty hen-shaped chocolate lollipops. They also sell fast food. Christmas trees are sold in December.

NEARBY ATTRACTIONS	
Heart Lake (10-min.)	p. 277
Belfountain (15-min.)	p. 353

Downey's Farm Market & Estate Winery
• North of Brampton
(905) 838-2990
www.downeysfarm.on.ca

C-2
N-W
of Toronto
45-min.

Schedule: Opens weekend prior to Easter and Easter weekend (Friday to Sunday, 10 am to 5 pm), then, May to December, 9 am to 6 pm. Pumpkinfest is during October weekends (plus the last weekend in September or first weekend in November). Call to confirm.

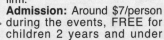

Admission: Around $7/person during the events, FREE for children 2 years and under (extra fees for craft activities).

Directions: 13682 Heart Lake Rd., north of Brampton. Take Hwy 401 West, then Hwy 410 northbound until the end, where it becomes Heart Lake Rd..

ALBION ORCHARDS

Picking and walking

A few things distinguish this orchard from others: many tall apple trees, ladders to reach the upper branches, and a long winding road running down the beautiful scenery of Caledon.

There's something about climbing up a ladder that adds to the pleasure of apple picking. The orchard closest to the entrance included taller trees than the ones I'm used to seeing in the region. My little picker was thrilled to climb hers and grab the red apples that seemed inaccessible from the ground.

The biggest part of the orchard is located much farther, hidden from our sight by a hill. Up the hill, we observe an intriguing little graveyard under the shadow of a very large tree, where the likes of A. Lawyer, I.M. Gone and Lou Zer were buried…

Going downhill, we can take in the panorama of the white gravel sinuous road contrasting with the greenery of the apple trees and pumpkin field, with a tiny touch of orange in the background.

TIPS (fun for 3 years +)

• Pick-your-own apples and pumpkins.

• Their market sells gift baskets, Christmas trees, pies, ice cream, hot dogs, and corn on the cob.

• I recommend you drive along Old Church Road, just north of Albion Orchards. It is as gorgeous a little country road as can be.

As we get closer, the orange spot turns into a giant pumpkin decoration sitting next to the remains of an old orchard, creating a picture perfect Halloween scene.

We stop to eat the sheep-shaped cookies we bought at the farm store and then off we go. We reach the entrance to the orchard where small red wagons to carry the apples (or the kids) are waiting for us. The tricky part here is to leave before the kids run out of energy. You still have to walk back up and down the hill to the starting point. A wagon ride can take you to the orchards during the weekends.

By the main building, there's a small play area where tires and hay are put to good use.

Albion Orchards
· Caledon East
(905) 584-0354
www.albionorchards.com

C-2
N-W
of Toronto
55-min.

Schedule: Open daily from end of August to just before Christmas, 10 am to 6 pm (closed on Monday from November 1).

Admission: FREE. You pay for what you pick.

Directions: 14800 Innis Lake Rd., Caledon East. Take Hwy 400, exit at Hwy 7 going west.

Turn north on Goreway Dr., it becomes Innis Lake Rd.. The farm is 15 km away, on the west side of the road.

NEARBY ATTRACTIONS	

SPRINGRIDGE FARM

Happy ending

Less than a 15-minute drive from other attractions in the Milton and Guelph regions (mentioned in this guide), you will find Springridge Farm on the way back to Toronto. It is ideal to loosen little legs, grab a snack and finish off your outing nicely.

Springridge's general store far exceeds what you would expect from a farm market. Inside the pleasantly decorated market you'll find a broad selection of seasonal decorative garden accessories, small toys, preserves and,

best of all: excellent pies, tarts, cookies, muffins, cakes, breads, hot soups and delicious sandwiches. All of which you can eat sitting atop large barrels.

Everyday, visitors can climb haystacks of different heights or enter the open mouth of a witch that leads to a corn maze they can explore. They can feed the greedy sheep, goats, hens and roosters. They can play with the trucks in the large sandbox, climb up the old tractor and fly down the slide. They can "milk" a cut out cow. All this for free.

Most weekends you can catch a pony ride or a tour of the property on a tractor-drawn cart for a fee. A section of the farmland is elevated, giving you a postcard perfect panoramic view.

In October, the wagon ride will take you to a huge corn **maze** you can't see from the farm.

TIPS (fun for 1 year +)

• Pick-your-own strawberries and pumpkins.
• Springridge closes at 5 pm. You will want to leave nearby attractions no later than 3 pm if you wish to include it in your itinerary.
• During the **Easter** 4-day weekend, kids may participate in a $7 egg hunt where plastic eggs are hidden by the Easter Bunny, which kids trade for treats and a little basket with hard-boiled chicken egg to decorate on the premises. Each child is sure to get one egg!
• Every weekend in October, **Halloween** activities are offered for a fee: pumpkin painting, scarecrow making and a visit to the Boo Barn (cute rather than scary) with some black-light effects and lots of details to observe.
• Every weekend from mid-November to **Christmas**, gingerbread making and glass ball painting are offered for around $5.

NEARBY ATTRACTIONS

Springridge Farm • Milton (905) 878-4908 www.springridgefarm.com	**D-2** **West** **of Toronto** **45-min.**

 Schedule: Open daily from mid April until Christmas, 9 am to 5 pm. If Easter falls in March, call to confirm if they will offer Easter activity.

 Admission: FREE (fees may apply to some activities).

Directions: 7256 Bell School Line, Milton. From Hwy 401, take exit #324/James Snow Pkwy southbound. Turn west on Derry Rd. and north on Bell School Line.

CHUDLEIGH'S FARM

Hay! You!

"Something's bothering me!" my farm boy insists. For the third time, I stop the car at the side of the road to look for small pieces of straw slyly lodged in his clothes. This time, I extract the last intruders... from inside his underpants! That's what happens when you spend an afternoon running, jumping, sprawling and rolling in the play area at Chudleigh's Farm.

The site is huge, but the layout of the attractions gives it the charming and intimate character of a village fair. I doubt that your kids will let you begin by apple picking, as there are so many other tempting activities on site. I prefer to allow them to let off steam first in the playground. (It is actually worth going to the farm for the sole reason of having your children enjoy it.)

A Twin Tower Hay Mow including two giant slides offers a breathtaking sliding experience. When we visited, it was surrounded by a thick carpet of straw, topped by bales of hay that children climbed as if they were mountain goats (hence the straw!). The petting zoo is fun and includes climbing goats.

Afterwards, my kids were thrilled to ride to the orchard in a wagon drawn by a mighty tractor. My 3-year-old apple picker was quite satisfied by a half-hour harvest coming from a few trees, an operation made easier by the small size of the apple trees. By the end of August, there's a wide maze built with bales of hay. During the fall, for an extra fee, you can take a 3-minute pony ride around a small orchard.

Chudleigh's Farm also grows pumpkins in a large patch by the orchard. After Thanksgiving, you can enjoy a wagon ride through the pumpkin patch to select your pumpkin.

Since our last visit, they've added a trail behind the bush with signs (to let your child guide you through the hardwood forest).

TIPS (fun for 2 years +)

• Pick-your-own apples and pumpkins.
• The admission fee to enter the orchard's entertainment area is refundable when you purchase either 20 pounds of apples (about two of their bags, moderately filled), two pies or one pie plus 10 pounds of apples.
• Giant hot dogs, European sausages and corn barbecued in its husk are sold during the fall weekends. At the tempting outdoor market you can buy delicious homemade soup and eat it while observing the golden fish in the new pond.

NEARBY ATTRACTIONS

Chudleigh's Farm
• Milton
(905) 878-2725
www.chudleighs.com

D-2 West of Toronto 45-min.

Schedule: Open daily end of June to October 31, 10 am to 5 pm. Retail store stays open Friday, Saturday and Sunday to December 24.

Admission: Fee to use orchard and entertainment area is $5/person or $16/family of 4, FREE for 3 years and under (see tips on refund).

Directions: 9528 Hwy 25, Milton. From Hwy 401 West, take exit #320/Hwy 25 northbound.

ANDREWS' SCENIC ACRES

Your pick

The first time we visited this farm, we picked strawberries. The ten-minute wagon ride led to the row assigned to us.

I must say my then 2-year-old son wasn't that fascinated by the picking itself. However, children 4 years and over seemed to be captivated by this activity. Furthermore, the rows of fruit were well spaced out, allowing little ones to run and explore easily.

After half an hour, our basket was full and my son's patience was coming to an end. Time to go back to the farm's big playground equipped with swings, a giant tire, an old tractor to explore and an animal corral inhabited by rabbits, goats, turkeys, ducks and pigs. Pony rides are offered for a fee during the weekends.

We returned in October to visit the small haunted forest located a short walk away from the playground. Don't expect a spooky trail but the winding trail created in the narrow forest made the experience interesting.

The mountain of straw was a hit with my family. There's real free play going on here. Try it! You'll be impressed by the straw's softness.

TIPS (fun for 2 years +)
• Pick-your-own rhubarb, asparagus, strawberries, raspberries, black currants, cherries, blueberries, flowers, elderberries and pumpkins.
• Wear comfortable, stainproof clothes. Don't forget hats and sunscreen.
• You can bring your own containers or buy them on site. As for the price of the fruit itself, it's about equivalent to what you would pay at your local store.
• The **haunted forest** trail is open most of September until end of October.
• Several picnic tables are located close to the playground. You can purchase delicious hot dogs and great cones of frozen yogurt. The farm market fills a large Mennonite barn with baked goods and produce as well as snacks.
• The farm is now producing a selection of 30 fruit wines through its Scotch Block Winery.

NEARBY ATTRACTIONS

Andrews' Scenic Acres Scotch Block Winery
• Milton
(905) 878-5807
www.
andrewsscenicacres.com

D-2
West
of Toronto
45-min.

Schedule: Open 7 days from May 1 to October 31, 9 am to 6 pm (longer hours during special events).

Admission: FREE ($1/person in September and October).

Directions: From Hwy 401 North, take exit #328/Trafalgar Rd. northbound, turn west on Ashgrove 10th Sideroad.

LONG LANE ORCHARDS

There's a beautiful and intimate country feeling to this nicely groomed farm. It will please those who want to avoid the big frenzy of other more popular places in Milton. There are some animals in a large cage by the store. The farm house, surrounded by trees, is gorgeous.

A big tree by the entrance was winking at us, another one by the pond was showing a funny face. I just love that kind of attention to detail.

The sandpit filled with toys, albeit nice, pales in comparison to the thrills given by a nearby old tractor and wagon and the suspended tire attached to a climbing structure. They sit next to a large spring-fed pond.

Apples anyone?

The week following our visit to Long Lane Orchards, I made two apple cakes, three apple pies, a batch of muffins... and my fridge was still jammed with apples. The kids had so much fun picking their own apples that we did not have the heart to stop them at one bag.

We pay for the apples by the bag. I know I'll get my money's worth from my son and his best friend as they enthusiastically fill their bags to capacity.

As for my 3-year-old daughter, it's another story. She won't be convinced to fill more than half of hers, for reasons that still elude me!

TIPS (fun for 2 years +)

• Pick your own apples. Fish for your own trout in their stocked pond. You have to bring your own gear. They say customers are seldom disappointed!

• During their **Easter** Festival, on Friday and Saturday, they offer 8 small activities including an Easter Egg Hunt where kids find plastic eggs with numbers inside they exchange for a prize. During their **Pumpkin Fest**, on Thanksgiving weekend (Saturday and Sunday) there's a corn maze, wagon rides, crafts and hay jumps. Small fees apply.

• McIntosh, Spartan and Empire are usually ready shortly after the middle of September. We visited in mid-October and most of the trees were bare by then.

• They sell tasty cider, doughnuts and more treats. You can observe through a large window the making of cider. There are many picnic tables.

• Check the panning place on p. 434.

NEARBY ATTRACTIONS

Long Lane Orchards
· Campbellville
(905) 854-2673
www.
longlaneorchards.com

D-2 West of Toronto 50-min.

Schedule: Open daily year-round, from 9 am to 6 pm.
Admission: FREE. It costs $7 to fill a 10lb bag with apples. It is $2 per rod in use to fish in the pond (refundable on cost of fish) and $4.80/pound for fish.
Directions: 2nd Line, Campbellville. From Hwy 401 West, take exit #312/Guelph Line northbound. Turn west on 15 Sideroad, then south on 2nd Line.

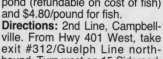

WILDFLOWER FARM

Do pick the flowers

To me, a typical city dweller with a shaded backyard the size of a handkerchief (not to mention a total lack of gardening skills), a patch of cutting flowers is pure fantasy. What a treat it is to be allowed to cut them by myself. It feels quite luxurious.

We visit this farm on a cold fall day when the sky is covered. It makes the colours stand out against the dried-grass background.

This place is a real artist's sanctuary, down to the last detail: from the branches woven into a railing in the tree fort or forming a gorgeous love-seat, to the fabu-

lous flower arrangements in the store.

We grab a bucket and clippers in front of the store and head towards the gardens. I am surprised to still see a good selection of colourful plants as we walk along the path meandering through the field. There are actually flowers in bloom throughout the season.

Sunflowers are twice as tall as my 3-year-old daughter. Unfortunately for me, she decides that she doesn't want to cut flowers! I choose to just stroll around and buy one of the superb pre-made bouquets on my way out.

Next to the store, an original playground awaits, with swings made out of half-logs and a slide framed by branches. In front of the building, we discover a fort in a wide tree. What a beauty!

I help my little donkey up the ladder and we start to re-enact the three little pigs story (I'm the wolf at the bottom of the tree). When I climb as well, I can admire the barn through the lace of woven branches.

On the store's second floor is a dark loft where plants are dried. Row upon row of aromatic bunches are suspended from the ceiling and dramatically lit by the natural light from a small window.

TIPS (fun for 4 years +)

• ATTENTION! As of May 2005, they will have moved to a new location in Orillia! The place will be in the same spirit but bigger. There won't be a tree fort but expect another funky and rustic playground. Call or look up their web site for exact new location and schedule.
• They usually hold a **Sunflower Celebration** on a mid-August Sunday (Sunday August 15 in 2004) with sunflower maze, sunflower crafts, floral headpiece making and more, $5/adult, $3/children, $15/family.
• There's a tea tent selling snacks and refreshments on the premises.

Wildflower Farm	C-2
• Schomberg	N-W
1-866-476-9453	of Toronto
www.wildflowerfarm.com	50-min.

Schedule: Open daily from May 1 to end of September, 10 am to 5 pm. ATTENTION: Read tips section about new location and schedule for 2005.
Admission: It costs around $38 to fill a bucket with the flowers of your choice (holding 50-100 stems). Average pre-made bouquets are sold for $18-$25.
Directions: R. R. 3, Schomberg. From Hwy 400 North, take exit #43 towards Nobleton. Take Hwy 27 North, turn west on 17th Sideroad, then north on 10th Concession.

PUCK'S FARM

This little piggy...

Looking for a farm event with a twist? Every weekend at Puck's Farm, pink pig races take place on a speed track and visitors can encourage the hogs to reach the finish line.

Puck's Farm is a site where you can wander freely while giving children the opportunity to experience a real day at the farm.

You will find a large barn with familiar animals (a few lucky ones will even experience cow milking). In the outside barn, you can pet lambs, cows and

goats. You can take a ride on a horse-drawn wagon that takes you through a picture-perfect countryside.

The admission fee includes unlimited access to activities such as singing performances and pony rides. The pony ride is unquestionably the best I've seen and it delighted my young cowboy. Here, no sorry lads turning endlessly around a minuscule carousel. Ponies travel along a path bordering a pond.

It was corn-picking season when we visited and ears of corn, picked by the visitors, were cooking in huge bubbling cauldrons and were to be eaten on the premises. We thought it was quite exotic to roam inside a 2-metre-high cornfield!

TIPS (fun for 3 years +)

• Pick-your-own crops such as peas, pumpkins, wild flowers and corn.
• After rainy days, it is difficult to manoeuvre strollers on the muddy terrain. The sticky mud can suck boots in and may curb your appreciation of Puck's Farm's activities, otherwise so enjoyable on a drier day. Call to check ground conditions the day of your visit.
• Show up early on **Easter** weekend! We went on Easter Sunday. It seemed the whole city came along with us, we had to park far away from the farm. Easter Egg Hunts take place, rain or shine, on the two weekends prior to Easter as well as during the 4-day Easter Holiday. Chocolate eggs are hidden all over the place by the Easter Bunny, 3 or 4 times during the day. I strongly recommend you attend during the earlier days of the event, when there are less visitors.
• Take along a picnic when visiting during the summer, but watch out for the hens as they'll keep an eye on your food. It's part of the fun!
• You can purchase hot dogs, as well as juice and ice cream.

Puck's Farm	C-2
• Schomberg	N-W
(905) 939-7036	of Toronto
www.pucksfarm.com	45-min.

    Schedule: Open two weekends prior to Easter and on Easter weekend (Friday to Monday), then weekends until end of June. Open daily from July 1 to Labour Day, then weekends only until Halloween, 10 am to 5 pm. Pig races go on from Victoria Day to Halloween.

Admission: $8/person, FREE for seniors and kids under 2 years old. Gives unlimited access to all activities.

Directions: From Hwy 400 North, take exit #55/Hwy 9 westbound. Turn south on Concession Rd. 11.

NEARBY ATTRACTIONS
South Simcoe Railway (15-min.)..p. 240
Albion Hills (20-min.)....................p. 278

DRYSDALE TREE FARMS

The kids enjoy the ride nonetheless, and we hop out to warm up by a bonfire. We will eventually get to the cutting area (in the back of the farmyard) on a large wagon fit to hold everybody's trees.

Back at the farm, we drag our designer tree to a counter, where we pay while a machine wraps our tree so it will fit on

That's the spirit!

It's the beginning of December and a snowfall has yet to happen. It is actually raining as my husband tucks under low branches on all fours, deep in mud, to cut our Christmas tree. He is on the verge of losing his spirits when the kids reward him with ecstatic exclamations as the tree finally falls.

Drysdale's Tree Farms is beautiful and very popular. The owner's house is picture perfect, all dressed up in decorative lighting. The parking lot is almost full when we arrive shortly after 3 pm. We catch a $1 ride on a horse-drawn wagon, expecting it will lead us to the cutting zone, only to find ourselves back to departure point some 20 minutes later.

top of our vehicle. Mr. and Mrs. Claus have their own little hut where families enter one at a time. They look like the "real" thing so bring your camera!

Afterwards, we reach the farm's **Christmas** store where we are greeted by an impressive herd of wooden deer and moose (for sale). It was redesigned since my last visit and offers an even wider selection of housewares, gifts and seasonal novelties as well as treats such as handmade chocolate and fudge.

TIPS (fun for 3 years +)

• During **Easter** time they do Easter Egg Hunts, wagon rides and magic shows. Kids look for plastic eggs to trade for generous loot bags (hence the admission price of $10). Call to confirm you're coming so they can plan enough loot bags.

• During October weekends, **Halloween** activities include: pick-your-own-pumpkins, wagon rides, magic shows and the one-acre-large hay maze. Call to find out the fees.

• If you intend to bring toddlers, remember it is difficult to cut a tree and care for highly mobile little ones.

• The farm will lend you a saw.

• During the tree-cutting season, magic shows are presented on weekends. There's a **Pizza-Pizza** concession on site and they sell snacks in the store.

Drysdale Tree Farms	B-2 N-W of Toronto 70-min.

Drysdale Tree Farms
• Alliston
(705) 424-9719
www.drysdales.ca

 Schedule: Open week prior to Easter and Easter weekend (Friday-Sunday), then daily from first week of May until December 24, 9 am to 6 pm (closes at 5 pm from October to December).

 Costs: FREE admission. Trees cost approximately $40.

 Directions: From Hwy 400 North, take exit #75/Hwy 89 westbound. Turn north on 7th Concession Road (Simcoe Rd. #56).

NEARBY ATTRACTIONS

HANES CORN MAZE

Fun at every corner

We had to think in three dimensions in order to figure out our position in the maze. "We're in the letter O!" understands my son, looking at the map. It turns out the framed letters on top of the map, which I mistook for a mere title, have actually been carved in the corn field. Amazing!

The corn stood ten feet high. The two 9-year-old boys I brought along couldn't get inside the 10-acre maze fast enough. They were armed with a map showing the contours of the five continents. Seven bullets on the map marked the places where they would find a box with codes: a series of letters and numbers plus interesting information about the

continent on which it "sat".

This elaborate activity took them over an hour, after which they found the keys to the codes on a board, obtaining seven syllables to sort into a message. How clever! They had to spin a wheel to claim their prize.

My 6-year-old daughter never wanted to get near the maze! She was afraid of getting lost and scared of potential spiders. Fortunately, Farmland, the other section of the farm was just perfect for her and we could explore it while the older kids finished touring the maze. She was excited to pet free-roaming animals. There were many more animals to watch in the big barn in the back: very cute bunnies with droopy ears, sheep, potbelly pigs, goats, and horses... She could play house in a tiny bungalow, ride in a few hand-made go-karts.

She could even "milk" a wooden cow by pulling its rubber udders, filling a bucket with the water spitting out of them. She was a very happy farmer.

TIPS (fun for 2 years +)

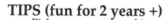

• Pick your own pumpkins.
• The **maze** experience can be fun for a 7-year-old if he's accompanied by older children. Otherwise, 9 years and over seems more appropriate. Don't enter a large maze with a young child if you are not convinced she could survive spending over an hour in it. I know dads who have found out it's a long time to hold a toddler on their shoulders. Bring flashlights for evening visits.
• There's a small farm market (closed on Sunday). Snacks and refreshments are sold at the admission stand.
• I noticed a fun place on our way back: the **Dutch Mill Country Market**, located on Road 505, east of Hanes Corn Maze, north of Hwy 5. This rustic market selling bakery, produce and crafts also serves lunch and comes with a funny outdoor playground with long wooden trains, Monday to Saturday, 9 am to 5 pm, (905) 689-7253.

NEARBY ATTRACTIONS
Christie C. A. (1-min.)....................p. 280

Hanes Corn Maze & Farmland • Dundas (905) 628-5280	E-2 S-W of Toronto 60-min.

Schedule: Open daily 10 am to 5 pm mid-August to Labour Day, then Friday 4 pm to 9 pm, Saturday 10 am to 9 pm and Sunday 10 am to 5 pm until end of October (last admission at 9 pm on Fridays and Saturdays). **Admission:** $8/adults, $5/5-15 years old, $2/2-5 years old, FREE under 2 years old ($2/person to access Farmland only).
Directions: 1001, Hwy 5, Dundas. Take QEW, then Hwy 403/Hamilton. Exit at Hwy 6 North. Turn west on Hwy 5. Located across from Christie C. A.

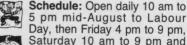

DYMENT'S FARM

Simply awesome!

Dyment's keeps you so busy you tend to forget you came to pick a pumpkin in the first place!

Every year, Dyment's celebrates the ritual of pumpkin picking by opening its doors to the public every weekend in October.

I strongly recommend this unique and delightful farm located in the Hamilton area, despite the 1-hr drive from Toronto. This outing is also a wonderful opportunity to view the colourful landscapes of fall as you head towards the Niagara escarpment where Dyment's is nestled.

A traditional playground including a "Retired Tractor" and "Tired Horse Swings" greets us at the entrance. I was taken by the Trike Track activity. The fun tricycle track, located close to the barn, is outfitted with a small bridge, a tunnel and some traffic lights which my young driver enjoyed obeying. Unfortunately, children older than 5 years old are often too big to fit the small tricycles.

Our kids were reluctant to leave the table filled with replicas (to scale) of farm machines to visit the other attractions: a small haunted cabin with cute light and sound effects, a Corn Bin with 10,000 yellow balls into which kids can plunge, a circuit offering bouncing ball races. There are also animals to pet, the Straw Fort filled with clean straw in which to frolic and they've added a mini putt.

En route to the hilly pumpkin fields, the tractor trail borders the Niagara

escarpment, offering a lovely view through the trees and providing one of the most enjoyable farm rides I can remember.

An interactive exhibit called Agri-Maze, where you can learn about the daily life of a farmer named Jim, is one of the farm's most interesting features. Full of amusing touches, including Jim with a television set as a head that speaks to the viewing public, the exhibit takes a little less than a half-hour to complete and is installed in the main barn.

TIPS (fun for 2 years +)

• Remember not to pick a pumpkin up by the stem or you risk seeing it come crashing down on your feet.
• You can purchase fast food and yummy snacks on the premises.

NEARBY ATTRACTIONS

Dyment's Farm
• Dundas
(905) 627-5477
www.dyments.com

E-2
S-W
of Toronto
60-min.

 Schedule: Open to the public during October weekends and Thanksgiving Monday, 10 am to 5 pm. (Open for Birthday Parties from May to October 30.)

 Admission: Around $6/adults, $5/children, FREE for children under 2 years old (does not include the pumpkins). Call to confirm.

 Directions: 416 Fallsview Rd. East, Dundas. Take QEW then follow Hwy 403 towards Hamilton. Exit Hwy 6 northbound, turn west on Hwy 5, then south on Sydenham Rd.. After the curve, turn right onto Fallsview Rd..

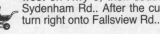

CHAPPELL FARMS

Did you see that?

I'm sure we looked like a bunch of hens in a red cage while riding a wagon through Chappell Farms' fields. Soon, our kids were competing to see who could spot the many surprises hidden in the cornstalks: pumpkin heads, old witches, a headless horseman and scarecrows who seemed to wave at us from their lawn chairs. This was no traditional wagon ride!

We arrived in the middle of the Pumpkin Festival. This means that in addition to the usual animal petting, cow milking sessions, entertainment, playground, maze, cut-out characters and seasonal displays the farm offers, we were also treated to a Boo Barn and a Haunted Barn.

I inadvertently entered the haunted barn with my 3-year-old, intending on the more suitable Boo Barn. Big mistake! Dimmed in light barely sufficient to appreciate the special effects, the place was so dark I could barely see my own hand, let alone the scary actors breathing

down my neck or the progressively narrowing fur-covered walls, with their unpredictable sharp turns.

The whole experience, successfully disorienting, left my younger one completely panicked, while my 7-year-old loved every minute of it. The Boo Barn, on the other hand, is lined with small friendly ghosts and funny characters.

The farm includes nanny mountain goats climbing around a silo, a big inflatable structure to jump in, knotted ropes to climb up, trike track and more. My little performer joined the show in another barn and was asked to assist the skillful magician during a good card trick.

This farm has been in the Chappell family for over 170 years!

TIPS (fun for 3 years +)

• Pick your own pumpkins.
• They usually offer **Haunted Hayride Adventure**s every night of the last week of October. Call to confirm.
• For **Easter**, the Egg'stravaganza event includes egg hunts (no more than 250 children at a time, scattered in a large area; kids are almost guaranteed to find candy), Billy Bunny Easter Barn, show and wagon rides. Of course, there's always Bunny Village, with its own school, church, windmill and all.
• The big Old Barn Shoppe is packed with seasonal goodies and crafts.

NEARBY ATTRACTIONS

Chappell Farms
• Barrie
(705) 721-1547
www.chappellfarms.ca

**B-2
North
of Toronto
60-min.**

Schedule: Open the weekend prior to Easter and on Easter weekend (Friday to Sunday, 10 am to 5 pm).The market is open daily from early July to October 31, 9 am to 8 pm. The Pumpkin Festival runs daily from last week in September to October 31, 10 am to 5 pm. (Magic shows and inflated castle on weekends only.)

Admission: During special events: $8/visitor on weekends and holidays, $4 on weekdays, FREE under 2 years old.

Directions: 617 Penetanguishene Rd., County Rd. 93, Barrie. Take Hwy 400 northbound, stay on centre lane onto Hwy 11, exit County Rd. 93/Penetanguishene Rd. westbound.

ROUNDS RANCH

Photos: Courtesy of G. Servinis

A round of applause

In this farm, you will find a special catapult that throws apples at a scarecrow. You'll see free-roaming rabbits and hens. Kids will ride on large pedal carts and families will be challenged with a well-planned maze adventure.

My dentist is a big fan of labyrinths. So when I mentioned this one, he had to check it out with his three children in tow. His family enjoyed it so much that I decided to include it even though I had not personally visited it.

When they visited, a pirate theme was going on. The next year, the theme was to be Australian Outback and the year after, Medieval Times.

The **maze** was shaped like a sailboat. At its entrance, a pirate greeted the family. Kids could dress up like pirates long enough for parents to take pictures. Everyone was given a map with different information to find the nine pirate stations throughout the maze. There were three different levels of difficulty. It took my dentist and his two boys over two hours to get out of the labyrinth. The goal was to collect letters at each station in order to form a code to access a special page on their web site!

His young daughter thought she was in heaven, petting the cute rabbits and other animals. The whole family eventually got onto the wagon to get a pumpkin from the field.

Back then, their maze covered 10 acres, including 5 km of pathways. Since they've reduced it to a more manageable 6.5 acres which should take no longer than 90 minutes to complete... And they've created a 6.5-acre horse trail ride through another corn maze!

Another small maze hosts pony rides. Then there's the colourful barnyard box-car... Imagine it, they've got it!

TIPS (fun for 2 years +)

• Pick-your-own strawberries, raspberries, other berries, beans, peas, tomatoes and pumpkins.
• Read tips about mazes on p. 150.
• Their **Easter** activities are unique. They offer 3 different concepts for egg hunts for different age groups, some quite elaborate. Their catapult shoots chocolate eggs into the air.
• On Fridays and Saturdays in October, they offer **haunted wagon rides** through the **maze**.
• There's a snack bar selling hot dogs, burgers, fries, corn on the cob and more.

Rounds Ranch	**B-2**
• Elmvale	**N-W**
(705) 322-6293	**of Toronto**
www.roundsranch.com	**90-min.**

 Schedule: Open weekend prior to Easter and Easter weekend (call to confirm which days), then weekends from Victoria Day until end of June. Open Wednesday to Sunday after that until Labour Day, 10 am to 6 pm (11 am to 5 pm on Sundays). Then, open Friday, 6 pm to 10 pm, Saturday, 10 am to 10 pm and Sunday, 11 am to 5 pm until October 31. Call to confirm.

 Admission: $9/maze + all attractions ($3 less if not visiting the maze), FREE for two years and under. Extra fee to use apple catapult and for fall craft activities. Pony rides $3/10 min. Horse $15/30 min. (minimum 48 inches).

Directions: 1922 County Rd. 92, 4km west of Elmvale. Take Hwy 400 North. Exit at Hwy 26/27 North to Elmvale. In Elmvale, turn west at the second set of lights, to County Rd. 92.

Bruce's Mill Maple Festival

Hop on the wagon!

My little lumberjack is dying to put a log on the huge bonfire all by himself. Not far away, white smoke escapes from the sugar shack's chimney. The fire gives off an odour that blends beautifully with the pancakes' sweet smell. It's the busiest time of the year at Bruce's Mill.

At other times, Bruce's Mill Conservation Area is a rather modest attraction, its main asset being its proximity to Toronto. So I was really surprised to discover how well it was set up during maple syrup season.

Bruce's Mill Sugar Bush Trail is the most manicured of all those that I visited. The trees are scattered, the areas where the self-guided trail signs are located are bare. It takes about 15 minutes to do the trail, nonstop.

The course is lined with some characters cut out of wood, illustrating the different methods of maple syrup production. When we visited, "Buddy" (a maple leaf bud character) was teaching us, among other things, that the maple syrup season ends once he and other

buds appear.

The children particularly enjoyed going in the tall teepee (not there every year), which reminded us that the natives discovered the maple sap's properties. The kids also liked to pet the real horse in its pen, a reminder of the time when sap was collected in large barrels pulled by such horses. A jolly fellow, clad in overalls and checkered shirt, offered us a taste of syrup, prepared in a huge pot the old-fashioned way.

On weekends and during the March Break, a horse-drawn wagon run around the site. Some years, they add a straw playground and animal pens.

TIPS (fun for 3 years +)
• More about **Bruce's Mill Conservation Area** on page 335.
• This sugar bush is my favourite when visiting with younger children. They can handle the short trail, and the wagon ride through the forest adds a feeling of adventure to the outing.
• The trails can be really muddy. Nice boots beware!
• They serve all-day pancake breakfasts during the festival.

Bruce's Mill Maple Syrup Festival
· Stouffville
(416) 661-6600, ext. 5203
or (905) 887-5531
www.trca.on.ca

| G-11 |
| N-E |
| of Toronto |
| 30-min. |

Schedule: The season may start early March and last to mid-April. (Call to check the exact dates.) During the festival, usually open Wednesday to Friday, 9 am to 4 pm, and weekends, 9 am to 6 pm.
Admission: Around $7/adults, $5/seniors and children, FREE 4 years and under.
Directions: Between Warden and Kennedy, Stouffville. From Hwy 404 North, take exit #37/Stouffville Rd. eastbound.

KORTRIGHT MAPLE FESTIVAL

No wonder maple syrup is so precious to us. Kortright Centre moves heaven and earth to educate us on the subject.

You can cover the path crossing the sugar bush in half an hour. It begins with a steep downward slope that seems difficult to tackle, but the secret is to go slowly. Kids won't resist the call of gravity and will go down at full speed. However, they'll surely stop before the big turn if tools were left to drill tap holes the old-fashioned way, using a brace and bit!

On the path, buckets have been installed lower than usual, allowing children to peek at the dripping sap. Pioneers cook maple sap inside huge pots. It's time to try the shoulder yokes.

Mouth-watering

The sugar content of maple sap is between 2 and 3%, while maple syrup has at least 66%. It takes up to 40 buckets of the former to produce one bucket of the latter. It's not surprising that the cost of syrup is so high. It's only made in North America and 80% of the world production comes from Canada.

Modern maple syrup production techniques are presented inside the sugar cabin. It's easy to see the modern maple sap collecting system and to explain its functioning to kids. My little engineer was fascinated by this gravity-fed system that moves the sap from the trees directly to storage tanks inside the cabin.

TIPS (fun for 4 years +)

• **March Break** is an excellent time to visit when weekend activities and entertainment are also offered on weekdays. They even offer an inflated jumping castle inside the main building, and crafts.
• During the Maple Syrup Festival, pancakes with syrup are sold at the centre's cafeteria. Tasty snacks made with maple syrup are sold in the shops.
• The first weekends of the festival are the quietest. Saturdays are quieter than Sundays. On weekdays during **March Break**, arrive after 2 pm when the school buses leave.
• The wagon rides are offered during the weekends only. I was disappointed by the ride as the course was uninteresting. On the bright side, the succulent maple popcorn we had bought kept my little companions' boredom at bay as we waited in the long line-up and the pleasant cart driver was very talkative. She taught us a lot about her horses and invited children to pet them.
• More about **Kortright Centre** on p. 332.

Kortright Maple Syrup Festival • Kleinburg (416) 667-6299 or (905) 832-2289 www.trca.on.ca	G-10 N-W of Toronto 40-min.

     Schedule: The season may start early March and last to mid-April. (Call to check the exact dates.) Open 10 am to 5 pm. (Demos stop one hour prior to closing time).
Admission: $7/adults, $5/seniors and children, FREE 4 years and under. Parking is $2.
Directions: 9550 Pine Valley Dr., Kleinburg. From Hwy 400 North, take exit #35/Major Mackenzie westbound, then turn south on Pine Valley Dr.

NEARBY ATTRACTIONS
McMichael Collection (10-min.)....p. 93
The Wave Pool (15-min.).............p. 384

BRADLEY MUSEUM

Condensed sweetness

The sugar bush may be the smallest I have seen but nothing's missing: maple trees with pokes, sweet maple water smell around the fire pit, maple sugar molding demonstration in the pioneer house, horse-drawn wagon and a craft activity in the barn.

Maple syrup time is probably the best time to visit this heritage attrac-

tion. It is located in a residential area but nestled among trees and charming.

Bradley House itself is not big. We used the maple sugar molding demonstration as an excuse to visit it but we spent most of our time outside. Our kids were just happy hiding in the teepee in the "Sweet Water Camp" section and checking out the maple sap level in the buckets on the trees.

We waited in line to catch a wagon ride (offered every day during the **March Break**). This reminded us that we are indeed in a residential area! Exploring Bradley House was a bit like time travel but the ride took us amidst modern houses and cars.

We grabbed a snack on our way back at the Anchorage Tea Room. That's where they serve pancake breakfasts on the weekends during their maple festival. Then we did some small crafts in the big barn in the middle of the place. All in all, this was a short and sweet outing.

TIPS (fun for 4 years +)

• Ask about their **Shakespeare Under the Stars** event presented by the Driftwood Outdoor Theatre Group, usually on the mid-July Friday and Saturday, at 8 pm (call to confirm). Suggested donation: $12/person, $25/family. Come early, it is very popular.

• In mid-September, there's the **Fall Fair** (call for exact dates). Saturday, from noon to 8 pm, there's musical entertainment, bake sale, children's area, wagon rides and contests. Sunday, from 10 am to 4 pm, there's a historic encampment, military re-enactments as well as historic demonstrations: horseshoeing, candle dipping, rug hooking... $5/adults, $1.50/children, $12/family of 6.

NEARBY ATTRACTIONS

Bradley Museum
• Mississauga
(905) 822-1569
www.museumof
mississauga.com

**I-8
West
of Toronto
30-min.**

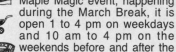
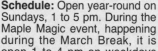

Schedule: Open year-round on Sundays, 1 to 5 pm. During the Maple Magic event, happening during the March Break, it is open 1 to 4 pm on weekdays and 10 am to 4 pm on the weekends before and after the March Break.

Admission: $6/adults, $4/seniors, students, $2/3-12 years, $15/family of 6.

Directions: 1620 Orr Rd., Mississauga. From QEW, take exit # 126/Southdown Rd. (Erin Mills Pkwy becomes Southdown Rd. south of the QEW). Turn east on Orr Rd. (south of Lakeshore).

MOUNTSBERG MAPLE TIME

Maple syrup time, with animals to boot

When you visit, if you are lucky, the hatchery in the Discovery Room might be bursting with little chirping chicks who undulate as one big yellow wave when children get close to them. What a great bonus!

The Mountsberg Conservation Area has a lot to offer during Maple Syrup Time.

Past the Visitors' Centre, there's a railroad crossing (it may be the first time your child walks over some tracks!) It gets us to a field from which you can walk to Mapletowne or wait for the $1 horse-drawn wagon. It will take you on a good ride through the sugar bush.

Mapletowne, a series of small, rustic houses, is in the heart of the action. In one of them, syrup is produced. In the next one, maple sugar is made (yes,

everybody can have a taste). Another one is a country shop.

The Pancake pavilion is an enclosed shelter with picnic tables. We enjoyed eating at our table while admiring the surrounding landscape with lively music playing in the background.

Scenes recreating different maple syrup production techniques through the ages are displayed around the pavilion.

Bring your skates, you might be able to skate on their pond by the trails (from January to mid-March, weather permitting).

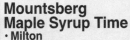

TIPS (fun for 3 years +)

• You can print a free child's admission from their web site.

• During **March Break**, live raptor demonstrations, normally offered only on weekends and holidays at that time of the year, are shown at 1 pm and 3 pm.

• On **Easter** Saturday, expect an Easter Egg Hunt, baby chicks in the Visitors' Centre, wagon rides, crafts and more.

• More on the **Mountsberg Wildlife Centre** on page 338.

NEARBY ATTRACTIONS
Hilton Falls (20-min.).....................p. 300

Mountsberg Maple Syrup Time
• Milton
(905) 854-2276
www.conservationhalton.on.ca

D-2 West of Toronto 60-min.

Schedule: Open every weekend from mid-February to mid-April and on weekdays during the **March Break**, from 10 am to 4 pm. Call for exact dates.

Admission: Around $5.50/adults, $3.75/5-14 years old, $1/wagon ride, FREE 4 and under (extra for pancakes).

Directions: From Hwy 401 West, exit #312/Guelph Line southbound. Turn west on Campbellville Rd., then north on Milborough Line to the park entrance.

See **Horton Original Farm** on p. 159.

Horton's Home Farm

cycle of such a tree, it is noted on a sign: "We hope to be able to tap this bush through many generations of our family." It turns out our guide is one of the children of the couple from the 70's you'll see in the laminated press clippings on the wall inside the shack. The maple sugar bush has been family-run since 1963.

On another sign, we're reminded that each taphole may yield 20-40 litres of sap in a season! A tree 25 cm in diameter will take one tap, three taps when over 45 cm. Among other things, the sign also states very clearly that "Tapping trees is a boring job!"

It's personal

No fancy educational program here, just a few very informative signs to read when self-exploring or the down-to-earth tour by a friendly guide. No big scale, the trail around the sugar bush is short. No bells and whistles, just a little sap and maple tasting in tiny paper cups. So why bother coming here? For the timeless charm of the place, I would say. For the "monkey tree" would claim my children!

Everything about this place is laid-back. Your kids really want to climb up the tall "monkey tree"? "Be our guest; you know your own child's limits." This is actually the best climbing tree I have seen in ages, with lower branches perfectly set to help one climb way up!

A lady clad in old-fashioned dress and cap serves us nice warm pancakes. The sun shining through the windowpanes inside the shack accentuates the warmth of the wooden walls and tables. Outside, it gives a dazzling glow to the snow.

Is it because it is so off-the-beaten track you have to go through 500 metres of mud by foot or be pulled behind a tractor to reach it? When you discover this rustic little sugar shack, you feel like you've found the best kept secret in the region. The oldest tree in their forest, the "grandfather tree", is 450 years old. It is noticeably larger than the maple trees we are used to. After explaining to us the life

Later, as I sat by a tree, I heard water dripping from the melting icicles and the laughter of the children involved in a snowball fight. It was so relaxing.

TIPS (fun for 4 years +)

• Don't confuse Horton's Home Farm with Horton's Primrose Farm or Horton's Magic Hill Farm. It is the only one with a sugar bush.
• There's a counter in the shack selling maple syrup, butter, sugar and popcorn. They sell pancakes, coffee and hot chocolate in the adjacent kitchen.
• You can count on wet snow or good old mud so you might want to bring an extra set of clothes for the way back.

Horton's Home Farm
· Stouffville
(905) 888-1738
www.hortontreefarms.com

G-12
N-E
of Toronto
40-min.

Schedule: Saturdays and Sundays from 9 am to 4 pm, usually from mid-March to mid-April. Call to confirm.
Admission: $4/adults, $3.50/students, $3/5-12 years old.
Directions: 5924 Slater Rd., Stouffville. Take Hwy 404 North. Turn east on Aurora Rd., then south on Warden Ave., and west on Slater Rd.

WARKWORTH MAPLE FESTIVAL

Have a taste of this!

"Her eyes are like maple syrup" declared my son as he closely observed his sister. A Canadian poet is born! Indeed, who else in the world would allude to this delectable brown gold that distinguishes us internationally? I must say that, thanks to the Warkworth Maple Syrup Festival, he had a taste of his first warm, amber-coloured ribbon, rolled around a wooden spoon. So he knows what he's talking about!

We parked in a field close to the **Sandy Flat Sugar Bush**. The snow was melting in the bright sunshine and getting mixed with the path's dirt. The resulting muddy cocktail would certainly prevent visitors from wearing their Sunday shoes to appreciate the event.

We'd just driven an hour and a half, leaving behind grey Toronto to go taste taffy poured on to white snow. (This activity isn't generally offered in sugar shacks neighbouring the city, as they suffer from a lack of the white stuff.) The country road we had been driving on for the last half-hour was charming and put us all in good spirits.

Our little traveller was thrilled by the ride in a tractor-pulled wagon, which took us to the sugar shack. The place is very popular; there was a short line-up at the entrance booth.

The warm and friendly ambience reigning over the site is contagious. By observing closely, one understands why. Retired people

from the area serve breakfast, boy scouts clean tables and local musicians play the violin. It seems that the whole Warkworth community is present!

All of the festival's activities revolve around a square, worthy of a postcard, where a happy crowd is gathered.

Here, onlookers watch how maple syrup is made, in the old-fashioned way and with the new method. There, two kids can't believe how lucky they are to be allowed to cut a slice off a log with a double-handled saw.

Farther on, a group of people is waiting to take a place in one of the horse-drawn sleighs on which they'll take a tour of the maple grove. We join them and hear the mischievous driver's comments: "One of the engines is backfiring!" he says, when the horse starts to… (I'll leave it at that!).

An original competition is proposed. Contestants are timed while they run in the snow between the maple trees, wearing snowshoes and holding a pail of maple sap. It's pretty funny to watch!

The excitement rises each time a new pail of delicious taffy is ready. Grown-ups and kids alike line up eagerly in front of troughs full of snow where they can have a taste of the delicious treat.

But this wasn't the only thing we had to eat! Abundant breakfasts were served outside, including pancakes, sausages and maple syrup.

While we ate, we watched spontaneous dancers move to the sound of the fiddler's jig. (Wasn't that my son I saw dancing on the stage?) During the festival, you might even see step-dancing on the small stage.

TIPS (fun for 4 years +)

• Since my last visit, the owners have created two trails allowing visitors to burn off some of those maple syrup pancakes! The short one takes 20 minutes to complete, the other is one mile long. They include little bridges and plaques with the names and uses of the different trees.

• Wear old boots and bring a change of clothes for the kids. At the end of the day, they'll be so dirty with mud you may refuse to let them get in the car without a good clean-up!

• During the Maple Syrup Festival weekend, activities are held in Warkworth Village, from 9 am to 5 pm on Saturday and 10 am to 4 pm on Sunday: craft show, antique show, art show, pony rides and petting farm.

• Every weekend after the festival until the end of April, you can also visit **Sandy Flat Sugar Bush** to taste taffy, go on a sleigh ride or to have breakfast in the little shack. When it's not festival time, the menu is different, even more diversified because there are fewer visitors to accommodate.

• Every weekend, chances are you'll see the owners and close relatives engaged in entertaining musical gigs in the rustic restaurant.

• Maple-flavoured cotton candy and many maple sugar treats are sold on site.

• I was told by a reader there's another sugar bush in the same spirit north of Peterborough. Check **Buckhorn Maplefest** at **McLean Berry Farm** at www.mcleanberryfarm.com or call (705) 657-2134. They offer taffy on the snow if fresh snow is available, musical shows, petting section, hay games, walking trail and much more during 3 weekends.

Warkworth Maple Syrup Festival • Warkworth (705) 924-2057 www. maplesyrupfestival.com	**B-6 East of Toronto 90-min.**

Schedule: The annual festival is held the second weekend in March, 9 am to 4 pm. The sugar bush is then open every weekend until the end of April.

Admission: FREE taffy sampling. Small fees apply for the wagon ride. Breakfast of pancakes and sausages with syrup costs $3 to $6.

Directions: Sandy Flat Sugar Bush, Warkworth. From Hwy 401 East, take exit #474/Hwy 45 northbound, then take County Rd. 29 eastbound towards Warkworth. Go to Burnley then turn left onto Noonan Rd. and follow the Sandy Flat Sugar Bush signs.

General tips about
Getaways:

• On the web sites of most major attractions listed in this guide, you'll find links to local hotels offering family packages and admission rebates to the attraction.

• A promising web site to find the perfect family getaway is **www.hotelfun4kids.com**. It focuses on Ontario destinations but is starting to think globally.

• Many hotels are awakening to the fact that single parents travel too! If you're a single parent or simply traveling alone with the kids, take advantage of the single parent rates certain resorts offer. Their kids' programs will give you a well-deserved break!

• Rule of thumb from a kid's point of view: better tacky with a pool than trendy without one.

• Travelling with pets? Check **www.petfriendly.ca** for a listing of pet-friendly accommodations, mostly in Canada but also in the United States.

GETAWAYS

See **About cottages** on p. 166.

ABOUT CAMPING

Not in my backyard

When putting the tent up in the backyard (or the living room!) just won't do anymore, maybe it's time to move on to the real thing!

Not too far

You can find decent campgrounds less than one hour away from downtown Toronto! See the **Glen Rouge Campground** (p. 349), **Indian Line Campground** (p. 33), **Albion Hills C.A.** (p. 278). **Bronte Creek P.P.** (p. 336) includes a campground located on an adjacent lot 5 minutes away by car.

Camping associations

The **Ontario Private Campground Association (OPCA)** has put together a camping directory of its 450 members and a web site. Both separate the province into areas, each with its own map with member campground location numbers. There's also an alphabetical list of the campgrounds. Among other things, each campground description includes phone numbers, e-mail and web site address, plus indication of services within a 5-minute walk.

CampSource offers a web site including 4,100 parks and campgrounds in Canada.

Great nature

Some places included in this guide were located in great natural settings and offered campgrounds so you could enjoy them even more. Younger families usually love **Rockwood C.A.** (p. 340). **Warsaw Caves C.A.** (p. 291) and **Haliburton Forest Wildlife** (p. 342) are really in the wild and unique.

Awenda P.P. (p. 288) and **Sand-**banks P.P. (p. 298) are among the most popular provincial parks with their great beaches. When you sleep in those parks, you get to enjoy sunsets or sunrises, quiet beaches before or after the day-visitor rush plus special activities organized by the staff. More about camping in provincial parks on p. 165.

Attractions & campgrounds

These attractions with adjacent campgrounds are worth visiting two days in a row: **Santa's Village** (p. 28), **Marineland** (p. 62) and **Emerald Lake** (p. 38).

Special sleepovers

Some attractions offer the unique experience of sleepovers, for a different perspective. Of course, you need to pre-register for all of these. Imagine having the **Ontario Science Centre** (p. 256) all to yourself during one of the only two nights when the centre invites the general public over, usually in February and May. **Toronto Zoo** (p. 46) opens its **Bush Camp** to families with children 6 years and over. You get to spend one night in the African Savanna! **Jungle Cat World** (p. 53) opens its doors to small groups. You really get to hear the animals through the night. I would be too excited to sleep!

OPCA
(519) 371-3393
www.campingontario.ca
Call Ontario Travel to get a FREE directory at 1-800-668-2746.

More sources
www.stlawrenceparks.com
www.campsource.ca
www.koa.com
www.greatlakesresorts.ca
www.campingquebec.com
www.camping-usa.com

ABOUT PROVINCIAL PARKS

Naturally yours!

Twenty of the 104 parks in Ontario listed in their brochure are located within a 2-hour drive of Toronto. Eleven of these are mentioned in this guide for their special assets: the golden dunes of Sandbanks, Rock Point's fossils, Earl Rowe's giant pool and beach... And that's just the tip of the iceberg!

One-day visitors might only want to focus on the beaches and nature trails but many provincial parks have much more to offer: kids' programs, guided hikes, campfires and star-gazing and myriads of special events.

TIPS (fun for all)

• Ontario Parks has put together an attractive free booklet packed with information titled: *Nearby and Natural*. Call **Ontario Travel** to get one mailed to you.

• If camping is not your thing, you can rent furnished all-season yurts (tentlike and mounted on platforms), rustic cabins or even cottages. Reserve way in advance!

• You can call 1-800-668-2746 for an up-to-date vacancy report of the Ontario provincial parks' campgrounds!

• A summer seasonal pass provides unlimited daily vehicle entry to all Ontario provincial parks. They are valid from early April to early November and cost $65. You can purchase it at any park. An annual pass is also available for $100.

Others might want to watch the Monarch butterflies gather at **Presqu'ile** (p. 319) for their autumn journey to Central Mexico. Others will want to visit **Bronte Creek** (p. 336) for its tobogganing, skating and original playbarn.

After a few years of day trips, my family is finally getting it. The best way to change a great outing into an outstanding family experience will be to turn ourselves into... happy campers.

About camping reservations

You can book a campsite in advance at 69 provincial parks (22 more are on a first-come first-served basis). You will actually have to book many months in advance for the most popular parks. For reservations, call 1-888-668-7275.

Even better, do it on-line! Click Reservations on Ontario Parks' web site. Then log in and use the New Reservation section where you enter your preferred dates, then selected park. Available campsites in that park will be marked with a green dot.

Click on a specific lot and you'll get information on site quality, privacy, shade, ground cover and more. Amazing!

Use Browse Maps if you don't know the parks. You then select a region. All parks in that area will show up. Click on specific parks for campground layout and specific lot information.

Ontario Parks Campsites
1-888-668-7275
www.ontarioparks.com

Ontario Travel
1-800-668-2746
www.ontariotravel.net

Schedule: Parks open, in general, from the second weekend in May until the end of October. Some parks, particularly those in the North, open mid-June until the end of the Labour Day weekend. Only 11 parks operate year-round.
Admission: Day-use vehicle permits vary from $6.50 to $12 per day. It does not include camping fees.
Other costs: Camping fees range from $18 to $28 per day depending on the facilities and services provided. They don't include the cost of the day-use vehicle permit.

ABOUT COTTAGES

You must have a vision!

Before you head out on a mission to rent a cottage for your loved ones, here's my advice: set your priorities! What do you fancy when you imagine your family in a cottage for a perfect vacation?

As an example, my priority for a summer cottage is to have beach access, making it easier for the kids to enjoy the water. In the winter, I long for a genuine fireplace. Anytime, I want panoramic views, and a place where no cat has lived for the last few years (I have a very allergic husband).

Word of mouth is probably the fastest way to find a cottage, although you must ask plenty of questions of colleagues, friends or family members who have supposedly found the "perfect" cottage. Your priorities and theirs might differ. Ask to see pictures or video footage, to get an idea of the surroundings, the water access and the inside of the cottage.

You can buy the *Tyler's Cottage Rental Directory* published three times a year and sold in major bookstores. It separates the listings into travel areas shown on a map. It compiles the owner's description of their cottage accompanied by a photo. Some rates are as affordable as $400 per week in high season. You can't only rely on the directory: call the owners and make arrangements to visit the cottage or see plenty of pictures.

I was talked into a cottage on Georgian Bay after looking at its owner's family album. The nice lady begged me to take very good care of her cottage. I did not think of asking if she had beige carpet all through her beautiful cottage. I spent the whole week policing my 3-year-old in order to keep the place spotless...

For another cottage, the "direct access to the beach, not for the elderly" was an 80-foot cliff by Lake Erie; not for anyone! (We rented it anyway, brought a rope ladder and had a ball, but it could have ruined another family's vacation.)

You can also deal with an agency such as **Cottage Country Travel Services** in Unionville, which carries video footage showing their listings (approximately 160 cottages) at a starting weekly rate of $700 in high season, including the agency commission. It could be a big time saver !

TIPS (fun for all)

• Ask the owners for a list of things you should bring (such as bedding, cookware, toys, tableware, lifejackets).
• Make sure you bring bug repellent!
• Check **www.rentcottage.com**, a rental company for Bruce Peninsula and Huron Shores area. You can search by location, price, availability and see photos of each of the 200 cottages listed. Their web site access is also free.

Tyler's Cottage Rental Directory
1-800-461-7585
www.tylers.ca
Cost: Each directory released in February, April and August retails for $9.95. Add shipping cost if you order from them (includes internet access to their web site for a trimester). Or you can pay $14.89 plus tax and shipping for a one-year subscription to their web site.

Cottage Country Travel Services
(905) 470-0385
www.cottagerental.com
Cost: No fees to use their web site (commission included in rental cost).
Directions: 209 Main St., Unionville.

ABOUT FARM ACCOMMODATIONS

A farming weekend

Some farms tantalize us with fresh eggs we can pick in the morning, or by their ducks wading freely in a pond before our eyes. Others boast about their 1850 vintage brick house or sunny veranda.

There are approximately seventy members of the **Ontario Farm & Country Accommodations Association (OFCA)**, with some fifteen located within a two hour drive of Toronto.

If you have a clear idea of the type of experience you wish for, it's best to ask the owner precise questions before you reserve, to avoid disappointments.

My family can be... loud. We are definitely more comfortable in farms offering the option of a separate house, with all the privacy we need. The first time we booked, the separate accommodation we rented (not listed anymore), turned out to be a depressing little bungalow at the end of an orchard on the side of the road; an ideal spot for students keen on enjoying the nearby ski hills, but unsuitable for those in need of a rest in a cozy nest. You bet I asked a lot of questions the next time around!

We subsequently spent a night in a lodging where we occupied half a rustic old house belonging to a farm (not listed anymore either).

There, we observed the cows returning home, ready to be milked. My daughter grabbed onto me, baffled at the sight of the 35 full-scale bovines. She warmed up to the idea of the farm when one of the assistants placed a small kitten in her arms. We had a picnic by the field. We pet horses and goats. And we watched the stars, away from the buzz of the city.

The best way to identify the farm which will provide the change of scenery you seek, is to obtain a copy of the **OFCA**'s directory. It is an excellent reference, and some 50 members are classified by region, with a complete description of the farm, including a photo as proof, as well as a general description of the site and a list of breeding and farming activities. It also includes information about the type of accommodation and services available, cost, and telephone number to make your reservation directly with the owners. You can also check the association's web site, which displays most of the information included in the directory.

TIPS (fun for all)

• Rental prices vary considerably. On average, a family should expect to pay around $80/per night for one room (or $100 for a separate accommodation).

ABOUT RESORTS

Resort to this!

To most parents of children under twelve, holiday rest is an oxymoron. Work actually feels like a vacation after a whole week of caring full-time for energetic kids... Unless you can treat yourself to an all-inclusive resort, which comes with in-house kids' programs, daycare, food, shows, etc...

Resorts Ontario, the Ontario resorts association, publishes a most useful tool: a yearly directory of the same name which promotes all of its members. It is divided into 4 sections: Resort Hotels & Lodges, Housekeeping Resorts, Country Inns and Fishing & Hunting Lodges.

Each section offers a chart listing the resorts in alphabetical order, along with the services they offer. Among others, we can find out if they have the following features: pool, beach, nature trails, mountain biking and, most importantly, kids' programs.

The directory includes the distance between each resort and Toronto and a reference to one of the Ontario travel areas shown on a map. This information is followed by advertisements from the resorts themselves, with a general description, colour pictures and information on how to reach them.

You still must call the resorts themselves for rates and availability, but the directory is a great comparison tool. Their web site is even more useful. It allows you to select a resort by name, location, region or type (cottage, inn, cabin, etc.). You may predetermine features that are important to you (beach, fireplace or horseback riding, for example) to narrow down the selection. And, it offers links to all the resorts with a web site.

TIPS (fun for all)

• The first time I looked for a family vacation in a resort, I must admit the rates freaked me out! Then, I crunched some numbers and realized that the cost of a week-long package was comparable to the added costs of hotels on the road, meals in restaurants, baby-sitting services, children's day camps, evening entertainment and equipment rental, without the hassle of driving from one place to the other...

Resorts Ontario
1-800-363-7227
www.resorts-ontario.com
Cost: To get the FREE directory by mail, call the association.

MARCH BREAK AT BAYVIEW

A real break!

Consider the snow melting all around the city, crowded major indoor attractions and the February blahs to shake off and all of a sudden, a few days at a resort seems like a good investment.

I'm sure Bayview Wildwood Resort is even better during the summer season but it delivered when we visited it during the **March Break**.

While Toronto had lost its white coat, there was just enough snow around the resort to try on their new snowshoes and ice was still strong enough to allow for broomball games. True, you never know what to expect during **March Break**: it could rain all week long or it could be freezing cold. One thing for sure, cabin fever is easier to handle in a resort with kids' programs.

We arrived on a Tuesday after lunch, just in time to join other guests roasting marshmallows by the lake. My kids were quite content by the novelty of

doing this in the winter and they served themselves many refills of hot chocolate.

Word to the wise: read the documentation they give to you at reception if you don't want to miss the fun! We missed the horse-drawn wagon ride and did not know about the Family Candy Bingo. But we got to stroll along the lake on modern snowshoes.

The Children's Programs had run in the morning but not in the afternoon because in the evening was the much appreciated Candlelight Dinner when families have to dine between 5:30 pm and 7 pm and then make way for the adults only dinner. Children's Programs kicked in again from 6 pm to 9 pm to allow this event. Now, that's a real break!

Evening activities were organized for children from 7:30 to 8:30 pm. They were followed by events catering more to the adults from which kids under 15 were banned by 10 pm. In addition to the buffet concept, most welcomed by kids, the resort offered: a cozy games room, an indoor pool open 8 am to 10 pm, a whirlpool, surrounding trails to explore, ping-pong tables and a movie listing available from a cable channel in our room. We supplied the pillow fights!

TIPS (fun for all)

• Even some of the cheapest accommodations are located by the lake.
• During the **March Break**, think muddy! Bring extra clothes and boots.
• The Children's Programs cater to three age groups. They are offered during **Christmas** and all winter weekends (running from January to the **March Break**) and during the summer.
• During the summer, residents have access to the resort's private beach. There are row-boats, canoes, kayaks and bicycles. Water skiing can be arranged for a fee. Evening entertainment is a given.
• Babysitting service can be arranged for parents who want to enjoy evening activities.

NEARBY ATTRACTIONS

SUMMER TIME AT WIGAMOG INN

Relax!

When I wake up before sunrise, the whole resort is still sound asleep and the first rays of sun shine through a screen of fog over the lake.

The raft equipped with a water slide is a real hit with the kids in the midst of a hot day, along with the water trampoline! We can use the free equipment put at the residents' disposal at the private beach: kayak, canoes, paddle boats, beach toys. We can also rent intriguing hydro bikes motor boats and Jet Skis. Water-ski rides, and rides on a pontoon boat suitable for the whole family, are also available for a fee.

TIPS (fun for all)

• You may try your luck any time but it is better to book 4 to 6 months in advance! They offer 25% off the week right after end of school.

• We stayed in a nicely decorated poolside studio which gave a good view. The economy rooms were more than decent, but had no country feeling to them.

• During the **March Break**, **Christmas** time, **Easter** and other long weekends, Kids Camp activities are offered in the morning (including Sundays). The Kids Dinner is available in the evening. Special family activities take place and the Kids Playroom, where you can leave your children, is open from 9 am to 12 noon and from 6 to 8 pm.

• The Kids Dinner accepts children 5 years and older, from 5:30 pm to 8 pm. Parents of children under 5 may feed their child at 5:30 pm and take them at 6 pm to the Kids Playroom. This leaves parents with up to 1 1/2 hours to enjoy an intimate dinner.

• Parents can arrange for babysitting service to enjoy the evening activities.

• In the winter you can use ice skates, toboggans, snowshoes, broom balls, binoculars. You can rent snowmobiles, cross-country skis or pay for **dogsledding**.

Mountain bikes, lifejackets, a variety of sports equipment, as well as board games can even be borrowed.

The Kids Camp Programs for six different age groups go full blast mornings and afternoons during the summer. They provide parents with free time to enjoy a wide list of activities... or a whole book!).

There are more activities for the whole family on weekdays: nature trail scavenger hunts, gladiator games, bingo, bonfires, casino with play money, movie nights. Nightly entertainment might include an impersonator, magician, one-man band, Yuk Yuk's Comedy (for adults only) or a cabaret performance.

We visited during the summer for a weekend only (Friday and Saturday nights) and did not have enough time to appreciate the camp programs. On the other hand, we enjoyed the great food, evening activities, the Kids Playground service, the Kids Dinner program and took advantage of the resort's equipment and, of course, the beach, until late Sunday afternoon, after we had checked out of our room. Can't believe we managed to miss the cool tree fort up in the bushes!

Wigamog Inn Resort	A-4
• Haliburton	N-E
1-800-661-2010	**of Toronto**
www.wigamoginn.com	2 1/2 hrs

Schedule: Open year-round.
Packages: All packages include dinner on the day of arrival, breakfast on the day of departure, and both breakfast and dinner every day in between. Lunch can be purchased at the Grill on site. Call for latest rates.
Directions: Take Hwy 404 North, exit Davis Rd. (exit #51, eastbound). Follow Hwy 48 North to Coboconk. Take Hwy 35 North to Minden (do not take Hwy 121 South to Kinmount!) Take Hwy 121 East towards Haliburton and follow it past the golf course to North Kashagawigamog Lake Rd.

NEARBY ATTRACTIONS
Haliburton Forest (30-min.)...........p. 342

WINTER TIME AT TALISMAN

Winter with a splash

"Hooo! Hooo!" exclaims my little dare-devil as he dashes through the snow in bare feet. Quickly, he shapes a snowball and returns to a snowball fight that has broken out at Talisman's... heated outdoor pool.

Hotel guests and non-resident visitors share the slopes. However, plenty of other activities, like the great outdoor pool, await the resort's residents.

There are rides in horsedrawn carts, obstacle course race in the snow, playroom, family casino, family shows...

The 18 slopes lining the Beaver Valley aren't very high. Yet a good half are intermediate-level and some offer sizeable challenges. Let's not forget the big half-pipe for snowboarders. Furthermore, the wait for ski lifts is short; amateurs can therefore have non-stop fun.

Talisman is renowned for the Kids Klub, with its daycare concept paired with a ski school. It boasts its own ski slope and lift, as well as varied half-day and full-day programs to answer the needs of all age groups.

Toddlers (18 months to 3-year-olds) play in a pretty, brightly coloured room filled with great toys. They are given the choice of crafts, storytelling, songs, a nap and even a ski-ing lesson (for an extra fee).

The 4 to 6-year-olds occupy a larger adjoining room, also colourful and well stocked with toys. They benefit from skiing lessons, perfectly adapted to each child's level. For bigger kids, the program loses its daycare status. It concentrates on teaching to different levels of skiers. There is even a program for those interested in snowboarding.

With the help of all these programs, parents can take to the slopes in peace while their children are handled by professionals. And the meals are taken care of before and after. Even more relaxing!

TIPS (fun for 2 years +)

• The least expensive "European style" rooms, with two double beds, are located in the main building, thus providing indoor access to all services.
• If with a toddler, you might want to choose a room without a gas fireplace with their burning-hot glass.
• All the meals included in the packages are served in the vast Tyrolean Dining Room. Some nights offer buffet. Breakfast is served 7:30am to 9:30 am on weekends, holidays and **March Break** (start at 8 am the other days).
• A babysitter can be reserved 48 hours ahead of time.
• Ask about their **Summer** packages with Kids Klub (18 months to 10 years), Power Pac (11-15 years), **water tubing**, horseback riding, fishing, climbing wall...
• **March Break** is a great time to go too, with the evening shows and outdoor pool. There is usually still enough snow on the hills. Call to confirm.

NEARBY ATTRACTIONS
Dogsled at Rob Farm (25-min.).p. 358
Adrenaline Alley (5-min. walk).....p. 379

Talisman Mountain Resort	B-1 N-W of Toronto 2 1/4 hrs
• Kimberley 1-800-265-3759 www.talisman.ca	

   Schedule: Open year-round. **Packages:** A minimum two night stay is required. Packages include accommodation and 3 meals a day (beginning with dinner upon arrival and ending with breakfast on departure day). Call for latest rates. **Directions:** 150 Talisman Mountain Dr., Kimberley. Take Hwy 400 North to Hwy 89, turn westbound (left) on Hwy 89 to Shelburne, then turn northbound (right) at the second set of lights onto Hwy 10. Continue on Hwy 10 to Flesherton, then turn east (right) at the lights onto Cty. Rd. #4. Follow #4 to Grey Rd. #13, then turn left towards Kimberley.

ALONG THE 401

Fun along the way

It takes over five hours to drive straight between Toronto and Montreal. It could be a boring ride or you could turn it into a fun (but more time consuming) adventure. Your call. But let me tempt you with a few suggestions for great stops along the road, to stretch their legs... and their patience.

My family drives back and forth Toronto-Montreal many times a year. For years, the blue signs promoting attractions along the 401 were teasing me. Experience has taught me that some of them are located as far as 50 km away from the highway! Many others are indeed less than two km from the 401, offering a nice two-hour stop that could make the day.

It is usually on our way back that we make a fun stop before going back to our routine.

beach is long and narrow, bordered with grass. Its sand is a bit rough with small pebbles but the bottom of the river isn't muddy and the water is shallow over a long surface and perfect for kids. There's a playground, paddle boat rental, snack bar and picnic tables. If you keep going on Long Sault Pkwy, you'll reach **Woodlands Picnic Area**. It is closer to the exit #770/Dickinson Drive. (If you take that exit southbound, you'll turn east at the end, County Rd. 2, and turn towards the lake at the West Gate of the park.)

I preferred this area. My kids could not resist climbing up the majestic weeping willows offering a great spot in the shade for a picnic. The round shape of the shore makes it more fun to explore. The beach has a bit of a crescent shape and the trees are closer. Here again, there's a playground, snack bar and a rental facility.

Upper Canada Village

This one is the next one on my list! Take exit # 758/Upper Canada Road, turn east on County Rd. 2. Upper Canada Village takes a pioneer village to the next level, with actors working in mills, artisan shops, bakery, cheese factory, tavern, livery, print shop, farms, churches and homes. They re-enact births, weddings and funerals! They organize events around planting (spring) and harvesting (fall).

Inside the village, we can travel by foot, on a horse-drawn carryall, or along the canal on a flat-bottomed boat! We can catch a small train ride outside the gates of the village. There's also a Children's Activity Centre offering 1860's games, toys and historical dress up. There's even a Photographer's Studio where we can dress up for a historical keepsake portrait. You can buy snacks, lunch in the restaurant or in the village's café.

Long Sault Parkway

This little parkway parallel to Hwy 401 looked so good on the map that I had to check it out. It is found some 90 minutes from Montreal and consists of a 10-km road crossing eleven islands belonging to the Parks of the St. Lawrence. Water embraces the road on both sides. It offers access to two beaches. Both entrance gates to the park are around 2 km from Hwy 401. Day use fees giving access to the small parkway and both beaches are set at a maximum of $10 per vehicle.

Mille Roches Picnic Area offers the first beach you'll encounter if taking exit #778/Molinette Road towards the river. (Molinette Road leads you directly through the East Gate of the park and the beginning of Long Sault Parkway.) The

Prehistoric World

Take exit #758/Upper Canada Road from Hwy 401 towards the lake and you're almost there. It is on your right side. You just have to see this place! Such a good attraction so close to the highway! What was great about it was that from the entrance of Prehistoric World, we could not see what lay ahead. Most of the over 50 prehistoric animals were hidden from our sight.

The first specimens we saw in the clearing were small. I thought the fossil pit (with over 20 different fossils to brush off under the sand) would be the highlight. Then, we entered the trail leading into the forest... Full size dinosaurs amidst the trees waited at every turn! The Brontosaurus was so tall I could not fit it in from head to toe in a single picture. The sculptures are very nicely executed and spread along the 1km trail. They keep

expanding so you might be lucky enough to witness the various construction phases of the latest addition.

In the midst of the summer, try to visit in the morning otherwise the sun can be nasty when walking through the clearing. Bring water!

We stopped for ice cream at the **Country Lane Diner**, down the Upper Canada Rd., at the corner of County Rd. 2.

TIPS (fun for 3 years +)

• Rush hour around Toronto starts to build at 7 am and 4:30 pm. Driving between Montreal and Toronto takes roughly six hours. If you leave Montreal no later than 10 am, you should not hit the Toronto traffic. If you leave after 11 am, I suggest you stop at one of the attractions along the road.

• You'll find two **McDonald's** offering indoor playgrounds around Kingston. Take exit #617/Division Street and drive southbound for a **McDonald's** with large play area and many other fastfood chains. Along Hwy 401 westbound, there's also the option of the first rest area past Kingston, a **McDonald's** with large indoor play area services it. Note that there's no play area in the **McDonald's** you encounter along the 401 when driving eastbound.

• Closer to Toronto: Some 90 minutes from Toronto is the **Big Apple** (exit #497), with giant apple, mini train, mini golf, animals and small trails, see p. 27. Ten minutes from exit #472, you'll find **Cobourg Beach**, the best beach in the area, see p. 283. Near Whitby (exit #412), some 40 minutes from Toronto, there's a **Chuck E. Cheese** (see p. 218) and a **Putting Edge** by the highway, just north of the 401 (see p. 21). There's also the indoor playground **Kidszone**, just a few minutes north of Hwy 401, (exit #410), see p. 223. Finally, 30 minutes from Toronto, there's a football field-size pool at **Petticoat Creek** (exit #394), see p. 385.

Long Sault Parkways
(exit #778 and #770)
www.stlawrenceparks.com
1-800-437-2233

Upper Canada Village
(exit # 758)
www.uppercanadavillage.com
1-800-437-2233
Hours: Open mid-May to mid-October, 9:30 am to 5 pm.
Admission: $17/adults, $16/seniors, $10.50/students, $7.50/5-12 years old.

Prehistoric World
(exit # 758)
www.c360.ca/morrisburg/pw
(613) 543-2503
Hours: Open June to Labour Day, 10 am to 4 pm (last admission 3:15 pm).
Admission: $8/adults, $6/seniors, $4.50/4-15 years old, FREE under 4.

General tips about
Holiday outings:

- Days without school are what's driving our lives, aren't they? This chapter offers a quick reference to seasonal outings or seasonal activities offered in year-round attractions.

HOLIDAY
OUTINGS

See **Cullen Gardens** on p. 202.

MARCH BREAK

It's baaack!

March Break is such a misleading name! The only good news about this break for many parents is that there will be no homework to supervise and no lunch to prepare.

This listing is for those who choose (or have no choice but to) take a week off to stay with the kids.

Outdoor outings are much underrated during March Break, the busiest period of the year in many of the major indoor attractions. Put on rubber boots, pack some great snacks and a change of clothes and flip through the **Nature's Call** chapter (pp. 265-353) to choose a destination. Then watch your kids turn into young explorers.

This is also maple syrup time; check the maple syrup places described on pages 154 to 161. **Horton's Home Farm** (p. 158) is the least crowded. Also consider **Lake Crawford Conservation Area** and its "Sweet Waters" event (p. 410), offering the advantage of great trails and the proximity of **Mount Nemo** (p. 297), with the best view from the Niagara Escarpment, to complete the outing.

Many local families choose to "get away" in their own city with **Stage West**'s family package of hotel, pool and dinner theatre (p. 84). The **Delta Chelsea** downtown Toronto also offers a very popular package with its large pool with 3-storey-high slide and activities (check www.deltahotels.com or call 416-595-1975). We've had successful March Break getaways at **Talisman Mountain Resort** (p. 171) and **Bayview Resort** (p. 169).

Note that March Break is usually the last week most ski and snow tubing parks are open, weather permitting (see pp. 376-379).

The pools normally offer extended hours during March Break (pp. 382-384).

This time of the year is the best time to visit the **Bata Shoe Museum** (p. 254), the **Textile Museum** (p.251), with their drop-in activities noticeably more interactive than usual. The **Historic Fort York** becomes quite attractive with its musket drills for children (p. 400).

Casa Loma is also a winner during this period (p.114), despite the fact it is quite busy; arrive early and enjoy special activities throughout the castle and a great musical.

I must say I have a soft spot for **AGO**'s special line-up of activities during March Break (p. 92). You can always expect a solid craft activity in the Family Studio and smaller ones in adjacent rooms, plus interactive activities related to current exhibitions and access to Off the Wall! **McMichael Canadian Art Collection** also offers drop-in craft activities (p. 93).

If you're looking for midways and big crowds, check the **Spring Fling** at the SkyDome (p. 356) and **Wizard World** at Exhibition Place (p. 25).

Finally, you'll find the best free activities in some of the **Toronto Public Library** branches (p. 94). Check their publication *What's On* to find one to suite your desire, they vary a lot from one branch to the next.

Note that all attractions offering some special activities or schedule during the March Break are marked with a calendar pictogram throughout this guide.

Easter

Say what?

Wondering when East-er falls this year? Sim-ple! It falls on the first Sunday following the first ecclesiastical moon (not astrological) that occurs on or after the day of the vernal equinox, that is March 21. Following me?

One thing for sure, it never occurs before March 22 and never after April 25. Even more simple, it will fall on March 27, 2005, April 16, 2006, April 8, 2007, and March 23, 2008.

The **Beaches Easter Parade** (man-aged by the Beaches Lions Club) is an obvious choice on Easter Sunday. Read the tips on p. 178 to get the most out of this cute family event. On a more reli-gious note, the **Good Friday Procession**, taking place in Little Italy, has been a Toronto tradition for over 40 years (p. 180).

A free visit to **Allan Gardens** green-houses will give you a jump-start into spring with their colourful and odorous display of spring flowers totally in the Easter spirit (p. 309).

Many farms create nice events dur-ing Easter weekend. Beware! When the holiday occurs in March, chances are the weather won't allow the farms to offer their event. But when it takes place in April, with a little help from Mother Nature, Easter activities at the farm can be lovely.

Also note that some of the farms start to offer Easter activities some week-ends prior to Easter while others only offer them one day during the Easter weekend. Rule of thumb: always call before you head to a farm.

I have visited all the farms described in this guide but not necessari-ly during Easter time. Based on their descriptions, I'm quite positive that **Rounds Ranch** near Elmvale offers the most original activities, with egg cata-pult, and hole poking in the maze with colour codes (read p. 153 to understand!) and free roaming rabbits.

We have been to **Chappell Farms** near Barrie during Easter and their range of activities was impressive (p. 152). **Drysdale Farms** near Allis-ton seems to be in the same line (p. 149). Both **Pingle's Farm Market** (p. 138) and **Springridge Farm** (p. 143) offer a nice craft activity. Both **Chappell** and **Pingle's** farms include a small Bun-nyville with little houses inhabited by real bunnies.

Puck's Farm is sticking to real chocolate egg hunts (p. 148) while the others choose to do a plastic egg hunt which kids exchange for treats. For a more intimate event, check **Long Lane Farm** in Campbellville (p. 146).

Easter time often overlaps with maple syrup time and **Mountsberg Wildlife Centre** is the best place to enjoy both (p. 157). It is also a good place to see cute little chicks.

Finally, **Cullen Gardens** is really a fun place to go during Easter (p. 116). The **Toronto Zoo** (p. 48) invites kids to collect stamps throughout the site to col-lect a treat, which adds to the pleasure of free parking at that time of the year.

Note that all attractions offering some special activities or schedule dur-ing Easter time are marked with a rabbit pictogram throughout this guide.

BEACHES EASTER PARADE

An Easter celebration

There could hardly be a better setting for a successful Easter parade: the Beaches, with its quaint, pleasant architecture, discreet storefront signs, wide sidewalks, and above all, community spirit. With the support of costumed volunteers, pastel-coloured balloons, vehicles decorated by enthusiastic amateurs, and with the participation of clubs and organizations of all kinds, the Beaches take on the atmosphere of a joyous celebration.

Of course, we're not talking about Stations of the Cross and resurrection... but rather about the Easter Bunny and coloured eggs. The Beaches Lions Club House has been organizing this parade for over thirty years. More modest than the Santa Claus Parade, it features majorettes, small marching bands, amateur gym-

nasts from the area, as well as Mounties and fire trucks.

Certain store owners and organizations create ambitious mini-floats. When we were there, we saw a pick-up truck topped by a giant Easter hat, a "steamboat", a travelling garden, a tractor pulling a multicoloured cart full of clowns, and even a tractor-trailer with costumed children.

Among those parading, there are children on decorated bicycles, boyscouts, preschoolers from local daycare centres riding in decorated wagons, clowns and mascots (Star Wars characters, when we were visiting; Darth Vader delighted many children!).

To sum up, it appeals to the community because the whole community participates! Encouraged by the Lions, a few people wear beautiful hats they made themselves, and some children hold on to their stuffed bunnies.

Don't be scared off by the small crowds gathering at either end of the course. In between, I found lots of room on Queen Street East, even close to **Kew Gardens**. I recommend that you stay close to **Kew Gardens** or the park located close to Glen Manor Drive.

TIPS (fun for 2 years +)

• More than one hour before the parade, a long stretch of Queen Street is closed to motor vehicles and the Queen streetcar line ends at Woodbine.

• For a religious event, see the **Good Friday Procession** on p. 180.

• See **Garden Gate** and **Sunset Grill** restaurants on pp. 435-436.

NEARBY ATTRACTIONS

Beaches Lions Club Easter Parade
(416) 693-5466
www.beacheslions.com

J-10 Dowtown Toronto 20-min.

Schedule: Easter Sunday at 2 pm, rain or shine.
Admission: FREE.
Directions: On Queen St. East, begins near Victoria Park and ends at Woodbine St.

On our way to **Glen Stewart Park Ravine** (p. 344).

GOOD FRIDAY PROCESSION

On a Good Friday

My daughter is given the image of a saint as we wait for the procession to come our way. I had not seen these in years! It adds to the retro feeling I get when I see the people pass in front of us, accompanied by the solemn music of a sombre band. It seems like we're back in the 50's.

Here, we're back in time, before the Easter Bunny became commonplace. I guess it's time for me to explain to my kids what Easter is all about!

Every year, the parish of **St. Francis of Assisi** organizes the mile-long march re-enacting the fourteen Stations of the Cross. It has been a tradition for ages.

Different religious associations take part in the procession. Followers walk behind banners held high. Many of these are beautiful pieces of craftsmanship that must see the daylight only on this specific occasion. The procession quietly proceeds with the display of banners, Jesus and Virgin Mary statues. Crosses are held on small floats, followed by a few shepherds and apostles in long robes.

The most impressive station is obviously the one featuring an exhausted Jesus bearing his cross, surrounded by Roman soldiers. My wide-eyed 5-year-old has to be reminded this is a re-enactment!

How we got from there to the **Easter** Bunny will be a hard one to explain...

TIPS (fun for 6 years +)
• If you're looking for the non-religious parade, check the **Beaches Easter Parade** on p. 178.
• It's a 5-minute walk from Queen Street East to **St. Francis of Assisi Church**.

NEARBY ATTRACTIONS	
AGO (15-min.)	p. 92
High Park (15-min.)	p. 322

Good Friday Procession (416) 536-8195	I-9 **Downtown** Toronto 20-min.

 Schedule: On Easter Friday, at 3 pm.
Admission: FREE.
 Directions: Starting point at St. Francis of Assisi Church at the corner of Mansfield Ave. and Grace St. The procession runs along Grace southbound, turns west on Dundas, goes north on Montrose, then east on College, south on Manning then back to the church.

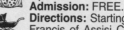

VICTORIA DAY

Spring is in the air

In Canada, the celebration of Victoria Day occurs every year on the Monday prior to May 25th. It is the official celebration of the birthdays of Queen Victoria and Queen Elizabeth II, established as a national holiday in 1901.

Victoria Day and Canada Day are the only two days when we're allowed to have our own little fireworks in the local parks. **Amazing Party & Costume Store** (p. 439) is the best store I know to sell pre-packaged kits of all sizes. Time to ask the neighbours to pitch in for a great local event kids will remember for the rest of their lives.

If you need a bigger fix, check one of the following public fireworks shows traditionally held during Victoria Day long weekend. **Canada's Wonderland** throws a big one on the Sunday of that weekend (p. 14), so does **Couchiching Beach Park** (p. 281).

On Victoria Day itself, check out the **Niagara Falls** fireworks (p. 302) or, closer to home, the one presented at **Ashbridges Bay Park** (p. 271), where a great ambience reigns on the beach while people wait and where the fireworks above the water give a great show!

Victoria Day is also one of the days when **Historic Fort York** is at its best (p. 400) and when **Black Creek Pioneer Village** gets even more interactive (p. 404) with its Fiddlers' contest and traditional games.

Don't forget that the **Milk International Children's Festival for the Arts** (p. 70) goes on for eight consecutive days starting on the Sunday of the Victoria Day weekend.

SIMCOE DAY

Last summer month!

The first Monday in August is a holiday in most of the provinces but it is in fact a municipal holiday called the August Civic Holiday in most municipalities. In 1968, the Toronto City Council officially called it "Simcoe Day" after John Graves Simcoe, first Lieutenant Governor of Upper Canada in 1791.

For some fireworks on Simcoe Day, check

Chinguacousy Park (p. 334). It is part of Brampton's Summer Festival, a whole day of family activities throughout the park (which already includes a pond, a petting zoo, a wading pool and mini-golf).

Historic Fort York marks the event with interactive activities including the popular musket drill for children (p.400). It is also a special day at **Gibson House Museum** (p. 403).

CANADA DAY

can go bigger! Note you need a 30 m by 30 m space to do it safely.

There's something magical about fireworks by the water. **Ontario Place** is back with ambitious fireworks a few evenings during the summer, including on Canada Day (p. 12). You can watch these from their grounds but they are also visible from the Lake Shore. Expect huge traffic after the fireworks!

Cobourg's Beach 4-day Waterfront Festival includes fireworks on Canada Day (p. 283) and so does **Couchiching Beach Park** (p. 281). Both locations are lovely and offer many family activities prior to the fireworks, along with a great beach and playground.

Canada's Wonderland (p. 14) and **Downsview Park** (p. 329) also throw a good one, with the big difference that you have to pay the ground admission price to enjoy Wonderland's while Downsview's admission is free (with a pay-as-you-play midway). Chances are **Mel Lastman Square** will also offer a free concert and fireworks on that day.

It's a blast!

Canada Day equals fireworks in my mind. Many attractions celebrate it with a blast. Whatever their size, you can always count on the fun of the collective anticipation and the exclamations of delights from kids and the young at heart.

Canada Day is the other day along with Victoria Day when we're allowed to blast private fireworks in local parks. I recommend **Amazing Party & Costume Store** (p. 439) as your fireworks supplier for their pre-packaged kits of all sizes. They come with a suggested order of launch. There's the family kit with noise, the family kit without noise, the driveway kit, the park kit, the cottage kit... You get the idea.

Last year, over eight households in my neighbourhood got together to buy the $200 park kit, with some extras. The kids had so much fun enjoying the (modest) show with all their friends, we decided to make it a tradition. Our local café even offered to sponsor part of it next year so we

Many local parks put together simple events that get kids really excited for the mere reason that they can enjoy them with their friends in the neighbourhood. **Jimmie Simpson Park**, located at the corner of Booth Avenue and Queen Street East is a good example. Last Canada Day, its baseball diamond was turned into a pony trail. A temporary stage was put up for local dance groups.

Belly dancing demonstrations were given in the adjacent community centre. Games and an inflatable structure were offered for a small fee. Arts and Craft tables were displayed; BBQs threw a great smell in the air and kids could create flags.

Add to this the wading pool and big playground at the other end of the park and you get good old-fashioned fun. Call (416) 465-7554 for details.

You may want to look at Toronto's web site www.toronto.ca/special_events and click Canada Day to find out about other parks offering events.

Last time I checked, among other activities, this page mentioned fireworks at **Stan Wadlow Park** (on Cosburn

Avenue off Woodbine, just south of O'Connor Drive) with a parade starting at 9:30 am at Broadview and Danforth, midway and music in the afternoon at the park, topped with fireworks. Call (416) 396-2842 for details.

Chinguacousy Park (p. 334) and **Cullen Gardens and Miniature Village** (p. 116) offer all-day family events complete with fireworks. **Milliken Park** (p. 327) offers fireworks only.

Other attractions include special Canada Day activities worth mentioning. The 4-day **CHIN Picnic** free event which always encompasses Canada Day is held at Exhibition Place, (p. 24). The **Hamilton Museum of Steam and Technology** offers rides on small steam engine locomotives (p. 243). **Downey's Farm and Market** throws a party (p. 141) and historic attractions **Fort York** (p. 400) and **Gibson House Museum** (p. 403) go the extra mile to entertain us.

In London, both the **London Children's Museum** (p. 262) and **Fanshawe Pioneer Village** (p. 421) offer special activities. Considering all the other attractions in the area, it is the perfect destination for a long weekend getaway during the Canada Day weekend (more on London accommodations on p. 31).

HALLOWEEN

Scary or cute?

It's always good to know where you're going during Halloween time. You don't want to traumatize your little pumpkin in the Barn from Hell but neither do you want to bore older siblings to tears in a cute Boo Barn.

I'll get straight to the point: the scariest farm we've visited is the **Magic Hill Haunted Adventure** in Stouffville (p. 185). They've honed their attraction for years. I would not go there with children under eight, not to all their attractions anyway.

I've seen the **White Rock Ostrich Farm** for their birds but never had a chance to check out their Screamfest event, which seems to have grown quite ambitious, judging by their web site (p. 55). I would also bet **Rounds Ranch's** haunted wagon rides are great (p. 153).

Screemers at the Exhibition Place (p. 13), the scary indoor attraction downtown Toronto, is also better suited for older kids.

The latest place I've visited that was lots of fun for the whole family is **Brooks Farms** near Mount Albert (p. 137). Their haunted hay-ride was funny. Their pumpkin cannon, zip-lines and pig races were great entertainment.

Other sure bets for their great range of activities when visiting with children of different age groups: **Downey's Farm** near Brampton (p. 141), **Chappell Farms** around Barrie (p. 152) and **Dyment's Farm** in Dundas (p. 151).

For the younger crowd, I strongly recommend the wacky wagon ride starring the owner himself, at **Archibald Orchards** (p. 139). **Pingle's Farm** musical puppet show (p. 138) and **Forsythe Family Farms'** Enchanted Forest (p. 140) are also very popular with young kids.

If you're into mazes, you have to check out **Hanes Corn Maze's** 10-acre labyrinth (p. 150) and **Rounds Ranch's** (p. 153). **Pingle's** also has a big one (p. 138).

Our favourite place to jump off straw mountains is **Andrews Scenic Acres** (p. 145), followed by **Springridge Farm** (p. 143). **Chudleigh's Farm's** slide into the straw is also a big hit (p. 144).

I love **Cullen Gardens** during Halloween time (p. 116). The whole attraction, decorated for the occasion, and the evening trick-or-treat stations throughout the natural setting are just great. Another natural setting we really enjoyed during Halloween time is **Bronte Creek Provincial Park's** decorated trail (p. 336).

On a more commercial note, the seasonal Halloween store of **Southbrook Farm**, combined with their great farm market is worth a visit (p. 134). **Harvest Fall Festival** at Riverdale Farm is also a fun event (p. 132). It includes Cabbagetown Arts & Crafts Sale.

Note that all attractions listed in this guide, which are offering some special activities during Halloween time (also pumpkin time) are marked with a pumpkin pictogram.

HAUNTED ADVENTURE

Courtesy of Magic Hill Farm

Good scare!

This is the best attraction of its kind in and around the GTA. It is located in the perfect setting of dark countryside, in woods and fields, and created by people with a real passion for entertainment, with the help of over 100 costumed actors.

When we got there on a Saturday at around 8:45 pm, it was so crowded that a policeman had to direct traffic on the small country road. By 9:30 pm, we were still far away from the living-dead cashier in the long line-up. My son was falling asleep as he stood waiting, so we headed back home.

The following Friday, we went back shortly before 7 pm. We found parking in the field right next to the entrance. Only 70 people were waiting ahead of us. When the doors opened at 7 pm, it was almost dark.

TIPS (fun for 8 years +)
• If you don't think you can get there around 7 pm, don't bother going with a child. Shortly after that, the line-ups are too scary! Or ask about their VIP Express Pass to by-pass the line for an extra fee.
• This attraction is not recommended for children under 8 years old. Don't make it your child's first experience with scary fun. You might want to avoid the Black Cavern with children under 10. I suggest you see the **haunted** barn when they are not too tired so they can stomach it. My son said he preferred the Howling Hayride, but I saw him react and laugh much more in the Terror Trail Trek.
• There is a snack bar.
• More on **Magic Hill Farm** during the winter on p. 136.

We were told to go straight to the **haunted** barn (the other attractions were not ready yet). As we waited our turn, we read one of the signs on the barn wall: "Rub the rock or you'll never see daylight again." My son kept bragging that he was not scared but I saw him rubbing the stone more than once!

The tour of the barn lasts less than 15 minutes. Among other things, we saw the kitchen from hell, a smoking electrical chair and sophisticated special effects. It ended with us being chased by a crazy man armed with a powered chainsaw!

Before heading in a wagon for the Howling Hayride through the Field of Screams, we were invited to shout at the top of our lungs, to practice for what awaited us: a morbid car accident, chains raking the metal roof of our wagon, and UFOs, to name a few.

My favourite was the Terror Trail Trek. The trail was beautiful, on top of a hill, with red spots in the bushes and the city lights in the background. "Monsters" jumped out of the woods at every turn, quicksand effects, a hung dead man, a tricky labyrinth and more made for a stimulating walk.

The Black Cavern had narrower walls, scarier situations. My son was not enjoying it anymore even though the staff toned it down when they saw his reaction. I was so busy "protecting" him from the scare that I hardly remember what I saw. We had a good scare!

CHRISTMAS TRADITIONS

Magic in the air
There's something magical about thousands of colourful light bulbs suddenly illuminating a huge tree. Christmas decorations on evergreens or at the mall, when skillfully done, are so pretty. Kids' excitement before a Santa Claus and the promise of gifts he represents is contagious. And, whatever your religion, a nativity re-enactment is a nice story to be told.

First things first, the biggest tradition to launch Christmas time in Toronto has been the **Santa Claus Parade** (p. 192) for a century! It is closely followed by the **Christmas Story**, a nativity re-enactment presented at the Holy Trinity Church for the last 60 years (p. 191).

The only other indoor nativity I've seen is the ambitious **Kids' Christmas Stable** in Burlington (p. 200). You'll find a list of all the other places offering nativity scenes in the index on p. 476 under **Nativity re-enactment**.

For a different kind of parade, have a look at the **Kensington Festival of Lights** (p. 196).

Colourful lights are the trademark for this jolly time of the year. The tree illumination launching the **Cavalcade of Lights** is quite exciting (p. 190). Throughout December, we can admire other **festivals of lights** where parks are adorned with structures covered by little lights (check the index for a list of these on p. 474). As far as I'm concerned, **Cullen Gardens' Festival of Lights** tops them all (p. 202), especially after a snowfall.

If you want to cut your own tree so your kids can see for themselves that they grow in fields, check **Magic Hill Tree Farm** (p. 136) or **Drysdale Tree Farms** (p. 169). If you want to see how far some people go to decorate trees, see the **Twelve Trees of Christmas** at the Gardiner Ceramic Museum (unfortunately back only in 2005 after the renovations) and the **St. James Cathedral Crèche Exhibit** (p. 194).

See what your options are if you want to take the kids to see **Santa at the mall** on p. 188. There's also the **Breakfast with Santa** on p. 187.

Looking for entertainment during this season? Consider the hilarious **Ross Petty Productions** or a traditional **Nutcracker** presentation (p. 193). **Famous People Players** always presents a fun show with huge puppets under black lights performing Christmas songs (p. 82). **Casa Loma**, at its best during Christmas time, usually offers a lively musical and a roster of other activities, in addition to a visit with Santa (p. 114).

On a more intimate note, there's the opening of the Victorian Christmas at **Allan Gardens** (p. 198), the small winter festival at **Humber Arboretum** (p. 330) and the Beaches Lions Club **Christmas Tree Lighting** usually held on the first Saturday in December from 5 to 7 pm at Kew Gardens Park (call (416) 693-5466 to confirm).

If you are into singing, there's **caroling in the park** at the Beaches (p. 344). The **Toronto Symphony Orchestra** makes room for some carolling as well during its Christmas performance (p. 103). For serious singing, however, try the impressive **Sing-Along Messiah** (p. 195).

Finally, let's not forget this is the time to share with **Operation Christmas Child** and other non-profit organizations (p.128).

There's more. Note that all attractions listed in this guide, which are offering special activities during Christmas time are marked with a Santa pictogram.

BREAKFAST WITH SANTA

See you in Court

It feels so weird to enter into the deserted Bay store at 9 am that it makes me doubt we are in the right building. Yet, when the elevator's doors open on the eighth floor, the Arcadian Court is already buzzing with the excitement of families gathering around their tables.

Even though there has been a restaurant on The Bay's eighth floor since 1889, I had never been to the **Arcadian Court** restaurant open daily to the public. The large white and cream room with high ceiling, suspended chandelier and marble floors offers the perfect setting for a breakfast with Santa.

Most girls did not want to miss a chance to dress up so we see a parade of

pretty **Christmas** dresses and the colour red reigns. People are still arriving at 9:30 am when the breakfast buffet opens. Don't go expecting fancy eggs Benedict or French toast soaked in maple syrup. Nevertheless, the buffet concept is enough to excite most kids and mine are thrilled at the sight of the scrambled eggs, sausage, bacon, small potatoes, pancakes, small muffins, fruit, yogurt and juice. Parents are content with the bottomless cups of coffee and tea.

As we eat at our table covered in fine linen, an interactive singer warms the place with his **Christmas** songs. Meanwhile, clowns are creating shapes with balloons and offering face paint to the kids between bites.

When Santa arrives, a stampede is contained by the promise that each table would be called in its turn to visit the jolly man waiting in his large chair (all tables were previously assigned a colour). By 10:30 am, all food is removed.

The Breakfast with Santa has become a tradition for many extended families to launch the festive season.

TIPS (fun for 2 years +)

• At this kind of event, kids will have more fun if they come with cousins or friends to dance and sing with.

• There is no need to rush to the line-up when they call your table's colour to visit Santa. Just make sure you show up when there are 20 kids or less left in line.

• You can access the **Eaton Centre** from the overpass on The Bay's second floor to admire the beautiful **Christmas** decorations (no need to put the coats back on). BEWARE! "Santa" is also there! Be prepared with a good explanation.

• The **Arcadian Court** is open for fancy lunches Monday to Saturday, 11:30 am to 2:30 pm (might be closed for private functions, call to confirm).

Breakfast with Santa	I-10
(416) 861-6611	**Dowtown**
www.arcadiancourt.ca	**Toronto**
	10-min.

 Schedule: Usually held on Saturdays, from the last weekend in November to the weekend prior to Christmas, from 9 am to 10:30 am. Call to confirm, the administration is considering adding weekends and Sundays. (Reservations are a must.)

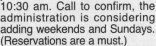 **Admission:** $16.25/adults, $11.65/12 years and under, all included.

Directions: In the Arcadian Court, on the 8th floor of The Bay, at the corner of Bay and Queen.

NEARBY ATTRACTIONS
Nathan Phillips Rink (1-min.walk) p.372

SANTA AT THE MALL

Spotted in shopping malls: he really exists!

Does your neighbourhood mall greet the real Santa in a magical setting? Does it house your favourite shops? Does it offer a drop-in child-care service? Other malls do but... which ones?

Starting mid-November until December 24th (inclusive), you can visit Santa Claus in several shopping malls. It is an adventure that requires some determination. Line-ups can be long and impatient children, who have waited for an hour, may decide to opt out at the last minute.

Sherway Gardens

The Santa Claus display is enchanting and colourful, and it is the only one I know which incorporates distractions into the line-up, year after year.

Last year, they've tried a new (and great) concept. They gave timed-tickets allowing group of kids to meet Santa for 45 minutes at once, for some interactive storytelling and song. No official photo sessions. Parents could take all the pictures they wanted of their kids in action. Call to see if they repeat the experience.

Sherway Gardens houses over 200 stores, including Holt Renfrew, The Bay, Sporting Life, Sears, Gymboree, Gap Kids and more children's clothing stores.

Square One

Less interactive in nature, yet the most spectacular, the tall Christmas Castle at this shopping centre enthuses every year. Above, a sleigh crosses a shower of lights and descends on the many turrets, and an electric train travels through the castle with its many colourful passengers. In the mall, you'll also find a small path where children find rides and many small moving cars (these attractions are accessible year-round).

Square One houses over 300 stores including The Bay, Sears, Wal-Mart, Zellers, Toys, Toys, Toys, as well as 12 children's clothing stores and **Cineplex Odeon Square One**, (905) 275-2640. **Coliseum Mississauga** sits across Rathbun, (905) 275-3456.

Eaton Centre

I recommend a ride in the glass elevator near the large water fountain in the Eaton Centre. It gives you a good view of the overall Christmas display: a large reindeer-pulled sleigh, travelling through a multitude of lights, suspended amidst giant Christmas trees and myriads of wrapped gifts above the Santa Claus Rotunda and the 4-storey-high water spray that spurts out at regular intervals.

This downtown mall is home to some 300 stores including Disney Store, Toys, Toys, Toys, Animal World, Gymboree, Gap Kids and more children's clothing stores. See **Eggspectation** on p. 436.

An overpass links it to The Bay. A good place to eat is the **Cityview Café** along the window side on the 8th floor of The Bay, with breakfasts and very affordable meals (Monday-Wednesday, 9:30 am to 5:30 pm; Thursday-Friday closes at 7:30 pm, Saturday closes at 4:30 pm; Sunday, noon to 4 pm).

Yorkdale Centre

Its Santa Claus Rotunda has been touched by the same refined aesthetic as the rest of the centre. Basking in beautiful light and dressed in wood and velvet, in shades of forest green and burgundy or red, it mirrors a picture perfect display in a Bombay Company's catalogue.

Here, you will find the **Rainforest Café** (p. 432), Holt Renfrew, The Bay, Sears, five children's clothing boutiques, as well as **Famous Players Silvercity Yorkdale**: (416) 787-4432.

Woodbine Centre

Located close to Pearson Airport, with some 150 stores, it includes The Bay, Sears, Zellers and some children's clothing stores, as well as the movie theatres **Rainbow Woodbine**, (416) 213-9048. It also houses the large indoor amusement park **Fantasy Fair** (p. 30). When we visited, the large Santa Claus Rotunda boasted a decorative merry-go-round topped with a tall Christmas tree.

Scarborough Town Centre

We enjoyed the large Christmas Castle and were seduced by Santa Claus' den with a Victorian living room and fireplace. Their daycare is more intimate than in other malls, **Kornelia's Korner**, (416) 296-0901. The mall is home to more than 200 stores, including The Bay, Sears, Wal-Mart, **Bear City** (p. 427), Gymboree, Gap Kids and more children's clothing

stores. It also hosts the **Famous Players Coliseum Scarborough**, (416) 290-6045.

Drop-off services

Drop-off services can come as life savers during the trying Christmas spree. In some malls that receive Santa Claus' visit, this service is offered for kids 18 months to 10 years, for a maximum two-hour period, at around $4.50/hour. Just enough time to purchase a few toys and hide them in the car or an old bag.

There's **Erin Mills Town Centre**, which stands out with its enormous tower dressed with clocks. Here you will find a **Where Kids Play/(905) 828-5893** daycare offering a drop-off service. The mall includes some 200 stores such as The Bay, Sears, Zellers, Gap Kids and more children's clothing stores.

See **Scarborough Town Centre**, previously mentioned. Finally, **J.J.'s Kids Centre** (p. 148) in North York's **Centrepoint Mall** is by far the most entertaining drop-off service.

Shopping centres
- **Eaton Centre/Toronto**
(416) 598-8700 (I-10 on map)
www.torontoeatoncentre.com
(Yonge St. and Queen St.)
- **Sherway Gardens/Etobicoke**
(416) 621-1070 (I-9 on map)
www.sherwaygardens.ca
(QEW, exit Browns Line, take Evans Ave.)
- **Yorkdale Centre/North York**
(416) 789-3261 (I-10 on map)
www.yorkdale.com (Hwy 401, Allen Rd. exit, take Yorkdale Ave. southbound)
- **Woodbine Centre/Etobicoke**
(416) 674-5200 (H-9 on map)
www.woodbinecentre.ca
(Hwy 427 North, exit Rexdale East)
- **Centrepoint Mall /North York**
(416) 222-6255 (H-9 on map)
(Yonge St. and Steeles Ave.)
- **Square One/Mississauga**
(905) 279-7467 (I-8 on map)
www.shopsquareone.com
(Hwy 403, exit Hurontario southbound)
- **Erin Mills Town Centre/Mississauga**
(905) 569-1981 (I-8 on map)
www.erinmillstowncentre.ca
(Erin Mills Pkwy., north of Hwy 403)
- **Scarborough Town Centre**
(416) 296-0296 (I-11 on map)
www.scarboroughtowncentre.com
(Hwy 401, McCowan exit southbound)

CAVALCADE OF LIGHTS

High spirited countdown

Our eyes are riveted to the lighted skating rink, shining in the frigid darkness. In less than one minute, the event we've all been expecting will take place. The 100,000 lights adorning the square's large trees and the tall Christmas tree will light up at once. Anticipation is building among the excited crowd.

Children delight in excited expectation and they, like us, marvel at the magical effect of this illumination. It's not surprising the City has been organizing this event for over 30 years!

You can arrive as late as a half-hour prior to the illumination, and easily find a spot in **Nathan Phillips Square's** large underground parking lot, and a viewing spot on the rink (providing you perch your little one on your shoulders). Those who wish to sit around the rink will make a point of getting there at least an hour in advance.

The Cavalcade traditionally follows the tree illumination with a performances of international calibre, usually a skating show complete with laser beam extravaganza and a light show.

A visit inside **City Hall** to view a model of the city also wins the enthusiasm of our little visionaries.

An **ice sculpture competition** (usually 2-3 consecutive days before New Year's Eve) is another tradition you won't want to miss. You can view the results on the days following the competition, providing temperatures remain at sub-zero levels.

Nathan Phillips Square is also host to a **New Year** celebration that begins after 10 pm on December 31.

NEARBY ATTRACTIONS

Cavalcade of Lights
(416) 338-0338
www.
toronto.ca/special_events

J-10
Dowtown
Toronto
10-min.

Schedule: Lighting celebration usually the last Friday of November (at 7:25 pm in 2003 but call for exact time this year). Cavalcade of Lights line-up of activities will take place many days until December 31.
Admission: FREE.
Directions: Nathan Phillips Square, Toronto (corner of Queen St. West and Bay St.).

THE CHRISTMAS STORY

A time for rituals

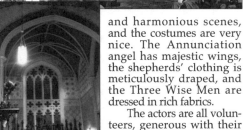

A tiny house of worship dating from 1847 is caught in a stranglehold by the buildings that have sprung up since then. For over 60 years, it has been telling the story of Christmas to Torontonians, with the assistance of its great organ, accompanied by a singing quartet and amateur actors of all ages miming the narrators' words.

The Christmas Story performances held at the **Holy Trinity Church** are certainly the most concrete way to explain to children the story of the nativity scene displayed at Christmas time. The Anglican church is modest but gorgeous. The great organ plays softly while we wait for the show to begin. The first two rows of pews, as well as two large carpets at the front, are reserved for young spectators.

Children hold their breath when all the lights go out, emphasizing the large stained-glass windows at the back of the altar, before a spotlight shines on the two narrators. For the remainder of the performance, the actors perform within islands of light standing out against the darkness. The amateur production offers studied

and harmonious scenes, and the costumes are very nice. The Annunciation angel has majestic wings, the shepherds' clothing is meticulously draped, and the Three Wise Men are dressed in rich fabrics.

The actors are all volunteers, generous with their time and enthusiasm, but they're confined in a relatively static formula. You don't attend "Christmas Story" for acting performances. However, I found King Herod was played quite convincingly, as well as Rachel, out of her mind with grief during the massacre of male babies of two years and under.

I was also charmed by many of the child actors: a pageboy with the giggles, a little angel forgetting to leave the stage, baby Jesus happily babbling as the myrrh is shown to him and quivering with joy during the offering of the third Wise Man, with the audience laughing. When I visited, Jesus was played by… eight-month-old twins, sharing the role according to their mood of the moment!

TIPS (fun for 5 years +)

• See **Holy Trinity Square** on p. 308.
• The performance lasts about an hour and combines perfectly with a short visit to admire **Eaton Centre**'s **Christmas** decorations (p. 188) and **Nathan Phillips Square**'s 100,000 lights and skating rink (p. 372).
• From the week after Victoria Day to Labour Day, you can enjoy music on Mondays at 12:15 pm in the church ($5 donation suggested, bring your lunch!).

NEARBY ATTRACTIONS
Cavalcade of Lights (2-min. walk) p. 190

The Christmas Story
(416) 598-8979
www. holytrinitytoronto.org

J-10
Downtown Toronto
10-min.

Schedule: Usually on the three weekends before Christmas: Friday and Saturday evenings, 7:30 pm. Saturdays and Sundays, 4:30 pm. (Call to confirm the exact dates and hours. It is better to reserve.)

Admission: Suggested donation: $10/adults, $5/children.

Directions: Church of the Holy Trinity. 10 Trinity Square, Toronto (west side of Eaton Centre).

TORONTO SANTA CLAUS PARADE

100-year old tradition

Kids are on grown-ups' laps, shoulders or in their arms, on stairways, windowsills or walls. Kids are everywhere, in small clusters in the foreground or packed 2 or 3 rows deep. Among this gigantic brood, brave adults tackle this event with a smile, initiating their little ones to the Santa Claus Parade.

1:30 pm – We settle at the corner of Yonge and Front. At the other end, the parade had begun an hour earlier. We've arrived in time to find a small but comfortable patch of sidewalk, but the rows are filling in all around us. We recognize seasoned members of the crowd by their gear: they're fully equipped with snacks, drinks, blankets, chairs, strollers, back-packs, toys and stuffed animals.

1:45 pm – Mothers distribute Smarties to occupy their little elves. The number of grown-ups returning to their stations with coffee in hand is multiplying. Security guards are starting to push feet back on the sidewalk. Are these drums we're hearing? The excitement is rising...

2:30 pm – Children squirm on their parent's shoulders. On the other side of the street, I see two grandparents grinning widely, warmly clothed and seated on their lawn chairs, delighted to mingle with the youngsters.

2:15 pm – The growing clamour is announcing the arrival of the parade. For an hour, we'll be seeing wonders: two dozen marching bands with majorettes, more than 1000 costumed volunteers and about twenty floats, with Santa's sleigh as the highlight.

In the past years, we've admired Captain Hook's huge crocodile leaping towards the crowd, a rabbit-magician that pulled a… man out of his hat, a dog-robot, a teddy bear picnic, a king with his dragon… and it's been going on for 100 years!

TIPS (fun for 2 years +)

• To obtain a vantage point suitable for children, it's best to arrive at a chosen spot at least an hour before the parade passes by.
• During the parade, postmen collect children's letters to Santa. Write the following address on the envelope: Santa Claus, North Pole, H0H 0H0.
• If you don't want to brave the traffic, the lack of parking and the cold, you'd better stay home and watch the parade on Global TV at around 4 pm on the day of the parade.
• See **Eggspectation** and **Marché Mövenpick** on pp. 436-437.

NEARBY ATTRACTIONS
Royal Ontario Museum (1-min.).. p. 252
Bata Shoe Museum (1-min.)....... p. 254

Santa Claus Parade
(416) 599-9090
(then press # 500)

J-10
Downtown
Toronto
10 to 30-min.

(This Toronto Transportation Infoline provides a recorded message about date and route of the parade by October.)
www.thesantaclausparade.com

Admission: FREE.
Schedule: The parade is held on the 3rd Sunday of November and now begins at 12:30 pm.
Directions: Starts at Christie and Bloor West and ends at Front and Church (the route usually runs along Queen's Park, University Ave., Queen, Yonge and Front St. but it is better to call to confirm the route).

ROSS PETTY PRODUCTIONS

Likeable villains!

For years, Ross Petty Productions has presented pantomime versions of fairy tales such as Robin Hood, Aladdin, Snow White and Peter Pan at the beautiful Elgin Theatre.

These presentations are pure entertainment for the whole family. Traditionally, they involve a villain (impersonated by Ross Petty himself), which everyone loves to hate and which is exactly what he wants the kids to do!

For the fun of it, performers take liberties from the original tale and talk directly to children as if they were part of the action. From songs complete with dances that are choreographed in a hilarious cartoon-like fashion, to elaborate costumes and decors, all contribute to making this goofy entertainment!

To avoid the extra charge of probably around $5 per ticket from Ticket Master, buy your tickets directly at the Elgin's box office. It is open Monday to Saturday from 11 am to 5 pm and prior to the shows. Buy in advance!

Ross Petty Productions · Toronto **(416) 872-5555** **(call Ticket Master, for schedule)** www.rosspetty.com	**I-10 Downtown Toronto 10-min.**

Schedule: Usually from early December to early January at around 7 pm with some matinees at around 2 pm. Call for exact schedule.
Admission: Around $49-$69/adults, $39/12 years and under.
Directions: Elgin Theatre, 189 Yonge St., across from the Eaton Centre.

THE NUTCRACKER

Pace yourself

Another Christmas tradition is the presentation of The Nutcracker.

The grandest rendition of this favourite story is obviously the one from the **National Ballet of Canada**, a pure enchantment with lavish sets and costumes. Tickets are expensive, but worth every penny... depending on the age of your children.

If this is your child's first Nutcracker, why not take her to a more modest version and save the more expensive production for later? Some years, I have noticed three other Nutcracker productions in the GTA alone! Check the family series programs of different performing arts centres or call the potential venues listed here to see if a Nutcracker version is being presented.

If you choose to attend the **National Ballet's** performance at the Hummingbird Centre, check if they still offer their Open House before one of their matinee presentations. It includes activities, sing-along, Nutcracker characters, Santa, and more.

Potential venues
· **Hummingbird Centre/Toronto**
(416) 345-9595 (Ballet box office)
www.national.ballet.ca
Cost: In 2003, prices ranged from $26 to $86.
· **City Playhouse Theatre/Vaughan**
(905) 882-7469 (Ontario Ballet Theatre's)
· **Markham Theatre/Markham**
(905) 305-7469 (Ballet Jörgen)
· **Leah Posluns Theatre/Toronto**
(416) 636-1880, ext. 258 (Academy of Ballet and Jazz)
· **College Street United Church Theatre,** (416) 929-3019
(Xing Dance Theatre)

ST. JAMES & CRÈCHE EXHIBIT

I spy...

Find the crèche made out of walnut. Which crèche figures are actually flutes? Where's the one with a pinecone roof? Can you see the shepherd feeding his sheep from a basket? These are a few of the items children are asked to find throughout the exhibition.

St. James Cathedral's annual crèche exhibit looks deceptively small when you first enter the room. But it actually features over one hundred Nativity scenes. Most of them are quite modest in size. This actually adds to the pleasure of the hunt!

They come from over forty countries and are made with every possible material: gingerbread, straw, clay, fabric, wool, stone, wood, shells, tin cans... They were knit, carved, modelled, painted, sewn or baked.

No need to be Christian to appreciate the lovely figures.

TIPS (fun for 3 years +)

• Every year, the St. James Archives and Museum puts together well searched exhibits. At the time of print, it featured a major exhibit on the life of St. James and the pilgrimage to Santiago de Compostela, including paintings of scenes along the road and photos taken by pilgrims during their trek.

• Don't forget to admire the daylight shining through the beautiful stained-glass window inside the cathedral! More on **St. James Cathedral** on p. 113.

• Check the **Marché Mövenpick** and **Eggspectation** on pp. 436-437.

NEARBY ATTRACTIONS
Eaton Centre (5-min. walk).......... p. 188

St. James Cathedral & Crèche Exhibit (416) 364-7865, ext. 233 www. stjamescathedral.on.ca	J-10 Downtown Toronto 10-min.

 Schedule: Open daily from early December to December 22, maybe beyond. Call to confirm.

 Admission: FREE.

 Directions: At the corner of King and Church St., Toronto. The exhibit takes place in the St. James Archives and Museum located on the second floor of the parish house, which you access from Church St.

SING-ALONG MESSIAH

Courtesy of Tafelmusik

Hallelujah!

As he's talking to us, Maestro Handel is interrupted by... a bawling baby. Tongue-in-cheek, he comments on the great potential of the future singer (while the mother sheepishly reaches the exit) and goes on introducing the great masterpiece we've all come to sing.

When we handed in our ticket at the entrance, we were asked in what register we sang. I used to contribute a thin soprano voice in a choir from my life b.c. (before children) but I was accompanying a friend of mine with his two young daughters so we opted for the mixed section selected by many families.

TIPS (fun for 8 years +)
• Arrive early if you want to buy a score (around $15). Consult the Sing-Along program to find out which portion of the score will be performed.
• Handel interacts with us again after the intermission. Remember it is only in the second part that you will be able to belch the famous "Hallelujah! Hallelujah! Halleeluujaaah!"
• The **Tafelmusik Baroque Orchestra and Chamber Choir** also present their *Messiah* (although not in the sing-along version) at the **Trinity St. Paul's Centre**. They usually offer a few performances mid-December. Call to confirm.
• During the intermission, you can buy frozen treats and beverages.
• Check **Eggspectation** on p. 436.

To reach it we had to climb way up through the narrow backstairs of the old 1804 **Massey Hall**.

From our seats, we could get quite a view of the happy crowd, most spectators eagerly holding on to their score. Later on, I realized that most of them had been there before and just could not wait for the magic to start.

The maestro, quite handsome in his overcoat and wig, encouraged us to "zing along" with his strong German accent and helped us warm up. **The Tafelmusik Baroque Orchestra and Chamber Choir** and special soloists were accompanying us.

Listening to thousands of voices joining in to present Handel's *Messiah* is an amazing experience. You literally become the music. One has to know that Handel composed his masterpiece in 21 days, partially paralyzed from a stroke!

At one point, I was totally lost and frantically flipping through the complicated score when I felt a gentle tap on my shoulder. Alia and Alex, aged 10 and 11, earnestly wanting to help, quietly pointed out to me the right spot on the right page. Hallelujah! (It makes one wonder what do they teach these kids in whatever school they attend?)

Sing-Along Messiah (416) 872-4255 (Massey Hall) www.masseyhall.com (416) 964-6337 (Tafelmusik) www.tafelmusik.org	**I-10 Downtown Toronto 10-min.**

 Schedule: Usually at 2 pm on the Sunday right before Christmas, call in October to reserve!

 Admission: $27/adults, $20/others.

Directions: Massey Hall, on Shuter St., just east of Yonge St. by Eaton Centre's parking lot entrance.

NEARBY ATTRACTIONS
St. James Crèches (5-min. walk).p. 194
Eaton Centre (1-min. walk)..........p. 188

KENSINGTON FESTIVAL OF LIGHTS

The longest night

On the night of December 21st, a wave of madness sweeps through Kensington Market, as the cars give way to pedestrians and to the joyous parade engulfing stunned passers-by.

Along the lively streets filled with musicians and people in disguise, everyone is won over by the spirit of the celebration.

Kensington Market is renowned for its coloured effervescence, but few people know about the Festival of Lights, an annual ritual now in its 15th year. We're not talking about standard, tiny Christmas lights. Rather, we mean the lights of sun and fire, symbolic or genuine: Hanukkah candles, the fire of Christian faith, the pagan celebration of the solstice, and the joyful party to salute Earth's last revolution of the year around the sun.

This is not a parade that people watch passively. We are the parade and move along, viewing shows as we pass by. On December 21st, all the people attending are warmly dressed, and walk the course where several attractions await. Playful families hold elaborate paper lanterns dancing over the crowd.

When we attended the event, the story of the people of Israel was told with theatrical humour. Giant marionettes mimed a solstice story. Actors (a real baby among them) acted out the Nativity scene... on the roof of a store. Then, we went on to Denison Square Park, where a giant sculpture was burned with cries of joy. After the parade, we enjoyed free soup and bread provided by the local businesses.

A different activity is organized every year to entertain children. Once it was a giant piñata filled with small toys; another time, the winter witch greeted them with sweets. As for adults, their gift is the spirited music of a live band.

TIPS (fun for 3 years +)

• The **Red Pepper Spectacle Arts** organizing the festival is a non-profit community arts organization and storefront production facility in Kensington Market. Its studio (at 160 Baldwin Street) offers drop-in lantern-making workshops where participants help create paper lanterns, sets and costumes. They take place every Saturday and Sunday in November and December leading up to the festival, from 1 to 6 pm and cost $6, for material and instruction. All ages and skill levels welcome.

• The parade begins at 5:45 pm, but by arriving at 5:15, you can borrow a paper lantern, hat or wings, to participate more actively in the celebration. You may also buy a lantern on site.

• Lately, they've started to organize a **Harvest Festival** in Kensington Market during the fall. Call for details.

Kensington Festival of Lights (416) 598-3729	I-10 Dowtown Toronto 15-min.

 Schedule: Every December 21st, at 5:45 pm. The parade lasts approximately an hour and fun continues until 8 pm.

 Admission: A voluntary contribution ($5 suggested) is requested from those who borrow lanterns and costumes.

 Directions: The parade begins at Augusta and College (Augusta, south of College is closed to traffic from 5 to 6 pm).

TWELVE TREES OF CHRISTMAS

A designers' Christmas

Every year, designers are given "carte blanche" to their wildest fantasies with the decorating of twelve christmas trees, which are then displayed on the two floors of the George R. Gardiner Museum of Ceramic Arts. The result is lavish, if somewhat loaded, with a myriad of lovely details that small eyes enjoy discovering.

While this is one of those places where the "do not touch" prevails, I mention it nevertheless for others who get swept away by glittering Christmas trees.

Every year has its own theme. When we visited, it was "Christmas through the decades", an exhibit where each designer created a tree evocative of a decade between 1888 and 2008. It included a tree reminiscent of 1938, decorated as a Monopoly game. I enjoyed the tree of 1908 with its dolls and "Anne of Green Gables" memorabilia. Children preferred the 1968 "Space Race" tree with its rockets, or the moving disco balls and plastic jewellery of the 1978 "Groovy Christmas", or again, the dozens of Beanie Babies on the 1998 tree.

While you visit, make sure to show your children the porcelain characters of the Commedia dell'Arte exhibit, displayed in their little theatre equipped with orchestra and small monkeys.

TIPS (fun for 3 years +)

• The **Gardiner Museum of Ceramic Arts** is adding a third-floor pavilion and reconfiguring other spaces. It will reopen in the fall of 2005. Meanwhile, it is maintaining its drop-in Family Sundays from 1 to 3 pm in a temporary location (60 McCaul Street). It is offered on a first come first served basis and involves work with clay. For an extra $3, our pieces can be glazed.

Gardiner Museum of Ceramic Arts (416) 586-8080 www. gardinermuseum.on.ca	**I-10 Downtown** Toronto 20-min.

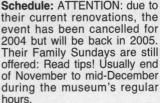

Schedule: ATTENTION: due to their current renovations, the event has been cancelled for 2004 but will be back in 2005. Their Family Sundays are still offered: Read tips! Usually end of November to mid-December during the museum's regular hours.

Admission: Family Sundays: $8/adults, $6/seniors, youth, $5/under 12 years old.

Directions: 111 Queen's Park, Toronto (across from the ROM, at the corner of Bloor St.). Closed for renovations until August 2005. Family Sundays temporarily located at 60 McCaul St. south of the Ontario College of Art building.

VICTORIAN CHRISTMAS

Allan Gardens' most interactive day

The opening day of Allan Gardens Victorian Christmas is the only time of the year when activities are planned for children.

The greenhouses have donned reds, pinks, greens and whites for a few months. Under the big glass dome, we admire a few Christmas shapes covered with plants (in the past, we've seen a toy soldier, a rocking horse and a fireplace).

During opening day, singers in Victorian costumes perform Christmas carols under that same beautiful dome.

A "make-and-take" activity takes place in the cactus room. More activities are held outside the conservatories.

When visiting, we could grab free Christmas cookies and hot cider and enjoy them in front of the bonfire.

We even caught a glimpse of a Victorian Santa (St. Nicholas) and took a horse-drawn wagon ride around the site.

There were a couple of farm animals to pet and a very pretty snowman and snowwoman with cut out holes to throw sandbags through. (Some Allan Gardens staff entertained the kids with that game.)

TIPS (fun for 2 years +)
• A craft activity is usually offered every year.
• More about **Allan Gardens Conservatory** on page 309.

NEARBY ATTRACTIONS

Adults and children even had a chance to toss balls into the air with a huge colourful parachute.

Victorian Christmas Opening Day
(416) 392-7288
http://collections.ic.gc.ca./gardens

I-10 Downtown Toronto 20-min.

Schedule: Usually first Sunday of December, 10 am to 5 pm. Call to confirm.
Admission: FREE.
Directions: Allan Gardens, 160 Gerrard St. East, Toronto (between Jarvis and Sherbourne, south of Carlton).

PIONEER CHRISTMAS

Victorian Christmas

During the Victorian Christmas, the village is adorned with decorations. Don't go expecting glittering frills and colours however, as decorations were humble and home made. The village's old houses are quite bare and pioneers certainly did not waste money on candles. As a result, it is likely your children won't even notice they are decorated!

When we last visited, we got to craft home-made presents and taste some treats. We toured the village muffled by the white snow. We also visited Santa's workshop in the Visitor Centre. (Call in November to find out if this activity will be offered this year.)

One of the most popular events at Black Creek Pioneer Village is the **Christmas By Lamplight** for which you need advance reservations. For the occasion, candles and lanterns lend a magical feel to the village. Singers dressed in costumes of the times present Christmas carols in the streets.

When we attended, chestnuts were cooked on a bonfire and hot cider was served. Kids could do make-and-take Christmas crafts, and have old-fashioned Santa accompanying them on wagon rides in the dark.

TIPS (fun for 5 years +)

• The **Christmas By Lamplight** event is so popular, try to reserve as early as July. They give priority to people booking the **Christmas** dinner as well (which I prefer not to attend with kids) but you can ask to be put on the waiting list!

• More on **Black Creek Pioneer Village** on p. 404.

NEARBY ATTRACTIONS

Black Creek Pioneer Village
• **North York**
(416) 736-1733
www.trca.on.ca

H-10
North
of downtown
35-min.

Schedule: The Victorian Country Christmas runs from mid-November to December 31 from 9:30 am to 4 pm on weekdays and from 11 am to 4:30 pm during the weekends (more activities offered on the weekends in December before Christmas). Christmas by Lamplight is offered the first three Saturday evenings in December.

Admission: Regular activities: $11/adults, $10/ seniors, $7/5-14 years, FREE 4 years and under, tax not included. Parking is $6. Christmas by Lamplight is $28/person without the dinner.

Directions: Located at the corner of Steeles Ave. and Jane St. (east of Hwy 400 and south of Hwy 407). The entrance is east of Jane St.

KID'S CHRISTMAS STABLE

Bethlehem live

There's a commotion when we pass the gates of Bethlehem as a woman is zigzagging through the crowd, her hands filled with stolen jewels. She's tying to escape the Roman guards running after her. The marketplace smells of lamb's wool, straw and olives. Everywhere we look, people are tending to their trade, making bread or pottery, fetching well water, weaving fabric and tending to the animals. It makes us forget we are indoors!

Kids Christmas Stable is an ambitious local event, which has become a tradition for hundreds of families in the Burlington area. And let me tell you they put on quite a show!

Our kids are given a small apron to collect tokens throughout the visit. It makes them look like little shepherds. Inside the city, I marvel at the fact that whole sections within the church building have been wrapped in painted canvas for the occasion. Dramatic lighting completes the overall picture.

After a long interactive tour of the marketplace with our guide, we spend half an hour in the animal corral (the beautiful animals of the Ken Jen Petting Zoo) before our group is lead through the second part of the adventure by an innkeeper.

What follows is a series of scenes with volunteers lip-syncing or simply acting to a voice-over. We see Mary, Joseph, baby Jesus (not a real one!), angels and shepherds, many of them children doing a good job.

We're taken to a carpenter's shop.

He's making crosses and explains how Jesus is the real Christmas gift, a message that is reinforced in a larger room where all the kids are invited to sit on the floor.

As I am wondering if many of those attending this event ever go to church, I hear our host asking the children if they know who Jesus is, and a 9-year-old boy answering: "Oh yeah, I saw him in a movie once and he killed lots of people!" The nice man didn't lose a beat, laughed and kept going.

One thing is for sure, whatever your faith, this event is a good way to start a family discussion on religion.

There's more to it than I can describe here: the "time machine" to get to Bethlehem, the centurions with handless phones, the collected tokens used to make bracelets, the free family magazines and small New Testament give-away...

When we reach a vast high-ceilinged room we are welcomed by the music of a piano player and volunteers awaiting us with plates filled with yummy desserts. Kids even get to decorate their own cookies.

Later on, we catch a cool play inside the impressive modern church.

Teenager actors were given great latitude for this play. They reach the stage on skateboards. They talk about "the three wise dudes" while explaining in their own way the ABC's of Faith. We also see a humourous sketch involving a family so busy with all the Christmas commercial hype they're missing the meaning of it.

Told you it was ambitious!

TIPS (fun for 5 years +)

• Their gift shop offers a great selection of **Christmas** and other spiritual books and music for the whole family.

• After your visit, I suggest you drive down Brant Street towards the lake to see the **Burlington Festival of Lights** in Spencer Smith Park. It usually starts on the first Sunday in December and goes until early January. It includes over 30 displays, some of them in motion. You'll see a helicopter, dolphins, seals, dinosaurs... (905) 333-9868, www. burlingtonfestivaloflights.com.

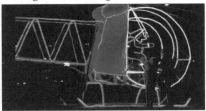

• See **Easterbrook's Foot Long Hot Dog & Ice Cream** on p. 435.

Kid's Christmas Stable
• Burlington
(905) 336-5445 or
(905) 336-0500 (church)
www.kidschristmas.org

E-2
S-W
of Toronto
50-min.

 Schedule: Usually on the first weekend of December, Friday from 5:30 to 7:30 pm, Saturday from 9:30 am to 5 pm and Sunday from 1:30 to 3:30 pm. Call to confirm.

 Admission: Around $10/adults, $6/children, $29/family.

Directions: Park Bible Church, 1500 Kerns Rd. in Burlington. Take QEW then exit at Brant St. northbound. Turn west at the North Service Rd. and north on Kerns.

Cullen's Festival of Lights

path, much to my little elves' delight, towards the least manicured attraction on site: a series of wood-carved Christmas characters displayed along the border of a small forest.

A large cage holding live deer marks the beginning of a trail that takes visitors along a series of scenes, complete with soundtrack, depicting the Bethlehem walk.

Festival of Lights

Cullen Gardens in winter is an altogether different and wonderful experience. Throughout the property, the walkways, bushes, pine trees and cottages are all lavishly dressed with Christmas lights that reflect their colourful hues on the snow. A large train of lights sits suspended above us, and everywhere the sound of Christmas carols accompanies us.

We were most impressed by the life-size scenes of Mary following Joseph on a donkey's back, and the shepherds under the gaze of an angel before them. Real sheep and donkeys bring to life a representation of the nativity.

A life-size replica of a deer and horse-pulled sleighs sit invitingly by the village exit. Further, a clever display of giant Christmas cards catches our attention. Here a "bonfire" glows against a starry night. There, a tree shimmers with decorations. We continue onto a steep

Our outing comes to an end with a visit inside Santa's workshop, where he and his elves await us. But not before enjoying an outdoor game of hide-and-go-seek and hilarious snapshots of my children posing behind a series of "faceless" wooden characters.

TIPS (fun for 3 years +)

• A visit to **Lynde House** is included in your entry fee. The 1856 residence is outfitted with animated mannequins. During **Christmas** time, *Twas the Night Before Christmas* comes alive .

• During the winter, I suggest you visit Cullen Gardens around 3:30 pm for good daylight photos. You may wish to have a second tour at 5 pm to enjoy the lights in their full splendour. Between the tours, visit Lynde House and Santa. Darkness falls as early as 5:15 pm. Be cautious as some paths can be slippery.

• Be warned. If like us, you visit after a snowfall, the miniature displays (built to 1/12 scale) may be covered by snow accumulation!

• There are **fireworks** on **New Year's Eve.**

• The Village snack bar is open throughout the year. There's nightly entertainment in it during the festival (except on December 24).

• More on **Cullen Gardens** on p. 116.

Cullen Gardens & Miniature Village	C-4 East of Toronto 45-min.
· Whitby (905) 686-1600 www.cullengardens.com	

Schedule: The Festival of Lights runs from mid-November to beginning of January, from 10 am to 10 pm. Closed December 25, closes at 9 pm on December 24.

Admission and Directions: See Cullen Gardens on p. 116.

JOURNEY OF LOVE

First Christmas

I wish I could tell you to go to the great outdoor re-enactments of the First Christmas I have seen in Stouffville, with the "Bethlehem Live" organized by the Christian Blind Mission or near Lake Simcoe, with the "Walk to Bethlehem" organized by the Cedarvale Church of the Nazarene. But unfortunately, these events are now things of the past.

On the other hand, I learned that the event which originally inspired the Blind Mission, Journey of Love, still takes place every year in Stayner. Here's your opportunity to enter into the Nativity story with your children. From my experience, it is bound to be an "interactive" show!

On the two occasions we attended such an event, we were "part" of a family going to Bethlehem, to see for themselves if rumours that the Messiah was born were true. A Good Samaritan or a "family member" led us. We were intercepted by menacing Roman soldiers controlling the roads by bonfires (which never failed to catch my kids' attention!).

Along our journey, we encountered costumed actors of all ages: shepherds, beggars, poor children, sick people and angels, all volunteers. (Both times, I tried

to make the gloomy tax collector laugh without success; some volunteers have real acting talents.)

After searching throughout Bethlehem, we would fail to find lodging for the night. Someone then would suggest we sleep in a barn, where we would be fortunate enough to meet the Holy Family, heated by a donkey or an ox... and heat lamps.

Both times, it was moving to see a genuine babbling infant in a manger, with his true parents (who had bravely agreed to play Mary and Joseph for the occasion) gazing at him. Any child having observed a crèche would make the connection!

Journey of Love is similar. A guide leads you to pay your taxes. Along the trail through the tall pine trees of a campground, you get to meet prophets, wise men, shepherds, angels and the Holy Family (without a real baby unfortunately).

Hot chocolate and cookies complete the half-hour-long outing, served in a welcoming ambience.

Journey of Love • Stayner (705) 428-2619	B-2 N-W of Toronto 95-min.

 Schedule: Usually the last Thursday to Sunday in November from around 6 to 9:30 pm.
Admission: FREE (donation box).
Directions: Evangelical Missionary Church Campground, 230 Scott St., Stayner. From Hwy 400 North, take exit #98/Hwy 27 then follow Hwy 26 towards Stayner and take Scott St. northbound.

TIPS (fun for 5 years +)

• I just learned about the nativity re-enactment at the **Country Heritage Village** in Milton, read the tips section on p. 406.

NIAGARA'S FESTIVAL OF LIGHTS

Courtesy of E. Ritson

An enlightening discovery

It's ironic that Niagara Falls should be a viable family destination given all the jokes that refer to it as the honeymooners' haven. Yet, this is what you get with the Winter Festival of Lights.

Created over fifteen years ago, the Niagara Winter Festival of Lights comes to life at dusk. Nightfall brings twenty lighted animated scenes (many representing Walt Disney characters), in a park facing the Falls.

The waterfalls themselves are lit by a powerful system, with sweeping colour spots that change throughout the evening. The light reflects nicely on the surrounding ice-laden trees.

It is preferable to take your car to view the scenes on **Dufferin Islands**, located south of the Niagara Parkway, bordering the Falls. Most visitors observe the displays from their car, and traffic is understandably slow on the small road that travels the islands. You can stop in certain areas along the road, if you manage to find a spot. In addition to the lovely displays (such as Noah's Ark), we spotted an owl in lights perched on a tree and a small sparkling doe behind a bush, when we visited.

TIPS (fun for 3 years +)

• The Festival of Lights includes an outdoor show on a stage next to the light displays most Saturdays at 7:30 pm.

• I strongly recommend you arrive in **Niagara Falls** at the beginning of the afternoon to enjoy the wealth of family attractions available in the area.

• I have visited many other festivals of lights (see **Burlington's** on p. 201). All of them offer smaller and fewer displays than Niagara's Festival. Regardless of the size, displays are done following the same concept of lights fixed on a metal frame outlining a flat scene. These smaller festivals are worth a visit when located near another attraction. They are pretty after a snow fall.

• My favourite festival of lights is at **Cullen Gardens**. It is small yet beautiful and includes a series of activities for a more interactive outing (see p. 202).

Niagara Falls Winter Festival of Lights
• Niagara Falls
(905) 374-1616

E-4
Niagara
Region
90-min.

www.tourismniagara.com

Schedule: From mid-November until mid-January, 5 to 11 pm.
Admission: FREE (voluntary contribution suggested during outdoor shows).
Directions: See Niagara Falls on p. 302.

FIRST NIGHT TORONTO

Happy New Year!

The first First Night originated in Boston in 1976. It was started by a group of artists who sought an alternative way to celebrate New year's Eve. The original concept has served as a model for over 130 similar events worldwide, one of which is here in Toronto.

Initially, First Night was held at **Harbourfront Centre**. There was something irresistible about little penguins falling on their bums during the ice skating performances. It just seemed to put us in the right spirit to start the new year.

In the last years, the event was taking place at the **SkyDome**. Those who thought the outdoor version was too cold welcomed the all-indoor celebration. Different venues offer

different advantages but you can pretty much count on an Imagination Market, in the spirit of the original concept, where families can create hats and masks for an eventual parade in the company of musicians, clowns, jugglers and maybe even giant puppets.

Several family shows are usually offered throughout the event such as wacky and dramatic magicians, famous children performers and special clowns.

The Children's Finale (actually a "mini-midnight") normally takes place on December 31 before 9 pm, to allow the youngest to celebrate. The one I attended was lively and engaged public participation by an entertainer wacky enough to make the audience dance until the "count down".

Those who wait for the real count-

down will be treated with some pyrotechnic effects following groovy musical entertainment. Happy New Year!

Both venues offered rides accessible for an extra fee (the **SkyDome** was obviously able to hold more of these).

First Night Toronto (416) 341-3143 www.firstnighttoronto.ca	**Dowtown Toronto**

 Schedule: Varies depending on the venue but always includes December 31. In the last years, it spread over 6 consecutive days. Call for exact dates.

 Admission: Will vary depending on the venue. Call to confirm. In 2003, it was $12.50/person per day plus cost of rides.

Directions: ATTENTION! The location of this event may vary from one year to the next but it always remains in the downtown Toronto area. Call for current location.

General tips about
Indoor playgrounds:

- Even in the middle of the summer when they're wearing sandals, always have socks handy for your kids when visiting an indoor playground. Some sell them on the premises but many don't!
- Most playgrounds' bread & butter comes from birthday parties so it happens that they close earlier to accommodate such parties. In some cases, the playgrounds create special events for the benefit of their regular customers, with an extra fee involved. They often request people book in advance for these events. Bottom line: always call before going to an indoor playground.

INDOOR
PLAYGROUNDS

See **Amazon Indoor Playground** on p. 212.

DROP-IN CENTRES

Just drop in!

My preschooler rushes to the sand box, what a treat given that we are in the middle of winter! She then embarks on a creative game with her 3-year-old friend, involving a doll house, an army of plastic animals and a tow truck. Meanwhile, I sit in the baby section surrounded by age-appropriate toys and play with my friend's infant who lies on a floor cushion.

Drop-in centres vary in size, activities and members' involvement. Yet, all offer an opportunity for preschoolers and their parents or caregivers to meet other children and grown-ups and enjoy informal playtime. Kids also love the opportunity to play with toys different from those at home.

In most of the drop-ins I have visited, there was a kindergarten feeling to the place; from the layout of the room with their craft and snack tables, to an array of well categorized toys. Most mornings, there is a circle time where adults and children are encouraged to sing or listen to a story. A healthy snack is usually provided in each of the morning and afternoon sessions.

TIPS (fun for 5 years and under)

• Call the **Metro Association of Family Resources Programs** to find the closest drop-in in your area. If it is not to your liking, try the next closest to you. Once you find one you like, adopt it! You and your child will eventually create a valuable network of friends.

• The biggest drop-in I have visited lately (the one shown in the pictures) is the **Applegrove Centre**, located at 60 Woodfield Rd., near Queen Street E., (416) 461-8143. It offers interesting craft activities, marker and play-dough tables, felt and magnetic boards, a painting corner, puzzles, all sorts of blocks, a ton of plastic animals, and baby and toddler toys. It also offers a toy and book library, a baby section outfitted with sofas, a room filled with costumes, climbing structures and short basketball nets. Call to confirm hours of operation.

Metro Association of Family Resources Programs
(416) 463-7974

Schedule: Many are open during school time only.
Admission: FREE.
Directions: All around Toronto.

PLAYGROUND PARADISE

A divine mural

Playground Paradise's walls and ceiling are covered by a magnificent painted birch forest. The mural successfully gives an intimate feel to this vast area. This meadow-like atmosphere brightens up gloomy days.

Two-thirds of the space is occupied by a two-storey play structure designed to get muscles working. Children can circulate underneath it. Inside, there is an 8000-ball pool with targets, as well as spiral and straight slides.

I was charmed by several of the place's original features: a rail to fly with, hanging on to the handle, a distorting mirror, big punching bags and long talk tubes used as a telephone system to chat from one crawl tube to the other.

The rest of the space includes a my-

riad of vinyl shapes used by children to build shelters. For preschoolers, there's a Duplo table, a wide activity board and a few abacus tables.

There are only a few benches for parents to sit on. Instead of sitting on the ground, you might as well... join the kids on the play structures!

TIPS (fun for 3 years +)
- Socks are required for everyone.
- This playground remains open during most of the **Christmas** holidays and through the whole **March Break**.
- They offer the cheapest birthday party package in town but you need to reserve way in advance.
- They have a small spray pad with a giant flower on the side of the building. Bring bathing suits... and sun screen (there's no shade).
- The playground offers an affordable snack bar and machines.

NEARBY ATTRACTIONS

Playground Paradise
· North York
(416) 395-6014

**I-10
North**
of downtown
20-min.

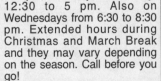

Schedule: At the time of print, hours were the following: Monday and Wednesday, 9:30 am to noon, Tuesday, 2 to 4:30 pm, Thursday and Friday,1 pm to 4 pm, Saturday and Sunday, 12:30 to 5 pm. Also on Wednesdays from 6:30 to 8:30 pm. Extended hours during Christmas and March Break and they may vary depending on the season. Call before you go!

Admission: (cash only) $2 per hour per child, FREE for accompanying adults.

Directions: 150 Grenoble Dr., North York. From Don Mills Rd. (south of Eglinton), turn east on Gateway Blvd.

KIDSWORKS

They'll dig that one!

Fifty tons of indoor sand untouched by cats, dogs or raccoons! Huge castle-like climbing structure with long slides to land in the sand complete with a twelve-foot climbing wall. All makes for a unique indoor playground.

I chose to include the place in my guide even though they're not open to the public most of the week because I loved their choice of covering half their playground with sand. There is plenty of sandy playground outdoors but the novelty of seeing it indoors makes it fun.

There's also a toddler centre with bouncing inflated castle, swings, wavy tracks (plastic slides toddlers ride down on sturdy vehicles) and train table. Stools are lined up along the sandy play area for parents' convenience. A dragon stares at the kids playing and lovely decorations adorn the reception area.

TIPS (fun for 8 years and under)

• Access to climbing wall's upper part might be restricted.
• They sell coffee and juices. They also put the next door caterer's menu up, from which you can order.
• One of the owners of this playground is also a partner in **Fantasy Castle**, a whimsical party place located next door! Their birthday packages are expensive but judging by the pictures on their web site, the space is gorgeous and parties allow for action and dress-up fun. Check www.fantasycastletoronto.com, (416) 422-2253, 105 Vanderhoof Avenue, Unit 8, Toronto.

NEARBY ATTRACTIONS
Vanderhoof Skatepark (2-min.)....p. 366

KidsWorks
(416) 483-1367
www.
kidsworkstoronto.com

I-10
North
of downtown
25-min.

Schedule: Open for drop-in Tuesday to Friday, 9:30 am to 3 pm (reserved for birthday parties at other times).

Admission: $7/first child, $5/for each additional child.
Directions: 105 Vanderhoof Ave., Unit 5, Toronto (one street south of Eglinton, east off Laird).

It's Playtime

Serious play going on

The narrow facade is misleading. The place is big, with an additional room attached to the back, giving us even more room to play. The range of activities is quite vast, from imagination games with a playhouse, small toys and costumes, to physical play, with climbing wall and wooden structure.

Here, the layout is different; more like a house school than an indoor playground. From the room with toys lined up on shelves, I see the costume corner and the furnished playhouse painted with leaves and wood. I can also peek into the adjacent room with sofa and large square table fit with small chairs.

Murals line the walls and a wooden climbing structure with slide stands in the middle of the main room, in front of the climbing wall. There's an aquarium with fish on the other side, right next to the karaoke machine playing kids' songs.

The owner is on the floor; unaware I'm here to write about the place. She's playing with a toddler and engaged in conversation with a preschooler while she keeps an eye on the baby sleeping in a bassinet. She's so good with them, I'm sure they're her kids! Then, I see their moms returning for them.

The place offers babysitting as well as Play Group allowing children to socialize without their parents! It involves singing, storytelling, playtime, and arts & crafts.

TIPS (fun for 7 years and under)

• You don't need to subscribe to the drop-off Play Group sessions for a series of days. Your child may attend only one half-day or the whole day (ending at 3:30 pm). They will take you on the spot if they have availability but I suggest you call ahead to reserve a spot.

• They offer different programs such as beginner's Mandarin classes and group piano lessons.

• Babysitting is $10 per hour for one child and $16 per hour for two children.

• They don't sell snacks. Bring your own.

It's Playtime
(416) 465-6688
http://members.rogers.com/itsplaytime

I-10 North of downtown 20-min.

Schedule: Open for drop-in Monday to Friday, 8:30 am to 5:30 pm (call ahead to confirm, sometimes open only from 9:30 am to 4:30 pm). Drop-off Play Group offered Monday to Friday, from 9:30 am to 11:30 am or from 9:30 am to 3:30 pm. Birthday parties during the weekends.

Admission: (Tax not included) Drop-in is $7/one child, $12/two children, Play Group is $17/morning or $32 for full day.

Directions: 1425 Danforth Ave., Toronto (on the south side of Danforth, west of Coxwell Ave.).

AMAZON INDOOR PLAYGROUND

They're at that stage...

I watch my little butterfly flash by me and disappear into the climbing structure. A moment later, she reappears in the... eye of a huge monkey's head.

This place is special. It is one of the few I have visited that offers costumes to play dress up and the only one with a small stage, complete with background curtains to fire up children's imaginations.

A puppet theatre comes as a bonus. This indoor playground also comes with the big climbing structure supporting the monkey head, ball pits, soft blocks and rider toys with some space to circulate.

I liked the large bay windows and pretty jungle decorations. Parents are allowed in the structure. Or they can rest on the large sofas.

TIPS (fun for 7 years and under)
- Socks are mandatory.
- They offer complimentary coffee and tea and sell candy.
- Check the ice cream shop **Dutch Dream** (10-minute walk away) on p. 433.

NEARBY ATTRACTIONS
Winston Churchill Park (5-min.)...p. 388

Amazon Indoor Playground
(416) 656-5832
www.
amazonindoorplayground.com

I-10
North
of downtown
25-min.

Schedule: Open September to June, Monday to Friday from 10 am to 3 pm. In July and August, open Monday to Thursday, noon to 4 pm. Note that additional playtimes or schedule changes are posted on their answering machine each week.

Admission: $8.50/first child with one adult, $5/for each additional child, $2/each additional adult, $5/under one year old.

Directions: 21 Vaughan Rd., Unit 108, Toronto (located on a v-shaped block south of St. Clair West, at the corner of Bathurst St., in front of Wychwood Library).

THE KIDSWAY

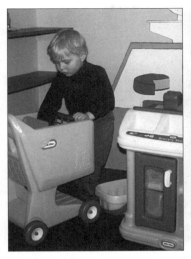

Life on a mini scale

When he was three years old, my little brother, seeing his mother suffering from a painful attack, hurried to get his medical kit to relieve her while the ambulance was coming. That's when I understood how seriously children take role-playing games. The owners of Kidsway also clued in to this, with the creation of an indoor street, scaled perfectly to its miniature visitors.

TIPS (fun for 7 years and under)
- Socks are mandatory.
- A **sitter service** is offered on Tuesdays and Thursdays, from 9:30 am to 3:30 pm, for 3 hours maximum; $10/hour for one child ($15/hour for 2 children). Available for children 2 to 7 years old. Call to reserve a spot.
- On Saturdays and Sundays, your child can also get a **haircut** for $12 on the premises, comfortably seated on a big chair strategically placed in front of her favourite video. Call to make appointment.
- The neighbourhood is packed with great boutiques, such as the superb children's bookstore **Mabels Fables**, only a minute walk west of Kidsway.
- Snacks are available.

Children fidget impatiently as they enter Kidsway; they sense this is a different kind of store. Those who can't stand the noise level of vast indoor playing fields can be reassured; the place is quiet, well-lit and intimate.

The concept is simple, yet not an obvious one. Lovely displays that incorporate the best products of the Little Tikes line, have been created to encourage creative play. You will find, side-by-side, a little house fully equipped with kitchen, dining room and living room on the second floor, a beauty salon that can accommodate a few clients, a garage (tools and hard-hat included), a grocery store (a real hit with my aspiring home economist) outfitted with food carts and produce displays.

You will also find a grey carpeted road, with its miniature cars and gas pump, sitting against a green carpet. Distorting mirrors, a couple of computers equipped with great software packages, games for the very young, a basketball hoop, a multicoloured ballroom and other similar outlets for energy surplus are also found at the Kidsway.

PEANUT CLUB (ETOBICOKE)

Nuts about play

Lots of kids know the club owner by his first name (which says a lot about the tone of the place).

The space is big and absolutely spotless, and is one of a few with children's books on a shelf. Great attention has been paid to the layout, with low walls and climbing structures placed in an angle that breaks the monotony of the big rectangular space.

The pretty mural featuring trees and animals is nicely placed by the picnic tables in the eating section.

This Peanut Club offers a virtual tour on their web site.

Peanut Club	**I-9**
· Etobicoke	**N-W**
(416) 245-1459	**of downtown**
www.thepeanutclub.com	**25-min.**

Schedule: Monday to Friday, 9:30 am to 3:30 pm. Saturday, 9:30 am to 12 noon. Closes at 1 pm on weekdays during the summer, call to confirm.

Admission: $7/per child for the day ($5 for one sibling).

Directions: 1500 Royal York Rd.,Etobicoke (north of Eglinton).

PEANUT CLUB (NORTH YORK)

Monkey fun

The climbing structure is original. Here, the train track runs around and under it, with pirate-like rigging and a spinning device above the ball section. An enclosure with a wall to wall castle interior holds all the toys to play house. It creates a feeling of intimacy quite appreciated by little homemakers.

Peanut Club	**I-10**
· North York	**N-W**
(416) 782-8735	**of downtown**
www.peanutclub.com	**25-min.**

Schedule: Monday to Friday, 9:30 am to 3:30 pm. Closes at 1:30 pm during the summer, call to confirm.

Admission: $8/per child.

Directions: 2788 Bathurst St., North York (south of Lawrence).

PLAY-A-SAURUS

Kids slide into the huge ball pit filled with turquoise, pink and purple balls that match the decor. There's enough room for the big plastic structures and children can move along easily in the small vehicles.

In the southern location, there's a huge central play structure with ball pit. A few motorized vehicles are put at the disposal of young drivers. In another corner, a playhouse is equipped with all imaginable household appliances and assorted accessories. Outside the playhouse, a fence gives the illusion of a garden. This area boasts games for toddlers. You'll also find an indoor merry-go-round.

So pretty!

In general, the largest, noisiest playgrounds do little to cater to the needs of preschoolers. Others choose to target this clientele. Both Play-A-Saurus playgrounds, under the same administration, are among the prettiest.

I fell for the zany murals that cover whole walls in each of them. In both places, the studied decor helps create an intimate ambience. An intelligent layout allows parents to watch their brood at all times, without difficulty.

Their northern location is lovely, from the turquoise ceiling to the colourful murals covering the walls. Huge dinosaurs relax on the couch painted above the parents' section. Other dinosaurs on the mural seem as busy as the kids on the floor.

As my friend's son fills up his car at the gas pump, my small paleontologist leads a team of prehistoric figures under the large climbing structure.

Play-A-Saurus
• Mississauga
South: (905) 274-1133
North: (905) 828-7088

Admission: $8/day for the first child, $4/siblings. Special May to September: $6 per child on Mondays and Fridays.

Schedule: Open Monday to Friday, 9:30 am to 3:30 pm (extended hours during the summer. Call to confirm).

Directions: South: The Shoppes of Lorne Park #9, 1107 Lorne Park Rd., Mississauga. Take QEW West, exit at Mississauga Rd. (exit #130) southbound. Turn west on Lakeshore Rd., then Lorne Park Rd. northbound (I-8 on map).

North: 3355 The Collegeway (Units 30 & 31), Mississauga. From QEW West, take exit #124/Winston Churchill northbound. Turn west on The Collegeway (I-7 on map).

TIPS (fun for 7 years and under)
• Socks are required at all times.
• The playgrounds regularly invite favourite characters for special days during **Halloween**, **Christmas**, **Easter** and more. On those days, admission cost is $10 per child ($13 if event includes food). Call for exact dates and to reserve. Also call around those dates to find out if regular drop-in takes place.
• They sell snacks.

NEARBY ATTRACTIONS
Rattray Marsh..............................p. 318

Also see **High Park** outdoor playground on p. 322.

KIDSPORTS

Fun network

Once again, a net partition separates us from our destination: a net corridor with deep holes filled with balls, located on the top level of the 3-storey-high structure. Finding the right entrance to get there is a real mind game and it's part of the fun.

Colourful houses dressed in turquoise, fuchsia, corals and blues mark the food area by Kidsports' entrance.

The apparent low height of the building from the outside is misleading because the interior is designed in split levels, with the play area actually nestled below ground level.

The impressive indoor climbing structure is topped with a bright papier mâché dragon. It is the best climber we have tried!

Adults and kids alike crouch to climb from one level of a net labyrinth to the next. It is the only way to reach the many slides, fire poles, tunnels, corridors outfitted with punching bags and ball rooms located in the vertical maze. (Grown-ups beware: the nets are hard on the feet.) Some twenty token machines are scattered around the structure, including an air hockey table which could make a few tokens go a long way!

There is a smaller structure for younger kids at the other end of the building, as well as a room filled with big toys and gym cushions ideal for toddlers.

TIPS (fun for 1 year +)

• The combination of hundreds of happy kids and token machines in action creates high decibels.
• Most machines reward the players with tickets they can trade for trinkets at a counter. This is an irresistible concept for kids over 5 years old. I strongly suggest you budget an additional $3 to $5 per child to give them the pleasure of winning something ($10 gets 40 tokens). Kidsports conveniently offers gadgets you can get for only a few tickets.

NEARBY ATTRACTIONS
Centennial Park (5-min.)..............p. 233
Pearson Int'l Airport (10-min.)......p. 234

Kidsports
· Mississauga
(905) 624-9400
www.
toronto.com/kidsports

**I-8
West
of Toronto
35-min.**

Schedule: Open 7 days, 10 am to 8 pm (June to September, closes at 7 pm on Sundays. October to May, closes at 9 pm on Fridays).

Admission: $8/children 3 years and up, $5/under 3 years, $2/under one year, FREE for adults.

Directions: 4500 Dixie Rd., Mississauga (south of Eglinton).

CHUCK E. CHEESE

Games on the menu

At first, the place looks like a well-staffed family restaurant (which it is). Then, the noise level reminds you this is an amusement centre above all!

As we get settled in a booth located by a huge maze structure of tubes and tunnels, we notice an army of kids free-roaming the site. Between the short, free-of-charge shows, the climbing structure (where adults are also welcome) and some 40 token machines (most of them requiring only one token), the kids had enough fun to spare (allowing me the luxury of a few chapters in the book I had the good foresight to bring!).

Food is ordered at the counter but

waiters serve at your table. Fries are served in a cone on a star-shaped holder with side dips (make them taste better), much to my little one's delight.

While her brother is enthralled by the machines, my daughter climbs next to Chuck E. Cheese and dances along as the big plush mechanical mouse sings a lively tune with its musicians. A video clip is shown on a couple of monitors by the stage and every song is followed by a five minute shut down of the mechanical band. Let's party!

TIPS (fun for 3 years +)

• Tickets are dispensed from the machines according to the player's skill. Tickets can also be exchanged for trinkets.

• I suggest you avoid these types of outings unless you are prepared to spend a few dollars on tokens. Even with dollars in hand, it seems you need loads of tickets to win anything remotely interesting (to you). As for my kids, all they really wanted was to win something... anything!

• We visited during **Christmas** time and the Chuck E. Cheese band's songs and clips were in the Christmas spirit.

• Pizza is Chuck E. Cheese's specialty. There is also a salad bar and hot sandwiches. Some value packages are real savers if you intend to buy tokens.

Chuck E. Cheese
www.chuckecheese.com

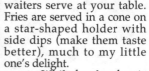

Schedule: Most locations are open daily, 9 am to 10 pm (closing at 11 pm on Fridays and Saturdays).

Admission: FREE (free refills on all soft drinks).

Directions:
Scarborough: 2452 Sheppard Ave. East (from Hwy 401, exit at Victoria Park Ave. northbound, turn west on Victoria Park), (416) 497-5224 (I-11 on map).

Mississauga: 4141 Dixie Rd., Rockwood Mall (south of Rathburn Rd.), (905) 602-5502 (I-8 on map).

Whitby: 75 Consumer Dr. (from Hwy 401, take exit #412/Thickson Rd. northbound, turn west on Consumer Dr.), (905) 430-7420 (C-4 on map).

Cambridge: 42 Pine Bush Rd. (from Hwy 401, take exit #282/Hespeler Rd. southbound, turn east on Pine Bush), (519) 621-7752 (E-1 on map).

NEVER-NEVER LAND

Never-never rest

It looks like the play area of a McDonalds's except in a much bigger version. The rooms are filled with colourful huge structures, tunnels, ball pits, slides, plexiglass spheres from which kids wave at their parents and lots of nooks and crannies in which to hide.

The two locations baring the same name offer the same concept of big rooms with large equipment to let kids' energy (and their parents') wind down. I visited the Dufferin playground with my daughter and she never rested for a moment. There was a corridor of punching bags, slides landing in ball pits, bouncing castle, large vinyl upholstered bumper slide and lots of new excited kids to befriend.

The Dufferin location has two rooms: one for kids up to 4 years and the other for children 5 to 9. The one on Jane Street includes three rooms: one for those under 3, a 3-7 room and a 5-10 years section.

TIPS (fun for 2 years +)

• They sell hot dogs, pizza and snacks. There are many tables.
• Near the Dufferin location, there's a big Italian family restaurant called **Park Place** offering a wide range of choices at affordable prices, 8700 Dufferin Street, Units 10 & 11, (905) 669-0366.

Never-Never Land Indoor Playground
• Concord
(905) 761-1166
www.
neverneverlandindoorplayground.com

H-10
N-W
of Toronto
35-min.

Schedule: Open for drop-in Tuesday to Friday, 10 am to 3 pm. ATTENTION! Jane location is closing for renovation. Call for re-opening date during summer 2004.
Admission: $6/child.
Directions: Both locations are located north of Hwy 407 and one block northwest of Langstaff Rd., at 8700 Dufferin St., Unit 20 and 8520 Jane St.

J.J.'s Kids Centres

J.J.'s Kids Centres "unlimited"

Kids sit atop a small stage in the movie viewing room, snacking heartily on their popcorn. Everyone is free to move around and re-stock on popcorn, slush, pop, and tea and coffee in the adjacent kitchen. A craft table nearby stirs their interest, and soon my children leave the video to begin a collage. Then, it's off to climb a fun play structure in the next room.

The play area is well organized and every inch is well used. It includes an original "beer roller" (a long slide made of metal rollers we sometimes see at the supermarket), which provides great acceleration.

From the multicoloured balls section, you can climb into small "secret" wooden houses. Since my last visit, the owners have added a system of pipes to allow kids to talk to each other. Among other things, you will also find fun rubber walls to bounce off.

To the delight of my "pre-adolescent" we realized that the admission fee gives us unlimited access to over thirty video games and pinball machines in a large room adjacent to the play area.

Younger children will enjoy a large abacus, a Duplo table, small Little Tikes vehicles, a log cabin, a well equipped kitchenette and, last but not least, shelving generously stocked with books and toys (replaced on a regular basis).

To top it off, children get a little free gift upon leaving, choosing from a large selection of items and treats. This great bonus helped me convince my little guys it was time to leave after two fun-filled hours.

Since our last visit, the owners have added fun new equipment, including a net allowing kids to climb from the floor to the ceiling.

TIPS (fun for 1 year +)
- Socks are required at all times.
- The admission fee includes **babysitting**! Parents with children aged 2 and over can opt to leave them under the care of playground staff. (I took advantage of this option once my child was used to the place.) It allows us to shop at The Bay, Loblaws, Canadian Tire, Zellers and some sixty boutiques at **Centrepoint Mall** (416) 222-6255. It is best to call ahead during Christmas and March Break.
- You access the playground via the entrance next to the **Pickle Barrel** restaurant. There is an elevator.

NEARBY ATTRACTIONS
Gibson House (10-min.)..............p. 403

J.J.'s Kids Centres
- North York
(416) 512-8122

**H-10
North
of downtown
35-min.**

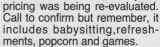

Schedule: Open Monday, Tuesday and Thursday to Saturday, from 10 am to 5 pm. Closed Wednesday. (Evenings and Sundays are available for private parties.)
Admission: At the time of print, pricing was being re-evaluated. Call to confirm but remember, it includes babysitting, refreshments, popcorn and games.
Directions: Centrepoint Mall, upper level, Yonge St., North York (south of Steeles Ave.).

WOODIE WOOD CHUCK'S

A kid-friendly interior

There's a major heat wave going on, and your house is not air-conditioned. The children are bursting with energy, but it's raining cats and dogs and the neighbourhood playground looks like a duck pond. So many good reasons to resort to the services of large playgrounds such as that of Woodie Wood Chuck's!

Neon lights, machine noises and children's screams bouncing off cement walls, all combine in a cacophony for the senses that makes me want to turn around as soon as we step in. A quick glance at my child's excited look convinces me we're here to stay... at least a couple of hours! Once I've come to terms with the idea, there are in fact several good surprises that await.

This indoor park is huge. It includes a section of sixty "pay-as-you-play" token machines, where you can test your throwing, pushing and hitting skills. Woodie Wood Chuck's main attraction, however, is its huge play area spread over two floors.

The imposing structure in itself is well worth the visit. Three large modules are connected by transparent tunnels or suspended bridges. All abound with hidden corners to explore. Ropes, slides, an enclosure filled with colourful balls, boxing cushions, tunnels and ladders; everything has been planned for the enjoyment of young climbers.

A note of caution however: it is very easy to lose sight of a child in this maze of corridors, and while adults are allowed on the structure, they can only go on when the playground is not too busy. Younger ones should therefore be encouraged to stay in the smaller playing area.

The place includes a small stage with mechanical characters playing in a band.

TIPS (fun for 3 years +)
• Socks are mandatory.
• Look carefully. You can't see the Scarborough location's facade from Sheppard Avenue. It faces Brimley Road.
• Both places sell pizza and include tables and booth sections. In the Scarborough location, there is also a large central area with tables, surrounded by bay windows. It is a great refuge for adults with sensitive hearing. They don't have one in the Mississauga location.

Woodie Wood Chuck's Indoor Playland
(416) 298-3555
www.woodiewoodchucks.ca

 Schedule: Monday to Thursday, 11 am to 9 pm, Friday, 11 am to 10 pm, Saturday, 10 am to 10 pm, Sunday 10 am to 9 pm.

 Admission: Only $1/child, FREE for accompanying adult.

 Directions:
Scarborough: 4466 Sheppard Ave. East (from Hwy 401 West, take exit #379/ Kennedy Rd. northbound, turn east on Sheppard. It is east of Brimley Rd (I-11 on map).

 Mississauga: 1248 Dundas St. East, west of Dixie Rd. (I-8 on map).

PLAYGROUNDS WITH INFLATABLES

Slam-bam fun

These have to be the noisiest places, with all those air pumps at work. Chances are your kids will accidentally knock each other's heads (my kids did) in the midst of such excitement! And yet, bouncing and jumping on the inflated structures remains a favourite of energetic children.

Such play centres can be a life-saver during cold winter days, and a welcome air-conditioned break during hot summer days.

Now under separate ownerships, the two centres offer similar attractions that include inflatable structures, token machines and a large food area filled with tables.

The Pickering one (the only one I have visited) also offers a glow-in-the-dark 9-hole mini-golf room with dark fluorescent mini-golf lit under black light. Beware, the mini-golf could be in use for birthday parties when you visit.

TIPS (fun for 4 years +)
• Socks are mandatory.
• Parents are not allowed on the inflatable structures. These could be suitable for kids under 4 years old only if they are very strong on their feet.
• Children have way more fun when attending places like these with friends.

Air Zone Party & Play Centre
• Pickering
(905) 839-1047

I-12
East
of Toronto
35-min.

Schedule: Open Monday to Saturday, 10 am to 8 pm. Sunday, 10 am to 6 pm.
Admission: (tax not included) $6 per child on weekends, $1 less on weekdays. Mini-golf is $3/12 years and under, $3.50/13 years and older.
Directions: 1095 Kingston Rd., Pickering (from Hwy 401, take exit #394/ Whites Rd. northbound, turn east on Kingston Rd.).

Airzone Cobourg
• Cobourg
(905) 377-9663

C-5
East
of Toronto
70-min.

Schedule: Open Monday 10 am to 3 pm (closes at 5 pm from July to September). Tuesday to Friday, 10 am to 8 pm. Saturday and Sunday, 10 am to 6 pm.
Admission: (tax not included) $6 per child on weekends, $1 less on weekdays. Tuesday special $2.50/child in play groups.
Directions: 900 Division St., Cobourg (from Hwy 401, take exit #474/Division St. southbound).

RAINBOW PLAYLAND

No hard sales!

The Rainbow Company sells fabulous wooden play structures that can be found in the best playgrounds. To help us test their products, the company opened Rainbow Playland, not a mere showcase but a genuine indoor playground.

A beautiful medieval mural, complete with castle, forest and dragons, covers the walls and ceilings of this large place and, of course, a huge Rainbow structure occupies most of the space. A movie-theatre-like video corner was set up. Several Little Tikes toys are also available. Smaller children will appreciate the padded area, equipped with a few toys and with cushions to climb on. It's conveniently located close to the area with sofas and tables set up for adults.

Rainbow Playland & Party Center • Richmond Hill (905) 886-0306 www.rainbowofontario.com	**H-11** **North** **of Toronto** **30-min.**

 Schedule: Drop-in Tuesday to Friday, 10 am to 3 pm. Call to check if not too busy!

 Admission: (cash only) $6 per child.

 Directions: 30 Fulton Way, units 5 & 6, Richmond Hill. Take Hwy 404 North, exit Hwy 7 westbound. Turn north on East Beaver Creek, then west on Fulton Way.

KIDS ZONE

Fun structure

The climbing structure in this playground is fun and original with two levels.

Among other things, it includes an area with a giant ball, a suspended bridge, a punching-bag "forest" and a pipe system allowing kids to talk from one tunnel to the next. Plus, adults are allowed to climb! The place also offers a section for smaller children with kiddie rides and arcade, a cafeteria with numerous tables and five birthday party rooms.

Since my last visit, they've added the Extreme Laser, a laser game for kids 8 to 15 years old (minimum 40 inches high at the shoulder).

Kids Zone Family Fun Centre • Whitby (905) 666-5437	**C-4** **East** **of Toronto** **40-min.**

 Schedule: Monday to Friday, 9 am to 8:30 pm. Saturday, 10 am to 8:30 pm. Sunday, 10 am to 6:30 pm. (during summer time, closes at 4 pm on Mondays and 9:30 pm Tuesday to Saturday).

 Admission: $7/child, FREE for accompanying adults. Laser game (for children 8 to 15 years old) is $7/one 30-minute session or $12 for two.

Directions: 12 Stanley Court, Whitby. From Hwy 401, take exit #410/Brock St. northbound, turn east on Consumer Dr., north on Garden St., east again on Burns St.; Stanley Court is on the right.

General tips about
Machines:

- In this chapter, you'll find attractions, events or simply places to observe things that roll, float, fly or work.

MACHINES

See **Big Brothers Soap Box Derby** on p. 232.

DOUBLE-DECKER RIDES

On top of things

"I have not had a good hair day since I started this job" claims the tour operator. I believe her. As we drive under the Gardiner, we feel quite a draft!

Olde Towne Tours (now called Hop-On Hop-Off City Tour) used to be the only ones offering this tour. Now, **Shop-Dine-Tour** offers a similar double-decker guided tour around the city, approximately 90 minutes long. **Hop-On Hop-Off** lasts two hours. Both include some 20 stops.

There are a few things you can experience only if you've taken a ride on the

top of a double-decker. You get to see the top of the TTC buses, your head is at times only a metre away from the traffic lights, and branches get close enough to brush your hair.

My daughter also enjoyed having a closer look at the CN Tower. She saw the huge characters fooling around on the SkyDome's balcony, bronze workers on top of a bridge, a restaurant's roof turned into a hockey table with rotating players and the Flatiron building's mural looking like a painting peeling off its facade.

Your ticket gives you the right to step on and off as you wish, throughout the day, at any of the stops. I recommend combining this ride with a visit to one of the attractions along the circuit: Harbourfront Centre, Hockey Hall of Fame, Royal Ontario Museum, Casa Loma and the likes (it would save you the parking fees!). Make sure you know the time of the last departure from that attraction!

TIPS (fun for 5 years +)
• You can call both operators in advance to reserve tickets and arrange for pick up at a stop along the circuit or reserve on line and print your tickets.
• Both operators tickets are valid for two consecutive days.
• This kind of ride is meant for tourists. As a Torontonian, I think too many stops take place in front of hotels in uninteresting areas to justify the ride for the sheer pleasure of admiring the city I live in. But it is really worth it if, like my son, your child has shown a fascination for double-deckers.
• **Shop-Dine-Tour** must have understood this because they offer a 50% discount to local customers who can prove they live within the 416 or 905 area codes, with a driver's license or other official piece of identification.

Shop-Dine-Tour Toronto (416) 463-7467 www. shopdinetourtoronto.com	J-10 Downtown Toronto by CN Tower

Schedule: From June 1 to mid-October, weather permitting. Check hours.
Admission: $29/adults, $26/seniors and students, $15/3-12 years old, $78/family of 4 (NOTE: 50% off for locals with proof of residency!).
Directions: Advisable to depart from the Hard Rock Café, 279 Yonge St. near the Eaton Centre.

Hop-On Hop-Off City Tour
(416) 594-3310
www.grayline.ca (click Toronto)
Schedule: From late April to mid-October, weather permitting. Check hours.
Admission: $34/adults, $30/seniors and students, $23/4-11 years old, $100/family of 4 ($15 for add. child).
Directions: Advisable to depart from Nicholby's Souvenir Shop, 123 Front St. West, near the CN Tower.

TORONTO HIPPO TOURS

It's a bus! It's a boat! No, it's a Hippo!

We notice something peculiar underneath the vehicle... Long wet weeds! You know, like the ones that can be observed at the bottom of Lake Ontario. The fact is, Hippo's drivers have to be licensed marine captains to be allowed to pilot the intriguing Canadian-made amphibious buses.

The kids are already excited by the overall look of the vehicle, adorned with colourful depictions of hippos in the water. Accessing the bus from a rear entrance just adds to the novelty. The windows are large and part of the ceiling is glassed so we know we'll get a good view of Toronto's tall buildings throughout the tour.

My young companions feel like royalty when they see the reactions our hippo gets from the people along the sidewalks. Kids are laughing and pointing at us as we pass by the Hockey Hall of Fame. We ride along Yonge Street, Parliament, University of Toronto then along McCaul Street by the AGO and the intriguing table-like architecture of the Ontario College of Art. Next, it's hip Queen Street to Bathurst and down to Ontario Place, our launching point.

It makes one feel uneasy to watch one's vehicle get nearer to the water than reason would dictate, then definitely too close... Then it's too late, we're in it with a splash, floating! We undertake our smooth ride on the lake amidst the elegant structures of Ontario Place. Our captain leads us up to the end of the channel opening into Lake Ontario.

Our guide, who's been commenting all along on Toronto's landmarks as we drove by, now cedes her front seat and microphone to a few young riders who pretend for a while they've got the job.

We leave the water with regret and

drive towards Harbourfront Centre, by Air Canada Centre and around the Sky-Dome before reaching the finish line on Front Street.

TIPS (fun for 5 years +)
• You can reserve by calling or booking on-line and printing a confirmation number.
• There's room to store strollers on the Hippo bus.

Toronto Hippo Tours
(416) 703-4476
1-877-635-5510
www.
torontohippotours.com

J-10
Downtown
Toronto
1-min.

Schedule: Open May 1 to October 31, from 11 am (last departure at 6 pm).
Admission: $35/adults, $30/seniors and students, $23/3-12 years old, $100/family of 4 ($15 for each additional child), FREE under 3 years if sitting on lap.
Directions: Departs from 151 Front St. West (near Simcoe St.), Toronto.

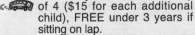

GO TRAIN RIDE

One, two, three... GO!

For children fascinated by anything on wheels, the GO Train offers the ultimate experience of a real train journey. Most importantly, it costs a fraction of the price of a regular train ride and you don't end up far from home. Lets not forget it's just as important to enjoy the scenery as it is to know where you're going!

Union Station, on Front Street, is a great starting point for a child's first ride on the GO Train. Suburban and intercity trains are next to one another and children get the chance to see imposing locomotives from up close.

Green and white signs lead us to the GO Train's ticket office and customer service department. When we stopped there to ask for information, they gave my son a few gadgets to celebrate his initiation.

After admiring a large mural decorating the outside of a railcar, we sat on

the train's second level in order to see farther. We were facing south to take in the view of Lake Ontario. Seats are very comfortable and each car is equipped with restrooms... A real train!

After analyzing GO destinations, we decided the most interesting was Pickering with the varied panorama of its itinerary: downtown skyscrapers, residential neighbourhoods, countryside and most of all, long stretches alongside Lake Ontario (and in our case, this line passes right in front of our house!). The ride to Pickering lasts 40 minutes and doesn't require a transfer. The train stops at six stations.

To prolong the excursion, you can take the local bus from Pickering Station up to the **Pickering Town Centre**. We went there to have a bite to eat, play with the toys in the Mastermind Educational shop and throw pennies in the centre's huge fountain.

TIPS (fun for 3 years +)

• A day-pass is sold at the cost of two single fares and allows one person unlimited rides between two specified zones throughout the day of purchase. This is perfect if your young travellers want to get off at different stations and catch the following train.

• To concentrate on the pleasure of the outing, I recommend that you avoid the stress of rush hour, favouring departures between 9:30 am and 2:30 pm. You'll be sure to get a window seat, as there are fewer passengers on board outside peak times! Little ones can be rambunctious without disturbing too much.

• See **Mövenpick** on p. 437.

NEARBY ATTRACTIONS
Hockey Hall (5-min. walk)..............p. 362

GO Transit (416) 869-3200 www.gotransit.com	**I-10** **Downtown** **Toronto** **10-min.**

 Schedule: Daily from early in the morning to late at night.
Costs: An adult day-pass for Union-Pickering-Union costs about $10. It is half the price for children under 12 years and FREE for one child 4 years and under per each accompanying adult.

Directions to Union Station: On Front St. (between Bay and York St.).

MODEL RAILROAD CLUB

Children are up to this attraction

Fascinated children of all ages are perched on steps running alongside the huge raised table. They watch small locomotives pulling long strings of rail-cars through villages, mountains and a harbour. Behind them, impressed adults admire the genius of miniaturization. This is the result of 180,000 hours of work by passionate people!

You can forget the metric system as everything displayed here is built to a one-forty-eighth scale! Railcars that measure 40 feet in reality barely make 10 inches. The entire set, inspired by the styles of the 1955-62 period, comprises the equivalent of 10 miles of track.

TIPS (fun for 3 years +)
• The association is located within a large complex of numbered warehouses. You can park your car relatively close to warehouse #8. You go down narrow stairs to reach the train room.
• As visitors circulate within a two-metre-wide corridor around the set, manoeuvering strollers is impossible. Comfortably nestled in my arms, my little one did not mind and was perfectly positioned to view the railway activity.
• If your kids are truly hooked and ask for more, make sure to read the association's posted notices advertising other similar events and activities held regularly by other regional associations.
• There is a food vendor on-site where beverages and snacks are available at a reasonable prices.
• More train shows on p. 442.

NEARBY ATTRACTIONS
High Park (10-min.).....................p. 322

The installation sits approximately a metre and a half off the floor. One has to actually walk around it to truly measure the magnitude of this ambitious set.

All the children in our small group easily found an observation point, changing places frequently so as to capture every angle of the fourteen moving trains. It took them more than an hour to get their visual fill!

Cargo and passenger trains, even circus trains, move along cliffs taken on by mountain climbers. They border a little harbour with its busy docks, construction sites, villages, factories and warehouses. Here, a fisherman indulges in his sport. There, a tow-truck is pulling a car out of the ditch.

Together, these contribute to making the installation incredibly realistic along with tunnels, huge suspended bridge, aqueducts, turntable, overpasses with real light signals and even a sound-track of moving trains!

Installed at the centre of the set with remote controls in hand, switchmen are directing railway traffic. They are members of the Model Railroad Club of Toronto, the over 60-year-old association responsible for this wondrous display.

Model Railroad Club of Toronto (416) 536-8927 www. modelrailroadclub.com	I-9 Downtown Toronto 15-min.

 Schedule: Call for the exact dates. Usually on the last three Sundays of February, 12 noon to 4:30 pm, call to confirm.
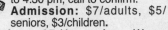 **Admission:** $7/adults, $5/ seniors, $3/children.
Directions: 37 Hanna Ave., Warehouse #8, Toronto. From King St. West, take Atlantic Ave. southbound, then Liberty St. eastbound.

KAJAMA, THE TALL SHIP

later, the Kajama left its mooring spot, motors on. The wind was blowing very gently. We headed towards Ontario Place.

Everything looked different from that angle: the amusement park, Toronto Islands, the CN Tower.

Many made a stop at the little bar to get a pop or a beer and some chips. My daughter undertook a thorough exploration of the 165-foot deck.

After a while, I noticed people were more cheerful and relaxed. Each small group seemed involved in its own little private party. Only then, did I realize the captain had shut down the engine and we were actually sailing!

Don't expect the soothing sound of the wind against the sails and the waves brushing the hull. We are in Toronto, remember? With hoards of motor boats in the harbour and planes landing and taking off at Toronto Islands Airport, when it is not helicopters flying over our heads.

Still, as my small crew member played hide-and-seek with her dad in the lower deck, I admired the sparkling blue water dotted with dozens of tiny boats right under the nose of the Kajama for the next hour. Now, that's my kind of outing!

Merely, merely...

My 5-year-old was not excited by the promise of the 7000-square-feet of sail we could potentially put up if the wind allowed, but she was thrilled when the captain summoned us with mock authority to help his crew pull the ropes to set sails!

We climbed aboard the Kajama, in the midst of a colourful and lively event at **Harbourfront**, accompanied by a whimsical chaos of music and vendors teasing the crowd, under a blasting sun. The illusion of playing tourists on some exotic cruise in the Islands was perfect.

As they came in, guests rearranged the chairs to their liking all over the large and unobstructed deck. Half an hour

TIPS (fun for 5 years +)
• Don't spend too much time trying to figure out the best spot to stay away from the sun. The boat keeps moving and so do the shadows. Bring hats!
• The return sail trip takes an hour and a half. I suggest you bring some toys if you sail with young children.
• There are many other boat tours offered in the harbour, some as low as $10, no need to pre-book. And there's always the ferry! (See **Toronto Islands** on p. 268.)

NEARBY ATTRACTIONS	
Harbourfront Centre	p. 68
Music Gardens (5-min. walk)	p. 307

Kajama
(416) 203-2322
www.tallship
cruisestoronto.com

J-10
Downtown
Toronto
5-min.

Schedule: Daily from July to Labour Day (call for schedule in June). Boardings at 11:30 am, 1:30 pm and 3:30 pm (departure half an hour later, sailing time is 90 minutes).
Admission: $20/adults, $18/seniors, $11/5 to 15 years old, FREE under 5.
Directions: Harbourfront Centre, Toronto (at the corner of Queen's Quay and Lower Simcoe St.).

See **Kajama** on p. 230.

BIG BROTHERS SOAP BOX DERBY

Big Brother is watching

The soap box cars are lined up along the top of Centre Road in High Park. Feverishly, Big and Little Brothers add the finishing touches to their creations: calibrating wheels, polishing hoods and fixing gadgets as they wait for the derby to start. Each in their own way, the kids are so proud; it is pure pleasure to read the emotion on their faces. What a fabulous project for them to undertake and for us to watch!

Two by two, in categories previously established in time trials, the young racers get ready for the signal. The small crowd at the bottom of the hill is already cheering.

The 10-year-old I am observing dries his hands on his pants before grabbing the steering wheel. His smile could not be broader. As he pushes his little racer down the hill, his Big Brother gently reminds him to lean forward to increase his chances with gravity. I laugh out loud as I read "Eat my Dust" on the Little Brother's bumper!

Many cars are pretty basic, built out of wood, screws and metal wire from a pre-made kit. This is usually a telltale

TIPS (fun for 5 years +)
• More about **High Park** on p. 322.
• More on **Toronto Big Brothers Big Sisters** on p. 126.
• See **Sunnyside Café** on p. 429.

NEARBY ATTRACTIONS
All Fired Up (15-min.)....................p. 424

sign of new Big and Little Brothers participating in their first race. Veterans have had all year to improve their vehicles.

Some cars are covered with silvery metal or aerodynamically-shaped fibreglass, others have flames painted on their sides. One ambitious Little Brother claims that next year, he'll have a radio in his car.

My son was so impressed by the cars that he started collecting recycled garbage in order to build a car of his own. Watching other boys driving cars at a soap box derby will do that to you!

Big Brothers Soap Box Derby
(416) 925-8981, ext. 4125
www.bbbst.com

I-9
West
of downtown
20-min.

Schedule: Usually a mid-September Saturday (September 11 in 2004). If raining, it takes place the following day. The whole Derby runs from 12 noon to 4:30 pm but the part where the Little Brothers compete one against the other starts at around 2 pm until 5 pm.
Admission: FREE.
Directions: Centre Rd. in High Park, Toronto (on southwest corner of Bloor St. West and Parkside Dr.).

CENTENNIAL PARK MINI-INDY

Step on it!

According to my young co-pilot, I drive my go-kart like a grandma on a Sunday outing. Since everybody is passing us, I must admit he has a point, so I step on it!

To drive on the 2km (1 1/2 mile) clover leaf track, one has to be at least 54 inches tall or 10 years of age and older. Anyone however, can be a co-pilot and ride for free.

Younger drivers (5 to 9 years old), can try their hand riding smaller cars on the kiddie track. Considering the expression on my pint-size Villeneuve, I would say he felt empowered by the whole experience!

After a couple of rides, we bought tokens to play with some 30 machines in the 3,000-sq.-ft. arcade by the ticket booth.

TIPS (fun for 5 years +)

• It is advisable to call ahead as the attractions are sometimes closed for private or corporate functions.

• At the south end of the park, you will find a big wading pool with spray pads, and a **greenhouse** you can visit for free. These are fun alternatives for little ones who can't accompany their older siblings on the go-kart rides.

• Ask about **401 Mini-Indy**, their indoor go-kart track with more powerful vehicles and Junior go-karts only children 10 to 15 years old can drive during Family Hours, located at 37 Stoffel Rd., Toronto, (416) 614-6789.

• More on **Centennial Park** during the winter on p. 389.

Centennial Park Mini-Indy
· Etobicoke

	I-9 N-W of downtown 30-min.

(416) 620-6669 (go-kart)
(416) 394-8750 (park)
www.mini-indy.com

  Schedule: Open daily mid-June through Labour Day, 11 am to 10 pm. Open on weekends in spring and fall. Call to confirm schedule when school is back.
Admission: $4/lap on the big track (passenger does not pay), $20/6 rides, $4/5 laps on the kiddie track.

Directions: From Hwy 427 North, take exit Rathburn Rd. westbound, turn north on Centennial Park Blvd. FREE parking on-site.

NEARBY ATTRACTIONS
Playdium Mississauga (20-min.)..p. 18
Pearson Int'l Airport (5-min.)........p. 234

PEARSON INTERNATIONAL AIRPORT

passenger waiting to board) is from the top of Terminal #1 parking lot (the longer you stay the more you pay).

The best way to view them for free is from Carlingview Street, a parallel street east of Hwy 427. Two

An outing that takes flight

"You're serious? You mean there is not one single viewing window in the entire airport?" I asked baffled. I squeezed my little guy's hand, glancing at him sideways checking for his reaction. Since morning I had been promising him beautiful planes and for the last half-hour had been dragging him around from one end of Pearson airport to the other, in search of an elusive viewing spot.

The disappointingly sad reality prompted me to investigate the issue. The only place in the airport where you can observe the planes (unless you are a

east-west runways share the bulk of flights. One of those borders the north side of Hwy 401. Planes that circulate on it fly just above Hwy 427.

The other east-west runway borders the south side of Derry Road and planes that circulate on it fly just above Airport Road. You can view them circulating on the ground from the huge parking lot, owned by McDonnell Douglas, adjacent to the airport. Judging by the number of cars during our visit, this is a well-known spot for serious observers with cameras.

TIPS (fun for 3 years +)

• You can see planes at closer range from outside the **Coffee Time** restaurant on Carlingview Street. Practical, isn't it? Between two planes, you can treat the kids to a snack. In the mid-afternoon to early evening, you might see a new plane every 4 to 5 minutes.

• Got a child passionate about aviation? Check the Prop Shop in **Buttonville Municipal Airport** in Markham. It is baffling to think there is no equivalent at Pearson Airport. Posters, clothes, models, pins, birthday cards, cake decorations, trinkets, puzzles, videos; it's all there, (905) 477-8100 (from Hwy 404 North, take exit #29/16th Avenue eastbound).

NEARBY ATTRACTIONS	

Pearson International Airport • Mississauga (416) 247-7678	H-9 N-W of Toronto 30-min.

Schedule: Heavy air traffic peaks daily between 3 and 7 pm, with most impressive sightings on weekends.

Admission: FREE admission to unofficial observation points.

Directions: Coffee Time is located at 215 Carlingview St., just east of Hwy 427. You reach it via Dixon Rd. eastbound. The parking lot at McDonnell Douglas is located on Airport Rd. (a west-end extension of Dixon Rd.). You reach it via Dixon Rd. westbound.

TORONTO AEROSPACE MUSEUM

This one takes off!

A huge grey aircraft with folded wings greets us at the entrance of the large hangar, the last Canadian tracker built at Downsview, initially used to detect submarines. Above our heads, an amphibian aircraft seems to fly into the adjacent hangar.

Other things displayed among the eclectic collection: the Ornithopter, an experimental craft designed by researchers from the University of Toronto to fly by flapping its wings, an aerobatic kit aircraft, a glider and a simulator from the 20's.

Volunteer staff involved with the museum are obviously skilled in collecting and restoring artifacts from the aviation heritage of the GTA but I was surprised by their visible effort to exhibit it in an interesting manner to the best of their capabilities.

If a staff member proudly shows you the full-scale replica of the Avro Arrow in construction, try to look in awe! Otherwise you're in danger of disappointing a dedicated volunteer. It turns out the Arrow has quite an intriguing story. Built around 1958, it was capable of

going at twice the speed of sound, still accelerating at over 1,000mph while climbing through 50,000 ft. Experts agreed that it was 20 years ahead of its time. Yet, the government of the time ordered the production stopped and destroyed all aircrafts and plans! An order that wasn't followed through apparently! When completed, visitors will be able to activate some basic controls on the replica.

You can watch the work-in-progress restoration of the Lancaster, a famous Second World War bomber Torontonians used to see on a pedestal in front of the CNE.

Kids will love to sit on the ejector seat but this is basically the only thing you can touch when self-exploring the museum.

In the "Blue Room" you'll find old machinery, some small jets and panels about early women pilots, competitive flying and more, along with rows of real passenger aircraft seats.

The museum is located in the original factory of the manufacturer The de Havilland Aircraft of Canada Ltd (currently Bombardier). Bombardier continues to use the adjacent runway for testing and delivery of aircraft.

TIPS (fun for 8 years +)

• Their small shop offers a wide selection of original trinkets, videos, books and models related to airplanes.
• Ask about their Summer Flight Camps for 10 years and older!

NEARBY ATTRACTIONS
Downsview Park (2-min.)..............p. 329

Toronto Aerospace Museum
(416) 638-6078
www.
torontoaerospacemuseum.com

H-10 North of downtown 35-min.

Schedule: Thursday to Saturday, 10 am to 4 pm. Sunday, noon to 4 pm.

Admission: $8/adults, $6/seniors, $5/students 6-17 years old, FREE under 6 (little extra for interesting guided tour).

Directions: 65 Carl Hall Rd., Toronto. From Hwy 401, take Allen Rd. North and turn west on Sheppard Ave. The Downsview Park's entrance is south of Sheppard and east of Keele. Take John Drury Dr. once in park and turn left on Carl Hall Rd.

RICHMOND HILL LIVE STEAMERS

I found the (rail) way!

The track site lies in a beautiful woodland setting, in harmony with the trees. From the road, we can barely see it, but can hear the whistles' wet hissing, as the small steam engines rustle along the 7 1/4-inch wide tracks.

On location, you see marvels of miniature trains, their steam puffing high; those little guys use real coal to produce their steam! At close range, you can even feel droplets coming down on your shoulders as they quickly condense; a refreshing mist on a hot summer day.

In addition to the miniature track, there are two larger tracks that cover the entire site. Many trains circulate on them, and they are conducted for the most part by contented retirees, outfitted with overalls and caps. Some of these hand-built steam engines range in cost up to $40,000. This is the achievement of some passionate members of the Richmond Hill Live Steamers, dedicated to the craft for more than twenty years.

On the central track, the shortest, the steam engines carry one passenger at a time. Conductor and passenger are literally straddling the small but solid locomotives. They go past a water tower and over a bridge. As for the track that surrounds the site, it boasts larger and stronger trains that can carry up to 16 passengers in their small cars, and travel through the forest site.

TIPS (fun for 3 years +)

• I recommend you arrive before noon to avoid long line-ups leading to the individual rides. Otherwise, we waited no more than 10 minutes for a ride on the larger train with wagons.

• For 2004, the association won't be able to welcome visitors as they used to do on Sundays from May to September, 12 noon to 3 pm, when we could find a few of the association's afficionados operating a locomotive of their creation and willing to offer a ride. Call in 2005 to see if the situation is the same.

• You can purchase juice and snacks on-site during the Open House events. Washrooms are also available.

Richmond Hill Live Steamers
• Stouffville
(416) 261-9789
www.geocities.com/
richmondhill_livesteam

G-12
N-E
of Toronto
45-min.

Schedule: Open Houses usually held the weekend after Canada Day and the weekend after Labour Day, 10:30 am to 4 pm (For 2004: July 10-11, September 11-12).
Admission: Donations appreciated.
Directions: From Hwy 404 North, take exit #45/Aurora Sideroad eastbound, turn north on McCowan Rd. (7th Concession Rd.). The site is on the west side.

CANADIAN AUTOMOTIVE MUSEUM

Hot wheels

This Museum is the only place I know where I could feed my son's passion for cars. It is probably the least interactive museum I've visited with children. But I couldn't resist including it in this guide. It is filled with over 60 vehicles from 1898 to 1980 displayed in an authentic car dealership.

The Canadian Automotive Museum (CAM) itself is not fancy. The first floor is made of cement, pipes run on the low ceilings and there's not much room for all the beautiful cars. How-

ever, memorabilia related to the different periods of vehicles make it fun to explore. Don't forget to raise your head at the entrance. You wouldn't want to miss the vintage red racing car pinned to

the ceiling!

The children who know the movie *Chitty Chitty Bang Bang* will think they recognize it in many of the cars displayed. There are also a couple of antique fire trucks.

On the second floor it's easy to observe the progression from horse carriages to cars. We can see wooden vehicles that were made by a carriage builder from Oshawa named McLaughlin. When increasing speed made the windshield a necessity, roofs were added and the look of cars changed dramatically from carriages (although it's funny we're still talking about horse power!).

TIPS (fun for 4 years +)
• The CAM was created for big kids with a driver's license! Don't go expecting interactive activities. In addition, the classy 1926 Bentley, sassy 1931 Alfa Romeo, gorgeous 1939 Rolls Royce, and all the other shiny cars are not to be touched, a rule which can be extremely frustrating for a young child.
• If you've come this far, pay a visit to the **Oshawa Aeronautical, Military and Industrial Museum**. In the last few years, they have reorganized the space around the time line of the origin and

evolution of the militia (King Louis X1V ordered Frontenac to create the first "milice" in Canada in 1669), with a focus on all

the generals up to today. Paul Dolly, who gives tours, is passionate on the subject. The museum owns 71 restored and working war vehicles, of which we can see some 30 around the site. Kids 7 years and older will appreciate these and displays of uniforms and weapons.

NEARBY ATTRACTIONS
Cullen Gardens (15-min.)............p. 116
Kids Zone (15-min.)....................p. 223

Canadian Automotive Museum
• Oshawa
(905) 576-1222

C-4
East
of Toronto
40-min.

Schedule: Open year-round Monday to Friday, 9 am to 5 pm. Saturday and Sunday, 10 am to 6 pm.
Admission: $5/adults, $4.50/seniors and students, $3.50/6-11 years, FREE 5 years and under.
Directions: 99 Simcoe St. South, Oshawa. From Hwy 401 East, take exit #417/Simcoe Stree northbound; the museum is on the east side.

Oshawa Museum
(Aeronautical, Military, Industrial)
(905) 728-6199
(905) 723-9930 (to book a tour)

Schedule: Friday, Saturday and Sunday, 1 pm to 5 pm.
Admission: $4/adults, $3/seniors, FREE 12 years and under.
Directions: 1000 Stevenson Rd. North, Oshawa. From the Automotive Museum, take Simcoe St. northbound, turn west on Rossland Rd., then turn north on Stevenson Rd.

YOUR FANNY DOWN THE GANNY

Among others, we admire a crew of eight rowers in their rail-car-boat, the Flintstones in their prehistoric craft and an airplane-shaped raft. But the golfers on a floating green, who'll reach the shore without getting wet, definitely take the cake!

About 20 years ago, the Ganaraska River burst its banks; Port Hope was officially declared a disaster area. Since then, during

That sinking feeling

A brave pooch barks frantically, running along the banks of the Ganaraska River. A small boat has just capsized in the current... to the audience's great delight! The good dog doesn't realize he's in the middle of Port Hope's annual event. He tries to rescue the laughing crew, who clumsily attempt to reach their home-made craft to finish the race.

To my little landlubber, a grown-up reluctantly immersed in cold water is the funniest sight he's ever seen! Most crews take the plunge. Their craft is usually precarious: pieces of Styrofoam, wood, metal or plastic barrels piled or tied together, sometimes quite artistically.

the sudden spring rise in the water level, the city has been organizing this race for canoes, kayaks and floating creations.

Each year, participants create their boat, inspired by a suggested theme. Usually, about fifty crazy crafts are expected, but they don't all finish the race. A technical error happens so fast!

The six-kilometre course followed by the boats ends downtown, where the crowd gathers to applaud the participants. The ambience is great; it shows that people know each other. After the race, everyone goes to Walton Street, where a few of the zany crafts are displayed.

TIPS (fun for 3 years +)

• Along Cavan Street, close to where it crosses Barrett Street, the banks are lined with flat stones and slope down gently. It forms a natural amphitheatre, stroller accessible with a great view.
• Many people bring blankets to sit on the ground, which can sometimes be muddy at this time of year.
• It's best to get to your observation point before 11:30 am. At 12 noon, the first boats can be seen from downtown.
• Temporary toilets are available. Stands sell hot dogs and coffee.
• Port Hope hosts the only "atmospheric theatre" in Canada. Built in 1930, the **Capitol Theatre**'s interior was painted like a medieval castle, with clouds projected on the ceiling. Check their web site for up-coming plays, films, and concerts at www.capitoltheatre.com or call 1-800-434-5092.

NEARBY ATTRACTIONS
Jungle Cat World (20-min.)............p. 53

Float Your Fanny Down the Ganny River Race	C-5 East of Toronto 60-min.

Float Your Fanny Down the Ganny River Race
• Port Hope
1-888-767-8467

 Schedule: Usually the first Saturday in April or the Saturday following Easter. Call to confirm. Starts at 11 am.
Admission: FREE.
Directions: From Hwy 401 East, take exit #464/Port Hope/Hwy 28 southbound (it becomes Mill St.). Turn right on Walton St., then left on Queen St. to find parking. On foot, go back to Walton St. (Cavan St. is located west of the River, north of Walton St.).

YORK-DURHAM RAILWAY

Chug-a-chug-a-chug-a... Choo-choo!

The train ride from Stouffville to Uxbridge can be summarized with the above words. It's a two-hour ride for the return trip on a 1900's diesel train. That's enough "choo-choos" to fill young railroad men's (and women's) ears for quite a while, believe me!

Don't forget this excursion's goal isn't to go somewhere, but rather to offer children the experience of a train ride.

If you can, visit the railcars before choosing one, as there are different types. I opted for one with wine-red upholstery.

TIPS (fun for 2 years +)
• Watch the children while they walk through the train. They could pinch their fingers in the joints between cars, as it moves with each bump.
• The Stouffville-Uxbridge railroad crosses many rural roads and has to blow its whistle each time. My two-month old daughter was stressed by the "CHOO... CHOO's" that delighted her brother!
• They sell snacks on the train. There's no food available at the Uxbridge station. However, you'll find portable toilets on the station's grounds and you have just enough time to walk to Brock Street to buy drinks and snacks for your return trip.
• Call to find out about the railway's special events: Teddy Bear Run, **Halloween** trains, Ride with **Santa** and more (must reserve seats).

NEARBY ATTRACTIONS

Its windows don't open very wide, but the car is comfortable and, above all, there's a space between the seats big enough for children to hide in.

There, my young Captain Kirk imagined a spaceship, while others saw it as a tent or a little house. At that age, it's impossible to look at the scenery for two hours!

Conductors are attentive to children and answer all their questions. They give kids a train-filled colouring book. I also recommend you take your children for a walk through the moving train. They'll love to watch the tracks from the last wagon.

The railroad passes through fields and woods. We only got off to stretch our legs at the last train station, in Uxbridge, and chose to catch our train back right away.

If you go on an early departure you can choose to stay in the small town while you wait for the next train (make sure there is a next train!).

York-Durham Heritage Railway • Stouffville (905) 852-3696 www.ydhr.on.ca	H-12 N-E of Toronto 40-min.

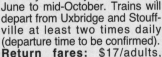
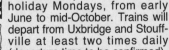

Schedule: Open weekends and holiday Mondays, from early June to mid-October. Trains will depart from Uxbridge and Stouffville at least two times daily (departure time to be confirmed).

Return fares: $17/adults, $13/seniors and students, $9/4-12 years, FREE for children 3 years and under.

Directions: From Hwy 404 North, take exit #37/Stouffville Rd. eastbound; the road becomes Main St. The Stouffville station is located east of 9th Line, on the north side of Main Rd.

SOUTH SIMCOE RAILWAY

Full steam ahead !

Here we are, my son and I, in the middle of nowhere, an hour away from Toronto. Fortunately, the return trip is included. We'll come back to our starting point after a charming, 45-minute ride in a vintage 1920's railcar pulled by a steam engine dating back to 1883.

You have to see the children's eyes when they watch the small train in the distance get closer and finally appear as the colossus it really is, with its whistle and its plume of steam.

TIPS (fun for 2 years +)

• It's best to get there 20 minutes before departure time. After you've parked and paid for your ticket, you'll be able to wait for the train to arrive (and hear it coming as well).

• Inside the railcars, don't expect luxury. Giving some of the seats a good knock could release a 50-year-old cloud of dust! Just in case, don't wear white pants...

• There's a small gift shop on the premises.

• Call to find out about their **Santa Train**. (You must buy tickets in advance.)

• On hot summer days, you'll be happy to take advantage of the **Tottenham Conservation Area**'s beach and playground, located less than 5 minutes from the train station on Mill Street.

Because there's only one track, the locomotive has no other choice but to move forward and then to back up. Mind you, it makes no difference from a passenger's point of view. For part of the ride, we see backyards full of flowers and a few commercial plots of land. Then comes the countryside, with farms, cows, cornfields and trees. Most trees along the track are deciduous and must take on beautiful colours during the fall.

When you're riding, try to make your children listen to what the conductor says, especially when he is telling the story of the train that disappeared into the river on a foggy night, a long time ago. To put us in the mood, the conductor stops the train and blows the whistle three times, hoping that the ghost of the missing train will answer back...

At the end of the line, we wait a few minutes before heading back. "We're waiting, because all the wheels must be reinstalled for us before we head in the other direction" the conductor seriously explains. It takes kids a few seconds to wrap their minds around that one!

NEARBY ATTRACTIONS

South Simcoe Railway
• Tottenham
(905) 936-5815
www.steamtrain.com

**C-2
N-W
of Toronto
60-min.**

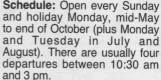

 Schedule: Open every Sunday and holiday Monday, mid-May to end of October (plus Monday and Tuesday in July and August). There are usually four departures between 10:30 am and 3 pm.

 Return fares: $12/adults, $10/seniors, $7/children 3-15 years, FREE for children 2 years and under.

 Directions: From Hwy 400 North, take exit #55/Hwy 9 westbound. Turn north on Simcoe Rd. #10/Tottenham Rd. then west on Mill St. (first set of lights in the town).

STREETCAR MUSEUM

On the right track

We climb into the first vehicle ready to leave. It is a superbly renovated passenger train car from the 1915 – 1960 period. It has elegant woodwork, velvet upholstery and copper tin ceiling decorations. Before long, the car heads towards a lavish green forest.

The Streetcar Museum differs from other railway attractions in the region. First, because its primary activity is the collection and renovation of trains, electric tramways and buses. Second, its track system is short (2km). Instead of offering long rides, the museum offers as many short ones as you wish, on any of the different vehicles available that day.

The museum's collection is large

and vehicles are primed for service according to drivers' availability. When we visited, we took a ride aboard the elegant "#8-Steel Car passenger", as well as an open-roof wagon replica of the 1890s, reminiscent of ancient carriages, in which we enjoyed a ride in nature.

Ten minutes later, our train reached the end of the line, not far from a lovely pond. The kids looked at some old abandoned railcars (most likely future renovation projects), including a run down, but amusing caboose that entertained children. Young visitors also enjoyed the opportunity to walk along the tracks.

Upon your return, you may jump into another train ready to leave, or hang around to admire those displayed in the warehouses or in the yards.

TIPS (fun for 2 years +)
- Make sure to pack some insect repellent; the little bugs are overtly present in the many bushes surrounding Meadowvale Station.
- Call to find out about their **Halloween** and **Christmas** special evening events.
- An ice cream stand, strategically located by the station and open on the weekends, adds to the outing's pleasure, while washrooms add to its comfort.

Streetcar Museum
· Milton
(519) 856-9802
www.hcry.org

**D-2
West
of Toronto
60-min.**

Schedule: Open early May until end of October, weekends and holidays only in May, June, September and October, 11 am to 4 pm, plus weekdays in July and August, 11 am to 4 pm.

Return fares: $9.50/adults, $8.50/seniors, $6.50/4 to 17 years, FREE for children 3 years and under.

Directions: 13629 Guelph Line, Milton. From Hwy 401 West, take exit #312/Guelph Line northbound.

PICKERING NUCLEAR CENTRE

Photos: Courtesy of M. Skuce

Power generation

When I entered the information centre of the nuclear generating station, I was quite impressed by the huge and elegant sculpture setting the modern tone of the vast display room. It happens my good friend Murray was responsible for the design of this centre so I congratulated him on the first occasion about the piece of art. "Nat! This is no sculpture, it is a life-size cutout of a Candu reactor!" Oops! Should have read the signs!

Open on weekdays only, it is hard for the general public to enjoy this information centre but we used a PA day to visit it. After all, Pickering's is one of the world's largest nuclear generating stations (with eight reactors producing enough energy to serve a city of two million) and kids are always big fans of mighty machines.

TIPS (fun for 7 years +)
• Check their web site under <u>Info Centre</u>, then <u>Learning Centre</u>, <u>Power Production</u> and finally <u>Nuclear</u>. You'll find a section called How Our Nuclear Stations Work. It includes simple explanations and a nice illustration of a Candu reactor with popping windows: a good thing to show kids 8 years and older prior to their visit.

Here's another one: at the end of the road leading downhill to the centre, you'll see a 30-storey-high wind turbine getting bigger and bigger as you approach. On top of the impressive 256-foot tower turn 148-foot-long blades to generate power for 600 households.

Inside, computer stations under large trees greeted us. They offered a few games. In one of them, kids would be quizzed with basic questions and loudly congratulated for their successes, the kind of gratification my 8-year-old companions thrive on.

The other displays explained different aspects of energy generation with the help of buttons to push, levers to handle or faucets to turn. They explain how the reactors produce heat by splitting the uranium atoms; how the heat is simply used to boil water, producing high pressure steam moving the turbines of electrical generators.

Most of them were way over the head of my 4-year-old, with all the reading involved. On the other hand, she had lots of fun with the jump-o-metre measuring the impact of her stomps.

NEARBY ATTRACTIONS
Cullen Gardens (15-min.)..............p. 116
Petticoat Creek (10-min.)..............p. 385

Pickering Nuclear Information Centre
• Pickering
(905) 837-7272
www.opg.com

**I-12
East
of Toronto
35-min.**

Schedule: Monday to Friday, 9 am to 3:30 pm.
Admission: FREE.

Directions: From Hwy 401 East, take exit #399/Brock Rd. southbound, turn west on Montgomery Park Rd.

HAMILTON MUSEUM OF STEAM

19th century techies

Our guide puts an oily paper hat on my nephew's head, turning him into one of the kids hired in the 19th century to keep the pumps well oiled. We all laugh at his funny "oiler" look until we are told this was the only protection those working children had when working in that environment. What about their little fingers?

The steam engines before us are quite impressive, at 70 tons each and 45 feet high. We're actually too close to see them in one shot as we look at them from the mezzanine. Canadian made, they're the oldest surviving examples in the nation and we can see them in operation under our nose.

Before we were allowed to see this phenomenon, our guide took great pains to explain to us the "beauty" of the technology involved by means of an interactive demonstration perfectly adapted for children. The tour lasted 40 minutes. At the end, kids are allowed to use a lever to make the huge wheel turn.

We could also admire a model of the pump house, in a large barn-like display room filled with charts explaining the system. Each of the 12,000 parts of this model were handmade by a Hamilton resident in the 80's and it is functioning.

In addition, there's always a temporary exhibit in the main building.

TIPS (fun for 5 years +)
• Every now and then from May to October, you can catch a ride on a miniature steam-powered locomotive (see the **Richmond Hill Live Steamers** on p. 236 to get an idea). On **Canada Day**, they always show up. Call for specific dates.
• During **March Break**, including the weekends before and after (and opening at 10 am) they offer more drop-in special demonstrations and craft activities.
• On the weekend before **Christmas**, they offer a special activity including two crafts and a craft bag to take home (for an extra fee). It shows that this museum's curator is the same who manages **Hamilton Children's Museum**!
• They offer some nice trinkets in their small gift shop. We bought a train whistle and a cute little tin boat moving with the heat of a candle!
• See **Baranga's**, **Hutch's** and **Lakehouse** restaurants on p. 431.

NEARBY ATTRACTIONS
Wild Waterworks (5-min.) ....p. 37
Children's Museum (15-min.)...... p. 259

Hamilton Museum of Steam & Technology
• Hamilton
(905) 546-4797
www.hamilton.ca

| | E-2 S-W of Toronto 65-min. |

Schedule: Open year-round Tuesday to Sunday, 11 am to 4 pm, from June 1 to Labour Day (opens at noon the rest of the year). Closed on Mondays.

Admission: $6/adults, $4/seniors and students, $3/children, $15/family of 4, FREE for 5 years and under.

Directions: 900 Woodward Ave., Hamilton. Take QEW towards Niagara, exit at Woodward Ave. and follow signs.

See **Canadian Warplane Heritage Museum** on p. 245.

CANADIAN WARPLANE MUSEUM

Down-to-Earth airplanes

When we arrive, children's imaginations are fired up by a real jet, its nose pointing towards the sky like a church steeple. More than twenty, genuine, functioning specimens await in the museum's immense hangar. Add cabins, cockpits, switches and buttons to explore and you get a great family outing!

Before entering the hangar, we saw a display on the use of planes in Canadian military history. Budding pilots appreciated watching the illuminated world map and operating the model airplanes. Then, we circulated among the impressive hangar's fleet bathed in natural light.

The wheels of certain planes were as tall as my future pilot. Part of the site is dedicated to the restoration of a few vintage models. It's an excellent occasion to appreciate aeronautical engineering while examining airplanes from every angle.

We're not allowed to touch most of the gleaming aircrafts, but don't worry, we can access a few specimens and their engaging cockpits: a real WWII trainer or a real CF-100 jet aircraft. We can also manipulate (from the outside) the array of controls in a Silver T-33 training aircraft. Not often do we get the chance to see a plane's landing gear in action! Children love the two-seat Flying Boxcar simulator, with its wall-to-wall switches and dials.

Stairs at the back of the hangar lead to an observation terrace, from which we have an overview of the museum's squadron.

Higher up the stairs, we can access the exterior terrace, from which other planes can be seen. At the bottom of the stairs is a vast room with tables, an affordable snack bar and best of all, a panoramic view of the outside. Paved roads connect with the Hamilton International Airport's runways, located 1 km away.

TIPS (fun for 4 years +)
• All aircraft are maintained in flying condition. On most days (weather permitting), you might have the chance to observe a vintage aircraft in flight.
• The museum's gift shop is well stocked.
• A great complement to the visit is located 5 minutes from the museum: **Killman Zoo**, open April to October 31, (closed on Tuesdays). I have not seen it but it has a large collection of felines and other animals. From the museum, take Hwy 6 south and turn east at Unity Side Rd to #237, (905) 765-5966.

Canadian Warplane Heritage Museum · Mount Hope 1-877-347-3359 www.warplane.com	E-2 S-W of Toronto 70-min.

Schedule: Open daily, 9 am to 5 pm.
Admission: $10/8 years and older, $8/seniors and students, FREE for children 7 years and under, $30/family of 4.
Directions: Hamilton International Airport, 9280 Airport Rd., Mount Hope. Take QEW West, follow Hwy 403 towards Hamilton, exit at Fiddlers' Green Rd. and follow the museum's signs.

WELLAND CANALS CENTRE

The ups and downs of a canal

A drawbridge lets the freighter go by with its iron ore cargo. The gigantic lock gates shut heavily behind the 225-metre-long ship finishing its course through the canal. Tons of water lift the boat. It gets even better when sailors working on the main deck wave at the children. The kids, confined to the observation platform, look at them with envy. Here in St. Catharines, at Welland Canal's lock number 3, we're swimming amidst a world of *Mighty Machines*.

The Welland Canal's eight locks allow ships from thirty countries to cross the Niagara escarpment, which brings about a 100-metre level difference between Lakes Ontario and Erie. Because of its ideal set-up for visitors, lock number 3 is the best place to initiate children to the science of locks. It boasts a snack bar, a restaurant, a souvenir shop and the great little **St. Catharines Museum**. And best of all, the lock's observation platform offers a breathtaking view.

A bulletin board can be found on site, listing the boats that will pass through the lock during the day. It mentions each boat's name, port of registry, length, destination, type of cargo it carries and its approximate time of arrival at the lock. This helps to put young minds to work...

A question of time

During our visit, a good half-hour went by between the moment we saw the arriving freighter passing under the drawbridge and

the time it entered the lock. The kids weren't expecting it to be so gigantic!

To help them pass the time while waiting for a ship, we went to the snack bar and explored the playground. We also visited the St. Catharines Museum. Don't hesitate to go there at any time, as speakers inside the museum will announce the arrival of each ship. You can then return to the lock and when the ship has finished passing through, resume your visit to the museum.

It took 15 minutes for the Canadian cargo, called the *Jean Parisien*, to immobilize itself inside the lock. This allowed us to admire it from every angle. The little sailors accompanying me brought up many questions: "Why is the bridge watered by those hoses? Why are there only a few life boats?"

It takes about 10 minutes for the lock to fill with water. The freighter was rising before our very eyes and the kids enjoyed identifying the objects that were getting closer. "Wow, look at the lifebuoy! Can you see the white stairs? And the blue basket?" Finally, the lock opened on the other side.

The freighter's engines restarted and caused the water to swirl around. The ship continued its slow course upstream. It was about time, as my little sailors' level of interest was beginning to sink dangerously low! We improved the situation by visiting the enjoyable museum.

TIPS (fun for 5 years +)

• The lock can remain empty for more than 5 consecutive hours. For a successful visit, it is best to call lock number 3's information service before you leave. It states the daily schedule, with the approximate arrival time of each ship. It is best to go to the site when three or four ships are scheduled to pass through the lock within a 3-hour period.

• The perspective is best when you watch a ship rising from "upbound", that is when it goes upstream from Lake Ontario towards Lake Erie.

• At the museum entrance, ask for a very interesting booklet called "ABC's of the Seaway", free with admission. Using simple terms, it describes the functioning of the locks that the kids have just seen live.

• There's a snack bar on site open from April to October.

• See **Lakehouse Restaurant** on p. 431.

The St. Catharines Museum

The museum includes various activities around the naval theme and several time-travel exhibits. The Lacrosse Hall of Fame comes with a shooting gallery, where kids can throw balls into a net. There are more hands-on pioneer artifacts.

My little inspectors fell for the captain's wheel with a moving landscape seen through portholes in the background.

We can watch a 15-minute video presentation to learn more about the four Welland Canals (we're at Lock 3, remember?)

Welland Canals Centre	**E-3**
• St. Catharines	**Niagara**
1-800-305-5134	**Region**
or (905) 984-8880	**75-min.**
www.stcatharineslock3museum.ca	

  Schedule: The museum is open daily, mid-March to mid-October, from 9 am to 5 pm and weekends only the rest of the year, from 11 am to 4 pm (ship traffic is interrupted shortly before Christmas and restarts around early April).

Admission: FREE admission to the centre. Museum admission is $4.25/adults, $4/seniors, $3.25/students, $2.50/6-13 years, FREE for children 5 years and under).

Directions: Lock 3, 1932 Government Rd., St. Catharines. Take QEW Niagara to St. Catharines, exit at Glendale Ave. West, cross the lift-bridge and turn right on Welland Canals Pkwy. (formally Government Rd.).

NEARBY ATTRACTIONS
Wild Waterworks (15-min.)...........p. 37
Niagara Falls (15-min.).................p. 302

General tips about
Museums:

- Museums change their exhibits on a regular basis. Points of interest described in this guide were accurate at the time of print.
- It is amazing that the biggest Canadian city still doesn't have its own children's museum, isn't it? **The Children's Own Museum**, which used to be beside the ROM, is still looking for a place to settle down. It is possible to check **www.childrensownmuseum.org** to find out about its current status or call (416) 360-1266. They accept donations to help built a state-of-the-art museum within the GTA.

MUSEUMS

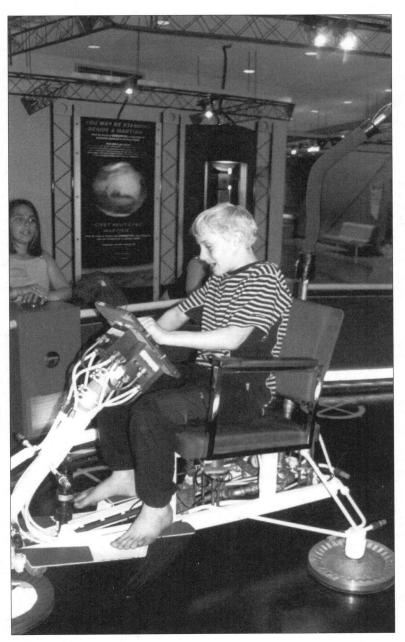

See **Ontario Science Centre** on p. 256.

TORONTO POLICE MUSEUM

Good guys, bad guys

Police work is so attractive and conducive to play-acting with its good guys, bad guys and elaborate gear, it will take children twenty years to realize the world of crime isn't cool at all. Until then, the Police Museum makes every effort to impress its visitors.

The architecture of the Police Headquarters building is magnificent. The museum, up with the best, offers plenty of activities which took us an hour to explore.

At the entrance, officers in uniform impressed my little citizen, but not as much as the gleaming police edition Harley-Davidson usually posted nearby. He happily (and legally!) hopped on the motorcycle. Mannequins display uniforms dating from the 1850's to the present. There's even a Mountie riding a life-size horse.

While your children inspect the genuine police car, read the captions inside the display cases containing exhibits from true criminal cases. Afterwards, initiate your miniature Sherlock Holmes to criminal investigation. You can show them several pieces of evidence: a drinking glass covered with fingerprints, a victim's jewels recovered from the murderer's house and nails stuck in garden hoses used by robbers to slow down the police during a chase.

Adults appreciate watching the short videos covering various topics. We all loved the interactive screen where we tried to draw the portraits of criminals previously seen in action on a video segment.

By touching the screen, we selected the shape of their facial features. The portrait was then compared to the corresponding criminal's face. It was not easy! An interactive fingerprint screen offered another interesting display.

A corridor leads to a prison cell, (which was unfortunately closed when we visited). Further on, my son saw his first real car wreck. It faces an officer on a 1950's road sign encouraging us to drive safely. The sign compares the number of automobile accident deaths from the current and previous year. The billboard is old, but the statistics are current and updated weekly! A display of police hats emphasizes the death of many officers. You see, kids, it's not as cool as it looks…

TIPS (fun for 4 years +)
• I suggest that your children watch the video segments about a woman calling 9-1-1 during an emergency. Three screens simultaneously show the woman, the officer on the line and the rescue services set in motion.
• Kids can ask for a free police button at the duty desk.
• They have a Cop Shop in the lobby, selling gift items, clothing (adult and children sizes), model police cars and more.

NEARBY ATTRACTIONS

Toronto Police Museum
(416) 808-7020
www.torontopolice.on.ca

I-10
Downtown
Toronto
15-min.

Schedule: Open Monday to Friday, 10 am to 4:30 pm. Also open on weekends in the summer, from noon to 5 pm. Book ahead if you want a guided tour.
Admission: FREE (donation) ($1 per person for groups of eight people and more, groups must call to pre-book.
Directions: 40 College St., Toronto (one block west of Yonge St.).

TEXTILE MUSEUM

Strong artistic fibre

In the Discover Fibre section, there's a discovery drawer to learn about the living things producing fibres. I really enjoyed the exercise but my five-year-old couldn't care less. She's too distracted by the alignment of colourful threads inside a large cage in the Discover Colour section.

It doesn't take long for her to rearrange the threads into an artful display. Then, she makes patterns using tessellating shapes (pre-cut patterns).

While she's busy, I can't believe I finally get to see what a silkworm looks like and touch real cocoons, so white and soft between my fingers. The Fibrespace education gallery within the Textile Museum is filled with such things to discover. There's also the Discover Textiles corner with a "knitted zoo", hooked rugs and lace making trials, and the Discover Meaning section where activities constantly change to coincide with specific exhibitions.

Exhibitions change twice a year. They're always intriguing and interesting for adults, like the one on geotextiles, which taught me how fabrics were used in construction and agriculture, or the one on the molecular structure of fabrics.

You can usually count on artistic installations involving fabric in some way. Once, a dramatic organza curtain pinned with thousands of rose petals by the artist stunned me. And the installation "I've got balls" was quite a sight, with its twenty-one white nylon legs suspended from clothes lines, heavy with baseballs in their feet, and one full pair of red nylons also with baseballs, nicely contrasting. Even my daughter reacted to that one.

TIPS (fun for 4 years +)

• The **March Break** is a great time to drop in with artsy kids who would like to create textile art! Special craft activities are then adapted to the current exhibitions.

• The store is filled with original works of some 50 artisans. It also carries a great selection of textile-related books, for adults and children (even some storybooks involving fabrics). Kids' stuff also includes textile-related kits, learning activity books and craft projects.

• Check their virtual exhibitions on their web site! It is exquisitely designed, very informative, both in English and in French.

• There's no restaurant on the site but the museum is only a 15-minute walk from the **Eaton Centre**.

NEARBY ATTRACTIONS	

Textile Museum of Canada
(416) 599-5321
www.textilemuseum.ca

I-10
Downtown
Toronto
20-min.

 Schedule: Closed Mondays. Open Tuesday, Thursday and Friday, 11 am to 5 pm, Wednesday, 11 am to 8 pm, Saturday and Sunday, noon to 5 pm.

 Admission: $8/adults, $6/others, and $22/family of 5, FREE for children under 5.

 Directions: 55 Centre Ave., Toronto. Just south of Dundas, one block east of University Ave.

ROYAL ONTARIO MUSEUM

You'll get their attention

The beauty of a Ming period vase and the mystery of ancient characters leave my son rather cold, as he's not inclined to contemplation. However, the ROM has many ways to get his attention: archaeological digging, discovery boxes filled with surprises, dinosaurs, volcano, costumes... Now, you're talking!

At the time of print, the ROM was undergoing major renovations so many galleries will be closed until 2005, including the favourite Discovery Gallery.

A temporary CIBC Discovery Room opened in March 2004, still across from the Dinosaur Gallery. It includes many of the elements of the former gallery and will remain open until December 2006, when the new CIBC Discovery Gallery will open in the southeast atrium on the main floor.

Meanwhile, there's still much to see. And Level 2 is still the most interesting floor for most children.

In the Dinosaurs Gallery, standing on prehistoric flora, embellished with great trompe-l'oeil, the skeletons are quite impressive. "Are they really dead?" asks my son innocently. Indeed! But they can be seen in action at the centre of the room, at the heart of the Maiasaura Project, with a giant screen showing computerized re-enactment.

The Bat Cave, where a swarm of fly-ing bats can be seen (and heard) from time to time, is a favourite but it will be closed in fall 2004 and is not scheduled to re-open!

In the Bird Gallery, tell the children to open the series of drawers located under the glass displays. They'll find one surprise after another. The drawers contain treasures: nests and eggs of all sizes, food for baby birds, bird beaks along with examples of food appropriate for their shape, hummingbirds and more. Alongside the Bird Gallery, a computer offers an amusing bird song menu, activated by touching the screen.

Then, a display of stuffed forest mammals (including a large moose!) leads you to the great Hands-On Biodiversity Gallery. Different sections, nicely laid out with display windows and discovery boxes, give us the impression of being on a field trip in Canada's lake and cottage regions. With guessing games, hands-on tables with skin, fur, bones and horns, beautiful costumes, a tunnel and real beehive, this section is a whole museum in itself.

TIPS (fun for 3 years +)

• There's a Toronto Parking Authority affordable parking lot on Bedford Street, north of Bloor Street, west of Avenue Rd.

• The ROM offers even more interactive activities during the **March Break** and around **Christmas** time, most probably including a show in their theatre on the lower level (they usually issue passes 15 minutes before each show outside of the theatre).

• All the gift shops (except for the small one by the entrance) are closed. In December 2005, a large gift shop will open off the new main entrance on Bloor Street. The small gift shop currently in the Rotunda will also be relocated there. A new Toy Shop will be located on the lower level.

• The museum's cafeteria on the street level is closed. For the moment, you can go to the smaller cafeteria on the lower level. By December 2005, there will be a large family restaurant on level 1 Below Concourse, in the Michael A. Lee-Chin Chrystal. By 2006, they will add a café in the restored rotunda (the former entrance to the museum).

• There's always the **McDonald's** west of Avenue Road on the north side of Bloor Street.

NEARBY ATTRACTIONS

You might want to see the mummy in the Ancient Egypt section on the third floor before heading back to the main level and the Gallery of Earth Sciences.

There, children will have to step into a large puddle of red lava in order to enter into the volcano. If they sit around the floor screen, they will watch an amazing short film about children diving to the centre of the earth!

We enter into the other room through an impressive crack made of quartz. There again is an interesting projection room where the image slowly moves from the walls to the ceiling and onto the floor.

Another section leads us through the history of our planet, from the Big Bang to the fossils, with the help of Trog (a rock character as old as the Earth and pretty dismayed by the appearance of bacteria on the planet). Beyond, there are small rooms to explore.

Royal Ontario Museum
(416) 586-8000
www.rom.on.ca

I-10 Downtown Toronto 20-min.

 Schedule: Open year-round, 7 days, Monday to Thursday and Saturday, 10 am to 6 pm, Friday, 10 am to 9:30 pm, Sunday, 11 am to 6 pm.

 Admission: $15/adults, $10/ seniors and students, $8/5 to 14 years, $35/ family, FREE for children 4 years and under. FREE on Fridays, 4:30 to 9:30 pm (excluding special exhibitions).

 Directions: 100 Queen's Park (at the corner of Bloor St. West). After the renovations, the entrance will be off Bloor St.

THE BATA SHOE MUSEUM

Little steps

Since the company has always focused on low-end products, I was quite curious to see what the Bata Shoe Museum had to offer. Well, I was impressed! The museum is gorgeous and Bata has shown great skill in putting itself into its young visitors' shoes to get their attention.

The All About Shoes permanent exhibition reviews the history of shoes, from prehistoric times until the present, using many props: art reproductions, informative text, mannequins, lighting effects and of course, fascinating artefacts.

The oldest closed shoe dates from the 1400's! Among other things, I learned that in 14th Century England, length of

the shoe tip was related to social status and regulated by law. That explains the disproportionately long shoes seen in some medieval paintings!

Children can't appreciate the historic value of ancient shoes. But they'll be impressed by the variety of footwear displayed here, especially if you explain the use of certain shoes to them. This one is for walking on burning sand; that one, to climb glaciers; this other one, to walk on the moon! And what can we say about the ancient Chinese shoes used to reduce the feet of the poor women victims of their time?

We then move on to the Star Turns display, showcasing some famous footwear: one of the Beatles' ankle boots, Marilyn Monroe's red pumps, Picasso's pony-skin boots. My little extrovert's favourite were Elton John's massive platform shoes.

Three other galleries feature special exhibitions under diverse themes. These have presented collections of dancing shoes, athletic footwear and Chinese shoes for bound feet, among others.

TIPS (fun for 5 years +)

• **March Break** activities are original. Last time I was there during that period, visitors could play with Brio-like tracks and "shoe" trains. They could create socks and shoes for a multi-legged dragon. They could try on firemen's boots and mules and dress up as Cinderella and Prince Charming.

• Check out their web site to find out about the original children's workshops they offer from time to time for a fee. When I visited, kids were painting a real Dutch clog!

NEARBY ATTRACTIONS
ROM (15-min. walk).......................p. 252

The Bata Shoe Museum
(416) 979-7799
www.batashoemuseum.ca

I-10
Downtown
Toronto
20-min.

  Schedule: Open Tuesday, Wednesday, Friday and Saturday, 10 am to 5 pm, Thursday, 10 am to 8 pm, Sunday, 12 noon to 5 pm. Open on Mondays in June, July and August.
 Admission: $6/adults, $4/ seniors and students, $2/5-14 years, $12/family of 4, FREE for children 4 years and under. FREE on Thursdays from 5 pm to 8 pm. Extra fee during March Break.
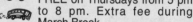 **Directions:** 327 Bloor St. West, Toronto (at corner of St. George St.).

JEWISH DISCOVERY MUSEUM

Filled with good faith!

"He'll read all this?" asks my son bewildered as he looks at the series of small papers inserted between the bricks of the "Wailing Wall". I just finished explaining these are children's prayers to God, after they've completed their visit to the museum. With that, he sits down before a blank page and....draws a plane (he'd like to go for a ride). He quickly slips his drawing in a crack in the wall.

Jewish or not, visitors equally enjoy the small interactive museum. It is dedicated to children between the ages of 1 and 8 and inspired by a precise theme: the history of the Jewish religion and its current life experience.

Thanks to a series of entertaining and original activities, parents who wish to introduce their children to notions common to all religions, such as compassion, empathy and a desire to do good, can do so with great simplicity.

The section People Help People recreates an emergency ward with a car-

diac intensive care unit. It includes accessories and costumes, complete with various organs to be reinserted in a dummy's chest.

At the entrance, the section Torah Time recreates a miniature synagogue, with objects for rituals that can be touched, as well as stories that can be re-enacted with felt accessories. My son played with a kitchen set to recreate a traditional Sabbath dinner. We ended our visit by making a crown in the crafts section.

Since our last visit, the museum has added a Tower of Babel to climb on. It explores the themes of communication and cooperation. Kids get to hear many different languages and record (and change) the sound of their own voice. There's also a whole new section taking us on a "trip" around the world.

They offer daily drop-in activities such as storytelling and crafts.

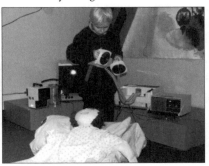

TIPS (fun for 8 years and under)

• Jewish holidays are celebrated on certain Sunday afternoons with a series of activities which could include art-making, games and prizes, performances, puppet shows, sing-along and storytelling. Call to confirm dates.

• There's a **Second Cup** coffee shop located in the entrance hall of the community centre that houses the museum. The centre also holds a well-stocked kosher cafeteria.

NEARBY ATTRACTIONS
Wild Water Kingdom (20-min.).....p. 33
Black Creek Village (15-min.)......p. 404

The Family Place @ The Jewish Discovery Museum
• North York
(416) 636-1880 ext. 242
www.bjcc.ca

H-10 North of downtown 30-min.

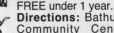

Schedule: Monday to Thursday, 10 am to 5 pm. Sunday, 11 am to 4 pm. Closed Fridays and Saturdays.

Admission: $2.50/person, FREE under 1 year.

Directions: Bathurst Jewish Community Centre, 4588 Bathurst St., North York (north of Sheppard).

ONTARIO SCIENCE CENTRE

The science of fun

What a unique playground! Leaf-cutting ants, 5-metre-high tornado, cave, shadow tunnel, human skeletons, bobsled race, space shuttle; the list goes on. Mind you, nobody has to see it all in just one visit!

I recommend starting the visit by taking the three escalators down to Level D and towards The Living Earth to your far right.

There is a 5-metre-high tornado which moves when you blow on it and a large cave with a TV monitor showing the visitors inside. Up the stairs you can lay on your belly and watch, through a visor, a short movie on a flight from the perspective of the flying bird!

Backing up a bit, in the humid tropical rain forest, don't miss the leaf-cutting ants circulating through transparent pipes.

At the time of print, renovations were going on in what used to be the Communication room and the adjacent Information Highway (now closed), at the centre of Level D. The new Weston Family Innovation Centre replacing it should have Hot Zone, its first phase, ready by December 2004.

From what I could gather this section will use unique and unexpected ways to explore current and emerging technologies. It will be followed by the construction of four other sections in the area currently called Technology Hall: the Media Studios (where, we are told, the boundaries between music, fashion, art, technology and science will blur), Citizen Science (in which our data will help real scientific researchers), Material World (looking at what fills our daily life in new ways) and the Challenge Zone (where we will be invited to create solutions to real-world problems).

These and more renovation projects will be completed by spring 2006. Welcome to the 21st century!

Still on Level D, the Science Arcade, farther in the back, is a favourite. It has a myriad of sound and visual activities: gyroscopes, electronic keyboards, jiggling sculptures, stroboscopes, steel drums, a Chinese percussion room and a screen on which you "see" your voice.

When you get in, you are greeted by the "cling clang" of metal balls rolling through intriguing circuits in a series of cause-and-effect reactions. It fascinates the children who may reload the balls themselves.

There is also a circular fabric room that turns around you to create the illusion that you are moving. In another small room, our shadow is projected on to a screen, coloured and processed using special motion effects. A good time to be silly!

The modules you will find there are quite daring, covering the reproductive system and all.

Ask your little explorers to stand in front of a smiling little girl's picture. Then, open the "window" around her face. Behind this opening, her face contracts and a hidden water spray system reproduces a noisy and generous sneeze. It's quite funny when you don't expect it. Just don't tell your kids!

On Level C, the Exploring Space is a favourite. It is worth waiting in line for a shot at the strange air-lifted vehicle (shown on p. 249).

Nearby, you'll find **KidSpark**, the latest addition replacing the old Food section. This new section has turned out to be so popular that at the time of print, the Science Centre had just decided to double its space (hence the relocation of Sports Hall to the lower level).

KidSpark is a real hit. This section is lovely. It was designed for kids 8 years and under, but my 10-year-old son really enjoyed it.

Finally, the Arcade is where you will find the famous hair-raising ball used during electrical demonstrations.

By summer 2004, Sports Hall, the other section to spend energy, will have been relocated into the current Transportation Hall, off the Arcade Hall.

Level E houses the Matter, Energy, Change Hall. Young children will either lack the height, strength or patience to obtain the desired results in most experiments. Still, try to make a large screen out of a layer of liquid soap with them and have their shadow printed on the walls of the Shadow Tunnel before heading towards the Human Body room.

Hard to say what my kids preferred, they tried everything: the stage with tunes to lip-sync while playing fake instruments and creating light effects, the construction site with lifts and blocks, the floating balls, the periscope, the water games or the pneumatic capsules to send messages.

By 2006, the Great Hall will be revamped into the Grand Central, to become the starting and end point of our visit. They promise a lush hanging garden, pillars of rock and minerals, a floor made of a mosaic of moving pictures, a vast aerial sculpture, stained glass panels, an enormous real-time image of our sun and a waterfall.

Until September 2005, the temporary exhibitions will keep being presented in the Great Hall. From then on, they will be featured in the vast room by the vast room by the Living Earth on level D.

TIPS (fun for 2 years +)
• See **Omnimax Theatre** on p. 98.
• To avoid disappointment if you intend to visit the **KidSpark** section, check if they are giving timed tickets as soon as you arrive on the premises.
• Don't be afraid to take young kids to this museum. Going down the three escalators to the lowest level will be an event in itself. They won't understand much but they will be elated by the concept of being allowed to touch everything. Just follow them!
• Picking up a map of the site at the entrance will allow you to orient yourself better. The place is huge!
• They offer even more activities during the **March Break**. Beware! It's their busiest time of the year.
• The gift shop on Level A (a **Mastermind Educational** outlet) is a fabulous place to buy educational toys, books and $10 gadgets on science. It offers a huge selection of activity books.
• By the entrance of Level D, there are several vending machines and a spacious cafeteria. In the summer, you can go outside and take advantage of the natural surroundings of the ravine... along with the raccoons.

Ontario Science Centre
• North York
(416) 696-3127
www.ontariosciencecentre.ca

I-10 North of downtown 25-min.

 Schedule: Open year-round, 7 days, 10 am to 5 pm (extended hours during the March Break, July and August).

 Admission: $14/adults, $10/seniors and students, $8/4-12 years, FREE for 3 years and under. Parking costs $8. Omnimax is $11/adults, $8/seniors and students, $7/children. Ask about combo prices for admission to the centre and a movie, save $4-$5 per person. Ask about their membership rates if you intend to visit more than twice in a year!

Directions: 770 Don Mills Rd., North York. Take Don Valley Pkwy., exit Don Mills Rd. North.

NEARBY ATTRACTIONS
Edwards Gardens (5-min.)...........p. 311

HAMILTON CHILDREN'S MUSEUM

Hamilton for kids

Don't be disappointed by the building's small size. The philosophy of the Hamilton Children's Museum is to maximize the use of space.

The museum is constantly reinventing itself. Every new edition, I have had to rewrite this page to follow the changes.

This time, I have to rely on the nice curator's descriptions and pictures to describe the latest activities.

Instead of offering a different theme for each room, each section now focuses on learning styles.

Whatever the concept, kids will explore it all anyway.

Their Muckabout room would satisfy my learning style! In that room, kids construct a ball course on a wall out of see-through pipes. They will find a weird canoe covered with faux-fur and climb into the 12-foot-high tree made out of recycled tires, pieces of carpet and other items. They'll use a periscope and a pulley system.

In Mary's Den, they'll play with horns, rocks, fossils and minerals which they will explore with microscopes, magnifiers, metal detectors and more.

There's also an Expression & Communication room with costumes, musical instruments, puppet theatre and so on.

TIPS (fun for 2 years +)

• The museum's visit lasts approximately one hour. It should be visited as a complement to a visit to another attraction in the area.

• There's a colourful room adjacent to the exhibition called the Sensorium. When it is not in use for birthday parties or pre-registered craft activities, young visitors can spend some quiet time in there.

• A small outdoor playground is located beside the museum. A very large playground including a wading pool and a spray pad is a 5-minute walk away, at the back of **Gage Park** on which the museum sits.

• There is no snack bar in this park but there is a **McDonald's** located on a parallel street in front of the museum.

Photos: Courtesy of Hamilton Children's Museum

NEARBY ATTRACTIONS
Warplane Museum (15-min.).......p. 245
Dundurn Castle (5-min.)..............p. 416

Hamilton Children's Museum · Hamilton (905) 546-4848 www.city.hamilton.on.ca	E-2 S-W of Toronto 60-min.

 Schedule: Open Tuesdays to Saturdays, 9:30 am to 3:30 pm. Closed Sundays and Mondays.

Admission: $3/2-13 years old, $1/adults.

 Directions: 1072 Main St. East, Hamilton. Take QEW West, then Hwy 403 towards Hamilton, exit Main St. East.

WATERLOO CHILDREN'S MUSEUM

Centre (see p. 256), with many scientific activities geared towards older kids and it is definitely worth the trip.

On the street level (emphasizing mathematics and patterns), the Geo-Terraces area by the giant kaleidoscope is quite popular with kids of all ages. Several building systems are at their disposal, not the least being magnetic rods to create geometrical shapes. Some young visitors figured out the potential of

New kid on the block

The yellow Swiss cheese slice covering the whole wall in the four-storey atrium certainly got our attention! It went perfectly with the two-storey moon-like projection on the round screen. A giant kaleidoscope was throwing its ever-moving light on it, while enlarged shadows of kids danced behind the surface. In a glimpse, I knew we would not be disappointed by the new museum!

Don't be fooled by the stiff facade of the building (except for the bouncing balls running upward through a series of long pneumatic see-through tubing). It used to be a department store, which sat vacant for 15 years.

To see its inner beauty, enter through the child-size doors (next to the full-size ones), go past the huge round reception counter and admire natural light pouring from skylights and the glass front, three mezzanines and a gorgeous tempered glass staircase bordered with glass guardrails, wooden floors and a line-up of creative activities.

The Waterloo Children's Museum opened in September 2003. It is a bit like a bigger version of the new whimsical KidSpark section in the Ontario Science

the nearby metal staircase and included it in their design.

Another hit is the carpeted TotSpot. Meant for toddlers and babies, the cocoon-like room is mesmerizing for anyone, with five bubbling water tubes lit in the dark and a ceiling covered with wavy mesh.

The second level focuses on mechanics and hydraulics. We loved the Construction Alley with its 138 sails of stretch-fabric panels we could hook with the help of 900 fasteners on poles to create labyrinths. The small pin wall next to it was a blast. Kids could leave a life-size impression on it. Beware, the wall is accessible from both sides so you want to be on one side when your child is imprinting her face into the opposite side, to make sure no other explorer is simultaneously pushing pins into her.

The Water Garden by the windows includes a 15-metre-long river where happy kids can pump water and steer boats between upper and lower sections. During the opening weekend, the "rain cloud" had not been put up yet. It is promising: suspended above the river, it should produce thunder and lightning effects and periodically rain over the distracted visitors.

The third level is dedicated to energy. Still pretty much under construction when we visit-

ed, it offered original temporary activities but we could already play with the Soundscape, creating music and animated movement on a backdrop by waving a special wand.

Once completed, you can expect the Energy Playground (exploring sound, electricity, magnetism, light, heat and X-ray through the use of projection systems on sail-like screens) and the Electric Wall (with circuits to connect in order to activate elements).

The fourth level hosts travelling exhibitions and a gallery space for artists' installations. It will eventually showcase exhibits focussing on communications.

More attractions, not ready on opening weekend, were on their way: the Metamorph (suspended robot body with stylized exoskeleton equipped with a camera and control consoles for kids to make it fly, laugh and flash), the Gear Wall (gears of varying sizes associated with musical notes, with a potential to create 117 rhythmic combinations) and the Hydraulic Swamp (which will make it possible to draw on mist with a laser).

We have to go back to check it out.

TIPS (fun for 1 year +)

- The gift shop offers a good selection of trinkets and toys.
- Ask about their birthday packages.
- Beverages and snacks are sold in vending machines. There's a **Williams Coffee Pub** outlet overlooking the fountain of Kitchener's City Hall on King (3-min. walk west of the museum). It offers a wide variety and a good kids menu.
- See **Chuck E. Cheese** on p. 218.

NEARBY ATTRACTIONS
Oktoberfest Parade (1-min. walk).p. 80
Shade's Mills C.A. (20-min.)........p. 281

Waterloo Children's Museum
- Kitchener
(519) 749-9387
www.wrcm.ca

**D-1
West
of Toronto
85-min.**

Schedule: Tuesday to Saturday, 10 am to 5 pm, Sunday, noon to 5 pm.

Admission: $7/person, FREE for children 2 and under.

Directions: 10 King St. West, Kitchener (despite its name, it is not in Waterloo). From Hwy 401 West, take exit#278/Hwy #8 West towards Kitchener-Waterloo. It becomes King St. The museum is in front of the downtown Shoppers Drug Mart. There's a parking lot on Duke St., just north of King St. and west of the museum.

LONDON CHILDREN'S MUSEUM

Fun space

The museum's large dimensions and its lovely setting inside a former three-storey school, enchanted me. When younger, my son loved its child-sized village. Now it's the new Space gallery that thrills him. See for yourself!

It took us more than two hours to explore the London Regional Children's Museum. On the ground floor, in a pretty room with bay windows, a huge hanging whale skeleton greeted us, floating over tables set up for lunch.

On one side, the prehistoric room boasts two complete dinosaur skeletons and a deep cave, with its dark and realistic nooks and crannies and prehistoric drawings on the walls. In the same room, you will find a cleverly designed sandbox, in which children can dig for stones with genuine fossils. A few dinosaur costumes and other educational activities complete the exhibit.

On the other side, you will find an Inuit room, complete with educational displays and a craft table where children can learn to write their name in the Inuit language. My kids fished magnetic prey through holes in the "ice" and climbed on the snowmobile.

On the second floor, from the Imagination Station (a mezzanine filled with preschoolers' toys), we got to take a closer look at the suspended whale skeleton.

The miniature rendition of a village is also located on the second floor. Its small buildings depict the decor, accessories and costumes of various businesses you'd find in any town.

The museum acquired a few "sponsors" so you'll recognize some company names. Kids can work out at the local Fitness Club. They can buy groceries and cash their friends through the check out, flip burgers and cruise around in mini cars on fun roadways.

Even before the renovations, one could marvel at the overall impression of this child-scale town and it was obvious the younger children were simply enthralled by it.

On the third floor, there's a room where kids can enjoy a huge tree that houses a slide and hiding places. The rest of the room was much in need of renovation when we visited.

There were a few other displays on the science of the senses but we did not explore them, the Space Gallery nearby was way too attractive!

Wow! What a beautiful gallery to look at and to explore too! You're inside a space station with a central control module with large bay windows and monitors allowing you to see the visitors in all the other sections of the station.

TIPS (fun for 2 years +)

• Bring your own lunch, as only snacks are sold on site. There is an interesting outdoor playground.

• Call the museum to find out about their special event during **Canada Day** and their Summer Carnival. They also offer special activities during **Easter**, **Halloween**, **Christmas** and **March Break Magic** (with guests, entertainment, magic, music and demonstrations).

• The **London International Children's Festival** usually runs for 5 consecutive days including the first or second weekend of June. It takes place in and around Victoria Park in London. Check www.londonchildfest.com or call (519) 645-6739. Might be a good time to do a little getaway to London.

Cargo, docking, experiment module and habitation module complete the gallery.

Staff members projected constellations in the dark on the dome-ceiling of the Observation Lab.

My kids looked like astronauts when they wore the silver costumes at their disposal. My daughter felt like a real one when she heard the noise after she had pushed the launch button in her space shuttle. Clever!

London Regional Children's Museum
· London
(519) 434-5726
www.londonchildrensmuseum.ca

E-1
S-W
of Toronto
2 hrs

 Schedule: Open Tuesday to Sunday, 10 am to 5 pm (closes at 8 pm on Fridays). Open Mondays also, May to August and holidays.
 Admission: $5/visitor, FREE under 2 years.
 Directions: 21 Wharncliffe Rd. South, London. From Hwy 401 West, take exit #186/Wellington Rd. northbound, turn west on Horton St., then turn north on Wharncliffe Rd. The museum is located between Springbank and Riverside Dr.

General tips about
Nature's call:

• Did you know poison ivy often climbs up larger trees? Me neither! In case you were wondering, here's what poison ivy looks like.

Look for shrubs with distinctive three-parted pointed leaves, the central of which has a longer stem than the two side leaflets. The edges of the leaves can be smooth or very jagged. It loves sunny areas along woods, roads and beaches.

The rash appears 24-48 hours after contact. Beware! You can get it from touching your pet if it has brushed itself against it in the woods.

We can complain about it but let's not forget it is a good source of food for fall and winter animals!

NATURE'S
CALL

See **Doris McCarthy Trail** on p. 294.

ABOUT CONSERVATION AREAS

Most affordable recreation!

Twenty-three conservation areas are described in this guide. Every single one we visited offered a good family outing under $20... and Ontario has over 300 of them!

Conservation areas were initially based on the Ontario watershed. Back in the early 1940's, wide areas of the province were strained by deforestation and erosion. Worsening spring floods were followed by low summer flows of polluted water. Eventually, the province encouraged the creation of locally based conservation authorities who were petitioned by municipalities to solve ecological problems. Dams and reservoirs were built.

Today, flooding has virtually been eliminated. The conservation authorities have broadened their activities to include restoration, recreation and education.

About Toronto Conservation

This conservation offers a **Conservation Area Site Membership** providing one year access to one only of the following conservation areas under its authority; see **Heart Lake** (p. 277), **Albion Hills** (p. 278), **Boyd** (p. 331), **Kortright Centre** (p. 332), **Bruce's Mill** (p. 335), **Glen Haffy** (p. 360), **Petticoat Creek** (p. 385) and **Black Creek Pioneer Village** (p. 404, that membership comes with free parking at **Black Creek**). The pass costs $35 for individuals and $65 for families (two adults and children under 18 years old), plus taxes. You still have to pay extra fees for cross-country skiing at **Albion Hills** and pool fees at **Petticoat Creek**.

Conservation Journeys Regular Membership costs $60 for individuals and $100 for families, plus taxes. It gives free general access for an entire year to all Toronto conservation areas plus some discounts on special events.

Both options are available in all the Toronto and region conservation areas or call their customer service at (416) 667-6295. You may also download membership forms from their web site.

TIPS (fun for all)

• **www.conservation-ontario.on.ca** is a portal to all Conservation Authorities. Click 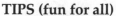Recreation to find the locations offering the recreation of your choice.

• **Conservation Halton** offers a $95 vehicle pass giving one-year access to its conservation areas, all mentioned in this guide; see **Kelso** (p. 280), **Rattlesnake Point** (p. 296), **Mount Nemo** (p. 297), **Hilton Falls** (p. 300), **Mountsberg Wildlife Centre** (p. 338) and **Crawford Lake** (p. 410). On a given day, admission to one conservation area gives you free access to any other conservation area under Conservation Halton's authority.

• **Credit Valley Conservation** vehicle pass is $88; see **Rattray Marsh** (p. 318) and **Belfountain** (p. 353).

• **Lake Simcoe Conservation**. **Whitchurch** (p. 275) and **Scanlon Creek** (p. 279) don't offer a pass.

• **Hamilton Conservation Authority** vehicle pass costs $85; see **Confederation Park/Wild Waterworks** (p. 37), **Christie Lake** (p. 280), **Webster's Falls** (p. 301) and **Westfield Heritage Village** (p. 414).

• **Grand River Conservation Authority** vehicle pass is $100; see **Elora Quarry** (p. 279), **Shade's Mills** (p. 281), **Rockwood** (p. 340) and **Elora Gorge** (p. 394).

Conservation Authorities

• **Toronto and Region Conservation**
(416) 667-6299 (info line)
(416) 667-6295 (customer service)
www.trca.on.ca
• **Conservation Halton**
(905) 336-1158
www.conservationhalton.on.ca
• **Credit Valley Conservation**
(905) 670-1615
www.creditvalleycons.com
• **Lake Simcoe Conservation**
(905) 895-1281
www.lsrca.on.ca
• **Hamilton Conservation Authority**
1-888-319-4722
www.conservationhamilton.ca
• **Grand River Conservation Authority**
(519) 621-2761
www.grandriver.ca

HANLAN BEACH

A taste of Paradise

At a glance, we take in the endless stretch of pristine water, with its swimmers frolicking against a backdrop of lazy white sailboats. On the right hand side of the beach, we can watch small planes taking off from the Toronto Islands Airport, stretched out against the city landscape. The CN Tower emerges behind the tree line, reminding us we are still in the heart of Toronto.

The sand is burning our feet on our way to the shore. By the water, it is cooled by the breeze and so soft our kids beg us to bury them in it!

The water is clear and refreshingly cool. It remains shallow for a great distance, reaching no higher than an adult's waist for at least 50 metres. The beach is well patrolled by lifeguards on shore and water.

When we last visited, the beach seemed relatively deserted. Further to our left however, a fenced area with the sign "you are entering a clothing optional area" attracted a larger crowd. Without being at close range, you see nothing out of the ordinary. Yet, those uncomfortable with the situation can move away along a wide stretch of beach to the right.

A small playground and a wading pool mark the entrance to the beach. Beyond the wading pool, a number of smaller sandy trails, some looking like real tiny dunes, branch off from the main trail leading to the beach.

TIPS (fun for all ages)

• More information on **Toronto Islands Ferry** on p. 268.
• From the paved trails beside the wading pool, plan on a 20-minute walk to reach the bicycle rental centre and another ten minutes to reach the **Centreville Amusement Park**.
• To have a nude section on Hanlan Beach is a voted decision made every year by the City. Call to confirm by June.
• The water along the south shore of the **Toronto Islands** is the cleanest water in the area. The Islands act as a filter. Environment Canada says we should not swim up to two days after a rain storm.
• Call the **Beach Hotline** to find out the water conditions, (416) 392-7161.
• A snack bar and washrooms are located near the wading pool.

NEARBY ATTRACTIONS
Centreville Park (30-min. walk)......p. 23

City of Toronto
(416) 392-1111
www.toronto.ca

**J-10
Toronto
Islands**

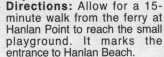

Schedule: Open year-round.
Admission: FREE, plus cost of ferry ride.
Directions: Allow for a 15-minute walk from the ferry at Hanlan Point to reach the small playground. It marks the entrance to Hanlan Beach.

TORONTO ISLANDS

Islanders for a day

Did you know that an amusement park existed in 1800 at the very same place today's Toronto Islands Airport sits? In 1909, a baseball stadium was added to this park. Did you know that it's in this very stadium that Babe Ruth hit his first professional home run?

The Toronto Islands might have lost their identity as centres of recreation after the 1930's when the stadium was closed, the amusement park demolished and the airport constructed, but they have since reclaimed the title with a vengeance, with over 1.2 million visitors a year.

Ferry ride

The adventure starts before you even reach the Islands with a 15-minute ferry ride, the only way to reach them.

My little sailor was tickled pink, unsure whether to check the panoramic view of the CN Tower and the tall buildings close to it, look at planes taking off from the Toronto Islands Airport, gaze at the white sailboats manoeuvring on Lake Ontario, or to simply explore the many bridges on the ferry itself.

Three ferry boats service the Islands. The ferry that reaches **Centre Island** brings you closest to the **Centreville Amusement Park** and the bicycle rentals. It is the most popular, crossing every 15 minutes on weekends (for most of the day). The **Hanlan's Point** ferry services the western end of Toronto Islands, while **Ward's Island** ferry reaches the eastern point. These two ferries cross every half-hour throughout the day.

Hanlan's Point

The **Hanlan's Point** ferry reaches the western end of the Islands. The amusement park is located approximately 3.5 km further, so I don't recommend you take on the walk with young children on a hot sunny day.

This part of the Islands includes the Toronto Islands Airport, tennis courts, 2 wading pools, a trout pond and 2 beaches including the superb **Hanlan Beach**, a 15-min. walk from the dock (see p. 267).

Centre Island

In addition to the popular **Centreville Amusement Park** (p. 23), Centre Island hosts the **Toronto Islands Bike Rental**, on the south shore of the island. It is located across the big bridge, at the end of the flower garden.

You can rent bicycles, tandems, double-seaters or 4-seaters to ride along 20 kms of **bike trails**.

TIPS (fun for 2 years +)

• More on **Centreville Amusement Park** on page 23.

• The **Centre Island** ferry won't allow bikes aboard on summer weekends but the other two ferries always welcome them.

• The Islands act as a filter and their beaches are the farthest away from the sources of pollution. Call the **Beach Hotline** to find out the water conditions on the day of your visit, (416) 392-7161. Environment Canada says we should not swim up to two days after a storm.

• From **Hanlan Beach,** plan on a 20-minute walk to reach the bicycle rental centre and another ten minutes to reach the **Centreville Amusement Park**.

• Throughout the summer, it is possible to rent a **fire pit** to make a bonfire by the lake. Call (416) 392-8188.

• A snack bar and washrooms are located near the wading pool by the entrance to **Hanlan Beach**. There are other snack bars throughout the Islands and the tearoom by the boardwalk on **Ward's Island** offers great homemade desserts during the summer.

NEARBY ATTRACTIONS
From Toronto Islands Ferry:
Harbourfront (10-min. walk)..........p. 68

Ward's Island

The eastern part of the Islands is where the year-round residents live. It is almost impossible to resist a nosy peek as you stroll by the little postcard cottages close to this boardwalk. Within a short walk of the dock, you can reach the boardwalk and the intimate **Ward's Beach**, interesting for its proximity to the boardwalk. This is not the only temptation here as one of us is always sent on a mission to fetch good coffees at the lovely tearoom by the boardwalk.

Toronto Islands	J-10
(416) 392-8193 (ferry) **(416) 392-1111 (city)** **(416) 203-0009 (bike rental)** www.toronto.ca	**Toronto Islands** **15-min.**

Schedule: During the summer, the 3 ferries operate from 8 am until 11:45 pm. Schedules vary on weekdays.

Admission: Return fare is $5/adults, $3/seniors and students, $2/2-14 years, FREE for children less than 2 years old.

Directions: The Toronto Islands Ferry Terminal is located on Queen's Quay West, east of Bay St. No cars allowed on the ferry.

BEACHES NEIGHBOURHOOD

recently and now offers a castle-like climbing structure built around the central mature tree. After playing hide and seek around the bandshell in the middle of the park, we head for **Kew Beach**, a 3-minute walk away.

It's a renewed pleasure each time I look at the water. It sometimes appears turquoise beyond the boardwalk that runs alongside. With the sand, pebbles and

When you hear the call

Queen Street East, enlivened by small shops, cafés and great parks along the waterfront, indiscriminately attracts three categories of people: those being pulled by their dog, those following their stroller and finally, those who can enjoy a long brunch.

We early risers always begin an outing to the **Beaches** by having breakfast at one of the district's restaurants in front of **Kew Gardens**.

We then explore the **Kew Gardens** playground. It was fully renovated

seagulls, you'd think you were staring at the ocean, as far as your eye can see. Towards the East, the boardwalk is lined with trees and you cross a few wharves projecting into the lake.

A long bicycle trail runs along the boardwalk. Towards the west, it connects to the **bike trails** of Cherry Beach, Lake Shore and Don Valley.

TIPS (fun for all ages)

• In the spring or the fall, bring an extra sweater. The breeze that sweeps across the beach makes it cooler than on Queen Street.

• Call the **Beach Hotline** to find out about the **Beaches** water conditions for the day (416) 392-7161.

• Fireworks are usually offered at Ashbridges Bay Park on **Victoria Day** and **Canada Day**. Call **Access Toronto** closer to the dates for events update, check www.toronto.ca/special_events or call (416) 338-0338.

• As of summer 2004, **Ashbridges Bay Park** starts hosting **Shakespeare-Works by the Lake**, a theatre company producing Shakespeare's plays. Check www.shakespeareworks.com or call (416) 463-4869. Their seasonal tent, offering the lake as a backdrop, will be dismantled at the end of each summer. BEWARE! The tent is 500-metres from the closest parking lot (golf carts will be there for those who require assistance). Around $25/person for evening performances; $15 for matinees; limited $2 tickets for 18 years and under.

• The Alliance **Beach Cinemas** are right behind **Woodbine Park**, at 1651 Queen Street East. It is our favourite theatre, with spacious seats, live jazz on Saturday nights, patio, café with lots of tables, chess games, puzzles and magazines at our disposal. And here, movies are hardly ever sold out, even on the day of their release! (416) 646-0444.

• You'll find a snack bar at **Kew Beach** and **Balmy Beach**.

• See the restaurants: **Boardwalk Pub** (p. 430), **Garden Gate** (p. 435) and **Sunset Grill** (p. 436).

NEARBY ATTRACTIONS

The boardwalk ends 20 minutes farther, eastbound, at **Balmy Beach**.

If you walk ten minutes westbound from **Kew Beach**, there's a playground located by the beach as well as the huge **Donald D. Summerville** outdoor pool. Along the way, if you're lucky, you'll see odd towers of rocks defying gravity, left by anonymous artists.

Beyond, the beach widens a lot and the sand becomes finer, you've reached **Woodbine Beach** from which we can see Ashbridges' fireworks during special events. After another 10-minute walk, there's another playground located close to the Boardwalk Pub and snack bar.

On the north side of Lake Shore Blvd., you'll see **Woodbine Park** with its rotunda and pretty pond welcoming the ducks.

The major parking lot for the Beaches is at the foot of Coxwell, also the entrance to **Ashbridges Bay Park**. This park offers huge stones on which older children love to leap about and tall trees as well as a scenic lookout.

When you park near Ashbridges Bay Park, it takes 10 minutes to walk to **Woodbine Beach**.

The Beaches	J-10
(416) 392-1111	**East**
www.	**of downtown**
beachestoronto.com	**20-min.**

Schedule: Open year-round.
Admission: FREE (during the summer weekends and statutory holidays, there is a parking fee to park in the Ashbridges Bay parking lot or around the Boardwalk Pub.
Directions: The Beaches neighbourhood is located between Coxwell and Victoria Park Ave., along the waterfront. Take Gardiner Expwy. eastbound to the end, exit at Lake Shore Blvd.

CHERRY BEACH

Cherry on top of the Sunday

Sorry for the easy pun but it was irresistible. It also describes very well our impression when we visited this beach on a hot summer Sunday when the Beaches area was overloaded with visitors and the Ashbridges Bay parking lot was full!

Unlike in the Beaches area, where beaches are wide open to the lake, Cherry Beach sits right in front of Toronto Islands so it offers a different panorama. You will see several small sailboats zigzagging between the two shores.

The sand is not as fine as the one you'll find more to the east but there are many pebbles worth prospecting, according to my kids. On the eastern part of the beach, many tall trees offer shady spots to gather large families' picnics.

Another great advantage is the direct access to the **bicycle trail** leading towards **Leslie Spit**, offering Toronto's least-crowded ride along the water. (This trail starts at the end of Leslie Street and reaches the light-house at the tip of the land, 5 km away.)

The place was already great when we visited but it will get better. It is the lead-in project to the more than 500 acres of revitalization planned for Toronto's central waterfront.

At the time of print, they were already in the process of doing an overall clean up, improving and adding to the Martin Goodman Trail, constructing a trail to Cherry Point (to the west), creating a grand entrance, restoring 1933 historic buildings, building a boardwalk and adding new benches, BBQ grills and picnic tables. Something to look forward to!

TIPS (fun for all ages)
• Cherry Beach is also known as Clarke Beach but the Cherry name is sticking with the locals since the beach is located at the foot of Cherry Street. Call the **Beach Hotline** for Cherry (or Clarke) Beach's water conditions at (416) 392-7161.
• There's usually a chip truck by the parking lot.

NEARBY ATTRACTIONS	
The Docks (2-min.)	p. 17
The Distillery (5-min.)	p. 44

Cherry Beach
(416) 392-1111
www.towaterfront.ca

J-10
Downtown
Toronto
10-min.

Schedule: Open year-round.
Admission: FREE.
Directions: Going eastbound on Lake Shore Blvd., turn south on Cherry St. Note that you can not turn south on Cherry St. going westbound. You'll have to turn north on Cherry and find a way to U-turn back southbound.

BLUFFER'S PARK

Cliffs from below

This beach, at first quite broad, narrows gradually. When dry, its sand is one of the finest I've seen in the area. My little lad threw himself down and made an angel with his arms and legs.

The beach spreads at the end of the fourth parking lot to the east. You reach it via a small road that borders the base of the cliffs which sit blazing in the summer light.

As you walk further east along the beach, you'll discover another source of playful inspiration in the pieces of polished beachwood lying here and there.

When visiting in early October, there was a multitude of red ladybugs every second step on the beach.

See **Rosetta Gardens**, a 20-min. drive away, on p. 313.

Check **Dogfish Pub** on p. 430.

City of Toronto · Scarborough (416) 392-1111 www.toronto.ca	J-11 East of downtown 30-min.

 Schedule: Open year-round.
Admission: FREE.
Directions: Take Kingston Rd. eastbound. Turn south on Brimley St. (east of Midland).

ROUGE BEACH

Spread of Rouge

We climb up stairs, cross over a bridge and arrive at a boardwalk where we get a superb panorama of the lake, with a strip of sand pointing out of the shore of Rouge Beach, not unlike the seashore during low tide.

The trail eventually takes off from the edge of the cliff, so we come down the path to get to the beach itself.

Rouge Beach is relatively long and wide, with great sand, and is equipped with changing rooms. When we were visiting, the kids had fun chasing nice tiny waves created by the wind.

Many people fish in the Rouge Marsh adjacent to the parking lot. Some launch their canoes into the small canals of Little Rouge Creek, visible from the shore. Others come from Lake Ontario into the creek. See **Rouge Park** on p. 348.

Rouge Beach · Scarborough (416) 392-1111 www.toronto.ca	J-11 East of downtown 30-min.

 **Schedule:** Open year-round.
Admission: FREE.
Directions: Take Hwy 401 East, follow Port Union signs, exit Port Union southbound. Turn east on Lawrence Ave., to the parking lot.

PROFESSOR'S LAKE

Spring-fed and urban

When I was told about this lake smack in the middle of a large suburban housing development, I envisioned... well, I just could not envision it! No wonder. The man-made lake is a first attempt of this kind in eastern Canada. It offers the best water in the region, a twisting water slide, a raft to jump from for the better swimmers and a large sandy beach. It is also surrounded by 750 housing units.

To access Professor's Lake, one has to go through a corridor in the recreation centre, which hides the lake from our view. When the beach revealed itself, I took in the panorama of the wide beach covered with pale sand, some 300 visitors (much less than I had expected for a great

TIPS (fun for all ages)
• You need to be 42 inches or taller to use the slide. Adults are welcome.
• An annual **Beach Party** run by the neighbourhood community group is usually offered on the last Saturday in June. You can expect water-ski shows, live entertainment, ice cream eating contests, maybe a sandcastle contest, and fireworks. Call to confirm.
• A trail runs around the lake outside of the gated area.
• A snack bar sells hot dogs, snacks, popsicles and slush.
• There is a **Famous Players Gateway Six** on Gateway Drive, just off Queen Street, (416) 646-0444. A family movie would be a nice way to finish a great outing (especially since the beach closes at 6 pm). You'll find many fast food chains and family restaurants in the area, a 5-min. drive from the lake.

summer day) and the 65-acre mass of blue water. My kids ran like wild horses to try the fun slide throwing happy children into the lake.

My 5-year-old spent the next four hours on the slide while her 9-year-old brother kept jumping off the raft, more than 30 metres from shore. Like many kids, mine could not care less about water attributes vital to me such as quality, temperature, colour or odour. Whatever water will do the job, as long as I allow them to swim in it.

I was really taken by the sensation of swimming in Professor's Lake, and so were the moms I introduced to this attraction. It felt... clean and refreshed!

There are many reasons for it. The former gravel pit is spring-fed. It offers a large shallow area but reaches 42 feet in its greatest depth. And unlike many lakes in the region, a storm drainage system was designed to bypass the lake so it is protected from water run-off from farms, houses and roads, following heavy rains.

Add lifeguards on the beach, at the raft and at both ends of the slide and you get a very relaxing outing for parents! Add a wide stable of canoes, kayaks and paddle boats for rental at affordable prices to take advantage of the lake, and you get an outing suitable for all ages and genders.

NEARBY ATTRACTIONS
Chinguacousy Park (5-min.).........p. 334

SUNSET BEACH ON LAKE WILCOX

Not bad at all!

If you can't bring yourself to trust Lake Ontario's water, you might want to mingle with the locals at the Lake Wilcox municipal beach.

The lake was big enough to show on the map, so we drove out to Sunset Beach

Park, which actually has a perimeter of almost 3 km. The beach is a long and narrow strip of rough sand, with the grass and trees almost touching the water in some places. The water is shallow along a vast area marked with buoys, so the place is perfect for young children.

A small road runs by the beach. You'll have to cross it to reach the beach from the parking lot. Show up before 11 am to find a place!

There's a snack bar and a playground by the parking lot.

Richmond Hill Parks & Recreation • Richmond Hill (905) 884-8013 www.richmondhill.ca	**G-11 North of Toronto 35-min.**

Schedule: Open year-round.
Admission: FREE.
Directions: Lake Wilcox by Bayview Ave. in Richmond Hill. From Hwy 404 North, take exit #41/Bloomington Rd. westbound. Turn south on Bayview Ave.

WHITCHURCH C. A.

Memories

When was the last time you saw a real frog? And a school of tiny fish? The intimate Whitchurch Conservation Area is a beautiful spot to enjoy the small joys of nature.

We stroll for five minutes on a trail before we reach a clearing. The pond is located down a small hill and we have to get closer to take it all in; it is beautiful! Tall trees and bushes on the other side of the water are reflected on the still pond's mirror-like surface. Everything is so quiet that we can hear the living creatures that surround us: the song of birds, the humming of insects and the funny

"Daow!" sound of a loud bullfrog.

As we get even closer, the kids jump on a thin strip of sandy shore behind a wild flower bush. They are not a big threat to the small quicksilver fish they try to catch with their bare hands. BEWARE! The water is not tested.

Whitchurch Conservation Area • Stouffville (905) 895-1281 www.lsrca.on.ca	**G-12 N-E of Toronto 35-min.**

Schedule: Open year-round.
Admission: FREE.
Directions: Aurora Rd., Stouffville. From Hwy 404 North, take exit #45/Aurora Rd. eastbound. The park is on the south side, between Warden Ave. and Kennedy Rd.

CEDAR BEACH PARK

A private matter

The sign atop the stone gate with its gothic lettering, brings to mind the look of a summer camp from the 50's. The entrance's iron doors frame a blue square of water, and as we reach the top of steep stairs, the wide private beach reveals itself, promising an afternoon of fun.

I can't believe our luck. It is a midweek hot summer day and we have the beach all to ourselves. Not for long. Our privacy is interrupted with the arrival of a school bus full of noisy camp kids. I kiss goodbye any hopes of a quiet day at the beach but my young socialites are thrilled!

The sand is lovely and works well for elaborate "engineering" projects of bridges and tunnels. The shores of Musselman's Lake are comfortably shallow for a distance, and the deeper water is well marked with buoys.

TIPS (fun for all ages)

• There's a slight algae smell to the water, typical in the midst of summer, though it was quite clear and refreshing when we visited. You might want to call and check the water conditions before you go.

• Kayaks and paddle boats are available for rent at the fully-serviced campground; ($11.50/hour + deposit). You might have to drive to the office to get a key to unlock the boat's padlock.

• The trailer park includes 41 **campsites** for tents.

• There's a snack bar on site. Picnic tables are lined up along the iron railing and we enjoyed eating there watching swimmers down below.

Cedar Beach Trailer Park & Pavilion
• Stouffville
(905) 642-1700
www.cedarbeach.com

G-12
N-E
of Toronto
50-min.

Schedule: The beach is open early April to late October, 8 am to dusk, weather permitting.
Admission: (cash only) $6/adults, $3/1-15 years old, FREE for babies.
Directions: 15014 9th Line, Musselmans Lake/Stouffville. From Hwy 404 North, take exit #45/Aurora Rd. eastbound, turn south on 9th Line (Regional Rd. 69).

NEARBY ATTRACTIONS
York Durham Railway (15-min.)...p. 239
Burd's Trout Farm (10-min.).........p. 359

Heart Lake C. A.

Dive into nature

Heart Lake's swimming hole is a well-kept secret. Its sandy beach is wide, and licensed fishermen can enjoy their sport looking for a few farmed trout, comfortably installed in the willows' shade. Beyond the area reserved for swimmers, paddle boats criss-cross the heart-shaped pond, escorted by dragonflies.

The valley's picnic sites bordering the parking lot closest to the lake offer an inviting panorama. There, you feel the urge to roll on the grass. Big families are gathering for large picnics and the air is filled with the appetizing smells of meat sizzling on the barbecues. Unfortunately, you don't get a view of the lake from those sites.

The lake is stocked with rainbow trout every spring. You may fish from the shore or rent a paddle boat to fish out on the water.

Half a kilometre from the parking lot by the lake, you'll find another parking lot that borders a lovely little path that rolls up and down. The whole family can stroll on it for 30 minutes, while enjoying the shady coolness of 40-metre-high trees.

TIPS (fun for all ages)

• The snack bar is not always open on weekdays; better to bring a lunch.

NEARBY ATTRACTIONS	

Heart Lake Conservation Area	**D-2 N-W of Toronto 35-min.**

**Heart Lake
Conservation Area**
• Brampton
(905) 846-2494
or (416) 661-6600, ext. 5203
www.trca.on.ca

Schedule: Open end of April to October 31, 9 am until dusk (variable closing time for each month).

Admission: $4/adults, $3/seniors, $2/5-14 years, FREE 4 years and under. Canoe/paddle boat rental is $13.80 per hour.
Directions: Take Hwy 410 North until it becomes Heart Lake Rd., then go 2 km north on Road #7.

ALBION HILLS C. A.

A quiet sandy hide-out

Albion Hills' beach is wide in certain areas, and sufficiently long to satisfy those seeking a quiet sandy hide-out at its far end.

At the end of the more quiet sandy point, you can take a trail running up the hill bordering the water.

From the highest point, you will get a great view and be able to go down a sandy slope bringing you to the shores of the small lake.

If you cross the road by the entrance of the trail, you'll reach the narrow Humber River, complete with picnic areas along the way. It eventually leads to the campground. You must take your car to access other hiking trails of 1.6 to 5.8 kilometre-long paths. You can rent a paddle boat or canoe to enjoy on the lake.

TIPS (fun for all ages)

• More about **Albion Hills** tobogganing in the winter on p. 392.
• During a visit in May, we observed hundreds of tiny tadpoles in the water!
• Albion Hills' trails are open for **mountain biking** from the end of April to the end of October, weather permitting. All trails start at Cedar Grove parking lot.
• Albion Hills offers over 230 **campsites**, quite close to one another, yet equipped with a lovely playground.
• The snack bar is mainly open during the weekends. You should bring your lunch on weekdays. There is a small playground by the beach.

Albion Hills Conservation Area
· Caledon
(905) 880-0227
or (416) 661-6600, ext. 5203
www.trca.on.ca

C-2
N-W
of Toronto
50-min.

Schedule: Open year-round from 9 am. Swimming is allowed June to Labour Day.
Admission: $4/adults, $3/ seniors, $2/5-14 years, FREE 4 years and under. Canoe or paddle boat rental is $13.80 per hour.
Directions: From Hwy 400 North, take exit #55/Hwy 9 westbound. Turn south on Hwy 50 and follow the signs.

NEARBY ATTRACTIONS
South Simcoe Railway (15-min.)..p. 240

SCANLON CREEK C. A.

No more

Oops, just before going to print, I learned this beach has closed. It was too late to reorganize my Nature chapter. Still, I thought its trail around the marsh lovely enough to keep it in this guide.

At the end of what used to be the beach, the trail runs over the body of water on a boardwalk across marshland. It climbs up a forest hill and goes down towards a bridge crossing the creek, leading us back to the beach at its other end. The whole walk takes less than 45 minutes. There are no more washrooms on the site. The sand remains but it is not raked clean of waterfowl droppings...

Scanlon Creek Conservation Area · Caledon (905) 895-1281 www.lsrca.on.ca	C-2 N-W of Toronto 45-min.

Schedule: Open year-round from 9 am to dusk.
Admission: $4/adults, $3/seniors, $2/children 5-14, FREE 4 years and under.
Directions: From Hwy 400 North, take exit #64/Simcoe Rd. 88 eastbound, turn north on County Rd. 4 (formerly Hwy 11), then east on 9th Concession.

ELORA QUARRY C. A.

body of water. Seen from the beach, the panorama is quite special. Last time we visited, our little amateur of antiques just loved the manual water pump, still in working order, located on the beach.

No jumping or diving is permitted due to insurance regulations.

Old fashioned hole

With the passing years, a basin has formed at the bottom of Elora Quarry, abandoned since the 1930's. On hot summer days, you can dive into this water fed by pure springs.

We accessed the quarry through a small beach offering an excellent view of the 12-metre-high walls surrounding the

Elora Quarry Conservation Area · Elora (519) 846-5234 www.grandriver.ca	D-1 West of Toronto 50-min.

Schedule: Open mid-June until Labour Day.

Admission: $3.75/adults, $2/6-14 years, FREE 5 years and under.

Directions: From Hwy 401 West, take exit #295/Hwy 6 northbound, then follow County Rd. 7 to Elora. Turn east on County Rd. 18 (also called Fergus-Elora Rd.). Elora Quarry is located between Elora and Fergus.

KELSO CONSERVATION AREA

Milton's water spot

For a successful outing in the Milton region, I recommend including a swim at Kelso Conservation Area.

Kelso Beach sits by a grassy park with lots of shade. The length of the beach is covered with long transparent wires hung some ten metres above, to prevent bird visits. Needless to say the sand is clean! It is the ideal spot for a picnic but expect hordes of visitors after 1 pm. With children 7 years and older, you may wish to hike all the way to the top of the escarpment. I have heard it takes more than 45 minutes to reach, but the panoramic view is amazing and you'll find an old quarry with **fossils** on the way! Kelso is known in the region for its series of trails for serious **mountain bikers**. More on this conservation area and the **Halton Region Museum** on p. 407! See **Glen Eden Snow Tubing** on p. 377.

Kelso Conservation Area · Milton (905) 878-5011 www.conservationhalton.on.ca	D-2 West of Toronto 50-min.

 Schedule: Open year-round (summer time, from 8 am to 8 pm). **Admission:** $4.25/adults, $3.50/seniors, $3/children 5 to 14, FREE 4 years and under. Bike fee is $6. Canoe, paddle boat or kayak rental is $12 per hour.

Directions: From Hwy 401 West, take exit #320/Hwy 25 northbound, turn west on Campbellville Rd., then south on Tremaine Rd., follow signs.

CHRISTIE LAKE C. A.

Check this out!

This sandy beach is 360 metres long and the swimming area is... chlorinated!

A fabric shield separates the swimming area from the rest. It protects the water from the pollution of bird droppings but the down side is that the muddy sand at the bottom stays suspended longer, giving a murky colour to that section. The truth is that happy bathers do lots of stirring in that water, never deeper than five feet, perfect for parents to toss their ecstatic kids like potato sacks into the lake.

You can rent large inner tubes to play on inside the boundaries, or paddle boats, canoes and... hydro bikes to explore the rest of the lake.

We're not allowed to eat on the narrow beach to keep it clean but we have our picnic on the grass right next to it. One of the trails runs around the lake for 5.6 km (get a map at the entrance).

Attention fishermen! Christie includes nine ponds for fishing (see p. 360).

Christie Lake Conservation Area · Dundas (905) 628-3060 or 1-888-319-4722 www.conservationhamilton.ca	E-2 S-W of Toronto 55-min.

 Schedule: Open year-round. **Admission:** $7.50 per vehicle and driver, $2.50/add. passenger, to a max. of $15. Canoe, paddle boat and hydro bike rental is $6 for 30 minutes.

 Directions: From QEW/403, take exit Hwy 6 North. Turn west on Hwy 5. Christie is on the south side.

SHADE'S MILLS C. A.

Paddle time

We were grateful for this nice swim almost right in town on our way back from other attractions in this region.

Regardless of the name, the beach is not in the shade but there are plenty of trees around the boat rental. Renting a canoe or a paddle boat was very tempting because of the shape of the reservoir, with a long water arm to explore, stretching out one side. It would have taken the whole day to try everything. The conservation area's map showed a footbridge and 12 km of nature trails (turned into cross-country ski trails in the winter).

Ask about their ice-fishing and heated Ice Huts for rental.

Shade's Mill Conservation Area · Cambridge (519) 621-3697 www.grandriver.ca	E-1 S-W of Toronto 75-min

Schedule: Open year-round.
Admission: $3.75/adults, $2/6-14 years old, FREE 5 years and under. Canoe or paddle boat rental, $10/hr.
Directions: 412 Avenue Rd., Cambridge. From Hwy 401 West, take exit #282 at Hespeler Rd. South. Turn east on Avenue Rd.

COUCHICHING BEACH

Summer treat

Ice cream, a playground by the beach, just a few metres from the water and soft sand. What more could a child want?

How about a miniature engine blowing its whistle in the park to invite the visitors for a $2 ride on a one-km-long track?

You can expect **fireworks** at dusk in the park on Sunday during **Victoria Day** and an even bigger celebration on **Canada Day**, also complete with **fireworks** at dusk.

The **Trans-Canada Trail** now includes a 9-km paved trail running through the City of Orillia.

Couchiching Beach Park · Orillia (705) 326-4424 www.orillia.com	A-3 North of Toronto 75-min

Schedule: Open year-round. The train runs weekends from Victoria Day to Canada Day, then daily until Labour Day.
Admission: FREE park access.
Directions: Take Hwy 11, exit eastbound on Coldwater Rd. Turn right on Front St., left on Mississauga St., to the Port of Orillia and the beach.

McRae Point & Mara Parks

Best family picnic

Lake Couchiching and Lake Simcoe are separated by a shallow strip of land called the Narrows. Mara Provincial Park sits right by the Narrows. McRae Point Provincial Park lays farther along the shores of Lake Simcoe.

We stopped for a swim at **Mara's** wide beach with shallow water and great sand. Picnic tables were set in the shade of tall trees; unfortunately, they were too far from the water for my liking. We preferred to spend the rest of the afternoon at **McRae Point** (10-min. drive).

We really fell for **McRae's** narrow beach bordered by grass, pretty trees and tables. As the day was fading away we had a great picnic, accompanied by the music of the lazy waves stroking the shore.

TIPS (fun for all ages)
• You can fish in both parks. Both provincial parks include **campgrounds**.

McRae Point P. Park	A-3
(705) 325-7290	**North**
Mara P. Park	**of Toronto**
(705) 326-4451 (seasonal)	**75-min.**
• Orillia	
www.ontarioparks.com	

Schedule: Mara opens mid-May to Labour Day. McRae opens mid-May to Thanksgiving.
Admission: $9.50/vehicle.
Directions: Take Hwy 400 North, then follow Hwy 11. Take Hwy 12 eastbound and follow signs. Mara comes first.

COBOURG'S BEACH

metres ahead of us, while my daughter embarks on a digging engineering project in the water. She soon joins new friends for a game of wave catching and burying in the sand!

Last time we went, we checked out their new spray pad right by the

Charge!

As soon as my little mermaid sees the wide and long beach at Victoria Park, she darts off, sure of her way, to a day of water fun.

It worked for her when she was three, and then again last time we visited, when she was six.

The shallow water is pleasantly refreshing, yet it warms up quickly in the middle of summer. Swimmers walk through the waves some 50

boardwalk. Lovely and colourful, it's a fabulous addition to this already great beach. There's also a **mini-golf** in the park.

The **Cobourg Waterfront Festival** returns every year during 3-4 consecutive days including **Canada Day**. It takes place in Victoria Park by Cobourg Beach and involves **fireworks** on July 1.

TIPS (fun for all ages)
• You'll find a snack bar selling great fries, slush and ice cream.
• There's also a nice ice cream parlour at the corner of Division and Charles Streets by the park.

NEARBY ATTRACTIONS

Cobourg's Beach
• Cobourg
1-888-262-6874 (festival)
or (905) 372-5831
www.cobourg.ca

C-5
East
of Toronto
70-min.

Schedule: Open year-round.
Admission: FREE.
Directions: Victoria Park, Cobourg. From Hwy 401 East, take exit #472/Regional Hwy 2 southbound. Turn east on King St., then south on Division St.

SIBBALD POINT PROVINCIAL PARK

Swimming, sand & snacks

People who aren't inspired by Lake Ontario can turn to Lake Simcoe, the next closest large natural lake in the Greater Toronto vicinity.

The Sibbald Point Provincial Park, located on the shores of Lake Simcoe, is quite busy. One goes there to mingle with the crowd rather than to return to nature. The decibel level in the park doesn't exactly make it relaxing, as motor boats are allowed on the lake. On the other hand, adult swimmers can take advantage of great waves challenging those swimming beyond the buoys.

The beach is long. The sand is mixed with a few pebbles, but you can easily walk on it with bare feet. There's a very nice playground facing the beach. The children in our group spent their time visiting it, in between a swim and an ice cream cone. Walking on the west side of Sibbald Point, across the farthest parking lot, you will find a tall pine and cedar forest where picnic tables are set up.

Various natural clearings reveal a narrow pebble beach, much more isolated and not marked by buoys. The waves are stronger and more fun for big kids who can swim well.

Here, people settle in the patches of sun shining through the mature trees. You can hear the sound of the waves and the birds singing. This area of the park is perfect for little trappers and for those who are looking for a quieter location.

TIPS (fun for all ages)

• See **About provincial parks** on p. 165.

• Sibbald Point offers more than 800 **campsites** made private by tall, deciduous trees.

• Several picnic tables await under the shade of tall trees by the most crowded beach. I recommend getting there before 11 am if you wish to use one.

• There's a well-stocked store and a snack bar by the main beach. They don't rent canoes or paddle boats anymore.

NEARBY ATTRACTIONS
Sharon Temple (25-min.)............p. 118

Sibbald Point Provincial Park • Sutton (905) 722-8061 www.ontarioparks.com	**B-3 North** of Toronto **60-min.**

 Schedule: Open mid-May to early October.

 Admission: Weekday Day Pass is $9.50/vehicle. Weekend Day Pass is $15.

 Directions: 26465 Hedge Rd., R. R. 2, Sutton West. Take Hwy 404 North to the end, take exit #51 (Davis Dr./Hwy 31) eastbound. Turn north on Hwy 48, then follow Rd. 18/Park Rd. northbound.

EARL ROWE PROVINCIAL PARK

Some water holes!

Beaches offer everything pleasing to children: space to run, sand to build castles and water to float and swim. Add to this a pool the size of a football field, and you get a feel for Earl Rowe Provincial Park.

Beaches at Earl Rowe Provincial Park are not as busy as those located around Lake Simcoe.

The two large beaches are connected by small wooden bridges straddling the reservoir. The bottom of the lake is slightly muddy.

TIPS (fun for all ages)

• More **About provincial parks** on page 165.
• There's a 4-km look-out trail at the northern part of the park.
• BEWARE! The beaches are closed on average twice through the summer due to high bacterial counts (lots of geese visit the park). Call before you go!
• Earl Rowe includes some 365 **camp sites**.

Children will enjoy crossing over the wooden bridge to reach the park store by the western beach. You may rent canoes and paddle boats, as well as bicycles, at the Information Centre.

Those who settle on the eastern beach will also enjoy the gigantic shallow pool (it took me 350 long strides to circumnavigate it), and a small playground.

Earl Rowe Provincial Park · Alliston (705) 435-2498 www.ontarioparks.com

B-2 N-W of Toronto 90-min.

Schedule: Open mid-May to Thanksgiving (pool opens end of June to Labour Day).

Admission: Vehicle day-pass is $9.50. The pool's entrance fee is $2.50/adults, $1.50/children, FREE 4 years and under. Canoe or paddle boat rental is $10/hour.

Directions: From Hwy 400 North, take exit #75/Hwy 89 westbound. Turn north on Regional Rd. 15.

NEARBY ATTRACTIONS

WASAGA BEACH

"The world's longest freshwater beach"

We only hear about the portion of Wasaga Beach which resembles an american ocean city on a March Break. This is only part of the reality. As a matter of fact, Wasaga Beach is 14 km long.

In some spots, the hot and soft sand is cooled by the shade from tall trees and it feels like paradise. Some other spots count bathers by the dozens instead of the hundreds. You'll even find a perfect playground if you go to the right section of the beach!

What makes Wasaga Beach so popular is that pretty much everywhere along the strip of beach, a 6-year-old can walk 100 metres into the water and still maintain her head above the water. In addition, being shallow, the water never gets as cold as the pristine water of Georgian Bay everywhere else.

The downside is if you want to have a good swim, you'll need to go quite far from the beach to have enough water to move in. But then, there's the threat of sea-doos and motorboats. On the bright side, those noisy vehicles make fun waves!

Beach Drive, which borders only the western side of **Beach Area 1**, is the hot spot with cars parked everywhere, traffic on the road as well as on the sidewalk, restaurants, ice cream parlours, beach shops, pierced navels and loud music.

As a rule of thumb, the farther you go east or west of **Wasaga Waterworld** (the water park in the middle of the action between Beach Areas 1 and 2), the less noisy and crowded it will be. You want to go there for a glimpse of the action but it's much better to move on in order to find a better beach spot to spend the afternoon.

The **Beach Area 1** access is at the foot of Spruce Street, to the right just after the bridge taking Main Street across Nottawasaga River. When I saw the beautiful white sand overflowing from the beach to the parking lot, it reminded me of ocean cities. Quite a change from Toronto!

There's no road along that part of **Beach Area 1** so it's much prettier than its western neighbour in front of Beach Drive. It is noisy from all the boats motoring around between the lake and the river but the shops are far away.

Away from the boardwalk, you will find tall birch throwing their most appreciated shade. Come early if you want one of those for your family. There are no more trees along Beach Drive. **Beach**

Area 2, accessible from 3rd Street, is already quieter than the western part of **Beach Area 1** because only dead-end streets reach it.

Beach Area 3 is narrower on its eastern part. Trees are back but they are shorter. You see bushes near the entrance and more grass on the eastern part of that area. It is accessible from 22nd Street.

You may access **Beach Area 4** from 24th Street. From then on, the sand is not as fluid, more packed.

Beach Area 5, which you access from 36th Street, might be your best bet with a young family. The children will split their time between the beach and its original playground amidst the trees (a nice way to cool down from the sun). I really liked its wooden structures. My kids enjoyed its many corners for hiding.

TIPS (fun for all ages)

• Even though the water is shallow, you need to keep a good eye on your younger children. When they fall, water does get over their head! There is also the problem of an undertow that can take away inflatable toys.

• If you feel like going to a water park, skip the small **Wasaga Waterworld** and go to their bigger location. Instead of just a few slides, you'll get speed slides, serpent slide, bumper boats, wave pool, whirlpool and more, call 1-800-809-0896 or check their web site www.wasagawaterworld.com.

• Special events take place at the **Beach Area 1**. We were there on Labour Day weekend and saw a dog show during the day and great **fireworks** on the Sunday evening (they called it the Memories of Summer Fireworks Display). Activities vary from one year to the next.

• Note most shops are closed after Labour Day weekend.

• The Beaches Loop, is a **10-km trail** of beaches and parks for bikers and hikers, sometimes running along a town road.

• If you are looking for a **campground**, it is a good idea to consider **Craigleith Provincial Park**, located 25 minutes from Wasaga Beach. It includes 165 campsites with a strip of slippery rocky shore on Georgian Bay. The advantage is that your vehicle pass to that provincial park saves you the $15 fee to access Wasaga Beach Provincial Park. There's also the **Cedar Grove Park**, self-described as family camping with 1000 ft of sandy beach, (705) 429-2134.

• See **Galaxie Diner** on p. 435.

Many large rocks were popping out from the water at **Beach Area 6**, accessible from 45th Street. The eastern beaches of New Wasaga and Allenwood, which I did not get a chance to check out, are respectively accessible from Albert Street and Concession 11. Locals go there.

Wasaga Beach is such a good get-

away destination, it is worth staying overnight. The plain motel room we rented last minute was expensive and off the beach, like most of the area's accommodations.

A good way to find an accommodation is through the web site **www.wasagabeach.com**. Click on Visitors, then in the Choose a page section, select Accommodations. Unless you are choosing an accommodation located near the beach or offering rustic charm and some privacy, I strongly recommend at least selecting something with a pool.

A few places caught my attention as I drove in the area (in the 705 area code): the cute green cottages Applebee Cottages, 444-9249, the rustic Bay Villages Cottages, also detached, 429-4008, the housekeeping units Polynesian Motel, 429-7679, Wedgewood Cottages surrounded by tall trees and Cedarwood Cottages, 429-2650.

Wasaga Beach Provincial Park • Wasaga Beach (705) 429-2516 (park) 1-866-292-7242 (town) www.wasagabeach.com	B-2 N-W of Toronto 1 3/4 hr

 Schedule: Open year-round (facilities available from mid-June to Thanksgiving).

Admission: $15/day per vehicle, good for all the park's parking lots ($9.50 after Labour Day).

Directions: Along Mosley St. in Wasaga Beach. From Hwy 400 North, take exit #98/Hwy 26/27 westbound, then follow Hwy 27 to Elmvale. Turn west on Hwy 92, it will lead you to Main St. and Mosley St.

NEARBY ATTRACTIONS
Rounds Ranch (15-min.)..............p. 153
Scenic Caves (15-min.)...............p. 290

AWENDA PROVINCIAL PARK

A clear choice!

One of the best ways to enjoy Georgian Bay's clear water is to visit one of the four beaches in beautiful Awenda Provincial Park.

The first beach you encounter, a short walk from the first and second parking lots, is our favourite, with gulls resting on rocks sitting above the water, and small pebbles nestled in the fine sand.

From there, you can walk to the second beach (also a short walk from the second parking lot), crossing over a small rocky section in the water. Last time we visited, the water had receded so much that what used to be a narrow stretch of pebbles had turned into a sea of rocks, great for imaginative play!

A half-hour walk from the second parking lot, along the wide and well-groomed Beach Trail (time to get the bikes!), you'll find the third beach.

Located in a small tree-sheltered bay, this beach is everybody else's favourite because of its emerald water and perfect sand.

There are some serious **bike trails** throughout the park.

The two pictures below were taken five years apart. Notice how we did not see the sand strip by the trees in the top one! The water has really dropped.

A 10-minute walk brings you to the fourth beach, for a completely different panorama that embraces a wide view of Georgian Bay. Good news: very few people choose to do the extra walking, and when we visited, we felt like we owned this sandy beach adorned with dunes and plants.

At last, on our most recent visit, we were able to pull the kids from the beach to explore Awenda's trails. We did the Dune's Trail, a 3-km trail which took us to a steep sandy slope. We actually walked to that slope and turned back, which was as much as my 6-year-old could bare; bring water!.

We also enjoyed the 1-km trail strolling around Beaver Pond and walked a bit on Wendat Trail around Kettle's Lake (a 5-km trail). You can bring your own canoe.

TIPS (fun for all ages)
• More on **provincial parks** on p. 165.
• Awenda Park's more than 320 **campsites** are really popular. Nicely set under tall trees, they offer great privacy. If you can't get a campsite there, you may try **Camping Lafontaine** on Lafontaine Rd., (705) 533-2961 or www.lafontaine-ent.on.ca It offers very decent campsites amidst trees. From there, you can return to Awenda Park for day use.

NEARBY ATTRACTIONS
Discovery Harbour (20-min.).......p. 418
Sainte-Marie (25-min.)................p. 420

Awenda Provincial Park
• Penetanguishene
(705) 549-2231
www.ontarioparks.com

A-2 Midland Region 90-min.

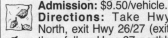

Schedule: Open year-round (facilities available from mid-May to Thanksgiving).
Admission: $9.50/vehicle.
Directions: Take Hwy 400 North, exit Hwy 26/27 (exit #98), then follow Hwy 27 northbound. After Elmvale, follow Simcoe Rd. 6 North. Turn east on Lafontaine Rd. Keep going on Concession Rd 16 and follow signs.

SCENIC CAVES ADVENTURES

Get to the bottom of it!

At the beginning of the path, you cross the Ice Cave, a natural fridge which maintains a cool 4 degrees Celsius in summertime. Even its exterior walls are cold. Hugging my small baby, I remain in the cave's narrow and cool vestibule, while father and son explore further down a corridor that descends into the even cooler part.

At the top of a path in the forest, iron railings sit at the opening of a large crevice, leading us some 20 metres below amidst magnificent rock formations and tender green foliage against the dark mossy rock face.

On a sunny day the sight is breathtaking. An information plaque tells us that some 300 years ago, Hurons used the natural fortress of the Scenic Caves to protect themselves from the enemy. That sparks the imaginations of young visitors!

The trail is filled with spots to explore and includes a few benches. You can easily recognize George Washington's profile, naturally sculpted by the shapes in the wall above our heads. While we didn't see any bears in the Bear's Cave, a small bat escaped. My young speleologist just loved the "Fat Man's Misery" passage. Its 36-centimetre width, at its narrowest, is not for everyone. Fortunately, there is an alternative path that circumnavigates the rock.

Since my last visit, they have added a 126-metre-long suspension bridge, the longest in Ontario, included with the admission to the caves. A wagon ride takes you there (or a 10-minute walk). It is 4 feet wide and I was told we feel lots of exciting sway in the middle, 25 metres above the valley and the stream. Wow!

TIPS (fun for 4 years +)

• The trail system is accessible for the entire family but not stroller accessible!
• Running or hiking shoes are a must, and take extra care when ground is wet.
• Equip your children with flashlights, it will enhance their explorations.
• The self-guided visit takes approximately one hour.
• There is a large pond filled with enormous trout you can feed. There's a mini-golf, along with a great "panning" structure allowing kids to find semi-precious gems from bags of mine rough.
• At the time of print, they were launching the **Eco Adventure Tour** involving a canopy trail in the spirit of **Haliburton Forest**'s without the canoe trip (see p. 342), but including zip lines (one of them 1,100 feet long) you slide down, hanging 40 feet above the ground. To reserve or for details, call (705) 446-3515 or check their web site. The 2 hrs 30 tour is $95/adults, $85/14 years old and under (min. 80 lbs, max. 250 lbs).

NEARBY ATTRACTIONS
Wasaga Beach (30-min.)..............p. 286

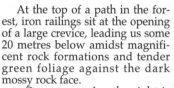

WARSAW CAVES C. A.

Underground experience

A while ago, I visited Warsaw Caves at the end of a cold afternoon, on a wet fall day, with a two-year-old and no flashlight. You might as well say I did not see them. Still, we were there long enough to assess what a unique underground adventure it offers to young explorers.

Some of the six biggest caves marked along the trails are up to 100 metres (300 feet) long. Some go as deep as 15 metres into the ground. Ice may be found in one of them all year round. The average temperature in the other caves is approximately 15°C.

The trail to the caves is indicated on a map by the parking lot. It starts out smoothly but is soon covered by large plates of rock (at times slippery), which offer a unique scene. We easily lose track of the trail but the caves are not too far apart.

Bright green touches of moss cover the stones, and straight tall trees have popped up wherever they can. Some have actually managed to grow from the bottom of 2-metre-deep crevices. Everywhere, there are natural nooks and crannies to explore.

Approximately 20 minutes farther, another trail leads to a lookout. Off the path, you will observe kettles, which are holes created by the movement of melting glaciers. They can be quite small but the biggest in the conservation area measures over 5 feet wide.

TIPS (fun for 7 years +)

• It is a must to bring flashlights and good shoes for everyone!
• You may explore on your own, but guides are often available to tour with you (call in advance).
• Our pint-size paleontologist never wanted to go deeper than one metre into the caves. The guide I talked to told me she recommends exploring the caves with children 7 years or older. They need to be a certain height to stroll more at ease in the underground corridors.
• During the summer, visitors can swim in a calm river only three feet deep, accessible from a beach where canoes and kayaks can be rented. There's also a campground in the conservation area.
• The staff sells ice cream bars and drinks during the summer. I was told there is a great chip truck in the town of Warsaw, five minutes away from the Warsaw Caves.

Warsaw Caves Conservation Area	B-5 N-E of Toronto 2 hrs

Warsaw Caves Conservation Area
· Warsaw
(705) 652-3161
Campground
1-877-816-7604
www.warsawcaves.com

Schedule: Open weekends from Victoria Day to Thanksgiving, open 7 days from late June to Labour Day.

Admission: (cash only) $7/vehicle. Guided tours cost around $30 for 6 visitors ($2 each additional visitor). Canoe and kayak rental is $7/hour or $32/day.

Directions: From Hwy 401 East, take exit #436/Hwy 35/115 northbound. It becomes Hwy 7 near Peterborough. Follow it east of Peterborough. Turn north on Regional Rd. 38 (2nd Line Rd.), then take County Rd. 4 to Caves Rd.

SCARBOROUGH BLUFFS

No bluffing!

The stunning Scarborough Bluffs can reach 60 metres in height. In some places, the sandstone cliffs are beautifully carved in such a way to have inspired the name the cathedrals. You'll add to your enjoyment of this natural phenomenon if you explore it from top to bottom in one visit.

To get the best panoramic view of the lake, visit the **Rosetta McClain Gardens** perched atop the Bluffs (see p. 313). But you'll get the finest lookout from the cathedral-shaped cliffs in Cathedral Bluffs Park a few minutes drive from the gardens.

Don't be put off by the simple look of the **Scarborough Bluffs Park**, as you can't readily see some fifteen benches sitting at the back. Nothing announces the breathtakingly beautiful panoramic view you'll get from each one. Try them all!

Facing us, the lake spreads endlessly. On the west side, we discover cliffs covered with trees, while the east side reveals the park's 400 acres, with its

marina and the cliffs with their rocky peaks.

On the park's eastern side, there is a lovely path that borders the cliffs. There, I noticed (just before it heads north), another steeper path going down towards **Bluffers Park**; a natural slide my son really enjoyed (don't try this with toddlers).

Last year, we discovered another way to explore the Bluffs from top to bottom: **Scarborough Heights Park**, just west of **Rosetta Gardens**!

Once again, the park doesn't look too appealing but as you get closer to the edge the gorgeous view of the lake emerges. This time, we took one of the improvised trails leading down the cliff. Boy! It was steep!

We loved it but I suspected there was a safer way down. There is! Between the park and Rosetta gardens is a closed road accessible from a small opening to the left of the gate.

The paved road faded into a compressed dirt road following the shore and bordered by huge boulders. We walked for 10 minutes and got a breathtaking view of the white cliffs, the best I have seen so far, completely surreal so close to Toronto.

The bushes along the trail were host to several butterflies.

Keep some energy to go up the slope on your way back!

TIPS (fun for 3 years +)
- More on **Bluffer's Park** on p. 273.
- I did not notice washrooms in these two parks.
- During a visit I made at the beginning of October, I spotted dozens of Monarch butterflies in a patch of wild flowers east of **Scarborough Bluffs Park**. The park is located on their migratory route. I was also intrigued by the multitude of red ladybugs I found every second step along the shore.
- As you stroll along Kingston Road, between Warden and Midland Roads, it is amusing to ask children accompanying you to spot the ten murals to be found there, commissioned by the Scarborough Arts Council. See if they can find the race car, ladies in gowns, a row boat and some tubas and drums. I particularly enjoyed the one with a row boat approaching the cliffs, while my young arts critic was awestruck by the military band.

City of Toronto | **J-11**
· Scarborough | **East**
(416) 392-1111 | **of downtown**
www.toronto.ca | **35-min.**

Schedule: Open year-round.
Admission: FREE.
Directions/Scarborough Bluffs Park: From Kingston Rd., take the short street west of Midland Ave. to access Midland southbound. Turn west on Romana St., then south on Scarboro Cr.
Directions/Scarborough Heights Park: From Kingston Rd., take Glen Everest Rd. southbound, then turn right on Fishleigh Dr., look for the pumping station.

NEARBY ATTRACTIONS

DORIS MCCARTHY TRAIL

A passage worth exploring

Nature was quite an artist. The turquoise shade of Lake Ontario I saw, walking down the trail, was mesmerizing with the sun lighting thousands of gems on the water. Powerful waves were brushing the shore. I was alone and everything seemed so exotic. Then, it revealed itself, at the foot of the trail, blending so lovingly with the surrounding: *Passage*, a work of art from one artist to celebrate another.

I had noticed a little sign announcing the Doris McCarthy Trail. Curious is my middle name, plus I'm always on the lookout for new ways to access the waterfront, so I engaged myself down the ravine, not expecting much from the trail.

It started predictably, enclosed by tall thin trees blocking the view. But very soon it widened and cleared to reveal the sky. Then, I heard the whimsical sound of a small stream. As I went down, I would peak through the bushes to watch it flow between large plates of rocks. The bed of the stream got eventually two metres lower than the level of the trail, forming an irresistible corridor I just had to explore.

I jumped into it and started to hop from one plate to another over pockets of water.

When I looked upstream, I saw that the layered plates created moss-covered stairs from which tiny falls fell. The blocks of rock framing the whole scene added to the impression of being amidst ancient ruins.

I'm not sure my 10-year-old would have appreciated the beauty of the site but I know for a fact that he would have loved this adventure on the bed of the small brook.

Down stream, the water pockets were getting larger and the plates fewer so I climbed back onto the trail. Moments later, I discovered the strange sculpture. The *Passage* stood like the remnants of an ancient canoe or the backbone of a strange aquatic mammal, overlooking the cliffs along the shore.

When I got home, I looked up Doris McCarthy on the Internet and was put to shame for not yet recognizing this amazing painter, now over 90 years old, who has spent her life capturing the beauty of the light on Canadian landscapes and passing on that passion to students.

It also turns out that she was the owner of the scenic property nestled on the **Scarborough Bluffs** east of the Doris McCarthy Trail: the Fool's Paradise. She has donated it to the Ontario Heritage Foundation along with funds to maintain the property as an artist's retreat.

This inspiring woman also wrote a biography titled *A Fool's Paradise*, relating her journey from childhood, in the Beaches neighbourhood, to a mature painter on top of the bluffs.

The trail was officially named after Doris in May 2001 and *Passage*, the work of Marlene Hilton-Moore, was unveiled in October 2002 in her honour.

TIPS (fun for 3 years +)

• It takes less than 15 minutes to go down the trail; more if you go the harder way, from the bed of the stream. BEWARE! There are thorns on the bushes bordering it. It takes longer to climb your way back up the trail, especially with tired children (not for under 8 years).

• There's a beach, east of the trail. I was told you could reach the **Guild Inn** property if you keep going in that direction.

• There's **Lick's**, a good hamburger joint, just west of Midland Av., at 2383 Kingston Road, (416) 267-3249.

NEARBY ATTRACTIONS

Doris McCarthy Trail
· Scarborough
(416) 392-1111
www.toronto.ca
www.dorismccarthy.com

J-11
East
of downtown
35-min.

 Schedule: The trail is open year-round.
Admission: FREE access.
 Directions: Take Kingston Rd. eastward, turn south on Ravine Dr. (which is named Bellamy Rd. on the north side of Kingston). You can park on the street past the sign marking the entrance to the trail off Ravine Dr.

RATTLESNAKE POINT C. A.

Shortcut

I first visited Rattlesnake Point with an energetic mom carrying her chubby baby on her back. I didn't dare bring my five-year-old explorer close to 25-metre cliffs before having inspected the surroundings first. What's the verdict? Well... With a firm hand and a strong heart, you can take children along to see the panorama from Rattlesnake, extending as far as the eye can see. The area's many assets are worth it.

The cliffs are a five-minute walk away from the first parking lot, giving children instant gratification!

The first parking lot is accessible via a small, one-way, loop road to the left.

TIPS (fun for 5 years +)

• You need good walking shoes. As soon as a child is less than ten metres away from the escarpment, you should hold his hand. A ratio of one adult per young child is advisable.

• Depending on which way the wind blows, your nose may be bothered by a smell emanating from a nearby mushroom-growing farm. Had to mention it.

• A most moving detail seen on the course: a 40-cm-wide flat stone with a plaque mentioning "Baby Nina Anna Glinny Copas, June 23, 1996". I was assured this child didn't fall off the cliff. Still, this is a real commemorative plaque placed by parents...

• Some readers told me they found small **caves** along the rock walls, barely noticeable through shady cracks.

• Remember to keep your Rattlesnake Point entrance ticket. During the same day, it gives you free access to other conservation areas such as **Crawford Lake** (see p. 410) and **Hilton Falls** (see p. 300), ten minutes away.

The path beginning in that area leads you directly to the Nelson observation point and to the stairway. The stairs lead down to the foot of the cliff. This gives visitors a totally different perspective of the rock. Furthermore, the rock formations in this area allow sturdy little explorers to climb enthusiastically, emulating the rock climbers who are most likely on the premises.

Rattlesnake Point is indeed a great spot for **rock climbing**. While walking along the path, you might spot seemingly abandoned backpacks, but look closely. You'll eventually notice brightly coloured ropes wrapped around trees, with climbers silently perched at their ends.

Before reaching the stairs, you'll notice a small path leading to the nearby Trafalgar observation point. You'll find another viewing point overlooking Nassagaweya canyon, a fifteen-minute walk away to the right, also accessible from another parking lot.

You'd have to walk another half-hour beyond that to reach the last observation point, Buffalo Crag, lengthening the return trek by about an hour. When you're accompanying kids, that's a serious consideration to ponder.

Rattlesnake Point Conservation Area
· Milton

D-2 West of Toronto 50-min.

(905) 878-1147
www.conservationhalton.on.ca

Schedule: Open year-round, from 8:30 am to dusk.

Admission: $4/adults, $3.25/ seniors, $2.75/5-14 years, FREE 4 years and under.

Directions: From Hwy 401 West, take exit #320/Hwy 25 northbound. Turn west on Campbellville Rd., south on Tremaine Rd., west again on Steeles Ave., then turn south on Appleby Line, to the park entrance.

MOUNT NEMO C. A.

Don't worry

From here, catch the most breathtaking views of the Niagara escarpment. Between the fragrant cedars, you can even admire the turkey vultures' wingspans while they silently glide at eye level, against a backdrop of checkered fields. Don't worry, there's very little chance that your little ones will fall from this 85-metre cliff without rails. The crevices will prevent this from happening!

Seriously, I was enthralled by the Mount Nemo Conservation Area when I realized that here, children could discover the natural phenomena of cliffs and crevices. During our last

visit, we accompanied two mountain climbers, aged four and five, who thoroughly enjoyed these famous crevices.

For little ones on foot or in strollers, there's a wide gravel path (Bruce Side Trail), a shortcut leading to the Brock Harris observation point in 10 minutes. From behind a solid, safe low wall, this belvedere offers a superb panorama. On a clear day, we can make out the **CN Tower**, 60 kilometres to the right.

The **crevices** most accessible to young adventurers are located just left of the belvedere. The two we explored were about 30 metres from the cliff. Their narrow openings slope gently. Five metres down, their bottoms are lined with large stones. Natural footbridges cross over the crevices and give access to the edge of the cliff.

Beyond the first two crevices, the path sometimes gets as close as two metres from the escarpment, and crevices abound. Incredibly tortuous, criss-crossed by roots, lined with moss-covered rocks, with spots of light piercing through the trees, this trail is one of the most beautiful I've seen. Its course is clearly marked by white paint on tree trunks. It leads you back to the parking lot in an hour.

TIPS (fun for 4 years +)

• With children 7 years and older, I recommend you take the North Loop (the first one to the left when you walk on the gravel path by the parking lot). Kids will love to spot the **Bruce Trail**'s white marks (two marks on a tree means that there's a turn). We found the South Loop less interesting.

• Accompanying adults who fear for their children's safety may want to stick to the first two crevices.

• Good walking shoes are a must; increased attention is required on certain slippery patches.

• You may use a stroller only on the gravel road leading to the belvedere.

NEARBY ATTRACTIONS
Kelso Beach (10-min.)...................p. 280
Crawford Lake C. A. (10-min.)......p. 410

Mount Nemo Conservation Area
· Mount Nemo
(905) 336-1158
www.conservationhalton.on.ca

D-2
West
of Toronto
45-min.

Schedule: Open year-round, 8:30 am to dusk.
Admission: $5/vehicle. Deposit the exact amount in an envelope provided at the entrance, or place your same-day entrance receipt to another Halton conservation area on your dashboard.
Directions: From QEW West, take exit #102/Guelph Line northbound. From Hwy 401 West, take exit #312/Guelph Line southbound. Turn east on Colling Rd. (north of Mount Nemo).

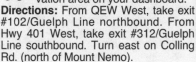

SANDBANKS PROVINCIAL PARK

Three beaches, three worlds

As soon as my son and his friends reached the top of the golden dunes overlooking the lake 30 metres below, they playfully fell on their knees, thanking Heaven like grateful desert survivors who just realized they're saved.

The first time I visited Sandbanks Park, I literally missed Dunes Beach. We went straight to Outlet Beach and stayed there for the whole day. Upon returning later, I was better able to appreciate the uniqueness of Sandbanks Beach and Dunes Beach which remained to be explored.

Dunes Beach

Dunes Beach is definitely unique. As you observe the tall dunes bordering the east side of the beach adjacent to the parking lot, you realize that your eyes are not accustomed to this kind of panorama. You must get closer to the lakeshore to better gauge the size of this natural playground.

You must then hike the highest peak of the dunes. The scenery is grandiose and conducive to daydreaming. Then, gravity calls and kids can't resist sliding down the silky slope all the way to the water. Others, of all ages, run wildly or simply tumble down with glee. The sandy water bottom is welcoming them.

Because of its location, the water of the beach at the feet of the dunes is the quietest of the Sandbanks Park. Located close to West Lake, it doesn't face Lake Ontario like the others (one has to consult a map to figure that one out). Well isolat-

ed, its water is warmer! This is great since I, unlike my little tomboy, found the water temperature at the other two beaches a little too cool for my liking. The shoal of small fish moving at our feet and the tiny frogs in the reeds added to the kids' enjoyment.

You can walk a lot farther through the dunes along the lake. The farther you go, the less crowded it gets, naturally. Don't forget bottles of water!

Outlet Beach

Outlet Beach's wonderfully fine and pebble-free sand is outstanding for building castles or digging a maze of interconnected waterways. Also, the very large area of shallow water along its shores is ideal for swimming toddlers, and great for parents' peace of mind. The Beach stretches along three kilometres, reaching depths of 30 metres in some places, which the surrounding tall trees can't completely shade.

The Beach's name changes to Camper's Beach, where it meets the River Outlet (which you can cross by foot). There's a specially designated pet area nearby!

Courtesy of D. De Oliveira

TIPS (fun for all ages)

• More on **provincial parks** on p. 165.
• If you want to go to **Dunes Beach** directly, don't follow the signs leading to the main gate; stay on Road 12 to reach Dunes Beach's parking lot and pay the admission at the automatic machine.
• The beautiful semi-wild **Outlet River Campground** holds 270 campsites. **Cedars Campground**, set further back from Outlet Beach holds 190 more sites. **Richardson's Campground** sits in a young and sparse forest near Sandbanks Beach, and offers less privacy than the two other sites.
• We overnighted at the **Bloomfield Inn**, a motel located in Bloomfield. A room with two double beds costs $100/double occupancy in summertime with a cost of $10 per person for additional guests (children up to 10 years old stay for free). The motel belongs to the owners of **Angeline**, a French gastronomic restaurant located on the same property. We also booked babysitting services to fully enjoy a great meal. See www.angelinesinn-spa.com or call 1-877-391-3301.
• Check **www.pecchamber.com** and click on <u>Business Directory</u> to find out about other accommodations in the area.
• A Visitor Centre and a Nature Shop are located at the entrance of Outlet Beach, close to Parking lots #1 and #2. This beach is well outfitted with picnic tables; you can easily get a hold of one before 11 am. A well-stocked snack bar is also located near Parking lot #7. There's another one at Dunes Beach.
• Last time we visited the area, we took the time to visit Picton's **Birdhouse City**. It is actually a vast park with a few trees here and there and over 100 bird-

houses mounted on poles. Most are miniature reproductions of historic buildings done as a community involvement project. The Friends of Birdhouse City have built, and maintain the houses, (613) 476-1659. From Main Street in Picton, take Union Street, it becomes County Rd. 8, the park is on the righthand side.

Sandbanks Beach

Sandbanks Beach offers 8 kilometres of sand; an obvious favourite for hikers. Lovely trails surround the slopes on these shores.

Here, the beach is not as wide as that of Outlet Beach. With a few pebbles here and there, its water is a bit deeper and nice waves usually form, greatly pleasing the young swimmers.

Last time we went, in the middle of a heatwave, hundreds of small silver fish were washed up on the shore, suffocated. If you think it would gross you out, call if you intend to go during such weather.

Sandbanks Provincial Park
• Picton
(613) 393-3319
www.ontarioparks.com

C-6
East
of Toronto
2 1/2 hrs

Schedule: Open April 1 to end of October from 8 am to dusk.
Admission: $7-$12 per vehicle for day use.
Directions: R.R. 1, Picton. From Hwy 401 West, take exit #522/Wooler Rd. southbound, then follow Regional Rd. 33 through Bloomfield. Turn south on County Rd. 12 and follow the signs. (Read TIPS!)

HILTON FALLS C. A.

Falls 101

We're on the way back. I'm puffing like an old locomotive while I pull my little "bundle", comfortably seated in the red wagon. I then hear his voice, somewhat concealed by the noise of wheels crunching on the gravel, chanting: "I think I can, I think I can." I burst out laughing when I recognize the chant from *The Little Engine that Could*. Those who know the classic tale will smile as I did when faced with my son's empathy. This goes to show how our children never miss a beat when we take them on outings!

The Hilton Falls are a 30-minute walk away from the parking lot. With good shoes, you can easily get close to the falls (there may be a cold shower included!). Here and there, makeshift bridges are made of tree trunks. If little explorers are able to cross the river on these, they're big enough to romp about in this natural playground: a cave, rock climbing and the discovery of a "secret" passage inside the ruins (even so, tell them to be careful on the sawmill wall).

Go for a short walk on the trail downstream from the falls. A huge round pothole was formed 12,000 years ago by the movement of rocks on the riverbed. It's quite safe for children to go down into it. However, they (and you) should be vigilant in areas closer to the cliff's edge.

From the belvedere in front of the falls, an unexpected view reveals the ruins of a 19th century sawmill. Farther ahead, along the **Bruce Trail**, stairs lead to the riverbank.

To return, I recommend taking the Beaver Dam Trail marked in orange until it crosses another trail. The red circles of the Red Oak Trail will then lead you to the parking lot. This trail crosses a small river that flows down into a wide reservoir.

TIPS (fun for 4 years +)

• More on **conservation areas** on page 266.
• During spring and summer, black-flies might swoop down on visitors as soon as they stop on bare trails: bring insect repellent. They're nearly absent close to the falls and in the woods.
• The gravel paths are wide and stroller-accessible except for the first hundred metres of the yellow trail going up hill.
• There are single tracks for **mountain bikes**.
• In wintertime, the falls surrounded by ice make for an original family outing. There's also cross-country skiing.

NEARBY ATTRACTIONS
Ostrich Farm (15-min.)................p. 55
Streetcar Museum (15-min.)........p. 241

WEBSTER'S FALLS C. A.

Double feature

A majestic gorge and powerful falls, plus the rainbow effect, the mist on our face and the gorgeous trail. I did not expect such a wholesome program! I'll just have to go by the usual cliché: this is the best-kept secret in the region.

Let your ears guide you to the falls from the parking lot but don't miss the tiny cemetery nearby to find out who they are named after.

You'll need to cross the cobblestone bridge to get a good view from the top and then to get to the trail leading down the falls. The adventure starts with the metal stairs, which are stiff and slippery (hold on to the smaller kids).

I just love the thundering noise of falls, and this is a good 79-foot one, with the bonus of a full rainbow when you look at the right place at the right time. The beauty of the trail bordering the river is that it is at the water level and the river cascades and dances all along. We walked for 30 minutes before

heading back (to maintain the children's momentum to the end).

A small sign from the parking lot indicated a trail leading to Tew's Falls. We were told it would take approximately 20 minutes to reach it but the kid had had it by that time so we drove to get there.

Many written sources described it as towering 41 metres, "only a few metres short of Niagara Falls"... It was tall indeed but nobody had mentioned that it was only a metre wide!

TIPS (fun for 4 years +)

• There's a trail along the edge of the escarpment accessible from the parking lot at Webster's Falls. It offers nice panoramas but the kids preferred the forested depths of the gorge.

• We were told the site is beautiful in the winter when part of the waterfalls are frozen and sparkling.

NEARBY ATTRACTIONS

Webster's Falls Conservation Area
• Dundas
(905) 628-3060
www.conservationhamilton.ca

E-2
S-W
of Toronto
60-min.

Schedule: Open year-round.
Admission: $5 per vehicle.
Directions: From QEW/Hwy 403, exit at Hwy 6 North then turn west on Hwy 5. Turn south on Brock Rd., then east on Harvest Rd. Turn south on Short Rd (it becomes Fallsview Rd.) to get to Webster's Falls or drive a bit further on Harvest Rd. to reach Tew's Falls.

NIAGARA FALLS

Fall for them

A couple of kilometres upstream along the Niagara Parkway, we observe the large cascades as they roar into the falls. Through the car's open window, we can hear their thundering sound and feel a slight mist blowing towards us.

Even though it is midweek on the summer afternoon we visit, we are caught in the long line-ups, and the closest parking space is located on Upper Rapids Drive, two kilometres away from the Niagara Falls.

Don't worry, it does not mean you will have to walk that distance or watch it all from your car! The **People Movers** all day pass you'll get as you pay the parking fees at the Rapidsview Parking gate, will allow your whole family to travel all day long in the air-conditioned buses going up and down the Niagara Parkway. They are simply the best way to enjoy the area if you don't find parking right away and kids love to ride them.

Upstream

The first bus stop upstream from the falls is the **Greenhouse**. Its admission is free... and so are the exotic birds flying over our heads. It is a good observation

Courtesy of E.Ritson

game for the children to spot them among the colourful plants.

A five-minute walk away upstream leads you to the **Dufferin Islands**. These are 11 little islands linked by small bridges. We got close enough to touch the dozens of wild ducks swimming around the bridges. Simply gorgeous during the fall.

At the Falls

The next bus stop is in front of the Table Rock Complex where **Journey Behind the Falls** is located. My children's favourite part of this attraction is the ride in the elevator down to the tunnels and the tunnels themselves. You may observe the white wall of water falling at 32 feet per second from a terrace or through the viewing portals behind the **Niagara Falls**.

We dared to take the kids to the **Table Rock Restaurant**, and it was a good move. The relatively affordable and edible meals are actually presented in a fancy manner. In addition, the view of the falls from the panoramic windows could not have been better.

A ride on the **Maid of the Mist** (905) 358-5781 is your surest bet to get in the middle of the action. I think "Maid of the Shower" would be a more accurate name for this boat. Don't go expecting not to get wet! After my ride, I started to notice all the visitors with wet pant legs. The plastic coats they give us before we get on the boat can't cover everything.

The truth is, you don't get to see much of the falls as the boat approaches them, because your eyes are shut to protect them from the water spray. But you get to hear them pretty well!

Our greatest surprise was the beautiful rainbow above our heads. Later on, as we took the 15-minute walk back to the Table Rock Complex, we could again admire a rainbow from the railing of the boardwalk.

The inclined railway across the Table Rock Complex costs only $1 per adult and 50¢ per child. It is a big hit with the children!

Downstream

I think the visit to the **White Water Walk** (formally called the Great Gorge Adventure), farther along the circuit of the **People Movers**, is underrated.

It is usually less busy than the other attractions and shows you the river from a different but equally powerful point of view. The elevator ride down to the dark and cool tunnel is as much fun for the kids as the one at **Journey Behind the Falls**.

It leads us to a boardwalk by the spectacular rapids. The river, being 38 metres (125 feet) deep at this level, makes the water gush down in large impressive swirls at the speed of over 60 km/h. Our 15-minute walk on the boardwalk was beautiful, safe and refreshing (in midsummer), without soaking us.

It takes approximately 10 minutes to walk from the gorge to the **Whirlpool Aero Car** (also accessible by bus). This car hangs 76 metres (250 feet) above the river. The track cable system that moves the car was invented by a Spanish engineer also responsible for the world's first computer (Leonardo Torres Quevedo). I have not tried it, but from what I saw, children would have to be five years and over to be tall enough to see above the railing of the car.

Further along, another attraction I want to visit next time we go is the **Niagara Glen Trail** which leads us down 60 metres (200 feet) to the water level in approximately 20 minutes.

Bikers and hikers can admire the gorge from the long **trail** running along the road.

Dry fun

The area is chock-a-block with attractions of all kinds in and around Clifton Hill Centre Street. **Guiness World of Records** and the **Ripley's Believe It or Not Museum**, despite some displays of questionable taste, are likely to strike children's imaginations, whether with "the biggest man in the world" or a sculpture made with one grain of rice. One! (Some displays of nature's anomaly can disturb kids under seven.)

Visits to the non-interactive wax and horror museums are too short for their cost. Last time my kids went, they loved the new **Niagara Falls Aviary** with free flying birds from around the world as well as bats, in a jungle setting with waterfall, open year-round, $15/adults, $10/5-12 years, 1-866-994-0090.

TIPS (fun for 4 years +)

• See the **Butterfly Conservatory** on p. 61.
• See **Niagara's Winter Festival of Lights** on p. 204.
• First time we went to the Falls, we visited the **Niagara Falls Imax Theatre**, at the end of the day, to watch the movie *Miracles, Myths & Magic*. I wish we had started our outing with it. The legends, accidents and stories of dare-devils, which were re-enacted on the huge screen, shed a new light on the falls. It would have made the children look a different way at the other attractions. The dare-devil artifacts shown in the lobby and the museum are fascinating when seen after the movie. It is $12/adults, $8.50/children 4 to 12 years, including access to the museum. Check www.imaxniagara.com or call (905) 374-4629.
• No need to wait in line-ups! You can buy timed tickets in advance at the attractions' ticket booths and show up 15 minutes before the booked time slot.
• Check their web site and click Plan a visit for information about **People Movers** and their **Adventure Pass** (including admission to **Journey Behind the Falls**, **White Water Walk**, **Maid of the Mist** and **Butterfly Conservatory** with your **People Mover** one-day transportation).
• My 3-year-old was a bit distressed by the showers of water falling over her on the **Maid of the Mist**. Kids normally scared by thunderstorms will probably not enjoy this noisy attraction. I don't recommend you go on with a stroller either.
• **Journey Behind the Falls** is your best option if you don't want to get too wet (but a lot depends on the wind). Otherwise, I would suggest you first catch a ride on the **Maid of the Mist** and then go down the dark tunnel of the **White Water Walk** downstream.
• Wondering how the Falls generate electricity? Tons of water are channelled through underground tunnels on each side of the river, into huge reservoirs behind the power plants downstream from the whirlpool. Water flows down the reservoirs to the generators during the day, when demand for power is at its peak; the reservoirs are filled at night, when demand reduces.
• Free **fireworks** can be seen every Friday and Sunday at 10 pm, from mid-

May to the first Friday in September as well as on **Victoria Day**, **Memorial Day**, **Canada Day** and **Independance Day**. They are preceded by concerts at 8 pm at the Illumination Stage. The falls are illuminated at night year-round.
• On Niagara Parks web site, click on Accommodation Partners for links to accommodation options in Niagara. Last Easter weekend, we chose the **Hilton Niagara Falls Fallsview** for its amazing pool and the kids had a blast! But everything comes with a price at Niagara Falls.
• See **Rainforest Café** on p. 432.

The Niagara Parks Commission	E-4 Niagara Region 90-min.

· Niagara Falls
1-877-642-7275
or (905) 371-0254
www.niagaraparks.com

 Niagara Parks attractions schedule: Journey Behind the Falls is open year-round. Other outdoor attractions are open at least from May 1 to mid-October, at least from 10 am to 5 pm. Call for exact dates and times.
People Movers schedule: From late June to Labour Day, the shuttles run daily from 9 am to at least 8 pm. (Variable hours for the rest of the season from early April to mid-October.)
Admission: All attractions are FREE for children 5 years and under. **Journey Behind the Falls** (6650 Niagara Pkwy) is $10/adults, $6/6-12 years. **Maid of the Mist** (5920 Niagara Pkwy) is $13/adults, $8/6 to 12 years. **White Water Walk** (4330 Niagara Pkwy) is $7.50/adults, $4.50/6-12 years. **Whirlpool Aero Car** (3850 Niagara Pkwy) is $10/adults, $6/6-12 years. **People Movers** all day pass is $5.50/adults, $2.75/6 to 12 years (or $13 for the whole family, including parking, if you park at Rapidsview Parking).
Directions/Rapidsview Parking: Take QEW towards Fort Erie, exit at McLeod Rd., turn left on McLeod Rd (it becomes Marineland Pkwy, formerly called Portage Rd.). Turn left at Rapidsview, it leads to Niagara Pkwy, where you turn north (left).
Directions/Rainbow Bridge: From QEW towards Fort Erie, exit at Hwy 420, continue on Falls Ave. until it turns into Niagara Pkwy (beware, this route was under construction at the time of print).

NEARBY ATTRACTIONS

HIGH FALLS

Small adventure

My son just loves exploring natural wonders full of nooks and crannies. High Falls is filled with these.

First, we tried to get as close as we could to the thundering High Falls. The powerful white body of water was fascinating to my then 5-year-old. In some spots, we had to jump more than one metre down onto lower rocks, to get closer.

All around the park, the ground is covered with big slabs of rock. Vegetation has tried to grow over and hold on to as much as it could with the help of really long running roots.

We slid down a steep hill filled with roots and followed a natural trail towards the water. We walked over a couple of miniature, natural bridges and small strips of rock with water on each side. It added to the feeling of adventure.

We explored the surroundings of a stream running into the woods. Part of the stream had enough water for it to expand into a nice wading pool among the trees. I wanted to stop for a while to listen to the musical sound of the water flowing over the stones, but my son felt like a pioneer, stick in hand and wanted to keep going.

TIPS (fun for 5 years +)
• The rocks and ground can be quite slippery. Bring rubber boots or shoes to better explore the stream.
• Bring insect repellent if you want to explore the stream.
• Since our last visit, the **Trans-Canada Trail** has reached High Falls. There is now a bridge running over High Falls offering a great panorama.

NEARBY ATTRACTIONS
Santa's Village (20-min.)...............p. 28

High Falls
· Bracebridge
(705) 645-5264

A-3
North
of Toronto
2 1/4 hrs.

 Schedule: Open year-round.
Admission: FREE.
Directions: North of Bracebridge. Take Hwy 400 North then follow Hwy 11 northbound. Take exit #193 (R.R. #117 on the east side, Cedar Lane on the west side), drive over Hwy 11, enter High Falls Resort and drive up the hill.

ROCK POINT PROVINCIAL PARK

On this rock, I will build... a park

Romantic picnic lovers and those longing for Cuban sand, stay away from Rock Point Park. Make way for miniature paleontologists, ornithologists, pebble collectors... and arachnid enthusiasts.

Courtesy of E. Ritson

When you arrive, ask at the gate for the trail leading to the fossils. On our visit, we parked not too far from a beaten dirt path which led us to the lake (where we intended to picnic...). What I saw was quite unexpected!

A rock floor covered the whole ribbon of "beach". The breaking waves were loaded with slimy moss and gave off a fishy smell. There was also the odour of the stagnant water evaporating from various natural basins carved in stone.

We had to choose between mosquito bites under shady trees and sunburn in open areas. At any rate, rock spiders heavily patrol the place.

If they don't decide to leave, park visitors are rewarded. From up close, we noticed that the fissures trapping the stagnant water were covered with **fossils**, dating back 350 million years!

Three-year-old tots aren't impressed by this discovery, but it will surely have an effect on older kids, especially if you do research before the outing. Personally, I was fascinated.

While I was examining the rocks, my two companions settled into a small, pebble-lined cove, fairly moss-free, where they "fished" with sticks for quite a while. Later, we walked to a viewing tower. We then drove to the beach on the other side of the park where beautifully rounded pebbles formed the lake bed. A great occasion to start a rock collection!

TIPS (fun for all ages)

- Beach shoes are a must to deal with the pebbles rolling under your feet in the water.
- The green space adjoining the beach by the parking lot is too bare for my liking; not what I would expect in a provincial park. There's a nicer beach accessible from the campground by the parking lot.
- Camping areas are surrounded by quite a bit of greenery. The level of privacy isn't great (campers have a direct view of neighbours camping across the road), but it's far from the sardine can concept found in several **campgrounds**.

Rock Point Provincial Park	
Rock Point Provincial Park · Dunnville (905) 774-6642 www.ontarioparks.com	E-2 S-W of Toronto 2 1/2 hrs

Schedule: Open mid-May until mid-October.
Admission: $9.50/vehicle pass.
Directions: Take QEW towards Niagara, exit Hwy 20/Centennial Park southbound (it becomes Hwy 56). Take Hwy 3 eastbound through Dunville, then follow the park signs.

TORONTO MUSIC GARDEN

Courtesy of R. Doyle

On a fun note

It seems nobody thinks to walk west of the popular Harbourfront Centre so this part of the water's edge feels like an oasis in the midst of the city.

The garden is developed following a dance theme. Accessible from Spadina, we first encounter the "Menuet", impressive with beautiful hand-made ornamental steel adorning its rotunda.

Walking down from the rotunda (kids will actually run), we reach a gentle slope of grass broken with grass stairs forming a sort of curved amphitheatre facing the water. At the foot stands a small stone stage. This whole section is called the "Gigue". Both the "Gigue" and the "Menuet" are the chosen stages for dance and music shows during the summer.

The "Sarabande" offers a small trail

spiralling down to a huge stone carved with a tiny pool of running water. Evergreen trees, turning this corner into a nice little retreat, surround the rock.

The "Courante" stands out with its tall Maypole spinning in the wind and competing with the CN Tower against the sky. It is surrounded by luscious borders of flowers attracting birds and butterflies.

Numerous granite boulders greet us in the "Prelude" section. It is also the best spot to observe the planes taking off and landing at Toronto Island Airport right across the water.

Across the street from the "Allemande", on the private ground of condominiums, don't miss the three 8-foot-high geese made out of mesh. Quite a sight! Just east of the Toronto Music Garden lies the Spadina Quay Wetland, an old parking lot transformed into a small marsh decorated with funny birdhouses.

TIPS (fun for 3 years +)

• It takes less than 5 minutes to walk along the garden on Queen's Quay West. **Harbourfront Centre** is 10 minutes east of the garden's entrance. The western part of the Music Garden is 2 minutes away from Bathurst Street.

• The **Marina Quay West** located south of the western entrance of the Music Garden offers underground parking at $7-$10. It is the place to rent headphones for a self-guided tour of the garden, (416) 203-1212.

• There's a well-supplied convenience store right in front of the rotunda, west of Spadina.

• Check the **Storehouse Pier 4** restaurant and patio on p. 430.

| Toronto Music Garden (416) 338-0338 (events) www.toronto.ca | J-10 Downtown Toronto 5-min. |

Schedule: Open year-round. Guided or self-guided audio tours and shows offered from June to September. Guided tour usually on Wednesdays.
Admission: FREE admission, $5 to rent headphones.
Directions: Runs along Queen's Quay between Lower Spadina Ave. and Bathurst St.

VILLAGE OF YORKVILLE PARK

with bistro chairs. Further is a marsh landscape complete with boardwalk and lanterns that illuminate the path in the evening. The idea behind the creation of this garden was to offer a patchwork of the various landscapes characterizing Canada.

Urban puzzle

The rock is approximately 1 billion years old. Its 135 pieces, each weighing between 500 and 2000 pounds, were removed by crane from the main formation in Muskoka and carefully labelled so the whole jigsaw could be reassembled in Toronto. Tell the kids it took 20 flatbed trailers to transport them!

There's no other little park like this one in the Toronto area. The rock sits next to a curtain of water meant to represent the gentle fall of rain and is flanked

The Village of Yorkville Park (416) 392-1111 www.toronto.ca	**I-10 Downtown** Toronto 20-min.

 Schedule: Open year-round.
Admission: FREE.
Directions: One block north of Bloor St. West, between Bellair St. and Avenue Rd.

TRINITY SQUARE LABYRINTH

Urban labyrinth

Step out of the Eaton Centre, through the west side door, and step into a sanctuary within the city.

This cobblestoned square includes tall trees, a fountain, the brick walls of lovely **Holy Trinity Church** and the **Trinity Square Café** (selling coffee, home-made snacks and light lunches).

For five years, the grass patch by the square has been cut into a labyrinth with a 70-foot diameter by a group of volunteers dedicated to maintaining a lasting labyrinth at **Trinity Square Park**.

At the time of print, the **Toronto Labyrinth Community Network** was confident that with summer 2005 would

come a permanent version of the grass labyrinth, maybe a painted paved one. You may call one of the volunteers at (416) 489-4471 for details.

A labyrinth is meant to symbolize a journey to the centre of ourselves. But my kids didn't know, so they ran through it to the point of getting dizzy. Laughter is another spiritual pathway, isn't it?

Trinity Square Park Labyrinth (416) 392-1111 (416) 598-2010 (café) www.toronto.ca www.labyrinth-toronto.ca	**I-10 Downtown** Toronto 5-min.

 Schedule: Café open weekdays, 9:30 am to 2:30 pm, June to October. **Admission:** FREE.
Directions: Between Bay St. and the Eaton Centre, north of Queen St.

ALLAN GARDENS CONSERVATORY

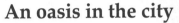

An oasis in the city

I tell my son we'll be visiting a greenhouse. "Is the house all painted in green?" he asks incredulously. "No, it's a house made out of glass and full of green plants that believe it's summer all year long!" I reply.

Talk about a greenhouse effect! Five buildings with large windows, covering over 16,000 sq. feet are filled with plants for all occasions. Some are filled with exhibits which gradually change into new ones according to the plants' life cycles. And it's free!

Enter through the building with the high palm tree filled dome. Stepping through a curtain of fine roots, you enter a tropical hothouse with hibiscus set amidst a tapestry-like leafy backdrop. Beyond it, a large selection of hairy, prickly, and fluffy cactuses await the little ones' impatient hands.

Retracing your steps to the other side of the dome, you'll find a cooler space with a small waterfall and a lovely red fish pond, with its penny-carpeted bottom, at the foot of a nymph statuette.

Further, the tropical mood is definitely on with its hot and humid climate. Here, orchids bloom against the roar of water going through a paddle wheel attached to a small house.

In winter, you can admire shapes covered with flowers installed amidst hundreds of poinsettias and palm trees.

For two weeks during **Easter** time, a new selection of flowers adds its sweet perfume to the conservatory. The first **Easter** we visited the hot houses, we were struck by the sweet bouquet and the visual richness of the settings. What a contrast with those of winter time!

Chrysanthemums bring an autumn look to the Allan Gardens, while December marks the return of the **Victorian Christmas** display.

TIPS (fun for 2 years +)

• More on their **Victorian Christmas** opening ceremony on p. 198.
• As we finished our visit, we played at guessing from which plant the fallen leaves belonged. A fun initiation to botany!
• There is a small free parking lot you can access from Gerrard Street onto Horticultural Avenue. Good luck!

NEARBY ATTRACTIONS
Riverdale Farm (5-min.)...............p. 45
Mt. Pleasant Cemetery (15-min.) p. 310

Allan Gardens Conservatory
(416) 392-7288
www.toronto.ca

I-10
**Downtown
Toronto
20-min.**

Schedule: Open year-round, 10 am to 5 pm.
Admission: FREE.
Directions: 14 Horticultural Ave.,Toronto (south of Carlton, between Jarvis and Sherbourne St.).

MOUNT PLEASANT CEMETERY

The circle of life

"Is it true?" asks my anguished son. A smart little girl had just concluded the dispute she had been having with him by striking with an ultimate, irrefutable argument, that had nothing to do with their quarrel: "Oh yeah? Well, girls live longer than boys!" My little live one was shattered when I confirmed this dire statistic. He was ready for a visit to the cemetery to help us approach this delicate but very natural topic in a more realistic fashion.

Few people realize that the Mount Pleasant Cemetery is far from being sinister. The setting is so pretty, it attracts walkers, joggers and cyclists.

Sculptures adorning numerous graves give the visit an interesting cultural quality. If you go to Mount Pleasant Cemetery with children, I suggest you try finding, by car or by foot, the works of art I've photographed for you.

Bayview Avenue and Yonge Street border the Cemetery. It's easier to enter by Yonge Street, north of St. Clair Avenue. Paved roads crisscross the site and cars can stop wherever they please. A tunnel allows vehicles to circulate under Mt. Pleasant Road, which separates the cemetery into two sections.

After reading for my son a few dates written on gravestones, I was able to discuss with him the random nature of death. Here, parents bid farewell to their child; there, a woman said good-bye to her husband waiting for the time she'll join him; farther away, an entire family was buried a long time ago.

Many tombstones from plots 37 to 47 even show a picture of the deceased. This confers a more concrete image to the experience. The cemetery really is a fertile ground for discussion.

TIPS (fun for 5 years +)

• A great variety of trees can be found in this cemetery. During the fall, it becomes a great harvesting ground for young leaf collectors.

• If you're into sculptures, you might want to get a copy of *Sculpture in the City* suggesting twelve walks in downtown Toronto to look at some 160 sculptures. This 138-page book was written by Torontonian Helen Nolan, an energetic woman I have personally met, with a passion for public sculptures. You will find her self-published guide in independent bookstores such as the **AGO** gift store or **The Distillery**'s visitors' centre, for $15.

Mount Pleasant Cemetery (416) 485-9129	I-10 North of downtown 20-min.

   Schedule: Open daily, year-round from 8 am to 8 pm.
Admission: FREE.
Directions: 375 Mt. Pleasant Rd, Toronto (entrance on Yonge St., north of St. Clair Ave.).

EDWARDS GARDENS AND BEYOND

The wheels go round and round...

When parents of young children feel the urge for a nature walk, it often means they have to drag wagon and stroller over roots and rocks. So, how about entering a forest of mature, brightly coloured trees, on a fabulous paved trail? How about crisscrossing a singing river that flows underneath several small bridges? You'll find all this in and around Wilket Creek Park, in the heart of Toronto.

OK, fine, I'm only telling you the pretty details. The Don River is polluted and in some areas isn't that crystalline, and several Sunday cyclists and runners rush through the trail. But even so, we really appreciated our invigorating stroll.

I recommend entering **Wilket Creek Park** at the entrance located at the limit of **Edwards Gardens**.

The weeping willows, the flowered rock gardens and the small valleys offer a charming rural panorama, complete

with dozens of ducks. Children love to watch them swim in the river.

Wilket Creek's wide paved trail takes shape at the end of **Edwards Gardens**. Along its course, you'll find a few benches, several bridges, smaller beaten dirt paths parallel to the trail, beautiful undergrowth facing the river as well as 30-metre-tall maple trees and several other species of deciduous trees that take on magnificent hues in autumn.

You need to walk a good half-hour for the path to cross the road going through **Sunnybrook Park** (where you can find washrooms).

Those who want to extend their stroll can add the **Serena Gundy Park** trail to their circuit. It is located across Sunnybrook Road, by the **Wilket Creek** path. You could also drive through **Sunnybrook Park** and park by the entrance of **Serena Gundy Park**. From there, it takes about ten minutes to reach the end of the little park. (The exit leads you to Broadway Avenue.)

The trees aren't as tall as in **Wilket Creek**, but the trail as a whole is pleasant. Among others, I passed two dog-walkers escorted by eight beautiful beasts and a quiet man demonstrating great patience as he was being used as a perch by birds eating out of his hand.

TIPS (fun for 2 years +)

• **Sunnybrook Park** is also accessible from Leslie Street. It includes an equestrian school with a small stand allowing visitors to sit while observing horses and riders at work.

NEARBY ATTRACTIONS
Paws in the Park (5-min.)............ p. 124
Ontario Science Centre (5-min.)..p. 256

City of Toronto	I-10
• North York	**North**
(416) 392-1111	of downtown
www.toronto.ca	25-min.

Schedule: Open year-round.
Admission: FREE.
Directions: Edwards Gardens' entrance is at the corner of Lawrence Ave. and Leslie St. There are a few pedestrian entrances to Wilket Creek Park on Leslie, south of Lawrence Ave.

JAMES GARDENS

viewpoint. A small pebble trail has been designed parallel to an asphalt one along the Humber River. It is reserved for pedestrians, so as to avoid collisions with cyclists and roller blade enthusiasts.

Heading towards the small forest of **Lambton Woods**, my aspiring botanist noticed several curiously

Cool picnic!

The flowerbeds full of tulips and other spring blooms don't impress my little thrill seeker. However, he really falls for James Gardens after he discovers the stairs. They climb 30 metres up towards the panoramic viewpoint overlooking the Humber River. To add to the picturesque character of this surprising city outing, we walk the trails through Lambton Woods and we head for a picnic on a bridge over the river.

The **James Gardens** are not particularly imposing, yet they have lovely symmetrical flower displays as well as several small ponds straddled by footbridges where ducks and chipmunks cavort here and there.

Small paths require the odd portage for those visiting with strollers, while a gentle slope offers a convenient alternative to the stairs leading to a terrace with a great

shaped and knotted trees and many tamed birds with red wings. We observed with great interest a female duck in her nest... perched atop the chopped trunk of what would have been a mature tree.

After a 15-minute walk, the path turns onto a long footbridge leading to a bridge with benches. We stopped there and enjoyed our picnic. Below, the river cascaded down, glistening in the sun. Some 40 metres above, trains rolled down tracks set on high pillars. The overall effect was stunning!

TIPS (fun for 2 years +)

•   **Lambton Woods** is well-known for spring wildflowers and the area is a favourite for birders.

•   If you picnic on the bridge, make sure to sit on the sidewalk stretching along its railing to avoid cyclists travelling in the middle on the **bike trail**.

City of Toronto
· Etobicoke
(416) 392-1111
www.toronto.ca

I-9
N-W
of downtown
35-min.

 Schedule: Open year-round.
Admission: FREE.
 Directions: From Royal York Rd. (south of Eglinton Ave.), take Edenbridge St. eastbound.

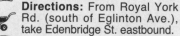

ROSETTA MCCLAIN GARDENS

Perched garden

If you're in Scarborough to admire the Bluffs, don't forget to stop by the Rosetta McClain Gardens, perched atop the cliffs. You'll catch a breathtaking view of Lake Ontario, 60 metres below.

You can go round the gardens' paved trails in about twenty minutes. In the centre, there are symmetrical raised planter beds adorned with a few large stones. A scent garden filled with fragrant plants will titillate little noses. Numerous benches allow visitors a chance to admire the landscaping.

Young visitors like to take refuge underneath a beautiful bandshell located at one end of the gardens.

I went with my family on a beautiful autumn day. The sun was shining on Lake Ontario and the ground was littered with large leaves in bright yellow and red hues.

TIPS (fun for 2 years +)

• During my first visit, on a rainy day, fog created a white screen that completely hid the lake from my view! The atmosphere was magical; I felt cut off from the rest of the world… but I did not get to see Lake Ontario.

NEARBY ATTRACTIONS

Rosetta McClain Gardens
• Scarborough
(416) 392-1111
www.toronto.ca

J-11
East of downtown 30-min.

Schedule: Open year-round.
Admission: FREE.
Directions: From Kingston Rd., access the gardens' parking lot, just before Glen Everest Rd.

ROYAL BOTANICAL GARDENS

Royal treat!

As we walk down towards the lilacs, the vivid greens among the tall trees of the luscious valley catch my breath. To top it off, a live jazz tune is filling the air along with the sweet fragrance of the lilacs. This is what I call a well-cultivated event!

The **Lilac Festival** is my favourite time of the year to visit the Royal Botanical Gardens (RBG). The weather is mild and the event takes us to the Arboretum, a large section 3 km from the RBG Centre, hosting lilacs and magnolias and surrounded by fun nature trails to explore with the kids. One needs to explore the Arboretum to begin to grasp how vast and wild the RBG really is.

The RBG is comprised of 30 km of nature trails, five separate gardens and four nature sanctuaries, one of which is the **Cootes Paradise Marsh**, right at the edge of the Arboretum.

You want to stop at the Arboretum's Nature Interpretive Centre, by the parking lot, to get trail maps and check out their interactive displays (with stuffed animals, microscope, live turtles and more) and their little shop, well stocked with trinkets.

During the **Lilac Festival**, we were handed a map of the lilac dell with sections indicated by letters (the letters are actually shown on signs in the valley). Don't fail to cross section "S" to get to section "T" where you'll find all the gorgeous yellow, pink and white magnolia trees. Bring your camera, the contrast between the dark branches and the delicate

petals when the sun is shining through is simply beautiful! You can access the North Shore trail from that section or from section "G". It runs along the **Cootes Paradise Marsh**. It was amazing to stop on the boardwalk just to listen to the birds and quite captivating to watch dozens of Cormorants hanging over their nests on the trees of a small island.

As a bonus for children, at different times and gardens throughout the year, the RBG displays interactive Discovery Carts filled with things to touch. During the **Lilac Festival**, kids could compare the odours of different lilacs. Some really stink! They were invited to draw a lilac flower, choosing from the numerous characteristics: single, double, small, medium or large with lobes cupped, flat or curled down. Then, they could check on a chart if it already existed and where they could find it in the lilac dell.

The Rock Gardens, much appreciated by the children, offered a different kind of fun. Built in 1929, it was the first major display at the RBG. The huge mature trees are a testimony to that. Tulips and rocks take over the show in that garden. Rock stairs leading to secret corners, rocks becoming small bridges over the pond, huge rocks to climb on. This is a great spot for little explorers!

The fish in the pond of the indoor Mediterranean Gardens were a hit along with some huge flowers. The outdoor Discovery Garden was fun with its giant leaves and hollow tree trunk. Both are accessible from the inside of the RBG Centre.

TIPS (fun for 3 years +)

• The **Lilac Festival** is usually held on the last two weekends of May but call before going to make sure the lilacs have blossomed. Last time I attended the festival, in its second weekend, the flowers were just starting to bloom. On the other hand, the magnolias were breathtaking!

• **Here's a calendar of some blooms to expect (but call ahead to confirm):** Spring flowering bulbs in April; lilacs, flowering trees, spring wildflowers in May; irises, roses, annual flowers in June; lilies in July and August. In September and October, you still can see annual flowers, roses, dahlias and chrysanthemums, (although not in their best!). From November to March, there's always the indoor Mediterranean Gardens in the RBG Centre.

• Rock Gardens, RBG Centre and Rose Gardens are stroller accessible. I would dare to push a stroller across the Arboretum and part of the South Shore when it is not too muddy. Expect to lift it over stairs here and there.

• There's a free (with admission) trolley service hopping from one garden to the next, including stops at the **Dundurn Castle** (p.416). It runs daily, every 30 minutes, from 10 am to 6 pm. Bear in mind that you might not be able to get on during very busy periods and the frequent stops mean it'll take the shuttle 25 minutes to go from the Rock Gardens to the Arboretum while you could do it in five minutes by car. (It took us 30 minutes to walk from the Rock Gardens to the Arboretum Nature Centre, following an unofficial narrow trail along the road.)

• For birthday packages, call the Nature Interpretive Centre at (905) 527-7962.

• There's no food service at the Arboretum. Bring your own water and snacks (including small nuts you could share with the chipmunks). If you are planning a picnic during the Lilac Festival, bring a thick blanket and some plastic garbage bags to line it! The ground might still be a bit wet.

• The Garden's Café at the RBG Centre is a bit too posh for my taste (when visiting with children). See **Easterbrook's Foot Long Hot Dog** restaurant and **Rock Garden Tea House** on pp. 428 and 435.

We have not had a chance to visit the other sanctuaries. There is the Hendrie Valley with 5 km of trails starting at the Rose Gardens parking lot. The Berry Tract is connected to **Cootes Paradise Marsh** and Rock Chapel by the **Bruce Trail**. Rock Chapel I have to see next time. It boasts a 25-m waterfall and 3.5 km of trails along the Niagara Escarpment, coinciding with the **Bruce Trail**).

The South Shore trails (not accessible from the North Shore trails) also seem quite interesting, with more hilly paths facing the Niagara Escarpment.

Royal Botanical Gardens
• Burlington
(905) 527-1158
www.rbg.ca

E-2
S-W
of Toronto
50 min.

Schedule: The outdoor garden areas are open from 9:30 am until dusk. The Nature Interpretive Centre near the Arboretum opens from 10 am to 4 pm. The RBG Centre opens from 9 am to dusk and the Mediterranean Gardens (the greenhouse inside the RBG Centre) are open from 9 am to 5 pm.

Admission: $8/adults, $2.50/5-12 years.

Directions: 680 Plains Rd. West, Burlington. Take the QEW to Hwy 403 West, then catch Hwy 6 North and take the first exit to Plain Rd. West.

See **Royal Botanical Gardens** on p. 314.

DON VALLEY BRICKWORKS

Surprise, surprise

The bricks mingle with the sand and pebbles on the path. They remind us there was a brick factory for a whole century on this site! It seems impossible. The place has become such a precious little enclave hidden in the big megacity. We could mistake the walls of the old quarry for a small natural escarpment shielding us from the urban noise.

Following the pleasure of observing the fish in the large pond amidst the water lilies, my little naturalist was ecstatic to discover a whole encampment of snails along the path of the Weston Quarry Garden farther in the back. We actually had to be careful not to crush them.

Bulrushes, wildflowers meadows, small creek with rocks to jump, small trails climbing up slopes; the place is perfect for young explorers.

Moore Ravine (see p. 345) is even accessible above the "West Wall" on the western part of the site.

TIPS (fun for 2 years +)
• My son's friend found a **fossil** among the rocks!
• Since my last visit, a lookout has been established at the top of the east slope.

Don Valley Brickworks (416) 392-1111 www.toronto.ca	I-10 North of downtown 20-min.

Schedule: Open year-round.
Admission: FREE.
Directions: 550 Bayview Ave., Toronto. It is on the west side of Bayview Ave. It is safer to access it going southbound on Bayview. The entrance is south of Pottery Rd. (a good way to access Bayview Ave. if you're coming from the east side of Don Valley Pkwy).

NEARBY ATTRACTIONS

RATTRAY MARSH C. A.

A real enclave

A marsh is an unusual site in a residential neighbourhood, yet, Rattray Marsh sits, sheltered deep within the conservation area sandwiched between Mississauga and Oakville.

Rattray Marsh, with its many viewpoints along tree-bordered walkways, attracts young explorers and bird watchers.

To reach it, you must first cross **Jack Darling Park**, on the shores of Lake Ontario. Those interested in visiting the marsh should leave their vehicle in the third parking area they will see.

Anticipate a 20-minute walk through several beaches and another interesting playground before you reach the conservation area. I have friends whose kids had so much fun in that part of the park that they never got to the marsh! (Read the directions for a quicker access.)

The path to your left that you cross just before you reach the marsh is worth the detour. It opens onto a wide pebble beach. It will take you a good half-hour to stroll along the boardwalk. More trails lead you through the marsh.

TIPS (fun for 3 years +)

• There are no washrooms at Rattray Marsh. The closest is located in **Jack Darling Park** and is closed in the winter.

• The long path that borders **Jack Darling Park** is stroller friendly. The boardwalk, however, has too many stairs for comfort. We left ours at the entrance to Rattray Marsh.

• Stay close to young children on the viewing platform bordering the marsh. While the boardwalks are solid, watch the children don't escape to the small slopes.

• Rubber boots are recommended after a rainfall.

• The marsh's shallow pond is partly turned into an unofficial ice rink by the locals during the winter!

• Make sure to stop from time to time and invite children to listen to, and locate, the many birds. Ornithologists have identified some 277 species on site! There is a wide range of wildflowers as well.

• It is possible to treat your family with a natural interpretation tour throughout Rattray Marsh by hiring your own nature interpreter from the Rattray Marsh Protection Association! For $30 an hour, Wendy Walker will provide all the information you want to know along some or all of the 3.5 km trail, (905) 823-6465.

Rattray Marsh Conservation Area
• Mississauga
(905) 670-1615
www.creditvalleycons.com

J-8
West of Toronto 30-min.

Schedule: Open year-round.
Admission: FREE (donation).
Directions: Take QEW West, exit Mississauga Rd. southbound. Turn west on Lakeshore Rd. Enter through Jack Darling Park on the south side. Or exit at Erin Mills Pkwy southbound, it becomes Southdown. Turn left on Orr, then left on Meadow Wood, and right on Green Glade and park in the school's parking lot. Access to the marsh is in the school's backyard.

NEARBY ATTRACTIONS

Presqu'ile Provincial Park

wind-swept beach on the lakeshore.

When we visited, the sand looked more like a neat harvested field than an idyllic beach. However, in places where the fine blond sand got licked by the waves, it had the tight and regular furrowed quality we prefer (it resists under the foot). It extends like this for more than 100 metres under shallow and warm water; just heaven for kids.

You must take your car again to reach the path that leads to the marsh's boardwalk, further along the peninsula. The narrow boardwalk is not too long (you reach the end with-

Bulrushes and sand on the menu

The appetizer: a smooth ribbon of sand separated from the shore by a natural barrier of shrubs (ideal for playing and picnicking). Beyond, the 200-metre-long beach leading to the main course: a vast, shallow, glistening body of water. To add a bit of green: a stroll among the bulrushes on the boardwalk overlooking the marshes. What a feast for the little ones' eyes!

The beach at Presqu'ile Park spreads for 2 kilometres along Lake Ontario. You can access it from four different entrances within the park. By entering via entry 2 and 3 you will take full advantage of all of the sites' appeal. Their parking spaces are located closer to the beach, which you access by going through a sandy enclosure bordered by bushes. The spot proved ideal for a picnic, and on a windy day, this secluded oasis was warmer than the nearby larger,

in a half-hour walk), and it is stroller-friendly.

The tightly pressed bulrushes bordering the pier reached taller than the head of my little naturalist. He was fascinated by the myriad of water lilies, adorned with yellow flowers, we could see at our feet.

My little boy agreed to stop and listen to the birds' various and surprising calls. They fascinated him. This marsh is a mecca for birdwatchers every spring and fall.

TIPS (fun for all ages)

• At the beginning of September, Presqu'ile serves as a meeting point for thousands of Monarch butterflies preparing for their migratory flight to Mexico. The event is celebrated by the **Monarch Weekend** held on Labour Day weekend.

• Presqu'ile includes two Interpretive Visitor Centres, an old lighthouse and 394 **campsites** surrounded by beautiful trees (some facing a pebble beach).

NEARBY ATTRACTIONS
The Big Apple (15-min.)..................p. 27

Presqu'ile Provincial Park
• Brighton
(613) 475-4324
www.ontarioparks.com

C-6
East
of Toronto
90-min.

Schedule: Open year-round.
Admission: $9.50/vehicle pass
Directions: R.R. 4, Brighton. From Hwy 401 East, take exit #509 to Brighton/Regional Rd. 30. Turn west on Regional Rd. 2, then north on Regional Rd. 66.

WYE MARSH WILDLIFE CENTRE

Water lily land

How about a canoe excursion amidst water lilies and turtles, paddling through corridors of tall grass and bulrushes? Interested? Then, Wye Marsh may be just what you need!

In July and August, you can reserve a seat on one of the seven-metre-long canoes that traverse the water of Wye Marsh. As father and son embarked on this one-hour adventure, I took off for a stroll with my younger one towards the beautiful boardwalk that spans the marsh.

As we approached the wooden trail, we could hear trumpet sounds blowing high and strong. As we moved closer to the large water hole, we discovered that, yes indeed, the noise came from spectacular white Trumpeter Swans, dozens of them, swimming through the channels. A three-storey-high tower afforded us a better view of the colony of birds.

On the boardwalk, we found a sheltered section with long landing nets to explore the marsh's bed. Quite a hands-on experience! In two places, the trail turns into a bridge and from there, my happy girl greeted her canoeist dad and big brother as they paddled along underneath us. My preschooler could not contain his excitement when he caught a glimpse of

some turtles between the water lilies and rocked the boat in a manner none of the other passengers appreciated!

On our way back, we spent some time at the Visitor Centre. There, we listened to samples of waterfowl calls and watched an interesting documentary on the Great Lakes (if not shown when you visit, you may ask for it specifically). My son fell for the poor canoeist who gets caught in time travel and many transformations of his environment (melting of ice, receding of water, etc). Ask for it!

TIPS (fun for 3 years +)

• Six years is the required minimum age for canoe trips with an adult. Five **canoe trips** depart daily, call for exact hours. You need reservations.

• Call to find out about Wye Marsh Parent & Tots programs, where young naturalists 5 years and under and their parents explore nature's wonder. The $4/child program includes a theme walk, craft, story, juice and cookies.

NEARBY ATTRACTIONS

Wye Marsh Wildlife Centre
• Midland
(705) 526-7809
www.wyemarsh.com

A-2 Midland Region 90-min.

Schedule: Open year-round, 10 am to 4 pm (open 10 am to 6 pm from May to Labour Day).

Admission: $6.50/adults, $5.50/seniors and children. FREE under 3 years. Canoe trip is $6/person ($10 on Sundays).

Directions: Same entrance as Sainte-Marie among the Hurons, Midland. Take Hwy 400 North, exit Hwy 12 westbound. Wye Marsh is just east of Midland.

LITTLE NORWAY PARK

Who knew?

I never expected to find such a tall and beautiful totem in such a secluded little park. And there was much more to discover as we walked further in. There's the intriguing metal bridge, a giant lion leaning on a slide, the small labyrinth, a little forest and the pier behind, overlooking the glittering water of Lake Ontario.

When you read the plaques by the entrance, you learn that this used to be a training camp for Norway's Air Force during World War II and that it was officially opened by the King of Norway in 1987. I

don't know when it fell into oblivion but this little park is a keeper.

There were many details to observe on the 12-metre totem, from the large whales at the bottom to the small people climbing stairs way up high. Then my little mountain goats explored the rock stairs under the metal bridge.

The playground, located by the water, was hidden from our view so the huge concrete lion adorning it came as a great surprise.

The long pier was accessible through the little patch of evergreens (providing nice shade for picnics). We walked on it towards the lake until we reached the open water of Lake Ontario sprinkled with tiny sailboats. Small planes landed on the runway at Toronto Island Airport as a bonus. It made us forget where we were!

TIPS (fun for 2 years +)

• There's no rail along the pier so you'll need to be extra careful with children. I don't recommend it with toddlers. The edges are too tempting...

• There's a wading pool in the playground. Bring bathing suits in case it should be open when you visit.

• The ferry ride to **Toronto Island Airport** is $5/adults, $2/children for the shortest ride ever: less than one minute.

• Parent and Child drop-in services (for children ages 0-2 and 3-5) are offered for $1 at the **Harbourfront Community Centre** just east of the park (627 Queen's Quay West). No need to pre-register but if you're interested, call to confirm their schedule at (416) 392-1509.

• You'll find a great convenience store at the corner of Bathurst and Queens Quay providing everything you might need for an impromptu picnic.

Little Norway Park
(416) 392-1111
www.toronto.ca

J-9
Downtown
Toronto
5-min.

Schedule: Open year-round.
Admission: FREE.
Directions: Runs along Queen's Quay between Bathurst St. and Little Norway Cr. There's public parking on the southwest side of Bathurst.

NEARBY ATTRACTIONS

HIGH PARK

Toronto's true nature

It's all a question of perspective. Previously, I associated High Park with romantic walks along Grenadier Pond and Shakespeare at the fascinating outdoor theatre. Now, when I think of High Park, I see a baby bison living in one of Deer Pen Street's many animal paddocks. I hear the little train's bell joyfully ringing through the park's 161 hectares and I see a castle...

There's a trackless little train operating on a nine-station circuit around the park from spring to autumn. You can get on the train at the station of your choice, get off where you want to, and stay as long as you wish before hopping back on. You have the privilege of getting back on at the same station or at the next one, to complete the circuit to your starting point.

The High Park train's flexibility allows visitors to build an itinerary suited to their schedule, to take advantage of the various pleasures offered at the Park. For us, it usually starts with the playground.

High Park's is simply the most original playground in town. Guess how long it took High Park volunteers to build it from scratch? Ten days! OK, fine, there were about three thousand volunteers and planning had been a long-term affair. Even so, I admire the results of what people can achieve when they put their heart into it.

The masterpiece is shaped like a fortified castle, decorated with engravings and mosaics of children's drawings. It occupies 10,000 sq. ft. A third of this area is dedicated to small children and is enclosed with a fence, for parents' peace of mind.

The section for smaller children is full of nooks and crannies to explore and includes an amusing vibraphone. The staircase in the area for older children gives a labyrinth-like impression (if you let small children go there, step up the supervision).

The playground is next to the big duck pond, the animal pens which house bison, goats, llamas and sheep, a snack bar as well as one of the train's stops.

When the children have played all they want, I suggest that you let the little train take you to Grenadier Pond, a few stations farther (about a fifteen-minute ride for young conductors).

In this corner of the park, the weeping willows that brush against the pond tempt visitors to picnic. Birds are so used to human presence that a Canada goose nearly left a few feathers between the fingers of my little rascal when he was only two years old.

After exploring this area of the park, you can hop back on the train to come back, ten minutes later, to your starting point. From there, you can visit Deer Pen Road's animals.

TIPS (fun for 1 year +)

• More about Shakespeare's **Dream in High Park** on p. 106 (see tips section).
• See **Big Brother's Soap Box Derby** in High Park on p. 232.
• More about **Colborne Lodge** and **Easter** activities at High Park on p. 401.
• BEWARE, from May 1 to October 1, on Sundays and holidays, the park can only be accessed from the Bloor Street entrance and you can only drive down to the restaurant.
• We prefer to enter the site through High Park Boulevard (accessible from Parkside Road) and turn left to park by the animal paddocks or at the end of Spring Drive. These parking lots are the closest to the High Park Adventure Playground. Otherwise, we park beside Grenadier Restaurant.
• The High Park subway station (on Bloor Street West) gives direct access to the park's entrance; it is located close to one of the little trackless train stops.
• High Park Children's Garden, near Colborne Lodge, offers FREE drop-in programs for families every Thursday from 10 am to noon, in July and August. It includes garden games, crafts and gardening activities for children 3 to 12 years old.
• High Park includes a large outdoor pool as well as a wading pool, closer to the Bloor Street entrance.
• There are snack bars in the park, one near the playground and one by the Bloor entrance. You can also eat at the **Grenadier Restaurant**, located at the centre of the park. There's a dining room and a take-out counter (great fries!). Open year-round, from 7 am to 10 pm during the summer, (closes earlier the rest of the year). Call (416) 769-9870.
• See **Sunnyside Pavilion Café** on p. 429.

City of Toronto

(416) 392-1111
(905) 652-6890 (train)
www.toronto.ca

I-9
West of downtown
15-min.

 Schedule: Open year-round. (The trackless train usually operates daily from early April to Labour Day, weather permitting. Hours are variable.

 Admission: FREE. Train ticket, cash only: $4/adults, $3/seniors and children 2 years and older, FREE under 2 years.

 Directions: At the intersection of Bloor St. West and Parkside Dr., Toronto (Parkside Dr. is accessible northbound from Lake Shore Blvd.). Read tips!

DUFFERIN GROVE PARK

with a laughing crowd. As we walked towards it, we discovered the best and most daring feature I have seen in a public park: a gigantic sandpit. It lay in front of us, complete with running water, gar-

Community centre without a roof

I was surfing through a very interesting site the other day: Project for Public Spaces, a non-profit organization dedicated to promoting great community places giving a new wholesome meaning to urban life. Guess what I found on their list of the 105 best public parks seen during their walk around the world in 1000 neighbourhoods, 46 states and 12 countries? Our own Dufferin Grove Park!

This park might have been considered a seedy one back in the 90's but those days are over! The Friends of the Grove, a neighbourhood association, turned it around.

As soon as we entered the park we saw acrobats casually practicing their walk on stilts along the sinuous path that runs up and down hill, with a canopy of leaves from mature tress in the background.

Families were busy fixing individual pizzas to cook in one of the two outdoor wood ovens. Isn't it the most clever idea to bring a community together? Some people had brought toppings they offered to share with us. There were toys for children and books near a colourful bench covered with kids' drawings. Another wonderful touch of colour in the vicinity: a huge border of tall sunflowers.

Further, a large playground surrounded by a split-rail fence (much prettier than the usual wire fence) was filled

den shovels and long logs.

Imagine what small engineers can do here! They build labyrinths of water streams and bridges. They dig holes. They create mini ponds...

It was so cute to see a bunch of preschoolers surrounding my 10-year-old boy scout, eager to help him as he undertook an ambitious bridge project. Many had the astonished look kids have when they can't believe their luck: "At last! A place where I'm allowed to get dirty and play with the garden faucet. Too good to be true; must hurry before someone stops me!"

TIPS (fun for 1 year +)

• You'll find free parking at Dufferin Mall across Dufferin Street. By the way, this mall includes Wal-Mart, Toys 'R Us and Winners, all under the same roof!

• There's a large wading pool right next to the playground.

• Weather permitting, the Pizza Days take place on Wednesdays from noon to 2 pm and Sundays from 1 to 3 pm (also on Tuesdays, noon to 2 pm in July and August). A piece of dough, tomato sauce and cheese are included in the $2 fee.

• From the beginning of May up to the middle of September, **Friday Night Suppers** take place. The park suppers are cooked in the community kitchen and served outside when the weather is good, lit with torches and candles. It costs $6. Call ahead by Friday morning to reserve a meal. There's at least one sitting at 6 pm. Sometimes, films are projected outdoors after the supper, at 8 pm, against the field house wall (on a bed sheet)... Can you get more retro than that?

• There's an organic farmers' market every Thursday from 3:30 to 7 pm, year-round.

• Native Child and Family Services has organized its annual **Children's Pow Wow** for the last six years at Dufferin Grove Park. It usually takes place on the third or fourth Saturday of September. Call (416) 283-7082 to confirm.

• The **Clay and Paper Theatre** has been involved with the park for years. Once a year, around October 31, they organize the interactive **October Night of Dread Parade**, starting and ending at the park and followed by a big bonfire, food and music. Call (416) 537-9105 or check www.clayandpapertheatre.org for the exact date and to find out about their drop-in mask-making workshops prior to the event.

• In the winter, if you go skating on the park's rink, you can buy buttered bread slices hot from their wood oven, soup and hot chocolate.

• The **Project for Public Spaces** web site includes valuable tips for those who want to improve their local park! Go to (www.pps.org). Click on Parks, Plazas and Civic Squares, then on More Parks & Public Spaces to access their lists of great streets, markets, parks and buildings as well as their hall of shame.

I saw some resigned parents who watched their kids getting covered with mud in their Sunday clothes. Had they known, they would have brought a change of clothes.

Another original initiative in this park: there are two **fire pits**, which you can use with a permit! Think about it! You can actually roast marshmallows in the middle of the city! Call to reserve; they'll charge $10-$15 for the cost of wood.

As a bonus, when we visited the park, there was the **Children's Pow Wow** going full blast on the soccer field, with huge teepee, traditional drummers and dancers, adults and children so cute in their elaborate regalia. For a small fee, we could make a button, a dance shawl or a necklace. Wow!

NEARBY ATTRACTIONS
Christie Pits Park (10-min.)..........p. 387

Dufferin Grove Park | **I-9**
(416) 392-0913 | **West of**
www.dufferinpark.ca | **downtown 15-min.**

 Schedule: Open year-round.
Admission: FREE access to the park.
 Directions: On the east side of Dufferin St., across from Dufferin Mall (two blocks south of Bloor St. West and the Dufferin subway station).

THOMSON & BIRKDALE PARKS

Paved with good intentions

While on a quest for stroller- and wagon-friendly paved trails, my wheels brought me to Scarborough. There I found great little asphalt paths in two adjoining parks: Birkdale and Thomson Memorial. Bathed in sunlight, the lush, leafy woods were abundantly laden with the autumn hues and shadows I enjoy so much. In addition, both parks offered a playground.

Usually, I'm not crazy about manicured parks. Nevertheless, I really enjoyed the intimate aspect of **Birkdale Park**. It is narrow, with plenty of curves and small valleys. The views are so diverse that you never know what awaits you around the next bend. It may be a small river, a pastoral valley, maple trees, either gigantically tall or short and stubby, or majestic weeping willows.

After a twenty-minute fun stroll, we got to a playground alongside Brimley

Street. Last stop! Everybody off the wagon to move a bit!

If you wish to walk some more, you can cross Brimley Street (unfortunately, there are no traffic lights at this location, so be careful) and join **Thomson Memorial Park** by taking the path across the street. You'll need to walk another 15 minutes before reaching the middle of this park. It has large picnic areas and woods carpeted with leaves. The trails along the border of the park are less interesting (at the east side exit, you pass under electricity pylons).

The picnic sites are pretty, and several are located under the trees. On the south side of the park, there's a small pond. It's a marvelously landscaped oasis located between two playgrounds and close to pens housing several farm animals (in July and August, depending on the City of Toronto's agreement with a private petting zoo).

When we were there, children were wading about in a brook emerging from the pond.

Grandparents sitting on a bench under the weeping willows were observing children hidden inside flowering bushes along the waterside. Simply lovely!

TIPS (fun for 2 years +)
• Both parks offer free parking.
• Thomson Memorial Park hosts the **Scarborough Historical Museum**, right next to its playground. During the summer weekends, costumed staff greet us in the four small buildings. On **Canada Day**, the museum usually offers a Strawberry Social.

NEARBY ATTRACTIONS
Woodie Wood Chuck's (10-min.)..p. 221
Agincourt Leisure Pool (10-min.)..p. 382

City of Toronto
• Scarborough
(416) 392-1111
www.toronto.ca

I-11
N-E
of downtown
30-min.

Schedule: Open year-round.
Admission: FREE.

Directions: Birkdale Park's entrance is on Ellesmere Rd., between Midland Ave. and Brimley Rd. Thomson Memorial Park's entrance is on Brimley Rd., between Lawrence Ave. and Ellesmere Rd.

L'Amoreaux & Milliken Parks

Ponds in the "hood"

For those short on time to explore the countryside, you can find a small oasis of nature in the suburbs.

Milliken Park offers paved trails, a large pond and a small island of trees. Those trees are mature and the variety of trails quite entertaining for young explorers. The forest sits next to the pond and a few picnic tables have been installed along the water under the trees.

The rest of the park is rather bare and offers little shade. We enjoyed, however, the nearby playground and its wading pool.

In the same region, you will find **L'Amoreaux Park**, adjacent to the community centre of the same name. It holds a treasure of small paved trails that border a large pond. Interestingly, the cranes

I saw resting along the edge seemed unaware they were in the middle of a residential neighbourhood!

Some of the paths lead to a small island of tall leafy trees that looks like some kind of a dense forest housing the neighbourhood's entire vegetation. It is circled by a woodchip covered trail (yet practical with a stroller), framed by trees. You can travel the entire trail in approximately 15 minutes, excluding the time to explore the selection of wild flowers.

TIPS (fun for 2 years +)

• L'Amoreaux Park South hosts the **Kidstown Water Park**. More about this great water playground on page 380.
• Read about the **Kitefest** at Milliken Park on p. 328.
• I don't recommend you go out of your way to visit these two parks. Should you find yourself in the area during the fall however, take the time to enjoy the colourful foliage. In winter, weather permitting, you can skate on the frozen ponds.
• There usually are **fireworks** at Milliken Park on **Canada Day**, at around 10 pm. Call to confirm.

NEARBY ATTRACTIONS
Woodie Wood Chucks (5-min.).... p. 221

L'Amoreaux & Milliken Parks	I-11
L'Amoreaux & Milliken Parks · Scarborough (416) 392-1111 or (416) 396-7757 www.toronto.ca	**I-11 N-E** of downtown **35-min.**

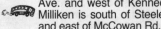

Schedule: Open year-round.
Admission: FREE.
Directions: Both parks are located north of Hwy 401. L'Amoreaux Park is north of McNicoll Ave. and west of Kennedy Rd., Milliken is south of Steeles Ave. and east of McCowan Rd.

INDUSTRIAL ALLIANCE KITEFEST

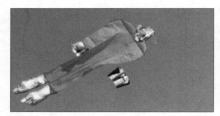

Go fly a kite!

Everybody's nose is pointing up. Everywhere we look into the open sky, there's a kite punctuating the blue background. I have never seen so many of them at once. One looks like an electric ray swimming above our heads. Others are huge and crazy. Every child wants to emulate the adults by making their own little kites lift up into the air in the open flying field.

The last time I visited **Milliken Park**, it was dwarfed by the huge sky. I thought it was a shame that all the tall trees were found in a tiny patch of forest by the pond, leaving the rest of the park without shaded spots. Now that I see it as the site of a great kite festival, it seems perfect.

TIPS (fun for 4 years +)
- More on **Milliken Park** on p. 327.
- The City staff have nothing to do with the organization of the festival. The park is rented by the Mandarin Club, a private group, for the occasion. Their official phone number, (416) 979-7110, in my experience has always led to a full mail box. Alliance has been the sponsor for some years. It could change in the future and therefore change the official name of the event. You can check **Toronto Kite Flyers'** web page, for a list of events: www.kites.org/tkf.
- It would be real torture for children to show up at such an event without having access to a kite. Traditionally, the festival offers a paper kite make-and-take craft activity for a minimal fee. Also, kite vendors are on the premises, offering affordable or unusual kites for sale.
- Snacks and Chinese food are sold on the premises.

NEARBY ATTRACTIONS
Woodie Wood Chucks (15-min.)...p. 221
Agincourt Pool (15-min.)..............p. 382

Kite flying is an art which originated in China many thousands of years ago. It is not surprising that the whole Chinese community seems to be meeting at this event. The KiteFest is organized by the Mandarin Club of Toronto (assisted by the **Toronto Kite Fliers**).

Industrial Alliance KiteFest includes professional kite flying demonstrations by teams from around the world, free kite flying classes for the public, international kite exhibits and kite design competitions.

We saw, floating in the air, a three-dimensional kite shaped like two gigantic legs with running shoes and shorts as well as a huge character dressed like Superman from a favourite children's television program.

The park's playground comes in very handy for parents who wish to try kite flying themselves (it keeps the kids busy!).

Industrial Alliance KiteFest • **Scarborough**	I-11 N-E of downtown 35-min.

 Schedule: Usually on a mid-September weekend, 11 am to 4 pm (for 2004: September 18 and 19). READ TIPS!
Admission: FREE (approximately $2 charge for material to build a small kite).
Directions: Milliken Park, Scarborough (at the intersection of Steeles Ave. East and McCowan Rd.).

DOWNSVIEW PARK

The missing link

The former military base was a bit of a no man's land for a while. It is slowly turning into an urban park. Tree City, the phased plan for Downsview Park's transformation, intends to integrate it into the system of wooded river valleys, ravines, parks and public paths already in existence in adjacent areas. Make way for the raccoons!

By the end of WWII, over 7,000 people worked at de Havilland Aircraft (currently Bombardier), completing 1.5 to 3 aircrafts every day. Now, 7,000 is the number of people taking part every week in soccer or volleyball-related activities in the hangar formerly used for aircraft assembly. Times change.

The Tree City project will be a very long time in the making. It will need to self-finance its implementation. Right now, the park doesn't look too appealing with huge fields of grass with very few mature trees. The project aims to add 25% forest coverage, meadows, playing fields and gardens. The first phase involves soil preparation, path making and planting.

TIPS (fun for 5 years +)
• See **Toronto Aerospace Museum** on p. 235.
• In addition to the **Canada Day** celebration, expect three other seasonal events: **Winter Wonderland** (usually on a mid-February Sunday), **Spring Fest**, (around **Victoria Day**) and **Fall Fair** (late October). Monthly community activities are also offered. They vary each year from Haunted Happenings, Holiday Lighting to Family Bike Day, to name a few. They usually put up an outdoor artificial skating rink. In 2001, their rink actually set the Guinness-sanctioned Canadian record! Check their web site or call for exact dates for current events.

Officials envision Downsview Park becoming to Toronto what Central park is to New York. It seems far-fetched but apparently, back in 1857, Central Park did not look better than Downsview does now. Meanwhile, and for the years to come, the main interest of the park is the special events it can host and year-round community programs and activities it can offer. Remember the Pope's visit to Toronto, drawing 800,000 pilgrims together? The Rolling Stones concert during the SARS scare? They took place in Downsview Park.

Since the land is owned by the Government of Canada, **Canada Day** is the obvious best time to visit the park. The free event presents a roster of stage performers and a large **midway** topped with an ambitious **fireworks** show.

When we visited, a circus had erected a tent on the site, for additional fun for a fee. A shuttle took us from the parking lot to the centre of the action. We only saw the fireworks but during the day, several children's activities had been offered: petting zoo, buskers, dog shows and the likes.

Downsview Park (416) 952-2227 (hotline) www.pdp.ca	H-10 **North** of downtown 35-min.

 Schedule: Open year-round.
Admission: FREE.
 Directions: Take Allen Rd. northbound (go north of Hwy 401). Turn west on Sheppard Ave., Then turn left on John Drury Dr. During major events, staff will direct you to the parking area.

HUMBER ARBORETUM

Urban ecology

A tiny house lies on a stump in the middle of the trail. As we approach, birds fly away and I explain to my 3-year-old that this is the local restaurant for birds. She collects seeds on the ground and intends to stand still until they come back to feed from her hand.

The nature trail leading to the woods by the Arboretum's gardens begins nicely with rustic stairs.

We spend some time in a small ravine near a curiously shaped old tree, then follow a path down to the meadow. We discover many nests in the high bushes and play with velvety cocoons from which seeds lazily escape, carried by their shiny umbrellas in the fall breeze.

The path leads us towards a large garden section. Its educational value seems most appropriate for a school trip. We prefer to wander informally in the gardens by the Arboretum entrance, with its pond, small pergola and little bridges.

Last time I visited, the visitor's centre was already an impressive sight with its hexagonal architecture. At the time of print, they were in the process of rebuilding it into a world class Centre for Urban Ecology. The new facilities will include a solarium, a Children's Nature Activity Centre, a Conservatory, a gift shop and furniture for both children and adults.

It will be supplied by wind turbine and solar panels. They will use composting toilets. They will use straw bales and a roof-top garden to insulate the building. State-of-the-art is the standard here!

TIPS (fun for 2 years +)

• The Arboretum organizes a free annual **Winter Festival**, usually the first Saturday in December in the afternoon. It includes hay rides, a visit from Santa Claus, **Christmas** tree sale and children's crafts.

• They offer a **Halloween** party with a walk through the forest to a Jack-O-Lantern tree.

Humber Arboretum
• **Etobicoke**
(416) 675-6622, ext. 4467
www.
humberarboretum.on.ca

H-9
N-W
of downtown
30-min.

Schedule: Open year-round.
Admission: FREE.
Directions: 205 Humber College Blvd., Etobicoke. Take Hwy 427 North, exit at Finch Ave. eastbound. Turn south on Humber College Blvd. Obtain an Arboretum pass at the college's parking kiosk, go to Lot #1.

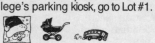

BOYD CONSERVATION AREA

Look Mom! Toads!

Some of the mature trees look impressive in these woods where the sun can't reach through the thick canopy of leaves. Many toads can be spotted on the dirt ground, as well as intriguing little man-made constructions of dead wood. The adventure begins!

A small playground greets us close to the parking lot at the end of the park's only road.

We walk back onto the road to the woods' first entrance, and

soon reach a fork. We opt for the left trail where our kids run wildly, until they are slowed down by a steep section with stairs made of running roots.

Soon, our little scouts are inspired by strange constructions made out of branches. Building their own becomes our family project for a good half-hour.

Back on this trail, we soon reach a picnic shelter. From there, we headed right onto the first little road along the river and discovered a great picnic spot. (You can also walk back to the gravel road, towards the parking lot.)

While the trail is a bit confusing, there's no fear of getting lost! Simply stand still, and the sounds of traffic on Islington Avenue will remind you this oasis sits in the middle of civilization after all!

TIPS (fun for 4 years +)
• We went with a couple of 3-year-olds, one of whom was scared by the darkness of the woods (made darker by cloudy skies). They both had a tough time exploring the steeper sections of the trail, but really enjoyed the toads!
• Bug repellent is a must, especially after a rain fall.

NEARBY ATTRACTIONS
Reptilia (10-min.)............................p. 49
Butterfly Conservatory (15-min.)....p. 49

Boyd Conservation Area
• Vaughan
(416) 661-6600, ext. 5203
www.trca.on.ca

H-9 North of Toronto 30-min.

Schedule: Open end of April to early October, 9 am until dusk.

Admission: $4/adults, $2/5-14 years, FREE 4 years and under.

Directions: Islington Ave., Vaughan. Take Hwy 427 North, exit Hwy 7 eastbound. Turn north on Islington Ave.

KORTRIGHT CENTRE

Seasoned activities

As the kids get older, one visit after another, families discover new aspects of this dynamic centre with the help of over one hundred events staged throughout the year.

There are enough trails throughout Kortright Centre to overwhelm newcomers. Fortunately, the centre puts great effort into the design of relatively short, self-guided trails.

From December to February, greedy birds of all kinds visit the numerous feeders on the Bird Feeder Trail.

The Wildflower Trail in May takes advantage of blossoming wild flowers. From June until September, the Honey Bee Trail leads us towards the bee house on the site. Kortright indeed includes a Bee Space which hosts over 2 million bees. During some summer weekends, children can taste fresh honey and learn the bee dance. It takes 15 minutes to walk from the Visitor Centre to the Bee Space.

There's also the Fall Colour Trail in October and finally, the Christmas Trail in December. On occasion, we've also wandered on the wooden trails surrounding the centre (where nature gets a little more imposing) and other paths running through the fields to a marsh.

In addition, kids can look at the interactive displays in the centre's exhibit section. My small naturalist really appreciated the display challenging him to spy on more than 30 insects and animals camouflaged in a recreated microenvironment.

TIPS (fun for 3 years +)

• The **March Break** takes place during the Kortright **Maple Syrup Festival**. More about it on page 155.
• See **Four Winds Kite Festival** on page 333.
• I prefer to visit the centre on weekends, when chances are the Visitor Centre will offer guided walks, demonstrations or crafts when more volunteers are present.
• Make sure you get Kortright's public events calendar at the Visitor Centre. It points out events of special interest to children. From dog sled races (end of January) to **Halloween** Night Hike, activities vary from one year to the next.

NEARBY ATTRACTIONS
Putting Edge (15-min.).................... p. 21
McMichael Collection (10-min.)......p. 93

Kortright Centre for Conservation
• Kleinburg
(905) 832-2289
or (416) 661-6600 ext. 5602
www.kortright.org

G-10
North
of Toronto
40-min.

Schedule: Open year-round, 9 am to 4 pm. (Opens at 10 am on weekends).

Admission: $5/adults, $3/seniors and children, FREE 4 years and under (small extra fee during special events). Parking is $2.

Directions: 9550 Pine Valley Dr., Kleinburg.Take Hwy 400 North, exit Major Mackenzie Dr. (exit # 35) westbound and follow the signs.

FOUR WINDS KITE FESTIVAL

The few times we attended the festival held at the Kortright Centre, the wind was rather timid! As a result, only the best participants managed to raise their flying apparatus into the air. The smaller amateurs' kites only went up slightly, thanks to air drafts generated by laughing children pulling on their toys' tight cords. We had a lot of fun, regardless.

Most young children remain within the small valleys surrounding the Visitor Centre. Farther, past

Flying high

Need to get out for some air (with the kids in tow)? During the first weekend in May, if Mother Nature bestows good winds upon us, you'll want to take advantage of this event. When decent wind is part of the picture, loads of large, graceful kites colour the sky.

TIPS (fun for 4 years +)

• More about **Kortright Centre** on pages 155 and 332.
• If it has rained for a few days prior to the festival, rubber boots are a must.
• During the festival, don't miss the "Teddy Bear Drop" during which a couple of furry creatures, equipped with parachutes, are dropped from flying kites and gently fall before young spectators' eyes. You can see them being launched in the competition field on Saturday and Sunday. Check the exact time of launching.
• Around **Kortright Centre**'s main building, kids pull small kites that they build themselves. The centre supplies little builders with the instructions, paper, balsam sticks, glue and string. This craft is suitable for children aged 4 years and up and costs about $5. The gift shop also sells some kites.
• Check the **Industrial Alliance Kite-Fest** held in September, on p. 328.

a vast field, is the site where real pros compete for two days. There's a section reserved for the amateurs on this site.

These artists, solo or as part of a team, create impressive ballets with their splendid kites, to the sound of music. The public can get a close-up look at their kites before they fly. There are individual precision and ballet disciplines, as well as "quad-line" kites (pulled by four strings), and team competitions.

Kortright Centre	G-10
• Kleinburg	**North**
(905) 832-2289	**of Toronto**
or (416) 661-6600 ext. 5602	**40-min.**
www.kortright.org	

 Schedule: Last weekend in April or the first weekend in May, from 10 am to 4 pm. Call to check the exact date.

Admission: $7/adults, $5/children, FREE for children 4 years and under. Parking $2.

Directions: From Hwy 400 North, take exit #35/Major Mackenzie Dr. westbound. Turn south on Pine Valley Dr., follow signs.

CHINGUACOUSY PARK

Anything else?

This park has everything! Animals? Check. Pony rides? Check. Pond? Yep. Splash pool? Got it. Mini-golf? Skateboarding pipe? Ski hill? Yes, yes and yes. Add a greenhouse, a teahouse, tennis courts, a playground, paddle boats, a band shell and a couple of ambitious events and you get a really dynamic municipal park indeed!

Chinguacousy Park is big but not so much that you could not walk from one attraction to the next. When visiting, we parked in the south lot off Central Park Drive and were seduced right away by the weeping willows throwing their shade over ducks on the sandy beach. A crane just happened to be standing there. It's always amazing to find spots like this in the middle of a city.

Right next to it, we saw several pens with different farm animals: pigs, lambs, goats, horses, hens and more. On the weekends, you can ride a pony for $3.

Further, we visited a large greenhouse amidst manicured gardens with a paved path leading to fields of grass. The teahouse with patio was adjacent to it.

Following the road back to the centre of the park, we found the snack bar, where you can rent the gear to play mini-golf. Closer to the bigger section of the pond, there was a busy splash pool within a fenced area and a playground. On that side of the pond, you can rent paddle boats to use on both sections of the pond.

Then, there were the skate-boarding features (two quarter-pipes and a slope) with the tiny ski hill in the background.

At the time of print, many of the installations in the park were a bit outdated and tired, but it still added up to a nice place to have a picnic and spend time with the kids. Most of all, it convinced me that any family event could be perfect in such a setting.

TIPS (fun for 2 years +)

• Call Brampton Parks & Recreation to find out about potential events in the park such as: **Canada Day** (with fireworks) and Brampton's **Summer Festival** (a whole day of activities with fireworks during **Simcoe Day** in August).

• Along Queen Street (Hwy 7) just southeast of Chinguacousy Park, between Bramalea and Airport Road, you'll find a strip of fast food outlets and family restaurants as well as a large movie theatre: a good combo after an afternoon at the park.

Chinguacousy Park
· Brampton
(905) 458-6555
(905) 791-1884 (teahouse)
www.city.brampton.on.ca

H-8
N-W
of Toronto
45-min.

Schedule: The park is open year-round. Most activities are available daily from late June to Labour Day weekend.

Admission: $1/child for wading pool; $3/mini-golf or pony rides. Paddle boat rental is $8/1/2 hr.

Directions: Take Hwy 427 North to the end of the road, turn west on Hwy 7. Turn north on Central Park Dr. Go into the first parking lot. It is the closest to the pond and animal farm.

BRUCE'S MILL C. A.

Conservation 101

The recreational pond created by the dam was affecting the natural watershed system, an important component of the Rouge River. So goodbye beach. Native grasses are overtaking the place.

TIPS (fun for 3 years +)
* More about **Bruce's Mill Maple Syrup Festival** on page 154.
* A local parent mentioned to me she always combines an outing to Bruce's Mills with a visit to **Applewood Farm**

Winery, located at 12442 McCowan Rd., a short distance north of Stouffville Side Road. You can pick your own strawberries, apples and pumpkins. They have a small playground (with an old functioning water pump) and wagon rides to take you to the fields as well as a small store; www.applewoodfarmwinery.com, (905) 640-5357.
* Nearby, we visited **Lionel's Pony Farm and Pet-**

ting Zoo at 11714 McCowan Rd., north of 19th Ave. It costs $3 for a pony ride
Monday to Friday, 10 am to 1 pm in July and August only. It is free to visit their petting zoo from May to November, 9 am to dusk (noon to 5 pm on Sundays), (905) 640-7669.

NEARBY ATTRACTIONS
Burd's Trout Farm (15-min.).........p. 359

We might have lost the swimming hole but it seems we are gaining a natural haven for bugs and tadpoles. There's not many of those around Toronto.

The conservation includes trails which fork into several paths covered with boardwalks in their most spongy areas. Staff was recently hired to maintain these but still, should you take the stroller along, be prepared for a few portages.

The park now hosts a driving range, past the gate on the left hand side. It is managed by a different administration.

Bruce's Mill Conservation Area
G-11 N-E of Toronto 35-min.
• Stouffville
(905) 887-5531
or (416) 661-6600, ext. 5203
www.trca.on.ca

 Schedule: Open early March to mid-October, 9 am to dusk (closes earlier in April and October).

Admission: $4/adults, $3/seniors, $2/5-14 years, FREE 4 years and under.

 Directions: Stouffville Rd, Stouffville. From Hwy 404 North, take exit #37/Stouffville Rd. eastbound (drive past Warden Ave.). If only going to the driving range, mention it at the gate so they don't charge the admission cost.

BRONTE CREEK PROVINCIAL PARK

Old MacDonald had a pool...

What a gorgeous summer day! Where can you go with children? To the farm? To the pool? There's no need to take a vote. Half an hour away from Toronto, Bronte Creek Park offers a great farm-pool combination, as well as many other sport and leisure activities.

Not only does Bronte Creek Provincial Park have the usual walks and nature centre, it also boasts farmyard animals, a Victorian-style farm where they work the soil in the traditional way, and a barn transformed into an original playground. To complete this unique mixture of activities, it offers one of the largest pools in North America.

In this vast park, wanting to try every activity in a single day would be too ambitious. Hardy walkers can move from one attraction to the other by taking the trails and roads laid out on the site. However, young families would be better advised to travel by car between activity centres, in order to spare everyone's energy.

Around Spruce Lane Farm

The Bronte Creek visit begins with a walk in the morning (while children are still full of energy!). Park at lot F to access the trails by **Spruce Farm**. On your way, you

have a good chance of seeing one-metre-long remote-controlled airplanes doing loops in a field reserved for that purpose.

The Half Moon Valley trail is an excellent starting point for the whole family. It offers a two-kilometre walk, and is bordered by wildflowers and old trees of unusual shapes.

In certain locations, the wide path runs alongside the wide Bronte Creek as well as the cliff over the ravine in which it flows.

The two storeys of **Spruce Lane Farm**, built in 1899, were laid out in accordance with the times.

During July and August, costumed actors move about, showing visitors a glimpse of rural life in the early part of the last century.

In the kitchen, there's usually a little something for us to taste.

The play barn

Turtles, snakes and fish await us inside the small nature centre near parking lot C. Bees go in and out through a long pipe connected to the outside. Not far from there, various buildings house rabbits, hens, chicks, pigs and horses.

All that becomes less interesting when kids spot the great **play barn** with its hanging bridges, tunnels, large tires to climb on and its second-storey platform from which children can jump into the big cushions, without breaking their necks. It even has a heated section for parents who are waiting while their kids go wild, during the colder months!

Take the plunge

The Bronte Creek pool, located near parking lot D, holds 1.3 million gallons of water spread over a 1.8-acre area. An adult must walk 500 steps to go around it! It is fabulous for children: no more than two metres deep in the middle, more than half its area is like a gigantic wading pool where little swimmers can frolic without swallowing mouthfuls of water.

Naturally heated by the sun, the pool's shallow water is very comfortable during the afternoon. Those who seek shade can plant their umbrellas on the grass around it. Several picnic tables and a snack bar are located outside the pool grounds.

TIPS (fun for 2 years +)

• More on **Bronte Creek** during the winter on p. 393.

• Bring mosquito repellent if you intend to stroll on the trails. We had some on and really enjoyed ourselves, but I've seen families fleeing from the woods because they weren't protected.

• Bronte Creek's **Maple Syrup Festival** is usually offered on March weekends and daily during **March Break**. It includes a pancake house, candy making demonstrations, syrup trail and horse-drawn wagon rides.

• During **Halloween**, we really enjoyed our "haunted" self-guided walk along the Trillium Trail. Funny things could be seen on trees at every turn: scary messages, bugs, snakes, bats and so on. In addition, the majestic forest in its fall coat was breathtaking! The visit to the "haunted" **Spruce Farm** turned out scarrier than my 6-year-old companions could bear. It was dark and dramatic with costumed staff enacting a creepy family. The girls urged me out!

• They offer a Victorian **Christmas** during the weekends of December, with baking, festive crafts and music.

• The park's **campground** is located 5 minutes away, on another piece of land. Its 144 lots are relatively secluded.

Bronte Creek Provincial Park
• Burlington
(905) 827-6911
www.ontarioparks.com

E-2
West
of Toronto
35-min.

Schedule: Park is open year-round, 8 am to dusk (play barn, 9 am to 4 pm). Farm and Nature Centre open May 1 to Labour Day,10 am to 4 pm (weekends only the rest of the year, 11 am to 3 pm). Pool opens July 1 to Labour Day, 11 am to 5 pm.

Admission: $4/adults, $3/ seniors, $2/4-17 years, or maximum $12 fee per vehicle. Additional fees to access pool: $2.50/adults, $1.50/4-17 years, FREE for 3 years and under.

Directions: 1219 Burloak Dr., Burlington. From the QEW westbound, take exit #109/Burloak Dr. northbound. To go to the campground, take exit #111/Bronte Rd. northbound, turn west on Upper Middle Rd.

NEARBY ATTRACTIONS
Coronation Park (10-min.)............p. 381

MOUNTSBERG WILDLIFE CENTRE

Wild!

I see a free roaming rabbit by the trees. Geese are flocking by the reservoir. After we've strolled through the Raptors Walkway including several cages with hawks and owls, we head towards a large field where the weird cry of the elks greets us! This conservation area is almost a zoo!

Many birds of prey are injured every year. Some fly through power lines or step in traps. Others are struck by vehicles or their nest is accidentally cut down by landowners. On signs, we could read about some birds' misfortunes: wing tip lost in wolf snare, permanent wing muscle deformity, etc.

The **Raptor Centre** at the Mountsberg Wildlife Centre site offers them a hospital with treatment and recovery areas. The birds we saw in the Raptor Walkway were non-releasable residents due to permanent injuries. Weather permitting, the centre holds live raptor presentations in a 6000-square-foot netted outdoor enclosure. Check out the round windows on the curved wall surrounding the enclosure. They allow you to peek into more bird cages.

Otherwise, presentations are held indoors, in the Aerie Theatre. We can also catch an audiovisual presentation in this theatre and peek into the Raptors' hospital through a one-way viewing window. The exhibit gallery artistically displays many mounted specimens.

Another time we went we were lucky enough to see the bisons staring at us impassively at the end of the short Raptor Centre Trail. Not this time. It seems the herd often hides in the backwoods of the vast field. But we saw an elk.

On our way back, we watched the ducks from the Lookout Blind by the reservoir (a good spot to see frogs).

The Lookout Trail is 6 km long but the observation tower overlooking the reservoir is less than 15 minutes away from the Visitor Centre. On our way, we notice Swallowville: a "village" of 25 birdhouses standing on poles. We walked 15 minutes more and could observe a flock of geese from a quiet spot by the shore.

Ten minutes further, we caught a trail to our right, going up a hill back to our starting point. It offered a very pretty view of the area.

Back to the Visitor Centre, we checked out their wonderful **play barn**. With fire fighter's pole, zip line, ladders, slides, climbing ropes and tons of straw, this was heaven for the kids! I was seduced by the picture perfect barn scenery of blinding rays of sunlight

shooting through the cracks of the wooden walls on the golden straw, like some laser beams.

The Visitor Centre will get a major make-over as of fall 2004. We should expect a bigger gift shop and more displays.

TIPS (fun for 2 years +)

• See **Mountsberg Maple Syrup Time** for **March Break** and **Easter** activities on page 157.
• During weekends in the Fall Harvest Season (end of September to end of October), there are $1 horse-drawn wagon rides, craft activities for kids, a 5-acre maze, pumpkin carving, straw piles and more.
• On the weekends from the end of November to right before Christmas, Mapletowne is transformed into Santa's **ChristmasTown**, with decorations and all. You can pre-book as early as beginning of September for this very popular event including Santa's visit, crafts, cookies and more, $14/adults, $10/children.
• From January to part of March, weather permitting, you can skate on the old farm's pond.

NEARBY ATTRACTIONS

Mountsberg Wildlife Centre

D-2
West
of Toronto
45-min.

· Milton
· (905) 854-2276
www.conservationhalton.on.ca

Schedule: Birds of Prey shows are at 1 and 3 pm on weekends year-round, holidays, March Break, and Wednesdays, Thursdays and Fridays in July and August. The area is accessible year-round, 10 am to 4 pm.
Admission: $4.50/adults, $3.50/ seniors, $3.25/ 5-14 years, FREE for children 4 years and under (they pay $1.50 if in a group of 6 or more).
Directions: From Hwy 401 West, take exit #312/Guelph Line southbound. Turn west on Campbellville Rd., then north on Milborough Line, to the park's entrance.

ROCKWOOD C. A.

Stunning!

Rockwood Park Conservation Area is a stunningly beautiful place that offers a complete change of scenery, with ruins, caves and natural reservoirs.

I still can't get over it: so much beauty, so close to Toronto and open to everyone. We're lucky...

As you arrive, take the first path on your left after Rockwood's entrance and you will reach large ruins; the site's first attraction.

This old windmill stopped functioning in 1925. It burned down in 1967 and only a few pieces of the stone walls remain today as my aspiring historian discovered. He was captivated by these explanations while he pursued his explorations of the site.

Another road, accessible by stroller, borders the ruins. It leads to two large **caves** a half-kilometre farther, which I found fascinating. Daylight enters the

grottos and children find them amusing to explore. Outside the caves, along the rock walls, make them shout and listen to the echo. It is amazing.

On the other side of the parking lot, you will discover a path that travels around dozens of potholes: some kind of natural tanks of all sizes created by the abrasive whirlpools from glaciers that melted over 15,000 years ago.

While you can't access it with a stroller, it is nevertheless safe and inviting as it turns into small wooden bridges here and there. It borders the Eramosa, a narrow river that runs lazily amidst a fabulous landscape of rock and trees. Visitors explore it with canoes and paddle boats,

which you can rent daily at the beach a little farther inside the park.

With young children, it is preferable to take your car to reach this beach. There, you will also find a small snack bar and washrooms. The beach is really nice with pleasantly smooth sand.

TIPS (fun for 3 years +)
• Bring a flashlight for the children to explore the small cave.
• There's a mini-golf course on the site. It is available at the cost of around $4, weather permitting.

NEARBY ATTRACTIONS
Kortright Waterfowl Park (20-min.) p. 56
Streetcar Museum (5-min.)............p. 241

Rockwood Conservation Area
· Rockwood

D-2
West
of Toronto
60-min.

(519) 856-9543
1-866-668-2267 (camp reservation)
www.grandriver.ca

 Schedule: Open from end of April to mid-October, 8 am to 9 pm.

Admission: $3.75/adults, $2/6-13, FREE 5 years and under.

 Canoe and paddle boat rental is $9 an hour.

Directions: From Hwy 401 West, take exit #312/Guelph Line northbound. Turn east on Hwy 7 to Falls St.

HALIBURTON FOREST & RESERVE

Walk in the clouds

"Wow! Hooking on to the web takes on a new meaning!" comments a guy in the group as he literally hooks himself to the lifeline some twenty metres above the ground.

As I carefully walk on the 12-inch wide boardwalk suspended in the air by an elaborate series of ropes knotted into a handrail, I realize I would be very nervous doing the same with my son, had he met the required minimum age of 10.

Our guide assures me he's never had to turn back because of a scared child, adding he remembers some kids who got bored by the experience! Bored?! If my children got bored by such an experience, it would be time to lock up the video games and throw away the key!

The four-hour round-trip starts with a 15-minute van ride through the reserve, catching a glimpse of some of the campsites located in semi-wilderness along beautiful lakes. We then take a 10-minute walk along a scenic creek before canoeing for 15 more minutes to a large stand of old growth White Pine. It would not surprise us to see a moose in such a landscape.

Our guide demonstrates how to put on our harness (to be hooked to a lifeline, a short walk from there). And we're off to the **canopy trail**.

It consists of half a kilometre of suspended boardwalk, painstakingly installed to ensure no harm comes to the tall White Pines. "The owner wanted to spruce up the forest trail" jokes the guide. We are each assigned a buddy before we hook ourselves and climb the ladder to our first section of boardwalk.

We walk from one tree to the next. Every time we change direction, we have to hook ourselves to a new lifeline while our extra hook remains attached to the line under which we stand. Taller buddies often have to lower the lines to allow shorter partners to hook themselves (that would be the tricky part for parents).

A large platform surrounds a very tall and straight pine, suspended from the tree top. We stop for a snack and to take in the amazing panorama while our guide tells us more about the crazy adventure in the building of this one-of-a-kind canopy boardwalk.

The Wolf Centre

The Wolf Centre, also located in Haliburton Forest, is only a few minutes drive from Base Camp. It was feeding time when we arrived (at around 1:30 pm).

A big line-up of visitors stood by the large bay windows overlooking a tiny part of the 15-acre enclosure, anxious to catch a glimpse of the wolves feeding on beaver carcasses. Through loud speakers we could hear the animals' growls as the leaders grabbed the best pieces and the tiny cubs patiently awaited their share.

TIPS (fun for 10 years +)

• Bring bug repellent during the spring.
• If you do the morning excursion, you will be back in time to attend the 1:30 pm feeding session at the **Wolf Centre** (best way to see the wolves). If you attend the afternoon excursion, try to book it on a Thursday, when Wolf Howl sessions are offered at 8 pm for a small fee (you might be lucky enough to hear the wolves howl with you).
• 17 of the 50 lakes, in this privately owned 50,000-acre forest, are accessible by car. It is possible to buy a day pass to access the park and swim in the lakes. This is a great family outing for children under 10 years old and their parents, while older siblings tackle the canopy trail. A detailed map is available on site.
• Haliburton Forest is renowned for its **mountain bike trails** (over 300 km). Bikes can be rented for $30 per day on the premises (15" frames and up).
• They now have a small wooden observatory the roof can roll off, equipped with two 10 and 12-inch telescopes and special star map. Presentations are offered from early May to Thanksgiving every Tuesday, Wednesday, Friday and Saturday evening at 9 pm, $15/adults, $10/under 18 years old (you need to call to preregister).
• These lakes host great **campsites** but most are leased annually, except for a dozen designated sites available for short term use. They also rent 2- or 3-bedroom housekeeping units for $49 per night, per person ($79 in the winter, half-price for children under 12 years) and log cabins for small groups. These are popular among the snowmobile amateurs. BEWARE! The roaring motors will trouble the quietness of the natural setting. Better rent during the fall to enjoy the colours.

Inside the Wolf Centre, there are many exhibits and some interactive displays, as well as a book section and an art gallery featuring works on wolves.

Haliburton Forest & Wildlife Reserve
• Haliburton
(705) 754-2198
www.haliburtonforest.com

A-4
N-E
of Toronto
2 1/2 hrs.

Schedule: Open year-round 8 am to 5 pm (extended hours in July and August and during the winter). The Wolf Centre is open daily from Victoria Day to Thanksgiving and Friday to Sunday only, the rest of the year, from 10 am to 5 pm. The Canopy Trail runs daily from early May to late October, starting at 9 am and 1:30 pm.
Admission: The daily use permit is $13/adult ($30 during the winter).Wolf Centre is $8/adults, $5/under 18 years old, $19/family.The Canopy Tour is $85/adults and $60/10-17 years old. (includes daily use permit and admission to Wolf Centre.)
Directions: R. R. #1, Haliburton. From Hwy 404 North, take exit #51/Davis Rd. eastbound. Follow Hwy 48 North to Coboconk. Take Hwy 35 North to Minden (do not take Hwy 121 South to Kinmount!). Take Hwy 118 East to West Guilford. Cross the bridge and take County Rd. 7 for approximately 20 kms to the Base Camp.

GLEN STEWART RAVINE

City trappers

As we happily complete our visit to the Glen Stewart Ravine, my son emerges from our expedition with muddy shoe soles, filthy elbows and knees, soiled pants and a sweater full of twigs, having climbed, slid, splashed about and crawled everywhere. We're perfect candidates for a detergent commercial!

TIPS (fun for 3 years +)

• See tobogganing at **Glen Manor Drive Park** on p. 386.
• To avoid exhausting your young travelling companion, I recommend you park on Glen Manor Drive East near the ravine entry. You'll find a place, even on weekends.
• Bring a small plastic or paper-made boat and follow its course down the stream. It won't be hard to retrieve when you are finished with the game.
• Warning! If you plan on returning thereafter to civilization on Queen Street, bring a change of clothes for the kids.
• Every year, locals enjoy the **Caroling in the Park** event by the rink, when hundreds show up to hear Christmas music in a magical setting. Usually on the second Tuesday before Christmas, 7:30 to 8:30 pm, (416) 694-0617.
• See **Garden Gate** and **Sunset Grill** restaurants on pp. 435-436.

Past the boutiques of Queen Street East in the **Beaches** and next to Glen Manor Drive, sits a gorgeous rock garden with many water fountains. From there, follow a path to a quaint and leafy park bordering the surrounding mansions.

Walk further, up the stairs and across Glen Manor Drive East, and you find yourself at the mouth of the Glen Stewart Ravine, a paradise worthy of any small Robin Hood! Its "unmanicured" qualities reminded me of the countryside forests of my childhood and won the interest of my young naturalist.

The small and narrow valley in the ravine is crossed by a log-straddled stream a few feet in width. Surrounded by steep tree-filled slopes, some paths and naturally-formed stairs are accessible and comfortably shaded by abundant undergrowth and sit desirably isolated from neighbouring houses.

Walking to the end of the main path bordering the ravine takes about fifteen minutes. Children love to climb the wooden stairs reaching the street, just for the sake of it.

The rugged terrain is not recommended for strollers, and I recommend vigilance with young kids as they can easily slide down (more fright than harm).

Glen Stewart Ravine (416) 392-1111 www.toronto.ca	**J-10** **East** **of downtown** **20-min.**

Schedule: Open year-round.
Admission: FREE.
Directions: Located by Glen Manor Dr. East, accessible from Queen St. East.

NEARBY ATTRACTIONS
Movies for Mommies (5-min.)......p. 99
The Beaches (15-min. walk)........p. 270

MOORE PARK RAVINE

Darkest corners of the city

The sun beats down on our heads. Our sandals barely shield us from the hot asphalt. On the street, the heat bounces from one building facade to the next, their walls blocking a breeze that would otherwise clear away the heat. Not to complain about summer, but we can't wait to hit the shade of Moore Park Ravine.

Moore Park Ravine is undoubtedly the jewel of Toronto's natural crown. You enter the ravine through a steep little path, towards a magnificent forest of spectacularly high trees. The underwoods are different from those at Glen Stewart Ravine, with bushier undergrowth.

Here, you'll find a large and powerful stream with birds' songs playing against the ruffling of leaves. There, a pond potentially inhabited by frogs, and farther, a large tree trunk inviting you to a moment's rest.

From this main path, many smaller trails depart, haphazardly fashioned by previous hikers. The main path travels under a couple of imposing bridges, and continues towards a large opening we reach after a half-hour walk. It runs along Bayview Avenue.

TIPS (fun for 3 years +)

• Be cautious when visiting with young children as some slopes are exceedingly steep and there are no railings. However, you can manoeuvre a stroller without much difficulty.

NEARBY ATTRACTIONS
Mt. Pleasant Cemetery (10-min.). p. 310
Don Brickworks (2-min. walk).......p. 317

City of Toronto
(416) 392-1111
www.toronto.ca

I-10
North
of downtown
20-min.

 Schedule: Open year-round.
Admission: FREE.
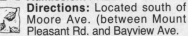 **Directions:** Located south of Moore Ave. (between Mount Pleasant Rd. and Bayview Ave.

SHERWOOD PARK RAVINE

Diamond in the rough

As you walk down the path from Blythwood Road, you'll discover what has to be one of the nicest playgrounds in the whole city! With new and interesting equipment, it sits like a jewel in the midst of tall trees, next to a beautiful wading pool adorned with giant water-spraying bulrushes.

It gets quite busy when summer camp children invade the place, but there is still plenty of room to comfortably roam the trails of this vast oasis.

The playground includes a small climbing wall much appreciated by the children.

After a good play and nice picnic,

we walked past the wading pool and reached long stairs leading up to a great trail.

Kids enjoyed the wooden stairs in the middle of the forest, and hopped from rock to rock over a shallow stream.

In all, it took us 40 minutes to complete the trail's return trip by foot.

TIPS (fun for 3 years +)

• The summer camps usually leave around 4 pm, perfect timing to enjoy the park for a couple of hours and a picnic dinner.

• Parts of the trails can be challenging for a 3-year-old, hold on to their hand.

• With a stroller, it took us over twenty minutes to cross Blythwood Road from Sherwood Park, and walk through **Blythwood Ravine Park** (not particularly interesting) to the **Alexander Muir Memorial Gardens** (on Yonge Street, south of Lawrence Avenue). The gardens are very pretty but hard to stroll around because of stairs.

NEARBY ATTRACTIONS

Sherwood Park
(416) 392-1111
www.toronto.ca

**I-10
North**
of downtown
30-min.

Schedule: Open year-round.
Admission: FREE.
Directions: Sherwood Ravine Park's entrance is off Blythwood Rd. (south of Lawrence Ave.), between Mount Pleasant Rd. and Bayview Ave.

MORNINGSIDE PARK

Morning glory

Very few things satisfy me as much as sunshine's glittery reflection on a stream. The stream that runs through Morningside Park is broad and long. With its short tree-filled hills, it is a wonderful site to explore with children.

For a guaranteed change of scenery, go to Morningside Park's farthest parking lot. From there, as you take the large path of fine gravel, you will hear the lovely sound of water running through stones. A few minutes later, you will discover Hyland Creek, a broad body of water some 20 metres wide, lying at the bottom of a valley, like a fine jewel nestled in a bushy bower.

The stream is shallow and its partly rocky shores attract hikers who can walk along it without getting wet. On one side, little clear rapids emerge through large flat rocks, while the water follows a more sinuous path between the big rocks on the other side. A few tree trunks provide children with ample distractions and many cyclists rest while admiring the shores from their trail above.

TIPS (fun for 4 years +)

• Sandals might not allow a sure grip on the rocks. However, in summertime we went barefoot along the stream, up to the muddier section (much to my little friends' delight). I nevertheless recommend rubber shoes to protect small feet in the water. While wet rocks can be slippery, fear nothing more serious than a wet bottom; you may want to pack a change of clothes. Rubber boots are ideal on colder days.

• They say it is an excellent site for cross-country skiing during the winter.

Morningside Park • Scarborough (416) 392-1111 www.toronto.ca	I-11 N-E of downtown 30-min.

 Schedule: Open year-round.
Admission: FREE.
 Directions: From Hwy 401 East, take exit #387/Morningside Ave.southbound. The park's entrance is south of Ellesmere Ave.

ROUGE PARK

So long, civilization

The trail had led us to the river; we heard the clear sound of splashing water. Standing still, we heard it again, this time identifying the source of this noise: a 60-cm-long trout, jumping upstream! It is a shame my 3-year-old could not appreciate the wonder of such a scene. Mind you, everything she saw that day was a first for her.

You can't explore Rouge Park in a single day. It is huge, with the Toronto Zoo occupying only a tenth of its area. It offers a wide variety of natural settings accessible from different points.

Resort Road access

I visited during the fall with my 3-year-old and I thought it was the perfect place to enjoy fall colours with a little one. A cascade of leaves would fall from the tall trees every time the wind blew, and the ground was covered with crisp leaves.

The easy trail runs along the river and, in many places, we had access to it through a wide strip of pebbles. The river is very shallow. I was flabbergasted to discover a huge dead fish on the pebbles! Observing the fish's sharp teeth, my little one declared it was nothing less than a shark. Later on, I learned that trout and pike, even though they don't travel upstream to spawn like salmon, still like to roam up and down the river.

We laid out our picnic on a fallen tree by the river. Further on, the trail was narrower and bushier so we turned back. We were only twenty minutes away from the parking lot.

I was told there is a trail along the Little Rouge River which would take us to Pearse House in approximately two hours.

Pearse House access

In the backyard of the pretty Victorian house that holds the Rouge Valley Conservation Centre, we found a circle of intriguing and nicely painted rocks between a tent made out of cedar branches and the entrance to the trail. The beginning of this trail was steep and winding, and lead to an easier stretch.

Our first glimpse of the Little Rouge River was simply gorgeous. The stream was shining like diamonds under the sun, framed by colourful leaves, with white cliffs and dark evergreens in the background.

Upstream, we explored the river banks. Large flat stones that popped through the shallow water allowed for a great hopping session. We reached the gravel road in twenty minutes.

Twyn Rivers Drive access

During the fall, Twyn Rivers is a real gem of a road in the midst of civilization! Breathtaking colourful leaves, white cliffs, a crossroad passing over two small bridges... and not a single house in sight!

The drive led to a large parking lot. From there, we took a trail along the river leading towards the bridge, which we crossed. Then we took the trail off the road. It eventually started to run up a steep hill to our right. For a little while, we explored the right-hand side of the fork up the hill. The path was really pretty, the dark trunks contrasting with a colourful patchwork of trees on a hill in the far background.

The left-hand side of the fork offered quite an interesting stroll. Roots were running across the path. We took the first downhill trail to our right, aiming at the river.

A strange vision of dark trees with peeling bark and tortuous branches among standing dead trunks awaited us. Soon after, following the sound of the river, we reached a postcard landscape of river and fall colours, complete with 50-cm trout jumping against the current! The manoeuvres required to succeed at this complicated task were fascinating. I just could not believe we could observe such a phenomenon so close to Toronto!

It took us approximately an hour to walk the whole loop back to the asphalt road and to the parking lot.

Kingston Road access

The path near the **Glen Rouge Campground** is the one that leads to the Riverside trail, which has the biggest trees. The high canopy scarcely allows sunbeams to penetrate the forest. At the height of the summer, it is a great place to hide from the heat of the day.

When we were visiting, the riverside trail was closed to be rejuvenated. The path we took, steep at times, ran through the forest and reached a clearing in half an hour. It would take approximately one hour to walk from Kingston Road to Twyn Rivers.

TIPS (fun for 3 years +)

• See **Rouge Beach** on p. 273.
• Check p. 391 to find out more about unofficial tobogganing by Twyn Rivers Drive.
• Exploring the shores would be even more fun with high rubber boots.
• The section of Rouge Park accessible from Twyn Rivers Drive is more fun to visit with energetic children 6 years and older with a taste for adventure.
• **Glen Rouge Campground** is located by the Kingston Road access. To reserve a camp site, call (416) 392-8188.
• **Toronto Kayak & Canoe Adventures** offers trips on the Rouge River, starting below Old Kingston Road, $50/person. Call (416) 536-2067 or check www3.sympatico.ca/tcordina.

Rouge Park • Scarborough (416) 392-1111 www.rougepark.com	I-11/12 N-E of downtown 30-min.

Schedule: Open year-round.
Admission: FREE.
Directions: Kingston Road access: From Hwy 401 East, take exit #392/Port Union northbound, turn east on Kingston Rd., the entrance is on the north side.
Twyn Rivers Drive access: Driving from Meadowvale, turn east on Sheppard Ave and take the first fork to the left (The Twyn Rivers Dr.). Pay attention, as this branch is easy to miss if you are coming from Sheppard Ave. eastbound.
Pearse House access: Go east on the overpass over Meadowvale Rd. (in front of the Toronto Zoo entrance).
Resort Road access: Take Meadowvale northbound, turn west on Old Finch, then north on Resort Rd. There is a small parking lot just south of Steeles. The park entrance lies at the end of a small clearing, not too far from the Little Rouge River.

NEARBY ATTRACTIONS

Toronto Zoo (5-min.)	p. 46
Petticoat Creek (10-min.)	p. 385

CREDIT RIVER

To Mississauga's credit

A friend of mine was anticipating the reaction of his sibling visiting from Quebec when he took him on a casual walk along the Credit River. It did not fail! His wide-eyed brother saw a man lure out of the water, right under his nose, the kind of salmon fishermen dream about. And this happened here, in the heart of the most urban part of Canada!

Credit River is a wild trout and salmon river where you can see huge fish swimming upstream into the shallow water.

We explored it from different access points all the way up to northern Mississauga, each offering a unique experience of the river, regardless of the season.

At the foot of Mississauga Road lies **J.C. Saddington Park**. Kids will enjoy exploring the large boulders along Lake Ontario's shore. I was impressed by the large area with picnic tables one can reserve for a large

family gathering by the lake. The park includes a cute stream not too far from a playground. The pond is lively with ducks, geese and a steering fountain, great willow trees almost brushing the water.

The eastern part of the park runs along the Credit River. We saw people fishing from the large rocks, under the watchful eye of a couple of swans. On Front Street, bordering the river, the boats of the companies offering fishing and cruising fares from spring to fall are located. You'll find the small and pretty **J.J. Plaus Park** on the east shore of the river.

Erindale Park is the best spot from which to observe fishermen during the month of September (the ride along Misissauga Road to get to **Erindale Park** is beautiful during the fall). The Credit River is less than a 5-minute walk from the vast parking lot. Downstream, right under Dundas Street Bridge, the shallow river joyfully cascades over the rock bed.

Upstream, the river is lined with high boulders overlooking deeper water. Many stone stairs offer lovely openings through the bushes leading to a large trail along the river, partly shaded by large trees. The trail is lovely and stretches past Hwy 403, approximately an hour-walk away northbound.

During the winter, we took this path, the **Culham Trail**, from Wellsborough Place, north of Hwy 403. I strongly recommend trying this winter outing. The sun shining on the stream bordered with ice and snow, with the added contrast of the dark rocks and trees, can be breathtaking! And it offers quite a playground for young explorers! It took us an hour to walk back and forth between the trail entrance and Burnhamthorpe Road Bridge, not counting the time allowed for exploration.

Streetsville Memorial Park is the access point to another lovely stretch of the **Culham Trail** going upstream along the Credit River. Mature trees are found on both sides of the river. We loved the colourful carpet of leaves during our fall visit. It includes a playground and an outdoor pool. I encourage you to get closer to the cluster of huge trees in the wide field, across the bridge. One of them forms an intriguing figure that really looks like a hooded person sitting by the trunk.

the river, for nice panoramas. One of them was running down the shore, to an appealing stone path crossing the shallow river (not suitable for pre-schooler!) At the end of the trail awaited the gorgeous **River Grove Community Centre** and its amazing indoor swimming pool (see p. 383).

It will take you 15 minutes to reach the Main Street Bridge if you stay on the western shore. You'll get a great view of the Credit River from that bridge. On the northeast side of it is located the entrance to **Timothy Park**. The trail is gorgeous and leads you in less then 40 minutes to the elevated part of **River Grove Park**.

Don't hesitate to take any little path leading to the edge of the hill overlooking

TIPS (fun for 3 years +)

• See p. 374 about **J.C. Saddington Park**'s skating pond during the winter.
• **Toronto Kayak & Canoe Adventures** offers trips on Credit River, starting at Dundas Street or Eglinton, $50/person (minimum 3 people). Check www3.sympatico.ca/tcordina or call (416) 536-2067.
• The **Streetsville Bread and Honey Festival** usually takes place at Streetsville Memorial Park on the first weekend of June (including parade, midway rides, petting zoo, kids' entertainment, main stage, crafts. Call (905) 816-1640 or check www.breadandhoney.com; $6/adults, $2/children 6-12 years old.
• A Fish & Chips restaurant and a Starbucks are conveniently located at the corner of Front and Lakeshore Road.
• I recommend a stop at the **Town Talk Bakery** at 206C Queen Street South in Streetsville, (905) 821-1166. It is closed on Sundays and Mondays but the other days, you can buy scrumptious pastries and lovely themed baked goodies according to the season.

Credit River • Mississauga (905) 896-5384 www.mississauga.ca	I-8 W & N-W of Toronto 30-min.

Schedule: Accessible year-round.
Admission: FREE.
Directions: J.C. Saddington Park: from QEW, take exit # 130/Mississauga Rd. South to the end of the road. **J.J. Plaus Park** is on the other side of Credit River, at the foot of Stavebanks Rd. South. **Erindale Park:** Take Mississauga Rd. North, turn east on Dundas St., the entrance is on the north side. **Southern access to Culham Trail:** Take Mississauga Rd. North, turn east on Eglinton Ave., then south on Inverness Blvd. Follow Credit Point Dr. to your left, turn left on Wellsborough Place. **Streetville Memorial Park:** Take Mississauga Rd. North, it becomes Queen St. South, turn east on Beech St. **Timothy Street Park:** Keep going on Queen St. South, turn east on Main St., it becomes Bristol Rd. The park's entrance is north of Bristol. There's a cemetery with parking space on the south side. **Northern access to Culham Trail:** Keep going on Bristol Rd., turn north on River Grove Ave. Park at the River Grove Community Centre. The trail's entrance is in the back of the centre.

HUMBER RIVER

Dam if you don't

I'm walking on a side trail bordering the cliff from which I can admire the river down below when a walker who just appeared on the edge of the cliff surprises me.

"How did you climb up here?" I marvel. "...I climbed" he says, matter-of-factly. I look closer to the edge and indeed spot very steep trails going down. I think I'll stick to my leafy trail.

A 15-minute walk west of the nice **Sunnyside Pavilion Café** by Lake Ontario is a footbridge you might have noticed when driving along the Gardiner. It is the passing over the mouth of the Humber River. Streets often interrupt the trail leading to the next access point to the river so I decided to drive to the next public parking lot by the stream at the end of Humber Valley Road.

Many use this parking lot as a starting point for bike rides. The scenery is not particularly pretty but if you walk 5 minutes, you reach the entrance of the trail by the Toronto Humber Yacht Club and some gorgeous spots overlooking the river. From there, it takes some 15 minutes to get to the Old Mill overpass. Nothing striking about this trail through **Kings Mill Park** but kids will find it intriguing to walk under the bridges.

The best way to appreciate the Humber River is to park by **Étienne Brûlé Park** right by the stream. Two **trails** follow the river, one **for bicycles** and one for pedestrians. The trail was bordered by tall tress and even cliffs on both sides at some points, creating unique intimate scenery.

Six low dams, spread along its course between Old Mill Road and Dundas Street, control the river's flow, hence the lovely sound of cascades we hear as we walk. With kids, it would take half an hour to walk to the Dundas overpass. The trail along the west shore of the river leads back to Old Mill Road Bridge. It offers one of the nicest **bike rides** for families. **Étienne Brûlé Park** gives way to **Lambton Woods** and **James Gardens**.

TIPS (fun for 3 years +)

• **Toronto Kayak & Canoe Adventures** offers trips on the Humber River, starting at Old Mill subway station, no minimum age, $35/person. Check www3.sympatico.ca/tcordina, click on Family Adventures or call (416) 536-2067.

• See the **Sunnyside Pavilion Café** and the **Old Mill Inn** on pp. 429 and 438.

Humber River
• Etobicoke
(416) 392-1111

I-9 West of downtown 25-min.

Schedule: Open year-round.
Admission: FREE.
Directions: Humber Valley Road: From The Queensway (north of the Q.E.W.), take Stephen Dr. northbound, turn west (left) on Riverwood Pkwy and take Humber Valley Rd. to your right. **Kings Mill Park:** From Bloor St. West (east of Royal York Rd.) take Old Mill Rd. northbound. The parking lot's entrance is just before the bridge.
Étienne Brûlé Park's entrance is just after the bridge, to your left.

BELFOUNTAIN C. A.

Small is beautiful

It's tiny. A 1.5-km trail goes round the park. However, it's so beautiful! No wonder so many people have their wedding pictures taken here.

It boasts a fountain, a pond, a "cave", a rumbling waterfall and a suspension bridge. The winding path starts up the escarpment and leads us into the depths of the ravine, towards another bridge crossing the crystalline river. Indeed, the park offers all the elements of a great family outing.

I stumbled upon Belfountain while driving on the beautiful Forks of the Credit Road during the fall. My young wanderer enjoyed this small, tree-lined country road built over several sizeable hills. It leads to Belfountain and to the Belfountain Conservation Area located just before the village.

Bringing a stroller along wasn't a great idea. I had to go down a long series of low steps leading to the river, then continue on rocky trails, while pushing my napping heavyweight angel.

Nice picnic spots lie at the bottom of the steps, by the waterside. Barbecues are available on site. Fishing and swimming were allowed at the time of our visit but the river is fed by springs, so the water is cold!

TIPS (fun for 4 years +)
• To make the most of the stream, bring along rubber shoes or boots.
• After leaving the park, if you head towards Belfountain, you should find a snack bar selling ice cream, the perfect grand finale to an outing. The village itself is small, but has a general store that seemed friendly and well stocked.

The original owner, who put up all the other existing structures at the beginning of the last century, built the park's dam. The fountain is a favourite spot for newlyweds. During our visit, we admired a bride with her elegant wedding party.

The man-made Yellow Stone "**mini-cave**" fires up fertile imaginations with its stalactites. The suspension bridge just downstream from the dam is long enough to impress children.

A stone path begins beside the fountain. It disappears under the trees and runs alongside the roaring river that lies 25 metres below. Now's the time to hold on to your little ones! At times, the path's inclination is quite steep. It eventually leads to a small boardwalk that stands one metre above a large stream. This area is magnificent during the fall. The kids stopped and played a good while with the stream's running water. The boardwalk continues on the other side and heads back to the suspension bridge.

Belfountain Conservation Area
• Belfountain
(519) 927-5838
or 1-800-668-5557
www.creditvalleycons.com

D-2
N-W
of Toronto
45-min.

Schedule: From late April to late June, open on Fridays, weekends and holidays, 10 am to 5 pm. From late June to Labour Day, open daily 9 am to 9 pm. From early September to mid-October, Monday to Friday, 11 am to 6 pm and weekends and holidays, 9 am to 7:30 pm.
Admission: $4/adults, $2.25/ seniors and 3-12 years, FREE 2 years and under.
Directions: 10 Credit St., Belfountain. Take Hwy 401 West, exit Hwy 410 North, turn west on Hwy 7 then north on Hwy 10. Turn west at The Forks of the Credit Rd.

NEARBY ATTRACTIONS

General tips about
Sports:

- Sunscreen, hats and enough bottles of water are a must during the summer sports.
- A change of clothes is always a good idea when playing outside where there's a potential for mud!
- Extra layers of clothes that you can add or take off could save the day during a winter outing. Bottles of water are also important!

SPORTS

See **Water Tubing at Elora Gorge** on p. 394.

SkyDome

Duck!

The two boys were only 4 and 6 but already great baseball fans; the time was ripe to take them to their first game at the SkyDome. They brought their little baseball gloves. When their dad shouted: "It's coming!" they never doubted the authenticity of the ball as he picked up a brand new ball (that he had bought for the occasion) off the floor! It was the best day of their lives!

TIPS (fun for 5 years +)

• Planning to attend a circus show at the SkyDome (or any other venue)? BEWARE! The cost of elephant rides and more is not included with the ticket and the intermissions are big commercials to promote $10 gadgets all kids want.

• SkyDome hosts the **Monster Jam** event on a weekend in mid-January. My 10-year-old has begged me to go for years! Demolition derby, biggest trucks in the world on the biggest wheels; the works! Just never had the time to go. It costs $15-$27. Check if they still offer their pit party ticket (extra cost of $5) to have access to the floor to get closer to the trucks two hours before the show.

• **Spring Fling** is the **March Break** event at the SkyDome. With the admission fee, you get to see the stadium and enjoy unlimited access to a large midway. Call to confirm if it's returning.

• See **First Night Toronto** on p. 205.

• See **Mövenpick Palavrion** and **Chez Cora** on p. 436.

NEARBY ATTRACTIONS
CN Tower (1-min. walk)................p. 110

I am not a baseball fan but when my dentist told me how he tricked his sons to create this magical moment, it made me want to rush to a baseball game, kids in tow. My son doesn't know anything about baseball but he is into buildings, models and how things work, so we had a SkyDome Tour Experience. We learned that the SkyDome required twice as much concrete as the CN Tower to build. This is enough concrete to stretch a sidewalk between Toronto and Montreal.

As we waited for the tour to begin, we watched a short film flash two years of building the SkyDome into a two-minute clip made from a time-lapse camera. The model of the SkyDome was not bad either. It helped us to understand how the four panels of the roof can retract in 20 minutes.

The tour began with a short movie in a small theatre, on the building of the SkyDome from the architects and the workers' points of view. We then had a peek at a giant baseball bat (picture time). The first glimpse into the huge stadium (with a seating capacity of 50,600 during a baseball game) is impressive! My then 8-year-old son was not thrilled by the tour itself, but he loved visiting the Hall of Fame box with its trophies and photos immortalizing the Blue Jays as they were winning the World Series.

SkyDome **(416) 341-2770 (tours)** **(416) 341-1234 (Blue Jays)** **(416) 341-2746 (Argonauts)** **www.skydome.com**	**I-10** **Downtown** **Toronto** **10-min.**

Schedule: Open year-round for tours when not in use for a special event. The baseball season runs from early April to late September.

Tour fees: $12.50/adults, $8.50/seniors and students, $7/5-11 years, FREE under 5.

Game fees: $2-$62 per person.

Directions: At the corner of Front and Peter St., Toronto (entrance to the tour is between Gates # 1 and 2).

Raptors at Air Canada Centre

"Thanks Dad!"

I had to see it to believe it: boys and girls, some barely five years old, eagerly following the game!

The truth is the enthusiasm of a roaring crowd is contagious and every minute when the teams are not competing is filled with action. When it's not the mascot Raptor fooling around with spectators by the aisles, it's the Raptors Dance Pack hitting the floor, or the halftime act. No wonder I heard a grateful boy exclaim, on the way back to their car: "Thanks Dad for taking me!"

A quick stop at the store to get some Raptors paraphernalia to show our support and another one to grab a mandatory hot dog and we were ready to find our seats. The Raptors and their visitors were already warming up and the mascot was stretching along with them. Then, a rain of metre-long balloons fell from the ceiling over the spectators in the Lower Bowl Endzone and Baseline Prime sections behind the visitors' basket. We later found out these were to be used by the Raptors fans to distract any opponent focusing on their free throws.

Foul play, rebounds, assists, running jump shots, one-handed jams... we saw it all. What we did not expect was the ever-present music and hilarious sound effects: sound of a bouncing spring when the ball would stray off the court, breaking glass noise when a player crashed into a panel.

We were lucky enough to be attending the game the Raptors won 84-76 against the Hornets during the 2004 season. Even for amateurs like us, it was a thing of beauty to watch Vince Carter do a half-court running jump-shot sinking into the basket as the buzzer announced the end of the third quarter.

That day, we saw the Raptors' 16-point lead melt down to six, two minutes before the end of the game. Talk about tension! And imagine the standing ovation when they won! But my guess is any Raptors game will always win the approval of young fans.

TIPS (fun for 5 years +)

• Parking beside Air Canada Centre during a game costs $25! We found a $5 spot in the parking lot on Windsor St., just north of Front St. and west of John St. (10-minute walk from the centre).

• We were in the first rows of the Upper Bowl seating area, at $52 per ticket, and had a ball. But I checked it out and can assure you you'll see well where-ever you sit in Air Canada Centre!

• Up to two hours before the game, ticket holders have free access to the Fan Zone and its baskets (different heights), video games and more.

• On Sunday home games, kids are invited on the floor after the game to throw once into the basket!

• The **Air Canada Centre Tour** was fun! It includes a visit to the suites, practice room (when no game is taking place), ground level and much more. Check out the size 18 shoes!

Air Canada Centre	J-10
(416) 815-5500 (info)	**Downtown**
(416) 815-5600 (Raptors)	**Toronto**
www.raptors.com	**10-min.**
www.mapleleafs.com	
www.theaircanadacentre.com	

Schedule: Basketball season runs from October to mid-April. Hockey goes from October to April. The tours are offered year-round, variable hours depending on the season.
Admission: The tours cost $12/adults, $8/12 years and under. Basketball tickets range from $11 to over $600! Individual hockey tickets are almost impossible to get. Try to call in September!
Directions: Between York and Bay St., north of Lake Shore Blvd. There's a covered passage to Union Subway Station, on Front St.

DOGSLED AT ROB ROY FARM

And, most importantly, I must slam on the brakes immediately if my sled starts to pass its own dogs or if our team threatens to charge the sled ahead of us!

"Don't worry" says a member of the staff, "everyone falls..." How reassuring! In fact, I did fall once. I didn't hurt myself, and had plenty of time to hop back on.

"Hike! Hike!"

Before seeing the Farm's Siberian Huskies, we hear their high-pitched barking. They're smaller than I expected, and are harnessed to the sleds in groups of three. They let out febrile howls, excited by the anticipation of an outing. However, they rapidly calm down when my little trail blazer pets them.

We walk towards a large clearing, where I receive my first sled-driving lesson. Meanwhile, my son takes his place in the front of the dog handler's sled, on the only passenger seat.

I learn basic concepts. I have to place my feet on the sled's skates. In order to turn to one side, I need to lean my body the right way. When I want the dogs to move forward, I must yell "hike!"

TIPS (fun for 5 years +)

• Young passengers have to be old enough to be able to hang on to both sides of the dog handler's sled. Young children are not allowed to ride alone with inexperienced parents.
• The braking manoeuvre is a bit difficult for children to handle but the owner assured me many succeed and drive a sled. If they don't, they can always be passengers.
• Expect an igloo, their new thing in the last few years!
• Bring your toboggan, there are some hills. They also rent snowshoes for $15/hour.

An employee rides a snowmobile behind us. He's there to catch up with the sleds that have lost their drivers. My son is clinging to his sled and loudly encouraging the dogs to go faster.

When the sled slides without resistance, the speed is exhilarating and the huskies' joy is contagious. The 2-km ride lasts around 25 minutes. It's not very long, but in my case it was intense enough to leave me the following day with aches and pains in several arm muscles I didn't even know existed!

Meanwhile, my 21-month-old daughter stayed in Daddy's arms. They admired the farm animals: a huge turkey, hens, goats, donkeys and horses. After the dogsled ride, we met at the barn and drank a hot chocolate.

Rob Roy Farm • Singhampton (519) 922-2706	B-1 N-W of Toronto 2 1/2 hrs

Schedule: December to April, weather permitting. Call for snow conditions.
Costs: 30-min. ride is $65/adults, $45/12 years and under.
Directions: 469358 Grey Rd. 31. From the Talisman Centre, take County Rd. #13 southbound, then take County Rd. #31 eastbound.

BURD'S TROUT FISHING

The line is busy

You need fishing gear? They rent it out. The very idea of putting a desperate worm on a hook grosses you out? They'll do the dirty work for you. And most of all, you're afraid your pint-size fisherman (or woman) might return without a catch? Well, you can't come home empty-handed with the thousands of trout that inhabit the ponds at Burd's Trout Fishing. From now on, nothing stands between your child and the intriguing experience of fishing.

The tree-lined farm is a pretty sight with its two, one-acre ponds, each adorned with a lazy paddle wheel that gently stirs the water. A small brick path runs alongside the bigger pond, allowing for strollers and wheelchairs to circulate.

The bigger pond, for general public use) is stocked every week. The other pond is reserved for group use.

There's a laid-back country feeling to the place. But don't be fooled: no stone was left unturned in order to cater to our needs. The employees, dressed in sweatshirts printed with the farm's logo, offer courteous service. There is also a rain shelter, washrooms, the sale of beverages (bring your own snacks) and, oh bliss, a small outdoor playground with sandbox (complete with toys!).

After weighing our catch, an employee killed, cut and cleaned our fish way too fast to trouble my little Nosey Parker, who was observing the whole scene with big... fish eyes.

Later on, we found out that the trout, being so fresh, were incredibly tasty. True, they weren't really a bargain compared to the market price, but watching my little guy frantically winding his reel to bring in the fighting fish was worth a million.

The proud look on his face while we were eating his catch wasn't bad either.

TIPS (fun for 4 years +)
- No permit required.
- One rod might actually be enough for two young children since one can bring the trout ashore with the rod while the other catches it with the net.
- Trout sells for 38¢ an ounce so you could run a high bill. Lucky for us, we're allowed to catch a maximum of five trout per rod in use.
- During our visit, the seven fish we caught measured between 18 and 25 cm and cost $27 altogether. The farm accepted payment by cash or credit card.

NEARBY ATTRACTIONS
Live Steamers (15-min.)............. p. 236
Bruce's Mill (10-min.).................. p. 335

Burd's Trout Fishing
· Stouffville
(905) 640-2928

G-12
N-E
of Toronto
30-min.

Schedule: Season runs daily May to September weather permitting (weekends only in April, October and November), 8 am to dusk (flexible).

Admission: $5/visitor, FREE for 7 years and under, $3/rod rental and bait.

Directions: 13077 Hwy 48, Stouffville. From Hwy 404 North, take exit #37/Stouffville Rd. eastbound. Turn north on Hwy 48, look on the east side.

ABOUT FISHING

Fun for shore!

I don't know about your children but as far as mine are concerned, fishing is the only fun way to remain calm for half an hour: there's the hope, the surrounding nature, and the thrill of the catch. So I've decided to get to the bottom of this sport to indulge their passion.

In years of visiting the region inside out, I have noticed people fishing everywhere, at all times of the year. I've always wondered if they were allowed, how they knew which fish was edible, how they got their permit, etc.

Fishing regulations

The bottom line is that kids and youth under 18 years old don't need a fishing permit. And if you just want to watch your kids fish, you don't need a permit either.

Only residents between 18 and 64 require a fishing license. Licenses are available from camps and lodges, summer camps, sporting goods stores or bait dealers. In smaller communities, they're often sold in general stores.

When buying a license from one of the 2,000 license issuers across the province, you fill out an Outdoors Card Application. An Outdoors Card bearing your one-year fishing license tag will be mailed to you. It is a plastic identification card good for 3 years, to which the fishing license is affixed.

Meanwhile, you'll get a temporary license on the spot. A renewal package is automatically mailed to you before your card expires.

If you want to fish with your kids, you'll need to get at least the $10-Resident One-Day Fishing License. If you intend to join them more than one day, you'll need to get the $19-Resident Conservation Fishing License or the $28-Resident Sport Fishing License, both good for one year and including the cost of the Outdoors Card Annual License. (In most cases, you'll be allowed to catch more fish with a Sport license.)

The daily catch limit varies a lot depending on the species, the location and time of year. For instance, in the Toronto area, there's no limit on Yellow Perch or Crappie year-round but you could catch only one Muskellunge with a Sport license (none with a Conservation one!).

OMNR publications

Could not distinguish one from the other? No problem! Get the **Ontario Ministry of Natural Resources (OMNR)** brochure *Recreational Fishing Regulations Summary* with a colour fish identification chart at the end.

This free publication is divided into five regions. Each is broken into fishing divisions, with specific regulations applying to them. There's of course more information than you'll need in it. For example, we learn that salamanders may NOT be used as bait. Yuck! The very idea they need to specify that!

Visit your local sporting goods store to get a copy or call the Ministry to have one mailed to you. You may also download it from their web site.

The **OMNR** has put together other great free publications which you can download or receive by mail. My favourite is the great 39-page brochure *Take a Kid Fishing*. It is filled with lovely pictures and very useful information for neophytes. It covers it all: tackle, hooks, sinkers, bobbers, bait, lures, etc. Illustrations will show you how to put together your tackle, how to make basic knots, how to cast. The last two pages include colour charts to identify your catch.

In it, I learned that the best beginner's fishing gear to buy for a child should be a light reel on a 4 1/2 to 5 ft. lightweight rod with 6- to 12-lb. line which should be easily found for around $30.

The pictures in their other publication, the 32-page *Fish Ontario*, are even more beautiful. Here, you'll have a better look at the different species, with some amazing pictures of prize catches that will make your young fisher dream. For each species, they give you the Ontario record catch, average size of fish, information on biology, temperature and habitat as well as concrete tips on bait and fishing techniques.

It mentions that Ontario includes over 400,000 lakes, roughly 15% of the world's fresh water. It also states that the record lake trout caught in an Ontario lake was 63.12 lbs. (28.65 kg)... Really!

Around the city

If you want to know where the fishing spots are in and around the GTA, you must get a free copy of the flyer *Urban Fishing Opportunities in Toronto & Surrounding Areas* put together by the Aurora District of the Ontario Ministry of Natural Resources.

It includes a list of the GTA fishing sites as well as the fish you're bound to find in them! Many of those sites are described in this guide: **Albion Hills C.A.**, **Heart Lake C.A.**, **Chinguacousy Park**, **Professor's Lake**, **Centennial Park**, Grenadier Pond in **High Park**, **Toronto Islands**, **Ashbridges Bay**, the mouth of the **Humber River**, **Bluffer's Park**, Rouge River Marsh by **Rouge Beach**, **Mill Pond**, **Willcox Lake**, **Bruce's Mill C.A.**, **Petticoat Creek C.A.**, **Pickering Nuclear Plant** and **Kelso C.A.**

TIPS (fun for 4 years +)

• Your surest bet to ensure your child will catch something is to go to a fishing farm, where you don't need a license to fish. Visit www.fishontario.com and click <u>Trout Ponds</u> for a listing.
• **Long Lane Farm** (p. 146) also has a stocked pond from which your kids are almost sure to catch fish. **Daniel's Ark** (p. 54) is another private place with a stocked pond.
• See **Christie C. A.** on p. 280.

A conservation area I don't describe in my guide but which is probably the best for fishing is **Glen Haffy** at 19305 Airport Road, north of Caledon East, (416) 667-6295. It has two trout ponds regularly stocked and fishing equipment for rent. It even hosts two private ponds for groups to rent!

Family Fishing Weekend

Ontario Family Fishing Weekend is an official three-day weekend of unlicensed fishing. Usually held on the second weekend of July, this event allows adults to fish without a permit. It is locally driven, meaning that what's done during this event varies from one municipality to the next.

Some locations offer games for the children and prizes, others offer free use of equipment and bait. Many will feature fly fishing demonstrations and give fish identification tips. Check their web site or call for details about local events.

On their web site, I learned that Ontario residents can now call or order on-line to receive a free "Introduction to Fishing" package including the four publications I described in these pages and much more. Must get that one!

Ministry of Natural Resources
1-800-667-1940 (info line)
1-800-387-7011 (for Outdoors Cards)
(905) 713-7400 (Aurora District)
www.mnr.gov.on.ca/mnr/fishing

Family Fishing Weekend
1-800-667-1940 (info line)
www.familyfishingweekend.com
Schedule: Usually on the first or second weekend of July, Friday to Sunday (July 9-11 in 2004 and July 8-10 in 2005).

HOCKEY HALL OF FAME

Shoot and score!

The Hockey Hall of Fame reflects the colourful palette of the world's many hockey teams and is as bright as any rink during play-offs. There is no need to be a serious fan to enjoy the many attractions displayed throughout the labyrinth-shaped path of discoveries.

The museum fills a large space in the underground of the eye-catching **BCE Place**. Devoted aficionados could easily spend an entire day reading the texts adjoining each window display (and manipulating CD-ROMs filled with histories, trivia and statistics), but there are also sufficient interactive displays to entertain children six years and older, particularly if they are hooked on this national sport.

My companions thoroughly enjoyed the NHLPA Be A Player Zone!

In the glassed rooms of the McDonald's Shut Out attractions, they positioned themselves in front of a goal and tried to intercept soft pucks thrown full blast by a virtual Marc Messier and Wayne Gretzky.

On the other side, they waited anxiously for their turn at the McDonald's Shoot Out, where they shot some fifteen real pucks towards a virtual Eddie Belfour guarding the goal. Data such as their speed, precision and reaction time would show up on a screen.

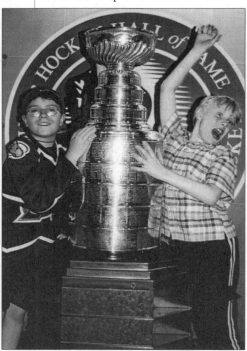

A mezzanine area overlooks the game zone. It is part of the TSN/RDS Broadcast Zone and includes several broadcast pods where visitors can transform into sports commentators. They watch clips of real games from a menu of classic moments as their comments are taped. (They find it challenging, except for yelling "He scores!") They can compare with the actual comments from legendary broadcasters. They also get a private access code to hear their play-by-play via www.hhof.com! It will stay on the web for 10 days.

The Production Mobile is for older kids (and adults). The simulator allows us to compose our own clip, selecting camera angles, audio mix, broadcast pace and more.

We liked our visit to the dressing room, an exact replica of Montreal's room in the 90's.

Make sure to photograph your aspiring players in front of the gleaming Stanley Cup, located in the Bell Great Hall. The room is capped by a dome 15 metres above, adorned with magnificent stained glass. The heavy doors of this ex-bank's vaults are an intriguing sight for children's active imaginations.

TIPS (fun for 6 years +)

• Parking at the **BCE Place** is expensive on weekdays but O.K. on weekends.
• Jerseys from most professional teams are available in small sizes in the boutique (strategically located at the museum's exit).
• There is a snack bar inside and a food court out of the attraction. Also see the **Mövenpick Restaurant** on p. 437.

NEARBY ATTRACTIONS
Toronto Buskerfest (10-min.)........p. 89
GO Train (5-min. walk)................p. 228

Hockey Hall of Fame
(416) 360-7765
www.hhof.com

I-10 Downtown Toronto 10-min.

Schedule: From end of June to Labour Day, Christmas and March Break, 9:30 am to 6 pm (opens at 10 am on Sundays). Fall/winter/spring, Monday to Friday, 10 am to 5 pm, Saturday, 9:30 am to 6 pm, Sunday, 10:30 am to 5 pm.
Admission: $12/adults, $8/seniors and 4-13 years, FREE for children 3 years and under.
Directions: BCE Place, Concourse Level, Toronto (at the North-West corner of Yonge and Front St.).

TORONTO CLIMBING ACADEMY

"There you go!"

"Is it the paparazzi corner?" teases a father. "Actually, we all work for the Globe!" I joke back. Truth is, if I am the only one writing about today's experience, I also have the least impressive equipment to catch the moment when my child conquers the 55-foot wall!

TIPS (fun for 6 years +)
• Shy children beware! Children climb with all eyes on them.
• I felt my tall 7-year-old's legs and arms were just long enough to reach the holds. A six-year-old in the group almost did not make it to the top. Bring good shoes or rent climbing shoes for $5.
• For $35, parents can be certified and learn how to supervise their child.
• If you want some down time while your child is in the program, just go five minutes east of Broadview on Queen Street, for a perfect croissant at **Bonjour Brioche** (812 Queen Street E., (416) 406-1250) or great coffee at **Joy Bistro** (884 Queen Street E., (416) 465-8855) where I literally wrote this guide while the zealous staff kept the coffee coming!
• **Joe Rockheads** at 29 Fraser Ave. offers the Kids Klimb program for $25/child, any time of the week (min. three, 8- to 13-year old kids). A good flexible birthday party solution! (416) 538-7670 or www.joerockheads.com.

I did not expect all parents to stay for the whole two-hour program. Most of all, I did not expect them to cheer each climber in unison!

The young supervisor coaches each child during the climb, with step-by-step instructions punctuated by plenty of "Awesome!" or "There you go!" encouragements. I read 5.4 at the bottom of the first wall. I am told 5 means "vertical", and 4, the degree of difficulty. Some impossible walls rate 5. 12!

The second wall (a 5.5) is 55 feet tall; more than twice the height of the first one. Those who reach the top hit a button which turns on a red light. Thankfully, all the kids succeed.

The third climb is a 5.7 corner wall. On his last climb, my son is bypassed by a spider woman on the "wall" above his head. She eventually falls, dangling safely at the end of her rope. "What happened?" asks a girl in the group. What did you expect? She was climbing on a... ceiling!

"Was it fun?" I later ask my little monkey when he comes down. "Yes!" "Does it hurt anywhere?" I inquire. "Everywhere!" is his reply. Go figure!

Toronto Climbing Academy
(416) 406-5900
www.climbingacademy.com

J-10 Downtown Toronto 10-min.

Schedule: Monday to Friday, noon to 11 pm. Saturday and Sunday, 10 am to 10 pm. **Kids Love To Climb** program Saturday from 11 am to 1 pm.

Admission: One Day pass $12/adults, $10/student, $6/6-12 years. Harness rental is $6.

Directions: 100A Broadview Ave., Toronto (south of Queen St. East, on the west side of Broadview Ave.).

NEARBY ATTRACTIONS
Cherry Beach (10-min.)................p. 272

SCOOTER'S ROLLER PALACE

Hold on!

It was a hot summer night outside when we visited the Palace so the light air-conditioning cooling the place was most welcome. A few minutes later, I was breaking a sweat just fitting my two kids into their skates. Still, it was nothing compared to what I felt the second I hit the rink!

Trying roller blades for the first time while holding the hand of my unsteady 6-year-old daughter on roller skates was a very bad idea! I held on to the boards and crawled back onto the carpet, went back to the rental counter and got myself good sturdy four-wheel retro leather skates.

There were very few people on that Wednesday night. The good thing about it was that it meant fewer potential collisions with fellow skaters. The bad thing was that there was nowhere for me to hide and preserve my dignity.

TIPS (fun for 6 years +)
• You can use a bike helmet. Knee and elbow pads are recommended.
• The more friends you take with you, the more fun your kids will have. It is actually a great place to bring a birthday party. You can rent a private room or the whole place for skating, blading or roller hockey parties.
• I was not impressed by the food at the snack bar. I suggest you stick to buying refreshments there. If a meal is part of the outing, you might want to go to Harvey's next door.

NEARBY ATTRACTIONS
Rattray Marsh (5-min.)..................p. 318

There's a "disco" feeling to roller-skating. Add a ceiling punctuated with colour follow-spots and a mirror ball reflecting on the shiny floor and you're back into the 80's... (or is it the 50's)! Add a couple of slow songs playing by the end of the evening and you might even get a flashback from your teenage years.

The dance floor is huge. Some loops are printed on it, for the keeners who want to practice routines. Scooter's Roller Palace actually offers affordable skating lessons for the young on Saturdays and for adults on some evenings. They also host "All Night" skating from time to time (going from 8 pm to 3 am!). I even heard about "Christian Gospel" skating nights!? The night we were there, the music sounded more like a very annoying radio station, not that I really noticed since I was in survival mode. Some nights, they have a disk jockey.

The place also includes some small bowling alleys and a few arcade machines. They sell glow pendants, bracelets and necklaces (from $1.50 to $2.50) which anybody aware of the roller skate culture knows is really cool when skating in a dark room under black lights.

Scooter's Roller Palace • Mississauga (905) 823-4001 www.scooters.on.ca	J-7 West of Toronto 30-min.

 Schedule: The schedule varies throughout the year. During the summer, "Family All Ages" sessions are Wednesdays, 6 to 8:30 pm, Fridays, 6 to 9 pm, Saturdays and Sundays, 1 to 5 pm, but more sessions cater to adults only. They are open for children on most holidays and P.D. days.

 Admission: $5.50 to $6.50.

 Rental: $1.50/roller skates, $3.50/in-line skates, $3/pads (limited inventory available).

Directions: 2105 Royal Windsor Dr., Mississauga. Take QEW, exit at Winston Churchill southbound, and turn east on Royal Windsor Dr. (an extension of Lakeshore).

ABOUT SKATEBOARDING

Join the club

It happens without warning. One day they're babies and the next they want wheels! So you take a deep breath and buy them their first skateboard... and skate shoes... and skate helmet (this sport doesn't come cheap!) Now, where's a skate park when you need one?

You owe this section to my buddy Cody, a very resourceful young expert I

TIPS (fun for 6 years +)
In my first weeks of indulging my son in his new passion I learned a few things:
• No! A $20 skateboard won't do! The cheap bearings make it very hard and frustrating for the new skater to learn to get some control. Better to start with $50ish ones.
• Try to borrow a board or find a second-hand one to verify how serious your child is about it before investing in the real stuff (new, it will cost over $200).
• By the way, whatever the look of your child's new board, it won't take long for it to look old! That's why they sell those huge stickers in the skate stores: to cover up the scratches. Stickers are part of the skate culture (sK8 for the insiders). When visiting a skate store, you can always ask if they give some away.
• Yes! Good shoes are a good idea! Skating is really rough on normal shoes and on tender heels.
• Ski helmets are way too warm for summer use. We tried!
• Make sure your young skaters always have a good supply of water with them. It is amazing how much this sport makes them perspire.
• Helmets and elbow pads are mandatory in most paying parks.
• In most of parks, roller blades and BMX bikes are allowed as well.

met at a skate park in Cobourg, after a nice day at the lovely beach there. It took him fifteen minutes to point me to all the good spots he'd been to around the GTA (with the help of a dedicated dad, I am sure!) and convince me that my research would not be lost on all the parents with kids with a strong inclination towards this sport.

On the following pages I describe the most popular parks we've visited around the GTA but they seem to be popping up more and more. Actually... THIS JUST IN! Just before the printing of this guide, a new one (and a good one) has opened in Toronto: the **Vandehoof Skatepark**, east of Laird Drive, two blocks away from the indoor playground KidsWork (p. 210) and one block from a Winners outlet (all located on Vanderhoof Avenue). It includes a great U-shaped bowl with an ambitious deep end, a separate section with ramps and stairs, and a paved path to link it all with a nice flow.

Your best bet to find the latest or closest skate park in your area is to call a local skate store. These guys usually know everything skateboarding-related that happens in the region! In these stores, you might even find some tapes offering an introduction to the sport.

You can also check the web site **www.skateboardparks.com**.

SHRED CENTRAL

Über cool

Some of you who reigned over an unfinished basement in your teenage years will know exactly what to expect at Shred Central. Those dusty hand-me-down sofas on the mezzanine (behind chain-link fence to protect the visitors) will bring back memories...

TIPS (fun for 6 years +)

• ATTENTION! A release form must be signed for the child by one of the parents on the first visit. They will then keep it on file for a year.

• One of the first skills a new skater will have to learn is to get out of the way as soon as he or she falls. The place is not as big as most outdoor parks.

• You may rent the space for birthday parties before regular weekend hours.

• Shred Central's small store is well stocked with shoes and other skate equipment. They have some vending machines for drinks and snacks.

• Your child does not need to be accompanied when skating on the premises. (There are a few cafés on Yonge Street, in the vicinity.)

• NEWS FLASH! One week prior to printing this guide, a new skateboard shop opened its doors in the Kensington Market area: **Adrift**, at 299 Augusta Avenue (south of College, west of Spadina). The shop includes an indoor mini skatepark, a lounge for kids and a gallery displaying skate art. It will pay special attention to the female market by always having an experienced female skater on staff and by offering girls-only clinics. It will host birthday parties. Check www.adriftskateshop.com or call (416) 515-0550.

Seriously, the place is über cool. And yet, the staff is really nice with anybody over thirty and under ten. Close to the time of printing, it was the only skatepark downtown Toronto.

In the winter, it's pretty much the only option for serious skaters (especially those who want to try out the new skateboard they got for Christmas!).

You access it through an alley. The façade is covered with large graffiti. Graffiti also covers the indoor walls, the columns, the pipes and the ramps.

I heard about **Commongrounds Skatepark**, another indoor skatepark located at 421 Rowntree Dairy Road in Woodbridge. Call (905) 264-8428 or check www.commongroundsk8.com. It looks great and relatively long. There too, skaters need a waiver signed by a parent. Admission is $15 for non-members.

Shred Central (416) 923-9842 www.shredcentral.com	**I-10 Downtown Toronto 15-min.**

Schedule: Tuesday to Friday, 3 to 9 pm. Saturdays, noon to 9 pm. Sundays, noon to 8 pm.
Admission: $10 for a day pass, minimum age is 7 years old. FREE for girls!
Directions: 19 Nicholas St., Toronto (a backstreet just west of Yonge and north of Wellesley St.).

NEARBY ATTRACTIONS

CUMMER SKATEBOARD PARK

Action!

When we approach the side of the skatepark, a guy we had not noticed flies off from nowhere and flips back in a flash.

As we observed his routine, we realized that there was a slope, farther and higher in the back, which allowed him and other dare-devils to gain an impressive speed before they threw themselves into what seemed like an empty pool and what I will learn to call a bowl.

This skatepark, adjacent to the **Cummer Community Centre**, is small but packed with features with which the skaters seem to be very creative: stairs, ramps, concrete corridors, different levels and the deep bowl. We can see it all in a glimpse.

It's around lunchtime and groups of teenagers arrive to watch their friends, armed with boxes of steamy pizza bought at the nearby strip-mall. The strip of concrete surrounding the park is quite narrow so we have to be careful to stay out of the way of the skaters in action. It's our first visit to a skatepark and we are learning as we go.

An older guy gives my 10-year-old son a tip or two after seeing him enduring a few painful-looking falls. I am immensely grateful to know that someone is watching over him because... personally, I can't watch!

When I dare to look at my newly extreme-sport-infatuated-one, he is as red as a tomato and soaked, I'm assuming from the adrenaline rush every time he tries a new move. Will he survive? An hour later, he's still at it!

Good news! There's a great indoor pool in the community centre, with giant slide and shallow area. I take a mental note to come back with my younger one for a swim next time I drive my son to Cummer Park.

In the back of the huge community park, there's also a small playground and four tennis courts.

TIPS (fun for 6 years +)

• **Cummer Pool** is open for family leisure swim Friday, 7:15 to 9 pm and weekends, 2 to 4 pm. More hours in July and August. Call to confirm.

• There's a snack bar in the community centre and some food outlets on the other side of Leslie St. We opted for the **Pickle Barrel** with its kids' menu, real "adult" food and acrobat-theme decoration.

Cummer Skateboard Park	I-11
Cummer Skateboard Park • North York (416) 362-1111 (City) (416) 395-7803 (pool) www.toronto.ca	**North** of downtown 35-min.

 Schedule: The outdoor park is open year-round. Call for the recreational swim schedule at the centre's indoor pool.

 Admission: FREE access to the skate park. FREE leisure swim.

 Directions: 6000 Leslie St., North York (north of Finch, just south of Cummer Ave.).

SPORTSVILLAGE SKATEPARK

Great pipes!

The features in this skatepark are all in wood with blue siding. It "looks" less harmful than concrete so the illusion has a very calming effect on me.
Even though it's a paying park, the place is lively with action on the numerous half- and quarter-pipes of different depths. My young skater and his friend hear the call of the mermaids and they're gone. It's our second time in a skatepark and I still can't watch. So I sit on the adjacent patio, order a glass of wine and bury my face into a good book for the next hour.

Sportsville is a sport complex including four indoor rinks busy with local hockey teams or private functions. In the back, there's the skatepark, a 30-foot climbing wall and visitors have free access to three 3-on-3-basketball courts and a 400-metre skate path for in-line skating during the summer or ice-skating in the winter.

There's a vast flat area in front of the patio leading to the sinuous concrete trail lined with some trees and grass.

The advantage of a free rollerblading path is obvious if you've come to this place with younger non-skateboarding siblings to accommodate your skater. There's also a small indoor arcade with a dozen games.

Sportsville offers group and private lessons for those who want to crack the code on skateboarding, BMX (you know, those bicycles with small wheels) or rollerblading. Group lessons are $20 per rider and one-on-one instruction is $40. Thinking about it, that's what I want for my next birthday: lessons for my son!

TIPS (fun for 6 years +)
• Helmets must be worn. You may rent one on site at the admission booth. Protective gear strongly recommended.
• The rollerblading path turns into a skatepath during the winter. See p. 373.
• Children under 18 years must submit a waiver signed by an adult once a season (you can download the waiver).
• It is possible to rent the skatepark for private parties during non-business hours for $200 plus tax, for two hours. Indoor ice rink rental is $150 per hour.
• There is a small food concession indoors as well a licensed restaurant with large tables surrounded by windows from which to watch the hockey games on one of the rinks. They service the outdoor tables near the skatepark.

NEARBY ATTRACTIONS

Sportsville
• Vaughan
(905) 738-7574
www.sportsville.ca

H-10
N-W
of Toronto
35-min.

Schedule: The season can start mid-April and end late November, weather permitting. At the beginning, weekdays only, from 5 to 9 pm and weekends from 1 to 5 pm and 5 to 9 pm. When school's out, both sessions are open daily. The skatepark is closed during or after rain until all surfaces are dry (no refund given if it rains).
Admission: $7 per skateboarding session. $60 for a 10-session pass. $250 per season's pass (including members' sessions, t-shirt and discounts). Helmet rental is $2. Climbing tower is $2/two tries. Free parking.
Directions: 2600 Rutherford Rd.,Vaughan (south of Canada's Wonderland, take exit #33 off Hwy 400 and go eastbound).

MISSISSAUGA SKATEPARK

a couple of adrenaline shots from trying (and missing) a few new moves on their board and you get well-cooked steamy skaters ready to throw themselves face first into the nearby snow bank formed by the Zamboni's discharge! (This park is located by **Iceland**, a complex with four indoor ice rinks.)

The municipal park includes a large bowl and there are slopes and quarter-pipes shaped into the gray concrete. Stairs and ramps look like those skaters love to ride around commercial buildings.

The park is unfortunately located along Highway 403, so it is a bit noisy. Good news is they've built a spray pad next to the skatepark, perfect for younger siblings waiting for big brother or sister to be ready to go back home!

Cool... but hot... but cool!

A sea of concrete waves is rippling before us. This skatepark seems bigger than the others!

There is ample room to ride from one feature to the next. Angles are not as accentuated as in other parks and slopes are not as high. As far as I can judge (from the humble point of view of a non-skater) the riders can't build as much speed here as in other parks but they can go for ever, not unlike a good back street lined with obstacles... without the cars. Oh! And did I mention it is free?

In the midst of summer, in 30-degree heat, the sun is burning hot. Add

TIPS (fun for 6 years +)
• You may rent the **Iceland** rinks for private functions. Call Mississauga Recreation and Parks Customer Service Centre for rental rates at (905) 615-4242. You may also call the **Hershey Centre** (home of the Ice Dogs), on the other side of Matheson Boulevard, to rent one of its three arenas, (905) 502-9100.
• There's a food concession indoors along with a small arcade.
• If you're waiting for your skater to be done and need to kill some time, visit the nearby mini-golf, **Bathgate Golf Centre**, also including a driving range: 600 Eglinton Avenue, off Cawthra. Open 9 am to 9 pm, $3/adults and $2/children. They also have a driving range. Call (905) 890-0156.

NEARBY ATTRACTIONS

Mississauga Skatepark
• Mississauga
(905) 896-5346 (City)
(905) 615-4680 (Iceland)
www.mississauga.ca

I-8
N-W
of Toronto
35-min.

Schedule: Skate park is open year-round (use at your own risk).
Admission: FREE access.

Directions: 705 Matheson Blvd. East, Mississauga. Take Hwy 403 West, exit at Eglinton westbound, turn right on Kennedy and right again on Matheson.

SHELL PARK

In a nutshell... loved it!

This is by far my favourite skatepark, strictly from an esthetic point of view. The place obviously belongs to the skaters.

I love the fact that the City of Oakville allowed colourful graffiti to blossom on the concrete instead of covering it with grey paint as soon as they appear. Let's hope nobody changes that! We've been to that park a couple of times and I could see that the graffiti is evolving!

The skatepark is contained in a large basin bordered by a large concrete sidewalk. When standing on it, you glimpse the whole park down below, with plenty of trees in the background. It is nicely laid-out with slopes, quarter-pipes and ramps.

The skatepark is located on the edge of a small forest with a trail and next to a playground and a lovely garden. It is a perfect spot for a picnic while you wait for your skater to throw in the towel.

If you feel confident enough to leave your capable skater behind, you can explore the trail in **Sheldon Creek Park** leading to the lake, on the other side of Lakeshore.

TIPS (fun for 6 years +)

• After the skating session, I recommend you take a 2-minute drive back towards Bronte Harbour, at the foot of Twelve Mile Creek Lands, to check out the little **Bronte Beach**. Turn south on West River Street (on the west side of the creek); you'll find a public parking lot

with access to the beach. We especially loved the western section of it, a secluded tiny sandy spot hidden by the trees. The small park on the east side of Bronte Harbour is also quite pretty.
• Check the **Fire Hall** or **Wimpy's Diner** on pp. 434-435.

NEARBY ATTRACTIONS
Coronation Park (5-min.).............p. 381
Kids Craft Café (15-min.).............p. 425

Shell Park
· Oakville
(905) 845-6601
www.oakville.ca

J-7
West
of Toronto
35-min.

Schedule: The park is open year-round (use at your own risk).

Admission: FREE access, FREE parking.
Directions: From QEW, take exit #111/ Bronte Rd. southbound, turn west on Lakeshore. Shell Park is on the north side.

MAJOR RINKS

By the lake

From one side, it looks as if the rink extends all the way to Lake Ontario. From another, the sun shines on the imposing CN Tower.

From the Lakeside EATS outdoor terrace, visitors observe skaters while sipping a hot chocolate. The Rink at Harbourfront Centre (currently called **Natrel Rink**) is decidedly a cool skating spot!

It is here, at **Harbourfront Centre**, that we decided to introduce our little one to the trials and tribulations (and fun) of outdoor skating. He was quite surprised when his blades hit the slippery surface...

In the hour that followed, as we pulled him along between us, he would drop like a dead weight – a prisoner being brought to death row. At least he was laughing!

Some object to skating in the crowd-ed conditions on the weekend. However, you won't find that many skaters at all between 10 and 11 am. Moreover, given the rink's odd shape, there are some secluded spots to be enjoyed by those not too eager on speed skating.

In the square

Nathan Phillips Square and **Mel Lastman Square** also boast large outdoor artificial ice rinks with rental services. They too are open from the end of November to mid-March, weather permitting, and their admission is free.

TIPS (fun for 4 years +)

• Don't count on cheering your dear one's arabesques, standing on the rink with your boots on. Skates only are permitted on the ice.

• The **Natrel Rink** offers blade sharpening service.

• The ice of these rinks is artificially maintained at freezing level, providing the external temperature does not exceed 10° C, and the sun doesn't shine too aggressively.

• More on **Cavalcade of Lights** at **Nathan Phillips Square** on p. 190 and **WinterCity Festival** on p. 90.

Major rinks

Schedule: Open from end of November to mid-March, 10 am to 10 pm (weather permitting).

Admission: FREE. Skate rental is usually around $7/adults, $6/seniors and children. Sharpening is $5.

Directions: Natrel Rink: 235 Queens Quay West, Toronto (west of York St., south of York Quay Centre). (416) 973-4866. **Nathan Phillips Square:** 100 Queen St. West, Toronto, west of Bay (416) 392-1111. **Mel Lastman Square:** 5100 Yonge St., North York (416) 392-1111.

SPORTSVILLAGE SKATEPATH

Skating trail

The ice-skating trail turns left and right around two molehills adorned by a few trees. It beats skating on automatic pilot mode at a rink!

There's a new technology that refrigerates cement paths so you get nice polished ice in the

winter when you water them. The first one I have seen is at Sportsville. It is 4 metres wide and 400 metres long. Another one I have heard of is in **London Story-Book** (see p. 30).

Year round, Sportsville hosts four indoor rinks used by local hockey teams, figure skating schools and for private rentals. Weather permitting, it opens a fancy skateboarding park for a fee (see p. 373).

The rinks are not open to the general public but there are great advantages to

the place for those who want to use the free outdoor trail. It includes a pro shop with skate sharpening service ($5), there's a food concession selling hot chocolate and a restaurant with large bay windows overlooking one of the rinks. You can put your skates on and leave your boots indoors near the back door of the building. The trail is located in the back of Sportsville.

Check the entertainment complex **Dave & Buster's** on p. 19.

Sportsville • Vaughan (905) 738-7574 www.sportsville.ca	H-10 N-W of Toronto 35-min.

 Schedule: Weather permitting. Call to check if the trail is functional.
Admission: FREE.
Directions: See p. 369.

CEDARENA

Old-fashioned way

Interested in a small rustic ice rink, managed by volunteers for over seventy years and located in the backcountry, thirty minutes from Toronto? Then head for Cedarena.

At first sight, we were charmed by the tortuous path that leads down to the Cedarena ice rink, which sits nestled amidst cedar trees.

At the end of the path, there is a small woodstove-heated cabin, where many families sit tightly against each other, as they put on their skates. Outside, an even smaller porch can hardly contain the overflow of eager skaters ready to embark on the ice.

It was a bit of a disappointment then to see boards surrounding the medium-sized rink, making it look somewhat

choked. In addition, when we visited, the ice was dented and the music rinky-dink. Yet, it did not keep skaters from having a great time. The intimate character of the place must have something to do with it. It has been a local tradition for over 77 years! There are washrooms on site and a little snack bar that serves cider and hot chocolate.

Cedarena • Markham (905) 294-0038 (seasonal phone number)	H-12 N-E of Toronto 35-min.

 Schedule: The hours depend on Cedar Grove Community Centre volunteers' availability and may vary from one year to the next. Usually open Sundays, 1 to 4 pm and some evenings, 7:30 to 10 pm, weather permitting.
Admission: Around $2.50/adults, $2/seniors and $1/children.
Directions: 7373 Reesor St., Markham. From Hwy 401 East, take exit # 383/Markham Rd. northbound. Turn east on Steeles Ave., then north on Reesor Rd.

POND SKATING

Bring on the shovel!

There's something about skating on natural ice... I think it is this mix of beauty and imperfection that gives us the feeling we're OK as we are and we fit into our environment. Plus, being surrounded by a wide surface of snow and trees certainly beats looking at rink boards!

Riverview Park

This park is buzzing with action! It is the unofficial town meeting place for those who love to play outside. In addition to pond skating, visitors can enjoy a good tobogganing slope. The skating pond is located on the western side of the Twelve Mile Creek in front of Riverview Park, where a marsh has formed (an official fish sanctuary).

On the day we went local families had cleared a dozen rinks in different sizes and shapes. Hockey games were going on the bigger ones and parents were initiating their toddlers on the smaller ones. The ice was not bumpy at all, the result of a fast-freeze overnight.

I found two fun restaurants in the area. Check out the **Fire Hall** and **Wimpy's Diner** on pp. 434-435.

Rattray Marsh Pond

This skating pond is much more secluded. I only know about it because of an acquaintance who lives right next to it. Two large rinks had been cleared on the day we went.

When you stand in the middle of the wide frozen marsh, there are only a few houses on the western side to remind you of civilization. Otherwise, you are surrounded by the wilderness of the conservation area, with Lake Ontario on the horizon.

You can't park in front of this pond. You have to walk five minutes along the trails of **Rattray Marsh Conservation Area** to get there. When you reach an elevated viewing point, follow a path in the snow left by previous skaters, leading down to the pond. (Sorry, my camera was out of film by the time I got there so you'll have to use your imagination with my fall picture of the Rattray marsh pond.)

Mill's Pond

The whole pond is cleared and managed by the Town of Richmond Hill. A sign indicates the ice conditions. You can call their Parks & Recreation Department to find out the conditions at (905) 884-8013.

There's an outdoor place to put on your skates and leave your boots as well as a small playground and some cages with geese and swans. There's even a parking lot and washrooms across the street from Mill's Pond.

A paved trail runs along the pond into a small forest. With gorgeous weeping willows brushing the pond, the place is a great picnic spot in the summer.

Read p. 91 about **Richmond Hill's Winter Carnival** held on the first weekend in February at Mill's Pond.

TIPS (fun for 5 years +)

• We need a couple of weeks with serious sub-zero temperatures in order  for the pond's ice to be safe. Rule of thumb: if dozens of people are already skating, it is safe. If you're first, scratch the ice to judge its state. If it is slushy, don't go there. Ice by the shore is always thinner.

• When you go pond skating, bring a shovel! If you're the first to show up, you'll need it! Or you can help widen an already existing rink and those who have cleaned the ice before you will be convinced of your good faith. If you are plain lazy (or have to hold a kid's hand instead of a shovel) I suggest you go on a Sunday. Chances are the other skaters will have worked for you the day before.

• Other potential sites for natural-ice skating: **Mountsberg Wildlife Centre** (p. 157), **Milliken Park** (p. 327) or **Centennial Park** (p. 389).

Saddington Park

The City of Mississauga manages this v-shaped pond. It is set by Lake Ontario and surrounded by trees. Hockey players seem to stick to one branch of the "v" while leisure skaters hang around the other one. See p. 350 describing this great park in the summer.

Pond skating

 Schedule: The ice is normally safe after two weeks of freezing weather. Our best bet is from mid-January to mid-February but it's all in Mother Nature's hands.

Admission: FREE.

Directions:

Riverview Park/Oakville: Take the QEW, exit at Bronte Rd. southbound. Turn west on Lakeshore Rd. and north on Mississauga St. The first street on your right is Riverview St. It is a dead-end leading directly to the front of Riverview Park. People park along this street.

Rattray Marsh/Mississauga: See p. 318.

J.C. Saddington Park/Mississauga: See p. 350.

Mill's Pond/Richmond Hill: Go west of Yonge, on Major Mackenzie St. Turn north on Trench St. to Mills St.

SKIING IN TOWN

The real thing!

From the "schlink" sound of the double chairlift, to the "swoosch" of skis scraping the slopes and the huge fireplace that sits in the ski chalet, Earl Bales looks like the real thing.

You won't see slopes running down to the **North York Ski Centre** as you would expect at a ski resort. That's because they run down a ravine behind the centre.

Hidden from view, you'll discover them when you walk over and stand at the top of the chairlift. There you'll find a gentle slope for beginners equipped with a rope tow. It is the best place to be introduced to this winter sport.

Don't expect great hills, but the high-rises you spot on the horizon are there to remind you this is the middle of the city. This ski centre is a little miracle in itself!

Centennial Park Ski Hill

Centennial Park Ski Hill is the ski centre located in **Centennial Park**. It offers two shorter hills equipped with a T-bar and a Poma Lift, and a slope for tobogganing.

TIPS (fun for 4 years +)
•   More on tobogganing at **Centennial Park** on p. 389.
•   Both ski centres have snowmaking equipment and night lighting. They also offer Alpine ski and snowboard lessons, and full sets of ski or snowboard equipment rentals as well.
•   Both centres have a snack bar on site.

North York Ski Centre & Centennial Park Ski Hill

I-9/10
North of downtown
35-min.

(416) 338-6754 (info & snow conditions)
www.toronto.ca/parks

Schedule: Usually from mid-December to mid-March.
Tow tickets: At North York, depending on number of hours of use: $8-$25/3-4 years old, $11-$25/5-14 years old, $14-$25/adults. Full set ski rental: $14-$25. Snowboard: $19-$25. At Centennial Park, tow tickets are around $5 less for all ages and it is $6 for a whole day for children 3-4 years old.
Directions/North York Ski Centre: Earl Bales Park, 4169 Bathurst St., North York (south of Sheppard Ave.).
Directions/Centennial Park Ski Hill: 256 Centennial Park Rd., Etobicoke (south of Eglinton Ave. West).

GLEN EDEN SNOW TUBING

Start here

Reluctant parents who've decided to give in and offer their enthusiastic kids the experience of snow tubing will love this one. It is the closest tube park to Toronto, and probably the one with the mildest slopes. Not that you could not gain some speed on these slopes. On a good night, the staff have seen people fly by at 80 km/h on radar.

The **Glen Eden Ski and Snowboard Centre** is located in the heart of **Kelso Conservation Area** in Milton. It opened its tube park in November 2003 including six parallel slides and one lift. The February weather was so mild, one of the staff

members was wearing shorts.

I thought the slopes a bit lame when I first saw them, but the ride down was quite fast. I was getting concerned by the acceleration that was building as I got really close to the end of the run when black rubber patches abruptly slowed me down. I recommend this tube park for parents of kids 5 to 8 years old.

Older kids know to visit the place in the evening, when the weather is colder and the chutes get icier. Younger kids will prefer day time, when warmer temperatures create more friction under the tube. Beginner skiers use the Galaxy Learning Centre, a series of mild slopes located on the north side of the train track. You access the ski hills on the south side of the track through a funny low tunnel right next to the rental shop.

A half-pipe awaits skiers and snowboarders on the west side of the hills. A smaller quarter-pipe is located on the eastern slope. Three lifts serve the ski centre.

TIPS (fun for 4 years +)
• See the **Halton Museum** on p. 407.
• Kids need to be a minimum of 42 inches (106cm) tall to ride. Only one person per tube is allowed but you can hold another rider's tube handles to ride down in duo (or trio).
• At the time of print, a walking bridge was being built to link the parking lot to the western part of the ski hills where the tube park is located.
• BEWARE! The farthest parking spot is located 1/2 km from the ski chalet, on the eastern part of the ski hills, and the Galaxy Learning Centre (it's a long way to walk back to the car with tired little skiers). The centre offers a shuttle service and there's a drop-off zone in the eastern part. When the bridge is ready, skiers will be able to buy their ticket at the western chalet, by the parking lot.
• There's a snack bar inside the eastern chalet and exterior food counters in both lodges.

Glen Eden Snow Tubing	D-2
	West
	of Toronto
• Milton	50-min.

Glen Eden Snow Tubing
• Milton
(905) 878-8455
www.gleneden.on.ca

 Schedule: Call to confirm when the season starts, it depends on the weather. Always call to confirm tubing runs are open. They're confident the season can go until end of March Break. Glen Eden is open for night use but closes at around 4 pm in the spring. Check exact schedule.

Admission: Around $3/one ride, $15/six rides. Note that unused rides can be used anytime within the same season. Ask about special nights.

Directions: In Kelso Conservation Area. From Hwy 401 West, take exit #320/Hwy 25 northbound. Turn west on Sideroad #5 (Campbellville Rd.), then south on Tremaine Rd. and enter Kelso C. A., west on Kelso Rd.

NEARBY ATTRACTIONS
Crawford Lake (15 min.)...............p. 410

SNOW VALLEY SNOW TUBING

Are you game?

The expanse of snow before us seems abruptly severed horizontally. **Beyond this divide, four long corridors stretch out, lined with a carpet of snow. Farther still, dark forests alternate with white fields. We need to walk right up to the edge of this imaginary line to discover a slope equivalent to a ten-storey descent.**

My six-year-old friends stamp their feet with impatience as they await the attendant's signal... but not me! In a split second, I feel like I am on a free-falling, four-storey elevator ride.

Then I am showered with snow that rushes from under my tube (all the more surprising because my eyes were shut and my mouth was wide open). I speed up even more, and my tube starts revolving around itself. I grasp my handles, barely catching a glimpse of my two lads standing alongside the slope, laughing at my adventure. My pint-sized Olympic bobsledders are already asking for more!

The tubes are covered with a thick canvas, equipped with a strap that you tie to the lift, to be brought up the hill. But you must be careful, it's not the time to wipe your glasses: you get to the summit faster than you think! Both your hands are required to hang on to the tube when it is unhitched from the lift.

TIPS (fun for 3 years +)

• Minimum height to ride down the slopes is 42". Smaller kids have two options: the Chicken Chutes (without a lift, where parents and kids can form groups to slide down) and the Kid Area (a miniature 3-chute tube park, without a lift, reserved for kids under 42"). They have kid-sized tubes.
• The "elevator" effect on the steep slopes is not as strong if we start sliding down while facing uphill.
• The first set of slopes is steeper. Tubers that choose a second group of gentler trails, located behind a row of trees, still come down at great speeds.
• On the day we visited, it took us ten minutes to go up, tube down and walk back to the lift. It was more advantageous to pay for a two-hour block of time. When there are long line-ups, it is recommended instead to buy a series of tickets, good for six descents.
• There are lockers and a cafeteria on site (and **Ski Snow Valley Barrie**'s ski **hills** right next door!).

NEARBY ATTRACTIONS

Snow Valley Snow Tubing Park
· Barrie
(705) 721-7669
or (416) 366-7669
www.skisnowvalley.com

B-2 North of Toronto 70-min.

Schedule: Open daily from mid-December to end of March (weather permitting). Call for exact schedule.
Admission: Around $15/person for 2 hours or $15 for 6 rides. Around $7 to use the Kid Area or Chicken Chutes.
Directions: From Hwy 400 North, take exit Dunlop St. (#96B) westbound, turn north on George Johnson Rd., then east on Snow Valley Rd.

ADRENALINE ALLEY

What a thrill!

When we visited the Talisman Ski Centre, we tried a thrilling activity, the only one of its kind in the area: snow-tubing by night. My family's two male inspectors had previously tested the trails in the St. Sauveur, Quebec area. They claimed that Talisman's trails had no cause to be jealous, and even said they were more entertaining because of their winding course.

Adrenaline Alley is open to **Talis-** man's guests as well as to the public. This park, adjoining the ski slopes, included about ten trails of various lengths and steepness served by two lifts when I visited it. It has now been reduced to five runs.

To ascend, we're lazily propped on chubby tubes, which are tied to the lift. We're going as fast as the adults who have decided to climb on foot beside us.

I was a bit scared to try so I found out the location of the easiest trails. Then, tied to one another on our respective tubes, my son and I leapt forward in the dark. We couldn't see the bottom of the slope due to its winding course.

I was happy to find that the tubes protect us well against bumps. In order to slow down, all we had to do was to lean on one side of the tube to steer it onto the trail's side. We bounced against the sides and turned round and round towards the bottom, where bails of hay helped us stop. On certain trails, those who choose to come down without touching the sides can accelerate up to 50 km per hour (not for me, thanks!).

TIPS (fun for 4 years +)

• Before paying a young child's admission fee, I recommend you test her interest. I sat my little one in the hole of a tube, and proceeded to take her for a little ride by sliding the tube from one side to the other. I also tried to push her from atop a tiny bump. The message was clear: she hated it! I saved $8 and Dad and I shared the privilege of tubing with her kamikaze brother.

• You can't go down with a child on your tube (the rule is one person per tube). However, you can hang on to another tube by holding each other's tube handles. Children must be 42 inches to use a tube.

NEARBY ATTRACTIONS

Talisman Mountain Resort........... p. 171
Dogsled at Rob Roy Farm............p. 358

**Adrenaline Alley
Snow Tubing**
• Kimberley
1-800-265-3759
www.talisman.ca

B-1
N-W
of Toronto
2 1/4 hrs

 Schedule: Open weather permitting (call by mid-December to find out about the snow conditions). Recently, the tubing park has opened on weekends only.
Cost: Around $2.50/ride or 5 rides for $10.
Directions: See Talisman Resort on p. 171.

KIDSTOWN WATER PLAYGROUND

A real bargain!

When you accompany young children, you can't expect much more for your money than what you get at Kidstown Water Playground in Scarborough.

This one is like the kid brother of **Ontario Place**'s water park. With water spurting whales, a water slide that ends in a wading pool, a large pirate boat armed with water pistols and corridor of spraying rings to navigate, this water park will thrill children 8 years old and younger. The older ones will be excited too, if they don't have high expectations from previous visits to larger commercial water parks.

The overall site covers approximately 2000 sq. feet and is surrounded by a grassy area with benches and picnic tables. Beyond the fence, there is a colourful playground and a lovely grassy hill down which my little stuntman and his new pals happily rolled.

Kidstown is part of **L'Amoreaux Park** but privately managed. A 15-minute walk across McNicoll Avenue will bring you to the large pond of **L'Amoreaux Park** where I have frequently seen cranes. Nearby, a small forest and many trails prove nice for family exploration. Since my last visit, they've added one of those structures with a large bucket of water periodically spilling on happy kids' heads. The sand box was taken away and they have traded the spurting bicycles with rocking whales.

TIPS (fun for 8 years and under)

• There are change rooms and the park is entirely framed by a fence. However, the entrance gate is always opened by incoming and outgoing visitors. It is therefore safer to keep a watchful eye on children.

• There is a food vendor on the site.

Kidstown Water Playground • Scarborough (416) 396-8325	**I-11** **N-E** **of downtown** **35-min.**

Schedule: Open daily, usually from end of June to Labour Day, 10:30 am to 7:30 pm, weather permitting (might close earlier in August when colder). Call to confirm.

Admission: Only $1 per child.

Directions: 3159 Birchmount Rd., Scarborough. From Hwy 401 East, take exit # 379/Kennedy Rd. northbound. Turn west on Finch Ave. and north on Birchmount Rd.

CORONATION PARK

Water playground with a view

The water sprays spurting out of the ground and out of posts planted in the pavement, wet the children playing on spring-mounted miniature horses and on the seesaw. Facing them, there's a pebble beach with Lake Ontario in the background, as far as the eye can see. No wonder a wise Mom had recommended this Oakville park to me!

I was seduced by the site's setup and by the choice of things to do. The spray pad is enclosed inside a fence, and is surrounded by a lawn and beautiful, tall trees with peculiar knots.

The children spent as much time refreshing themselves under the water sprays as they did inventing games with the thousands of plump pebbles in the shade of wide trees.

The large toy truck we brought along worked well. A skipping stones contest kept us busy and I'm still congratulating myself for the pebble I threw that skipped five times.

A paved trail leads to the pebble beach. A very nice playground is located on the premises. It includes two stimulating structures, one of them wooden with a hanging bridge and a tunnel-shaped slide. They have also added three small climbing walls, perfect for small kids.

TIPS (fun for 2 years +)
• More about the **Oakville Waterfront Festival** in June on p. 88.
• A funny tradition in Coronation Park is the annual **New Year's Day Polar Bear Dip** involving over 400 dippers and some 5,000 spectators to raise money for World Vision. For details, see www.polarbeardip.ca or call (905) 609-0218.
• See **Fire Hall** and **Wimpy's Diner** on pp. 434-435.

NEARBY ATTRACTIONS
Rattray Marsh (5-min.)..................p. 318
Shell Skate Park (5-min.).............p. 371

Town of Oakville
• Oakville
(905) 845-6601
www.oakville.ca

J-7 West of Toronto 30-min.

 Schedule: Open year-round.
Admission: FREE.
 Directions: From QEW West, take exit #116/Dorval Dr. southbound, turn west on Lakeshore Rd.

AGINCOURT LEISURE POOL

Under the palm trees

We often crave turquoise water and palm trees. The Agincourt Recreation Centre pool offers an innovative alternative. It includes aqua-coloured water, water slides, an adjoining Jacuzzi, a waterside restaurant and... coconut trees as a bonus!

As soon as we went in, the aquatic complex's originality, revealed by wide bay windows, caught my little one's admiring eye and made him walk towards the admission counter, wriggling with impatience.

It wasn't long before my son and other little pirates launched an attack on the fun, ship-wreck-shaped waterslide. It is ingeniously sheltered under four towering coconut trees, whose fruit fill up with water before dumping it over our heads.

Behind the wading pool is the small, intermediate pool, perfect for introducing children to swimming.

Farther to the right, swimmers 48 inches and over are going down the gigantic, spiral-shaped waterslide into a small pool lined with tall palm trees. They are greeted with a loud SPLASH!

To the left, adults can soak in the warm water of the Jacuzzi, reserved for bathers aged 12 years and up. Nearby, there's a sauna.

Tables are especially set up for swimmers in their bathing suits, overlooking palm trees and the pool area. They can order off the counter from the adjacent **Country Style** concession! When we visited, the illusion of being down South would have been perfect if observers hadn't been standing on the other side of the bay window, wearing their winter coats!

TIPS (fun for all ages)
• Bring your own lock if you wish to use the changing room lockers.
• The slide is open during the programs: Recreational Swim, Family Swim and Youth Swim (reserved for 11 to 17 years old). Call for the schedule of the day.
• The Parent and Tot program is reserved for adults accompanying children 6 years and under. It is usually less crowded.
• The **Country Style** is usually open on Saturdays, and daily in July and August. Call (416) 899-5841 for details.
• **Birchmount Pool** is similar with huge slide and tables by the pool. It is located at 93 Birchmount Road, call (416) 396-4311 for information.

DOUGLAS SNOW CENTRE

Me Tarzan

I don't know of any other public pool with a Tarzan rope everyone can use to swing into the air before bombing into the water. A big hit? You can say that again!

What a beautiful pool! O.K., I admit I had special permission to take pictures when leisure swim time was over, so don't go dreaming your family will have the pool all to itself. It will be you and dozens of other happy swimmers.

The huge pool offers a wide section with beach-like access, perfect for younger kids, and a profusion of water toys at your disposal in a separate room (you just need to ask the staff). They even have duck decoys!

Bigger kids will spend their time at the Tarzan rope, the long, bumpy white slide and the huge flume slide with a few loops. The Tarzan rope is, of course, above deep water but those who use the two slides land in the shallow section.

Only those who pass a deep-end test will be allowed to use the flume slide. Both slide and Tarzan rope are available during Recreational Swim.

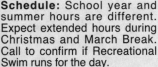

| **Douglas Snow Aquatic Centre** • North York (416) 395-7585 www.toronto.ca | **H-10 North** of downtown 40-min. |

  Schedule: School year and summer hours are different. Expect extended hours during Christmas and March Break. Call to confirm if Recreational Swim runs for the day.

 Admission: FREE (fees for lane swim).

 Directions: 5100 Yonge St., North York. Turn west on North York Blvd. (north of Sheppard). The pool is at the corner of Beecroft Rd. (public parking).

RIVER GROVE AQUATICS

Lighten up!

The nature is so nicely framed by the glassed wall and the whole architecture of the pool that one would think they are swimming inside the McMichael Canadian Art Collection building!

Very high wooden ceiling, smooth arches and huge bay windows catch the daylight, beautifully filtered by the tall trees. Quite a setting for a community pool! Kids just love the triple loop red slide ending in shallow water and the blue one in the deeper end. Most of the pool is actually shallow. Balls, floaters and life jackets are provided. A big whirlpool completes the experience. A large mezzanine on the second floor allows parents to watch their kids.

There are vending machines on site. The **Culham Trail** running along the **Credit River** is accessible from the back of the community centre (see p. 350).

| **River Grove Community Centre** • Mississauga (905) 615-4780 (pool) www.mississauga.ca | **I-8 N-W** of Toronto 35-min. |

 Schedule: School year and summer hours are different. Expect extended hours during Christmas and March Break. Call the pool number to confirm if Family and Fun Swim programs run for the day (when the slide is open).

Admission: $3.75/person, $9.75/family of 5.

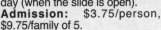 **Directions:** 5800 River Grove Ave., Mississauga. From the QEW, take exit #130/Mississauga Rd. North. Turn east on Main St. (in Streetsville), it becomes Bristol Rd. Turn north on River Grove Ave.

THE WAVE POOL

Courtesy of The Wave Pool

Surf's up!

I had often heard of the Richmond Hill Wave Pool: a huge indoor pool with 4-foot-high waves. I was in no hurry to go there with my son. Every time I thought of it, I imagined a heavy swell filled with excited kids who would menace my little tadpole.

How far I was from the truth! Not only is this aquatic complex very secure and exciting for little ones, it's as much fun for older kids.

The spacious Wave Pool aquatic complex forms a harmonious whole, bathed by natural light. Funny fish decorate the ceiling.

A few tables covered with umbrellas and lined with palm trees are aligned near the bay window. The centre supplies toys and life jackets.

With the irregular shape, the wave

pool looks like a shallow bay you go into gradually, just like at the beach. Over a large 5,000 sq. ft. area, the water doesn't go higher than our knees. In this shallow section, the waves are calm, and have the perfect level of turbulence to entertain young children.

The big waves sweep across the rest of the pool. The 160-foot-long waterslide is reserved for users at least 48 inches high.

What a surprise! Beside the wave pool is a superb whirlpool delighting young and old alike. It is 70 cms deep and it is kept at a temperature of 96 degrees F.

TIPS (fun for all ages)

• Services offered at the pool include a sauna, one changing room for families and lockers for 25¢ and $1.
• There's no snack bar on the premises. You can eat your own lunch on the glassed-in mezzanine equipped with tables and vending machines.

NEARBY ATTRACTIONS

The Wave Pool • Richmond Hill **(905) 508-9283** www.richmondhill.ca	**H-10** **North** **of Toronto** **40-min.**

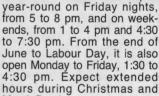

Schedule: Wave swim is open year-round on Friday nights, from 5 to 8 pm, and on weekends, from 1 to 4 pm and 4:30 to 7:30 pm. From the end of June to Labour Day, it is also open Monday to Friday, 1:30 to 4:30 pm. Expect extended hours during Christmas and March Break.
Admission: $6/16-54 years, $3.50/3-15 years and seniors, $13.25/family of 5, FREE for children 2 years and under (price for one period, those who want to go swimming twice in the same day need to repay their admission fee).
Directions: 5 Hopkins St., Richmond Hill. From Yonge St., turn west on Major Mackenzie Dr., south on Arnold Cr., then east on Hopkins St.

PETTICOAT CREEK C. A.

Not a petty pool!

The Petticoat Creek wading pool is huge and nicely surrounded by green lawn and small trees! It took me over 350 full steps to circumnavigate the edge of this blue wading pool.

We found ourselves a spot in the shade of a coniferous tree and we watched our kids run wildly into the shallow water. Some lines drawn at the bottom of the pool mark the vast shallow area. There's enough water to allow bigger kids to swim in the centre of the pool (where I had water below the shoulders).

Petticoat Creek is located on the shores of Lake Ontario. Outside the fenced pool area are picnic tables and a trail leading to the lakeshore below the bluffs. The view from above is great, however, don't go expecting a fabulous shoreline.

TIPS (fun for 2 years +)

• The pool's water isn't heated and remains quite cool in the deeper areas. The sun warms up the shallow section by the afternoon. If you think of bringing along some water toys, it will be heaven for the kids.
• There are no railings at the edge of the cliff facing Lake Ontario along the Waterfront Trail.
• There are changing rooms and a snack bar on the premises.
• There are similar football field sized pools in **Bronte Creek** (p. 336) and **Earl Rowe** (p. 285) **Provincial Parks**.
• I have not visited them but you'll find more of those huge pools under the Grand River Authority, both including **campgrounds**. **Byng Island Conservation Area** is located near Dunnville. Its pool is deep enough in the middle for diving; (905) 774-5755. **Brant Conservation Area** is in Brantford; (519) 752-2040.

Petticoat Creek Conservation Area • Pickering (416) 661-6600, ext 5203 or (905) 509-1534 (weather conditions) www.trca.on.ca.	I-12 **East** of Toronto 35-min.

 Schedule: Park is open from mid-May to Labour Day, 9 am to dusk. Pool opens early June to Labour Day, 10 am to 7 pm.
Admission: Maximum $10 per vehicle, around $3/person to use the pool.
Directions: From Hwy 401 East, take exit #394/Whites Rd. southbound.

NEARBY ATTRACTIONS

TORONTO SLOPES

Off the beaten tracks

When snow finally graces our city, it's time to run to the slopes.

Glen Manor Drive

After a hearty brunch on Queen Street East in the Beaches, I recommend you drive to Glen Manor Drive, and continue the day at **Glen Stewart Ravine** (p. 344). On the north side of Queen Street, Glen Manor divides in two at the beginning of the ravine.

There, an ice rink has been installed (somewhat bumpy when we visited).

A little farther, the ravine deepens and the two facing slopes are sufficiently steep, despite their lack of length, to entertain kids of all ages.

From the top of the stairs at the entrance to the ravine, you can catch a lovely view of the area and the gorgeous residences and mature trees that overlook the slopes. Read about **Caroling in the Park** on p. 344.

Riverdale Park East & West

On a different scale, Toronto's most challenging slope sits at **Riverdale Park**, west of Broadview Avenue. It is quite broad, steep and long, and offers a stunning view of downtown Toronto's skyline.

Hang on to your hats though if the slopes are even just slightly icy! In fact, it is best to avoid the area altogether when the shiny crust covers the slopes, as it becomes nearly impossible to climb back up.

The western face of Riverdale Park, on the west side of the Don Valley Pkwy, is not as broad but is equally fun and challenging. Plus, it includes shorter sections, better for younger kids. The **Riverdale Farm** is a 5-minute walk from this slope (see p. 45).

Lawrence Park Ravine

Beautiful **Lawrence Park** (see above picture) is hyperbolic-shaped, free of obstacles in the middle and surrounded by mature trees.

You can access the slope from all sides. The height varies so the site is suitable for different age groups. Bigger kids usually manage to create huge bumps to challenge themselves on the slope adjacent to Yonge Street.

Christie Pits Park

Snow was pretty much gone on the steep slope next to the rink but I still could see the toboggan tracks. This hill must be a thrill for big kids, but beware of the poles 15 metres apart at the bottom of the hill. This is not where most people go.

Rather, they will use the wide slope near the corner of Bloor and Crawford (see pictures below). The youngsters go down a gentle slope in front of the playground.

There are snack machines in the Christie Pits Centre and the rink might be open for free skating when you are visiting so bring the skates.

TIPS (fun for 3 years +)

• You will easily find parking on Glen Manor Drive along the park of the same name, as well as on Broadview Avenue along **Riverdale Park**.

• **Riverdale** and **Glen Manor Parks** have no washroom facilities. **Christie Pits** does. **Lawrence Park** visitors could use the George H. Locke Library Branch (at the corner of Lawrence Ave. and Yonge St.) where kids could warm up as they choose some books to take back home.

Toronto slopes
(416) 392-1111
www.toronto.ca

Schedule: Weather permitting.
Admission: FREE.
Directions:
Riverdale Park: On Broadview Ave., between Danforth Ave. and Gerrard St.
Glen Manor Park: North of Queen St. East, between Glen Manor Dr. East and West, five blocks east of Kew Gardens.
Christie Pits Park: 779 Crawford St. The slope is just north of Bloor St., between Christie and Crawford Streets. Rink: (416) 392-0745.
Lawrence Park Ravine: South of Lawrence Ave., at the southeast corner of Yonge St. and Weybourne Cr.

SIR WINSTON CHURCHILL PARK

Prime location!

The snowy slope is endlessly winding down. When I looked at it from the bottom of the hill, I was impressed by the white panorama stretching high in front of me. That's a long and wide slope for the energetic ones.

When I checked this slope, I did not have my young inspectors with me but I saw a whole class with their teacher joyfully walking from their local elementary school, armed with toboggans.

The upper part of the hill is blocked with fences. The lower section is shorter and less steep on the eastern side, more suitable for younger kids. From wherev-

er you attack the slope, it is so long, the snow will slow you to a stop before you can hit anything. On the down side, kids will need to take a good walk back up the hill. Not for the lazy ones!

The small Roycroft Wet Forest lays at the bottom of the hill. In other seasons, it offers quite a change of scenery from the big city: a 5-minute walk amidst native shrubs and wildflowers and tall trees.

Under the bridge taking Spadina over the ravine, I discovered stone stairs leading to Russell Hill Drive. When my daughter was exploring them, in the middle of the summer when it was invaded by plants, it looked like she was climbing the ruins of an ancient Mayan city.

TIPS (fun for 3 years +)
• A hot chocolate in the café of the **Forest Hill Market**, the Loblaws on St. Clair just west of Spadina, is the perfect way to start or finish this tobogganing outing (see p. 428). The grocery store offers plenty of parking (to its loyal customers) and you can catch a 5-minute trail leading to the park in front of it.
• Also check the ice-cream parlour **Dutch's**, open year-round, on p. 433.

NEARBY ATTRACTIONS
Casa Loma (5-min.).....................p. 114

Sir Winston Churchill Park
(416) 392-1111
www.toronto.ca

I-10 North of downtown **25-min.**

Schedule: Open year-round.
Admission: FREE.
Directions: At the southeast corner of St. Clair Ave. West and Spadina Rd., in Toronto. There's street parking on Ardwold Gate just south of the park.

CENTENNIAL PARK

Off the record

At Centennial Park, there's the designated tobogganing area, and then there's the unofficial one where a sign, at the bottom of the hill, reads: "No hang-gliding or parasailing permitted." You get the picture.

When you, along with fifty other people, use the unofficial slope, you do so at your own risk. The hill is really steep, lasts a long stretch, and has a great panorama at the top.

The official hill is located next to the parking lot accessible from Eglinton Avenue. The slope is not steep but it goes down forever (which means parents will feel they are climbing up the hill forever with their younger child's toboggan in tow). It is lots of fun for the young crowd with a good toboggan.

TIPS (fun for 3 years +)
- See skiing at **Centennial** on p. 376.
- It is better to go on the steep hill only with children old enough to know better than to take their time at the bottom of the hill. You don't want your

child to be hit by a full-speed teenager on a tube!
- There is a greenhouse in Centennial Park, located by the parking lot closer to Rathburn Road. It offers a nice contrast to winter, with colourful flowers, cactus, fish and turtles in a pond. An exotic way to end the outing.
- The outdoor pond in the park is often icy enough to allow people (willing enough to shovel) to skate on it.

NEARBY ATTRACTIONS
Fantasy Fair (15-min.)....................p. 26

Centennial Park
· Etobicoke
(416) 392-1111
www.toronto.ca

| I-9 N-W of downtown 30-min. |

Schedule: Open year-round.
Admission: FREE.
Directions: Centennial Park Blvd., Etobicoke. Take Hwy 427 North, exit Rathburn Rd. westbound, turn north on Centennial Park Blvd. The official hill is at the southeast corner of Centennial Park Blvd. and Eglinton Ave.

RICHMOND HILL LIBRARY

One for the books

The slope by the Richmond Hill Library is long, moderately steep and... facing Atkinson Street.

Dare-devils can't resist the part of the hill where big bumps give enough speed to require them to "put on the brakes" before they reach the street.

You will want the younger ones to use the safer slope closer to the parking lot. Inside the Library, a café sells great hot chocolate and coffee to warm up. There are washrooms.

See **The Wave Pool** on p. 384.

Richmond Hill Central Library	H-10 North of Toronto 20-30 min.

· Richmond Hill
(905) 884-9288 (library)
www.richmondhill.ca

Schedule: Weather permitting.
Admission: FREE.
Direction: 1 Atkinson St., Richmond Hill. From Hwy 404 North, take exit #31/Major Mackenzie Dr. westbound. The hill is south of the Library (at the corner of Yonge).

APPLEBY COLLEGE

This hill gets an A+

When we saw this slope as we were driving by on Lakeshore, we just had to join the fun. It was wide and long. Trees were surrounding it and we could admire the blue lake on the horizon.

This gorgeous spot certainly is a favourite in Oakville, judging by the dozens of local families with kids of all ages enjoying it. But it's wide enough that everybody spreads nicely. There's a large visitor's parking lot on the college's grounds. During the weekend, we could even park closer to the hill, on the western part of the school.

A one-minute drive away to the east, on the prettiest strip of Lakeshore Road in Old Oakville, there are lots of nice cafés selling hot chocolate, to top off the outing.

See **Wimpy's Diner** or **Fire Hall** restaurants on pp. 434-435.

Appleby College	J-7 West of Toronto 35-min.

· Oakville

Schedule: Open year-round (use at your own risk).
Admission: FREE.
Directions: Take QEW, exit at Dorval Dr. southbound, turn west on Rebecca St., then south on Suffolk. Appleby College's entrance is just across Lakeshore Rd. West.

ROUGE PARK

Unofficial fun

"Now I understand why there are so many broken toboggans along the slope!" comments my 7-year-old, rubbing his bottom after his first try from the top of the very steep hill.

In the midst of winter, everybody walks over the frozen (shallow) river to get to the hill located next to the parking lot off Twyn Rivers Drive in Rouge Park.

Trees buffer the noise of the city. Two hills are separated by a line of trees. One has to be in good shape to walk up the steep slope.

From above, it is a real pleasure to admire the forest panorama and to hear the laughter of the families sliding down the unofficial slope (at their own risks, I might add). Many teenagers go down on their snowboards.

For the next two hours, my son and his friend will feel more comfortable sticking to the lower half of the hill.

TIPS (fun for 6 years +)

- More about the **Rouge Park** trails near Twyn Rivers Drive on p. 348.
- There are no washrooms on site.

NEARBY ATTRACTIONS
Toronto Zoo (5-min.).....................p. 46

Rouge Park
· Scarborough
(416) 392-1111
www.toronto.ca

I-12
N-E
of downtown
5-min.

Schedule: Open year-round.
Admission: FREE.
Directions: From Hwy 401 East, take exit #389/Meadowvale Rd. northbound (keep to the right lanes as soon as you reach Morningside to catch this exit), turn east on Sheppard Ave. and take the first fork to the left, Twyn Rivers Dr. (easy to miss when you are driving eastbound on Sheppard). You'll see a parking lot on your right.

ALBION HILLS C. A.

Panoramic tobogganing

It took us 40 minutes to reach Albion Hills, where I had been assured we'd find great tobogganing hills. Indeed, a long and wonderful slope awaited us, sitting against a breathtaking panorama! It promised an even acceleration without being too risky, and I know my little appraiser would have loved it... had I been able to wake him up! Kiddies' naps and snow conditions are undoubtedly the two unpredictables for family outings!

Our son did not bat an eye for the two hours of our visit but we tested the site ourselves. The slope's incline was long enough to provide lots of excitement, and not too steep to make the climb back unpleasant.

TIPS (fun for 3 years +)
• More about **Albion Hills Conservation Area** during the summer on p. 278.
• When Toronto's snow begins to melt, call Albion Hills to enquire about snow conditions, as the tobogganing season is often prolonged for another few weeks in that region.
• You can park your car not far from the centre's admission booth, close to a sign indicating "tobogganing". The slope is located on the left. Then drive to the ski chalet (follow the signs), where you will find washrooms, a snack bar, and ski rentals. They rent toboggans for $5!

The day we visited, while Toronto's tobogganing hills were icy at best, those at Albion Hills boasted a lovely coat of fresh snow, completely enjoyable for sliding afficionados, perfect for cross-country skiers, many of whom passed us with beaming smiles!

Albion Hills Conservation Area · Caledon (416) 661-6600, ext. 5203 or (905) 880-0227 www.trca.on.ca	C-2 N-W of Toronto 45-min.

 Schedule: Open year-round from 9 am to dusk.
Admission: $4/adults, $3/seniors, $2/children 5-14, FREE 4 years and under (more than double this price to use the cross-country trails).
Directions: From Hwy 400 North, take exit #55/Hwy 9 westbound. Turn south on Hwy 50 and follow the signs.

NEARBY ATTRACTIONS
Kortright Centre (25-min.)............p. 332

BRONTE CREEK PROVINCIAL PARK

Hill addiction

Each time we go tobog-ganing, it's the same story. At the top of the hill, our little adrenaline addict smiles with antici-pation, then lets out a long happy shout as he toboggans down. At the end of the descent, he bursts out with the laugh of victory, only to be towed back up (thanks to the private chairlift he finds in his stamina-filled daddy), again and again, happy to relive the experience.

Bronte Creek Park is a great summer outing. In the winter time however, our attention shifts from the big pool to the large, well-maintained ice rink.

The rink's natural surroundings are quite pleasing.

There is a wide path climbing to the top of a hill overlooking the park. Its two faces hold much to be enjoyed by young toboggan fans. The view is far-reaching from both sides of the hill, offering ath-letes an unusually rare panorama.

TIPS (fun for 3 years +)
• More about **Bronte Creek** on p. 336.
• Skate and cross-country ski rental services are available.
• A washroom and small snack bar are available close to the rink. Wash-rooms are also available next to the visi-tor centre.

NEARBY ATTRACTIONS
Festival of Lights (20-min.)...........p. 201
Riverview Park (10-min.)..............p. 374

You can access these activities via the park's parking lot D.

After the winter sports, I sug-gest you drive to parking lot C, and walk to the farm's playground in a barn and its area with various farm animals. I strongly recommend you dress warmly as the barn is not heat-ed in winter time. On the other hand, they've added a heated room within the barn for the parents patiently waiting for their kids to be done.

Spruce Farm, the visitor centre and animal barns are open in winter.

Bronte Creek Provincial Park · Burlington (905) 827-6911 www.ontarioparks.com	E-2 West of Toronto 35-min.

Schedule: Open year-round from 8 am to dusk. Most activi-ties are offered on weekends only during the fall, winter and spring.
Admission: $4/adults, $3/seniors, $2/4-17 years, FREE 3 years and under, maximum $12 per vehicle.
Directions: From QEW West, take exit #109/Burloak Rd. northbound and fol-low signs.

ELORA GORGE C. A.

For your inner child

For years I have noticed people floating down the river on innertubes as I watched from above the trail at Elora Gorge. I always thought they were just marginal people, looking for adventure and braving the natural elements on their own. I was wrong... There is actually a whole crowd of them, seeking thrills, with the full consent of the conservation authority's administration.

Which explained the sign "Tubing Sold Out" at the gate when we got to Elora Gorge at 1 pm on a Saturday, planning to try out tubing ourselves. (As I found out later on, there was a way out of this disappointing situation.)

First, let's say that tubing down this river is not as adventurous as it seems from above. My 9-year-old thought the one-hour long descent did not offer enough action as real whirlpools formed only in three spots (maybe more earlier in the season). Still, it beats floating down the lazy river in any water park.

Adults really enjoy the relaxing sight-seeing, offering a totally different view of the cliffs.

Children 42 inches tall and over are allowed to ride and I have seen parents on their tube with a child on their laps.

The equipment consists of a helmet (hockey style), a vest and a tube. You can bring your own, but it can be rented at the beach house. Unfortunately, the activity is quite popular on hot summer weekends when tubes can be sold out by 9 am!

We waited over an hour before some tubes became available. My patient husband spent the time in the line-up, a good book in one hand and a sandwich in the other, while we swam in the small lake by the beach house.

of greenery closely frame the river. The water is cold but the current is really slow at this point so it offer a great spot to swim for those who are just accompanying... Unless they want to rush back to the trail to take a picture when their friends' tubes pass under the bridge where the cliffs reach a height of 70 feet.

Once you have your equipment, you can catch the school bus serving as a shuttle from the beach house to the launching area. Instead, we chose to drive following the tubing signs along the park's road. We easily found a parking spot and the opening through the bush to the trail leading down the river (also indicated by a little sign). It was hilarious to follow the line of gigantic black tubes through the woods.

The section of the river where everyone gets in the water is simply gorgeous! High walls of rocks with splashes

TIPS (fun for 5 years +)

• BEWARE! During periods of high water flow, water tubing could be cancelled. Call for the current conditions.

• Some farms in the vicinity announce tubes for sale, knowing about the limited number of tubes for rent at the park. Tubes generally sell for $15, with $5 back if you return them. When we were visiting, the beach house allowed people to use their air pump to put air into their own tubes.

• The tubes are huge! Kids under 9 will hardly fit on top of them. We could only fit one in our trunk and I had to wear the other one around my waste inside our 4 X 4. Bring bungee cords to creatively tie them on to the roof.

• Wear shoes while tubing, to prevent your feet from scratching against the rocks. The segment of trail leading to the river is lined with slippery rocks. Flip-flops beware!

• Bring a waterproof camera for some amazing pictures as you go down.

• This conservation area includes 550 **campsites**, some nicely secluded.

• There's a snack bar at the beach house.

Elora Gorge Conservation Area
· Elora
D-1 West of Toronto 65-min.

(519) 846-9742
1-866-668-2267 (camp reservation)
www.grandriver.ca

Schedule: Open 7 days, from end of April to mid-October, from 8 am to dusk.
Admission: $4/adults, $2.50/5-14 years, FREE 5 years and under.
Directions: From Hwy 401 West, take exit #295/Hwy 6 northbound, then follow County Rd. 7 to Elora. Turn left at the first light on County Rd. 21. Elora Gorge is on the right.

General tips about Time travel:

- All these places involve staff members or volunteers dressed in period costumes to play the part.
- You too can dress up! It will add to the experience and you'll get a good reaction from the staff, volunteers and other visitors.

TIME TRAVEL

See **Crawford Lake** on p. 410.

MEDIEVAL TIMES

"A thousand years ago…"

"Is that real metal?" asked my son, pointing towards the spear held by the knight greeting us. With just enough authority, the guard scraped the blade on the stone wall. Gritting our teeth, we concluded that the metal was definitely genuine. "Mi'lady, may I help you?" asked the ticket office attendant, before showing us the way to the table where we would all be crowned.

We found ourselves inside the "castle" antechamber, in front of a camera, alongside a count and countess (we were then pushed gently towards the next activities). During the meal, the photo they took was presented to us, which we are free to purchase. It did appeal to us, with its medieval-style frame and our hosts' superb costumes!

Inside, the 110,000 sq. ft. space has been turned into a dark, 11th Century castle, complete with coats of arms and murals depicting chivalry scenes.

To the right of the grand hall, the stables are equipped with windows allowing us to admire the stallions with braided manes. On the other side, royal thrones are surrounded by suits of armour. With great pomp, those who pay an extra fee are knighted during a short ceremony.

We attended an afternoon presentation. At around 3:45 pm, the master of ceremonies, to the sound of genuine resounding trumpets, invited us to enter the 1350-seat banquet hall. Wearing yellow crowns, the colour of the knight that we would be rooting for, we headed for the tables bearing the same colour.

Over the sand-covered arena, powerful spotlights projected an entertaining ballet of coloured lights on a smoke screen. This captivated us until the show began.

We see an act featu-

ring well-trained horses. Then, the handsome, long-haired equestrian warriors were introduced. Guests in each section were greeting their knight as noisily as possible. Everyone burst out laughing when the master of ceremonies described the people greeting the green knight as "scum" from the bad part of town, invited only thanks to the king's great generosity.

In the cheering department, we could not manage to outdo the blue section, completely filled by a group of friends, who encouraged each other to produce a happy clamour.

The knights confronted each other at games of skill, and the queen rewarded the best with a flower, which they promptly threw at a beauty sitting in the audience.

At around 4:40 pm, costumed waiters invaded the field, armed with chicken-covered trays. "You will love the taste of baby dragon!" our waiter confided to my incredulous son. We were also served spareribs, followed by coffee and dessert.

The story line has changed since my last visit but it remains the justification for games, joust and a tournament to choose a new champion. In the former version, the champion was needed to fight the revengeful son of an enemy killed by the king. Now, it's the king himself who's seeking revenge for his brother's death.

When the knights fought each other in mortal combats (what a waste!) to determine the champion, my son very nearly climbed on his chair to better cheer for our yellow knight.

"Is he really dead?" anxiously inquired my young humanist when our knight collapses on the floor after a fatal blow.

In the darkness, real sparks were flying from swords clashing together.

Photos: Courtesy of Medieval Times

I must say that the fights resembled a choreography, which had to be well orchestrated! It is obvious that the well trained actors could easily suffer serious injuries while manipulating the really heavy weapons.

When the final confrontation took place between the champion and his enemy, *Carmina Burana* was thundering as a musical background. I was told the new musical core of the new version is even more dramatic. Expect a grande finale!

At 5:45 pm, when we returned to the hall, we got down on the dance floor to the beat of non-medieval music!

Despite the fact that Medieval Times is an expensive outing (even more so with all the extras that can be purchased), the experience is worth the trip, thanks to dynamic actors and a very entertaining show.

TIPS (fun for 6 years +)

• I recommend avoiding the small dungeon with an exhibit of reproductions of medieval torture instruments. Accompanied by graphic drawings, these apparatus bear witness to horrors very difficult to explain to children. After a fabulous show, visiting this dungeon left a bitter taste in my mouth.

• The gift shop area is chock-full of varied "medieval" goods, from small accessories for children priced at $7 to metal swords going for more than $500.

• You can print a rebate coupon from the Medieval Times web site. They also often offer interesting specials during **March Break**, Mother or Father's Day and other such occasions.

• The meal is served with soft drinks or water and we eat with our fingers. You will eat to your heart's content, but do not expect a gastronomic feast. (Alcoholic beverages are also available for an additional cost.)

NEARBY ATTRACTIONS

Medieval Times (416) 260-1234 1-888-935-6878 www.medievaltimes.com	**I-9** **Downtown** **Toronto** **10-min.**

 Schedule: Open year-round, Wednesday to Sunday. Usually on Wednesdays and Thursdays at 7 pm, Fridays and Saturdays at 7:30 pm, Sundays at 3:30 pm. Call to find out about additional shows or any change in the schedule.

Admission: (tax not included) Show is $60/adults, $42/12 years and under. Parking fees vary throughout the year. You can upgrade your ticket for $8. The upgrade includes preferred seating, cheering banner and commemorative program.

Directions: Medieval Times building is on the west end side of Exhibition Place, Toronto. Take Lake Shore Blvd., go north on Strachan Ave. There is a parking lot right next to the building.

HISTORIC FORT YORK

Kids hold the fort

Little soldiers learn how to hold the wooden rifle, to walk in step, to present arms and to fire at the order of a lenient officer. Giggles are guaranteed; bring out your cameras!

When they discover the historical and archaeological wealth of this Fort, Torontonians are surprised, as they've been passing by for years without noticing it. Nestled between buildings and highways, Fort York is in fact, one of Toronto's well kept secrets.

On this site, the City of Toronto, initially named Fort York, was founded in 1793, following the demise of the French Fort Rouillé around 1750.

Historic Fort York really comes to life in July and August with its daily historic military demonstrations of music, drill and artillery, all performed by costumed employees. You're also treated to an historic tasting in the kitchens.

You can explore the basement of the Officers' Brick Barracks, built in 1815. More than 12,000 artefacts were found during the archaeological digs performed there from 1987 to 1990.

The Blue Barracks houses the military museum full of arms and uniforms from different times.

TIPS (fun for 4 years +)

• Fort York's favourite activity for children, the drill, is only offered during special events. Dates to remember: **Victoria Day**, **Canada Day** and **Simcoe Day**, when they usually offer special activities.

• During the **March Break**, Fort York is very active with the "Time Machine" event for children 10 years and under (also including a kid's drill).

• Fort York usually offers one battle re-enactment during the year. Call to confirm dates. For more **battle re-enactments**, read tips section for **Black Creek Pioneer Village** (p. 404), **Battle of Stoney Creek** (p. 412), **Westfield Heritage Village** (p. 414), **Discovery Harbour** (p. 418) or **Fanshawe Pioneer Village** (p. 421).

NEARBY ATTRACTIONS

Historic Fort York
(416) 392-6907
or (416) 338-3888 (events)
www.toronto.ca

I-9
Downtown Toronto
10-min.

    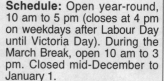

Schedule: Open year-round, 10 am to 5 pm (closes at 4 pm on weekdays after Labour Day until Victoria Day). During the March Break, open 10 am to 3 pm. Closed mid-December to January 1.

Admission: $6/adults, $3.25/seniors and students, $3/6-12 years, FREE 5 years and under (slightly higher rates during the March Break). Parking is FREE.

Directions: At the end of Garrison Rd., Toronto. Take Lake Shore Blvd., go north on Strachan Ave., east on Fleet St.

COLBORNE LODGE

Easter traditions

Last spring when we visited High Park, several geese were walking over the pond ice and kids warmed up in the gorgeous nearby playground. The year before, the sun had been warm enough to melt the little chocolate eggs fallen from the kids' baskets on their way back from the egg hunt. Easter time is a tricky time of the year but one sure thing during this period is the Easter fun at Colborne Lodge.

Colborne Lodge was built in 1837 and still contains many of the original artifacts, but the adults better appreciate this. The best time to visit the historic museum is around Easter, for their traditional Easter activities.

First, there's the **Spring Egg Fun Day** on Palm Sunday, one week prior to Easter. The event's activities vary from one year to the next, depending on the volunteers involved. You can always count on egg dyeing in the lodge's kitchen, for a small fee, and chocolate egg hunts divided by age group in and around the Children's Garden by the lodge.

The **Easter Traditions** activities are usually offered on a few consecutive weekends around Easter time. The event has been so popular lately that, at the time of print, they were reconsidering the concept to better accommodate visitors next time. It will definitely include egg dyeing in the historic kitchen, using natural vegetable dye, but you will have to call for the latest information on the concept, dates and costs.

TIPS (fun for 3 years +)
- See **High Park** on p. 322.
- During **Easter** time, you can enter the park from High Park Blvd. off Parkside Rd. and park by the animal pens. An unofficial trail leads up the hill to Colborne Lodge. Anytime of the year, you can also park by Grenadier restaurant and take a 5-min. walk to the lodge.
- During **Christmas** time, you can pre-register for $12.50 for half-day Christmas trimming activities. In February, they offer very popular Family Baking half-day classes ($15/person, pre-registration required).

NEARBY ATTRACTIONS
All Fired Up (10-min.)....................p. 424

Colborne Lodge
(416) 392-6916
www.toronto.ca/culture

**I-9
West
of downtown
15-min.**

 Schedule: Open weekends only from January through April. Open Tuesday to Sunday during March Break and from May through December, noon to 4 pm (closes at 5 pm May to September and at 3 pm on Christmas and New Year's Eves). Closed on Mondays. Spring Egg Fun Day is always on the Sunday before Easter, usually noon to 3 pm).

 Admission: $4/adults, $2.75/seniors and students, $2.50/children (a bit more during Christmas time). Spring Fun Day costs around $2/person.

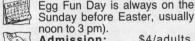 **Directions:** Located in the south end of High Park, see High park's directions on p. 322.

SPADINA STRAWBERRY FESTIVAL

Garden party

It feels like the whole family has been invited to the garden party of very rich relatives. After behaving nicely when visiting the elegant Spadina House, children run wild under the shade of the huge trees to burn off energy. Others stroll with their kites in tow under the indulgent gaze of proper ladies. They have all donned their fancy hats for the occasion.

Spadina House is a gorgeous 19th-century home set on an enormous property by Toronto standards with adjoining gardens.

Only a few hundred very privileged guests could rate doing the same back in 1900 when the Austin family was holding its annual private strawberry social.

Now, many line up to get refreshments and a piece of strawberry shortcake drowned in whipped cream.

Old-fashioned activities are offered during the event: tossing games, stilt walking, shaker making and ice cream making demonstrations.

A more ambitious craft activity was taking place in the basement when we visited: kite making presented by the Children's Own Museum. Live musicians entertained children on the lawn.

There's no better time to visit Spadina House... with kids.

TIPS (fun for 4 years +)

• I recommend you buy your food or refreshment tickets as soon as you get in. There's a line-up to buy tickets and another one to actually get the food. Strawberry Shortcakes sell out before the end of the event! Consider bringing a blanket to sit on the grass for the picnic.

• Another Strawberry Social takes place in Mississauga at the **Benares Historic House**, normally on the same date, and this event is free. The house, restored to the 1918 period, was home to four generations of Benares and is furnished with original family possessions. It is located at 1507 Clarkson Road North, between QEW and Lakeshore West. Call (905) 822-1569 or check www.museumsofmississauga.com.

Spadina Museum
(416) 392-6910
www.toronto.ca

I-10
North
of downtown
20-min.

Schedule: The Strawberry Festival is usually held on the third or last Sunday of June, from noon to 4 pm. The museum is open for tours year-round on weekends, noon to 5 pm. Also open Tuesday to Friday from early April through December and March Break, noon to 4 pm.

Admission: The festival's admission is $3/person, FREE for 3 years and under, plus the cost of food. At other times, admission is $6/adults, $4/6-12 years old, FREE under 5 years.

Directions: 285 Spadina Rd., Toronto (located just east of the Casa Loma).

GIBSON HOUSE MUSEUM

Hands-on history

The Gibson House Museum is the historic house offering the most hands-on activities. In the minds of young visitors, the museum's great discovery room for children makes the actual visit to the 1851 house look like a mere bonus.

Our costumed guide looks and sounds like a benevolent grandmother, with all the patience in the world for the children's questions. The Gibson House's staff members and volunteers are used to dealing with young visitors.

We are allowed to touch a few old-fashioned toys, peek into a few bedrooms and stop at the kitchen for a taste of hot cider and a cookie.

Usually, in most other historic houses, once visitors have no more questions for the guide, the visit is over. Here, we head towards the modern-looking discovery room, where the real fun starts for children.

Some fifteen boxes, each bearing a label describing its contents, await us on the shelves. In the "Sheep" box, you'll find real wool kids can glue on a drawing of a sheep and take back home! In the "Rug Braiding" box are strips of fabric, scissors, needles and instructions to create a small rug for a dollhouse.

I loved the quilt puzzles with wooden triangles and quilt designs to reproduce. Then there's the weaving box with materials to create our weaving device from scratch, great drawings to colour and more.

Boys' and girls' clothing and accessories are available next to full mirrors. Beside a beautiful mural are two heavy buckets with a yoke.

Once your children have tried to carry this apparatus, tell them that on a regular day, the Gibson children had to carry 15 buckets for cooking, many more for laundry water or baths, and as drinking water for people or animals. The very idea should make their bed-making, toy-tidying and pet-feeding chores more bearable!

TIPS (fun for 3 years +)
• More free activities on **Canada Day** (including free ice cream) and on **Simcoe Day**.
• On selected days during **March Break** children can register for a $17 full-day activity-filled program, usually involving more hands-on fun in the old kitchen. $10 half-day programs are offered some days during **Christmas** time.

NEARBY ATTRACTIONS

Gibson House Museum
• North York
(416) 395-7432
www.toronto.ca

H-10
North
of downtown
35-min.

Schedule: Open year-round, Tuesday to Sunday, noon to 5 pm (also open on holiday Mondays). Closed to the public in September.
Admission: $3.75/adults, $2.25/seniors and students, $1.75/2-12 years (50¢ more from mid-November to end of Christmas activities).
Directions: 5172 Yonge St., North York (at Park Home Ave., south of Finch Ave., on the west side of Yonge).

BLACK CREEK PIONEER VILLAGE

Sneak in!

Here, the blacksmith hammers hot red iron; there, a weaver hums as she works. Elsewhere, a homemaker in her long dress bustles about in front of her ovens, while the harness maker handcrafts leather articles. This is Black Creek Pioneer Village: a fascinating replica of a small cluster of some 35 houses and businesses of the 1860's.

In fact, Black Creek Pioneer Village satisfies the "voyeur" within each one of us. Here, you can enter anywhere without bothering to knock! (I make sure to point this out to children when we visit.) I found it captivating to watch my young explorer open doors by himself and discover new territories.

Many of the rooms, inside the houses you'll visit, cannot be entered. You may however, view them from the doorway. Thankfully, there is generally an area inside these buildings where you may roam freely and feel as if you are truly in a private house.

If you come with younger children (as I did with my then 3-year-old son), anticipate their attention span will not exceed 15 seconds for a woodworker silently planing down a plank in the making of a barrel, or a weaver calmly working at her loom.

Other details however, will satisfy their curiosity. For instance, there are farm animals in various parts of the site, and after all, the blacksmith makes lots of noise as he hits the red hot iron! We can't forget the treats sold at the old post office!

Every day, you can smell fresh bread baking in the kitchens of the village's Half Way House restaurant.

Not all houses are open daily, it all depends on the volunteers' availability. Sometimes, you may have the chance to listen to a choir in the old church, or you may observe the shoemaker or the broom-maker at work. You never know!

TIPS (fun for 4 years +)
• See **Christmas** activities and **Christmas by the Lamplight** on p. 199.
• Wagon rides are offered during special events only.
• Black Creek Village offers much old-fashioned family fun during special events: Fiddlers' Contest on **Victoria Day**, the Battle of Black Creek (with re-enactment) on Father's Day weekend, and the Pioneer Festival on the second or third weekend of September, the Howling Hootenanny, usually on the weekend prior to **Halloween**, and more.

NEARBY ATTRACTIONS

Black Creek Pioneer Village
• North York
(416) 736-1733
www.trca.on.ca

H-10 North of downtown 35-min.

Schedule: Open only May 1 to December 31, at least from 11 am to 4 pm (extended hours during the summer and some weekends). Call to confirm. **Admission:** (tax not included) $11/adults, $10/ seniors, $7/5-14 years, FREE 4 years and under. Parking is $6.
Directions: See p. 199.

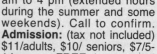

MONTGOMERY'S INN

Tea is served

Some events are more interactive than others at Montgomery's Inn, but you can always count on their tearoom experience to complement your visit to this old Inn, dating from the 1830's.

Most historical buildings that can be visited in the region used to be private houses. The Montgomery family lived and made a living at Montgomery's Inn. The rooms' settings are therefore different than historical houses.

There is a worn-out floor in front of the bar counter, with tables and checkerboards. There's a small ballroom, and guest rooms with many beds (in those days, you rented a place in a bed, not a room!).

We visited during a special program requiring pre-registration during **Christmas**, when crafts and games were organized for young visitors. These might change year to year, but the spirit remains the same.

The kids made New Year's crackers. They created a game from the old days, made out of a button and a string, to take home.

They had fun making a bed (!), rearranging the straw mattress, feather mattress and heavy blankets. They never dared to slip on the itchy wool nightgowns. They tried their hand at old-fashioned games: cup-a-ball, marbles and "traumatropes".

They crunched spices, grated lemon and cinnamon and rolled dough in the kitchen, supervised by a cook in costume. They could not taste the tarts they helped make, because these were to be sold in the tearoom. It became our obvious next stop.

My 3-year-old was thrilled to have her lemonade transferred into a teacup on a plate. The small pastries were delicious. I rediscovered the pleasure of pouring myself some good tea from a teapot.

TIPS (fun for 4 years +)

• Call to find out about special events involving storytelling, usually during **Halloween** and **Christmas** time (advanced registration required, fees apply, call to confirm dates). No drop-in activities during March Break but they offer camps.

• In the tearoom, they serve tea and snacks for $4 per person. On special occasions, they serve seasonal treats (apple or pumpkin pie or other special pastries) for a higher fee.

NEARBY ATTRACTIONS

Montgomery's Inn
· Etobicoke
(416) 394-8113
www.
montgomerysinn.com

**I-9
West
of downtown
35-min.**

Schedule: Open year-round, Tuesday to Sunday, 1 to 4:30 pm (closes at 5 pm on weekends). Closed on Mondays. Tea served from 2 to 4:30 pm.

Admission: $3/adults, $2/ seniors and students, $1/11 and under, $8/family. Tea with pastry is $4/visitor.

Directions: 4709 Dundas St. West, Etobicoke (east of Islington Ave., on the south side of Dundas).

COUNTRY HERITAGE PARK

A close shave!

A big sheep, held firmly in the grip of a farmer, sits, literally, on the cushion of her own wool, ready for "a close shave". As soon as she starts to bleat, the sheep in the pen walk towards her as if offering moral support.

When the newly shaven beast joins them, they all push her away. Really concerned for her well-being, the kids ask why this is. "They don't recognize her odour", explains the farmer. Poor thing!

TIPS (fun for 4 years +)

• You can hop in and out of the tractor ride as much as you want, which turns out to be really handy for the site is huge.

• Activities vary from one year to the next. At the time of print, their calendar of events included a kids' weekend with heritage toys, games and crafts, an Antique Tractor and Toy Show and even an American Civil War re-enactment. Call for specific dates.

• They are also open during the year for some special events. I will have to go back to check out their **Walk to Bethlehem**, a re-enactment of the nativity throughout the site, ending with **Christmas** carols in a barn. It is held on four consecutive days (In 2004: December 3 to 6, from 6:30 to 9 pm). Ask about their **Parade of Lights** in November with tractors decorated with lights, music in the barn and Santa's visit.

• There's a snack bar and a small gift shop on the premises.

It was "Sheep Day" when we showed up at the Country Heritage Park, formerly The Farm Museum (itself formerly the Ontario Agricultural Museum). Around the central pavilion, dogs bark at a herd of sheep during another demonstration.

The kids tire quickly with the slow performance and we head towards the nearby school. A teacher in a long skirt invites us to write with a gray stone on a black slate. We eventually sneak out to catch a tractor ride around the farmstead.

There are some thirty buildings on site. Located in one area of the park, the "Dairy Industry Display", the "All About Apples" barn and the "Steam Power" buildings offer the most interaction. There, my little farmers "drove" a dairy delivery truck, and felt the suction of a milk pump (for cows, of course). They observed the workings of a steam machine, tested a hay bed, pressed and peeled apples the old-fashioned way and pet animals in the small pioneer farm. They were not allowed however, to climb on the antique tractors located in the tractor barn, which was pure torture for my 7-year-old. That's life...

Country Heritage Park	D-2 West of Toronto 45-min.

Country Heritage Park
• Milton
1-888-307-3276
or (905) 878-8151
www.countryheritagepark.com

Schedule: Open to the public weekends only, in July and August, noon to 5 pm.

Admission: (cash only) $7/adults, $6/seniors, $4/6-12 years, FREE 5 years and under, $20/family of 5.

Directions: 8560 Tremaine Rd., Milton. From Hwy 401 West, take exit #320/Hwy 25 northbound. Turn west on Regional Rd. 9, then south on Tremaine Rd.

NEARBY ATTRACTIONS

HALTON REGION MUSEUM

... and surroundings

On my way back from the snow-tubing park located in the Kelso Conservation Area, I decided to check out the museum on site. When I entered the large red barn bearing the museum's name in big letters, I almost turned back right away. Although it seemed like a beautiful banquet room to rent, it didn't look like much to visit. It's a good thing a nice staff member insisted on showing me the place!

TIPS (fun for 4 years +)

• More on **Kelso Beach** on p. 280.
• More on **Glen Eden's Snow Tubing Park** on p. 377.
• The third floor is maintained at a cool temperature to better preserve the artifacts. It offers a great break for the kids to cool down after some time under the sun at the beach. It is open upon request during the museum hours, don't be shy!
• This whole park encompasses 16 km of overlapping trails for hiking and/or mountain biking with three levels of difficulty. You can get a detailed map at the park's entrance or at the museum's Visitor's Centre. Bikers might prefer to access the trails from the summit parking lot at the corner of Bell School Line and Steeles Avenue.
• When I asked about the trail to the top of the cliff, I was told that a 25-minute walk on the way up, we would find an old quarry with lots of **fossils**! That would make it worth the trip for young paleontologists. The top is only minutes away from then on. You access the trail from the cute tunnel by the ski chalet.
• Ask about their **Autumn Colour Skyride** at least three weekends in October. It allows us to catch a ski lift ride up the escarpment to admire fall colours.

We had been here numbers of times to enjoy the lake. Each time, the kids were so involved in water fun that I never got to visit the museum or stroll along the trail leading to the top of the Niagara escarpment.

Turns out that within the first room I entered, there was an interesting display of the turbine developed by the Alexander family in 1898 to generate waterpower and electricity, using water from a natural spring up on the escarpment. The museum is actually located on the former site of the Alexander family farm. This family settled in 1836 and farmed the land until 1961!

A few galleries featuring carriages, lamps and lanterns was found on the second level but the real fun was on the third floor. There awaited a casual showcase of some of the 35,000-artifact collection of the Halton Region Museum. I noticed many antiques kids would like to see: wreaths made out of dried flowers and human hair, chairs made out of buffalo horns or branches, seats with a hole (adult-size potty chairs), ancient washing machines and antique toys, to name a few. All are stored by categories on shelves, in a warehouse fashion.

More artifacts are currently stored in other buildings on the site. All will eventually be relocated into a new Artifact Centre the museum is planning to build.

Halton Region Museum
• Milton
(905) 878-5011
www.conservationhalton.on.ca

**D-2
West
of Toronto
50-min.**

Schedule: Open year-round Monday to Friday, noon to 4 pm (also open on weekends from noon to 5 pm from Victoria Day to Thanksgiving. The park is open year-round from 8:30 am until dusk.
Admission: FREE, with Kelso Park's admission.
Directions: See **Kelso Conservation Area** on p. 280.

NEARBY ATTRACTIONS
Country Heritage Park (5-min.)...p. 406

ONTARIO RENAISSANCE FESTIVAL

Playing in the royal court...yard

Upon eyeing the size of our watermelon, the village apothecary exclaims (in renaissance English): "It's certainly not produced locally." He collects the seeds from the piece we had offered to him, anticipating their medicinal properties. A damsel, all trussed up in her bodice, interrupts our picnic claiming to have stolen the ring of King Henry VIII's new wife, Queen Anne, while they were shaking hands. Before fleeing, she begs us not to breathe a word about this to anyone. Indeed, there's a lot of action at this festival.

In 1999, it was all about Henry VIII. In 2001, the action built around Elizabeth I. In 2004, the Mayor of Trillingham wants to impress the queen with riches of his sea expedition but some pirates could ruin the feast. In all, there are over fifty actors at a time on the festival site, very well costumed and scattered in small groups throughout the village.

In old English, they shout out false confidences intended for everyone's ears. If you smile at them, they interact with you, but continue to play their part.

There's an arena of course, to go along with the spirit. Here they hold authentic jousting matches where knights, in full armour, fight one another with spears. They also hold birds of prey demonstrations. During our visit, public entertainers gave Molière and Shakespeare performances for the whole family. Period music was very much in evidence, with minstrels wandering throughout the village.

Half of the village huddles up against the edge of a shaded forest. This gives us the impression that we are close to the Nottingham Forest.

Some 50 artisans present their merchandise: glass blowers, blacksmith, sculptors and more. Some crafts are really eye-catching: beaded crowns made of flowers and long ribbons, butterfly wings or wooden armour to dress up as a fairy or a knight.

For a few dollars more, several other activities are offered: archery, ax and spear throw, rope ladder climbing, arm tattoos and wax hand-castings. The wooden horses on a zip line are a must! Children four years and older will really enjoy this. They'll charge on horses, spear in hand, aiming at a small ring as their mount slides along a rope up in the air.

The Human Chess match was by far our family's favourite activity! The "pieces" had previously been recruited from among the audience. The people chosen stood on a giant chessboard. Their moves depended on the outcome of several fights between actors, each one funnier than the last and guided by a narrator amidst general chaos.

TIPS (fun for 4 years +)

• At the entrance, a plan of the site is given out. It contains a detailed schedule of all the shows.

• Those interested in jousting should arrive at least 15 minutes before the show to have a seat in the stands, unfortunately placed in the sun.

• Hats are a must, since more than half the site is in the sun.

• If you don't want to spend more than the admission fee, take a deep breath and be on the defensive when you and the kids pass in front of the shops selling Renaissance articles: shields, wooden swords, flower crowns... they're all so tempting!

• By taking advantage of many shows, we definitely got our money's worth!

• Some families, already familiar with the ways of the festival, dress up for the occasion. We saw little knights and princesses strolling behind mothers clad in long skirts... and dads who didn't dare to be crazy and dress up!

• Giant smoked turkey legs, which taste like ham, won't necessarily appeal to young palates, but you may buy other fast food on the site.

NEARBY ATTRACTIONS

Ontario Renaissance Festival

D-2
West of Toronto
35-min.

· Milton
1-800-734-3779
www.rennfest.com

Schedule: Weekends only and holidays, usually from third weekend in July to Sunday of Labour Day weekend, from 10:30 am to 7 pm. Call for exact dates.

Admission: (tax not included) $12/adults, $11/seniors, $4/7-15 years, FREE for children 6 years and under.

Directions: East of Trafalgar Rd., on Height Line, Milton. From Hwy 401, take exit 328, head south for 2 km, turn left on Derry Rd., continue for 1 km, then turn right on Height Line. (Alternate way: take exit 118 from the QEW, head north for 11.3 km, turn right on Britannia for 1 km, then turn left on Height Line.)

CRAWFORD LAKE C. A.

An Indian village

Walking into the fortified village through a corridor lined with 5-metre-high stakes is like entering another world. From the top of the palisade, my young warrior inspects his territory with a watchful eye. In such a setting, it's easy to imagine the life of native people who lived here in the 15th Century.

Inside the palisade is the Crawford Lake Indian Village, which was reconstructed using data collected during an extensive archaeological dig.

Lifestyle

It is believed that initially, there were five Iroquois longhouses. Unlike traditional teepees, they were shaped like long, windowless hangars and each one housed several families. Two of them have been rebuilt on the site.

The Turtle Clan House stands close to the central square. With an austere exterior, it doesn't reveal the exoticism of its interior layout: roof openings to let the smoke out and the sunshine in, fur-covered sleeping areas, animal skins hung here and there, tools, clothing and jewellery.

My little one stuck her nose in the soft beaver pelt and pulled on the raccoon tails, while her big brother examined the forerunners of toboggans, hockey sticks and moccasin slippers, with a puzzled expression on his face. Little cooks could even crush corn at the bottom of a large wooden mortar.

When we visited, a native story-teller was answering questions triggered by this journey back in time. Inside the second longhouse, the Wolf House, a short educational film was shown in a mini-theatre. My little busybody didn't stop to watch the movie, preferring the indoor archaeological site reproduced close by.

He was quite disappointed when he was told visitors couldn't dust the displayed archaeological artefacts.

A third of the Wolf House has regained its original look. To help visitors visualize the daily life of the Iroquois of yesteryear, big family clan pictures are hidden behind large pelts. Children enjoy peeking through the holes to discover these worlds.

Where's the lake?

Because of the Conservation Area's name, we were surprised not to see a lake beside the village. We even hypothesized that Crawford Lake didn't exist anymore and that it had been revealed by excavations. It actually was the other way around: the lake revealed the village!

It is well explained in the pretty Visitor Centre (which abounds in interactive information). The village's presence was discovered after analyzing Crawford Lake's bed. When corn pollen was identified in a sedimentation sample, it became evident that there had been agriculture close by. Research confirmed the hypothesis, and the remains of the village were then unearthed.

A well marked trail leads to Craw-

ford Lake. You can go around it by taking a wooden trail, relatively safe for young children. The walk lasts about half an hour. A couple of picnic tables are available by the lake.

Opposite to the lake trail, a stroller-accessible path leads to a belvedere offering a view of the Niagara escarpment in about fifteen minutes. Another winding path offers a one-hour return hike into the forest, between roots and crevices, to the viewpoint. Ask for a trail map at the Visitor Centre.

TIPS (fun for 4 years +)

• You can ask for free craft material to make a small object.

• During the weekends of the "Sweet Water Season" at the native village, you can watch maple syrup being made from sap, sitting on a log around the fire. A staff member prepares and cooks corn flatbread that can be dipped in syrup at the end of the presentation.

• Call to find out about Sweet Water Season (March), the Indian Summer Festival (September) and Autumn on the Escarpment Celebration (Thanksgiving). During autumn, the colours are magnificent! During the Snow Flake event in February, you'll roast marshmallows!

• If you present your Crawford admission receipt at other Halton Region conservation areas, you can visit them for free on the same day. Our favourite outing consists of a visit to Crawford Lake, followed by a visit to **Mount Nemo Conservation Area**, 10 minutes away by car (see page 297).

Crawford Lake Conservation Area
· Milton
(905) 854-0234
www.
conservationhalton.on.ca

D-2
West
of Toronto
45-min.

Schedule: The site is open year-round. Full access to all facilities is offered weekends and holidays year-round and during the March Break, from 10 am to 4 pm.
Admission: $6/adults, $5/seniors, $3.50/ 5-14 years, FREE 4 years and under.
Directions: From Hwy 401, take exit #312/Guelph Line southbound, then follow the signs.

NEARBY ATTRACTIONS
Springridge Farm (15-min.).........p. 143
Hilton Falls C. A. (10-min.)...........p. 300

BATTLE OF STONEY CREEK

Time travel at its best!

Upon your arrival, you'll notice the military encampment, with its small white tents facing the Battlefield Museum. Women under their umbrellas, gather around campfires with their long dresses, while soldiers practice formations. Costumed children play with antique toys, and Native Warriors, in full makeup regalia, add a touch of authenticity. We find ourselves deep in 1813.

For the sole pleasure of acting, volunteers from all over Canada (some flying from the States) join in and don their costumes, put up their tents, prepare their authentic food and most of all, get ready to re-enact the Battle of Stoney Creek, which involved about 3000 Americans and 700 British troops in 1813.

As a general rule, tents with open doors mean you can sneak in and admire the historic furniture, made without nails, and different objects for daily use these passionate people have gathered.

The powder bullets, used with historic muskets, explode in a muffled sound as they are shot during the military drills.

The muskets were good for one shot for each charge. Still, there is lots of firing and many artillery shots during the re-enactment. The noise creates quite an atmosphere with, of course, many soldiers "dying" on the battlefield.

Don't expect any hand-to-hand combat however, as soldiers of the time moved slowly and in straight lines towards the enemy, stopping to shoot or recharge as they went.

Next to the battlefield is an amusing section with old-fashioned games: fishing pond, haymaze, wooden muskets firing rubber bands and wooden frames to entrap prisoners' heads and hands (for a small fee).

Other attractions include the high monument to climb, the museum with costumed staff handing out cookies from the kitchen, horse and wagon rides and shooting demonstrations.

Battle of Stoney Creek
• Stoney Creek
(905) 662-8458
www.battlefieldhouse.ca

E-2 S-W of Toronto 65-min.

Schedule: Usually takes place the first weekend of June (call for exact time and date). When we were there, there were re-enactments on both afternoons plus Saturday evening (at 8:30 pm, followed by fireworks). The museum is open year-round, Tuesday to Sunday, 1 to 4 pm (opens at 11 am from mid-June to Labour Day).

Admission: (Museum) $5/adults, $4/seniors and students, $3/7-12 years, $15/family of 4. (Battle re-enactment is $5/adults, $2/students and FREE for 12 years and under.

Directions: 77 King St. West, Stoney Creek. From QEW towards Niagara, take exit #88 (Centennial Pkwy/Hwy 20) southbound. From Centennial, turn left on King St. (museum is on your right).

TIPS (fun for 4 years +)
• There's no parking on site. Free parking and bus shuttle service are available at the St. David's Elementary School, on Centennial Parkway. Follow signs or ask the locals.

NEARBY ATTRACTIONS

See **Westfield Heritage Village** on p. 414.

WESTFIELD HERITAGE VILLAGE

Wonderful events

If our visit on Anne of Green Gables Day reflects the quality of all events organized at the Westfield Heritage Village, my family could easily become addicted to the place.

At the fence, a trio of Anne of Green Gables look-alikes are greeting arriving friends, similarly clad. We look around and see dozens of young Annes. Later on, we'll be able to admire 45 of them, all lined up by the train station, where they will be presented to the judges. Big ones, Lilliputian ones, with genuine red hair or wigs and period dresses, all are trying their luck at the look-alike contest.

Much of the Anne of Green Gables movies and TV series created by Sullivan Film Productions were filmed on site at Westfield Village, which explains the special day. The truth is… this is a girls event; there are not many boys around.

During the whole visit, my son begs me to return to the very amusing old-fashioned game section. He has spent thirty minutes there, learning to walk on

tin cans. He has engaged in a race, holding an egg on a spoon between his teeth. I thought it was hilarious to watch a bunch of girls, sporting straw hats with red wool braids, compete in a tug-of-war game.

Alongside the village bandshell, people line up to dance to the fiddle. My daughter also shakes it up, until a parade of antique cars and horse-drawn carriages starts to race around the place.

We go for a ride on a big wagon to catch an overall look at the village's 33 buildings before we visit a few of them.

At the General Store, we buy candy in a surprise bag and play with old wooden toys. At the Doctor's house, we take a look at the old-fashioned pill-making technique; my son promises not to fuss around next time he has to take modern cherry-flavoured medicine.

Farther, I am not able to convince my little girl to catch a ride in the wheelbarrow pushed by a nice boy in old-fashioned attire. She's

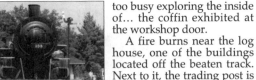

too busy exploring the inside of... the coffin exhibited at the workshop door.

A fire burns near the log house, one of the buildings located off the beaten track. Next to it, the trading post is interesting, with pelts to touch and traps used by pioneers to catch animals. We walk across a covered bridge to return to the action.

TIPS (fun for 3 years +)

• Sundays in March as well as some weekdays during the **March Break**, it is maple syrup time with demonstrations of native, pioneer and modern methods all around the site. They serve pancakes at the restaurant.

• There usually is a battle re-enactment at the village but not in 2004. Call to see if it is coming back in 2005. Considering Westfield's setting, it should be an amazing event.

• Some activities are traditionally offered: **Halloween** evening (end of October) and **Christmas** evenings in the Country with carol singers, toy makers and Santa's visit (the three Saturdays before Christmas (for 2004: December 4, 11 and 18, 5 to 9 pm) at the cost of $12.50/adults and $6.50/6-12 years).

• There is a restaurant on the premises.

NEARBY ATTRACTIONS

Westfield Heritage Village
· Rockton

E-2
S-W
of Toronto
70-min.

(519) 621-8851
or 1-888-319-4722
www.westfieldheritage.ca

Schedule: The village is open and alive with staff in period dress any Sunday and holidays from early April to late October, 12:30 to 4 pm (also open weekdays during the March Break and other selected days for special occasions). Anne of Green Gables usually on third Sunday in September (for 2004: September 19).

Admission: $6.50/adults, $5.50/seniors, $3.50/6-12 years, FREE under 6.

Directions: Take QEW West, then Hwy 6 North. Turn on Hwy 5 westbound. It becomes Hwy 8. Turn north (right) on Regional Rd. 552 (past Rockton). The Village is on the west side.

DUNDURN CASTLE

Yes, Sir!

Outside the 1832 building, a woman in a long dress is plowing the garden. To go inside, we have to walk through an interior courtyard. At the entrance, children play with antique toys while waiting for the guided tour to begin.

Dundurn Castle is in fact a superb manor that once belonged to one of Ontario's first Premiers, Sir Allan Mac-Nab. The building has been preserved with much of its initial splendour, with magnificent furniture, trompe-l'oeil walls and original artwork.

The guided tour, which lasts a bit more than an hour, allows us to admire the manor's three floors. Not interactive enough for my then 5-year-old son, he made us leave after 30 minutes. It's a shame! During the last third of the visit his patience would have been rewarded

TIPS (fun for 4 years +)

• The gift shop is usually well stocked with children's books on castles.
• During **March Break**, expect an Activity Centre with a dress-up area, puzzles and games.
• From the end of November until the beginning of January, Dundurn Castle puts on its **Christmas** finery: cedar garlands, red ribbons and flowers add to the Castle's rich Victorian ambience.
• At Dundurn's restaurant, **The Coach House**, the atmosphere is a bit quiet for children but they offer a kids menu.
• The gift shop sells snacks.

when visitors get to the Castle's underground passages.

These stone-floor corridors are the part of the manor that younger children will readily relate to a true castle. At the end of the visit, they're expected in the kitchen for a snack of cookies served by employees in period dress.

Back outside, children inevitably stop to look at the large cannon sitting by the **Hamilton Military Museum**. Small but efficient, this museum traces military history from the War of 1812 until World War I, using many photos, military uniforms and artillery pieces.

At the entrance, children are given a sheet of paper with pictures of objects they have to find on the site. This treasure hunt is guaranteed to excite them.

Inside the museum, in a small, dark corridor, a trench has been reconstructed. The sound effects are very effective; you will have the uneasy feeling of really being at war!

The **Military Museum** also offers an outdoor Spy Game where kids are given instructions to look all over the historic complex to find five words forming a secret message.

Dundurn Castle & Hamilton Military Museum
• Hamilton
(905) 546-2872
www.hamilton.ca

E-2
S-W
of Toronto
60-min.

Schedule: Open from Victoria Day to Labour Day, 10 am to 4 pm. The rest of the year, open Tuesday to Sunday, noon to 4 pm (Military Museum opens 1 hour later and closes at 5 pm).

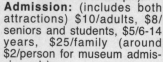
Admission: (includes both attractions) $10/adults, $8/seniors and students, $5/6-14 years, $25/family (around $2/person for museum admission only).

Directions: 610 York Blvd., Hamilton. Take QEW West, then Hwy 403 towards Hamilton, exit York Blvd. and follow the signs.

SIMCOE COUNTY MUSEUM

To explore inside out

Maybe I was just lucky but when I was there, the soft light of the fall sun bathing the historical small village made everything look picture perfect. It was the last week in the season to visit the buildings and there were hardly any other visitors. The carpet of red needles on the ground muffled my steps. The tall trees ruling the parkland hid the highway. For a moment, I thought I was back in good old 1870's.

I was glad I made an impulse stop to this museum on my way back from another attraction in the area. I had noticed it several times over the years, being so close to Hwy 26, so it was now or never.

Imagine my surprise when I discovered a full-size Huron long house inside the main complex. A (fake) salmon was installed over the fire for smoking. Corn was drying in a corner and fur lay on furniture made out of branches. Nearby was a small activity centre with archaeological digging bins.

Around the corner awaited a strip of a Victorian street lined with shops. Through the window, I could see a Santa consulting a list of names. In another were antique toys. Further, a vast room was filled with antique furniture, arranged to reconstruct whole Victorian rooms.

There was a display of musical instruments and old cameras. There was a model bridge and miniature trains. A number of Victorian craft sheets completed the range of activities. After all this, the fifteen outdoor historical buildings felt like a bonus.

Right by the tiny school was a large bell one could ring. Some basket weaving was going on in a barn. The train station was funny, with just a few metres of track in front of it. One could explore the Spearin House, which was home to Barrie's Spearin family for over five generations.

During the summer, they offer demonstrations and activities with a different historical theme each week.

TIPS (fun for 4 years +)

• Enquire about their events. In 2004, they plan a weekend-long Quilt, Rug and Craft Fair in September. On a few evenings during **Halloween**, visitors play Bean the Bat and Bowling for Tombstones. Whatever that is, it sounds fun. And they get treats. **Easter** Eggstravaganza, on evenings as well, is held during Easter. During the Victorian **Christmas** in December, expect roasted chestnuts, crafts and Christmas carols accompanied by the organ in the little church.

NEARBY ATTRACTIONS

Simcoe County Museum	**B-2** **North** **of Toronto** **70-min.**
• Minesing (705) 728-3721 www.county.simcoe.on.ca	

Schedule: Open Monday to Saturday, 9 am to 4:30 pm and Sunday, 1 pm to 4:30 pm. The outside buildings are open to the public from May 1 to the end of November.

Admission: $4/adults, $3.50/ students & seniors, $2.50/4-12 years old. FREE for 3 years and under.

Directions: 1151 Hwy 26, Minesing. From Hwy 400, take exit #98. Follow Bayfield St. North and then Hwy 26. Look on south side.

DISCOVERY HARBOUR

Past and present in the same boat

My son had heard about feathers being used as pens, so he was intrigued by the real one on display in the office of the "Clerk-in-Charge". He could hardly believe his luck when the guide invited him to dip it into the inkwell and write his name in the official register. From then on, my child was hooked for the rest of the excellent guided tour of Discovery Harbour.

In the Sailor's Barracks, the guide introduced us to sailors' sleeping habits as she hopped into one of the hammocks that hung one metre over my preschooler's head.

He tried a few times before settling into one. We then played a tossing game the sailors used to play. In the kitchen, attached to the Commanding Officer's House, my young cook pretended to mix one pound of this and one pound of that to make a pound cake.

In another barrack, he was absolutely thrilled to sit at a workbench and work with old-fashioned tools, while my youngest one was seriously "re-arranging" the logs in the shed.

Trotting through the Assistant Surgeon's House, the Home of the Clerk-in-Charge, the Naval Surveyor's House and Keating House with its long table set for a family, we visited one intimate interior after another and observed a wide range of artefacts from the daily life of the 19th Century.

At the outer limits of Discovery Harbour (a full 30-minute walk from our starting point), we found the site's sole remaining original building: the impressive Officer's Quarters, built in the 1840's. The children loved to stroll along its many corridors and climb up and down the stairs.

For my part, I was impressed by the collection of period furnishings.

After the tour, we explored two replica schooners, *Bee* and *Tecumseth*, moored at the King's Wharf, on our own.

We explored the vessels' nooks and crannies, tackled the bells and examined more hammocks in the ships' holds. Meanwhile, my little toddler was busy "re-organizing" the ropes' tight spirals on the bridge...

TIPS (fun for 4 years +)

• When muddy, it is hard to push a stroller on the slightly sloped trails; a wagon would be a better option.

• Special activities are offered Tuesday to Saturday such as quill pen making and writing, historic dance, rigging and ropework, naval demonstrations or others in the same spirit. Ask to find out when they are doing croquet and tea or soldier's drills.

• On Tuesdays, early July to Mid-August, costumed staff role-play specific situations during the First Person Days.

• There's a gift shop operated by the Georgian Bay Métis Council, selling aboriginal items.

• A few years ago, we could sail on a tall ship on Georgian Bay but not anymore.

• There's the **King's Wharf Theatre** on site, presenting summer dinner-theatre as well as Sunday High Tea, check www.kingswharftheatre.com or call 1-888-449-4463 for information.

• Their restaurant serves light lunches and snacks but you might want to stop at the **Dock Lunch** in the port of Penetanguishene, for tasty fast food and ice cream at outdoor tables by the water, (705) 549-8111.

Discovery Harbour
• Penetanguishene
(705) 549-8064
www.discoveryharbour.on.ca

A-2 Midland Region 90-min.

Schedule: Open Monday to Friday, 10 am to 5 pm, from end of May to mid-June and weekends as well after that, until Labour Day. Last admission at 4:30 pm. Open Wednesday evenings for the Lantern Tours offered end of June to end of August. (Re-opens a few days for special Halloween and Christmas events).

Admission: $6.50/adults, $5.50/seniors and students, $4.50/6-12 years old, FREE 5 years and under, $20/family of 4.

Directions: From Hwy 400, take exit #121/Hwy 93 to Penetanguishene, turn right at the water and follow ship logo.

SAINTE-MARIE AMONG THE HURONS

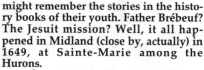

Kids on a mission

Those who received a Catholic education might remember the stories in the history books of their youth. Father Brébeuf? The Jesuit mission? Well, it all happened in Midland (close by, actually) in 1649, at Sainte-Marie among the Hurons.

This unique site is a vibrant testimony to the far-reaching impact of European cultural influence and the Christian religion. Judging by the multitude of languages heard during our visit, Europeans know about this and the word-of-mouth mill is going strong!

On the other side of the fence, we found costumed attendants busying themselves with chores reminiscent of the times. A (pretend) Jesuit father was praying in the candlelit chapel and a (real) native storyteller was talking with a few visitors while stirring the contents of a large pot.

Children loved to explore the buildings freely. We adopted their rhythm and therefore, did not see everything. Yet, we took time to view the river from above the bastion. The little ones were intrigued by the canoes built in the old tradition. We climbed up and down the stairs inside the Jesuits' residence, and tried their small beds.

Everything here was sculpted in wood, even the plates. We tried on clothing in the shoemaker's shop. My young trapper was flabbergasted by the small fire an attendant started in the hearth with sparks that flew from two stones he was hitting against one another. Children loved the teepee and three-metre-high sunflowers.

At the end of our visit we enjoyed the **Sainte-Marie Museum** and its refreshing coolness. It is decorated with great refinement, even in the texture of its wall coverings. The result of careful and extensive research, the museum harmoniously blends and juxtaposes expressions of 17th Century French culture, the frugal materialism of Canada's early settlers and the native culture.

TIPS (fun for 4 years +)

• Get a map of the site at the entrance. Before you begin your visit, you may wish to view a 20-minute film to get yourself in the mood.

• Various craft activities are offered daily to kids in July and August. There's also a Family Activity Day on Wednesdays from early July to mid-August with even more activities and demonstrations.

• On Thursdays, early July to mid-August, costumed staff role-play specific situations during the First Person Days.

• It's the second year that a **Pow-Wow** is offered in the park across from the attraction in September (for 2004: September 11 and 12). A new tradition?

• The main building includes a cafeteria.

Sainte-Marie among the Hurons	A-2 Midland Region 90-min.
· Midland (705) 526-7838 www. saintemarieamongthehurons.on.ca	

Schedule: Open early May to mid-October, 10 am to 5 pm. Additional public tours offered at 1 and 3 pm from early April to mid-May and early October to early November.

Admission: $11/adults, $9.50/ seniors and students, $8/6-12 years old, FREE for 5 years and under, $32/family of 4.

Directions: From Hwy 400 North, take exit #147/Hwy 12 westbound. The Mission is located just east of Midland, across from the Martyrs' Shrine.

FANSHAWE PIONEER VILLAGE

Back to the past

Here, kids can actually operate an old sewing machine and scrub to their hearts content at the washboard. They can even climb onto a chuck wagon, like in the Far-West. Quite the life!

Many of the twenty-five buildings at Fanshawe are open to the public, displaying various antiques within reach. Little pioneers absolutely adore the fire station, with the bell they can ring and the 20-metre-high tower, used for drying water hoses, which they can climb to the top.

The Fanshawe School, built in 1871, is charming with its rows of small wooden desks. Make sure to read the rules observed by the pupils of the time! In a replica of the *Canadian Free Press* Building, a predecessor to the *London Free Press* founded in 1853, children can look at typesetting letters and engravings that were patiently set for the printing of the newspaper.

My little one enjoyed exploring the kitchen of London-born Canadian painter Paul Peel's childhood house, with its utensils and fridges of another era, and other curiosities. Last but not least, was a pedal-activated sewing machine.

The log house is a good example of the type of house built by the settlers who arrived in 1865. The Pioneer Farm shows the type of house they subsequently built, on wooden foundations this time, once they were better settled on their land. The Jury's House, for its part, displays all the comforts available at the end of the 19th Century.

TIPS (fun for 4 years +)

• Call the village to find out about special events. For 2004, they plan a **Canada Day** event, a Harvest Fest in late August, a 1812 re-enactment end of August, **haunted** hay rides the last three weekends of October with a Pioneer Pumpkin party on the last weekend, and **Christmas** activities on December weekends.

• **Fanshawe Conservation Area** is located right next to the pioneer village. It includes a nice and long unsupervised beach and over 600 campsites. We really enjoyed it after our visit to the village.

• The **London Museum of Archaeology** is located at 1600 Attawandaron Road. See www.uwo.ca/museum or call (519) 473-1360. It includes indoor exhibits, a longhouse and on-going excavation of a 500-year-old native village, open to the public.

Fanshawe Pioneer Village	E-1

Fanshawe Pioneer Village
• London
(519) 457-1296
www.fanshawepioneervillage.ca

E-1
West
of Toronto
2 1/4 hrs

Schedule: Open from Victoria Day weekend to Thanksgiving Day, Tuesday to Sunday and holiday Mondays, 10 am to 4:30 pm (also open at other times for special events).

Admission: $5/adults, $4/students and seniors, $3/3-12 years old, $15/family of 4.

Directions: 2609 Fanshawe Park Rd. East, London. From Hwy 401 West, take exit #194/Airport Rd. northbound. Turn west on Oxford St., then north on Clarke Rd. to Fanshawe Park Rd.

General tips about this
Totally arbitrary section:

- The purpose of this section is to pass on a few good addresses I have come across in the last nine years I have spent exploring Southern Ontario.

None of these places paid to be listed. It is in no way an exhaustive list of fun stores, restaurants or services.

If you want to share with other parents your own good addresses, contact me at (416) 462-0670 or **mail@torontofunplaces.com**, I'll find a way to pass on the information.

TOTALLY ARBITRARY
SECTION

See **Dutch Dreams** on p. 433.

ALL FIRED UP

Crazy for pottery!

My budding artist is smitten with a true replica of a mouse, while her older brother opts for a monster truck-shaped piggy-bank. As for me, I sway between a cake and cone-shaped box.

It takes us a good half-hour to select our piece, decide on colours and wait for the assistant to bring it all to our work table. My kids are told that they will have to limit their colour selection to four, while adults can use as many as they want.

Highly focused, my 7-year-old meticulously paints away, while my young daughter embarks on a 15-minute splash that will leave her mouse (and herself) covered in (washable) paint. While she is delighted with her work, I must admit the end result is not pretty, and she'll eventually insist on painting it all over again. These will be glazed, fired and ready in five working days. They feature finished pieces in their large windows. Before returning for pick-up, I suggest you call to make sure that your pieces are on display. Your kids will be so proud!

All Fired Up • Etobicoke (416) 233-5512	**I-9** **West** of downtown 20-min.

   Schedule: Tuesday, Thursday and Saturday, 11 am to 6 pm. Wednesday and Friday, 11 am to 9 pm. Sunday, noon to 5 pm. Closed on Mondays.
Cost: Kids' studio fee: $7/for piece $25 or less ($12 if piece over $25). Pieces: $5 to $50.
Directions: 8 Brentwood Rd. North, Etobicoke (west of Royal York Rd., north of Bloor St. West).

YOUR FIRED

For young apprentices

My daughter goes for a cat. I opt for a sunflower plate. We're going to be here for a while...

The huge room can seat over 100 people. The selection of pieces to paint is vast, with lots of animals and smaller $8 options. You're charged a fixed price to use paints on the premises, whatever the size of your piece. It is the best way to go if you want to launch yourself into the painting of a set of mugs or the creation of a complex design.

Check out their bathroom! Its walls are covered with individually designed tiles. The overall effect is quite whimsical!

They sell snacks but we chose to stop after at the **3 Coins Open Kitchen**, at 10140 Yonge Street, for an all-day breakfast in the spirit of the 50's: juke box, chrome, vinyl and so on. It is open from 6 am to 4 pm, Monday to Saturday, and 7 am to 2 pm on Sundays, call (905) 884-0643. See **Mill's Pond** on p. 374.

Your Fired • Richmond Hill (905) 737-8944	**H-11** **North** of Toronto 35-min.

 Schedule: Open Tuesday to Friday, 3 to 10 pm (last admission at 8:30 pm), Saturday and Sunday, 10 am to 6 pm.
Costs: $6/adults and $3/children to use the place and paints, plus the cost of the pieces. Add $1 for the glazing.
Directions: 10178 Yonge St., Richmond Hill (right in front of a little park).

KIDS CRAFT CAFÉ

One of a kind

My daughter and her friend's attention are fully focused on their craft. This could take more than 30 minutes. It would be plenty of time to read a chapter while drinking my coffee but instead, I choose to explore an amazing selection of very creative art supplies for sale, covering the whole wall.

The place calls itself a café (but don't expect a cappuccino). This is mainly an artsy place and it looks like what it is: a hands-on retail craft store with the goodwill of parents and kids at heart.

Interesting craft samples are displayed here and there to inspire us. In the back of the room, a birthday party is taking place and a group of kids is involved in craft making. Kids do crafts on low tables under the supervision of friendly staff while the guardians can have a coffee at the nearby tables.

Valentine's Day is a few weeks away and the choice theme for the weekly drop-in craft. My two artisans are creating a Heart Friend out of pink and purple foam sheets, pipe cleaners, beads and sprinkles.

A different craft activity is supervised every week. Have a Kids Craft Café card punched (and stored) and your 8th craft will be free.

In the coming weeks, kids will be able to make a special dish to fill with candies, a clock to "Spring forward" and a pot of gold for St. Patrick's Day. Birthday Party packages offer other craft options to suit different age groups. Fifty-two craft projects per year for many years ahead, I am sure! It takes crafty people to think up so many craft projects!

TIPS (fun for 3 years +)

• Call to find out about their affordable birthday packages and loot bags ($5 for a bag filled with art supplies and a free drop-in session!). They can host special events, workshops and camps.
• The plaza includes a Loblaws, the second-hand outlet Once Upon a Child, a Subway and a Pizza Hut. Across Trafalgar Road, there's a Wal-Mart, a huge dollar store and the restaurant Kelsey's.
• At the south-east corner of Trafalgar and Dundas, you'll find **Funtastic Kids**, an indoor playground with a Brio-train table, bouncing castle, puppet theatre and Mastermind toys. Check www.funtastickids.com, (905) 257-6500.

NEARBY ATTRACTIONS
Coronation Park (15-min.) ....p. 381
Appleby College slope (15-min.).p. 390

Kids Craft Café	I-7
• Oakville	N-W
(905) 257-7002	of Toronto
www.kidscraftcafe.com	40-min.

  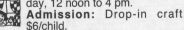

Schedule: Open Tuesday to Saturday, 10 am to 5 pm (closes at 6 pm on Friday) and Sunday, 12 noon to 4 pm.
Admission: Drop-in craft $6/child.
Directions: 2387 Trafalgar Rd., Trafalgar Ridge Plaza, Oakville. Take QEW, exit at Trafalgar Rd. North, look for the plaza with a Loblaws on the east side.

UPSTAIRS AT LOBLAWS

Here's what's cooking

The trick here was to convince my child not to eat the batter, the blueberries, the filling or the decorations. I did a good job so my young cook was able to take home a plate filled with muffins and mini tarts to proudly show around. For once, her big brother was more than happy to compliment her on her good work. He showed his appreciation by licking the plate clean.

Many of the biggest outlets of the grocery chain Loblaws have a second level with rooms to offer their trademark Upstairs at Loblaws cooking programs. Add this to a large café on a mezzanine overlooking the colourful fruit and vegetables section, live musicians on the weekend, more classes on different topics and you'd think you're in a fancy community centre.

Our first experience was within the **Forest Hill Market**, which I love for its café with a view (see p. 428). We arrived early so we had a bite while we waited... Big mistake! In the

cooking room, we were offered coffee, juices, cookies and brownies before starting the class. And during the cooking lesson, the kids would taste the dough, the blueberries, the decorations... By the end of the activity, everyone was full!

I chose a Parent and Tot class (for ages 3-5) built around a storybook. Forest Hill Market was the first to offer this original concept. Other outlets have followed the trend since. To begin the morning, the cook-in-chief read the story *Blueberries for Sal* by Robert McClosky. It got the young apprentices into the right mood to make blueberry tarts and muffins.

A *Curious George* story would lead to banana muffins; kids would cook bat cookies following *Arthur's Halloween*; *Miss Spider's Tea Party* would be the perfect match for tea sandwiches.

Some Loblaws are stronger on Parent and Tot classes, others focus more on after-school programs. Age requirement varies from one outlet to the other. Some places even offer junior programs for ages 11-15. I noticed really fun classes such as "Squeeze bottle pancakes" or "Diner is on the kids" for 6 and up. Some programs allow you to book for only one class while others only come as a series.

By the way, adult classes sound like as much fun: "Gourmet Babies", "Boys night out", "Rodney's oysters", "Mushrooms demystified", "Knife skills", etc. The selection is actually amazing!

TIPS (fun for 3 years +)

• The pre-registration classes are popular. You need to book as soon as you get the new *What's Cooking* booklet released three times a year from the cashiers. You can register in person or on the phone through Customer Service. For details, you can call the outlet's coordinator. Both numbers are in the local booklets.

• All the Upstairs at Loblaws offer gingerbread workshops for kids of all ages before **Christmas**. They supply an already-built house with candies and equipment. All of them offer much-appreciated birthday party packages.

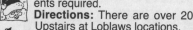

BUILD-A-BEAR WORKSHOP

Bear in mind

My daughter pumps the little red heart to bring it to life. She holds it against her own and kisses it before inserting the silky organ into her new favourite toy: a plush beagle baptized Buddy, as written on his birth certificate.

Buddy was carefully chosen from among dozens of cute stuffed animals of varying prices: leopards, unicorns, pink poodles, rainbow bears, rabbits, etc, exposed on shelves. My 6-year-old picked Buddy's shapeless fur lying in back under the samples. Then it was stuffed with the help of a friendly staff member by pressing on a floor pedal to blow acrylic filling through a pipe into the animal.

Following a cute ceremony to pledge their friendship to their new pals, kids (and some adults!) inserted a little heart through an opening left in the fur, for the staff to sew down. Then, it was up to the bath section to blow and brush fluff bits away.

Meanwhile, someone at the counter rang a bell to get our attention! Everyone in the store was invited to repeat their promise to take good care of their animal. Responsibilities are not taken lightly here! I was impressed by the selection of outfits and accessories! One can definitely get carried away in this store: sports kits, career outfits, casual wear, evening wear, sleep wear, camping gear, dog bed, leash, Sketchers shoes, even four-wheel roller skates to add to the shoes.

The experience would not be complete without a stop at the computer station to print the new family member's birth certificate. Finally, the animal is handed to the child in a cardboard doghouse. Perfect final touch to a great concept!

TIPS (fun for 3 years +)

• You can pick a sound device to insert into the paw of your animal before stuffing it. You can even record a short personalized message on it! Keep in mind that every time the child presses the paw, the sound will be heard.

• **Bear City**, a Canadian chain, now follows the same concept. They have two locations, one in **Scarborough Town Centre** (store near Wal-Mart, (416)279-1400) and the other in **Centrepoint Mall** (store next to Zellers, (416) 224-1020) or check www.bear-city.com. This means a different selection of bears and more outfit options. It is a new company so their merchandising has not reached the polished level of Build-A-Bear, established for some years in the States before it came here. Let's just give them some time!

• Relatives and friends asking for gift ideas for your child will find accessories to suit any gift budget. The three stores always come up with new products to keep consumers on their toes.

• A new Build-A-Bear is opening in September 2004. Call for exact address.

NEARBY ATTRACTIONS
Mississauga Festival (2-min.)...... p. 78
Santa at the mall..........................p. 188

Build-A-Bear Workshop
· **Mississauga**
(905) 270-3609
www.buildabear.com

I-8
N-W
of Toronto
40-min.

Schedule: Open Monday to Friday, 10 am to 9 pm, Saturday, 9:30 am to 6 pm, Sunday, noon to 6 pm.

Costs: Animals/$15-$39, sound device/$5-$8, outfits/$12-$24, shoes/$8-$11.

Directions: Square One Shopping Centre, Mississauga, just

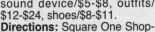
south of Hwy #403 and west of Hurontario St. (located on the upper level, near Sears).

RESTAURANTS WITH A VIEW

Horizon's Café
(416) 868-6937 (J-10 on map)
www.cntower.ca
Hours: 11:30 am to closing of **CN Tower**
Directions: 301 Front St. W., Toronto.

The Horizon's Café is not the expensive revolving restaurant on top of the CN Tower. It is the one located right underneath the latter.

On its menu, you'll find a few choices that will appeal to children: fancy nachos or tasty chicken fingers. You could go just for the yummy desserts and refreshments with CN Tower-shaped stirring sticks.

It will cost over $10 per person but I think it is an excellent investment considering the fun they'll have admiring the Lilliputian cars circulating on miniature highways and trying to identify Toronto's well-known buildings.

The **360 Restaurant**, one floor higher, takes 72 minutes to complete a full rotation. It offers a gastronomical menu (with matching prices). The dress code is smart casual. You don't pay for the elevator ride when you're having a meal at 360. Call (416) 362-5411 for reservations.

There' no kid's menu but children under 12 may order half portions (at half the price) from the regular menu. They have high chairs.

I have eaten there a few times and it was always excellent. Desserts were as spectacular as the view.

The best way to enjoy the experience is to arrive before sunset and see the lights on the streets and the buildings slowly transform Toronto into a glittering jewel!

Forest Hill Market
(416) 651-5166 (I-10 on map)
Hours: Usually opens at 8 am.
Directions: 396 St. Clair St. W., Toronto.

Many Loblaws include a café on their second level, most adorned with a fake tree with wide foliage. My favourite is the one in Forest Hill. The large bay windows overlooking the canopy of trees in the adjacent park, added to the garden furniture, parasols and fake ivy on a trellis creates the impression of being in a garden. They sell snacks and light lunches we buy on the first floor.

Rock Garden Tea House
(905) 522-7399 (E-2 on map)
www.rbg.ca
Hours: Open from warm Spring to Labour Day, 10 am to 4 pm (closes at 6 pm on weekends and holidays).
Directions: See **Royal Botanical Gardens** on p. 314, Burlington.

From the elevated terrace, you can embrace the whole Rock Garden. There are tables inside the small restaurant but it is so lovely to sit under the sun. I think it worth waiting until an outdoor table is free. You can order light meals. My favourite on their menu is the scrumptious scones accompanied by hot tea.

SUNNYSIDE PAVILION CAFÉ

Someone pinch me, please!

I'm seated in a café. Facing me, the blues of sky and water merge in an unending horizon. I gaze at two swans flying over the shoreline, hearing the rustle of their majestic white wings. Thirty metres away from me, my son is building a short-lived dam in the fine sand. Beside me, my little one is asleep in her stroller. Sighing with contentment, a flavourful cappuccino in hand, I'm getting ready to relax. Where am I? Here in Toronto, at the Sunnyside Pavilion Café!

Along Lake Shore Boulevard West, you will notice a large, white building beside a long municipal pool. If you venture to the other side of this building,

you'll discover a facade with arches and columns and a terrace full of tables topped by umbrellas. The structure efficiently muffles the roar of motor vehicles circulating on the adjacent boulevard! Only the boardwalk separates the terrace from the beach.

An inner courtyard boasts other tables set amid fountain, trees and flowers. A beautiful mural completes the illusion of being at a European café. It makes you feel like writing postcards to friends you've left behind.

The restaurant offers an elaborate choice of hearty breakfasts. You can order coffee any way you like it. Salads are large and fresh. Gourmet pizzas are delicious. The terrace is the perfect spot for adults with children. Parents can finish their meal while watching their little ones play on the beach.

TIPS (fun for all ages)
• On rainy days, the restaurant might be closed. When the weather is grey, it is better to call before you go.
• Call the **Beach Hotline** to find out about the beach's water conditions at (416) 392-7161.
• East of the restaurant (beyond the huge outdoor public **Gus Ryder/Sunnyside Pool**) you'll find a great shaded playground, a large wading pool and a few dinosaurs to climb on! Let's not forget the ice cream stand and snack bar on the west side of the café.

NEARBY ATTRACTIONS	
Ontario Place (15-min.)................p. 12	
High Park (5-min.).........................p. 322	

Sunnyside Pavilion Café
(416) 531-2233

I-9 West of downtown 25-min.

Schedule: Usually open daily from May through September (weather permitting), with variable hours, usually from around 9:30 am to at least 11 pm during the summer. Call to confirm.
Admission: FREE admission to the beach (you will pay around $8 for a fancy burger, $11 for a pizza).
Directions: 1755 Lake Shore Blvd. West, Toronto. If on Lake Shore westbound, drive past Ellis Ave. and take the exit for Lake Shore East to your left. A few parking lots are located on the south side of Lake Shore Blvd.

WATERFRONT RESTAURANTS

Boardwalk Pub

(416) 694-8844 (J-10 on map)
www.boardwalkpub.com
Hours: Open year-round, 11 am to 11 pm minimum.
Directions: 1681 Lake Shore Blvd. E., Toronto (at the foot of Coxwell).

This is the only restaurant on the waterfront in the **Beaches** neighbourhood (p. 270). I like it for their nice terrace in the shade (although far from the beach). There's a large playground right across the park's trail. The restaurant serves fancy burgers, good salads, pizza, pasta, etc. They will reimburse your parking fees if you spend $10 and over on their premises and park in the section in front of their restaurant.

Stokers Patio Grill

(416) 461-3625 (J-10 on map)
www.thedocks.com
Hours: Open in May weather permitting, from noon. Kids allowed until 9 pm.
Directions: See **The Docks**, p. 17, Toronto.

Nowhere else will you get this view of Toronto's landscape. There's lots of action to watch on the water by day. It is even better when the colourful city lights start reflecting on the water and torches and candles are lighting the tables. The music is quite loud... nothing is perfect. The patio offers a kids' menu.

Pier 4 Storehouse Restaurant

(416) 203-1440 (J-10 on map)
www.pier4rest.com
Hours: The restaurant is open year-round. The patio is open weather permitting, from 11 am to around 10:30 pm.
Directions: 245 Queen's Quay W., Toronto (just west of Harbourfront).

When visiting **Harbourfront** (p.68), cross the foot bridge on its west side, walk around the corner and you'll see a great spot to eat burgers and fries by the water (beware of the seagulls!). Their patio overlooks the action in the harbour.

The indoor restaurant serves seafood, fish, meat and poultry and a kids' menu. Some of the tables offer a great view of the lake. The whole place is packed with nautical memorabilia.

Dog Fish Pub

(416) 264-2338 (J-11 on map)
www.bluffsparkmarina.com
Hours: Open beginning of June until end of summer, from 11 am (kids are allowed until 9 pm).
Directions: See **Bluffers Park**, p. 273. In Scarborough.

This is a plain restaurant located right under the fancier seafood restaurant Bluffer, in the marina by **Bluffers Park**. It serves nice affordable hamburgers and fries. The inside is nondescript, but the outdoor terrace offers a delightful view of the cliffs, the forest and sailboats.

Hutch's Dingley Dell

(905) 545-5508 (E-2 on map)
Hours: Open year-round, 11 am to midnight (closes at 10 pm after Labour Day until just before March break).
Directions: 280 Van Wagner's Beach Rd., Hamilton (take QEW Niagara, exit at Centennial Pkwy towards the lake, turn left, North Service Rd. becomes Van Wagner's Beach Rd.).

Loved the 50's feeling, loved the booths by the large bay windows, and loved the fries. You order, wait a lot while you play music from the jukebox or watch the seagulls teasing people on the beach. Then your number gets called and you pick up your steamy food. Yummy and affordable! There's also a great dairy bar.

Lake House Restaurant

(905) 562-6777 (E-3 on map)
www.lakehouserestaurant.com
Hours: The restaurant is open year-round, from 11:30 am to 10 pm (opens at 10:30 am on Sundays). The patio opens weather permitting.
Direction: From the QEW (coming either way) take exit #57 to Victoria Avenue, drive towards the lake and turn right on North Side Rd, in Vineland Station.

This restaurant offers a gorgeous view of the lake. You can sit at their elevated patio and order real food for you... and the usual suspects from the kids' menu for them.

Baranga's on the Beach

(905) 544-7122 (E-2 on map)
www.barangas.com
Hours: Open from spring to December 31, from 11:30 am.
Directions: 380 Van Wagner's Beach Rd., Hamilton (take QEW Niagara, exit at Centennial Pkwy towards the lake, turn left, North Service Rd. becomes Van Wagner's Beach Rd.).

When I noticed this restaurant on my way from **Wild Waterworks** (p. 37), I just had to check it out! Exotic music was playing, candles were already lighting the vast patio and the lake in the background was coloured in blue and yellow hues from the sunset. The overall impression was that of a beach restaurant by the ocean. They definitely have the best waterfront patio around Toronto... and good food too, judging by the plates waiters were hustling out of the kitchen.

Expect fancy Greek food, salad combinations, pasta, finger food, copious brunches and more. Not the cheapest but many affordable options. Definitely worth the drive! They have a kids' menu.

RAINFOREST CAFÉ

Under the tropics...

**Our "guide" talks to us about para-
keets as we watch three superb,
multicoloured birds. While we
throw coins into a pond from
which vapours are escaping, we
seem to awaken the hippo that is
napping in the water. Then we
walk underneath an arch-shaped
aquarium. Its wonderful, live tropical fish greet us before we enter
the restaurant, inside of which a
furious tropical storm is erupting!**

Looking up at the ceiling, we
notice a starry sky surrounded by a
thick canopy of foliage. In fact, the
restaurant's creeping vegetation over-
flows from all directions. We sit close to
two huge elephants that will come to life
every 12 minutes.

We are busy reading the menu
when the lights start to flicker. Another
tropical storm begins. Lightning bolts
project their stroboscopic reflection on
the foliage and thunder drowns out the
exotic music. From where we are sitting,
we can see a wall of rain separating the
restaurant from the gift shop. This phenomenon will repeat itself intermittently
(about every half-
hour).

The overall per-
spective of the
restaurant is impres-
sive. All over the
room, aquariums
diffuse their blue
light. Here, a wide
fountain flows,
there, perched in a
tall tree, a lazy (and
fake) leopard swings
its tail. A bit farther,
two gorillas are
making a scene.
Everywhere, we catch a glimpse of cock-
atoos, monkeys, lizards, butterflies and
frogs, hidden by a camouflage of leaves.

After the meal, my son gets lost in
the jungle for a few minutes ... That is,
the commercial jungle of the restaurant's
luxuriant gift shop. For sure, its merchandise is very attractive! It even boasts
a talking tree bearing an expressive face.

TIPS (fun for 4 years +)

• The restaurant's thunderstorms
may upset those children who are afraid
of violent natural phenomena. My little
one wanted to get out!

• Before 5 pm, we didn't have to wait
to get a table at the restaurant.

• I was not impressed by the entrées
or the Kids' meals but I really loved their
warm dips and enormous desserts with
flashy presentation. You could just stick
to those expreience Rainforest at a lesser
cost.

• There is a **Famous Players Silvercity Yorkdale** next to the restaurant. Call
(416) 787-2052 for movie listing.

• Check out the huge **PJ's Pet Centre**
near Holt Renfrew, right under the food
court, just for the fun of watching the
wide range of animals they host!

• There's another Rainforest Café in
Niagara Falls at Clifton Hill and Falls
Ave., (905) 374-2233.

NEARBY ATTRACTIONS

Rainforest Café
• **North York**
(416) 780-4080
www.rainforestcafe.com

**I-10
North
of downtown
30-min.**

Schedule: Open year-round,
Monday to Thursday, 11:30 am
to 9:30 pm, Friday and Satur-
day, 11:30 am to 10:30 pm,
Sunday, 11:30 am to 9 pm.
Admission: Desserts cost $6.
Dinner for 2 adults and 2 chil-
dren, excluding wine, would
cost no less than $60.
Directions: Yorkdale Shopping Centre,
North York. Take Hwy 401 West, exit
Allen Rd. (exit #365) and follow York-
dale Rd.

THEME RESTAURANTS

Captain John's

(416) 363-6062 (J-10 on map)
www.toronto.com/captainjohns
Hours: Open year-round, 11 am to 11 pm (closes at 1 am Friday and Saturday, opens at 10:30 am on Sunday).
Directions: 1 Queen's Quay W., Toronto (at the foot of Yonge St.).

I had to check out this floating restaurant, which had teased us for years on our way to nearby attractions. So we showed up for dinner on a nice summer weekend evening. What a fun experience for the kids! But I learned the hard way this seafood place is really expensive if the whole family wants to have lobster! Had we gone for lunch, weekday evening or Sunday brunch, it would have been affordable and my kids would have enjoyed it as much. Live and learn!

The moored boat stands very tall. By the entrance, a cutout features Captain John and a crew member (with a hole so kids can put their face there). Inside, there's plenty of brass devices and nautical theme objects. The dining room is plush and cozy. There are options on the menu for those who don't like seafood or fish.

While in the area, check the embedded copper letters on Queen's Quay's sidewalk at the foot of Yonge Street. They point out the fact that you are at the beginning of the longest street in the world. Walking towards the west, you'll read the name of major cities located along this street (with distances). As we were reading aloud the inscription *Thunder Bay, 1893 km, Rainy River*, a stunned tourist looked at us and exclaimed he was from Thunder Bay!

Dutch Dreams

(416) 656-6959 (I-10 on map)
Hours: Open year-round (closed on Mondays during the winter), from noon to midnight during the summer, from 3 pm to midnight when weather starts cooling down and from 5 to 11 pm during the winter.
Directions: 78 Vaughan Rd., Toronto (take St. Clair, turn north on Vaughan Rd., just west of Bathurst).

If you've never noticed this funky ice cream parlour off St. Clair, you're in for a treat! The facade in itself is candy for the eye, covered with colourful sculptures, signs and other objects. The inside is even busier, with a Dutch theme emphasis: cows, windmills, clogs and Holland scenes.

They make their own waffle cones and the basic cone comes overloaded with ice cream, topped with whipped cream and fruit. They serve huge banana splits, sundays, frozen cakes, waffles, and the likes. The ice cream is so decadent that we all agree to pay the price (money and weight-wise)! Imagine how exotic it would be to visit this place in the middle of the winter!

Love ice cream? If you drive 15 minute to the west on St. Clair, you reach **La Paloma**, the best place in town to eat Italian gelato. We had just come back from Italy when I discovered the place and I swear their Sicilian Pistachio gelato was as good as the one I tasted in the best outlet in Florence. There are dozens of flavours. The stuff is expensive but heavenly. Located at 1357 St. Clair W., Toronto, (416) 656-2340. Open year-round, from 9 am to 11 pm.

Lahore Tikka House

(416) 406-1668 (I-10 on map)

Hours: The small restaurant is open year-round, the patio is open weather permitting, noon to 1 am.

Directions: 1365 Gerrard St. East, Toronto (on the south side).

On a nice summer evening, the strip of Gerrard east of Coxwell is always warmly lit in a festive way. Lahore Tikka House extends into a beautiful covered patio draped with silky fabrics and wrapped in Indian music. In front of it, my daughter hops on one of those three-wheelers adorned with flowers and pompoms typical of India. My sizzling chicken Tikka arrives in a heavy pan. (Ask to hold the spices for the children!) We gorge on their tasty homemade naans (flat bread straight from their outdoor clay oven). My daughter is delighted by the mango popsicle.

We then head for a walk on Gerrard. Beautiful colourful saris are displayed in the large windows. There's more music bursting from welcoming open-door shops. We enter into one of them and my little princess chooses pretty metal bracelets from a bin (they're 10¢ each). Along the sidewalk, street vendors offer exotic food: corn on the cob, sugar cane juice mixed with lime, coconut water directly from a freshly cut shell...

The "panning place"

Directions: From Hwy 401, exit Guelph Line (exit # 312) southbound. It becomes Main St. in Campbellville. There should be a snack bar in the red brick building located at the northwest corner of Main St. and Campbell Ave. (D-2 on map).

This snack bar has changed owners and name so I can't be more precise but it has been offering a panning activity for $5-$7 for years. Take a chance when you are in the neighbourhood.

Fire Hall

(905) 827-4445 (J-7 on map)

www.thefirehall.ca

Hours: Open daily from 11 am to 1 am.

Directions: 2441 Lakeshore Rd. West, Oakville (take QEW westbound, exit at Bronte Rd. and go south, the entrance is on Bronte Rd. by Lakeshore Rd.).

They really play the fire hall theme here, with fire hydrants, firemen's gear, hoses, small fire truck ride and pictures of real fires on the walls. The menu boasts items such as extinguisher dip, fire crackers, three alarm chicken fingers or engine red pasta dish. Food is tasty. They offer a kids' menu. They even sell kid-size fire-fighter hats for $6 and any kid wearing those on Monday nights eats for free.

Fire & Ice

(905) 947-1900 (H-11 on map)

Hours: Open daily, from 11:30 am (opens at noon on the weekends).

Directions: Located on the south side of Hwy 7, between Woodbine and Hwy 404 (take Hwy 404, exit at Hwy 7 eastbound), Markham.

The interior looks like a grotto with stalactites hanging from the ceiling and torches hanging on the walls.

The concept is fun! There are different stations to choose from to fill your plate before giving it to the chef: meat, shrimp or fish, soft veggies, hard veggies, pasta, condiments and sauces. First, you get an order confirmation from your server. Then, you visit the stations. While they cook your stir-fry, you can help yourself to the bread and salad bar. We opted for blackened snapper combination. My kids went for the sausage and veggies. Kid-size plates are less expensive than the already affordable regular stir-fries.

50's RESTAURANTS

Garden Gate

(416) 694-9696 (J-10 on map)
Hours: Open daily, from 8 am to at least 11 pm.
Directions: 2379 Queen St. E., the Beaches in Toronto (past the busiest area, in front of the **Fox Cinema**).

This is the kind of family restaurant that reigned before the fast-food chains started to impose their happy meals on us. Think Norman Rockwell! Where else can you buy a peanut butter sandwich for $1.50? It has large bay windows, an open-kitchen concept and many booths (two of them large enough to accommodate a 12-person group). They serve a wide choice of good and affordable Chinese (even Szechuan), Canadian food and all-day breakfasts.

Galaxie Diner

(705) 422-1182 (B-2 on map)
Hours: Open year-round, 8 am to 9 pm.
Directions: 288 Main St., Wasaga Beach.

So many little things to look at! There's a large collection of retro Coca-Cola ads, small cars from the 50's, B & W tiling  with chrome and booths with individual jukeboxes. The menu is typical of a 50's diner, with affordable prices. It was our favourite place to eat during our weekend at **Wasaga Beach** (p. 286).

Wimpy's Diner

(905) 337-9667 (J-7 on map)
Hours: Open year-round, 8 am to 8 pm (closes at 10 pm Thursday to Saturday).
Directions: 150 Lakeshore Rd. W., Oakville (between Dorval and Kerr).

 They have 23 other locations spread over the territory covered in this guide, including a franchise at 3555 St. Clair Ave. and 199 Sheppard Ave. in Toronto. Call 1-888-594-6797 to find the closest Wimpy's.

The small place is plastered with old records and posters. Their specialty is their charcoal-broiled hamburgers. My daughter and her friend loved the burgers, fries and milkshakes ($5 from the kids' menu). I had a decent Caesar salad with grilled chicken. Their thick menu offers a huge selection, including all-day breakfasts.

Easterbrook's Foot Long Hot Dog & Ice Cream

(905) 527-9679 (E-2 on map)
Hours: Open year-round, 9 am to 9 pm (opens at 11 am on Sundays).
Directions: On Spring Garden Rd., near parking lot at the **Royal Botanical Gardens** Centre (p. 314), Burlington.

The spot to go in the area for great fast food. Think of anything that can be put on a hot dog, they've done it: dozens of foot-long hot dogs to tempt us. Add fries, burgers, ice cream, shakes. They have some tiny booths and a counter, plus a few picnic tables at the side.

BREAKFAST RESTAURANTS

Eggspectation

(416) 977-3380 (I-10 on map)
www.eggspectation.ca
Hours: Open daily from 6:30 am to 9 pm.
Directions: 220 Yonge St., Toronto (by the Eaton Centre, entrance at street level).

Recently opened in Toronto, this franchise is part of a very popular chain in Montreal. One visit to the place and you'll understand why. Their all-day breakfast menu offers a wide variety of tasty and fancy breakfasts, as well as salads, sandwiches and wholesome meals; a great place to have breakfast before going shopping at the **Eaton Centre** (it opens at 6:30 am!). They also have a kids' menu printed with activities and supplied with crayons.

Two-levelled, it catches plenty of natural light with large bay windows. It is best to arrive before 10 am on the weekends. Check out the washrooms with egg beater-handles and oval mirrors and make sure the kids find the CN Tower on the mural in the staircase.

Sunset Grill

(416) 690-9985 (J-10)
Hours: Open year-round, 7 am to 4 pm (closes at 5 pm on weekends).
Directions: 2006 Queen St. East, the Beaches in Toronto.

Located in the heart of the **Beaches** area (p. 270), it is a favourite among the locals. On the weekends, it is better to show up before the line-up (around 9:30 am). We prefer to sit in the back, in the elevated section under the skylight. The open kitchen restaurant serves all-day affordable and plentiful breakfasts as well as burgers and salads, with bottomless coffee as a bonus. Cash only.

Mövenpick Palavrion

(416) 979-0060 (J-10 on map)
www.movenpickcanada.com
Hours: Open daily from 8 am.
Directions: 270 Front St., Toronto (right across from the CN Tower).

This Mövenpick offers waffles and omelettes made in front of you, sausages, good croissants and much more. Light meals and full course dinners served the rest of the day. Their freshly brewed coffee and house muffins are great.

The southern part of it is multi-levelled. It offers table service (for a little extra). The decorations in that section are worth the detour. Actually, the best part is the corridor leading to the washrooms and the washrooms themselves!

Chez Cora

(416) 598-2672
www.chezcora.com
Hours: Open year-round from 6 am to 3 pm (opens at 7 am on Sundays).
Directions: 277 Wellington St. West, Toronto (entrance off Blue Jays Way).

Also from Quebec, very popular Chez Cora's colourful menus and whimsical all-day breakfasts are now available downtown.

Yum! Think fruit! Think eggs, crêpes and waffles, and think big! When a breakfast combo comes with fruit, expect a sculpture on your plate. They serve real old-fashioned oatmeal, huge fruit cups with English cream and signature breakfasts. They also serve lunches and they have a kids' menu with $3.50 suggestions. There are options for around $5 but most of the items cost around $8.

Check their web site for other locations in Mississauga (4120 Dixie Rd.), Brampton, Oakville and Newmarket.

LE MARCHÉ MÖVENPICK

Market analysis

My family and I really enjoy going out to eat, for the change of scenery and crowd immersion it provides (two reasons that suit my little explorer just fine). And there's the sheer pleasure of having someone else cook for us ("Is there another way?" wonders my little guy). The uniqueness of this concept and an ideal location have made Mövenpick Market our preferred choice for a family brunch.

There are no endless waits on your chair here. Simply pick a table and venture out into the profusion of chef-manned stations, where your order will be prepared in front of you. The overall setting is bliss for the senses with its lavish displays of cooking ingredients and tempting presentations.

The sizzling sound of cooking omelettes or roasting potatoes and the freshly baked smell of danishes, small breads and warm crêpes are married to the full-bodied aroma of freshly brewed coffee that teases your nostrils. The sweet bouquet of apples mixes with the tempting smells of crisp vegetables blending with delectable sauces in a skillet. All combine in an invitingly appetizing experience. Hard to imagine a child ever getting bored in such a place!

The Market is located in the heart of **BCE Place**. The large hall (which connects Yonge and Bay streets) with its majestic vaults crossing harmoniously some hundred feet above, the imposing marble water fountain and granite paving stones and the multitude of stairs, escalators and hiding nooks, combine to create a truly exciting playground.

When the hall holds no more secrets, simply turn to the specialized magazines at adjacent Great Canadian News.

TIPS (fun for 2 years +)

• You can access **BCE Place**'s indoor parking lot via Wellington St. It is quite expensive on weekdays but the weekend flat rate is reasonable.
• Before 5 pm, waits at the door of the restaurant are seldom more than 15 minutes.
• Everyone (kids included) is handed a white card at the entrance. You carry this with you and the server puts a stamp on it when you order a dish. This way, the cashier knows what to charge when you exit. You may run a high bill, although the Marché now offers a cheap menu for kids.
• One of us (generally me) always manages to enjoy the quiet pleasure of a hot coffee and a newspaper, while the other takes off to explore the **BCE Place**.

NEARBY ATTRACTIONS

Le Marché Mövenpick (416) 366-8986 www.movenpickcanada.com	J-10 Downtown Toronto 10-min.

Schedule: Open daily from 7:30 am to 2 am.
Admission: FREE admission to BCE Place. Average cost of a meal is $15-$20/person, kids menu is around $4.
Directions: BCE Place at the corner of Yonge and Front St., Toronto.

RESTAURANTS WITH BUFFET

Mandarin

(416) 486-2222
www.mandarinbuffet.com
Hours: Open daily, noon to 9:30 pm (closes at 10:30 pm on Fridays and Saturdays). Hours vary by location.
Directions: 2200 Yonge St., Toronto, south of Eglinton. Call for other locations.

I love the look of their colourful buffet, with plenty of fresh veggies and bite-size desserts. We were greeted with great earnestness by the courteous staff. My whole family found something to their taste amidst the wide selection of the buffet.

It is better to reserve if you want to go for dinner or on a weekend. Children 5-12 years old pay half price, children 4 years and under pay $2. Lunch buffet is $9/weekdays, $13/weekends; dinner buffet is $16/Monday-Thursday, $23/Friday-Sunday. **Famous Players Canada Square** is in the same building, (416) 646-0444.

Frankie Tomatto's

(905) 940-1900 (H-11 on map)
www.frankietomatto.com
Hours: Open daily at least from 11:30 am to 2:30 pm and from 5 pm to 10 pm (closes at 9:30 pm on Sundays). Better to call!
Directions: 7225 Woodbine Ave., Markham (take Hwy 404 North, exit at Woodbine, the restaurant is north of Steeles, on the east side.

The place is noticeable for the Leaning Tower of Pisa. It offers an all-you-can-eat Italian buffet that my kids really enjoyed. The affordable food is presented in 14 different stations made to look like a small Italian village and you can choose from several rooms, each with it's own style. Kids 11 years and under pay 1/2 price except on Saturday nights.

The Old Mill Inn

(416) 236-2641 (I-9 on map)
www.oldmilltoronto.com
Hours: Sunday Brunch starts at 10:30 am; Sunday Family Dinner Buffet starts at 5 pm. When we arrived at 10:30 am for the brunch, 8-10 people were already in line; by 11:45, the place was relatively full.
Directions: 21 Old Mill Rd., Toronto (take Bloor St. West, off South Kingsway Rd., turn north on Old Mill Rd.).

The Old Mill Inn is a boutique inn built in the spirit of Old England. A favourite location for wedding banquets and corporate events, its large dance hall hosts buffets on Sundays.

The dance hall and surrounding room are luxurious, with white tablecloths, warm decor with wooden floors, brick walls, French windows and comfortable upholstered chairs.

The buffet's layout is appealing. After cleaning the plate from her first serving, my daughter asked permission to go back to "explore the food". The buffet is more than decent, with a wide selection including a seafood and fish table with cold lobster, shrimp, a meat table with roast beef, a warm breakfast station, salad tables and dessert stations.

Sunday brunch costs $26/adults, $12/6 to 12 years old; dinner buffets are $28/adults, $10/6 to 12 years. Both are free for children 5 years and under. They supply kids with a small activity book and crayons.

Ask about their special **Christmas** or **Easter** buffets. They seem to be the tradition for many families!

FUN SUPPLIERS

Creative Bag
(416) 631-6444 (H-10 on map)
www.creativebag.com
Directions: 880 Steeprock Dr., Toronto (west of Allen Rd., south of Finch). Call (905) 670-2651 for Mississauga outlet.

This warehouse carries all sizes of bags and boxes, in all kinds of materials, as well as ribbon, tulle, tissue paper, gift wrap, etc. The best place I know to buy cute tiny clear loot or candy bags.

The Amazing Party Store

(416) 259-5959 (I-9)
www.
amazingpartystore.com
Directions: 923 Oxford St., Toronto (take QEW, exit at Kipling southbound, turn east on Evans, north on Eastwick and west on Oxford).

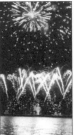

Best place in town to buy fireworks. They sell street kits, park kits, cottage kits and more, with firing sequence suggestions. They're also the place to buy or rent costumes for Halloween, Christmas, Mardi Gras or Easter, with accessories and make-up. You can count on a large selection of related trinkets, decorations, tableware and so on as well as balloons and helium rental.

Party Packagers
www.partypackagers.com
Toronto: 125 Orfus Rd., west of Dufferin, south of Hwy 401, (416) 785-4035 (I-10).
North York: 1225 Finch Ave. W., west of Dufferin, north of Hwy 401, (416) 631-7688 (H-10).
Mississauga: 3050 Vega Blvd., north of Dundas, west of Winston Churchill, (905) 607-2789 (I-8).
Scarborough: 29 William Kitchen Rd., east of Kennedy, south of Hwy 401, (416) 293-2339 (plus locations in Ajax, Ancaster and Brampton) (I-11).

My favourite place to buy items for loot bags and gadgets to create themed activities for birthday parties or school fairs!

Miko & Samko
(416) 532-1114 (Samko) (I-9 on map)
(905) 771-8714 (Miko) (H-11 on map)
Hours: Usually open early October (a bit earlier at Miko) until a few day prior to Christmas, Wednesday to Saturday.
Samko directions: 11 Peel Ave., Toronto (take Queen St. W., turn north on Gladstone Ave. (east of Dufferin), then turn west on Peel. There's free parking at the foot of Gladstone, less than a 5-minute walk from the warehouse.
Miko directions: 60 East Beaver Creek Rd., Richmond Hill (take Hwy 404 north, exit at Hwy 7 westbound, turn north on East Beaver Creek.

Both warehouses offer the same merchandise: end of line brand name toys (Little Tikes, Fisher-Price, Mattel, Crayola, Barbie, Tonka, etc), craft activities or gadgets that might catch your fancy, all at really affordable prices. I love to go there to stock up on toys under $10 for last minute birthday or Christmas gifts and loot bags. BEWARE, no infants, or kids under 16 are allowed in the Samko location. Miko accepts everyone.

The Palmer's Group
(905) 670-7999
www.palmerkids.com

Louise Kool & Galt
(416) 293-0312 (I-11)
www.louisekool.com
Directions: 180 Middlefield Rd., Scarborough (east of McCowan Rd. and south of Finch).

Order these two suppliers' catalogues! They're full of affordable craft material we don't always see in retail stores. **Palmer's Group** requires a minimum order of $150, no delivery charges. **Louise Cool & Galt** charges delivery but requires no minimum. In addition, they open their warehouse to the public. They also carry toys, playroom furniture and more.

R. Hiscott Theatrical Supplies

(416) 977-5247 (I-10)
Directions: 435 Yonge St., Toronto.

You might have noticed in the past the great artists of Kromatic turning children's faces into masterpieces at the **Milk Festival** or **Toronto Buskerfest**. I asked them where I could find the make-up they use to paint on skin and they sent me to this place. I found great colours in small compacts, perfect sponges and fabulous glittering powder so fine it is 100% safe to use on kids' faces. They also carry a wide selection of fancy Halloween make-up supplies like scars!

Sassy Bead

(416) 488-7400 (I-10)
www.sassybead.yp.ca
Directions: 2076 Yonge St., Toronto.

This great store sells beads of all types. Every time I have been there, a great number of bead creations were displayed to inspire us. For bigger kids you could buy material to make spring or elastic bracelets. The tiny bead boxes allow you to line-up a 2-metre-long string of beads. There's a vast selection of fancy metal charms for under $2. For younger kids, I bought a $25 bag of large beads shaped like teddy bears (perfect for making necklaces with pre-schoolers). I noticed many $10-$15 bead kits to create animals. Ask about their birthday package.

Loots

(416) 787-5668 (I-10)
www.lootsonline.com
Directions: 896 Eglinton Ave. West, Toronto (just west of Bathurst).

This is a funky small store! Plush on the ceiling, vibrant colours, hanging disco ball and chandeliers define the look. Shelves are packed with gift items and the walls are covered with loot bag suggestions presented by age group. They used to offer a wide variety of crafty loot bags but their current selection is now in the line of ensembles of small toys. Check out their back room! Even funkier, it is where they hold birthday dance parties. Ask about those. Kids love them!

Chocolicks

(416) 485-2047 (I-10)
www.chocolicks.com
Directions: 573 Eglinton Ave. W., Toronto.

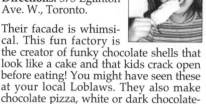

Their facade is whimsical. This fun factory is the creator of funky chocolate shells that look like a cake and that kids crack open before eating! You might have seen these at your local Loblaws. They also make chocolate pizza, white or dark chocolate-dipped marshmallows on a stick, giant fortune cookies again dipped in chocolate and more.

Sandylion Stickers

(905) 475-6771 (H-11 on map)
www.sandylion.com
Directions: 400 Cochrane Dr., Markham (take Hwy 404 North, exit at Hwy 7 westbound, turn south on Cochrane).

Kids adore their stickers and parents adore the Sandylion warehouse bargains! You have to buy a minimum of $14. Every possible theme of stickers is available. It also carries sticker books, activity books and large stickers for decoration.

Vivid Tiles

(905) 804-9203
www.vividtile.com

Until these guys find a permanent location, you can order through their web site, sending artwork or scanned photos over the Internet. Many people use their services to create kitchen or bathroom tiles but I used them to create personalized gifts. I had a friend's art printed on tiles to be used as coasters. I had one of my best travel pictures printed on an 8" by 10" tile as a decorative plate. For a literary contest at my kids' school, we printed the winners' texts on large tiles as an award... They offer glossy, satin, matte finish porcelain or tumbled stone (more durable). Tile 4.25" by 4.25" costs around $8; 8" by 10" costs $21-$24. Call for details.

Efston Science

(416) 787-4581 (I-10 on map)
www.escience.ca
Hours: At least from 10 am to 6 pm. Closed on Sundays.
Directions: 3350 Dufferin St., Toronto (just across the street from **Yorkdale Mall**, on the west side of Dufferin).

The store is hard to miss with its gigantic telescope on the roof. It is of course the place to buy serious astronomical material (and great books for stargazing) but amidst the merchandise on the three other floors, I found many intriguing trinkets and original toys or gadgets to give as special gifts.

The large glow-in-the-dark section, located at the educational toys level, offered a wide selection ranging from $4 glow-in-the-dark paint to a $120 Star tunnel. When visiting, I noticed a funky $40 inflatable radio on that floor that really worked.

On the last level are the chemistry kits, gems, and activity books, among other things. Different quality of rock tumblers caught my attention.

My favourite level was the third one. There, you'll find solar batteries, electronic circuits, magnets of all kinds, everything involved with robotic: the dream place for the beginners and the more serious hobbyist. They have a glassed showcase including non-expensive fun stuff such as balls that make an explosion sound when they knock each other!

Mastermind

(416) 422-0434 (I-10 on map)
www.mastermindtoys.com
Directions: 770 Don Mills Rd., Toronto.

The Mastermind located in the **Ontario Science Centre** (p. 256) is the best choice to find cool educational gadgets for fancy loot bags. It offers a wider selection of activity books and toys under $10 than the other Mastermind outlets. When you get to the parking lot gate, mention you just want to go to the store. They normally will assign you a temporary place to park without charging you.

Wonders of the Earth

(416) 396-4043 (community centre) (I-11)
www.scarbgemclub.ca
Schedule: Usually on the second or third weekend in September (for 2004: September 18-19) at least from 11 am to 5 pm.
Admission: $3/adults, $1/children.
Directions: Mid-Scarborough Community Centre, 2467 Eglinton Ave. East, Scarborough (between Kennedy Rd. and Midland Ave.).

This gem show has been organized by the **Gem & Mineral Club of Scarborough** for the last 35 years. It is a great starting point for young mineralogists.

My kids were thrilled by their Kids Quarry where we could get a sandbag of minerals for 50¢. They would dump its content into a sifter and discover at least 6 specimens. A little plastic pouch included contained labels to identify the rocks. There were also hands-on soapstone carving and fossil preparation.

The show is held in a large gym. Many members exhibit their collections. You can watch lapidary work and jewelry making, gem faceting, soapstone carving and fossil preparation.

There's also a Mineral Identification Table where your child can take the "precious" stone he found for the experts to identify (but maybe he doesn't really want to know...).

There were many 50¢ to $1 minerals to choose from. My daughter went for a $2 fabric surprise bag holding three stones. We could buy strands of fresh water pearls for $5.

To find your local gem club, check **www.canadianrockhound.com**, a free web-based geological magazine for collectors, beginners and educators. Click Clubs and then choose by city or name. Check their Junior Rockhound section!

MODEL TRAIN SHOWS

Adults play too!

My action-driven son is fascinated by the small trains riding full speed on parallel tracks. His friend, the observant type, is absorbed in the examination of detailed small-scale landscapes. My young daughter is delighted by every display featuring a cow in a field. Whatever their personality, a child's attention is sure to be caught at a train show.

Neither of the two 60,000 square-foot shows I have visited this year had a unified look to them. But each model railway association represented there was a small world in itself.

One association tested children's observation skills by providing a list of funny details to spot on the landscape and allowed them to pick chocolate balls from the display. Another was quite interactive, allowing visitors to play with remote controls moving lifts up and down, handle baggage, control the saw mills and more.

One long train track was set on the floor. We saw a couple of miniature circuses by the railway in small towns.

Some buildings along the track in some exhibits were real pieces of art. We could even observe some exhibitors in the process of building copper trains from scratch. Such shows could easily become more interactive but let's not forget that their main purpose is not to amuse small kids. It is to delight the child within big people...

TIPS (fun for 3 years +)

• I saw a dad carrying a little stool for his 4-year-old. It is a great idea since many displays are 48" high, preventing the younger ones from seeing without help.

• Not all exhibitors have the same attitude towards children. Some get really nervous with them. Make sure you are in control of your little ones' hands unless you want to see a grown man cry!

• There was nothing really "festive" about the **Toronto Christmas Train Show** (except for a few small Santas here and there) but it offered more train displays than the **Toronto Model Railway Show** held in March (which seems to be a favourite among those serious about their hobby).

• There are tables and a snack bar on both premises.

• For a good list of train shows around the GTA, I suggest you check **www.railtronics.com** and click on <u>Schedules</u>.

Toronto Christmas Train Show
	H-9
• Mississauga	N-W
(905) 945-2775	of Toronto
www.antiquetoys.ca	30-min.

Schedule: Usually in November (for 2004: November 20-21, at least from 11 am to 4 pm). Call for following years.
Admission: Around $10/adults, $4/6-14 years, FREE for 5 years and under.
Directions: International Centre, 6900 Airport Rd., Mississauga. Take Hwy 427 North. Exit Dixon Rd., turn west on Dixon, it becomes Airport Rd.

Toronto Model Railway Show
• Mississauga
(416) 536-2894

Schedule: Usually held a weekend in March. Call for specific dates.

Admission: Around $9/adults, $4/6-14 years, FREE for 5 years and under.

Directions: Usually at the Toronto Congress Centre (650 Dixon Rd., Mississauga, east of Hwy 427). Call to confirm.

ALL ABOUT PETS SHOW

A pet project

I would not trade my very allergic husband for a great dog or beautiful cat. I would not even add the weekly cleaning of a lizard's stinky cage or the troubled water of a fish tank to my already hectic schedule. So we are not about to get a pet. All this said, we love animals, so a pet show turned out to be a nice outing.

All About Pets Show is actually more ambitious than the pet show I visited with my kids a few years ago (which doesn't exist anymore). I have not seen it personally but this one is bigger, with over 180 exhibitors and experts, and has been going on for 12 years.

This kind of show obviously offers the latest pet products and services, and as we anticipated, there were plenty of dogs, cats, birds, and fish. On the other hand, we did not expect to see hedgehogs, the cutest pets ever. There's no guaranty you'll see some when you go, exhibitors change from one year to the next, but you'll see plenty of rabbits (including the **Easter** Bunny).

Next to the exhibition hall is a dog demonstration ring which can seat 2,000 visitors. It offers continuous activity: dog shows, parade of breeds or dog fashion. The kind of action we won't see at our local pet shop.

This show also includes a Pet Adop-

tion Area coordinated by the SPCA. (Don't expect to leave with an animal on the spot.)

In another section (as far as possible from the dog shows) visitors find the World of Cats and its well attended Championship Cat Show.

One thing for sure, this is the right place to find out what you're really getting into if you are considering adding a pet member to the family (or why you shouldn't... yet).

All About Pets Show	H-9
• Mississauga	N-W
1-800-250-3080	of Toronto
www.pets-show.com	30-min.

Schedule: Usually Friday to Sunday on Easter weekend, from 10 am to 6 pm, closes at 5 pm on Sunday. (For 2005: March 25-26-27). Call to confirm exact date for following years. Note hours differ when not taking place on Easter weekend.

Admission: Around $10/ adults, $7/seniors and students, $6/5-9 years, FREE 4 years and under.

Directions: International Centre, 6900 Airport Rd., Mississauga. Take Hwy 427 North. Exit Dixon Rd., turn west on Dixon, it becomes Airport Rd.

TIPS (fun for 3 years +)
• Snacks, fast food and hot meals are sold on the premises.
• Dog lovers want to see **Woofstock** and **Paws in the Park** on pp. 44 and 124.

NEARBY ATTRACTIONS
Pearson Airport (5-min.)...............p. 234

PARENT RESOURCES

Help We've Got Kids
(416) 444-7678
www.helpwevegotkids.com

This publication is a yearly directory of children's resources put together by two dynamic Toronto mothers. It is your best bet if you're totally lost when looking for services, programs, camps, party products suppliers, doctors, insurance, education funds and so on in the GTA. It includes coupons and is sold in bookstores and other outlets for $14.

They also have a web site where you can search their book's information by city, category, company name or key words. It also includes a calendar of events.

www.toronto4kids.com

This is a new free portal for parents in the GTA, another initiative from a Toronto mom. This web site is quite user-friendly. It is a cross between a directory and a magazine. The founder will be adding useful tools such as checklists, tips on travelling with kids, finance tips for kids. Check her exhaustive monthly listing of events with links!

Parent Help Line
1-888-603-9100
www.parenthelpline.ca

This service is the parents' arm of the great **Kids Help Phone**. It is a national, bilingual telephone and on-line service you can turn to for confidential support from trained counsellors. Talking helps!

Parentbooks
(416) 537-8334 (I-10 on map)
www.parentbookstore.com
Directions: 201 Harbord St., Toronto (just east of Bathurst St, south of Bloor St.).

This is the only bookstore in town focusing on books aiming to help parents do a better job. They offer thousands of titles but their main asset is the expertise of their staff. They're the main source for parents and professionals.

www.campsearch.com
(416) 588-6375

This web site includes camps from 32 countries. When I clicked Canada, then selected Ontario, day camp, 11 years old, under $250 and 1 week, I found 49 suggestions. For residential camps in the price range of $250-$500, I found 67 suggestions.

www.canadiansitter.ca

This is a web site you can subscribe to in order to have access to hundreds of names of babysitters in your area. You can look it up to have an idea of the kind of list they could provide (lists by city with street intersections).

We need to subscribe for the phone numbers to show on the list. You can subscribe for three months for $40, or pay $80 for a full year access to their network.

Beach Hotline
(416) 392-7161

This one comes in handy when you live in the GTA. It gives you a daily report on the water conditions for major beaches managed by the City of Toronto.

Environment Canada says we should not swim up to two days after a rain storm.

www.cinemaclock.com

This one is used on a regular basis in my family! It is my favourite movie listing. Go there, click Toronto (if you live in the GTA, but they do listings for all major cities in Canada). Then, search by movie or by theatre. They will show the times, price, rating, etc. They also provide a top-10 list, a section describing the new movies and another one mentioning upcoming movies.

They even include an alphabetized list of older movies, some with symbols indicating when presently playing in a theatre or available in DVD, with description, pictures, actors, directors and even trailers!

CALENDAR OF EVENTS

JANUARY

New Year's Day Polar Bear Dip at Coronation Park 381
on New Year's Day
Monster Jam at the SkyDome 356
on mid-January weekend

FEBRUARY

Barrie Winterfest 91
usually first weekend of February
Richmond Hill Winter Carnival 91
usually first weekend of February
Winter Wonderland at Downsview Park 328
usually a mid-February Sunday
WinterCity Festival 90
usually two weeks in February,
including the 2nd
Model Railroad Club Show 229
usually the last 3 Sundays of February
Penetang Winterama 91
usually a Saturday in mid-February
Orillia Winter Carnival 91
usually 2nd weekend of February

MARCH

MAPLE SYRUP TIME
Potentially from early March
to mid April. See pp. 154-161.
Warkworth Maple Syrup Festival 160
2nd weekend of March
St. Patrick's Day Parade 73
always on a Sunday, before or after
March 17, noon to 3 pm
MARCH BREAK
 Around mid-March. See p. 176.
For more March Break activities,
look for the pages in this guide
with a calendar pictogram.
Casa Loma March Break Show 114
on March Break week and maybe
weekends before and after
Spring Fling at the SkyDome 356
on March Break week and maybe
weekends before and after
Wizard World at Exhibition Place 25
on March Break week, plus weekends
before and after
March Break drop-in fun at AGO 92
Tuesday to Friday
March Break drop-in fun at Bata Shoe Museum 254
Tuesday to Friday
March Break drop-in fun at Fort York 400
on March Break weekdays

March Break drop-in fun at McMichael 93
on March Break weekdays
March Break drop-in fun at the ROM 253
on March Break weekdays
March Break drop-in fun at the Science Centre 258
on March Break weekdays
March Break drop-in fun at Textile Museum 251
Tuesday to Friday
EASTER
 Can fall any time between
March 22 and April 25!
See pp. 177-180.
For more Easter activities,
look for outings with a rabbit
pictogram.
Easter Tradition at Colborne Lodge 401
A few consecutive weekends
around Easter time
Spring Egg Fun Day at Colborne Lodge 401
on Palm Sunday,
one week prior to Easter
Easter Procession in Little Italy 180
Easter Friday at 3 pm
Beaches Lions Club Easter Parade 178
Easter Sunday at 2 pm
All About Pets Show 443
usually Easter Friday and Saturday
Easter activities at Cullen Gardens 117
Usually Friday and Saturday
of Easter weekend
Easter activities at Toronto Zoo, 46
Usually on Easter Sunday
Float Your Fanny Down the Ganny 238
usually the first Saturday
following Easter

APRIL

Sprockets Film Festival 100
on 10 consecutive days
usually from mid-April
Hot Docs 100
on 10 consecutive days
usually around last week of April

MAY

Four Winds Kite Festival 333
last weekend of April or first of May
Toronto Doors Open 108
usually first weekend of May
Bell Walk for Kids 123
usually on firstSunday of May,
from 10 am

Special activities at
Jimmie Simpson Park 183
on Canada Day
Special activities at
Scarborough Museum 326
on Canada Day
Summer Carnival at
London Children's Museum 263
on Canada Day
Fireworks at Ontario Place 13
before and after Canada Day
Kidsummer 85
July 1 to August 31
ShakespeareWorks by the Lake 271
all summer
Richmond Hill Live Steamers'
Open House 236
weekend after July 1
Toronto Street Festival 87
first or 2nd weekend of July
Ontario Family Fishing Weekend 361
3-day weekend,
usually the second of July
Sunfest in London 31
a 4-day event
usually around mid-July
Shakespeare Under the Stars 156
a Friday and Saturday in mid-July
Ontario Renaissance Festival 408
weekends only and holiday Monday
Monday, usually from the 3rd in
July to Sunday of Labour Day
Junior Caribana 71
usually one week prior to Caribana

AUGUST
Shakespeare in the rough 106
usually Wednesday to Sunday
in August
Caribana 71
usually first Saturday of August
SIMCOE DAY
First Monday of August. See p.181.
London Balloon Festival 31
on Simcoe Day weekend
Special activities at Fort York 400
on Simcoe Day
Special activities at
Gibson House Museum 403
on Simcoe Day
Summer Festival at
Chinguacousy Park 334
on Simcoe Day
Art Naturally Festival 107
usually on weekend
following Simcoe Day
CNE 24
on 18 consecutive days ending
on Labour Day Monday

Sunflower Celebration at
Wildflower Farm 147
usually on a mid-August Sunday
Toronto Buskerfest 89
usually on weekend
before Labour Day

SEPTEMBER
Toddle for Tots 125
usually on a Saturday in September
from 9 am
Paws in the Park 124
usually on a Sunday in September,
from 10 am
Canadian Int'l Air Show 13, 24
on Labour Day weekend
Fiesta del Sol in London 31
on Labour Day weekend
Monarch weekend at
Presqu'ile Provincial Park 319
on Labour Day weekend
Fireworks at Wasaga Beach 287
on Sunday of Labour Day weekend
Pow Wow at Sainte-Marie
among the Hurons 420
early to mid-September weekend
Cabbagetown Arts & Crafts Sale 132
weekend after Labour Day
Richmond Hill Live Steamers'
Open House 236
weekend after Labour Day
Riverdale Farm Fall Festival 132
on weekend after Labour Day
Six Nations Annual Fall Fair 79
on weekend after Labour Day
Fall Fair at Bradley Museum 156
a mid-September Saturday
Big Brother Soap Box Derby 232
usually on a mid-September
Saturday from noon to 4:30 pm
Alliance Toronto KiteFest 328
usually a mid-September weekend
Word on the street 96
usually last Sunday in September,
11 am to 6 pm
Wonders of the Earth 441
usually 2nd or 3rd weekend
in September
Doggie Day Afternoon Festival
at Jimmie Simpson Park 44
usually third Saturday of September
Anne of Green Gables
look-alike contest at Westfield 414
usually on third Sunday
of September
Children's Pow Wow at
Dufferin Grove Park 325
usually on 3rd or 4th Saturday
of September

OCTOBER

HALLOWEEN

 Pumpkin time and Halloween activities in the farms usually start end of September. See p. 184. For more Halloween activities, look for the pages in this guide with a pumpkin pictogram.

Magic Hill Haunted Adventure 185
  usually last Friday and Saturday
  of September and Friday to Sunday
  in October

Ghostly Ghoulish Gala at
  Toronto Zoo 48
  a few days in October

Blessing of the Animals at
  St. James Cathedral 113
  one day in October

Oktoberfest Thanksgiving Parade 80
  on Thanksgiving Monday, at 8:30 am

Toronto French Book Fair 95
  usually first or second week
  of October

Screemers at Exhibition Place 25
  13 nights ending October 31

Autumn Colour Skyride at Kelso 407
  at least 3 weekends of October

Screamfest at the Ostrich Farm 55
  usually over 3 weekends in October

Fall Fair at Downsview Park 328
  one day late October

October Night of Dread Parade 325
  on the evening of October 31

NOVEMBER

CHRISTMAS TRADITIONS

 Many start in November. Most attractions are closed on December 25 and January 1st. See pp. 186-204. For more Christmas activities, look for the pages in this guide with a Santa Claus pictogram.

Parade of Lights at
  County Heritage Park 406
  one night in November

Christmas Train Show 442
  usually one weekend in November

Royal Agricultural Winter Fair 133
  10 consecutive days, usually from
  first Wednesday of November

Cullen Gardens Festival of Lights 202
  mid-November to early January

Niagara Festival of Lights 204
  mid-November to mid-January

Toronto Santa Claus Parade 192
  third Sunday of November
  at 12:30 pm

ChristmasTown at Mounstberg 339
  usually on weekends from end of
  November to right before Christmas

Journey of Love 203
  usually the last Thursday to Sunday
  of November

Canadian Aboriginal Festival 72
  usually last Friday to Sunday
  of November

Cavalcade of lights 190
  usually starts last Friday
  of November with tree illumination

12 Trees of Christmas at the
  Gardiner Ceramic Museum 197
  usually from end of November to
  mid-December (cancelled for 2004)

Casa Loma Christmas Show 114
  end of November to early January

DECEMBER

Walk to Bethlehem at
  County Heritage Village 406
  usually 4-day in early December

Crèche Exhibit at
  St. James Cathedral 194
  usually early December to a few
  days before Christmas (maybe more)

Winter Festival at
  Humber Arboretum 330
  usually the first Saturday
  of December

Kids' Christmas Stable 200
  usually on first weekend
  of December

Burlington Festival of Lights 201
  starts first Sunday of December

Opening of Victorian Christmas at
  Allan Gardens 198
  first Sunday of December
  from 10 am to 5 pm

Caroling in the Park at the Beaches 344
  usually on second Tuesday before
  Christmas from 7:30 top 8:30 pm

The Christmas Story 191
  usually on the three weekends
  before Christmas

Sing-Along Messiah 195
  usually on the Sunday
  before Christmas at 2 pm

Kensington Festival of Light 196
  on December 21st at 5:45 pm

Bugfeast at Wings of Paradise 60
  last week of December
  through early January

Fireworks at Cullen Gardens 117
  on New Year's Eve at dusk

First Night Toronto 205
  on December 31 and probably
  a few consecutive days prior to
  New Year's Eve

TOP 10 FOR TODDLERS

The Beaches: p. 270

Microkids (Ontario Place): p.12

Fantasy Fair: p. 26

Toronto Zoo pavilions: p. 46

Yorkville Park: p. 308

Enchanted Forest (Forsythe Family Farms): p. 140

Drop-in centres: p. 208

Waterloo Museum: p. 260

Agincourt Pool: p. 382

The Kidsway: p. 213

TOP 10 FOR 3-5 YEARS OLD

High Park: p. 322

KidSpark (Ontario Science Centre): p. 256

Spooktackle (Archibald's): p. 139

Kidstown Playground: p. 380

Glen Stewart Ravine: p. 344

Santa's Village: p. 28

Splash Island (Toronto Zoo): p. 46

Centreville (Toronto Islands): p. 23

Children's drill (Fort York): p. 400

Off the Wall! (AGO): p. 92

TOP 10 FOR 6-9 YEARS OLD

Hilton Falls C.A.: p. 300

African Lion Safari: p. 58

StoryBook Gardens: p. 30

Casa Loma: p. 114

Royal Ontario Museum: p. 252

Ontario Place: p. 12

Brooks Farm: p. 137

Burd's Trout Fishing: p. 359

Milk Festival: p. 70

Snow Valley Snow Tubing: p. 378

TOP 10 FOR PRE-TEENS

Renaissance Festival: p. 408

Water tubing (Elora Gorge C. A.): p. 394

Laser Quest: p. 20

Emerald Lake: p. 38

Ontario Science Centre: p. 256

Shell Park in Oakville: p. 371

Haunted Adventure: p. 185

Hanes Corn Maze: p. 150

Scenic Caves: p. 290

Playdium Mississauga: p. 18

TOP 10 FOR TEENAGERS

Warsaw Caves C.A.: p. 291

Sing-Along Messiah: p. 195

Hockey Hall of Fame: p. 362

Wonderland: p. 14

Vanderhoof Skatepark: p. 366

Wasaga Beach P.P.: p. 286

Drive-in theatres: p. 97

Haliburton Forest: p. 342

Medieval Times: p. 398

Rock climbing: p. 364

TOP 10 WITH GRAND-PARENTS

Wings of Paradise: p. 60

Toronto Symphony Orchestra: p. 103

Stage West: p. 84

Warplane Museum: p. 245

Allan Gardens: p. 309

Bowmanville Zoo: p. 52

Sprockets: p. 100

McMichael Canadian Art: p. 93

Cullen Gardens: p. 116

Easter Parade: p. 178

TOP 10 PICNIC SPOTS

Sandbanks Beach: p. 298

Doris McCarthy Trail: p. 294

Ward's Beach: p. 269

Bluffer's Park: p. 273

Coronation Park: p. 381

Royal Botanical Gardens: p. 314

Streetsville Memorial Park: p. 350

McRae Point P.P.: p. 282

Elora Quarry C.A.: p. 279

Whitchurch C.A.: p. 275

TOP 10 FREE OUTINGS

Santa Claus Parade: p. 192

Don Valley Brickworks: p. 317

Kensington Festival: p. 196

Douglas Snow Centre: p. 383

Soap Box Derby: p. 232

Float your Fanny Down the Ganny Race: p. 238

Toronto Police Museum: p. 250

ROM (Friday night): p. 252

Cobourg's Beach: p. 283

Dufferin Grove Park: p. 324

My vision...

(Six months prior to publication)

So many good ideas, so little time...
But all is not lost! There's always my web site.

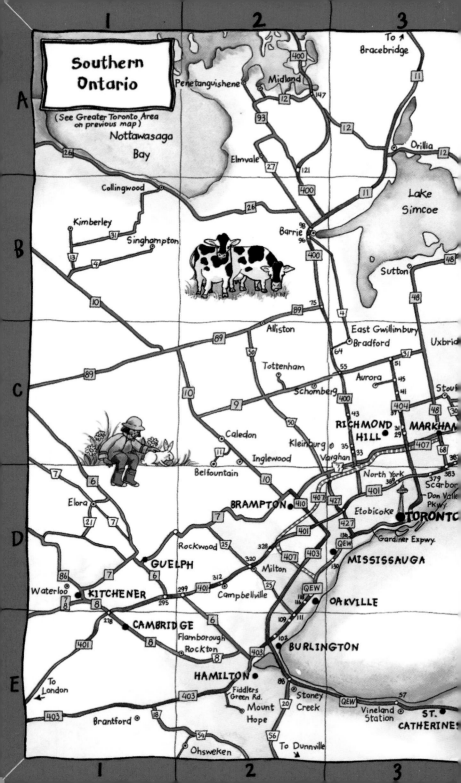

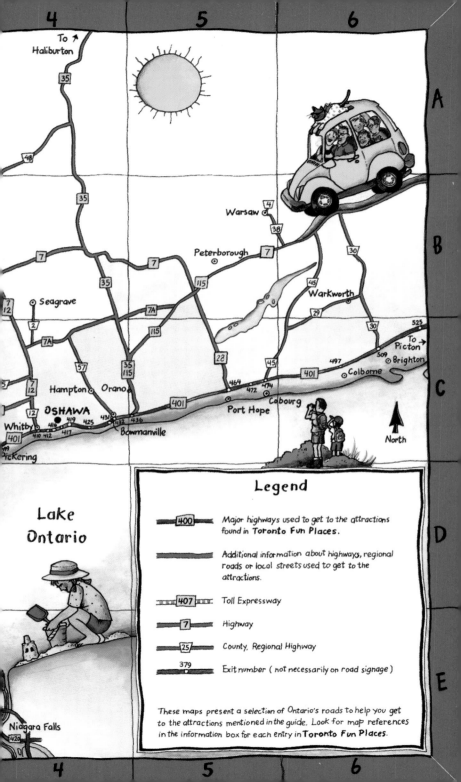

Legend

400	Major highways used to get to the attractions found in **Toronto Fun Places**.
	Additional information about highways, regional roads or local streets used to get to the attractions.
407	Toll Expressway
7	Highway
25	County, Regional Highway
379	Exit number (not necessarily on road signage)

These maps present a selection of Ontario's roads to help you get to the attractions mentioned in the guide. Look for map references in the information box for each entry in **Toronto Fun Places**.

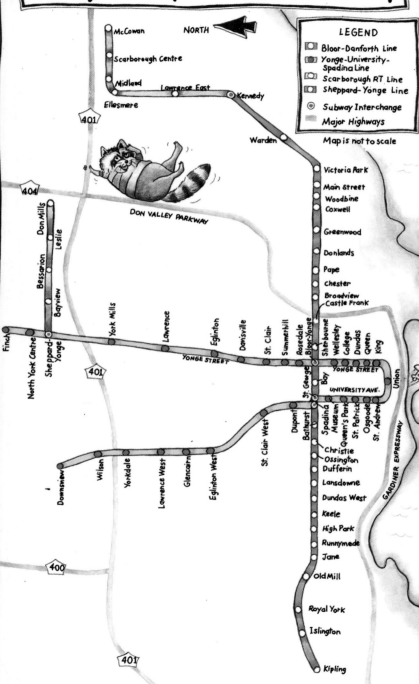

About the TTC

- FUN PLACES bearing the bus symbol offer TTC public transportation (subway, bus or streetcar) in their vicinity. Those without might still be reached by another local public transportation system.

- To find out about the TTC access to a FUN PLACE, call TTC infoline **(416) 393-4636** (press "0" to reach someone in person from 8 am to 5 pm).

- Check your Yellow Pages for a a subway map and a map showing the major TTC surface routes, with their numbers. You will need the route number to find out the itinerary and schedule through the TTC automatic telephone system or on their web site **www.ttc.ca.**

Map Reference Index

CITY LOCATION INDEX

ALPHABETICAL INDEX

NEED A GUEST SPEAKER?

Nathalie Prézeau, the resourceful author of
TORONTO FUN PLACES
and radio columnist for the French CBC
radio station in Toronto,
gives lively speeches on family outings
tailored to your needs.

It is a unique occasion for your group to:
• talk with the self-published mother whose first editions
sold over 18,000 copies throughout the GTA
• hear first-hand information about outings
• get copies of the 482-page guide at a discount price!

Contact Nathalie Prézeau:
Tel.: **(416) 462-0670**
mail@torontofunplaces.com
Fax: **(416) 462-0682**

TO ORDER A COPY

If you would like to order one copy (or more!)
of TORONTO FUN PLACES
through the mail, simply fill out the form below
(or a photocopy of it) and send it with payment
to the attention of: Word-of-Mouth Production.

Word-of-Mouth Production will pay shipping
and handling charges for you!

You should receive
your guide(s)
within 3 days
after we receive
your order form!

Mailing address:
Word-of-Mouth Production
299 Booth Avenue
Toronto, Ontario M4M 2M7

Tel.: **(416) 462-0670**
Fax: **(416) 462-0682**
mail@torontofunplaces.com

TORONTO FUN PLACES	QUANTITY	PRICE	TOTAL
	_____ X	$19.95 =	_____
GST in Canada 7 % ($1.40 per guide)		+	_____
(Total per book: $21.35)		TOTAL	_____

Name : _____

Address : _____

City : _____ Postal Code : _____

Province : _____ Telephone : _____

e-mail : _____

Payment : ☐ Cheque   or   ☐ Money Order